THESE UNITED STATES

THESE
UNITED STATES

PORTRAITS OF AMERICA
FROM THE 1920S

Edited with an Introduction by

DANIEL H. BORUS

CORNELL UNIVERSITY PRESS

ITHACA AND LONDON

First published 1992 by Cornell University Press, by special arrangement
with *The Nation* magazine/The Nation Company, Inc.

Illustrations courtesy of International Museum of Photography
at George Eastman House, Rochester, N.Y.

International Standard Book Number 0-8014-2747-9
Library of Congress Catalog Card Number 91–39031
Printed in the United States of America

Library of Congress Cataloging-in-Publication Data

These United States : portraits of America from the 1920s / Daniel H. Borus, editor.
  p.   cm.
  Includes bibliographical references and index.
  ISBN 0-8014-2747-9 (alk. paper). — ISBN 0-8014-8026-4 (pbk. :
alk. paper)
  1. United States—Description and travel—1920–1940—Views.
  2. United States—History—1919–1933. I. Borus, Daniel H.
E169.T43   1992
973.91'4—dc20   91-39031

⊗ The paper in this book meets the minimum requirements of the
American National Standard for Information Sciences—Permanence
of Paper for Printed Library Materials, ANSI Z39.48–1984.

For Irving Halle

CONTENTS

x   *Contents*

ACKNOWLEDGMENTS

THIS BOOK OWES much to two University of Rochester colleagues. Christopher Lasch first called my attention to "These United States." Lasch discovered the series while leafing through bound volumes that had been replaced by more "advanced" microfiche technology. Since microfiche and laser disks don't invite browsing, the incident serves to illustrate his thesis that progress is a concept not borne out by history. Although his stimulating interpretation of the series in *The True and Only Heaven* differs at points with my own in the introductory essay, his encouragement and generosity are constant reminders that collegiality need not be a meaningless platitude.

Robert Westbrook patiently answered my questions about the 1920s, heard a number of false renditions, read the essay, and made trenchant criticisms that honed its points and polished its prose.

Thanks are also due to Howard Brick and Casey Blake, who read the manuscript with their usual rigorous intelligence and deep commitment. Joan Rubin helpfully commented on a lecture that formed the basis of my essay. In addition, I profited from discussions with Celia Applegate, Richard Kaeuper, William McGrath, Kathy Peiss, Michael P. Steinberg, and Stewart Weaver.

Robert Schumann and Eric Anderson-Zych undertook the crucial and painstaking task of ferreting out the biographies of some of the lesser-known contributors to "These United States" and the more obscure references.

Peter Agree of Cornell University Press supported the project from its inception and escorted the book over the hurdles from vague enthusiasm to hard type.

The Nation, one of the country's few remaining journals of opposition, was gracious in granting permission to reproduce "These United States."

Joseph Struble of the International Museum of Photography at the George Eastman House, Rochester, directed me to the Underwood and Keystone stereographs that illustrate the volume.

This book is dedicated to Irving Halle. In 1933, while living in Riga, he decided that for all its faults, these United States offered the last, best hope for his

family. Like many of the contributors to the series, he managed to combine criticism with a deep and abiding love of his new country. Many of those faults still
remain and new ones have emerged, but I see no reason to deny the wisdom of
his choice.

DANIEL H. BORUS

Rochester, New York

ABOUT THE ILLUSTRATIONS

THE ILLUSTRATIONS have been chosen from a collection of stereographs made
by the Keystone View Company of Meadville, Pennsylvania, between 1915 and
1930. Stereographs were taken with a dual-lens camera that produced two nearly
identical images. When viewed through a device known as a stereoscope, the
two prints gave the illusion of a single three-dimensional view. The Keystone
View Company was founded in 1892 and possessed over two million negatives
by 1920. These holdings allowed the company to dominate the lucrative stereograph market. Keystone stereographs were sold in boxed sets for classroom and
home educational use and were intended to give viewers guided tours of distant
places. Following the conventions of the day, Keystone stereographers often selected images of work and industry as representative of a place. This emphasis
affords an unusual, but not inaccurate, view of the 1920s.

THESE UNITED STATES

The Unexplored Twenties:
"These United States" and
the Quest for Diversity

CERTAIN NOTIONS ABOUT the American past seem unshakable, even in the face of overwhelming evidence to the contrary. These convictions persist because they appeal to a sense of the picturesque or flatter us that we are more enlightened than our predecessors. We are certain that the Gilded Age was intellectually and culturally barren, even if the years between 1870 and 1890 witnessed the maturation of literary realism, the beginnings of pragmatism, and the painting of John Singer Sargent, Thomas Eakins, and Winslow Homer. We term the 1890s gay despite the presence of the most severe economic crisis the nation had yet experienced, the revolt of agrarian radicals, and major strikes on the rails and in the coal fields. We take as given that the 1950s were conformist and repressive, regardless of the prevalence of abstract expressionism and the rise of two of the least conformist political movements of the twentieth century—civil rights and nuclear disarmament.

As much as any decade, the 1920s has an enduring reputation. Historical currents rarely have the courtesy to begin in a year ending in 0 and subside in one ending in 9, but any decade that starts with the "return to normalcy" election of Warren G. Harding and concludes with the Great Crash in 1929 is a likely candidate to constitute a special unit. Termed the "Roaring Twenties" or the Jazz Age, the decade is known as a mélange of new fads and mores, uncontrolled consumption, and political conservatism. One can hardly envision the 1920s without thinking of flappers, prohibition, bathtub gin, rumrunning, radio, movies, all manners of crazes (flagpole sitting remains inexplicable), petting, and fundamentalists. Its unique character seems forever preserved in the political campaign rhetoric that stressed the "normalcy" of the enjoyment of private satisfactions, the advertising that promoted new consumer goods for their psychic rewards rather than their utility, and the social movements that opposed what many Americans regarded as a threatening modernity of loose morals, runaway science, and absurd and futile social engineering.

I

These familiar images are central to our view of the decade as a struggle between modernists, who favored liberation from restraints, and traditionalists, who insistently demanded conformity to long-standing mores. Rarely has the cultural divide seemed so stark or so unbridgeable. So striking are the decade's extravagances and eccentricities that they dominate our conception of its social and cultural life. Even when we concede that not all the young carried hip flasks and that most of the petite bourgeoisie rejected the Ku Klux Klan, we still view the decade as a combination of levity and repression. By treating the twenties as an exotic interlude, an anomaly between the Progressive and Depression eras, we scarcely credit other, equally important aspects of the past.

The view of the 1920s as a strange mix of release and restraint dates from the decade itself, but on the evidence of "These United States," a remarkable series of articles that began to appear in *The Nation* on 19 April 1922, not all Americans thought their times so easily categorized. Intended to demonstrate that a "gratifying divergence" among the states constituted a valuable source of resistance to the lamentable trend toward "regimentation" and "centralization," the forty-nine essays (one for each state and New York City) were the work of men and women who, for the most part, knew their subject matter intimately.[1] The editors imposed no political conformity or standard format on their contributors in the hope that the results would be as diverse as the country the articles purported to represent.

There was good reason for such optimism. Among the contributors were many of the most prominent names in American letters: Sinclair Lewis on Minnesota, Sherwood Anderson on Ohio, Theodore Dreiser on Indiana, Willa Cather on Nebraska, W. E. B. Du Bois on Georgia, Dorothy Canfield Fisher on Vermont, Mary Austin on Arizona, and Edmund Wilson on New Jersey. The widely diverging perspectives of the contributors make the series compelling reading both for its challenge to our received notion that the twenties were a decade of cosmopolitan sophistication and for its revelation of the country's extraordinary variation in architecture, cuisine, education, ethnic composition, industry, and manners.

Founded in 1865 as a forum for northern intellectuals and former abolitionists, *The Nation* quickly established itself at the center of late-nineteenth-century intellectual life. Under its first editor, E. L. Godkin, the journal combined an unyielding advocacy of Manchester liberalism with a disdain for the new commercialized mass culture to create a distinctive form of cultural custodianship. When Oswald Garrison Villard, son of the railroad baron Henry Villard and grandson of the famed abolitionist William Lloyd Garrison, became the editor and publisher in 1918, the magazine dropped its conservatism for an eclectic brand of left-wing politics and cultural criticism. Despite the national conser-

---

[1]New York City received special treatment because the editors thought the metropolis had little intrinsic relationship with New York State and hence deserved an article of its own.

vative tide, *The Nation* published a broad spectrum of social democrats, anarchists, and liberals and continually championed civil liberties, feminism, and pacifism throughout the 1920s.[2]

"These United States" originated with Ernest Gruening, the magazine's managing editor, who wanted a critical assessment to acknowledge the diversity most contemporary analyses ignored. Initially he planned to include treatments of the District of Columbia and six major U.S. possessions—Alaska, Hawaii, the Philippines, Puerto Rico, the Virgin Islands, and the Canal Zone—but this ambitious scheme proved unworkable. In examining the country state by state, Gruening hit upon a special facet of the American experience. Although its political boundaries may be, as the editors admitted in their introduction to the series, "somewhat arbitrary," the American state combines social and cultural characteristics and generates an intense pride of place in a way that few political subdivisions do. Attachment to place is, to be sure, a common human experience, but it seldom coincides with political boundaries. Departments in France, for example, are simple administrative units and German *Heimaten* are not political divisions.

"These United States" is not travel literature. Eschewing panoramic coverage for personal impression and telling detail, contributors sought out the distinguishing kernel that made each state unique. Foremost among the descriptive emphases of the series is the country's geography. Many of its depictions of the vast array of geographic formations reveal the pervasive influence of a new environmental consciousness that developed in the 1920s. Stressing the power of the natural environment to shape social relations and to counter the rootlessness of industrial life, such writers as Benton MacKaye and Aldo Leopold argued that a proper respect for the land restrained the ruthless drive for mastery which destroyed resources, despoiled the landscape, and exploited human beings. Numerous essays gloried in the power of the deserts, plains, forests, mountains, and rivers to awe observers and to affect the way men and women constructed their lives. Even Theodore Dreiser, who took pride in his rejection of the sentimental, pointed to the soil and light of Indiana as the determining factors of the quality of life in the state. Other essays, including Charles H. Chapman's (Oregon) and Easley S. Jones's (Colorado), complained bitterly of the sale of beauty to tourist and extractive industries.

The series most evokes a sense of place in its detailing of the human environment of customs, beliefs, and practices. At their best, the essays convey in a sentence or a phrase the elusive sense of how it felt to live in a specific locale. Edmund Wilson's condemnation of New Jersey's suburban life, for instance, takes on new force with his observation that the state is a place "where people

---

[2]Villard was a founding member of the National Association for the Advancement of Colored People, an active participant in the suffragist counterinaugural march in Washington in 1917, and a staunch opponent of U.S. intervention in World War I. A collection of feminist autobiographies that *The Nation* published in the late 1920s has appeared under the title *These Modern Women: Autobiographies from the Twenties* (1978).

do not live to develop a society of their own but where they merely pass or sojourn on their way to do something else.'' Ludwig Lewisohn's observation of the
grandeur of Charleston's homes and streets strengthens his lament for the passing of the civilized ways of the South Carolina aristocracy. And Anne Martin's
description of families ''stoically enduring life in little hot cabins in the heart
of a burning desert'' reinforces her thesis that the central factor of Nevada life is
the struggle for control of water, not the better-known triad of easy divorce,
prostitution, and gambling.

''These United States'' allows us a glimpse of a version of the past that we
rarely encounter. Not all its pages are populated with flappers and fundamentalists or reveal a nation in thrall to mass media or mass hysteria. Better written
and more nuanced than other contemporary explorations of national life, the series acquaints us with Americans who valued past practices for their ability to
confer a valuable sense of order and rootedness. The twenties portrayed in the
most perceptive of the essays does not take its tone from the covers of *Life* or the
sermons of Billy Sunday. Nor are all the voices that resound in ''These United
States'' those of the fabled ''lost generation'' of alienated intellectuals. Many
contributors demonstrate an attachment to the people they chronicle. This less
graphic, less familiar view of the decade bears out the editors' belief that viable
local allegiances slowed the numbing homogeneity of mass society.

The better-known aspects of the 1920s are certainly not ignored in ''These
United States.'' In Texas and Oklahoma the Klan rules through terror. Ohio displays an abundance of deadening materialism. Montanans and New Yorkers agitate to remove professors whose views are unconventional. Salesmen permeate
the entire fabric of Michigan, and Kansas is in the grip of prohibition. While
much of the series appeared before the twenties truly roared, George P. West
notes both the libertine morals of San Francisco's Bohemian colony and the
dreamland, make-believe quality of southern California, already home to an assortment of cults. Clara G. Stillman, Gruening's sister, concentrates on the land
boom and the vacation colonies in Florida, not yet a haven for retirees and Latin
American émigrés. The entire country feels the impact of the automobile; Dakotans and Nebraskans, for instance, seem to have at least one car per family.

One major contribution of the series is its disclosure of an enduring, if dam-
aged, political and social opposition unacknowledged in our conventional
images of the 1920s. The withering of the Progressive movement and the degeneration of the left into sects of true believers by 1920 is usually thought to
have made possible the Republican ascendancy that liberated business from governmental restrictions and promoted a vision of the good life as dependent on
ever-increasing consumption. By formulating a public policy that matched private desires, the conventional interpretation holds, politicians catered to the
public's rejection of the politics of economic justice and reform and furthered
one centered on mores. ''These United States,'' however, indicates that a dissenting political culture dedicated to restraining the harmful effects of uncontrolled accumulation of capital had a continued presence in the early 1920s.

Clearly in decline, this political culture nonetheless had strength enough to define the agenda in a handful of states and to keep alive the hopes of some of the contributors. The left-wing sympathies of *The Nation* in the immediate postwar years lead us to expect radical analyses, but the depth of the documentation suggests that the survival of a left-wing current cannot be dismissed simply as wishful thinking or ideological distortion.

For many Americans who lived in the 1920s, Washington State meant Seattle, and Seattle meant the infamous general strike. Along with the steel and Boston police strikes, the Seattle action was part of the 1919 strike wave that helped fuel the notorious Red Scare. Most Americans considered the strike an aberration, and this view seemed to be corroborated when quiet returned to the state. Robert Whitaker, in "Washington: The Dawn of a Tomorrow," disagrees. The strike, Whitaker argues, was neither the creation of ideologues and outside agitators nor a fluke. It resulted instead both from the oppressive working conditions in the orchards and on the docks and from workers' realization that only by acting collectively could they exercise their fair claim to the natural wealth of the land. Rejecting a revolutionary optimism that imagines a truly heroic radicalized working class on the verge of another attempt to seize power, Whitaker does insist, however, that the defeat shattered only its organization, not the dream of using the land for creative labor or the conditions that made that dream so appealing.

Whitaker's portrait of labor solidarity complements Robert George Paterson's picture of agrarian radicalism in North Dakota. There Nonpartisan rule revived the old Populist notions of community control of the conditions of exchange and the use of wealth for social ends. Terming the Nonpartisan revolt "one of the century's outstanding political events," Paterson traces the influence of the Nonpartisan League on the entire fabric of the state. Attracting reformers from as far away as New Zealand, Nonpartisanism altered North Dakota's educational and legal systems and thrust its government into a new role as chief financier. Paterson laments some of the League's antidemocratic enthusiasms but cannot imagine the state as tranquil ever again.

The general strike and Nonpartisanism were fresh memories in the early 1920s; southern Populism was not. Yet W. E. B. Du Bois, in his elegant and insightful "Georgia: The Invisible Empire State," detects its lingering presence in the home state of the revitalized Ku Klux Klan. Only the fear among the state's ruling classes that the black-white alliance that Populism augured would raise wage levels for both races, Du Bois argues, can account for the manipulation of racism that marked Georgia life. "The central thing is not race hatred in Georgia," Du Bois observes, "it is the successful industry and commercial investment in race hatred for the purpose of profit." As long as even the faint possibility of a union of the dispossessed existed, racism will be found in Georgia. Although many of the white founders of Georgia Populism abandoned its goals as unworkable, Du Bois concludes that its prospects are not completely moribund. As he views the shacks of white tenant farmers from a train window,

Du Bois writes, "somehow it seems to me that here in the Jim Crow car and there in the mountain cabin lies the future of Georgia—in the intelligence and union of these laborers, white and black, on this soil wet with their blood and tears. They hate and despise each other today. They lynch and murder body and soul. They are separated by the width of a world. And yet—and yet, stranger things have happened under the sun than understanding between those who are born blind."

Few of the writers in the series had Du Bois's ability to perceive radical potential. Radicalism, after all, has always been a minority persuasion. Progressivism, on the other hand, had until World War I claimed the allegiance of the majority of Americans. As late as 1912 all three major presidential candidates presented themselves as authentic Progressives. Corporate disenchantment with the wartime management of the economy and the general postwar disillusionment with the possibilities of reform, augmented by the Republicans' reliance on corporate trade associations rather than government agencies to achieve the Progressive movement's goal of rational organization of the economy, weakened national Progressivism. On the state level, however, Progressivism did not wilt so quickly. According to Zona Gale, Wisconsin, where even conservatives styled themselves "moderate Progressives," should be placed at the head of the column of holdouts. She pays tribute to the continuing significance of the "Wisconsin idea" that government and the university should jointly put knowledge to social and democratic uses. The backlash from fiscal conservatives eager to restrain the cost of Progressive programs in the state did not repeal any important legislation or prevent the passage of a landmark equal-rights law that attempted to preserve special protections for women workers while guaranteeing them equal access to positions from which they had been barred by hours limitations.

The "gratifying divergence" is most apparent in those states where the authors stress cultural rather than political resistance to the commercial logic of the New Prosperity. The distinctive character of such states rested on their citizens' commitment to traditions and institutions that were at odds with the dominant temper of the decade. Valuing the subtle rewards of producing for oneself and for one's community rather than the thrill of purchasing the latest fashionable goods and stressing concern for the lot of others over the quest for personal liberation, the traditions of these states placed a premium on the maintenance of community solidarity and fostered attachments to the particularities of place which did not lead to a narrow parochialism. Despite the inroads made by national media and industry, these ways of life flourished (or at least persevered) because residents felt that they owed part of their basic identities to the special nature of their states.

In an era known for the celebration of consumption, Dorothy Canfield Fisher's frank defense of Vermont's poverty in "Vermont: Our Rich Little Poor State" strikes a discordant note. Untouched by large-scale investment, her state was the land of what was formerly called the "competency," the condition in which each independent citizen held a moderate share of the available resources.

An economy organized around the competency stressed balance rather than growth. "There is so little money to make in Vermont," she writes, "that few people are absorbed in making it. . . . It is very rare when anybody in Vermont fails to secure a fair amount of shelter and clothing and food and education; and it is equally rare when anybody secures very much more than that. There are, so to speak, no accumulated possessions." Maintaining this equilibrium was the basis of classical republicanism, and not surprisingly, Fisher finds much evidence for the virtues honored in civic humanist thought of the seventeenth and eighteenth centuries. Vermont tradition rescued Vermonters from two central anxieties of the modern world: fear of poverty and worry over social standing.

Murray E. King's "Utah: Apocalypse of the Desert" highlights a religion-based communalism, which King both condemns and appreciates. Long regarded in liberal circles as the cult that ran a state, the Utah Mormons faced intense national scrutiny and persecution during much of the nineteenth century. Their polygamy, the common ownership of most forms of productive property, and their belief in the truth of the Book of Mormon ran against the dominant liberal and evangelical currents of the nineteenth century. King, a lapsed or "jack" Mormon, details the church's control of the state, its antiliberal insistence that religion not complement daily life but govern it, and its opposition to labor unions—all qualities that have never been popular with *The Nation*'s readers. King's account is not Mormon bashing, however. Explaining the justification for polygamy, he emphatically denies the common fantasy that it was equivalent to promiscuity. Nor does he countenance the notion that a belief in miracles makes the average Mormon a disoriented soul. The typical Utah resident he asserts, is a "practical, common-sense, shrewd, fairly human and neighborly individual interested in a great many worldly, materialistic, and modern things."

Mormonism also commands a cooperative community, which, though regimented, provides roots, connections, and purpose. "There is little isolated rural living in Utah. The man who cultivates the soil is the main pillar of a highly structured town life, a life that is indeed tinged with communism. Many towns have cooperative stores, creameries, cheese factories, and canneries. The irrigation system is owned and administered cooperatively. Milch cows and work horses graze placidly on a common pasture. The church has a communal provision against indigence. Part of the 'tithing,' Relief Society, and fast-day 'offerings' is used to provide for those who are unable to provide for themselves."

Gentile influences and modern organizations, King predicts, will soon spell the end of old Utah. As Mormons ignore those religious doctrines that do not square with the material and intellectual environment, he notes bittersweetly, the state will resemble the rest of the nation. However shaky the future of Mormon communalism, many of the authors who write on surrounding Western states admire its accomplishments. Anne Martin, the Nevada historian and National Women's Party member who twice ran for the Senate as an independent, had no reason to admire the church's stand on gender issues, yet she praises its ability to manage large land and water holdings for the public good. Easley Jones recognizes that Utah, unlike Colorado, is not easy prey for opportunistic companies that want to commercialize its natural resources. New Mexican communalism, Elizabeth Shepley Sergeant observes, results not from mimicking Utah's but from the state's mix of three ancient cultures.

In recalling the cosmopolitan and multilingual Nebraska of her youth, Willa Cather demonstrates pluralism in practice. "The early population of Nebraska was largely transatlantic. The county in which I grew up, in the south-central part of the State, was typical. On Sunday we could drive to a Norwegian church and listen to a sermon in that language, or to a Danish or a Swedish church. We could go to the French Catholic settlement in the next county and hear a sermon in French, or into the Bohemian township and hear one in Czech, or we could go to church with the German Lutherans. There were, of course, American congregations also. . . . I have walked about the streets of Wilber, the county seat of Saline County, for a whole day without hearing a word of English spoken."

Accompanying this cosmopolitanism is a pioneer spirit that values the hard work of subduing the wild lands to make them habitable. Hostile to Populism, which she treats as a political movement of slackers, Cather champions a temper that takes pride in accomplishments achieved by one's own efforts. Modern Nebraska pleases her less. Its obsessive "Americanism" mandates the teaching of a single language, and its materialism has replaced the pioneer spirit with a mean-spirited utilitarianism. Modern Nebraska values the results of prosperity, not the effort to achieve it. In contrast to most contemporary analysts, Cather treats economic modernity as provincial because its driven consumerism limits experience, and the frontier ethic of community and work as truly liberating because it enriches experience. She consequently regards old Nebraska as more tolerant and cosmopolitan than modern Nebraska. Aware of the attractions of appeals for liberation from restraints, Cather, like Fisher and Robert Herrick (Maine), touts those restraints as the antidote to the false promise that it is easy to live happily.

Since it seems to explain our current mores and to provide a ready-made set of heroes and villains, the image of the 1920s as the Jazz Age is likely to persist, whether one celebrates the ethos of liberated personal expression or decries the fall from traditional values. Yet, as "These United States" indicates, the conventional interpretation ignores much that is significant about the decade. Not all struggles were between a narrow parochialism and a sophisticated urbanity; some were between a constricted modernity and local attachments that provided sources for personal and social development. A decade animated by such contests does not fit easily into neat categories or conform to our vivid images of the twenties.

Just as vivid as the Scopes trial or prohibition in our conception of the twenties is the alienation of intellectuals. Dominated by tales of the "lost generation," our notion of twenties literary life emphasizes those who rejected America as provincial, aesthetically shallow, and repressive. Convinced that they were a class apart, the prominent writers of the day sought refuge on the Left Bank and in Greenwich Village or renounced exact representation for a modernism of internal states and self-reference. Even those who did not choose exile shared the detachment of those who fled. Many intellectuals seemed to specialize in savage portraits of the United States during the twenties. Two of Sinclair Lewis's titles, *Main Street* (1920) and *Babbitt* (1922), entered the American vernacular as terms of derision for the Middle West and its culture. It may be counted as another of the virtues of "These United States" that it also reveals authors reaffirming and redefining their connections with the American people.

The degree to which writers felt estranged from the rest of American society in the 1920s was indeed unprecedented. Never before had alienation seemed an essential, rather than accidental or tragic, condition of literary men and women. Early in the nation's history, many Americans had seen literary accomplishment and political leadership as complementary. The founders had assumed that because the writer was the articulator of social values, mastery of polite letters was a precondition of political rule. Even during the nineteenth century, when political leadership and literary accomplishment were no longer so firmly linked, such American romantics as Nathaniel Hawthorne, Ralph Waldo Emerson, Henry David Thoreau, and Herman Melville envisioned literature as serving society by upholding the life of the mind against crass commercialism and cold calculation. It was the duty of the writer to portray alternatives to current social and cultural conditions. Speaking to and for Americans, romantics, however much they quarreled with America, never abandoned it.

As romanticism waned in the years after the Civil War, a new conception of the literary vocation took hold. Most established writers regarded the ideal author as a genial member of the middle class who defended the best that had been thought and written against interlopers. For all their grousing about the poor taste of the American people and the commercialism of the book trade, few late-nineteenth-century authors repudiated American culture or society. Some saluted the contributions of capitalist-inspired economic growth to civilization and even found it refreshing to mix with businessmen in private men's clubs. Beneath the surface affability, however, some more perceptive writers discerned the dilemma of the free-floating intellectual in the late nineteenth century. In "The Man of Letters as a Man of Business" (1893), William Dean Howells argued that because writing was a form of work, the author ought to be allied with others who produced things of value. Unfortunately, Howells lamented, most literary men and women thought the people too pedestrian to be the source of fine art or an audience for it. For their part, the common people saw the mark of luxury in a fine novel and, since they toiled so ceaselessly, admired only books that promised amusement and relief from drudgery. The upper classes bought and read books, but their support provided authors with no true satisfaction. Writers, Howells concluded, were suspended between the classes, at home nowhere in the world.

This state of suspension was not the radical estrangement of the 1920s. Howells neither courted rejection nor imagined authors as separated from the rest of
American life. With their economic and social victories of the early twentieth
century, however, businessmen no longer felt a need to justify their position by
values other than their own. Increasingly they scorned literature as impractical,
except as it supplied needed relaxation to recharge tired minds for yet another
round of commercial struggles. Simultaneously, many authors ceased to share
Howells's perspective. Refashioning their sense of craft, they carved out a new
understanding of both the purpose of art and their relationship with the American public. Whereas most nineteenth-century writers had regarded art as a pure
reflection of nature, twentieth-century modernists saw literary work as a social
invention. Drawing upon new conceptions of time and psychology, modernists
rejected the dominant realism as stale, uncreative, and naive. Whereas authors
had formerly prided themselves on their social responsibility, the new generation paraded its awareness that art was about nothing so much as the act of artistic creation itself. The deliberate subjectivity and experiments in form made
the new literature less accessible, and the literary rebels of the early twentieth
century began to court those whom they regarded as the appreciative few rather
than the unenlightened many. The outrage that greeted the Armory Show
(1913), Theodore Dreiser's *The "Genius"* (1915), and James Branch Cabell's
Jurgen (1919) only seemed to confirm modernists' sense that true art was beyond the reach of the masses.

What simmered before the war boiled over after it. Although some writers
were loath to adopt the rhetoric of alienation, others took it with enthusiasm.
"These United States" includes many essays of estrangement. H. L. Mencken's
"Maryland: The Apex of Normalcy" is a virtual primer on the complaints of the
literary intelligentsia. Maryland suffers from complacency and the relentless desire to shape nature to industrial ends. "In brief, Maryland bulges with normalcy. . . . It is safe, fat, and unconcerned." Life, as a consequence, is "dull"
and "depressing," and "steadily grows worse." All of the original character of
the place has vanished. "Regimentation in morals, in political theory, in every
department of thought has brought with it a stiffening, almost a deadening in
manners, so that the old goatishness of the free democrat . . . has got itself exchanged for a timorous reserve, a curious psychical flabbiness, an almost complete incapacity for innocent joy." Mencken's culprit is the industrial system,
which "shifted the center of gravity from the great estates to the rushing, pushing, dirty, and, after awhile, turbulent and hoggish town of Baltimore, and so,
bit by bit, the old social organization fell to pieces, and the very landscape itself
began to lose its old beauty."

The terms in which Mencken phrases his criticism of the corrosive effects of
industrialism indicate the new attitude toward business among the new breed of
critical writers. Unlike the nineteenth-century critics of capitalism who emphasized its oppression, twentieth-century critics stressed the repressive nature of
the economic system. In the new critique, capitalism had an inherent tendency

to stress work over play, to harness both outer and inner nature, and to suppress what it could not regiment. Business in the 1920s stood opposed more than ever to the aesthetic values that many members of the intelligentsia championed. The cultural strain by which this repression spread was denominated as Puritanism. Twenties intellectuals little understood actual colonial New England practices and beliefs; for them the term designated attitudes of extreme prudishness and rejection of beauty in favor of utility. Summarized in Mencken's remark that the Puritan lived in fear that someone somewhere was having fun, the concept melded economic and cultural currents into a single creed, which was regarded as the central vice of American life.

The popularity of the "Puritan" analysis is evident throughout "These United States." William Allen White does not hide his distaste. It was Puritanism that enabled Kansans to create a commonwealth in which regulations both eliminated injustice and destroyed diversity. "What we lack most keenly," White writes in a passage typical of the aesthetic critique of the 1920s, "is a sense of beauty and the love of it. Nothing is more gorgeous in color and form than a Kansas sunset; yet it is hidden from us." It is a form of Puritanism as well that motivates Leonard Lanson Cline's Michigander salesmen. The Detroit Art Museum secured its collection of paintings only by arguing that "pictures increase in value and are most profitable investments." It is not the scenery that attracts Sunday drivers, but the driving itself. "On his Sabbath outings [the salesman] drives fast, taking the same straight, flat roads week after week, the roads everybody else takes. When he gets home he squints at the speedometer to see if he has had a good time; how many miles has he traveled?" And it was the Puritanism of transplanted Midwesterners in southern California that had "wiped out a Homeric society of Latins and Indians and replaced it with a Gopher Prairie de luxe."[3]

Although the South could not reasonably be labeled "Puritan," it too was an obstacle to the achievement of the civilization that many of the intelligentsia sought. The literary portrait of the region stressed its collection of grotesques, demagogical politicians, fundamentalists, and antievolutionists, as befitted Mencken's designation of it as "the Sahara of the Bozart." The home of lynching and disease, cursed by a colonial economy, the South was the United States's backwater, thoroughly resistant to the flexibility that writers admired. So deeply embedded was this attitude of southern crudity that some of the essays in "These United States" make the southern states seem virtually indistinguishable. Had place names not been provided, one might not be able to tell Arkansas from Tennessee or either from Kentucky. The brunt of Ben Lucien Burman's article is that life is cheap in Kentucky and killing the norm, as if the

[3]George West, author of the California article and himself of New England stock, was at least willing to acknowledge that criticism of Puritanism was "the literary habit of the hour." He notes that in southern California, "where the orthodox American genius has proved itself not merely acquisitive, but creative as well," Puritanism coexists with what he calls a "vast assortment of odds and ends of humanity."

St. Valentine's Day massacre had taken place in Lexington and Leopold and Loeb were privileged sons of Louisville. C. L. Edson's Arkansas is a proletarian paradise, but not one that would warm the heart of a radical. Having no opposition from the better elements, Arkansas rednecks, in Edson's view, run riot. The counterparts of Arkansas rednecks in James M. Cain's West Virginia are miners, whose battles are not so much signs of labor solidarity as proof of a deeply ingrained, irrational desire for vengeance.

Condemnation of the South did not lead to sympathy for African Americans. For all the white intelligentsia's fascination in the 1920s with the Harlem Renaissance, blacks are rarely mentioned (no article on the North notes the Great Migration, a demographical fact of some consequence), and when they do appear, most writers treat them as inert objects. Beulah Amidon Ratliff breezily blames Mississippi's blacks for the failure of Reconstruction. Their "childish ignorance and egotism . . . made their disgraceful contribution to the misery of the situation." Noting the frequent whippings that black field hands still receive, she qualifies this observation with another. "The life of the Mississippi plantation Negro is toil, ignorance, hopelessness, animal stupidity, and bestiality. He is a filthy, stolid, unloved and unloving creature, as far from the 'merry, singing hoehand' of fiction as is the dirty, diseased reservation Indian from Cooper's 'noble redman.' " City blacks do engage her sympathy, but she implies that their "civilized" behavior results from their proximity to whites. Clement Wood's sensationalism, revealed in his offensive assertation that a black woman who "accepts" a white lover "obeys the deep biological law that woman chooses a master superior to herself," mars his recognition that the fear of miscegenation haunts white Alabamans. White hypocrisy, not black suffering, dominates his essay.

A land permeated by Puritanism and southern backwardness held little appeal for many of the literary intelligentsia. Rejecting any connection to a people prone to emotional outbursts, enslaved by ancient habits, and fearful of experimentation and creative thought, literary rebels took pride in an alienation that freed them to criticize at will. This stance departed from past critical positions of the left and right, both of which also identified with and defended some portion of the life of the masses. Left-wing critics had recognized that the workers or the people could be misled and act in destructive, unprogressive ways. They had not, however, assumed that this condition was either permanent or natural. Leftists from Eugene Debs to Daniel De Leon to Tom Watson took it for granted that some form of popular power would be the foundation of national reconstruction. However undemocratic their means or inaccurate their assessments, American leftists based their criticism of American life on their identification with the political and economic interests of the American people. Right-wing critics, on the other hand, detested popular rule as unworkable anarchy but championed the prevailing mores against industrial transformation and the revolution of social relations. Suspicious of equality, which they dismissed as a vain hope, American rightists nonetheless had no doubt of the value of popular religion, family life, and community morality. Critics as diverse as George Fitzhugh and Orestes Brownson found much to admire and support in the masses' embrace of particularisms and traditions.

The literary rebels of the 1920s rejected both the left's defense of democratic rule and the right's advocacy of popular customs as threats to independent critical thought. Neither left-wing political action nor right-wing defense of community promised to advance either artistic expression or the position of the intellectual. This posture was not without its consolations. In a time of retreat, a self-chosen alienation made a virtue of necessity. In place of a politics of struggle, with its inevitable defeats and setbacks, many members of the literary intelligentsia engaged in a politics of self-validation. This attitude is widespread among the essayists of "These United States." By dismissing American life as retrograde and treating it solely as an object of derision, such contributors as Burman, Cain, Cline, Edson, Mencken, and White could reassure both themselves and knowing readers of their sophistication and separation from the herd.[4]

Not all the contributors indulge in the sarcasm of alienation. Refusal to belittle, although not to refrain from criticism, is evident in the essays of the upholders of the left-liberal faith; in those of such writers as King, Fisher, Herrick, and Du Bois, who respect and at times admire the struggles of the American people; and in less obvious quarters as well. Although George West loves San Francisco for its striking types, constant variation, and tolerance, he regards its lack of a Puritan heritage as a drawback. Without it there is little passion and iron, only seduction. "It might be instructive to our legions of young people who indolently blame Puritanism for everything banal to come and live for a time with these anti-Puritans of the Golden Gate. They would find the Good-Fellow tradition as stifling in its way as the Puritan, and harder to escape."

The essays of the famous writers with reputations for being at odds with the country are among the most startling to readers expecting the predictable and stereotypical. The contributions of Sinclair Lewis, Sherwood Anderson, and Theodore Dreiser belie the usual perceptions of their work. None of the three produced an uncritical report, and the acerbic wit for which each is known is in evidence. These are not Chamber of Commerce pamphlets. Yet all three are a bit nostalgic about places they acknowledge they continue to carry with them. Each of these essays is, in effect, an attempt to understand that mysterious connection.

For a writer credited with virtually inventing the Middle West as a metaphor for rigid conformity, Lewis shows a surprising appreciation for Minnesota's virtues. Protesting his reputation as a literary rebel and nay-sayer, Lewis stakes out a position as a radical Tory, or, as he puts it, "a yearner after . . . ivied cottages." In light of his later proclamations, one might well take this assertion to

---

[4]Why did Mencken stay in the United States if he found it so dreadful? "Why does a man go to the zoo?"

be a literary pose, but his essay has the ring of authenticity. Irritated that his state is considered featureless and homogeneous, Lewis sets out to refute accumulated misconceptions. Minnesota is not entirely flat and it does produce something other than wheat. Fortunately, in his view, its population includes more than Yankees and Swedes. Although he lauds the ethnic diversity, he has special praise for the Swedes. Contrary to popular belief, they are not "helots and somehow ludicrous and tribal." Swedes have long populated the most progressive organizations in Minnesota. They have been the leaders in the women's suffrage movement, in labor unions and cooperative societies. These achievements, however, have not come without a price. Forced to counter the prejudice of the Yankee middle class, "Swedes 'Americanize' too quickly," forfeiting the best of their traditions.

There are few Gopher Prairies in Lewis's Minnesota. Written while he was at work on *Babbitt*, "Minnesota: The Norse State" details a fascinating mix of admirable souls. The diversity of the state is in marked contrast to the dullness he often portrayed in his fiction. He praises the former professor of history who "cheerfully grows potatoes in a backwoods farm among the northern Minnesota pines and builds up cooperative selling for all the farmers of his district," the kindergarten teacher who "does something of the work of a Montessori, with none of the trumpeting and anguish," and the Chippewa mechanic who "actually understands ignition," an accomplishment that anyone who has visited an auto mechanic can appreciate.

Even the businessmen of Minnesota are spared ridicule, receiving instead measured praise. "There is one merit not of Minnesota alone but of all the Middle West which must be considered. The rulers of our new land may to the eye seem altogether like the rulers of the East—of New England, New York, Pennsylvania. Both groups are chiefly reverent toward banking, sound Republicanism, the playing of golf and bridge, and the possession of large motors. But whereas the Easterner is content with these symbols and smugly desires nothing else, the Westerner, however golfocentric he may be, is not altogether satisfied; and raucously though he may snortle at his wife's 'fool suffrage ideas' and 'all this highbrow junk the lecture-hounds spring on you,' yet secretly, wistfully he desires a beauty that he does not understand."

Sherwood Anderson does not seem to share Lewis's admiration for the hidden spirit of the Midwestern businessman. Indeed, he deliberately sets out to reveal that nothing approximating a soul resides in the businessmen's breast. Writing in the voice of a booster, Anderson portrays an Ohio whose bourgeoisie relentlessly denies all that is beautiful in its never-ending quest to convert all of nature into a commodity. "We Ohioans tackled the job and we put the kibosh on that poet tribe for keeps. If you don't believe it, go down and look at our city of Cincinnati now. We have done something against great odds down there. First we had to lick the poet out of our own hearts and then we had to lick nature herself, but we did it. Today our river front in Cincinnati is as mean-looking a place as the lake front in Chicago or Cleveland." This attitude has created a modern inferno. "Have you a city that smells worse than Akron, that is a worse junk heap of ugliness than Youngstown, that is more smugly self-satisfied than Cleveland, or that has missed as unbelievably great an opportunity to be one of the lovely cities of the world as has the city of Cincinnati?"

The callousness and obtuseness of tone are deceiving. Beneath the broad satire and the damning criticism, Anderson draws a more sympathetic and deeper portrait. The narrative voice, both of Ohio and beyond it, reveals a Midwesterner more self-aware and self-critical than was common in the typical portraits of Middle Border self-satisfaction. What Anderson sensed was that Ohioans were less mean-spirited than tragic, so set on mastering the visible world that they had lost another, the inner world. Anderson's beginning, "I have always thought of myself as an Ohioan and no doubt shall always remain, inside myself, an Ohioan," suggests that his own acknowledged dreaminess is meant to signify a truth about the state as well.

Theodore Dreiser, too, shows fondness for his native state. Unsparing in his criticism of those features of Indiana for which he feels little sympathy, he duly notes its traditions of trusts and union-busting, "its social devotion to dogmatic religion, . . . its rather pharisaical restfulness in its assumed enlightenment and knowledge of what is true and important to the world at large, its political somnolence as suggested by its profound and unchanging devotion to the two ancient and utterly platitudinous parties." Yet Dreiser cannot let the matter rest there. "But perhaps," he remarks, "this is not the type of thing that should be registered of Indiana. Despite a long and happy intimacy with it, it is entirely possible that I have not even suggested or have entirely missed its truer spiritual significance, as we are wont to say of so much that is but deeply human."

Much of the essay is devoted to identifying this "truer spiritual significance." Noting the state's atmosphere of earnestness and sincerity, what he terms "a kind of wistfulness that is the natural accompaniment of the dreams of unsophistication," he explains his attraction to his native state by its ability to combine contrasting qualities into a complex whole. He sees the particular combination of soil and light in the state as providing the impetus for such a melding. The essence of Indiana is its embodiment of human nature, "a manifestation of forces which unavoidably assume opposite phases, which same we label good or evil, but which really are found to be supplementing each other in any manifestation which can be labeled life."

Recovering the historical importance of the essays requires understanding the context in which they were written. That context encompasses not only the events and conditions of the 1920s but also the intellectual tradition of national criticism. Indeed, the editors hoped that "These United States" would make a "valuable contribution to the new literature of national self-analysis." From the colonial period onward, the American tradition has depended upon a unique conception of the national essence. Although debates over national essence have often assumed the United States to be a "white man's country," American thinkers have rarely located the core of the nation either in a presumed common ethnic or racial heritage or in an ancient historical act of founding. Analysts in most other national traditions have taken for granted the existence of such sources, no matter how invented or contested. Even in such countries as France and Russia, the internecine warfare of revolution has not destroyed the role that prerevolutionary elements play in constituting national identity.

American writers and thinkers, by contrast, have long located the roots of national identity in the national acceptance of uniquely American principles and beliefs. Few countries have the equivalent of the infamous House Un-American Activities Committee, which had the power to deprive the holder of supposedly subversive creeds of national status. Other nations treat dissidents as dangerous or even dupes, but not as beyond the national compass. Despite declarations to the contrary, the truth of American creeds has not been self-evident. Much of American history has revolved around disputes over the meaning of the founding documents. Because the ideas at the center of American life have been sources of contention, both the national analysis that has tried to ascertain them and the national unity that they were to guarantee have shown signs of strain. The evanescent quality of American ideals has virtually ordained that the analysis of the national condition would be incessant.

The United States has certainly had no monopoly on national fragility, but even challenges to its national unity differ from those in other traditions. Separatist and autonomy movements such as those in Eastern Europe, Ethiopia, Scotland, and Wales have based their claims to nationhood on traditional historical or ethnic grounds, contending that the previous definitions of the nation suppressed their historical and ethnic particularity and promulgated a spurious unity. Other movements have challenged the basis of national unity on the grounds that the inherent irreconcilability of interests in a class system makes union specious. This position has had little effect on the U.S. tradition, since the generally accepted view is that class in the United States is an individual, not a social, characteristic and is in any event easily changed.

National self-analysis has invariably entailed a view of the meaning and purpose of national history. Two of the earliest forms of historical narrative, both of which predate the actual establishment of the United States, have been among the most compelling in the American tradition. In the epic of the New World, both the North American continent and the United States figure as sites of unlimited possibilities for the construction of a new form of humanity and a new set of social arrangements. For a significant number of European writers and thinkers, what made the New World new was not simply its recent discovery (itself clearly a European conceit) but also its potential to liberate men and women from the restrictions of the past. Americans quickly refined the myth Europeans originated. The presumption that Americans could make history as they pleased has sunk deep into the dialogue on the national condition. Americans have never denied the presence of flaws or problems, but those for whom the New World myth is a description of reality rather than a literary device have viewed these shortcomings as minor and temporary setbacks. Evidence to the contrary has not prevented Americans from envisioning life in the United States as beyond intractable conflicts, full of the promise of unlimited upward mobility, embodying a destiny of progressive expansion, and free from institutional limitations.

The cheerful optimism of the New World tradition has coexisted with the pessimism of the jeremiad. The Puritan sermon of inevitable decline accused the present generation of abandoning the pure intentions of the founders for the lure of material gain and self-indulgence. On first hearing, the jeremiad detailed national failure. Since the world as it appeared to the senses had to be interpreted for what it revealed about inner grace, the jeremiad countered the New World strain's tendency to judge the national condition by material measures. In its recognition of the sinful nature of human beings, it functioned as a brake on uninhibited optimism and complacency. Where the New World tradition hinted at the transcendence of history, the jeremiad spoke of the inescapability of pain and limits. Yet those who issued such calls did not simply judge the nation to be irredeemable. Jeremiads were intended to spur listeners to greater efforts at holiness, an intention embodied in William Dean Howells's famous remark that given the prevalence of social injustice, he was angry at the United States because it would not let him love it more. Without the presumption that some reform was possible, the jeremiad had no purpose.

The "new literature of national self-analysis" of the 1920s contained elements of both the jeremiad and the New World epic.[5] Alternating between a belief in the unlimited possibilities of the nation and a sober recognition of the constraints that history had placed on the country, the new cultural criticism focused on deeply held patterns of thought and their social consequences. Rejecting as cold the tendency of late-nineteenth-century inquiries to use systematic observation to construct rigid laws of social and personal behavior, early-twentieth-century critics drew on the romanticism of Emerson, Thoreau, and Walt Whitman and developments in other disciplines (especially the emphasis of the English geographer Patrick Geddes and the American anthropologist Franz Boas on culture as a totality of relations and practices). Nurtured in the "little magazines" of the 1910s and exemplified by Van Wyck Brooks's *America's Coming-of-Age* (1915) and Randolph Bourne's "Trans-National America" (1916), the new form combined literary experimentation with an urge to map more than the empirically verifiable. Since it emphasized a state of mind rather than historical origins, it resonated well with the tendency to regard America as an idea as much as an entity. Quarreling with their country for its failure to live up to its best principles and for its adoption of less felicitous ones, the new

---

[5]Not all 1920s analyses of the national condition regarded the essence of the United States as a set of principles or told its history in the terms of the New World epic or the jeremiad. Vernon Louis Parrington's *Main Currents in American Thought,* for instance, envisioned American history as a struggle between two dialectically opposed camps over issues of power. Parrington did favor what he christened the "Jeffersonian" democratic strain, whose ascendancy he associated with a form of progress. There was nothing inevitable, however, about the result.

cultural critics simultaneously embraced ethnic pluralism, spiritual wholeness, and the possibilities for personal growth.

The 1920s were an auspicious time for a new form of national examination. Signs of the century-old consolidation of a relatively unified national culture from a coalition of local ones were increasingly apparent after World War I. The spread of such mass media as radio and movies and the success of new mass-consumption industries in supplanting local production led to complaints (and, for that matter, approval) of the growing standardization of American life. The decline of local production had made the local practices and relations that had sustained it less viable. Under such circumstances, the distinctiveness of place seemed less salient.

In the forty years before 1920, national consensus had been especially fragile. Despite the much-ballyhooed success of the post–Civil War industrialization, the economy had performed erratically. Prone to crisis, it had faltered in the middle of each decade between 1880 and 1910. This performance fostered a series of challenges aimed not only at redistribution of the social product but at the conditions of production itself. Both Populists and workers had mounted serious attacks on the industrial order. Their efforts had not deterred the accumulation of capital or prevented the rise of the corporation, but they had made both exceedingly difficult. Nor were all problems of national stability and purpose found in the economy. A resurgent feminist movement both demanded the vote and proposed a revamping of the arrangements of home and gender, widely regarded as the underpinning for all other social relationships. Immigration restriction, the defeats of labor, and the suppression of the left during World War I and its immediate aftermath exhausted much of the opposition to corporate power and opened the way for the construction of a new basis of social unity.

In the years leading up to the 1920s, a significant number of writers and thinkers had advanced the ability to consume freely as the essence of American life. Shunting aside as settled such questions as who should own property, the defenders of material abundance stressed the unique contribution it made to democratic life. By enabling a self-governing people to make choices as consumers, the mass culture of consumer goods both realized the promise of American life and made moot those differences that had long threatened the American social fabric. The Boston retailer Edward Filene and the advertising executive Bruce Barton, whose *Man Nobody Knows* (1925) presented Christ as the world's greatest salesman, justified the social order not on the nineteenth-century grounds that existing arrangements embodied the natural rights of individuals to use their property as they pleased but on the grounds that they ensured an equal right to purchase from an ever-increasing basket of goods. Although contemporary studies suggested that the national wealth was maldistributed, such slogans as the famous "chicken in every pot" ratified the belief that the American dream of unlimited wealth was the democratic basis of the new American order.

Although increasingly prevalent, defenses of consumerism were still relatively novel and provoked unease at and resistance to the sweeping reorientation they proposed. Given the unsettled nature of American goals, it is not surprising that analyses of the national condition proliferated in the 1920s. Perhaps the best known is *Civilization in the United States* (1922). Edited by Harold Stearns, an aspiring cultural critic fresh from Harvard, the volume consisted of thirty-three essays that together constituted an encyclopedic examination of the culture. Deliberately designed as a position paper on American life, *Civilization* has earned a reputation as the definitive critical statement of the period. Because the essays found little of value in the United States and Stearns settled in Europe immediately after the book's publication, one frequent verdict was that it would have been more accurately titled *The Absence of Civilization in the United States*.

The conclusion is perhaps overdrawn, but not fundamentally incorrect. Page after page detailed a shallow community life, the absence of democracy, the lack of fit between techniques and ideals, a culture that failed to engage the best minds, and a business-dominated civilization that sanctioned acquisitive materialism. Although in his introduction he denied a muckraking intent, Stearns drew three major indictments. First, the ideals and practices of the culture did not coincide, producing not a general feeling of hypocrisy but a fear of being found out. To this sure sign of decadence Stearns added the widespread delusion that the nation was predominantly Anglo-Saxon. Since Stearns used "Anglo-Saxon" as a term of derision, a synonym for dull, predictable, stodgy, limited, and repressed, the pretense of cultural uniformity by his lights had disastrous consequences for valuable diversity. Finally, Stearns saw social life as "emotional and aesthetic starvation, of which the mania for petty regulation, the driving, regimenting, and drilling, the secret society and its grotesque regalia, the firm grasp on the unessentials of material organization of our pleasures and gaieties are all eloquent stigmata. We have no heritages or traditions to which to cling except those that have already withered in our hands and turned to dust. One can feel the whole industrial and economic situation as so maladjusted to the primary and simple needs of men and women that the futility of a rationalistic attack on these infantilisms of compensations becomes obvious."

Although Stearns called for "an entirely new deal of the cards in one sense," he and his contributors offered no political solutions and could not envision any. In the essay on political life, H. L. Mencken concluded that politics was a simple scramble for election which at best produced mediocrity. Drawing on his idiosyncratic reading of Friedrich Nietzsche, Mencken propounded his notion that the fundamental ill of modern society was the restrictions that the masses place on men of truly extraordinary ability. Conspicuously absent from the volume was any extended discussion of labor organizations, farmer revolts, or community associations, an absence that reverberated with the contributors' sense that the enlightened individual could redeem civilization. Even the organization of business and work were only lightly analyzed. George Soule's chapter on radicalism alone made an effort to detect what organized group could possibly reverse the dreadful decline of American civilization, and it dwelt primarily on the psychological and programmatic confusion of radicals.

Stearns advised Americans to acknowledge "our spiritual poverty," and he hoped that the nation would grow up through "the self-conscious and deliberately critical examination of ourselves, without sentimentality and without fear." These critical functions happened to coincide with the collective self-image that *Civilization*'s editors and contributors had assigned to themselves. The less than enthusiastic response from the general public to this critique only reconfirmed their sense of the justice of their analysis and the hopeless condition of the culture.

Civilization did create a stir in intellectual circles. The editors of *The Nation* deemed the book so important that they devoted a six-page symposium to it in the issue of 22 February 1922. The mixed reception that *Civilization* received from the magazine's editors revealed differences that reappear in "These United States." Some found much to admire in the book, singling out its diagnosis of the spiritual malaise that resulted from the combination of technocratic expertise and the vacuum of ideals and its call for revitalization through the intellect. Carl Van Doren's opening piece commended the impulse to penetrate Americans' self-congratulatory mists. Freda Kirchwey, who in the course of her career served as the magazine's managing editor, literary editor, editor, and ultimately publisher, hailed those articles that condemned the nation's anti-intellectualism, although she dissented from Stearn's peculiar characterization of that condition as the result of "feminization." Other editors, however, has reservations. Villard scorned Mencken's treatment of politics as immature. Norman Thomas labeled the work "a rebel's Chautauqua hand book," claiming that the authors were "employing in the name of revolt—polite revolt and not at all violent—the intellectual short cuts of your typical American in search of culture."

Gruening's belief that the indictment in *Civilization* was too sweeping and failed to locate alternatives to the current malaise prompted the appearance of "These United States" two months later. Organizing the series was not easy. The success of the series depended on his ability to locate suitable authors. Many states had no assigned author when the series began appearing. Some choices had been obvious: White for Kansas, Mencken for Maryland, Dreiser for Indiana, Cather for Nebraska. Other states were not intimately associated with well-known authors, and Gruening and his fellow editors were forced to call upon journalists who had only the briefest familiarity with the states about which they wrote. Other contributors were relatively unknown men and women who had never before written for a national publication. These problems forced Gruening to accept work he regarded as deficient. The Kentucky article, for instance, prompted an interoffice protest from Villard. Gruening's response suggests some of the immense difficulties that he encountered in putting the series together. A number of authors whom Gruening thought more suitable were unavailable or were not offered the opportunity to write the essay. The article had been sent back for revision. "How that article managed to get in when there were five or six perfectly good articles in type from last fall, how it was rushed in way ahead of schedule, how it could get by you and everybody else when they knew that you wanted to see it is certainly a mystery to me.''

Popular among the magazine's readers and critics (Bruce Bliven of *The New Republic,* then friendly rival of *The Nation,* lauded the series as a landmark in national criticism), the series was published as a book in two volumes (1923 and 1925) by Boni and Liveright, in part to provide new funds for the financially ailing journal. The financial returns proved less magnificent that expected. The intellectual returns, however, were quite substantial. Much as the editors had hoped, "These United States" helped define the terms of a national debate about the condition of the republic. In the years that followed its publication, geographical-cultural examinations were a prominent form of national self-analysis. *The New Republic* initiated a series of essays on American cities, *The American Mercury* combined cities and states, A. Philip Randolph's *Messenger* addressed a conspicuous absence in *The Nation's* series with "These 'Colored' United States" (1925), and journalists contributed their own versions, including Irvin S. Cobb's *Some United States* (1926) and Robert Littell's *Read America First* (1926). None had the literary grace or intellectual range of the original. In sociology and social thought, the related concept of regionalism gained new prominence. In 1923 Lewis Mumford, a contributor to *The Nation,* and others created the loosely organized Regional Planning Association of America, which was dedicated to linking social arrangements to the specificities of place. In 1929, Howard Odum set up shop at the University of North Carolina, where he sponsored studies that stressed the regional determinants of social behavior. The discipline of history weighed in with Frederick Jackson Turner's *Sections in American History* (1932), a collection of essays written primarily in the 1920s which extended his famous "Significance of the Frontier" (1893) by arguing that sectionalism and regionalism were the keys to the meaning of the American past.[6] In the 1930s the Federal Writers' Project published the better-known and more inclusive WPA guides with a rationale similar to that of "These United States.''

Although the essays were not intended as prophesies or predictions, they almost inevitably invite a judgment on the persistence of state distinctiveness. Conclusions on the matter depend upon personal experience, and experience, of

---

[6]The conceptual underpinnings of "These United States" and those of 1920s regionalism differed in one major respect. Although the regionalists rejected national homogeneity, they did not account for the power of and loyalty to states. Odum's regions paid little heed to state boundaries. Turner treated the section as a congregation of states with like interests, denying entirely the notion of state loyalty. Judging state loyalty by the saliency of states' rights, Turner argued that "state sovereignty . . . has in fact never been a vital issue except when a whole section stood behind the challenging state. This is what gave the protest reality." Because of the size of the United States, Americans have looked upon their country through "sectional spectacles. We think sectionally and do not fully understand each other." This danger prompted Turner to separate good sectionalism from bad. Loyalty to place was admirable, but not when it caused people to mistake the nation as a whole for their section writ large and to discredit opposing views and interests.

course, varies from reader to reader. My own youth in St. Louis (and not Missouri, as we shall see), graduate education in Virginia, and teaching positions in New York City and Maine suggest that at least some of the atmosphere that each of these places summoned up in the 1920s still remains. Exercising the prerogatives of the editor, I here offer a highly selective and subjective judgment of how well the sense of place that the Virginia, New York City, and Maine articles evoke has persevered in the face of nearly three-quarters of a century's worth of historical changes.

One could hardly find three places in the United States more diverse than Virginia, New York City, and Maine. Their political economies, cultural resources, and mores bear little resemblance to one another. Each has a distinctive character that has long been part of the national discourse on cultural differences. To say that Virginians venerate the traditions and manners of the past, New Yorkers live in a permanent impersonal hustle, and Mainers are stolid borders on cliché; exceptions to these commonplaces are easily found. Yet something of these qualities contributes to the special flavor of each place. These characterizations are not necessarily at the crux of what constitutes Virginia, New York City, and Maine, but residents (or more precisely a portion of the residents) have internalized the qualities as a distinctive part of state or local identity. If the test of the character of a place is the response to a request for directions, the conventional appraisals have some validity. New Yorkers do seem to take a special pride in their rudeness, Mainers in their terseness, and Virginians in leading you directly to where you want to go. The challenge for Douglas Freeman, Ernest Gruening, and Robert Herrick was to breathe a measure of specificity into these mundane observations.

Freeman's essay has much of the southern progressive in it. Although "name and blood" did not dominate Virginia life as they had once done, Freeman was concerned about the ways in which veneration of the past still distorted Virginia life. Virginia high society could not command with the unchallenged authority of antebellum days, but it could still require potential entrants to pay homage to its past. Deferential to money, however made, the remnants of the landed gentry created a culture that had its skeletons (disenfranchisement) and its obsessions (the famed "Lost Cause" of the Civil War). Freeman was convinced, however, that the passing of those who remembered the war and a dynamic educational system would destroy the grip of nostalgia. He was also aware of how those memories of a triumphant aristocracy contributed to the unique quality of Virginia social life—the renowned politeness of its citizenry. "Whether a mountaineer on the side of a wretched little clearing or the inheritor of a great name chatting over his first editions, the average Virginian displays an inherited thoughtfulness for the sensibilities of another. He dislikes to say unpleasant things or to touch a sore spot, and his is equally anxious not to have his own bruises handled or his own feelings hurt."

Nearly seventy years have passed since Freeman wrote. Neither he nor anyone else could possibly have envisioned the rambunctious growth of the Washington suburbs or the impact of the civil rights revolution. In many situations, the famed manners of the gentry still prevail in towns and on farms, and for much the same reasons that Freeman offered. Northerners often suspect such exaggerated politeness and are made uneasy by the deference to tradition, but beneath the manners lies Virginian reserved more often that Virginian hypocrisy.[7] Contrary to Freeman's liberal hope that education would dissolve the fixation on the past, however, the University of Virginia often seems committed to preserving in its entirety its heritage as a training ground for gentlemen. The insistence that the campus be called the "grounds" and professors "Mr." (and now "Ms."—a break with tradition that the university had to be forced to make) because that was how Mr. Jefferson referred to them distinguishes UVA as one of the few universities in which the practices of the past so thoroughly frame present-day campus debates. Even in the turbulent 1970s, antagonists on both sides of issues ranging from expulsion of the ROTC to the number of credit hours that should constitute a major began and ended their arguments with what Mr. Jefferson said on the subject or what could reasonably be inferred that he might have said had he lived.

If Virginia had its eyes fixed only on the past, New York in Gruening's rendition rushed only to the future. Gruening's New York is a machine for living, the embodiment of the principle of modernity. In New York, ceaseless motion, constricted space, and the destruction of nature have reached their greatest intensity. "Here civilization is creating its own code and manners, its language variations, new ways of life, new diseases, a new human species. New forms of beauty, too. These canyons, these pinnacles and spires, these airy wire-hung bridges over which multitudes thunder daily, this skyline—these million lights, blinking massed and scattered through the city's vast night—these achieve a poignant beauty of line and atmosphere which stirs the emotions deeply and has in it something almost spiritual."

Gruening is not the only writer to have looked at the city from the Staten Island ferry or the Empire State Building and wondered in reverence and horror what humankind has wrought. Nor is he the only writer to have registered the city's impersonality or to note that many of its residents feel so unconnected to its *real* life, a life so immense that one can never grasp it whole. Three sentences make the point: "New York has no monuments for her dead. She alone survives. Neither has she thrones for her living." Gruening's New York, however, is midtown Manhattan. It is the famous grid plan that attracts his interest as the source of regimentation, an argument that Lewis Mumford made earlier in the year in his essay on American cities in *Civilization in the United States*. Gruening does mention the diverse neighborhoods of New York, but asserts that the hodge-

---

[7]Not all Virginia politeness is free of hypocrisy. State legislators refused a Martin Luther King state holiday on the grounds that King was not a native son—a reasonable position, but no one thought a Nat Turner holiday would be in order. As a compromise, some offered a proposal of dubious historical merit: to put the King holiday on the day the state set aside to commemorate Robert E. Lee and Stonewall Jackson.

podge allows none to stand for New York itself and permits no combination to give the city any unity. "Long before the city achieved its metropolitan bulk . . . it appeared careless of its localism, indifferent to its civic entity. It was as if the city had been aware somehow of a national, a cosmic role, which made local concerns, local pride mere provincialism." This contention is the literary equivalent of the sign that greets travelers coming over the George Washington Bridge from New Jersey. One arrow points south and says "Downtown"; the other points north and says "Upstate." Those who live in the Bronx may be forgiven if they think something is wrong here.

Whereas the experience of New York City is constant motion and constricted space, that of Maine, in the words of Robert Herrick, is "not so much reactionary as stationary." Little changes in Maine, except its two seasons: winter and road repair, as the joke goes. As late as the 1920s, wresting sustenance from nature was still its residents' fundamental experience of life. Herrick saw virtues in the struggle but emphasized the tenuous quality of the effort. For all the lists of Maine's natural resources of land and sea, the product is not easily taken or made. The Maine that tourists do not see, post–Labor Day Maine, is often harsh. Its winters create an often desolate and uninviting beauty. Maine differs from the other New England states in significant ways. Considerably poorer, largely unsettled (over 50 percent of Maine land consists of unorganized territories owned by lumber companies, outside the jurisdiction of any local government), and having a lower population density than neighboring states even in the settled areas along the coast, Maine has a frontier quality that the rest of New England does not possess. What was true in the twenties is true today: "The backwoods, the wilderness and the frontier, also a stern ocean, have never been far from man's consciousness in this easterly province." Herrick's description of the typical Maine farmhouse encapsulates the quality of Maine life. It is "a strong plain affair, too steep in the roof (to stand heavy snowfalls), too heavy and angular, perched on big granite blocks, connected by a long shed with an even larger barn, equally homely. Even in the older inland towns size and substantiality count for much more than grace of line and proportion. Timber is cheap, winters long and rude, and the Maine man is not given to adornment, to prettiness."

Herrick intimates that there is regionalism within Maine but makes little of it. Although "Down East," a term taken from the direction of the ocean currents, is applied to the entire state, many residents of the two easternmost counties, Washington and Hancock, stake their claim to exclusive possession of it. One can hear Kennebunkport and other vacation spots somewhat contemptuously referred to as Northern Massachusetts. These differences aside, the historical isolation of the state has forged a common identity. Such is not the case of the relationship between St. Louis and Missouri. Many in the city barely acknowledge that they are part of the state. Few governors hail from the city, and until reapportionment, the rest of the state dominated the legislature. I do not recall a St. Louis television station that had a full-time correspondent in Jefferson City to cover news of the state government. Contrary to the reports of the 1985 World Series, St. Louisians by and large did not acknowledge an intrastate rivalry with Kansas City. Their eyes have long been directed eastward. Or as Manley O. Hudson summarizes the matter, "Even the postal clerks know it as St. Louis, U.S.A."

Today such differences seem to be remnants of another time. The pervasiveness and homogeneity of our national media, the uncanny resemblance of nearly all our airports to shopping malls, and the nearly identical characters of our white, middle-class suburbs make it hard to imagine the hopes that the editors of *The Nation* placed in "gratifying divergence" to combat the consolidation of American culture in the aftermath of World War I. Except for ceremonial occasions and travel advertisements, geographical differences are today not usually considered of much consequence. Current discussions of diversity concentrate on race and gender, two minor emphases of "These United States," despite the contributions of the noted feminists Austin, Gale, and Martin. Yet the men and women who wrote and compiled the series were not entirely naive in their understanding that one of the most important aspects of the idea of the United States is that we have never accepted "universal sameness" without resistance. Read today, "These United States" reacquaints us with a time when this distinctive part of our national heritage seemed able to stem our loss of distinction and open up a different form of national reconstruction.

Divided We Stand

THE EDITORS

APRIL 19, 1922

IT IS SAID in the Purple Book of Nommag that one of the more pedantic of the archangels argued in Heaven to something of this effect: The Civil War in America, said he, was fought over a point of grammar, and that point was whether the Americans should say "the United States are," as used to be the practice, or "the United States is," as is now almost universally the mode. The process was the same, this grammatical archangel insisted, as that which went on between the time when New York said "the Fifth Avenue," still conscious of the article, and the time when "Fifth" had become not a numeral but a name and had declared and achieved its independence of all and any articles forever. Look, urged the archangel, to the instinctive grammar of a nation for the true evidences of its unity. Foreigners may say "the United States are," in their various languages, and here and there some purist at home may do the same archaic thing; but the overwhelming bulk of those whose testimony is most valuable say "is" and thus reveal their sense that the welding is finished, the fusion complete.

> Were you looking to be held together by the lawyers?
> Or by an agreement on a paper? or by arms?
> —Nay—nor the world, nor any living thing, will so cohere,

chanted Whitman at the end of the war. Indeed, the lawyers with their agreements on paper have done nearly as much to hold the States disunited as to unite them. Consider the differing statutes as to incorporation, insurance, divorce, and a hundred matters which hinder the nation's unity; consider the blood and sweat which the Interstate Commerce Commission has had to shed. But these are the technical and the trivial aspects of union, hardly to be weighed in the same balance against that increase of similarity which in spiritual and intellectual affairs has standardized the land. The United States "is" said to be now one vast and almost uniform republic. What riches of variety remain among its

27

federated commonwealths? What distinctive colors of life among its many sections and climates and altitudes? How far does it justify that other line of Whitman:

> Always the free range and diversity; always the
> continent of Democracy?

In search of an answer to these troubling questions *The Nation* has asked a group of keen observers to set down, each of them, the impression which he or she has of some given State—defining, describing, acclaiming, arraigning, analyzing, creating an image out of fragments, whatever the particular case demands. These observers will speak for themselves, one by one; but *The Nation* would like to preface the series with a statement of its hope regarding the union of These United States which has prompted the investigation. That hope is that whatever is artificial in the distinctions drawn between State and State may, in keeping with the current process, be assimilated, but that there may be the least possible surrender of the essential differences which soil and weather, social habit and ethnic stock, experience and ambition have raised up among the varying regions of the country. Though centralization and regimentation may be a great convenience to administrators, they are death to variety and experiment and, consequently, in the end to growth. Better have the States a little rowdy and bumptious, a little restless under the central yoke, than given over to the tameness of a universal similarity:

> A party in a parlor, all silent and all damned.

ALABAMA

A Study in Ultra-Violet

CLEMENT WOOD

JANUARY 10, 1923

THE SPANIARDS marched raggedly into Alabama before 1540, and then blundered on. The French fortified Twenty-seven Mile Bluff on the Mobile River in 1702, and in that neighborhood they have stayed. English traders of Carolina bored into the valley of the Alabama River in 1687, and radiated and settled throughout the four-square richness of the State. They found almost infinite variety: Florence perched upon its palisaded bluegrass plateau, Dothan drowsing in the sluggish shadows of palmettoes, Livingston crowning the fertile western muck of the Black Belt, Opelika baked in the sandy eastern lowland. There were no igloos and icebergs, no grand canyons, no fire-breathing Popocatepetls; but there were hill and valley, river and gulf coast, chill uplands, baked midlands, lush tropical lowlands: a land superbly endowed to be an abiding-place for the soul of man. These English traders dragged over the Blue Ridge with their wagons, floated in flatboats down the Tennessee to Muscle Shoals, and pushed on packhorses to the bottom of the State; they overflowed along Gaines's Trace and the Natchez Trace in the North, and the "Three Chopped Way" in the South. Not only traders came: planters pushed behind them, with their household goods and Negro chattels. In 1820 the Negroes were nearly a third of the total population; in 1870, they constituted 47 per cent; in 1910, 42½ per cent. Negroes compose more than 75 per cent of the population of the eleven counties in the Black Belt; "free and unterrified white Anglo-Saxon Democrats" constitute the remaining quarter. In ten of the upper mountain counties there are practically no Negroes. It was these counties that gave birth, in 1860, to the stillborn proposal to form a neutral State to be called Nickajack. They went with the South in the end; and the problems arising from the commingling of colors are theirs, as well as Alabama's, and the South's, and the nation's.

Alabama is the center of the sisterhood of Southern States: Montgomery was therefore the first capital of the Confederacy. Topographically these are the most fertile States in the Union; if we are still to judge a tree by its fruit, mentally, spiritually, they are the most sterile. What is true of Alabama is largely true of

Georgia and Mississippi, of Tennessee, the Carolinas, Florida, northern Louisiana, and Arkansas. It is perhaps more true of Alabama than of any of these.
Hers is a static sterility; observing the stubborn medievalism that possesses her
merely, one may well credit a surviving saurian in Patagonia. For years there
was one Darwinian—in Alabama argot, "atheist"—on the faculty of the State
University; the fact, in spite of the professor's popularity, was a whispered scandal. Darwin to many Alabamians is Lenin and Landru in one, assuming that they
have heard of either or both. The State is saturated with a provincialism that
prefers the *Demopolis Gazette* to the New York *World,* and the Capitol at Montgomery to Notre Dame. This may be due to shrewd common sense; as a hoe is
worth more to a field hand than a Stradivarius could be. It is a land where G. K.
Chesterton's ideas would be considered advanced; none but an Alabama radical
considers advancing them.

   Alabama has the largest production of pig iron among the States, and the third
highest percentage of illiteracy. She is fourth among the States in the production
of cotton, and one of the heartiest encouragers of child labor. Apologists for the
State point to the drain of the Civil War and the anguish of Reconstruction: both
of these were by-products of the vaster blight of slavery, whose price the State
is still paying. Her story is the story of Romulus and Uncle Remus, the white
man and his darker brother. In the old story, the autocratic city-builder slew his
brother; this facile ending was only in the fable. Alabama is still looking for the
answer to the questions: What will she do with him; and what will he do with
her? There are other problems as definitely hers as this one; but, since it is the
most important and the least understood, the others must be ignored, with mere
acknowledgment of their existence.

   An after-growth of slavery—that is Alabama today. And slavery, as Helper's
Impending Crisis decisively established, is the most costly form of industrial organization yet devised. "If slavery continues," a Southern Representative admitted in Congress, "they will soon be advertising for runaway masters, instead
of runaway slaves." "Free" Negro labor has not served the State better; although free Negro labor might. How many throughout the Union know—how
many Alabamians guess—that the average value per acre of farm land in Alabama dropped from $11.86 in 1860 to $8.67 in 1900? A more recent figure
might show again an upward trend; but the decline was the product of the forty
years' wandering in the wilderness of black emancipation.

   The Negro question permeates every phase of Southern thinking. It wakes
with the Southern white, walks with him, keeps him from sleep; it is never absent from the Southern black. It drugs Alabama's educational system. How
can it be otherwise, when a typical Black Belt county spends $17.35 on each
white pupil, and ninety cents on each colored pupil? It determines Alabama's
economic thinking. The per capita wealth of the Southern white is $885; that of
the Negro, $34, or one-twenty-fifth as much. It splits the labor movement. Shall
Negroes be admitted to unions, and how; and if not, what about strike time?
Long before the country voted to go dry it saddled prohibition on Alabama and

the South in the attempt to divorce the Negro from the intoxication of gin. It retarded woman suffrage. "Would you want your wife and daughters to be forced to jostle Negro washwomen, and worse, at the polls?" This, by the way, was typical American political logic; since Negro men are as prominent at the polls as Eskimo pies in Hades. It may retard any general exodus from Alabama to Heaven, at least until the unsullied Anglo-Saxons are assured that the Negro there will know his place. And, speaking of the unsullied Anglo-Saxons, the catch phrase applied by rural Southern statesmen to their white audiences, the mind directly recalls that the Negro problem affects the sex life of the whole South. White women shiver at its feline menace; white men arm and klan against it, even while its siren voice hums a constant invitation; many Negro women smile with satisfaction at it, many more shrink from it; Negro men watch it, sometimes reach an arm over the wall for its forbidden fruit, and sometimes burn for it.

"What is the solution to the Negro question?"

"There's only one: amalgamation." The man who said this to me was then an Alabama Congressman, conservative, non-alarmist, who still stands high in State and nation. "But, above everything, don't quote me! My political life wouldn't be worth that, if you did. . . . You see," he continued, "it's going on now. . . . All the time. It always has. Read your statistics on the increase of mulattoes. It's a pity that it's the lowest elements of both races that unite; but . . . it's going on."

How far was this Congressman right? A few scattered facts may materialize the problem. A Democratic candidate for governor was speaking at a rally in Montgomery, some twenty years ago. He finished his set speech; an excited man rose in the rear of the hall, shaking a lean, accusing finger at the orator. "What about your family of black bastards, Governor?" The distinguished Alabamian came forward to the challenge, and pointed an index finger straight at his questioner. "I've raised 'em, and educated 'em, and made decent, law-abiding citizens of 'em; and that's a damn sight more than you've done for your black bastards!" There was wild applause at this; the interrupter was thrown out. The story spread from end to end of the State; the candidate was elected. Spoken like a true white Southerner; for the ethics of old-time Southern chivalry included this treatment of the black race. In what other section of the Union could a man have been elected to public office, after such a confession?

In slavery, a state of concubinage between the master and comely slaves was permitted. The master was owner of the bodies of his slaves; can not a man do what he will with his own? There are those who state that certain strong-minded white mistresses played the same game, as a fitting payment to their catholic spouses. Certain leading white men had two families, the white and the near-white. There was a State Senator who was half-brother to a Negro door-tender at the Capitol—a Negro so light that visitors mistook him for the white brother. In slavery, it was to a large extent the better class of each race which intermingled. For years, in both races, the drift has been away from this. In many circles

The skyline of Birmingham, Alabama. Contrary to the beliefs of many Progressives, the industrial growth of the "Pittsburgh of the South" did not eradicate the racially proscriptive codes of the region.

the white man who has a colored mistress thereby has lost caste; the better class of Negroes no longer admit to the circle of their peers the Negress who is a white man's by-wife.

And yet, the mixing continues. There are still the double families, in scattered locations. There is still the occasional case where the white woman accepts a Negro lover. Among white boys of all classes there is much of this denial of the color line. This is less in the cities, and more in the country: for the cities offer white prostitutes, and in the rural districts loose white women are scarcer, or more difficult of approach, than Negro girls. The condition at the State University is not untypical. It is located in a small town, Tuscaloosa, with few slack white women; and the Negresses are "easy." More than a dozen of the writer's classmates and intimates at this institution have explained to him that their first direct sexual experience had come with one of the willing Negro girls; the prevalence of the relationship there was a byword.

When it comes to Southern white men of the better families, it must be remembered that in slavery many men openly cohabited with Negro mistresses; now as a rule only the boys of college age do this and in many places a strong movement has grown up against it. The practice has shrunk from an accepted custom to a wild oat. But the mixing is not confined to boys today. There are certain white men, usually not from the better classes, who live exclusively with Negro mistresses, or who maintain families in both races. It is told on good authority that in one town the long-suffering white wives met in indignation, and delivered the ultimatum to their husbands that they must choose between their white wives and their black mistresses. The husbands refused to leave the mistresses.

The white woman occupies a peculiar position, in thus sharing her man, not with an equal, but with one who in her eyes is little removed from the animal. How does she react to the situation? For one thing, she denies that it exists; just as the white man, until he becomes confidential, denies it. The generation of the white mother of yesterday and the day before—I speak of the so-called higher-class women especially—was so saturated with that forthright denial of life and its truths that we call Victorianism that she did not know of the dual racial experiences of her menfolk; that she would not hear of them, and can say little concerning them. Such a woman led a life sheltered and remote, even as compared to the Northern white woman of the same period; she kept to her bedroom, her kitchen, her parlor, and had no eyes and no ears for what happened in the servants' quarters. But the men knew; and the Negroes knew.

It was—it is—a life of strange inconsistencies, of eerie contradictions. There is the stream of unsullied Anglo-Saxon blood; there is the casual byword that no Negress has virtue. There is the denial that the races intermingle to any extent, with laws and klans to extirpate the odd case; there is the fetish that loose morals among Negro women protect the purity of white girls. Everybody knows that it is, and that it isn't. It is like life in the fourth dimension, which the mathematicians tell us touches our familiar three dimensions at all points, and yet is wholly intangible. It is in this impossible and omnipresent world that the Southern whites and Negroes dwell. Perhaps it would be apter to say that they inhabit a world illumined by the light rays beyond the violet of the spectrum—rays invisible to the eye, but more active and, wrongly used, more maleficent than the visible. These are the rays of powerful chemical action; they share qualities with the dynamic Roentgen or X-rays, which penetrate through the garb of flesh to the bone beneath. They are rays that cure—or kill. It is in this infra-twilight world, never seen, yet always just at hand, just beyond the corner of the vision of the eye, that the races meet and mingle. It is no shrinking violet of a world: it is a land of gusty and pernicious forces, driving furtively to their perverted, unrecognized matings.

We have spoken of that postulate of Southern white thinking, that a Negro woman has no virtue. The Southern white man today knows only the lowest type of Negress—the type largely in the majority. More than two hundred thousand Negro women work in Alabama; almost as many workers as the Negro men. Seventy-one per cent of these are field hands, and 26 per cent domestic servants. The white man comes in contact with these, and generalizes his denial of virtue to the race from them. But there is a growing class of cultured Negro women, sheltered from the Southern white, of whom this is increasingly incorrect. The truth lies at some distance from the casual byword. The low-class Negro woman attaches less value to her chastity; and in accepting a white lover, she obeys the deep biological law that woman chooses a mate superior to herself. This slackness is not confined to the Southern Negro girl; there is much of it among white mill girls, perhaps the largest low white class in Alabama.

Worst of all, from the standpoint of the white man's welfare, there is, in the South, apparently no acceptance of responsibility in such a relationship, on the part of the man. The Negro girl, it is said, has no legal recourse. The law in certain States recognizes no such thing as a bastardy proceeding of a Negress against a white man. The very intimacy is outlawed; no rights may spring from it. It is no wonder that the Negro girl is easy game; there is no closed season against hunting her. It is easy for the white man to accept the relationship; he assumes no risk. Illegitimacy is always an anomalous relationship; but elsewhere there is a recognized stigma on the father. This abnormal freedom from responsibility is true only of the South. As long as it continues, we may except this furtive tasting of the flesh-pots of Ethiopia.

The case of the cultured Negro woman is rather apart from the others. She is sheltered from all Southern white men, as far as may be; yet her problems come too. The wife of a Negro doctor, quite well-to-do, confided to a friend: "I would never dare tell my husband or brothers half of the things white men say to me. Whenever I enter a store, the clerks make insinuations or outright proposals. . . . '' No comely girl of this class escapes solicitations from white men. One Negro father sent his daughter North to Columbia University to separate her from the attentions of a white admirer. The man followed her to New York. Such a woman, in the main, is sheltered; she is never safe. Advances come to her; there is little law to which she can appeal, if a white man invades her home. It is at the risk of his own blood that her husband dare even lay hands on a white man to protect her. Grandfathers have been lynched for protesting against mistreatment of their young colored granddaughters. The situation of the Negro husband, father, or brother, under these not infrequent occurrences, is a hideous dilemma: dishonor or death are the proffered choices. And there is always the threat of the black hour of a race riot, started by some isolated breath of white lust.

What is the status of the breathing product of these alliances between the races? Is he white, or black, or both, or neither? He is really both; but man itches to checker-board the universe, and pigeon-hole everything as this, or that—never half this and half that. It hardly irks him that what he calls the laws of nature are against him; let the legislature pass a law that it is day until 5:59 P.M., and night the next second; and all will be well. Is there any problem our American Solons cannot and have not solved? The legislature of Texas has decreed how long sheets must be, the Assembly of Maryland has fixed by ukase the length of women's skirts, the Houses in Pennsylvania have banned a cinema kiss beyond thirty feet or so, and prohibit a scene showing a mother sewing on baby clothes, before the baby is born: the element of surprise in life must be maintained, at any cost! By a majority of one, the Kentucky Legislature recently decided that Darwin was right, and that man evolved from the animal. A million years' slow incubation of the wonder of life could have been changed by a switch in the vote of the tobacco-chewing gentleman from Alfalfa County. It is interesting to see what the law says of the children of the dusk. Edwards's *West Indies* declared that in the Spanish and French West Indies there was no degradation of color beyond the quadroon. In Virginia, before 1860, a colored person was one who had a fourth or more of Negro blood; in Carolina, an eighth or more. The Louisiana law was stricter; no amount of white blood could emancipate the offspring of a slave. A Louisiana war legislature considered a bill to legalize marriages between white and black, and rejected it; later her law defined the white man living with a Negro woman as a vagrant. The law in many Southern States defines as a Negro one who has one-eighth or more of African blood; but the census enumerators since 1790 have followed the popular conception which classes as Negro all persons known or believed to have any admixture of African blood. All such persons are subject to the discrimination of Jim Crow cars, Jim Crow restaurants, Jim Crow theater balconies, and to a social standing that means ostracism in its kindest hour.

If this were all—this crazy-quilt of racial intermingling—it might not be worth while to put it down on paper. But this is not the half. The great misfortune is not that there are mulatto children in Alabama; it is that Alabama, the State itself, is the offspring of two races, united so furtively and blunderingly that she is immeasurably the loser by her joint parentage. The mental and spiritual sterility of the land has been catalogued with devastating impertinence by H. L. Mencken, and stated by others. Two-fifths of the population are stigmatized as inferior, and kept illiterate; their every effort at individual and racial progress is obstructed and bitterly contested. The races are in daily contact; and each is affected by the contact. The white imparts to the Negro something of his outlook on life and its problems—an outlook lifted and corrected by contact with the progressive thought of the world. The Negro imparts to the white his ignorant, superstitious attitude on the same questions—an influence that is not recognized, that may be scoffed at, but that takes root and grows to noxious height. Let us not have this or that benefit, lest the Negro share it. "Inasmuch as ye have done it to the least of these—" Alabama is both races. If she forgets this, the cost to herself will be desolating.

This cost she is paying: and it is not a small thing. What is the State's—or the South's—contribution to the absorbing world of science, that handmaiden of man in his progress from beasthood? What is the State's—or the South's— contribution to music, to drama, to sculpture, to painting, to literature? Where are the State's, and the South's, critical reviews, publishing houses? Some slight answer might be made to all these questions. But Alabama leads the States alphabetically; and it is time she awoke from her lotus doze, and accepted man's responsibilities, out of which grow man's achievements. It is easy to follow the old ruts, to keep alive old attitudes of hatred, prejudice, ill-treatment; it is hard to think, to weigh courses and adopt the stranger, fairer way: but this is the price of full living. That land does not prosper, half of whose citizens are kept from wisdom, and in economic, mental, and spiritual poverty. That land cannot speak her word, nor sing her song, when half is bound and half is free. But when has good counsel brought forth sweet fruit? Are there any teachers but the lash of experience and the red scorpion of time?

ARIZONA

The Land of the Joyous Adventure

MARY AUSTIN

APRIL 4, 1923

IT WOULD BE easier to treat of Arizona as a Dominion than as one of these United States. Not that there is any question about the swift and wholehearted allegiance of Arizona, but there are distinctions. Her territory is about equal in map miles to the combined areas of New York, New Jersey, Delaware, Pennsylvania, and Maryland, which means, taking the mountainous nature of the country into account, that there are about as many more miles standing straight in the air, lying at the bottom of deep canyons, or doubling in immeasurable folds of crumpled rock. To this dramatic variety of contour is added color and a play of light and atmospheric effect which for pure splendor and subtlety is not elsewhere matched. This superlative intention exhibited in the topography is reflected in the history of Arizona to an extent that makes it obligatory to add -est to every adjective that describes it. Not only is its Grand Canyon the grandest and its cotton staple the longest in the world, but it is the newest State and the seat of the oldest civilization within the territory of what is now the United States. In Arizona one finds the scale of amazing things running from petrified forests to common weeds that produce rubber in what promises to be commercial quantity.

First of all we hear of this country emerging from a cloud of legend in the report of one Cabeza de Vaca who had come first to Florida with Narvaez, was thence wind-driven in an open boat as far as the coast of Texas, and wandering, in the longest walk ever recorded by a European, heard of—and possibly touched—what is now Arizona, as a land of many-storied cities, true prototype of the modern American skyscraper, using gold as common metal, having door lintels crowned with turquoises. Later its wilderness was certainly traversed by Estevan, a Barbary Moor, slave of that Dorantes to whom were given the five emerald arrows, and by Fray Marcos de Niza, who confirmed the report and enlarged upon it in the manner of all subsequent visitors. Of all the joyous adventures undertaken there since Coronado's to find Seven Cities of Cibola, no report of failure, hunger, thirst, or torturing savages has dimmed the bright

appeal of Arizona's beauty and mystery. There can be no adequate discussion of
a country, any more than there can of a woman, that leaves out this inexplicable
effect produced by it on the people that consort there. It is an effect that primitive men seem to have responded to as readily as moderns, for a cut across the
human history of Arizona reveals almost as many stratifications as the banks of
the Grand Canyon. When the Mormons built their first irrigating ditch at Mesa,
they saved $20,000 by utilizing the gradients laid down by prehistoric peoples,
so ancient that the traditions of the present Indians have no reference to them,
and every spade that the archaeologist puts into the soil puts back the record of
the dust of another cycle.

It is the peculiarity of the human history of Arizona that its strata seem not to
show those interpenetrations of the diverse elements which, in other environ-
ments, make up the amalgam of State character. Indian tribes in Arizona are as
distinguishable from one another and from Indians elsewhere as Frenchmen
from Italians. The Spanish-speaking Arizonian is removed in type from the
Spanish-speaking New Mexican as the Scotch are from the English. And yet nowhere is the State type more definitely localized. Somehow the land has found
a way of imposing its free dramatic quality on the inhabitants, which gives them
a likeness to itself more evident than their likeness to one another.

It is reported that during the late unpleasantness in France an Arizona teamster, delivering ammunition to the firing line under cover of darkness, lost the
road and ran into a listening post from which he was frantically warned to turn
back and not to speak above a whisper while he was doing it. "Whisper, hell!"
said the Arizonian. "I got to turn four mules around!"

Something of this clear concentration on the task in hand and a magnificent
unawareness of any reason for not proceeding directly to its accomplishment
is the note of Arizona. It is always coming to the surface of the political and
social life of the people in ways inexplicable to communities in which the lack
of sharp structural lines in the environment has permitted the local character to
run into a somewhat flavorless plasticity. There is a story that when Arizona
applied for stateship, President Taft objected to certain items of the proposed
constitution. Did that worry Arizona? Not that you could notice. "Rip 'em
out," was the general verdict, "and as soon as the first legislature meets we can
put 'em in again." Which was done to the satisfaction of all parties. In much the
same spirit of adaptation of immediate issues to an ultimate good, woman suffrage and prohibition were put through far in advance of communities that
prided themselves on their sociological sophistication. Both woman suffrage
and prohibition contributed to place social control in the hands of the superior
racial groups, and neither the rancor of sex antagonism nor the moral fanati-
cisms which retarded these movements elsewhere played very much part in the
Arizona decisions. Something of the same values were expressed in Arizona's
election of a labor governor. Nothing could be more mistaken than the conclusion drawn by the political friends of organized labor, that Arizona was thereby

committed to its program, or viewed its objective with a self-same eye. Almost nothing, indeed, can be prophesied of Arizona on the same basis that makes prophecy possible in older communities. The most, and by no means inconsiderable, comfort that can be drawn out of such incidents is the assurance that nothing is going to be retarded in Arizona by the fear of newness.

The one thing that might retard the necessary free experimentation in economic adjustments natural to a unique natural situation would be the settled determination of the rest of the country to regard them as the fruit of policies and agitations to which they bear only passing resemblances. Like Kim, confronted with the soul-loosening vistas of the Himalayas, Arizona has "flung its soul after its eyes." Its economic horizon is as vast, as vague, as absolutely unterrifying as its landscape. It can afford to experiment in local devices, just as a man going from Flagstaff to Dokoslid can afford to take any promising detour without fear of missing the mountain. This quiet certainty of having all the room they need to turn their mules around in, rather than the persistence of any given party or policy, is the key to the political development of Arizona.

To understand how, without theatricality and with very little intellectual sophistication, such a common consciousness comes about among such dissimilar elements as make up the population of Arizona, we must turn again to the interactions of history and topography. Arizona is protected on the east and south by pure desertness, screening out of successive waves of invasion all but the types in whom the pull of adventure is stronger than most other considerations. The many-colored dragon of the Colorado Canyon, curving about the north and west, prevents the overflow eastward of the complacent and comparatively commonplace cultures of the Pacific coast. The Indian tribes incorporated within the State are most of them of superior type. With the exception of the diminishing Hopi, none of the Arizona tribes have been communistic to the degree that has made of the Rio Grande tribes an economically satisfied and socially inbred people, incapable of assimilation except by a slow and wasteful process of absorption into the Spanish-speaking population. In Arizona more individualistic cultures have made possible a more citizenly type of coordination, in which the Indians give promise of becoming, as an intelligent Navaho once put it to me, "a pulse in the side of the white race." They have contributed the largest quota of place names, their trails have become automobile roads, their ancient ruins are public monuments, their dances and festivals are occasions of general entertainment. All this must eventually be felt as a formative influence in the art and literature of the State. If the rule holds good here that, in Europe, produced the most outstanding cultures out of a successful intermingling of aboriginal and conquering peoples, we would be justified in expecting more of the Arizona of the future than of any other single State. But for the present the aboriginals live alongside the invading settlements with, except for the brief period of Apache wars, a remote but amiable toleration. The Navaho and Hopi together cut out a section of the northeast about the size of Connecticut. The Haulapai

Alfalfa harvesting in Arizona. Arizona's frontier individualism required considerable effort to adapt to the state's sometimes inhospitable environment.

and Havasupai are distributed along the Grand Canyon, the Apaches in the
White Mountains, the Pimas in the Gila Valley, the Papagoes and other remnants
along the most senseless bit of boundary in American history.

The political stupidity which deflected the southern boundary of Arizona
from its original intention of proceeding directly from Nogales to the Gulf, thus
giving us a deep-sea outlet, no doubt altered the whole course of political and
economic development in the Southwest and probably in Mexico also. Its chief
result has been to make of southern Arizona, which was naturally laid out to
produce an agrarian and mercantile culture comparable with that of ancient
Egypt or the valley of the Euphrates, a landlocked commercially introverted
community.

The interactions between Arizona and Mexico, checked by this illogical political interference with a natural, trade-provoking situation, have nevertheless
been a considerable item in the commercial prosperity of the southern towns.
During the Mexican revolution gold shipments to Tucson were not uncommon
and much of the Mexican Government's banking was carried on through the local banks. Settlement from Mexico never flourished within the territory of Arizona as it did in New Mexico. In the Rio Grande country, pioneer colonization
carried two distinct strains: scions of old Spanish aristocracy and peasant colonists who intermarried first with native Mexicans and later with local New
Mexican tribes. The result was an almost feudal social organization which persists in the economic and political life of New Mexico to this day. But in Arizona
settlement was much more a matter of individual adventure than of political en-

terprise. There are many more squatter's rights than royal grants among the early land titles. The Jesuits and Franciscans during the first hundred years of Spanish occupation both tried their hands at establishing missions among the Indians, which were somewhat feebly enforced by colonization. The remnant of Mexican population drawn to Arizona in their wake functions chiefly as a medium for ameliorating the social environment for reserves of labor drawn across the present border. Mexican labor properly handled is likely to prove a steadily appreciating factor in the development of southern Arizona. A Sonoran Yaqui will do twice as much work as a white laborer and show a steadier sense of responsibility toward his job.

The bulk of this Spanish-speaking population is centered around the Gila River and its tributaries. At Tucson the lovely mission of San Xavier del Bac preserves the best of Spain's contribution to the Southwest, a style of architecture so right in its relation to the conditions of church and home building that it has become part of the Southwest's contribution to America, and a tradition of an intimate and releasing art of life and decoration.

Impinging on the Spanish-speaking culture, often in direct conflict with it, came successive waves of adventurous overflow from the United States. As early as 1803, when the Louisiana purchase had made what was then known as Nueva Mexico contiguous territory, American trappers began to explore the lower spurs of the Rocky Mountains. Incidents bearing the names of Kit Carson, Lieutenant Beale, Zebulon Pike, Frémont, the Pattees, Captain Cooke leave a rich detritus of romance; filibustering episodes, Apache raids and counter-raids, lost mines and lucky strikes. Stuff of this nature, drawn out of the history of their own community, is excellent filling for the imaginations of the younger generation. Actually the new romantic period of Arizona, which lasted from about the beginning of the nineteenth century until the separation of the Territory of Arizona from New Mexico in 1863, has left fewer visible traces on the life of the State than the period of the old romance, which began with the exploration of Fray Marcos and Estevan the Moor in 1539, and lasted until the death of Maximilian. Mexican interest and influence dwindled rapidly during the years between the founding of the Mexican Republic and the Treaty of Guadalupe. American settlement had already begun when annexation took place. Development since the separation of the Territory of Arizona from that of New Mexico has been so rapid that, to all appearances, the pioneering period has been completely submerged by it.

Over all the social and commercial life in the larger communities of Arizona has been spread that shining surface competency made possible by rapid transit, the wide use of electrical appliances, popular magazines, and the possibilities of mail-order shopping. The uninquiring stranger might spend months in the cities of Arizona without discovering anything that distinguished them from other American cities except a faint Spanish flavor kept alive chiefly for the delectation of the tourist. I have addressed a teachers' institute in Tucson without finding it any less competent or any freer from conventional teaching limitations

than similar groups in Kansas or Pennsylvania. I have lectured to Arizona women's clubs on precisely the same subjects that make club programs elsewhere,
and with almost identical reactions. Arizona women are a trifle less familiar
with the "patter" of culture east of the Mississippi; they are also a little more
accessible to new points of view. But this is a distinction that can be made in
other Western States in direct ratio to the distance from New York.

The things that are peculiarly Arizona's are expressed in the quality of the
attack on the environment, rather than in the surface forms of culture. To many
people Buckey O'Neill and his Rough Riders are the quintessence of this Homeric Arizona strain, but even to get the full flavor of that, one must know such
nuances as that the redoubtable Buckey himself fainted at his first sight of a legal
execution, and that the massed church choirs and a chorus of normal-school
girls saw him off from the station to the Spanish War singing "God be with you
till we meet again."

Perhaps this native attack on the environment is best described in material less
Homeric and easily assembled out of the annals of trade in almost any small
Arizona city. The freight rate for Tucson, for instance, included at one time
charges to some point on the Pacific coast and back, as, in the days of Frank
Norris's *Octopus,* used to be the case with all points in California. But the Arizona merchant wasted no time in raising an Iliad of woe over his situation. He
shipped his goods in bond through to Guymas, or some point in Mexico which
has a water rate: shipped back to Nogales and hauled them the remaining seventy
miles in wagons.

All around Tucson and Phoenix and Prescott you will find the evidences of
true American normalcy, wide streets, beautiful homes, orange orchards, cotton
fields, crop rotation, automobiles and Rotary clubs, but, underlying them, strat-
egies and toils of the dimension just quoted, rooted in the rich stock of pioneering life of no more than a generation or two ago.

If you examine any list of names of those pioneers you will find English,
Scotch, and Virginia-Irish names—a great many Southerners drifted in that direction after 1864—and in any collection of pioneer likeness you will find one
type of physiognomy predominating, tall-bodied, broad-browed, wide between
the eyes, and in spite of the Viking mustachios and long curls which gentlemen
of that period generally favored, a look of almost childlike mildness. You will
find a good many faces of that type looking out at you from any group of University of Arizona students, with the far-fixed gaze of generations who have
"stretched their vision" over the great spaces of the arid West. They were hard
livers, those Arizona forebears, slow talkers, quick doers, chivalrous toward
women, and within their concept of justice and honesty, incorruptibly just and
honest. But it will be another generation or two before the stock comes to flower.

This Arizona which I have described, with its agreeable and promising mixture of modern American "pep," pioneering fiber, and Spanish-Mexican flavor,
is concentrated almost wholly in the river valleys south of the Rim, the cutting
edge of the Mogollon Mesa, running slantwise of the State between the Hualapai

and Fort Apache Indian reservations. Northward the character of the land changes to vast stretches of sage-brush and bunch-grass country, sparsely dotted with cedar and piñon, cut with great gorges and outcrops of brown and ocher and vermilion rocks. The Rainbow Bridge is in this country, the Painted Desert, the Hopi pueblos, and the most interesting of the cliff-dwelling remains. It is also a cattle country within which is nourished, almost as much apart from the rest of Arizona life as if they did not occupy adjacent and overlapping territories, one of the three C's—cotton, copper, and cattle—which keep up the economic life of the State.

Cotton is raised in the valley of the Gila and in irrigated lands under the Roosevelt Dam; cattle are raised chiefly north of the Rim; and copper, together with silver and lead, is produced out of widely distributed mountain regions. Between these three industries there is only the thinnest integument of commercial interchange. Any one of the three could fall out altogether without in any way affecting the entity that is Arizona. In times like the present when every one of these industries has experienced a slump, the personnel items shift and are replaced as the land calls its own out of the most unlikely quarters, calling "Come and find me!"

The relation of the great mining industries of Arizona to the features that have just been described requires a certain amount of explanation. Productively their output must be credited to the wealth of the State, but actually they are mere isolated spots of infection, of industrial enterprise or corruption—as your point of view inclines you to regard them—taking their life from New York. Whole towns spring up overnight or are depopulated by mandate. Clashes between employer and employed take place in their streets, motivated by issues at stake in the capitals of the world. Only occasionally Arizona takes a hand in the proceedings. When it does everybody knows it, as in the case of the Bisbee deportations.[1] Also everybody else is more worried by it than the native Arizonians. In spite of the effort of organized labor to make of what happened at Bisbee an item of capitalist strategy, it remains in fact a characteristically Arizonian incident. There was at Bisbee at that time real apprehension of Mexican raids. There were also at Bisbee certain representatives of a not much-loved labor organization making the juxtaposition of the tinder pile to the Mexican match. Promptly, efficiently, and wholly illegally the native Arizonians removed the tinder to a less threatening neighborhood, and nothing in their experience surprised them more than the fuss that organized labor and the liberal element generally made about it. In the press the incident was made to appear as a result of hysteria engendered, according to the political bias of the organ, either by I. W. W. or by the mining interests in an effort to discredit organized labor. But so far as the social consciousness of Arizona at large was concerned, the truth

---

[1]During a 1917 strike of an IWW-affiliated union against Phelps-Dodge, vigilantes deported 67 IWW members and two days later 1,200 "disloyal" people. The first were deposited on the California border, the second placed in a detention camp in New Mexico and held under government guard. [D. H. B.]

of either, or both, or neither of these allegations did not enter in the determining degree. The deportees were handled much more in the spirit which, in the old days, made it obligatory on the other gentlemen present to throw the drunken cowboy out of the dance, without inquiring too closely who paid for his liquor, than, as it was generally treated by the press, as an incident of the welter of our civilization in the bog of economic stupidity. Politically it harked back to the period in which the *jefes* and *governadoras* of remote communities were allowed to dispense justice and equity in all cases except the most overt to their satisfied tribesmen, as might be easily deduced from the nature of reactions in the State at large. The Governor, á Republican in an overwhelmingly Democratic State, lost no votes by his public utterances as to the extra-legality aspects of the affair; and the most public of trials, with actions in State and Federal courts, with no avoidance of the facts, brought no convictions, in accordance with a prevailing public sentiment.

There does not appear any immediate reason for thinking that Arizona will outgrow her right to the Joyous Adventure. The irrigated valleys are due to become opulent. But a rod beyond the furthest ditch the desert waits with immeasurable beauty and mystery. New mountains not yet worn down to the soothed contours of maturity lift the vision and color the aspirations of men as they stain the air with splintered light. Beyond the rim of Mogollon, irreducible spaces of open wood and wide-sculptured rock and ancient ruins intrigue the imagination.

There is an effect of beauty upon the spirit of man that escapes measure and definition. So much of Arizona is by its natural constitution conditioned to be always beautiful, and to serve only by its beauty, that we cannot suppose that it will fail ultimately to produce some equivalent uniqueness among its inhabitants.

ARKANSAS

A Native Proletariat

C. L. EDSON

MAY 2, 1923

"THE ONE STATE in the Union that I still have a seething curiosity to visit," wrote H. L. Mencken recently, "is Arkansas." If the relentless hunter of the Americano should ever reach this last Carcassonne of his critical desire he would at last have one wish-fulfilment that was up to expectations. For Arkansas is our most distinguished State. It is the one member of our glorious Union that has accomplished all that it set out to, has lived up to its highest ideals, and stands today the only commonwealth of its kind on earth.

What then are the ideals of this State? The motto in Latin on her State seal says: "The People Rule." They do. But to what end? Arkansas has its own popular motto and it is this: "I've never seen nothin', I don't know nothin', I hain't got nothin', and I don't want nothin'." These fundamental aims the people of Arkansas have achieved in every particular. Therefore the Arkansawyers are happy, the only happy and successful people in America. But it was luck that did it. Happy is the State that has no history—and Arkansas has none. It was not founded by a pious Æneas, nor fought over by Hannibals and Scipios. It just grew up out of seepage. While the ports of Louisiana, Florida, Carolina, and New Amsterdam were being struggled for by Frenchman, Spaniard, Dutchman, and Britisher, old Arkansas, having no port and lying on the road to nowhere, was free to grow up without a history. The Mississippi River, highway of the old adventurers, lies broadside the whole length of the State but there is no landing place. Mississippi has Vicksburg, Louisiana has New Orleans, Tennessee has Memphis, and Missouri has St. Louis. But where is the old port of Arkansas; where its ancient capital of Creole days? A belt of mud, a hundred miles wide in places, prevented Arkansas from having a port as well as a metropolis, a civilization, and a history.

A people who were willing to foot it a hundred miles through the muck to get nowhere founded Arkansas and achieved their aim. Mighty planters, greedy merchants, daring pirates with beautiful hot-blooded women—these came not to Arkansas nor founded there an aristocracy of strength and cunning. But the kind

45

of folk that pirates terrorize, and merchants cheat, and planters impress into peonage were the wandering sheep that grazed their way into Arkansas to establish
there a morons' paradise. No strong men arose to oppress them because the
pirate-merchant-planter breed was not in them. They could not raise up strong-
arm Caesars among themselves because there were no Caesar chromosomes in
their blood. They were an infiltrate, and in seeping into Arkansas through a mud
filter the Caesars had been strained out.

The Arkansawyers are of the type of the old Hoosiers, Crackers, Pikers, and
the Big Smoky mountaineers. The Hoosiers themselves were descendants of the
bond-servants of Colonial days and being of low degree sought their own kind
while the great migration going "out West" moved along the Ohio. They settled
in the malaria swamps of Indiana and Illinois, but that was on the highway to
empire and civilization drove them out. They colonized again in Pike County,
Missouri, and made the name "Piker" notorious throughout the West as denot-
ing a fellow of feeble wit and feebler initiative. Other migrations of the bond-
servant stock found their way into Arkansas, and as no strong tribe followed
them into this retreat they were never driven out again. "Crackers," descendants
of the Georgia convict colony, also found refuge in Arkansas. The mountain people, too, came gradually onward, proliferating in their beloved highlands till
they crossed the Mississippi and peopled the Ozarks. But these people are not
mentally dull nor physically inefficient. They are simply a highland race that
loves solitude and scorns comfort, literature, and luxury.

These three strains, the mountain people, the Crackers, and the Piker num-
skulls, have united to make the Arkansas nation; for they are a nation, as distinct
from the other peoples in America as is a Swede from a Dane. Whenever Arkansawyers appear in Kansas, California, South Carolina, or Texas the natives
hold up their hands in horror, fearing that their Spartan State will be erased
by the obliterating helot swarm. The high wages in the agricultural Northwest
during the World War drew a few Arkansawyers to Nebraska whither they
took their dogs and women, their customs and ideals—and labored for the
Swedish and Teutonic farmers. The sturdy Nebraskans (from North Europe)
were shocked by the general worthlessness of the Arkansawyers and were heard
to declare: "If they keep on letting that kind of people into this country, America has gone to hell." The Arkansawyers are a race compounded as we have
seen of three strains of American roughneck blood with no trace of gentility, no
Cavalier.

There is one great quality that is not an attribute of the superior classes, and
that is wit. The Arkansawyers have it. It reaches its highest notch in such blithe
fellows as Will Rogers and Tom P. Morgan. To be an immortal wit is no mean
distinction. But wit is so common in Arkansas that it does not distinguish a
man—not while he is in Arkansas. It is the tradition of the land. No nation so
young as Arkansas has produced as great a mass of comic legend and genuine
native humor. But its people are not a literate people and you seek in vain to find
their glory on the printed page. Perhaps one can best approach this pathless sub-

ject by facing about and going back to Davy Crockett. Crockett was a Tennesseean by birth who roved through Arkansas and made his mark in Texas. He
spent some years in Congress. Crockett was severely in the Arkansas tradition.
He boasted that he was so rough that he could take a porcupine under one arm,
and wild cat under the other, and climb a thorn tree without getting a scratch. He
was a dead shot with the rifle and a rough-and-tumble virtuoso of the bowie-
knife. He loved the wild, hard life of the pioneer woodsman, saw the fun and
poetry in it, and was equally at ease when clowning from the stump before
his backwoods "constituents" and when speaking at an Ambassador's dinner
in Washington. London had discovered the American backwoods through the
writings of James Fenimore Cooper, and the literary spotlight swung this way
and provoked the inquisitive visits of Dickens and Thackeray. The stage was
set for an American Leatherstocking, and Davy Crockett stepped out and "took
his bows."

There spoke the spirit of Arkansas. "Wild and woolly and full of fleas, I've
never been curried below the knees." Imagine a Massachusetts statesman or a
Carolina gentleman making such a claim. But such course boasts are the glory
of the Davy Crocketts. The smart Londoners were "charmed," as they are
charmed by a woolly rhinoceros, and Davy Crockett was all the rage. He was
genuine, he was American hickory with the bark on; and he was so witty that his
every word was caught and saved and became a treasury of Americana, recalled
for a generation and not wholly forgotten now. Typical was his best-remembered
boast from the lecture platform that he was recognized as such a faultless marks-
man by all the denizens of the woods that a coon in the tallest tree, seeing Crockett priming his rifle, would cry: "Don't shoot; I'll come down."

Such humor is the common intercourse in Arkansas, but when it penetrates to
the polite world it is believed to be fabulous. Will Rogers, the jewel of the New
York Follies, was born in Arkansas and has carried on the Arkansas tradition.
Cracking jokes about princes, prime ministers, and metropolitan foibles while
he does miracles with his cowboy lasso and loudly chews his "chawin' gum" he
is but the reincarnation of Davy Crockett, who could skin a panther with his
bowie-knife while making quips to set the gilded capitals of Europe laughing.
These feats build no triumphal arches nor give new work for the map-makers,
but they are no easy accomplishments. The men that do these tricks have
achieved heights of mental agility that few attain. And the race that can produce
such men is as salty as the race that flowers in Napoleons and Fochs. Arkansas
is that race. One such wit might be an accident. But Arkansas repeats.

Uncouth audacity is the tradition of Arkansas. The trick of the Arkansawyer
is to capitalize his boorishness. It solves his problem in a flash. Why did no
other race think of this solution? What medicine for the New Englander fighting
his "inferiority" until it drives him crazy? The Arkansawyer says: "Look, I am
a buffoon. With one hand I drive my mule, with the other I toss off epigrams."
He therefore has no desire to ape gentility; he knows he is as good as anyone.
Even as the Southern Negro long believed that the white race was made for

him—to amuse him, shelter and feed him, and protect him from his enemies, so the Arkansans believe that the duller race of Rome and Paris and all the glittering world of white shirts, table linen, chefs, opera, tiaras, and taxicabs were made for them—made as a background and a setting for their inspired buffoonery. There is no Freudian grouch in the soul of Arkansas. This is the unique distinction that makes the tribe worth while. They have not, in all their philosophy, any complaint against anything. They are the only white tribe among us that habitually fiddles and sings.

But why has the Arkansawyer never pushed this claim? He doesn't know it. What then does he glory in? He's a joiner of high-sounding, meaningless societies. He prides himself in the fact that "Albert Pike, American's most illustrious Mason, reached the zenith of his career while a resident of Arkansas," and that "the post laureate of Masonry, Fay Hempstead, is a native Arkansan," and that "the only man ever invited to speak before the New York Lodge of Elks, not a member of the lodge, was an Arkansan." These claims were put forth in the *Congressional Record* last year to show what Arkansas has accomplished in eighty-six years of statehood. The non-member that appeared before the New York Elks was probably Will Rogers. His appearance before the Elks seems to the Arkansans a greater distinction than that his wit has made him a favorite with the smartest audiences of a world metropolis. Another claim that the Arkansas Congressman makes is that Arkansas was the "first State to pass the bone-dry law." But this is typical Arkansas ignorance. Maine and Kansas voted dry a generation ago, while State-wide prohibition came to Arkansas during the World War. But the Arkansawyer's scorn of history and letters and of all things outside of Arkansas has long been the trait that distinguished him in the eyes of other peoples.

So here is a civilized tribe—civilized in the sense of the "Five Civilized Nations" of the Iroquois—that has no literary tradition. Few can read in Arkansas, and those who can, do not. Their own legends, jokes, and coon-skin fables suffice them. They hark back to no classics. They have as little use for Greek culture as a Nevada dry farmer for the canals on Mars. An Arkansas printer named Fields recently removed to Orangeburg, S.C., and there started a paper, the *Daily Field*. At the beginning of each editorial stood the caption in black letters: "Fields Says:" And what Fields said was distinguished, but one perceived he did not write the stuff himself. He told me that he simply couldn't write general editorials. But in an old house he had found a book full of the sayings of Bacon, Swift, Johnson, Addison, Thackeray, and Lamb. These he ran in his editorial columns as original matter. The Arkansawyer supposes every one to be as unlettered as he is. This "editor" had never heard of Addison and Thackeray and supposed that his Carolina readers were equally ignorant.

The unwritten lore of Arkansas is self-reliant, witty, and grotesque. Its utter vulgarity may be explained by the lack of any strain of gentility in the Arkansas race. The "Speech of Senator Jones," known to every adult in the State, and treasured by him as the New Englander treasures the Ride of Paul Revere, begins: "Mr. Speaker God damn you, Sah, I've been trying for half an hour to get your eye"—and proceeds amid the most unutterable coarseness, phrased in rounded periods, the eloquence of the hogwallow, to argue heatedly against the bill to change the name of Arkansas to Arkansaw. Who was Senator Jones and where did he make this classic address? Who composed the endless ballads, fables, and droll tales that constitute the Arkansas legend? We do not know. There is no scholarship to expound them.

The Arkansawyers have a legend, a ceremony, and a ballad for every occasion, from the planting of a turnip to the cutting of a bee tree. When I was buying shoes preparatory to shaking the dust of Arkansas from my feet, the merchant laid business aside for the moment and sang me that twenty-verse ballad: "When I Left Arkansas." It is full of pathos as well as rollicking fun, and concludes with:

> And I got drunk as a boiled owl when I left Arkansas.

Every old Southern State has produced scholars, except Arkansas, according to Mencken's dictum, and no man of first-class intellect was born in Arkansas, lived there, or even passed through that State. That is why he has a curiosity to go and look upon that peculiar human kennel. And why shouldn't he? For it is high time that some critical mind turned inquiringly to these people and added to the American archives their short and simple but not uninteresting story. Washington Irving crossed the State of Arkansas, but merely to enjoy the beauties of its natural scenery. Arkansas has mountains of quartz that glitter in the sunlight with every color of the rainbow. It has marble of all kinds and colorings, the outcrop of a single marble bed being visible a hundred miles along the White River. There is no part of Arkansas save where man pollutes it that is not beautiful, no spot that is not a veritable mine of wealth. Its soil is rich and varied, its forest covering is of the choicest woods, cypress, white oak, red oak, hickory, and pine, and its mineral wealth is unbelievably diverse and vast. Arkansas is the only State that produces diamonds, and its output of pearls is greater than that of all the others. To enjoy this natural splendor, Irving came with Audubon, who was classifying the birds. It is time for someone to come and view those rarer specimens, the people.

A region as rich as Arkansas would long ago have been exploited by the soldiers of fortune and the planter-entrepreneurs had it not been segregated from the routes of the world. The captains and founders of first families having passed by on the other side, the buck privates inherited Arkansas. Blood will tell, and it told. The struggle of history saw other States rising to the rank of general officers, but first sergeant is as high as Arkansas ever got. But as every soldier knows, good sergeants are the backbone of every successful army. And Arkansas has moved steadily ahead in population, wealth, and industry. Whence came this population of nearly two millions? There is no immigration. Arkansas has fewer unmarried men than any other State. It got its population as it got everything else it has—manufactured it at home. In Arkansas men build their own

houses, cobble their own shoes. It is what makes these people bold. In the highland half of the State there is probably not a man over forty who has not once or
twice gone into the woods and hewed out a home, that is, purchased a tract of
wild timber or received it as a gift from the government, and with his own hands
cleared the ground, split the rails (or "busted 'em open makin' rails" as they
call it, the word "split," although used by Lincoln, being unknown in rural Arkansas), hewed the logs for his house or muled them to a saw-mill, carved
wooden hinges, made the doors, and riven the shingles by hand with a frow. In
a word, Arkansas is a land of raw materials and raw people. The people take
hold of the materials and fashion themselves such wealth as they desire. And
their desire is the only limit to their wealth. They own it all in fee simple; there
are no masters to oppress them and they occupy without molestation a land unbelievably rich and a climate most favorable. But they desire little. No ambition
consumes them. Their wants are limited to their needs and normal human needs
are not much after all. Hence their merry motto: "I ain't got nothin', and I don't
want nothin'." In the great war of man against nature, science against ignorance, Arkansas has remained a neutral.

Were it not that Arkansas is incorporated in the United System of Go-getters
it would have remained like the Balkans, a land where men have had forty centuries of farming without a step of progress, that farming being the same as
Rome's and Rome's the same as Adam's. But Federal bulletins and State agricultural college bulletins and Ford's tractor bulletins are everywhere, and some
of the farming done in Arkansas is scientific. Besides the opulence of timber,
soil and water, minerals and precious stones Arkansas was blessed with upland
rice. The planters in that State grow fabulous fields of it, ten bushels more to the
acre than any other State, according to their claim. It is grown on flat prairie
land underlaid with a water-tight clay. They dike it and flood it with pumped
water, which because of the hard pan stays there like water in a saucer. When the
rice ripens, the water evaporates and the farmers roll in with great harvesters—
the machinery of the wheat country—and bind up wealth so fast as to startle the
world. The farmers in that region pay the highest income taxes of any like area
in this country.

At the opening of the World War, Arkansas was for Germany to a man. The
people were still in the mood their fathers were when they threw the British out
of New Orleans. They had to make a complete about-face when they were
drafted. There is no foreign population in Arkansas to speak of. Yet the Union
Station in Little Rock has a great "immigrant section" occupying three-fourths
of the station, and it is filled with ragged, ill-smelling, greasy men and women
with sacks, bundles, and bedding, with dogs and innumerable, miserable young.
This mass of nondescript humanity sleeps huddled on the station floor as best it
can and remains herded there until the trains they are awaiting are announced
and Red Caps lead them in bewilderment to their cars. These "immigrants" are
the native Arkansawyers! In Hot Springs, Arkansas, the Government maintains
one of the world's great resorts, and visitors from all the civilized sections come

there in rolling Pullmans. En route they behold around them the mangy herd of Arkansawyers and they shrink away shocked and questioning: "In the name of God, what manner of men are these?" In this inadequate essay I have tried to suggest the answer. Here is the dictatorship of the proletariat in America. These scrub-stock people have been free to work out their own destiny under ideal conditions. They have had no intelligent class among them to prey upon their dulness. Capitalism has not laid a heavy hand on them, for they have been always in touch with free land, free water, and all raw materials free. And where labor is free and land is free there can be no capitalism. The lumber companies and the railroads in the past have tried to exploit these simple folk, but you can't lay hands on a land-scratching people roving through forests of free land. Like a greased pig, they elude you. Money has been kept down by barter—corn and pork being used as an exchange medium when there was no cash. For tax-money the people could always trap a few coons and sell their hides. Some of the more obliging officials as late as five years ago would accept coon skins in lieu of taxes due, and cash the furs in the best market. This is in the highlands of the State. The lowlands have their cotton and rice to sell.

How rich is Arkansas? About the same as boastful Kansas or the once mighty South Carolina. In population also she ranks with these. But Kansas is almost totally literate and was peopled by militant New England idealists. South Carolina was the cradle of aristocracy and literature on these shoes and once contained the richest landed society in America. These were the rice planters of the coastland. Arkansas, the land that has no history, the land of illiterates, Arkansas the moron sister, see, she walks saucily abreast of them now. The richest landed society is in Arkansas today! These are the facts; what can your philosophy do with them? Is it brains or luck that makes America?

CALIFORNIA

the Prodigious

GEORGE P. WEST

OCTOBER 4, 1922

CALIFORNIA lies wide and luminous and empty under the infinite blue between the high Sierra and the sea. Horizons are not miles but counties away, and between distant mountain sky-lines the land, lustrous and radiant in pastel shades of blue and green and golden brown, swims in warm sunlight. A physical entity seven hundred miles long and two hundred and fifty wide, California is cut off from the nearer West by a high rampart of mountains, with the sea on its other flank, while on the north its contact with Oregon lies across a wild tumble of mountains and forests, and on the south there is only the trackless mountainous desert of Mexico's Lower California. Inside these limits lies a land larger than Italy and Switzerland, as richly endowed with beauty and natural wealth as any in the world, with a climate of a semi-tropical friendliness that robs the mere business of sustaining life of its rigors and leaves human energy free for whatever other tasks the spirit may conceive. Within itself in stimulating variety are great deserts; noble mountain ranges where peaks of 14,000 feet go unnoticed; vast stretches of rich farming land in valleys flat as a billiard table; gentler mountains along the coast, where immigrants from northern Italy cultivate the vine or descendants of the Spanish conduct cattle ranches larger than Eastern counties; great regions in the north where mountain and valley are black with forests of giant pine and redwood, and bear lope across the logging road ahead of the infrequent stage; endless miles of glittering sea-coast where the lazy blue Pacific crashes and pours at the foot of tawny brown hills; gold mines and placer diggings in the lower canyons of the Sierra; valleys and foothills that at certain seasons are one vast flare of blossoming fruit trees; broad belts of olive-green orange and lemon orchards and of silver-green olives.

For northern Europeans made somber and astringent by a centuries-long struggle with obdurate soil and unfriendly climate to stumble upon such a land and discover it empty and waiting was in itself a dramatic episode in the life of the race. The people who call themselves Californians are not yet over their surprise. A sense of the prodigious abides with them. They are like children let loose in a new and wonderful nursery, and their enjoyment lies still in the contrast of its spacious magnificence with the meagerness into which they were born. The joy of the discoverer still exhilarates them, and stimulated and organized as their "boosting" is by the land speculator and the hotel-keeper, its swelling chorus voices also a generous eagerness to share the new-found blessings with friend and neighbor. They live in the radiance of a great destiny, which envisages the taming and the diverting of the torrents of the high Sierra, so that valley after valley and desert after desert now lying parched and empty shall become so many gardens for the culture of children and roses. The Californian of today is a pioneer in the task of turning water onto virgin soil and transforming wheat ranches, grazing land, even desert, into patinas of orchards and vineyards and truck-gardens.

But only the map-makers and politicians still think of California as an entity. In its human aspects it is sharply divided into north and south. There is San Francisco and there is Los Angeles, each with a million people within an hour's travel. Between the two stretch nearly five hundred sparsely settled miles of mountain and valley and desert, and a spiritual gulf wider still. These two communities *are* the State, in a cultural sense, and they are farther apart, in background and mental habits, than New York and San Francisco, or Chicago and Los Angeles. For ten years there has been a movement to write southern California with a capital S. Its people are as different from the older Californians up San Francisco-way as Cromwell's Roundheads were different from the Cavaliers and the seventeenth century successors of Falstaff. It is a difference of origins.

San Francisco's beginnings have been sufficiently celebrated. In an epilogue to *Two Years Before the Mast,* Richard Henry Dana describes in diary form a visit to San Francisco in 1859. Here, set down more than sixty years ago, are observations that remain true of the city of today. "It is noticeable," he writes, "that European continental fashions prevail generally in this city—French cooking, lunch at noon, and dinner at the end of the day, with *café noir* after meals, and to a great extent the European Sunday, to all of which emigrants from the United States and Great Britain seem to adapt themselves. Some dinners which were given to me at French restaurants were as sumptuous and as good, in dishes and wines, as any I have found in Paris."

It is a picture of the one pioneer American community where Puritanism was never permitted to intimidate the gusto and the zest for living of healthy men. Dana meets "a man whom I had known, some fifteen years ago, as a strict and formal deacon of a Congregational Society in New England. . . . Gone was the downcast eye, the bated breath, the solemn, non-natural voice, the watchful gait, stepping as if he felt himself responsible for the balance of the moral universe! He walked with a stride, an uplifted open countenance, his face covered with beard, whiskers and mustache, his voice strong and natural, and, in short, he had put off the New England deacon and become a human being."

Thus Dana in 1859—and still today the north holds all that is natively and distinctively Californian. It faces San Francisco, and celebrates the Argonauts of forty-nine as New England the Mayflower Pilgrims. It is a lusty, cosmopolitan community that has drawn its later increments of population largely from Ireland and northern Italy, and that maintains with undiminished gusto the Good-Fellow tradition instead of the Puritan. It cherishes a romantic, conventional aestheticism, drinks wine habitually, despite the Eighteenth Amendment, feels a vast tolerance toward weaknesses of the flesh, nurses a sense of the great world, a feeling of kinship with New York and Paris, a contempt born of utter ignorance for Chicago and the Middle West, a touch with the Orient, a love of the sea, a quick eye for the picturesque and the romantic. It loves fetes and pageants and froths with uncritical sentiment at the slightest provocation. There is a regard for the past such as you will hardly find in Boston. "The days of old, the days of gold, the days of forty-nine" live again in the imagination of every school-child. Yet this San Francisco which holds an undisputed eminence over the older California belongs rather to the world and to the sea, which pierces the coast here through the narrow straits of the Golden Gate, between steep cliffs, and spreads out then into a bay of vast extent. One arm of it runs south for twenty miles and leaves between it and the sea a mountainous sliver of land with San Francisco crowded onto its northerly tip. The city's half-million live on wind-swept and seagirt hills, now drenched with fog, now bathed in a sunlight that is opalescent and sparkling and bracingly cool in reminiscence of the sea-mist that here never quite surrenders to the California sun. They live for the most part in the innumerable downtown hotels and apartments, or in solid blocks of wooden houses and tenements, standing flush with the sidewalk, painted white or gray, ugly with scroll-work. Here and there through the town a cluster of charming houses in Italian renaissance cling incredibly to some steep hillside and look sheerly down over the red-brown roofs of gray tenements to the blue Bay. But the city would be hideous if its streets were not forever marching up sheer hillsides or plunging down from dizzy heights to the flashing sea, so that the poorest Italian on Telegraph Hill knows the imminent glory of far-flung waters and encircling hills, and breathes clean winds from afar.

Contrast and surprise lurk around every corner, and the city's people are sensitive and untiringly appreciative of every beauty, every contrast, every grotesquerie. They love their city as a man loves a woman of many moods and surprises. And the town is incurably bizarre and exotic. Cool trade winds blow down its streets every summer afternoon, and toward 5 o'clock a fleecy white billowing sea-fog, chill, eerie, palpable, drifts eastward over its hill-tops, hugging the land, bringing the feel and smell of the sea like a presence. It throws a glamor over the cheaply built wooden tenements, mile after mile of them. It makes of summer evening interiors so many cozy havens from its chill and sinister mystery, and accounts in part for a cafe life that for generations has been normal and habitual. People of every race and nation meet on an equal footing in the restaurants and on the streets. For San Francisco belongs to Europe and the Pacific Islands and the Orient and Latin America and the wanderers of the sea as well as to California.

Market Street, San Francisco. The city's reputation for diversity and Bohemianism often obscured recognition that its business district differed little from those in other cities.

Chinatown is now adored by a people who stoned Chinese a generation ago, only to discover, after the exclusion act had removed them as an economic factor, that they are a singularly honest, humorous, and lovable folk. The Japanese might be more popular if the large Japanese colony weren't so colorless. Perhaps we should be touched and flattered by their eagerness to discard everything Oriental and adopt every Western banality of dress and custom. It would take a Freudian to explain why the intensely proud, nationalistic Japanese should do this while the Chinese persist in their own ways. San Francisco owes its Oriental flavor to Chinese who came before the exclusion act, or were born here, or smuggled in.

For the rest, San Francisco is distinguished by its startlingly radiant women with their superb health and their daring color; by its swaggering working men; by its rowdy and disreputable politics, nourished by an underworld that remains institutional and arrogant in spite of prohibition; by the imminence of the sea and the life of ships; by its dozens of odd characters, past and present, such as the monkey-house bar where an old man in a plug hat sold liquor amid the chattering of birds and beasts from the Pacific Islands—a long-vanished phenomenon that is yet somehow eloquent of the town today.

Here, in this district about the Bay, is the California of Bret Harte, Mark Twain, Joaquin Miller, Charles Warren Stoddard, John Muir, Robert Louis Stevenson, Frank Norris, Ambrose Bierce, Edwin Markham, Henry George, Gertrude Atherton, Henry Morse Stephens, Gelett Burgess, Lincoln Steffens,

George Sterling, the Irwin boys, Jack London; the California of Stanford and California universities; the California of the Vigilantes, Nob Hill, the Big Four of the Central Pacific; Abe Ruef and the graft prosecution; the Mooney case; the California of Hiram Johnson, Fremont Older, William Randolph Hearst, David Starr Jordan, Herbert Hoover.

San Francisco has always been a favorite with those who rail against a Puritan and regimented America. Yet it might be instructive to our legions of young people who indolently blame Puritanism for everything banal to come and live for a time with these anti-Puritans of the Golden Gate. They would find the Good-Fellow tradition as stifling in its way as the Puritan, and harder to escape. There is a celebrated club in San Francisco the very name of which is a protest against Philistinism. It admits writers and artists without fee, and proceeds then to kill them with kindness. It has blunted more than a few men of first-rate talent by acclaiming them to the clink of glasses, drowning them in an easy and bibulous success, censoring in them any impulse to self-expression not compatible with the *mores* and taboos of the Good Fellow. Each year it presents an elaborate masque in blank verse in a noble grove of giant redwoods. Words and music are written by members, and the most successful business and professional men of the town compete for part in the caste. The plays celebrate friendship or portray the burial of care. Usually they are rather conventional and dull, full of "What Ho!'s" and "Who Is Without?'s" but the members sit through the performance with a touching religious fidelity, proudly conscious of their role as patrons of the arts and further assuaged for the tedium of the performance by a warm hazy alcoholic glow. For all that it is a brave and handsome enterprise. But when Witter Bynner, sojourning in California and admitted to membership, signed a plea for the release of political prisoners, the heavens fell on him and there was such a club row as reverberated for days in the newspapers of the town.

Yet it is hard to be critical of a town where George Sterling is as popular as Edgar Guest in Detroit,[1] where a tiny Spanish galleon with golden sails, set in the center of a public square between Chinatown and the Barbary Coast commemorates Stevenson's sojourn, where successful business men even pretend an enjoyment of the arts. Many young people here are without that hard-boiled quality, that contemptuous sophistication, which blights so many American youngsters of the prosperous middle class. The minority who have escaped the cultural sterility of a nation that worships salesmanship is perhaps a little larger, in proportion, among native Californians than among Americans generally.

But because Puritanism never did prevail here, one misses certain advantages of the Puritan temperament. In the East young people find it exhilarating to make their rebellion. There is passion and iron in it. California youngsters miss

[1]The poet George Sterling was a mainspring of the Western literary flowering of the early twentieth century. His deliberately cultivated aestheticism earned him the praise of Ambrose Bierce and Theodore Dreiser. Founder of the Carmel artist colony, Sterling retained his popularity in San Francisco in the 1920s despite Eastern critics' charges that he was out of date. [D. H. B.]

some of that thrill. They grow up in a society congenial enough to seduce them. Where good fellows are not barbarians there is a tremendous temptation to be one. In more than one respect living in California is like being happily married to a very beautiful woman, a placid, maternally wise, mentally indolent woman of the classic traditions, whose mere presence allays restlessness by making it seem gratuitous and a little ridiculous. In California one worries and squirms for fear one is not worrying and squirming enough. It is not only the need of a market that sends creative youngsters scampering to New York. From a California hill-top, much of the eager striving and rebellion afoot in the world get to seem mere stridency, much of the hard discipline of creative effort so much senseless drudgery.

Nor must anything here set down show San Francisco in too rosy a hue as a sparkling oasis in an America, in a world, that seems so often these days the desert of this metaphor. What Dana's outnumbered New Englanders could not accomplish in the fifties has been, to an extent, accomplished by the leveling and regimenting processes of our industrial civilization, so that here as elsewhere men and women go about too much as though listless and driven, as though bound on the wheel. And a nationalism that in this one of its effects seems suffocating and unnatural brings San Francisco within the workings of the Prohibition amendment, where its Latin spirit flutters, crippled and bewildered, like a bird in a church.

Not so the wide region at the other end of the State that calls itself the Southland. Wine was never honored in this heaven on earth set up and maintained by the great Mississippi Valley as a dazzling reward for thrift and piety. Southern California is an amazing achievement in colonization, an achievement not of California but of the Middle West. It stands there flaunting its testimony to the wealth and the overflowing population of what was yesterday our Middle Border. They discovered it when the first trains rolled westward over the newly completed Santa Fe and Southern Pacific in the eighties. It lay empty before them, except for a few negligible and benighted Spanish-Americans. Real estate speculators and health-seekers and the elderly retired came first. They were mostly New Englanders of modest savings, confirmed in their Puritanism by a generation or two of hard work and drab living in the Middle West. And they were not to be seduced by anything in the air of California or the ways of its shiftless caballeros. Among them there was no turning of backs on the familiar. They brought their household gods and all their mental baggage with them, and set them up in California without missing a prayer-meeting. They accepted the mountains and the sunshine as their due from God for being thrifty, Republican, Protestant, and American, but they did not neglect to give thanks regularly at the churches which they promptly erected. Most of their social life still centers about these churches, which remain amazingly untouched by any profane idea or discovery that has come into the world in the past hundred years. Of the New England that flowered in the great Unitarians, in the Abolitionists, in Phillips Brooks, in Thoreau, in William James, there is scarcely a trace.

Easter services, Hollywood Bowl, Los Angeles. Discovered to have perfect acoustics in 1919, the awesome Hollywood Bowl was typical of the pastiche quality of southern California culture. Both symphony concerts and fundamentalist revivals used the site.

The preempting by these people of southern California, a land drenched in sunshine and fragrance and sensuous, languorous beauty, is poignant irony. Contemplating one of their towns, with its trim bungalows and shrewd Yankee faces and many churches, it is easy to conjure up the gho;tly figure of an ancient caballero, sitting graceful in his saddle under the moorı, a brown-paper cigarette in his lips, long tapaderos brushing the ground, the moonlight glistening on the heavy silver trimmings of his bridle, gazing scornfully, wonderingly, sadly down from a hill-top over the electric-lighted rectangles of these victorious aliens. In a short generation they have wiped out a Homeric society of Latins and Indians and replaced it with a Gopher Prairie de luxe.

To write thus of the Yankee strain that predominates for the moment in rapidly changing southern California is to fall into the literary habit of the hour. Some day, as the drubbing continues, those of us who come of that stock will feel a pricking of latent pride, a call to arms. And we shall find, then, and reaffirm in new terms, certain brave victories for the human spirit, certain unique conquests of happiness and even of beauty. Probably we shall always feel that they were bought at a frightful price of suppression and perversion, a price demanded not alone by the racial heritage of northern Europeans, but also by the hard conditions of pioneer American living. But the victories are real. They are to be seen today in southern California, where the orthodox American genius has proved itself not merely acquisitive, but creative as well, by bringing into being towns and countrysides that in homes, and schools, and gardens, and in every sort of community enterprise show a taking of thought, an intelligent care, a vast competence, a striving for a kind of life from which, if the free and diverse and inquiring impulses are banished, so also are the ogrish and the sensual. One may not disregard the community taboos. But by regarding them one may feel the community enveloping one in a kind and neighborly and even gracious concern. Out of the agglomeration of diverse and unoriented elements that make up southern California came, a decade ago, the major impulse behind most of the political progress associated with the six years of Hiram Johnson's governorship. True, it was in essence the orderly and moralistic impulse of comfortable, privileged commoners intent on putting down the heathen. The same people seemed in 1920 utterly satisfied with Mr. Harding. They destroyed the corrupt, generous, disreputable old railroad machine that had ruled the State for forty years. But they jail radicals and squelch labor organizers with more gusto still, with the same pious resentment once detected by the writer in one of their typical individuals, a retired farmer, who had discovered a cat that didn't belong there under his garage, and forthwith brought out a shotgun with moral and sanguinary intent.

Along with the elderly and the moderately prosperous who represent the virtue of the Middle West, the climate has attracted a vast assortment of odds and ends of humanity—poor souls in sick bodies, victims of all manner of starvations and suppressions and perversions. Every weird cult and -ism flourishes on the patronage of these pitiful refugees. Large areas of the community are stamped with shoddiness—the shoddiness of "folksy" real-estate men who station forlorn women on the sidewalks to hand cards to passers-by, or who advertise free turkey dinners at the opening of their new additions; of wornout farmers and their wives from the prairie States who move about blinking in the unaccustomed sunlight and take refuge in their churches; of a horde of petty venders and mountebanks who prey on them. Bible Institutes flourish, and the thousands who flock to them are aroused to excitement by the reaffirmation of such doctrines as the second coming of Christ. Here, too, have come in increasing numbers the camp-followers and veterans of such professional sports as baseball and boxing and automobile-racing and of less reputable trades, so that Los Angeles is acquiring an underworld and a half-world of startling proportions, which shades into the lower reaches of the movies.

That serpent crawled into this garden unnoticed, tawdry bands of adventurers from "the show business" who took up quarters at third-rate hotels, twelve or fourteen years ago, and began making "Westerns." Today there are ten thousand actors alone in and around Los Angeles, including all who are listed with the central casting bureau from millionaire stars to drug-addicts used for "atmosphere" in plays of the underworld. The movies spend hundreds of millions a year for salaries and materials. They have profoundly changed the tone of Los Angeles, a sprawling, formless city with an underlying population of Middle Western villagers, and their influence reaches into every home of the Southland where there are boys and girls. In Hollywood, Puritanism out of Iowa lives neighbor to this demimondaine of the arts.

But California, like any youngster, is chiefly interesting for what it may become. As they go about the State and comprehend its natural resources, men of any imagination at all are able to foresee here a great society. Other States no older have already begun to "settle down," but here the seventy-five years of American occupation have made only a beginning. Development has been slow because a fuller use of soil and climate has waited always upon finding and conducting new water at enormous expense, and upon adapting tropical or semi-tropical plants at the cost of endless experimenting. No decade passes now without an excited planting of hitherto neglected acres to a new fruit or nut or a new variety, discovered usually by some obscure putterer in experimental gardens maintained by the State or Federal Government and then promptly exploited by shoals of land salesmen. And ceaselessly, in the high mountains, first engineers and then workmen concentrated in great temporary camps perform prodigies of tunneling and damming to get more water for irrigation and more hydro-electric power for the cities and for pumping more water still from the beds of the valleys. Instead of the four millions who inhabit the State today, every Californian confidently looks forward to the time when there shall be twenty or thirty millions, and these visions are shared by the disinterested and the skeptical by such authorities, for instance, as Dr. Elwood Mead.[2] This sense of a great future is a challenge to every citizen with an instinct for state-building or social engineering. (One uses terms hateful to the individualist, who indeed will find it hard going for a long time to come in a State where even tilling the soil requires organized community enterprise in getting water and in marketing its peculiar crops.) The future is a challenge, equally to the conservative and the radical, each of whom wishes ardently to build the greater community according to his pattern. Today California is eminently a child of privilege, the largess of its climate and soil increased at the expense of the rest of the country by means of high tariffs that give its growers almost a monopoly and so keep half a dozen delicacies off the tables of the poor. The benefits are promptly capitalized in land values, so that citrus and walnut orchards bring as much as $5,000 an acre. Unimproved land fit for tillage is held at $200. Nearly as much more is required to prepare it for planting and irrigating, to provide the minimum in equipment and living quarters, and to sustain life until the first returns. It is a situation that has already checked development and made a fruit-growing or farming of any sort a rich man's game. And the tariff corrupts the State's participation in national politics, by making of its congressmen so many log-rollers in collusion with special privilege everywhere.

One thing California has achieved already: a body of water law, in statutes and decisions, that establishes the principle of beneficial use as a condition to

[2]Mead (1858–1936), head of the California Land Settlement Board, pioneered cooperative group settlements on irrigated land. [D. H. B.]

possession, and that decides as between users in favor of the greater number. And this year the private control of hydro-electric power by half a dozen great companies is being challenged by the influential and widely-supported sponsors of an initiative act substituting state development and operation—a socializing of this vital necessity that may be safely predicted for the near future even if it is defeated this year. There remains the land. A constitutional amendment limiting tenure by the single tax method, in accordance with the principle of beneficial use, received a quarter of a million votes in 1916. It has been more decisively beaten since then. If one were not hopeful, if one did not cling to the belief that it is too late in the day, one might foresee California becoming another Italy, the Italy of a generation or so ago, with beggars and an aristocracy. The beggars it would be easy to manage, in time. It requires more imagination to see our land speculators, with their Rotary badges and Elks buttons on belted khaki coats, metamorphosed into anything corresponding even dimly to the Italian aristocracy. To prevent that sort of thing there are a fair number of local H. G. Wells's—such men and women as are now pushing the Power Act—with a generous following. And, far off, new winds are blowing, and gently, oh, so gently, stirring the minds of the people of the Golden State.

COLORADO

Two Generations

Easley S. Jones

May 16, 1923

THE SNAP of the whip over the six-horse stage where it bowled between red cliffs, laughter of bar-rooms louder than the ring of poker chips, the volley of dynamite opening the gold wealth of the hills: these voices of the frontier are gone, and in their place have come the purr of taxis, the chatter of tourists, the rattle of tea cups in the summer hotels. In fifty years the rip-roaring life of gold, adventure, cowboys, pistols, ran to its climax and subsided; the mines, yielding their richest ores, were abandoned on a thousand hills, the forests were hewn down, the prairies fenced with barbed wire. The restless, kindly, spendthrift pioneer has given place to a still genial, but a calculating, penny-saving race; Colorado has become a taker-in of summer boarders, another Switzerland, flaunting the sign Rooms for Rent under the shadow of every mountain.

While it lasted no State had ever a more spectacular youth. The sense of conquest, the marching of caravans into unexplored forests, the exhilaration of active life in the clear mountain air, the prospect of wealth to be made overnight, the springing-up of mushroom settlements gave a zest that has not since been rivaled, and the glitter of firearms served to keep nerves tingling. Liquor was strong; a lusty music animated the dance halls; it was a commonplace to shoot the clock and pay the fiddler with a pinch of gold dust. The world was not only young, but on the eve of fortune. Beggars might be lords before another sunset. In the rudest camp of pine-board saloons, canvas hotels, and sod houses every penniless rogue assumed the manner of a milllionaire, spoke a language of gross exaggeration, and indulged in flamboyant humor, even at his own expense. The names the early adventurers gave their mines reflect the expansive spirit of the day, mouth-filling or defiant names: Golconda, Mantinomah, Onandaga, Brazilian, Ace of Diamonds, Newsboy King, Invincible, Silver Serpent, Revenge. For a score of years, shifting its center from camp to camp with each new rumor or discovery, the turbulent life of the frontier reeled upon its headlong course. It seemed impossible to believe that the enthusiasm roused by gold could ever have an end. But it did.

As the mines failed or became worked out the names of the lodes gave evidence of the change: Last Chance, Hard Times, Grubstake, Esperanza, Hungry Dog, Up Grade, Blue Monday. The decline of the price of silver in 1893 was a heavy blow. And in another twenty years the increase in the cost of living, which is to say, the decrease in the value of gold, reduced the metal industry to one-fourth its activity in palmy days. Neswpapers periodically announce that "Mining in Colorado is about to enter upon an era of great prosperity"; but no one is deceived. Shaft-houses and mills now sprawl upon the steep slopes, picturesque in semi-ruin, with sunken roofs, sheet-iron swaying to the winds, logs up-ended and overgrown with clematis, ore-dumps covered with berry bushes where scamper fugitive chipmunks. The great camps, Cripple Creek, Leadville, Black-hawk, Silverton, Ouray, Creede, have become ordinary lauguid villages, piled about with red and yellow worthless heaps of mineral, waiting for a revival that never comes. In the two decades following 1900 the annual production of gold, silver, zinc, lead, copper declined from fifty to twenty million dollars, and the value of agricultural products rose from seventeen to 181 millions. The irrigated areas produced grain, alfalfa, and sugar beets; "dry farming" on the high lands above the ditches, at first timid, experimental, attained unexpected success. Smelters were established in Denver, steel works in Pueblo, sugar factories in the prairie towns; the mountain torrents were harnessed for electric power. The era of high spirits passed; the devil-may-care swagger had served its turn; the hair-trigger guns so long worn and used in the open day were put on the shelf. The influx of new migration gave the population more and more the character of the States eastward along the fortieth parallel: Nebraska, Iowa, Illinois. The Wild West was overrun by the tame Middle West, tempered with its practical wisdom and forethought, its shrewdness, its concern for proprieties and amenities.

Another destiny overtook Colorado when tourists began to flock to the State in armies outnumbering those which followed the discovery of gold. In 1922, against a native population of one million, the tourists numbered three-quarters of a million, and the wealth left by them was something like forty-five million dollars. Since the war the number of visitors has doubled every two years. If the increase should continue at the same rate, in 1925 the tourist army will be larger than was the American military force in France, an army to be housed, fed, entertained, and sent away satisfied. Every year in June the deluge begins. From Texas, Oklahoma, Kansas they come, from the central States sweltering in heat; on trains, in automobiles; school teachers, clerks weary of the counter, business men sick of ledgers, and not the ultra-rich, but the middle class grown prosperous since the war. They come with endless questions, and not a few misconceptions. They expect to discover Indians, cowboys, prairie schooners; they find instead electric interurban trains, and Chautauqua lectures by Dr. Steiner and Lorado Taft. They are sure that Pike's Peak is the highest summit in the State, and are surprised to discover at least two dozen peaks higher. They whirl through Estes Park in taxis, taste the mineral water at Manitou with a wry face, and buy gorgeous post cards of "Sunset behind the Spanish Peaks." They write eloquent letters home, how they scaled Sierra Blanca (on horseback), how they slid down snowbanks in August. The men wade in cold streams with rod and line, where the trout are long since grown wise or scared to death. The women throw aside their georgette waists for flannel shirts, and appear transformed, but still charming, in khaki trousers and shoes full of little bright nails. The children ride burros, throw stones until their small arms ache, or shout madly where down both sides of the street race irrigation ditches full of shining water. The tourists go frankly in for pleasure; they uproot wild flowers; they prefer movies to books; they are indolent enough to want to climb hills by automobile; yet for all this they have a certain eager sparkle of curiosity; the mountains have not ceased to be for them a splendid novelty.

The ironical fate is that of the natives, sons of the free, strong race that Mark Twain wrote about—and Bret Harte and Eugene Field and Walt Whitman and Horace Greeley—tied to the treadmill of shop and boarding-house, fated to become the keepers of a nation's playground. For in comparison with Bret Harte's men, breakers of the wilderness, founders of cities, the present generation appears to shrink in stature. One perceives a change even in the names of mountains, streams, and towns. These the pioneers created from the first material at hand, careless, homely names: Wildhorse Creek, Dead Man Gulch, Lost Lake, Quartz Hill, Riflesight Notch, Rattlesnake Butte, Three Cottonwoods, Rabbit Ear Peaks. The later generation of small business men, the race that had read Tennyson and Harold Bell Wright, sought purring, soothing, or bookish names, like Idylwilde, Brookvale, Ferndale, Glenwood, Rosemont, Montrose; or some bit of cleverness to scrawl upon a cabin door, like Seldom Inn or the Jazz Whisper. Many of the pioneer names they made over. They turned Skunk Canyon into Bluebell, Red Bull Draw into Antelope Glen. A prize was offered for a name for an upland park, and the best that came forth was Panorama. The greatest modern triumph was Mount Sanitas, triumph because people could really be persuaded to repeat the word, and the mountain thus libeled is standing yet. One has only to let the mind sweep along in time, from the earliest Spanish names that blazoned the snowy peaks with memorials of Christ and the saints: Sangre de Cristo, San Miguel, San Juan; from the Indian names of as stern dignity as that of the hills themselves: Navaho, Arickaree, Oglala; from the pioneer names which, lacking dignity, had still the smack of an outdoor energetic life: Powderhorn, Dripping Rock, Lone Pine; to the culmination in Ingleside, Sanitas, to get an impression of a late generation feeble in invention, yawning beside the fire, jaded by comforts the frontier never knew, reading the ten best sellers, tired and tiresome. The pioneer, if we are to believe a hundred legends, was a prince in hospitality, and scorned to take a penny. His sons show an increasing desire to take all they can get. Such comparisons lead one to believe, not that the race has degenerated, but that it has at least passed from an adventurous, generous, impulsive life to a shrewdly reasoned, narrow one. The mind of the frontiersman occupied itself with uncounted herds of cattle ranging over ten square miles of

Railroad in the Royal Gorge of the Colorado River near Canyon City, Colorado. Once the immense technological problems of building the machine in the garden were overcome, the railroad became a conduit of tourism. The train stopped here to allow tourists to gape (for a price) at the natural wonder.

pasture, with the need for bridging a roaring forest stream, his only domestic care being to provide the four staples—whiskey, coffee, bacon, bread. The modern mind is occupied with minute complexities and hesitancies: whether the salad shall have caper sauce or only mayonnaise, whether to play bridge whist or see Salome in the movies, and (this particularly) what the neighbors think about it all. In the face of natural beauty that towers half up the sky, it is still possible for human nature to be servile. In streets pleasant with flowering hollyhocks under the beetling mountains gossips meet and snigger, repeat contemptible trivialities, virulent pin-pricks of rumor, concealed weapon of enslaved minds. Blue through the orchard-tops, eagle-haunted summits shimmer in the slant of sun, or darken with forests and the purple shadows of clouds, home of mystery and adventure, a challenge to the imagination forever. In front of a barbershop a man buries his head in the Denver *Post,* the most ill-mannered and vindictive yellow newspaper that money can buy. The tragedy of Colorado is that her race cannot measure up to the scene which it inherits. The stage is set for heroic action, or a theme of beauty, but the actors are raising the room rent or winding the phonograph. The race is dwarfed by the epic mountain theater where its life is cast.

Or do we deceive ourselves in making sharp the contrast between two generations—one romantic, dare-devil, open-hearted, the other humdrum, nicely moral, calculating? Is the difference only subjective, our mistaken feeling that the race has changed? Or is it part subjective and part actual? Was the pioneer

truly a "prince of hospitality"? Was he not, as much as any now, a conniving
rascal, except that we have chosen to forget the petty element and remember
only the glorious feature of his rascality? Was his era a true youth of the race,
or only the rawness (often mistaken for youth) of an old race greedy for gold?
Was his largeness of spirit born only of speculation, waste, wealth easily got?
Do boardinghouse-keepers lack strong will, generous impulse, the free, large
mind we attribute to the earlier day? If we push the inquiry only a little, we find
qualities of the pioneer which are active at the present time. Even the wildness
of the frontier reappears in curious ways. For let the news fly to tungsten or oil
shales discovered, or free lands opened in remote corners of the State, and the
old fever returns, the phenomena of the frontier repeat themselves on a smaller
scale; the same frenzy is astir as when George Jackson discovered gold in Idaho
Springs. Exactly as in 1859 one may hear men say: "Here's where we make a
strike. Let's drop all, take bag and baggage, and go." The outdoor tradition,
too, maintains itself in the midst of an indoor age. Camping, anywhere, is a natural impulse; but in Colorado it is a mania, a compelling influence in the blood,
perpetuating in men the ways of their fathers who tramped the granite peaks and
slept under the blazing stars. The expansiveness of the gold-mining era, its
frankness, its democracy, its humor are met today in unlikely places, even in the
summer hotels. The Western landlord does not bow the knee before the tourist;
he baits him, or meets him as an equal. The mountaineer does not covertly smile
when the Eastern schoolmistress asks questions: he laughs aloud. "What is that
feather you have in your hat?" "That, madam, is a woodchuck feather." "A
woodchuck? Why, I didn't know woodchucks had feathers." "Ah, yes, madam,
at certain seasons. In winter their plumage is pure white; in spring, green; in
autumn, red and brown. This feather, as you can plainly see, was picked in the
autumn." Thus the tourist is received, not as a lord to be fawned upon, but as a
lineal descendant of the greenhorn, the tenderfoot of the earlier day.

These and other sturdy qualities of the frontier remain. Actually there has
been a gain in comfort, manners, intellect. It is not reasonable to compliment
one generation at the expense of another. Both share certain virtues. Both have
in common many faults. The raw, wealth-greedy pioneer could not mine ores
less rich than forty dollars a ton; more than half his gold he wasted in the process
of extraction. He slaughtered part of the forests and set fire to the rest. He
impoverished the soil. He could only exploit nature, rob her, and he sometimes
robbed his fellow-men. His record is a continuous story of colossal waste. And
the son of the raw pioneer is still an exploiter, except that he has no bonanza or
forest, easily accessible, rich, to waste. It takes hard work and thought to exploit
ten-dollar ore, without labor wars. He therefore sinks into small business, establishes a factory in which the employees are always threatening to strike, or
exploits the most available resource, the tourist. The generation that shall merit
compliment, at the expense of both pioneer and present age, is one that shall
conserve and build—that shall learn to extract the gold from ten-dollar poor ore,
or even five-dollar ore (without labor wars into the bargain), that shall make

forests grow, one foot of clear timber for every foot cut down, that shall return chemical values to the soil and conserve the moisture of the arid lands, that shall conserve childhood and manhood, that shall establish tolerable factories, and make the conditions of industry human.

Colorado as an industrial battlefield has furnished the nation at intervals during thirty years with spectacles of violence amounting almost to civil war. The most bitter conflict was the coal strike of 1914, directed against the Rockefeller interests, marked by brutality on the part of both operators and miners. The culmination was Ludlow, a settlement of wretched tents and hovels on the bare prairie where more than twenty miners and women and children lost their lives. Ludlow is the contribution of Colorado to the list of scenes of industrial terror, the black list that includes Homestead, and Herrin, and grows longer year by year. One feels the tragedy of such warfare less keenly when any permanent good results, and the lessons of the strike of 1914 were not lost. The operators undertook to improve the conditions of living at the camps, and succeeded beyond anyone's expectation. More important still, the public conscience was, at last, profoundly stirred. The most amazing feature of economic struggles is the haste with which public opinion jumps to a conclusion on the first false rumor, and the reluctant slowness with which it arrives, when the facts are sifted, at a just decision. The question public opinion immediately asked concerning Ludlow was, who fired the first shot? Popular judgment was based largely on this question; yet it was a cheap and superficial inquiry. The underlying issue was not who fired the first shot, or even who accumulated guns and bullets. The issue was, what grievances and tyrannies had accumulated, over a period of years, that could make men want to break the law.

Other ugly social phenomena occur in Colorado, as elsewhere, and the wonder is not so much that they occur as that they are so little regarded or remedied. Abuses of political power pass usually without much protest. Mineral and timber lands, sources of water power, are unscrupulously gobbled up; the beet-sugar corporations haggle to escape taxes. Freedom of speech is so far from being realized that a labor organizer, scheduled to give in Denver the same speech he had delivered in Eastern cities, was seized by police and dumped across the border upon a neighbor State. A millionaire makes a present of a building to some college and nominates himself for the United States Senate. Educational institutions have been a football of politics since the founding of the State in 1876. In those earliest days when institutions were passed out as plums by the legislature, Cañon City, so the story goes, was offered a choice; she might have either the penitentiary or the university. And looking on society as it was then constituted, Cañon City chose the institution which was already a thriving concern, and whose future was not threatened with uncertainty. She elected to take the penitentiary, and the State university fell into the lap of Boulder. The penitentiary has today only one-third as many inmates as the university has students. One may smile, indeed; but it is perhaps too early to laugh. Cañon City's day may come, if the citizen lets public issues drift. For his attitude appears on first observation to be this: Let the politicians be as vicious as they please; business is good, our scenery matchless, the climate perfect. The physical conditions of life are so pleasant that he is deceived into the belief that the world is going well, when so far as the social aspect is concerned it may be going badly, and going fast. From his mountain vantage ship subsidies and tariffs seem small disputes of lowland minds. The hills lull the senses with a false impression of security.

But this view of her citizenship is only half the truth. Colorado adopted the eight-hour day, equal suffrage, prohibition, and had ceased to talk about them before they became national issues. For every name of ill odor, like that of Guggenheim, there is some brilliant name, like that of Judge Ben B. Lindsey, whose juvenile court was one of the first and best of its kind, or that of Miss Emily Griffith, whose Opportunity School in Denver is a model for a new idea in education.[1] Neither the Republican nor the Democratic Party has been able to maintain control of the State, the vote shifting from one to the other according to the issue. Whenever money and privilege become insolent, the people overstep party lines and elect a liberal governor, even an advanced liberal of the type of William E. Sweet. Whenever the political hierarchies of Denver become flagrantly, notoriously corrupt, the district attorney, Philip Van Cise, leads a popular revolt, and sends a score of speculators, confidence men, tourist-fleecers to our large and comfortable penitentiary.

The Western mind still overrides not only trifles, but hardships, the downright slaps of fate. Things which loom large on the horizon in New England, like a misspelled word, or a breach of formal etiquette, or exclusion from a social set, or even losing a job, give short pause in the rush of Western progress. Here where distances are vast, where between bristling mountain ranges the eye sweeps over valleys deep and wide, into which a Delaware or Rhode Island could be dropped and never missed, the frontier habit of thinking in big terms persists in some measure despite the trivial occupations of a modern day; the imagination, surrounded by scenes of beauty, flatters itself with the delusion that human nature is largely good also, and that what is not good can be dismissed with a clutter of other useless things not worth one sober thought.

The climate encourages this large and easy way of taking life. The greatest distinguishing feature of the State is a subtle atmospheric stimulus, hardly capable of description, further than to say that its immediate effect, experienced by everyone, is a feeling of buoyancy. The clear, dry air prolongs one's cheerfullest moods, releases energy. Its extreme effect is even a kind of nervousness. The phlegmatic, plodding human creature often found in Mississippi Valley regions of sticky days and muggy nights hardly exists in the mountain States; the usual temperament of the high altitudes is sanguine, buoyant, excitable. The

---

[1] Ben B. Lindsey was the first judge to try juveniles separately from adults. During the course of his career Lindsey's support for liberalized divorce laws, companionate marriage, and birth control made him a hero to the Progressives. [D. H. B.] Emily Griffiths's Opportunity School provided adults with a wide variety of course selections. [D. H. B.]

teamster shouts a greeting to every stranger in the road; in commercial clubs business men extend the hand before they think of introductions; in a few weeks one calls a new-made friend by his first name. In every physical aspect the country is one of light and color. Nowhere is one confronted by any moldy symbol of decay. Reaping machines remain in the field for weeks without danger of rust; an unroofed wooden house endures without rot the weather of two decades. The cliff-dwellings stand much as they did centuries before the white man turned his thought toward America, not ruins in any usual sense of the word; the charred sticks on their hearthstones look like embers of fires extinguished yesterday. Even the graveyards assume a cheerful appearance, always small, with glistening sharp corners of new stone, no lichen, no tarnishment of decay, no moldering wall, no biting of the tooth of years.

At the end of September there is a freakish burst of weather, a premature frost, or a flurry of snow on the range. The last of the tourists, fearful, get their reservations, and in Colorado Springs and Loveland the outgoing trunks are piled high as the station roof. Then only does one see the outdoor world at its best. From mid-September to mid-December is an interval for which Indian summer is too pale a word. The mountains, as if to make ridiculous the flight of tourists, assume another mood, and cloak themselves with color. In the first weeks of October the quaking aspens on the higher summits turn, interlacing their yellow and gold fantastically with the dark green of the pines. Every night the frost descends; every morning the margin of color creeps lower until it reaches the plain; the maples glow, the sumac bushes are like flame. Everywhere this glimmer of leaves is seen through a blue veil; a vapor, whether from moisture or smoke of forest fires, drifts across every valley. The mountains, cut from their base, appear to float upon the vapory element; ridge behind ridge they lie, each outlined in a deeper shade of blue; the steep remotest peaks lose themselves in clouds, or hang suspended in the sky. Threads of gossamer drift free; the wings of insects glitter; the sounds of railways, of city traffic, of hammers building new homes come back from the cliff in echoes miraculously far off.

In a small college town beneath these mountains young men and women pass in merry groups. "How many students do you have on the hill this term?" "Two thousand seven hundred now." Yet there are scores of men living who remember to have seen herds of elk pasturing on the open prairie where now the university stands. The suburbs reach toward the mountains, and far beyond the last house concrete walks pierce the surveyed field, and streets are ready for travel, as if no one made question of growth. Hammers ring out clear; a new bungalow is going up; the owner stands in the street to watch. "Isn't the air crisp and clean?" he volunteers. And after a moment's talk: "You wouldn't think, to see me now, that I'd ever had weak lungs. Why, before I left Chicago, the doctors told me I had just two months to live. I came out here to die." "Well, did you?" A grin is his first answer. "Not very fast. That was—let me see; I forget—ten long years ago." The hammers rap more lustily; a meadow lark, in sheer defiance of the calendar, trills a downward slur of notes; an irrigation ditch flows by, brimming full. Some children play beside it, building with little stones, the same red stones that tinge the mountain ramparts and give the State its name, building elaborate ground-plans, one after the other, on a scale too ambitious to be finished. Children of a third generation, heedless of the voice of time.

CONNECTICUT

A Nation in Miniature

DON C. SEITZ

APRIL 18, 1923

CONNECTICUT has been humorously described as "ninety-five miles long and seventy-five miles thick," these being roughly the State's geographical dimensions. Contiguous to Long Island Sound for the entire length, its bare ledges and deep valleys are credited with contributing their top soil to the making of Long Island itself, the detritus having been swept to sea in the days of the glacier, taking away much fertility and leaving mainly the picturesque behind. But picturesque the State is to an extent undreamed by the traveler who shoots through on the railroad touching mostly factory towns and glimpses only occasional views of water and nothing of the hills. The interior is singularly wild. There are long reaches of forest, great areas of idle land, vales that rival those of Cashmere, less its mountains, and that of Yumuri without its palms. Three noble rivers find their way through it to the sea, the Housatonic, the Connecticut, and the Thames. Of these the Connecticut travels farthest, its springs almost touching the Canadas and glorifying four States with its pride. As the country rises from sea level to the Berkshires on the west, or follows the rivers in the east, it develops great ridges, some of which are backed by hills, the chief of which, Bear Mountain of Litchfield County, reaches the respectable altitude of 2,355 feet. Eminences of from 500 to 1,200 feet are plentiful and high uplands border wide valleys that spread out refreshingly to the eye.

The artists discovered the charm of Connecticut years before the automobile gave people in general a still neglected chance to see and know this miniature wonderland. More than a quarter of a century ago John H. Twachtman, Childe Hassam, Harry Fitch Taylor, A. F. Jaccacci, Leonard Ochtman, and Elmer L. MacRae located Cos Cob, and George Wharton Edwards later visualized Greenwich. The art colonies at Saybrook and old Lyme have become famous. Other groups inhabit Westport, Norfolk, and Silver Mine.

In the rough country made by the broken terrain are stored quaint villages, untouched by the rush of the day, lakes unpolluted, and here and there fat farm lands enriching their owners with an exotic plant—tobacco. Once the "Connecticut filler" was a plebeian. Under improved breeding it has become an aristocrat, as a "wrapper" for the finer-flavored brands of Cuba. In warm summer days to ride among the plantations is to scent the dreamy narcotic and to know why Sir Walter Raleigh loved the weed at first sight. Beyond tobacco the farms contribute little. Connecticut raises only enough mutton to meet its needs for a single day, enough beef for eight days, and enough potatoes for fourteen. The rest of the supply must be imported and to procure this, cunning artisans in brass, silver, and fabrics toil in many towns. Some industries the State has made its own. The copper of Anaconda and Cerro de Pasco becomes clocks, rods, and sheetings of brass in Ansonia, Waterbury, and New Haven, while the hats of Danbury, Bethel, and Norwalk cover many heads. Stamford and New Britain put hinges, locks, and knobs on our doors. Manchester specializes in silk, Glastonbury in soap, and Willimantic in thread. In Bridgeport the typewriter, the corset, and the cartridge rule. In Meriden the silver spoon and its counterfeit began their lives. Far away New London and Stonington recall through stable fortunes the whale fishery and the seal hunting of the Antarctic, with not a few shekels wrested from the sea by venturesome privateers in 1812. In sleepy Middletown, now noted for Wesleyan University, money gathered by merchant mariners still earns its increment and shall it be said echoes the scandal of the wooden nutmeg and the basswood ham!

The "factory towns" can be put by as blots on the landscape, though not all are to be condemned for their abasement to utility. One of them, Stamford, is a model of what a complete city can be without smothering its soul in size. Its 35,000 people enjoy a fine theater, clubs, schools, library, commodious, handsome churches, the best of fire departments, and indeed all the elegancies as well as the comforts of life. How better it would be if the United States could possess 5,000 Stamfords, rather than the congested centers of New York, Chicago, Philadelphia, and their lesser kind into which our people are packing!

Despite the Puritan grimness of its birth-throe Connecticut became the father of the circus in its modern magnificence. If P. T. Barnum is not truly one of the immortals it is because there is no justice in the process of selection. Bridgeport built itself around him and his fame, and though the genial exhibitor long since passed away he left in its parks and public works a monument to his memory. And this is not all. The Greatest Show on Earth still winters there. The local boys take kindly to acrobats and are indifferent to elephants.

Hartford is a gay combination of Life Insurance and Death, for here the former had a pioneer foundation that has brought in great accumulations of cash, while Samuel Colt's "revolver" has grown into "Browning guns" and many forms of deadly repeaters that wipe out a regiment at a discharge. A dip into history reveals that the warehouse of one Major Selleck, of Stamford, sheltered a share of Captain Kidd's much-hunted booty, while a contumacious person named Clark acted as agent for the whilom pirate in defiance of authority and to the great wrath of the Earl of Bellomont, King William's Colonial Governor.

But the State can be truly described as a nation in miniature. It has made itself. It could be argued that Connecticut, not Necessity, was the mother of invention. Eli Whitney produced the cotton gin and Elias Howe the sewing machine, the two greatest advances in civilization after steam and before electricity. It has been claimed that the Yankee did not invent so much from innate ingenuity as laziness. He wanted a machine to do the work and save muscle.

Behind all this varied industry and energy stand Education and Congregationalism in high companionship, adding to the sum of wisdom and salvation. Although Elihu Yale—

> Born in America, in Europe bred,
> In Africa traveled, in Asia wed—

hanged his servant in India for misusing a favorite horse, his dollars laid the foundation for one of the greatest of universities, whose charter is firmly imbedded in the constitution of the State. Article 8 provides that "the Charter of Yale College as modified by agreement with the corporation thereof, in pursuance of an Act of the General Assembly, passed May 1792, is hereby confirmed."

There is much in this constitution that is notable besides giving shelter to Yale. Its first two sections contain all that need be said of the Rights of a People in establishing a government, viz.:

> 1. That all men when they form a social compact, are equal in rights; and that no man or set of men are entitled to exclusive public emoluments or privileges from the community.
>
> 2. That all political power is inherent in the people, and all free governments are founded on their authority, and instituted for their benefit; and that they have at all times an undeniable and indefeasible right to alter their form of government in such manner as they may think expedient.

Alas, that this clear and potent view can no longer seem to prevail among us! It is no more in force in Connecticut than elsewhere in these United States. The sturdy independence of the Charter-makers that began when Joseph Wadsworth concealed the first one in the famous oak is not echoed in the practices of their descendants. They can still resent mandates from without as they withstood the orders of Massachusetts Bay in Colonial days. When the suffrage amendment reached Hartford the legislature was not in session. The ladies were eager to have the then Governor Marcus H. Holcomb call a special session to secure its acceptance and so give them the vote at once. The Governor could see no exigency and declined at first to act, but as the legislature in Connecticut can summon itself when need be, he yielded to the prospect that it would do so and convened its members. The Governor, true to the traditions, thought that prohibition and suffrage were questions that belonged by right for the State alone to determine. So far as prohibition is concerned, the amendment has been three times rejected, while the "concurrent" act, passed to fit the Volstead law, makes it illegal for the police to interfere with a citizen who may be transporting less than five gallons of liquor at a time!

The political processes by which the American people have been separated from their liberties have ground over Connecticut as the glaciers did long ago, leaving a sterile "freedom" behind. In the beginning Church ruled State. The much vaunted "Blue Laws" were not so blue as many that prevail on the statute books today. They were merely enforced. When the church ceased to have political power parties contended with some diverseness until Insurance came to the fore and its magnates in Hartford took over the legislature, as later the same sort did in New York. When all their needs in lawmaking were satisfied, the control was handed over to the "Consolidated," that being the local name for the Interstate Railway combination, better known as the New York, New Haven and Hartford Railroad, reversing the New York order, where the law factory was first owned by the Central interests.

This lasted until the dethronement of Charles S. Mellen as the railroad head. For a few years the legislature has been free of corporations, but like a prisoner released after long confinement does not know what to do and sits blinking at the light save when the "boss" calls upon it to obey.

The cities are not permitted to dominate the towns. Though sixty-one of the latter have but one legislator, the remainder send to the Capital two each, and the large centers of population receive no consideration for numbers. Two is their allotment. This is a grievance with the big communities, but the little will not yield them more. The total membership of the Lower House is 262; that of the Senate 35. Representatives receive $300 a session and meet biennially.

The Master of the Legislature is J. Henry Roraback, the Republican "leader" of the State, and its National Committeeman. He comes from the pleasant land of Canaan up in the hills, is president of a big water-power company, which is taking 35,000 horse-power from a new development on the Housatonic, and is secure in his saddle. For some years he was assailed by the rivalry of John T. King, a carpet-bagger from Brooklyn who rode into control of Bridgeport on a public works contract. He followed Roosevelt and came down, not to earth, but alighted neatly in Wall Street, where he is reputed to serve in some way a great financial combination. The antithesis of political leadership with Roraback is the Democratic National Committeeman, Homer S. Cummings, of the silver voice and velvet paw. But he, it must now be told, is an exotic—born in Chicago. Both gentlemen are careful to see that no real harm comes to each other.

Although the Republican margin of votes is normally small, Connecticut has had but two Democratic Governors in forty years, Thomas M. Waller and Simeon E. Baldwin, both of whom owed their success to discontent in the opposition. Each did much for the State, Governor Baldwin taking the roads out of politics in such a way as to keep them out up to date, the State Highway Superintendent, Charles J. Bennett, whom he appointed, being a sound engineer with a policy that has developed permanent pavements laid on trunk lines, where his predecessor spent millions on useless sections of temporary construction scattered to please localities and doing no one good.

The State has been chary in the past about enacting general legislation. It is less than ten years since it passed a banking act. The general railroad act was wiped out when Mellen moved in. Petty judges are appointed by the legislature, members not infrequently naming themselves for the honor. The constitution's plea that there should be no monopoly of office-holding is often grossly disregarded. Though the faithful be plenty, there are many cases of double place-keeping that pass unrebuked. Clifford E. Wilson, Mayor of Bridgeport for many years, enjoyed three terms as Lieutenant Governor, while holding his city job, and another genius in office getting contrived to be State senator, State treasurer, and county judge in one overlapping period of bliss. Local officials are constantly picking up State or county jobs under this kindly system of respecting their several terms.

The electorate, it may be sadly said, is corrupt. I myself, in the course of several political adventures, have been three times offered the "control" at the polls of the richest community under town government in the United States. The offer was made in good faith by a man quite competent to carry it out. The poor towns are just as bad as the rich in this respect. Election Day is a biennial harvest. The Republicans are the usual purchasers. The practice began in a desire to save the country and become permanent as part of the process of saving themselves. One factor in the corruption of Connecticut local politics is the system of minority representation. A town Board of Selectmen consists of three members. Four candidates run. The three highest win. An aggressive nominee for the minority is readily beaten by a deal with the majority which can head him in the poll. So good men who might truly represent rarely win. The third man is usually a dummy or a conformer. The same method applies to the choice of assessors and justices of the peace. Well meant, it leads to party treachery and individual chicane through which the minority often has worse than no representation.

Under a system of privilege-selling the citizens of the State have been deprived of much that was their own. For example, nearly all of the long waterfront with its rocks and beaches, bathing facilities and the liberty to dig shell-fish in the sand has passed into private ownership to the great hardship of the people at large. Maine, Massachusetts, and Rhode Island, with jealous eye, have guarded "fisherman's rights" and so have preserved access to the sea. The proudest estate at Bar Harbor, Nahant, and Narragansett must provide a pathway to the shore. In Connecticut "No Trespass" signs mock the people. From Byram shore to Stonington the story is about the same. Greenwich has preserved to itself a waterfront fifteen feet wide, and Sound Beach, imposing as is its name, is little more than a few grains of sand for the public. Here and there a town has salvaged some of its former possessions. Stamford, though it lost possession of the glorious shores of Shippan Point, has established a park on old meadows and

given it a sandy shore, and Westport makes the proceeds of a town-owned bathing beach pay a good slice of its expenses. The State also suffers scenically from
the invasion of the rich. The segregated shore front, where the "villa" prevails,
is further monopolized by the planting of trees and shrubbery, so as to cut off the
view. Even on the uplands, where the wealthy have come to live, the roads are
girded with walls of stone or hedges of privet, so that one can no longer look
across the land.

Industry, too, has dealt hardly with nature. The rivers and bays are polluted.
The shad that once crowded the Connecticut come in scant schools, where once
they were legion, and the salmon come not at all. Menhaden exterminators have
driven bluefish, striped bass, and weakfish from the Sound and the minor species suffer from the sewage in the harbors and the poison in the streams. In remote shore spots lobsters still hide amid the reefs and command metropolitan
prices when caught. A few men live by an occupation that once supported many.

Beyond this the franchises of railways, water, and light are mainly in outside
hands. It was considered "slick" to unload them as was so generously done during the Mellen regime. The result was not so satisfying. So great a burden was
laid upon the New Haven road, in which many had their hoard, as to crush its
earning power, while the costs of travel, of light, of water, and of power have
gone up. These the public pay. Their increment in the main goes elsewhere. The
State's system of justice does not work for the general advantage, but since the
railroad quit naming the judges the bench has greatly improved. The jury system
continues bad. Jury lists are compiled by the town selectmen, who reward all
too often men of poor caliber with a chance to earn the fee. The Town of Greenwich was a conspicuous sinner in this respect, so much so that Chief Justice
George W. Wheeler found it necessary not so long ago to warn the selectmen
that he would punish them if better material were not forthcoming.

Grand jurors are elected by the towns, but do not sit as a County body to consider complaints and hand down indictments. Their functions are limited to
transmitting information of law infractions to minor jurists and the powers given
are so limited as to be practically nil. The ordinary run of criminals pass through
the hands of a town prosecutor; important cases, through those of the State's
Attorney, who serves the county. The decision of guilt rests in their hands. This
leads sometimes to extraordinary miscarriages that need not be listed here. Cor-
oners are appointed by the judges of the Superior Court upon the recommenda-
tion of the State's attorney. Persons reporting the finding of a body dead from
violence are rewarded with a tip of fifty cents. An appeal from a local to the
county court begins the case *de novo*. The State's Attorney decides whether or
not he will go on, regardless of the local official. So the accused has always
what is pleasingly called "a chance." This power sometimes becomes visible in
local politics. In capital cases only, a grand jury summoned by the Sheriff considers and indicts.

Taxation is, on the whole, light. There is an elaborate personal-tax provision,
but it is not enforced by penalty, so it is generally disregarded. Four dollars per

$1,000 is levied annually on bonds held in the State. There is no remedy for non-compliance until death, when the State steps in and collects five times the amount and retroacts it for five years. So it gets something. Under its charter the New York, New Haven and Hartford Railroad is expected to turn all its earnings above 10 per cent over to the State. In its most prosperous days the prudent management always contrived so that nothing accrued to the commonwealth, but it found that it was much easier to deal with a surplus than a deficiency. One thing the Mellen regime did besides electrifying the line to New Haven deserves remembering. It planted both sides of the track from Mount Vernon on for many miles with ramblers of the Dorothy Perkins variety. These have flourished in sand and cinders, in all the hard soil along a railroad cut, so that in the month of June the path of the commuter is strewn with roses, even if there are none for the stockholders. It is a moot question whether the obligation to pay the State all returns above 10 per cent does not constitute an obligation that would annul the wrecking of the road's earning power by loading it with worthless properties, like the unlawful dissipation of assets by a creditor, making the lines eligible for seizure by the State as in violation of contract. No lawyer or citizen has ever taken steps to test the point, while of course the State government itself is supine as usual in corporate matters. The Attorney General is seldom selected for aggressiveness.

The communities are curiously self-centered. The many excellent newspapers circulate closely at home. There is no journal with a statewide distribution. New York to the west and Boston to the east smother them. This does not mean that they are not profitable. Usually they are—some of them very much so, like the pair in Hartford, which probably earn more per capita of population than any other sheets in America. They simply do not reach out and there is no covering editorial influence. In the paternal days of the railroad management the train service was so arranged as to keep the New York and Boston papers back until the news grew cold as a form of protecting the local press and keeping it amiable. This ceased during the Spanish War, when the city papers bought train service, which later became regular, not the least to the disadvantage of the home journalism, so far as profits go. It has prospered since as never before. A misfortune it is that some of the cities are dominated by journals grouped together by the National Manufacturers' Association; not that this does their owners much good. It is simply against the interests of the community if there is any merit in the theory of a free and untrammeled press.

The cities have become strongly foreign. The country is still strongly native. The melting process is slow, because the large immigration to industrial centers broods together by nationalities. Italians are the strongest force industrially, the Irish politically. The Democratic mayors of New Haven, Waterbury, Hartford, Meriden, and Middletown are of Celtic descent; New Britain's ruler is Italian. In some of the rude reaches of the north, middle, and east bordering Rhode Island, where the scenery is best, dwell grades of people whose minds and habits make the observer regret the extermination of the Mohegans and Pequots. It seems to be the mood of nature when on show to breed the poorest samples of mankind. These back countrymen are not influenced by newcomers of wealth or by the nearness of cities. When a traveler expressed astonishment at one living but an hour away from New York who had not "been thar" for eighteen years, he replied: "Why should I go—I've plenty to do here." And he had!

The State is New England in epitome. It has character, often too latent in these latter days. That this will soon reassert itself through the coming of women into political life is my profound belief. Just as Barbara Frietchie "took up the flag the men hauled down," the new owners of the franchise will surely elevate its political morals, abashing the careless and corrupt males and lifting up the parties above sordid office-getting and the selling of popular rights. These women of Connecticut who have picked up the gage are not "flappers" or notoriety seekers. They are the sort a real man likes for a mother.

Incidentally it may be added that Connecticut has mothered much. The now overcrowded Dartmouth College began as Dr. Eleazer Wheelock's Indian School in Lebanon, with Joseph Brant, the "cruel Mohawk," as one of the first pupils. She mothered Ohio, whose "fire-lands" given to pay the State for British raids during the Revolution became the Western Reserve of Connecticut, giving it and us the Shermans, the Tafts, and other worthy names. She mothered the assault on Ticonderoga during the early hours of the Revolution, when Ethan Allen with Connecticut troops took the stronghold in "the name of the Great Jehovah and the Continental Congress." Her soldiers under Israel Putnam and his like followed the English flag to Quebec and the Havannah. She built a navy of her own to aid the Continentals as bravely by sea as her men had done by land, and the graves of her dead lie thickly in the fields of France.

A land of steady habits, not all good, but her own!

DELAWARE

The Ward of a Feudal Family

ARTHUR WARNER

SEPTEMBER 6, 1922

LEGALLY ADOPTED or wantonly kidnapped from the Sisterhood of the Forty-eight, Delaware has become the ward of a feudal family and the victim of a family feud. Of no other child of these United States is one family so closely in control; upon no other have the actions, the aspirations, and the quarrels of a single family had so profound a repercussion.

The visitor is apprised of the dominance of the Du Ponts the moment he descends from the train in Wilmington. He is driven, as a matter of course, to the Hotel Du Pont. He discovers it to be part of the huge Du Pont Building, which dwarfs all other structures and contains, besides the hotel and corridor of offices, one of the city's principal theaters. In addition to the executive offices of the great explosives company, with its numerous offshoots and graftings, the newcomer notes the existence of the Du Pont Country Club, the Du Pont Gun Club, and the Alexis I. Du Pont School; he learns that there is a North and a South Du Pont Street in Wilmington and not far outside of it a town of Dupont and a fort of the same designation. The Wilmington City Directory for 1921–1922 lists twenty-eight persons or organizations bearing the family name.

These are merely superficial evidences of the infiltration of Dupontism. Investigation reveals more vital and surprising saturation. Since 1906, when Henry A. Du Pont broke the long legislative deadlock caused by the stubborn candidacy of John Edward Addicks and was seated in the United States Senate, the leadership of the Republican Party in Delaware has been in the Du Pont family. Since 1921, when T. Coleman Du Pont went into the United States Senate by a trade with the Democratic incumbent, Josiah O. Wolcott, the Democratic Party in the State has been disorganized and divided, unable to present any adequate opposition. In addition to large holdings of real estate and the great power exercised through the explosives company, the Du Ponts have sapped in numerous directions into Delaware finance. Lammot Du Pont is the largest single stockholder in the powerful Wilmington Trust Company while Alfred I. Du Pont and his cousin William control the Delaware Trust Company, with its home office in Wilmington and a half-dozen branches in other towns.

Even more important in the process of Dupontization than political and industrial power—though far less understood and appreciated in Delaware—is the hold of the family upon the means of influencing public opinion in the State: newspapers, welfare organizations, and the schools. All of the three daily newspapers printed in Delaware (the Wilmington *Morning News,* the *Evening Journal,* and the *Every Evening*) are in Du Pont hands, together with the *Delmarva Star,* the only Sunday newspaper of general circulation published in Wilmington. Since 1918 a body known as the Service Citizens has become the leading—and to some extent the engulfing—welfare organization of the State by grace of an annual subsidy of $90,000 given by Pierre S. Du Pont. Under his presidency and under a director selected by him, the Service Citizens have conducted educational campaigns to create popular sentiment for a variety of purposes, having been especially active in promoting Mr. Du Pont's most cherished and ambitious civic project: rebuilding the public schools. The Delaware School Auxiliary Association, headed by the director of the Service Citizens, has been organized to administer a school building fund given by Mr. Du Pont. A complete reconstruction of the State's school buildings for Negroes is under way at a cost of a million dollars. The work is expected to be finished in 1923, while it is planned to expend about two and a half millions—in addition to money raised by local communities through taxation—to give modern structures to the white children.

This program is the outgrowth of a movement for better schools which has been the overshadowing political issue in Delaware for the last four years. A survey by the United States Bureau of Education in 1917 placed Delaware thirty-ninth among the States in its school opportunities. A year later the report of a commission appointed by the General Education Board showed the defects in detail. Largely as a result of this report, a new school code was put through the legislature, but partly because of expense and partly because of interference with certain ancient local customs the new law became the vortex of one of the most turbid political whirlpools that has ever stirred the State, and has been changed twice since. It was the outcry against the expense of the State's school program that led Mr. Du Pont to undertake the job at his own cost.

Although formerly a member of the State Board of Education, Mr. Du Pont has nothing to do now with the administration of the schools and I am convinced that his rebuilding program is inspired by the most sincere and disinterested motives. At the same time it has given him an indirect influence upon a fundamental process in the development of public opinion—the training of the young mind—and it is charged that in carrying out his school projects underlings have used the power of his money to coerce or buy action according to their wishes. The fact that the Delaware School Auxiliary Association may grant or withhold its funds for building in the case of any community obviously gives it a powerful lever which, some say, it has not been backward in using. Its stipulation that its own architects must be employed and that school equipment must be purchased through it are also criticized. Mr. Du Pont's activities embrace not only the whole public-school system, but he has also given largely to Delaware University—the only institution of higher learning in the State—among the trustees of which his friends and relatives are well entrenched.

No family in America of equal wealth has stuck more tenaciously to its ancestral home or been more closely identified with the land than the Du Ponts. Neither for administrative nor residence purposes has New York been able to lure them away. Predominantly they are still to be found within a few miles of the original powder mill which Eleuthère Irénée Du Pont de Nemours, their progenitor in this country, set up on the banks of Brandywine Creek, near the present city of Wilmington, in 1802. The close identification of the family with Delaware during all this period is the more remarkable when one considers that the manufacturing establishments of E. I. Du Pont de Nemours and Company have of necessity gone elsewhere, the last one in the State—the original mill on the Brandywine—having been abandoned this year.

The Du Pont family has been self-contained, clannish, and on the whole respected, if not loved, by its neighbors. The third generation has come and mostly gone without the proverbial transition from shirt-sleeves to shirt-sleeves. But for the Du Ponts the second hundred years will be the hardest. During the first century the family took little part in public life and even up to now only two members of it—ex-Senator Henry A. Du Pont and the present Senator T. Coleman Du Pont—have gone into politics as politics. It was solely because of a family squabble that Alfred I. Du Pont took his spectacular plunge into the political pool of Delaware several years ago. Just as, until recently, the family kept out of politics, so it kept out of any business but its own. But the forces of the Twentieth Century which have been fusing politics with business, and squeezing both into molds prescribed by the banks, have carried the Du Ponts with them. The war, with its Midas touch, was a great stimulus. The company expanded from 5,000 to 100,000 employees and its profits bulged in proportion. For the year 1916 the company paid 100 per cent on its common stock, while in consequence of the war that stock ran the gamut from about $20 to $1,000 a share. Naturally these fabulous profits accelerated a transition already begun in the careers of the Du Ponts—from makers simply of explosives to captains of industry interested in dyes, automobiles, and a host of other products; then from captains of industry to politicians, bankers, and directors of public opinion.

The living Du Ponts who have come most into public notice are four: Henry A., Alfred I., T. Coleman, and Pierre S. All are cousins, the first named belonging to the third generation of the family in this country and the other three to the fourth. Henry A. Du Pont, the ex-Senator, is the titular head of the family, receiving the first call on New Year's Day and the consideration due his eighty-four years among relatives where feudal traditions are strong. Henry A. Du Pont is known as "the Colonel," while T. Coleman (now Senator) has raised himself to the rank of "the General." The title of "the Colonel" is a legitimate one descending from service in the Civil War. So far as can be learned, the only fighting front upon which "the General" has served is the sector at Dover occupied by the staff of the Governor of Delaware. It seems a bit incongruous that a Civil War veteran of eighty-four should be only a colonel while his junior adorning a Governor's staff should be a general. But when picking a title for yourself, you might as well choose a good one.

"Cherchez la femme." As already suggested, the evolution of the Du Ponts from small to big business and from big business to industrial politics has been part of a process going beyond them or their State. The unique results in Delaware are due partly to its smallness and partly to a woman—or, rather, to two women. In 1907 Alfred I. Du Pont, having divorced his first wife, married again. But the Du Pont family refused to ratify the divorce and declined to receive the new wife. In some families and in some States this would scarcely have mattered. Among the Du Ponts and in Delaware it did. Retaliation and a family quarrel ensued which have been largely responsible for the orgy of vote buying that Delaware has recently experienced and the present demoralization of the Democratic Party. T. Coleman Du Pont, having decided to get out of the explosives business, offered his stock for sale to the company. It was refused by the company on the advice of its president, then Pierre S. Du Pont. The latter subsequently organized a pool in the family—in which Alfred I. Du Pont was not included—and bought the stock. Alfred I. joined in a suit to prevent the sale of the securities to the pool. Eventually the courts sustained the arrangement, but in the meanwhile the family had become divided and the political debauchery of the State which Addicks began had been carried to a new stage. For Alfred I. Du Pont jumped into politics as a means of sabotaging his opponents in the family squabble. The term of Colonel Henry A. Du Pont as United States Senator was to expire in 1917. Failing in an effort to prevent his renomination, Alfred I. Du Pont put an independent Republican up against his cousin and succeeded in throwing the election to the Democratic candidate, Josiah O. Wolcott. In connection with his political fight Alfred I. Du Pont bought the Wilmington *Morning News* and obtained the control of several influential weeklies down State. By 1918 he had come almost, if not altogether, to control the Republican State machine. Is it necessary to add that money was burned like gunpowder in achieving these results?

But at this point Alfred I. Du Pont became involved financially. Pierre S. Du Pont came to his assistance, obtaining for him a loan from J. P. Morgan and Company. One of the conditions—or, at least, consequences—was the surrender by Alfred I. of the *Morning News* and other newspaper properties. About the same time the *Every Evening*, the only Democratic daily in the State, with a tradition of independence and ability, came on the market and was purchased by a brother-in-law of Pierre S. Du Pont. The *Evening Journal* had been acquired a little earlier by others of the family. This publication and the *Morning News* were placed under centralized control, but for the sake of appearances the *Every Evening* was leased to a Democrat who makes a certain show of conducting it in opposition to the other two. The most immediate consequence of the Dupontization of the daily press of Delaware has been not so much to deprive the State of independent political discussion—which few communities enjoy—as to put a stop to the useful revelations that grow out of partisan journalism elsewhere. Amidst the myriad and often conflicting interests of the Du Ponts the editors of their newspapers find it hard to discuss any vital questions and are most at home when deploring, or pointing with pride to—the weather.

Now let us move forward to 1921. Senator Wolcott, elected on a fluke, had never cared for the job. He did want to be Chancellor of Delaware, the highest judicial office in the State. On the other hand T. Coleman Du Pont wanted to go to Washington. His business is largely outside of Delaware—he has a string of hotels and other interests—but he has given four million dollars for a north and south highway through the State and has liberally subventioned the Boy Scouts, Consumers' League, and other organizations of Wilmington. So the strange spectacle was witnessed of a Republican Governor appointing a Republican as United States Senator while asking a Republican legislature to confirm the nomination of a Democrat for Chancellor. It was done; but against the vehement protest of one wing of the Democratic Party, that led by ex-Senator Saulsbury, the adherents of which openly charge that the arrangement was an over-the-counter cash transaction, even going so far as to name the amounts that various persons received. In any event the affair further split the already disorganized Democrats, and is the latest chapter in the political corruption begun by Addicks and continued by Dupontism—a debauchery so general and direct that, in the southern part of the State especially, farmers have come to regard their votes as a staple crop, legitimate as sweet potatoes, and to market them almost as shamelessly.

As indicating the vagaries of Du Pont journalism, it may be noted that the *Evening Journal* and the *Morning News,* which, of course, are supporting T. Coleman Du Pont for election in November for a full Senatorial term, are condemning the appointment a year ago of Mr. Wolcott—which was for the sole purpose of creating a vacancy for their candidate.

So much for the Du Ponts. Now what of the fabric of the State upon which they have embroidered their lives? Delaware is the second smallest State in the Union both in area and population. Politically speaking, one may question whether it ought to be a State at all. The fact that it has two Senators and only one Representative in Congress shows how illogical its situation is. Geographically, industrially, and socially, there is even less reason for its statehood. It is an artificial slice of the peninsula that lies between Delaware and Chesapeake bays. This region, locally known as the Delmarva Peninsula, is an almost perfect entity in its geographical situation, its industries, and its inhabitants. But Fate has decreed that the southern tip of this peninsula shall belong to Virginia, the western part to Maryland, and the rest to Delaware. And in spite of all reasons to the contrary, so it will probably remain.

This whole Delmarva Peninsula lies only a few feet above sea level. The watershed between Delaware and Chesapeake bays is so inconspicuous that even

Nature scarcely knows where to find it. Rivers that run—or drag their way—toward the Chesapeake are so interlaced at their source with those going in the other direction that they must often get wretchedly mixed. Brother and sister currents in the same rivulet may find themselves deflected by a pebble or a tuft of grass, not to meet again until they hail one another in the great Atlantic, one having arrived via the Chesapeake and Cape Charles, the other by the Delaware and Cape May. These level acres make wonderful fruit and vegetable gardens. Yes, you exclaim, the Delaware peach! Ah, but disease brought the peach orchards near to extinction several years ago; for a time peaches became as scarce in Delaware as cowboys in the streets of Chicago. They have returned somewhat, but tend to be overshadowed now by apples. Meanwhile the strawberry flourishes, encouraged by Prohibition and the seething and multiplying soda-water fountain. Some twenty million quarts are picked in a good year—at 2½ cents a quart! At least that was the pay proffered in Wilmington at the beginning of the 1922 season. It is the same as, or only half a cent better than, the rate twenty years ago when farmers were glad to sell their berries at six to eight cents a quart instead of twenty to twenty-five. The answer is: child labor. The State has a child-labor law which forbids the once prevalent employment of children under fourteen years of age in canneries, but like most such legislation the statute does not apply to farm work. Thousands of children are employed—and kept out of school in the meanwhile—to gather strawberries, tomatoes, sweet potatoes, and other products of the vast garden from which Delaware largely subsists. Without such assistance it is argued—doubtless justly—that the farmers would be well-nigh helpless. Which raises another problem.

Despite the fact that it lies on the Eastern seaboard midway between North and South, Delaware is one of the least visited of our States—one of the least disturbed by the winds of controversy, cult, and progress that roar over the rest of the Union. Thousands of persons pass through the northern tip of the State every week on the two great railway routes between New York City and Washington, but if they stop at all it is only in Wilmington. And Wilmington is no more like the rest of Delaware than New York City is like the rest of the United States. Wilmington contains nearly half of Delaware's 223,003 inhabitants, but it does not rule its State as certain other large cities of the country do theirs. It has only two of seventeen members in the State Senate and five representatives among thirty-five in the lower house. It is by no means allowed to hog the political plums, custom decreeing that the Governor, the two United States Senators, the one Representative, and other officials be passed around among the three counties of the State according to a regular rotation.

When one leaves the trunk railways at Wilmington and heads southward—as few but commercial travelers seem to do—he begins to penetrate the real Delaware. If he goes in springtime, as I did, he sees in progress a vast and omnipresent assault upon the soil, a mass attack upon the earth with plow and harrow and seed drill. Acre upon acre of pink, freshly turned ground. Peach orchards waving leaves of shiny yellow-green. Apple orchards with nodding boughs of cool gray-green. Fields lying fallow, brilliant with crimson clover and golden patches of blossoming wild mustard.

Dover is the smallest State capital in the United States and with two exceptions the only one of less than 5,000 inhabitants. Its shady streets are restful and its public square, or Green, carries one well out of the toil and moil of this Twentieth Century. Planted with towering sycamores, elms, and maples, the Green is surrounded by still more ancient buildings, among which stand out the Court House and the State Capitol, both of mellow saffron brick with milk-white columns, porticos, and cupolas, reminiscent of colonial days in the old South. The buildings that are not Court House or State Capitol gleam with brass plates carrying the names of lawyers sufficient for the whole of Delaware. To be a lawyer caged behind a glass door in an iron-ribbed New York office building has always seemed to me a job I should enjoy not having; but to sit behind a brass plate, put my feet on the desk, and look out over Dover Green—well, there could be worse occupations, particularly if not interrupted by too many clients.

If Delaware is little disturbed from without, it is even less so from within. Settled originally by English and Dutch stock, its population has been largely self-perpetuating with remarkably little of the later foreign infusions which have transformed or created so many of our other States. The old English law prevails in Delaware more intact perhaps than anywhere in our country, together with the ancient legal vocabulary. Delaware still has its courts of chancery and of oyer and terminer. The pillory existed up to recent date and the whipping-post still survives, uniquely among the States. The political division of the hundred—corresponding to a township—persists, as does the levy court with its levy courtmen (the latter administrative, not judicial, officers).

Like all self-contained and ingrowing communities, Delawareans look with suspicion upon persons coming to live among them who have been so ill advised as to be born somewhere else. Sometimes years of residence can hardly remove the taint from the carpet-bagger. The head of a philanthropic society, who had come from another State, told me that after urging some action upon a public officer the latter said to him kindly but as if actuated by some great principle: "I like you, but I sha'n't vote for the appropriation because you're not a Delawarean."

Wilmington is the spot in the State, if any, where one would expect to encounter an eager intellectual life. Does one? On the half-mile stretch of Market Street from Christiana Creek to the Du Pont Building—the city's chief business artery—I discovered only one bookstore. Wishing to know where the others might be, I consulted the City Directory and found only one other listed for all of Wilmington! The automobile, the five-and-ten-cent store, the movies, and the pineapple nut sundae have entered Delaware with their standardized virtues and vulgarities, but of mental stimulus the State seems to produce little and to import less. A young woman in Wilmington (a carpet-bagger from New England) confessed to a liking for the newer poetry, but said she had found nobody who cared to discuss it with her. "They think my interest in it is just the eccentricity of a Boston highbrow."

Delawareans generally deplore the political corruption of their State and some look with apprehension on the growing financial ascendancy of a single family. But they are almost unanimously unaware even of the facts of, much less the danger in, the control by the Du Ponts of press, welfare work, and education. When these things are called to their attention they plead as excuse the State's poverty and backwardness, heedless that such conditions are intensified and solidified by the stifling of independence and initiative. In this, of course, the people of Delaware are not alone. They are children of a generation pathetically and universally eager to barter permanent spiritual values in return for opportunist material advantages. The Dupontization of Delaware is not a unique development. It is an advanced stage of a process under way in the United States as a whole. All along the line existing governmental organization—Federal, State, and municipal—grows increasingly impotent before the important questions of the age. It is baffled to find either the money or the intelligence to attack big problems in a big way. On the other hand the last twenty years have seen a vast augmentation of private benefaction and the establishment of various foundations the interest charges upon whose great funds are a controlling lever upon the work—and thus the lives—of thousands of men and women yet unborn. If a sparse scattering of Carnegie libraries and Rockefeller colleges is good for the rest of America, why is not the State-wide, all-inclusive educational plant promised to Delaware by Dupontism a superboon? Either Delaware is right, or the rest of the country too is wrong. We must be willing to consider a new industrial basis for society or to drift on in the direction of an oligarchy ruled not by supermen but by superwealth.

If this is to be the destiny of the Sisterhood of the Forty-eight, then credit as the leader of a new Americanism—not blame as a backslider from the old—belongs to Delaware under the dynasty of the Du Ponts.

Meanwhile the aroma of the strawberry and the fragrance of the peach perfume the State; the Green at Dover is a tonic for fretful minds; and the potato biscuit which I ate at Lewes survives in memory as a work of art which ennobles a whole State—a deed of piety for which some woman ought to be canonized.

FLORIDA

The Desert and the Rose

CLARA G. STILLMAN

OCTOBER 31, 1923

A FLAT, SANDY, sun-bathed plain sprinkled with a sparse monotony of pine, punctuated here and there with vague swamplands and thick, rich forests intricate with interlacings of hardwood, scrub, and vine, and jeweled with thousands of sparkling lakes, streams, and fountains—such is Florida, a paradise for invalids, sportsmen, and naturalists. To the east the far-flung coast line harbors still other waterways, great salt rivers and lakes formed by shallow sandbars and peninsulas lying parallel with the mainland. To the south stretches the vast region of the Everglades, eight thousand square miles of swamp and partly submerged prairie bristling with rapier-edged saw-grass eight feet high, a panoplied wilderness only recently penetrated by white men, through which Indians have traveled swiftly from time immemorial. The west coast, curving widely around the gulf, crumbles away at its southern end into the archipelago of the Ten Thousand Islands, a land of mystery, a labyrinth of woods, swamps, mud flats, beaches, bays, and fierce tidal rivers that has never been completely explored. Most of the southern shore, too, is a little-known wilderness. Florida preserves for us, though probably not for long, our last remnant of virgin soil.

No other State thrusts down into the Tropics. No other contains so many kinds of climate and soil, such an elongated and diversified coastline, such a widely distributed and easily tapped water supply, such varied luxuriance of native and naturalized vegetation. As a final unique gesture there are the Keys, that exotic flourish beyond the mainland's southern tip, of coral and limestone reefs and prickly island jungles, swept and sculptured into jagged grotesqueness by wild tropic tides, eternally being built up and dissolved away by wind and sea—remote repositories of curious and entrancing forms of life.

In 1513 came Ponce de Léon seeking the fabled island of Bimini, its fountain of youth and its mythical treasure far surpassing the known splendors of Mexico and Peru. Then for three hundred and fifty years the smiling region remained a wilderness, tossed from Spain to England, from England back to Spain, from Spain in part to France, finally from France and Spain to the United States. It became a territory distracted by Indian wars, then a State entering the Union only to secede a few months later, then a State once more, enfeebled by civil war and racked with war-born hatreds and maladjustments. In its history there has been little continuity or coherence. Of British and Spanish occupation hardly a trace persisted. During the Revolution the State was a base for loyalist plots. Seven thousand Tories fled there. The wilderness beyond the frontier became a refuge for fugitive slaves and other outlaws. To the more accessible regions there was a trickle of immigration from the North, from Alabama and Georgia, mainly a low grade of white squatter, but conditions were not such as to attract wealth or culture. Such germs of social life and refinement as existed at all were concentrated in the great cotton plantations and the few small towns in the north. Here were some magnificent homes and such wealth and fashion as the State could boast. The least-developed territory admitted to statehood, Florida was at the outbreak of the Civil War the poorest of the Southern States, with the fewest towns, plantations, and slaves. It had no social, political, or religious traditions such as went to the founding of Massachusetts, Maryland, Virginia, or South Carolina, and no homogeneous group of citizens bound by common ideals to develop it in any particular direction. Immigration for the culture of oranges and the taking up of land for homes began seriously about 1870. In the eighties were discovered the great potash fields of the southwest. And long before that St. Augustine and the St. Johns River had been centers of winter travel.

But it was in the nineties, with the beginning of the great railway systems— the East Coast, of which Henry M. Flagler was the presiding genius, and the Atlantic Coast Line, carried down to Tampa by Henry B. Plant—that Florida's history as a modern State actually began. As they pushed south the railroad companies built the huge, elaborate hotels so well known to all tourists, at least from the outside, which were to be the last word in comfort, elegance, and expense. Plant died before completing all that he had planned, but the Flagler system pushed on, passing beyond the last small pioneer settlements to tame wildernesses and plant palaces in lonely deserts and jungles. Palm Beach arose to snatch from St. Augustine its social eminence as the Winter Newport. By 1896 the railroad had reached Miami, dropped another hotel into the wilds, and proceeded on its way to perform one of the most appealing of modern engineering feats—the Overseas Route that joins Key West and the intervening keys to the mainland, snaring wild islands and binding turbulent seas with concrete and steel, and stopping finally only because there were no more keys to conquer.

Now began a period of sensational economic development. Tourists overran the State. East coast, west coast, and center sprouted resorts like mushrooms. A thousand and one agencies sprang up to cater to their needs. A huge floating population of invalids and pleasure-seekers that had to be housed, fed, clothed, doctored, nursed, entertained. A secondary throng of floaters arriving to help serve the first. A great stock-taking and overhauling of regional resources. A hectic competition of road-building and developing schemes. Great swamp areas drained and turned into fertile farm and fruit lands. The most ambitious of these projects, the draining of the Everglades, has been going on for some eighteen years, and is not yet completed. While tourists continued to be enthusiastically cultivated, settlers and investors were and still are a greater need. For in spite of the large volume of immigration from other States, there are still only 17.7 inhabitants to the square mile, and planned improvements are constantly outstripping taxes and bond issues. Hence an endless, vociferous campaign of real-estate enterprise, of building and boosting, of speculations and bonuses and invitations to free trips with luncheons and eloquence thrown in.

Perhaps because of an inferiority complex due to her long history of frustration and her lack of traditions. Florida has suddenly discovered an unlimited pride and faith in herself, an enormous appetite for wealth and power. Her climate is unrivaled, her soil unsurpassed. She can produce three crops a year and some that can be grown nowhere else in the country. To her long list of products and manufactures—fish, sponges, cigars, lumber, turpentine, potash, tobacco, citrus fruits, peaches, pineapples, potatoes, tomatoes and other vegetables, sugar and forage grasses—items are constantly being added. For her growing commerce she is busily deepening harbors. Nothing less than everything that any other State has, with a few slight exceptions such as mountains and glaciers, and as many things as possible that other States have not is her economic ideal. A great world playground. But this is not enough. A great agricultural commonwealth unrivaled in the quantity, quality, and variety of its products. But this is not enough. A great focus of world trade with opulent cities strewn along its splendid coasts, cities that shall combine 100 per cent industrialism with 100 per cent American home atmosphere and 100 per cent opportunities for luxury and pleasure. If anything has been omitted, let the reader supply it and be sure that Florida includes that too in her vision of greatness.

Material greatness, of course. For Florida, mixture of infant prodigy, spoiled prima donna, and *nouveau riche,* has the engaging and disheartening qualities of all three. Forced into adult ways beyond her years, what wonder that she frequently lapses into corners to play with dolls or make faces, what wonder that like the slattern beautiful only for company she decks herself gorgeously according to her lights, in her tourist centers and rich agricultural regions, with wastes of slovenly, burned-out, swamp-gutted rural destitution and decay between. Nothing can exceed the forlornness of some of her aspects, with windowless cabins and crazy lean-tos in the midst of a sandy waste containing a few stricken pines, anemically sharing a bog with weedy, undaunted razorbacks and discouraged cattle mournfully nosing among inhospitable cypress roots. Then there are Florida's beautiful schoolhouses—for her white children—which she has scattered about with a prodigal hand. Only the best is to be good enough for them. And naively to her the best is always something to be seen, touched, and financially rated. But school terms are short, teachers few and poor, and money for their salaries not always forthcoming. Here is the antithesis of the little red schoolhouse of New England tradition with its meager equipment dedicated to high purposes.

Nothing distinguished has yet emerged from Florida, whether in statesmanship, scholarship, letters, or arts, and whatever comes in the future will have to struggle through a pall of American provincialism, economic ruthlessness, and Protestant obscurantism. Florida took William Jennings Bryan to her bosom with the instant mutual recognition that they were made for each other. But Florida is a melting-pot of all the States. So what one finds there is after all not only typically Southern but a composite of small-town and rural Americanism with an infusion of pioneer crudeness and youthful bumptiousness. The States and sections of the country are, however, not equally represented. The Southern cracker type still rules in politics, which are narrowly local and unprogressive. Florida, after years of agitation, still retains the antiquated open range for cattle, still finds in abuse of the Negro the master key to political office, and would still be farming her county prisoners to the highest bidder had not recent sensational disclosures, made by another State, of the murderous brutalities practiced upon her unhappy convict slaves forced her only a few months ago to abolish the lash and sweep the leasing system out of existence.

There are in fact many Floridas within the boundaries of the State, and some of them know little of some of the others. There is, for instance, the proposed political division along geographical lines which frequently comes up for discussion. The northern part of the State was settled long before the rest, the center is but of yesterday, the south barely of today and partly of tomorrow. United only in their common jealousy of California, whose minutest blizzard, seismic tremor, or other liability or peccadillo is enthusiastically featured on every Florida newspaper's front page, these parts are jealous of each other. The north has the State capitol and all the public institutions. In 1885, when the present constitution was established, representation was according to population, which was much denser in the northern counties, and no change in the ratio has since been made in spite of strenuous efforts of the southern counties to bring it about. In the last twenty-five years the increase in population in the southern half of the State and in its political and economic consciousness has been phenomenal. South Florida feels that it is different, unique indeed among all parts of the Union in climate, aspect, agricultural and structural possibilities. It is developing a regional self-consciousness and dreams of a regional culture. So one hears talk sometimes of a separation into two States—North and South Florida—and even into three—part of northwestern Florida to become part of Alabama so that Alabama may have a larger access to the sea and the north gulf coast a better representation.

The jealousies of Florida, however, exist not only between north and south but between east and west coast and individual resorts in the same or different regions. Miami and Jupiter "merely cling to the outer skirts of Palm Beach," a booklet informs us, which compares Palm Beach to Egypt, Venice, Honolulu, Algiers, Mandalay, Constantinople, Greece, and Mecca, "the Mecca of the pilgrim with his face turned toward Society, and perhaps praying equally as fervently as his Bedouin brother," a Mecca, moreover, to which one does not merely travel in a Pullman but makes "a journey of de luxe idealism." But tourist Florida is not all extravagance and fashion. It may be a small room with a kitchenette in which a Northern farm couple are passing a thrifty and comfortable winter. One sees them mainly in the center and on the west coast—for the east goes after bigger game—but actually they are everywhere, strong, ungainly, weather- and work-worn, or cadaverous and pale, sitting about on park benches, pitching horseshoes in shirt sleeves, or forcing huge fists to guide treacherous pens over the gay stationery provided by paternal boards of trade. They are from Vermont, New Hampshire, Iowa, Michigan, Kansas, from everywhere where farmers in winter sit by the stove behind the snowdrifts. They have found a better way to wait for planting time. "Like it? Wall, I guess I do. Four feet o' snow to hum," and they smile, crinkling little red eyes, sharing with you the picture and the subjective shiver in the rosy well-being of sun-warmed blood and appeased "rheumatics." Yes, they'd like fust rate to settle if they was twenty years younger. "But there 'tis. Ma 'n' me's too old to start fresh." Sometimes they do settle, fail wretchedly, and are fortunate if they can return to their frost-bound Northern haven. Sometimes with efficiency and luck they reap a golden harvest in spite of the real-estate man. For these and for the many others who need the sun Florida is all golden.

Then there is the naturalists' Florida, far different from that of the railroad folder and the realtor's snappy blurb, unimproved, unmanicured, devoid of sleekness and comfort, full of hardship, danger, adventure, and beauty, now being pushed ever farther south and fast disappearing. The stories of these men are hidden from the public gaze in the journals of museums and scientific societies. Only one that I know of, Charles Torrey Simpson, a veteran explorer of thirty years' standing, has emerged into the open with a delightful book, *In Lower Florida Wilds,* which is at once a paean to the wild life he knows so well and a protest against its passing. Through its pages one may come to see in the vanishing tropic and semi-tropic forests, the rich, wild hammocks, Florida's unique treasure, whose like is not in any other State, and will soon be little more than a memory in this. His is a voice crying for the wilderness fast turning into tomato farms, pineapple fields, and cocoanut groves, and with him one learns to mourn the departing mangrove, most human of trees, whose primitive methods of land building are giving way before the concrete sea-wall, the dredge, and the suction pump; the flamingo, the roseate spoonbill, the gentle, colorful race of tree snails, and other wild things that die in the presence of civilized man.

Still another Florida, least known of any, through which most travelers and natives walk blindfolded or upon which they bestow the cursory attention and facile generalizations of the "car-window sociologist." This is the colored man's Florida, which differs more from all the other Floridas than they do from each other. What does Florida mean to its Negro inhabitants? It is "the best of the bad States," one will tell you. On the whole it used to be better before there were so many people and so much competition. Of course this means some increase in economic opportunity, but also increased discrimination and bitterness. In

Miami, the wonder city, pride of South Florida, where some of its citizens dream a new culture is to be born, we have this extraordinary situation, extraordinary even for the South: a curfew regulation. No Negro except those needed as night bell boys, porters, and the like by hotels allowed out of the colored section of the city after 9 P.M. No Negroes permitted to act as public chauffeurs, or, in the winters at least, in any but unskilled jobs connected with building. In winter, when building is at a standstill in the North, northern workmen, "snow birds" or "white doves" in Negro parlance, flock south. Work must be found for the white doves, so out go the blackbirds. It is hardly within the power of any builder to retain his colored workmen, even if he wishes to. Pressure is too strong. In summer when pressure relaxes one may find Negro workmen again on the job, but the uncertainty and seasonal character of the work discourage them, as it is intended they shall. Miami is proud of its "solution" of the race problem. They "keep them down" and "You must hand it to the Southerners," remarks many an admiring Yankee, "they know how to treat the niggers." Odd, this, for Miami is anywhere from 75 to 85 per cent Northern. What becomes, then, of the pleasant myth that the presence of so many Northerners in Florida has perceptibly lightened the Negro's lot? It continues to be a pleasant myth.

Miami is of course the extreme. As everywhere in the South, the Negro's condition varies greatly in various sections. Places are "good" and "bad" from the Negro point of view, and it is not always easy to know why some should be one and some the other. Thus Miami is bad, Tampa is good. St. Augustine is good, Jacksonville less so. In the northwest there is a certain amount of peonage—white peons as well as black, caught in the net of tenant farming with all its attendant evils in remote rural districts where conditions are always at their worst. If the white schools throughout the State are poorly developed except architecturally, colored schools have not even architecture to boast of. Brick buildings are rare and matter for some pride. In all the State there is not a single standard colored high school. In all South Florida there is only one high school, so called, for colored children, the one at Tampa, which shares a somewhat down-at-heel brick building outside the city limits and its principal with a grammar school. The equipment for this school did not include chairs. The money for these was recently raised by colored citizens. They still have no desks for some classes. They have themselves put in electricity, so they can use the building for evening meetings. Chemistry is in the curriculum, but it has to be taught theoretically because there is no apparatus. School terms are everywhere shorter than those of the white schools, which are themselves in some cases shorter than they should be. There are several counties that have no colored schools at all. The Florida Agricultural and Mechanical College, the State College for Negroes at Tallahassee, has a Carnegie library, and at Jacksonville there is a Negro reading room in the Public Library building containing some eight thousand volumes, which cannot grow because there is no budget for its expansion. This is the only public library provision for Negroes in the State.

The colored public school system is supplemented by several large educational institutions supported by denominational and individual contributions. These schools are the soil for a certain timid and delicate growth of optimism that is beginning to raise a somewhat paradoxical head among Florida Negroes. It consists of the feeling that although racial conditions are growing worse, they are also growing better. Violence and lesser forms of oppression have of late years increased, but there is also an increasing number of Negroes technically and intellectually equipped to improve the primitive social conditions under which most of the race lives. There is the rising financial status and the growing spirit of racial responsibility and self-help, so much needed, which is fostered by these schools. If increased education and prosperity sometimes bring with them an increase of persecution, this is to be faced and overcome with still further progress.

Taking it all in all, Florida is physically and spiritually both the desert and the rose, and, strangely, when it appears to be one it often turns out to be the other. Its gray sands and malarial swamps are potential treasure houses of fertility and health; its bustling surface life, its expansive self-satisfaction hide a profound mental and spiritual sterility. There is no reason why we should expect it to be different from other States. Fine climates do not necessarily make fine peoples, and the best States in the world, like the most beautiful woman of the French proverb, can give only what they have.

GEORGIA

Invisible Empire State

W. E. Burghardt Du Bois

January 21, 1925

GEORGIA is beautiful. High on the crests of the Great Smoky Mountains some Almighty Hand shook out this wide and silken shawl—shook it and swung it two hundred glistening miles from the Savannah to the Chattahoochee, four hundred miles from the Appalachians to the Southern sea. Red, white, and black is the soil and it rolls by six great rivers and ten wide cities and a thousand towns, thick-throated, straggling, low, busy, and sleepy. It is a land singularly full of lovely things: its vari-colored soil, its mighty oaks and pines, its cotton-fields, its fruit, its hills.

And yet few speak of the beauty of Georgia. Some tourists wait by the palms of Savannah or try the mild winters of Augusta; and there are those who, rushing through the town on its many railroads, glance at Atlanta or attend a convention there. Lovers of the mountains of Tennessee may skirt the mountains of Georgia; but Georgia connotes to most men national supremacy in cotton and lynching, Southern supremacy in finance and industry, and the Ku Klux Klan.

Now, all this is perfectly logical and natural. Georgia does not belong to this nation by history or present deed. It is a spiritual borderland lying in the shadows between Virginia and Carolina on the one hand, Louisiana on the other, and the great North on the last. It is a land born to freedom from a jail delivery of the unfortunate, which insisted passionately upon slavery and gave poor old Oglethorpe and the London proprietors many a bad night because they tried to prohibit rum and slaves. But Georgia was firm and insisted: "In Spight of all Endeavours to disguise this Point, it is as clear as Light itself, that Negroes are as essentially necessary to the Cultivation of Georgia, as Axes, Hoes, or any other Utensil of Agriculture."

The sweep of the cotton kingdom drove the listless, the poor, and unlucky back to the hills above and around Atlanta and kept on-coming hillmen from descending; while below Macon the great plantation system spread. Away to the south and west stretched this black land—the ancient seat of the cotton king-

94

dom, the granary of the Confederacy. Swamp and twisted oak and mile on mile of cotton are neighbored by the new pecans, tobacco, and peanuts. Below and to the left Brunswick and Darien sleep and decay beside the water that looks on the Caribbean. Below and to the right, the massive flood of Chattahoochee parades to the Gulf with muffled music.

When catastrophe came, Georgia was among the first to see a way out. While other States were seeking two impossible and incompatible things, the subjection of the blacks and defiance of the North, Georgia developed a method of her own. With slavery gone the slave baron was bankrupt and two heirs to his power had rushed forward: The poor white from the hills around and above Atlanta and the Northern speculator—"Scalawag" and "Carpet-Bagger" they were dubbed—sought to rebuild the South. In the more purely agricultural regions this involved a mere substitution of owners and black laborers. But the development of Georgia was to be more than agricultural. It was to be manufacturing and mining; transportation, commerce, and finance; and it was to involve both white and colored labor. This was a difficult and delicate task, but there were Georgians who foresaw the way long before the nation realized it. The first prophet of the new day was Henry W. Grady of Atlanta.[1]

Grady's statue stands in Atlanta in the thick of traffic, ugly, dirty, but strong and solid. He had Irish wit, Southern fire, and the flowers of oratory. He was among the first to incarnate the "Black Mammy" and he spoke in three years three pregnant sentences: in New York in 1886 he made a speech on the "New South" that made him and the phrase famous. He said: "There was a South of slavery and secession. That South is dead." The North applauded wildly. In Augusta, in 1887, he added: "In her industrial growth the South is daily making new friends. Every dollar of Northern money invested in the South gives us a new friend in that section." The South looked North for capital and advertised her industrial possibilities. And finally he said frankly in Boston in 1889: "When will the black man cast a free ballot? When the Northern laborer casts a vote uninfluenced by his employer."

In other words, Grady said to Northern capital: Come South and make enormous profits; and to Southern captains of industry: Attract Northern capital by making profit possible. Together these two classes were to unite and exploit the South; and they were to make Georgia not simply an industrial center but what was much more profitable, a center for financing Southern enterprises; and they would furnish industry with labor that could be depended on.

This last point, dependable labor, was the great thing. Here was a vast submerged class, the like or equivalent of which was unknown in the North. Here were a half-million brawny Negro workers and a half-million poor whites. If they could be kept submerged—hard at work in industry and agriculture—they

---

[1] Henry W. Grady was the editor of the Atlanta *Constitution*. [D. H. B.]

Turpentine farm, Savannah, Georgia. Such workers did not enjoy the fruits of industrial progress. Victims of a racism fostered to keep wage levels low by preventing a multiracial alliance, according to W. E. B. Du Bois, African-Americans in Georgia often toiled under the eyes of the Ku Klux Klan.

would raise cotton, make cotton cloth, do any number of other valuable things, and build a "prosperous" State. If they joined forces, and went into politics to better their common lot, they would speedily emancipate themselves. How was this to be obviated? How were both sets of laborers to be inspired to work hard and continuously? The *modus operandi* was worked out slowly but it was done skillfully, and it brought results. These results have been costly, but they have made Georgia a rich land growing daily richer. The new wealth was most unevenly distributed; it piled itself in certain quarters and particularly in Atlanta— birthplace and capital of the new "Invisible Empire."

The method used to accomplish all this was, in addition to much thrift and work, deliberately to encourage race hatred between the mass of white people and the mass of Negroes. This was easy to develop because the two were thrown into economic competition in brick-laying, carpentry, all kinds of mechanical work connected with the new industries. In such work Negroes and whites were personal, face-to-face competitors, bidding for the same jobs, working or willing to work in the same places. The Negroes started with certain advantages. They were the mechanics of the period before the war. The whites came with one tremendous advantage, the power to vote. I remember a campaign in Atlanta. The defeated candidate's fate was sealed by a small circular. It contained a picture of colored carpenters building his house.

Hoke Smith in his memorable campaign in Georgia in 1906 almost repeated Stephens[2] of forty-five years earlier:

> I believe the wise course is to plant ourselves squarely upon the proposition in Georgia that the Negro is in no respect the equal of the white man, and that he cannot in the future in this State occupy a position of equality.

A white labor leader, secretary of the Brotherhood of Timber Workers, wrote about the same time:

> The next cry raised by the bosses and their stool pigeons is the "Negro question," and so we are often asked, How will the brotherhood handle the Negro and the white men in the same organization? Answer: How do the capitalists or employers handle them? To the employer a workingman is nothing but a profit-producing animal and he doesn't care a snap of his finger what the animal's color is—white, black, red, brown, or yellow; native or foreign born; religious or unreligious—so long as he (the worker) has strength enough to keep the logs coming and the lumber going—that is all the bosses want or ask. It is only when they see the slaves uniting, when all other efforts to divide the workers on the job have failed, that we hear a howl go up as to the horrors of "social equality." Not until then do we really know how sacred to the boss and his hirelings is the holy doctrine of "white supremacy."

On the other hand, once the laborers are thrown into hating, fearing, despising, competing groups, the employers are at rest. As one firm said in 1901, comparing its black labor with white: "Do the same work, and obey better; more profit, less trouble."

In agriculture poor whites and Negroes were soon brought into another sort of indirect competition. The Negroes worked in the fields, the poor whites in the towns which were the market-places for the fields. Gradually the poor whites became not simply the mechanics but the small storekeepers. They financed the plantations and fleeced the workers. They organized to keep the workers "in their places," to keep them from running away, to keep them from striking, to keep their wages down, to terrorize them with mobs. On the other hand the Negroes worked to own land, to escape from country to city, to cheat the merchants, to cheat the landholders.

Then in larger ways and more indirectly both groups of workers came into competition. They became separated according to different, but supporting and interlocked, industries and occupations. Negroes prepared the road-bed for the railroads; whites ran the trains. Negroes were firemen; whites were engineers. Negroes were porters; whites were mill operatives. Finally there was the Negro servant stretching all the way from the great mansion to the white factory hand's hovel, touching white life at every point.

---

[2] Alexander Stephens was a Southern Whig and vice president of the Confederacy. [D. H. B.]

Soon the subtle rivalry of races in industry began. Soon, to the ordinary Georgia white man, the Negro became a person trying to take away his job, personally degrade him, and shame him in the eyes of his fellows; starve him secretly. To the ordinary Georgia Negro, the average white man was a person trying to take away his job, starve him, degrade him, keep him in ignorance, and return him to slavery. And these two attitudes did not spring from careful reasoning. They were so coiled and hidden with the old known and half-known facts that they became matters of instinct and inheritance. You could not argue about them; you could not give or extract information.

It is usual for the stranger in Georgia to think of race prejudice and race hatred as being the great, the central, the unalterable fact and to go off into general considerations as to race differences and the eternal likes and dislikes of mankind. But that line leads one astray. The central thing is not race hatred in Georgia; it is successful industry and commercial investment in race hatred for the purpose of profit.

Skillfully, but with extraordinary ease, the power to strike was gradually taken from both white and black labor. First the white labor vote was used to disfranchise Negroes and the threat of white competition backed by the hovering terror of the white mob made a strike of black workers on any scale absolutely unheard of in Georgia. Continually this disfranchisement went beyond politics into industry and civil life. On the other hand, the power of a mass of cheap black labor to underbid almost any class of white laborers forced white labor to moderate its demands to the minimum and to attempt organization slowly and effectively only in occupations where Negro competition was least, as in the cotton mills.

Then followed the curious and paradoxical semi-disfranchisement of white labor by means of the "white primary." By agreeing to vote on one issue, the Negro, the normal split of the white vote on other questions or the development of a popular movement against capital and privilege is virtually forestalled. Thus in Georgia democratic government and real political life have disappeared. None of the great questions that agitate the nation—international or national, social or economic—can come up for free discussion. Anything that would divide white folk in opinion or action is taboo and only personal feuds survive as the issues of political campaigns. If real issues ever creep in and real difference of opinion appears—"To Your Tents, O Israel"—Do you want your sister to marry a "nigger"?

What induces white labor to place so low a value on its own freedom and true well-being and so high a value on race hatred? The answer involves certain psychological subtleties and yet it is fairly clear. The Southern white laborer gets low wages measured in food, clothes, shelter, and the education of his children. But in one respect he gets high pay and that is in the shape of the subtlest form of human flattery—social superiority over masses of other human beings. Georgia bribes its white labor by giving it public badges of superiority. The Jim Crow legislation was not to brand the Negro as inferior and to separate the races, but rather to flatter white labor to accept public testimony of its superiority instead of higher wages and social legislation. This fiction of superiority invaded public affairs: No Negro schoolhouse must approach in beauty and efficiency a white school; no public competition must admit Negroes as competitors; no municipal improvements must invade the Negro quarters until every white quarter approached perfection or until typhoid threatened the whites; in no city and State affairs could Negroes be recognized as citizens—it was Georgia, Atlanta, the Fourth Ward, *and* the Negroes.

In return for this empty and dangerous social bribery the white laborer fared badly. Of modern social legislation he got almost nothing; the "age of consent" for girls in Georgia was ten years until 1918, when it was, by great effort and outside pressure, raised to fourteen. Child labor has few effective limitations; children of twelve may work in factories and without birth registration the age is ascertainable with great difficulty. For persons "under twenty-one" the legal workday is still "from sunrise to sunset," and recently Georgia made itself the first State in the Union to reject the proposed federal child-labor amendment. Education is improving, but still the white people of Georgia are one of the most ignorant groups of the Union and the so-called compulsory education law is so full of loopholes as to be unenforceable. And black Georgia? In Atlanta there are twelve thousand Negro children in school and six thousand seats in the schoolrooms! In all legislation tending to limit profits and curb the exploitation of labor Georgia lingers far behind the nation.

This effort to keep the white group solid led directly to mob law. Every white man became a recognized official to keep Negroes "in their places." Negro baiting and even lynching became a form of amusement which the authorities dared not stop. Blood-lust grew by what it fed on. These outbreaks undoubtedly affected profits, but they could not be suppressed, for they kept certain classes of white labor busy and entertained. Secret government and manipulation ensued. Secret societies guided the State and administration. The Ku Klux Klan was quite naturally reborn in Georgia and in Atlanta.

Georgia is beautiful. Yet on its beauty rests something disturbing and strange. Physically this is a certain emptiness and monotony, a slumberous, vague dilapidation, a repetition, an unrestraint. Point by point one could pick a poignant beauty—one golden river, one rolling hill, one forest of oaks and pines, one Bull Street. But there is curious and meaningless repetition until the beauty palls or fails of understanding. And on this physical strangeness, unsatisfaction, drops a spiritual gloom. There lies a certain brooding on the land—there is something furtive, uncanny, at times almost a horror. Some folk it so grips that they never see the beauty—the hills to them are haunts of grim and terrible men; the world goes armed with loaded pistols on the hip; concealed, but ready—always ready. There is a certain secrecy about this world. Nobody seems wholly frank—neither white nor black; neither child, woman, nor man. Strangers ask each other pointed searching questions: "What is your name?" "Where are you going?'' ''What might be your business?'' And they eye you speculatively. Once satisfied, the response is disconcertingly quick. They strip their souls naked before you; there is sudden friendship and lavish hospitality. And yet—yet behind all are the grim bars and barriers; subjects that must not be touched, opinions that must not be questioned. Side by side with that warm human quality called ''Southern'' stands the grim fact that right here and beside you, laughing easily with you and shaking your hand cordially, are men who hunt men: who hunt and kill in packs, at odds of a hundred to one under cover of night. They have lynched five hundred Negroes in forty years; they have killed unnumbered white men. There must be living and breathing in Georgia today at least ten thousand men who have taken human life, and ten times that number who have connived at it.

Of religion as it exists in present-day Georgia one may well despair. Georgia is already religious to overflowing. Everyone belongs—must belong—to some church, and really to ''belong,'' one should be Presbyterian or Baptist or Methodist. Episcopalians are unusual, Unitarians gravely suspect, Catholics and Jews feared and hatred. But all these are within the range of understanding and misunderstanding. The hottest of hell-fire is reserved for any so unspeakable as to hold themselves freethinkers, agnostics, or atheists. Georgia's religion is orthodox, ''fundamental.'' It continues to wash its ''miserable sinners'' in ''the blood of the Lamb,'' but the blood of the mob's victim lies silent at its very doors. But outside of the church religion has its uses! When the Ku Klux Klan sent out its official instructions to delegates to the State convention, the Grand Dragon said: ''It is the earnest desire of Mr. McAdoo[3] to elect his friend Mr. John S. Cohen as national committeeman. Mr. Cohen is a high-class Christian gentleman, a member of the North Presbyterian Church of Atlanta.'' No, there is little hope in Georgia religion despite a light here and there.

Nevertheless, there are brave men in Georgia, men and women whose souls are hurt even to death by this merciless and ruthless exploitation of race hatred. But what can they do? It is fairly easy to be a reformer in New York or Boston or Chicago. One can fight there for convictions, and while it costs to oppose power, yet it can be done. It even gains some applause and worth-while friends. But in Atlanta? The students of white Emory College recently invited a student of black Morehouse College to lead a Y.M.C.A. meeting. It was a little thing— almost insignificant. But in Georgia it was almost epoch-making. Ten years ago it would have meant riot. Today it called for rare courage. When the Southern Baptists met in Atlanta recently they did not segregate Negro visitors. Such a thing has seldom if ever happened before in Georgia. It is precisely the comparative insignificance of these little things that shows the huge horror of the bitter fight between Georgia and civilization.

---

[3]William McAdoo of California, secretary of the treasury under Woodrow Wilson, lost the 1924 Democratic presidential nomination on the 103d ballot, in part because of his links with the Ku Klux Klan. [D. H. B.]

Some little things a liberal public opinion in Georgia may start to do, although the politico-economic alliance stands like a rock wall in the path of real reform. A determined group called "inter-racial" asks for change. Most of them would mean by this the stopping of lynching and mobbing, decent wages, abolition of personal insult based on color. Most of them would not think of demanding the ballot for blacks or the abolition of Jim Crow cars or civil rights in parks, libraries, and theaters or the right of a man to invite his black friend to dinner. Some there are who in their souls would dare all this, but they may not whisper it aloud—it would spoil everything; it would end their crusade. Few of these reformers yet fully envisage the economic nexus, the real enemy encased in enormous profit. They think reform will come by right thinking, by religion, by higher culture, and do not realize that none of these will work its end effectively as long as it pays to exalt and maintain race prejudice.

Of the spiritual dilemmas that face men today I know of none more baffling than that which faces the conscientious, educated, forward-looking white man of Georgia. On the one hand is natural loyalty to what his fathers believed, to what his friends never question; then his own difficulty in knowing or understanding the black world and his inbred distrust of its ability and real wish; there is his natural faith in his own ability and the ability of his race; there is the subtle and continuous propaganda—gossip, newspapers, books, sermons, and "science"; there is his eager desire to see his section take a proud place in the civilized world. There is his job, his one party, his white primary—his social status so easily lost if he is once dubbed a "nigger lover." Facing all this is lynching, mob murder, ignorance, silly self-praise of people pitifully degenerate in so many cases, exploitation of the poor and weak, and insult, insult, insult heaped on the blacks.

Open revolt comes now and then. Once Tom Watson tried to unite labor. He organized the Populist Party in Georgia and invited the blacks to help. It was a critical situation that developed in the early nineties, when it was increasingly difficult to keep the Negro disfranchised illegally and not yet possible to disfranchise him legally. In the first campaign it was easy to beat the Populists by the fraud of "counting them out." Immediately thereafter the captains of industry mobilized. By newspaper, by word of mouth, by lodge communications it was conveyed to the white workers that not only would Negroes benefit from any attempt to better the present industrial situation, but they would gradually displace the white workers by underbidding them; that any benefits for white workers must come secretly and in such a way that Negroes could not share in the benefits. Thus immediately the emphasis was put on race discrimination. And this race difference grew and expanded until in most cases the whole knowledge and thought of the workers and voters went to keeping Negroes down, rather than to raising themselves.

Internal dissension in the labor ranks followed. The Negroes were then blamed for not voting solidly with white labor, for selling out to capital, for underbidding labor. The whole movement swung into intense Negro hatred; and the net result was that the white labor vote turned eventually into a movement finally and completely to disfranchise Negro labor. The mob shot down Watson's Negro leaders in their tracks and the only way in which he could survive politically was to out-Herod Herod in his diatribes against Negroes and in coining new variants of appeals to prejudice by attacks on Catholics and Jews. To his death he kept a dangerous political power and even reached the United States Senate, but with his labor party cut in two and forced into additional disfranchisement by the "white primary" he could not menace the "machine."

A second way toward emancipation may lie through dissension in the high seats of power. When in Cleveland's day Hoke Smith opposed "free silver" he was read out of Georgia Democracy and his path to the United States Senate was blocked. Immediately he espoused the cause of "labor" and made a frontal attack on capital and the great corporations of Georgia. The white labor vote flocked to him, and instead of the "white primary" being the ordinary parade a bitter internal political fight developed. Smith and his opponents quickly came to terms. In the midst of the campaign Smith dexterously switched his attack on monopoly to an attack on Negroes as the cause of monopoly, and since this old game had often been played, he played it harder and more fiercely. He went so far that the State was aroused as never before. Race bitterness seethed, and white labor took the bit into its teeth. It demanded economic disfranchisement of the Negro to follow political. The Negro must be kept from buying land, his education must be curtailed, his occupations limited.

This was overshooting the mark and destroying the whole bi-racial labor situation upon which the Secret Empire of Georgia is based. Quick action was needed. The minds of the mob must be turned again and turned from political and economic thought to pure race hatred. Immediately the sex motif arose to leadership. All subconsciously, sex hovers about race in Georgia. Every Negro question at times becomes a matter of sex. Voting? They want social equality. Schools? They are after our daughters. Land? They'll rape our wives. Continually the secrecy, the veiled suggestion, the open warning pivot on sex; gossip rages and horrible stories are spread. So it was at the culmination of the Hoke Smith campaign. All restraint was suddenly swept away and submerged in wild stories of rape and murder. Atlanta papers rushed out extra editions, each with a new horror afterward proved wholly fictitious or crassly exaggerated. On a Saturday night the white Atlanta laborers arose and murdered every Negro they could catch in the streets. For three days war and rapine raged—then the streets of the Empire City sank into awful silence. Hoke Smith became Governor and Senator, and the industrial and political systems were intact.

All these occasions of revolt against the present political and industrial situation have thus ignored the Negro as an active factor in the revolution. But he cannot be ignored. In truth there can be no successful economic change in Georgia without the black man's cooperation. First of all the Negroes are property holders. Sixty years after slavery and despite everything, Georgia Negroes own two million acres of land, a space nearly as large as the late kingdom of Montenegro. Their taxable property saved from low wages and systematic cheating has struggled up from twelve million dollars in 1890 to over sixty million today; and now and then even the remnant of their political power strikes a blow. In 1923 in Savannah a fight within the "white primary" between the corrupt gang and decency gave twelve hundred Negro voters the balance of power. Efforts were made to intimidate the Negroes. Skull and cross-bones signed by the Ku Klux Klan were posted on the doors of eight of the prominent Negro churches with the legend, "This is a white man's fight; keep away." Warning slips were put under the doors of colored citizens. In vain. The colored voters held their own political meetings, financed their own campaign, went into the election, and of their twelve hundred votes it was estimated that less than a hundred went for the gang; the reform mayor was elected.

I am in the hot, crowded, and dirty Jim Crow car, where I belong. A black woman with endless babies is faring forth from Georgia, "North." Two of the babies are sitting on parts of me. I am not comfortable. Then I look out of the window. The hills twist and pass. Slowly the climate changes—cold pines replace the yellow monarchs of the South. There is no cotton. From the door of hewn log cabins faces appear—dead white faces and drawn, thin forms. Here lives the remnants of the poor whites.

I look out of the window, and somehow it seems to me that here in the Jim Crow car and there in the mountain cabin lies the future of Georgia—in the intelligence and union of these laborers, white and black, on this soil wet with their blood and tears. They hate and despise each other today. They lynch and murder body and soul. They are separated by the width of the world. And yet—and yet, stranger things have happened under the sun than understanding between those who are born blind.

IDAHO

A Remnant of the Old Frontier

M. R. STONE

JUNE 13, 1923

"GALLOP YOUR HORSE," wrote Joaquin Miller, "as I have done hundreds of times, against the rising sun; as you climb the Sweet Water Mountains, far away to the right you will see the name of Idaho written on the mountain top—at least, you will see a peculiar and beautiful light at sunrise, a sort of diadem on two grand clusters of mountains that bear away to the clouds, fifty miles distant. I called Colonel Craig's attention to this peculiar and beautifully arched light. 'That,' said he, 'is what the Indians call E-dah-hoe, which means the light, or diadem, on the line of the mountains.' "

For all of Miller's romantic explanation of the origin of the name, the fact remains that the State of Colorado was originally called Idaho, and at a time years before the poet and his friend Colonel Craig, of Craig's Mountain, Nez Percé, rode together to Oro Fino. Whether or not the name may mean "the gem of the mountains" or "shining mountain" is difficult to establish; but such a definition must have appealed to the first settlers who were attracted to the State by the shining gems of the mountains—gems far more tangible and valuable to them than the sunlight on the crests.

The early history of the State is inextricably united with the gold discoveries of the sixties. This movement laid the foundation for one of the two traditions that to this day are largely instrumental in molding public opinion and character in the State. Gold was first discovered in the territory now known as Idaho in the bed of Canal Gulch, a tributary of Oro Fino Creek, in 1860. The following summer the banks of all the tributaries of the Clearwater were lined with the tents of thousands of prospectors. This was the first inrush of settlers into the hitherto uninhabited region embraced by the vast, sweeping bend of the Snake River. There followed, in rapid order, the strikes on Elk Creek; on the Salmon River, known as the Florence mines; and in the Boise Basin.

It was 1862 that gold was first washed out from the gravel of Grimes Creek, a small stream in the basin. Today, at the foot of the low range of mountains that mark the southwestern rim of the basin, is the city of Boise. The census accredits it with twenty-odd thousand inhabitants. Sixty years ago it was a barren field of sage-brush bordering the willow-lined Boise (wooded) River. At that time the population of the basin was equal to that of the present city, while today there are not two thousand persons in the entire county that includes the site of the old mining camp.

It is difficult now, so far as any physical vestiges that remain, to reconstruct a picture of the teeming civilization that had its center in the Boise Basin over half a century ago. It is known that a stage made four trips a day between the busy mining centers in the basin and could not accommodate the passengers; that daily stage service was maintained with Umatilla, 285 miles away, at the head of navigation on the Columbia; that the main printing office ran day and night, for ail that kerosene was nine dollars a gallon. The largest camp, Idaho City, possessed three theaters: the Jenny Lind, the Forrest, and Kelly's Varieties. In the latter the musicians were placed on a suspended platform, swung above the heads of the patrons, so as to be out of the line of fire.

Mining still is one of the leading industries of the State. Some of the largest lead and zinc and copper producers in the nation are located in Idaho, and there has recently been uncovered what promises to be one of the largest copper deposits in the world. The vast interior of the State, remote from any railroad, is an immense reservoir of mineral wealth. This fact more than anything else tend to prolong the pioneer spirit in the citizens of the State. But many of the renowned old mines have played out. Of these, the ones around Silver City, in the Owyhee Mountains—still preserving the original spelling of Hawaii, O-why-hee, in honor of some Kanakas engaged in the early workings—were, perhaps, the most famous.

The State today possesses little that is tangible to remind the observer of their existence, and yet their romance and glamour still colors local thought and action. It is a tradition of easy-won wealth, of native riches respondent to the luck of the prospector, of a democracy based, not upon work or merit or power, but upon the impartiality of chance. This legend of placer gold has preserved the gambler's spirit, which is not as reprehensible a characteristic as may be imagined, especially when there are difficult things to be undertaken in the face of heavy odds. The willingness to take a chance, coupled with its corollary, the appreciation that tomorrow your poorest neighbor may be a man of wealth, is a great preservative of sincere democracy.

With the decay of the first mining impulse there came the era of the sheep and cattle man—the days of the rustlers and vigilantes. The vast, dusty ranges were dotted with thousands of heads of live stock. The water holes were claimed and counter-claimed, guarded and worked as fervently as ever the mines. This was a transitory era, soon to be followed by the period of the homesteader. There is an element of tragedy in the story of this valiant but visionary newcomer, living in squalor but in high hopes on his barren tract of land. The conquest of the desert was a cruel, hard fight; if not long in years, interminable in the number of humans lives and hopes sacrificed.

Sheep herding on the Idaho range. "However restless its citizens may be, they find plenty of opportunity to express themselves in overcoming the immediate problems of nature. However prosaic their ordinary daily activities may appear, back of them there is the knowledge that over the hill or beyond the valley lies the wilderness and the romance of the unknown."

The present green and fertile fields, the scene of so much hopeful industry, are actually battlefields, as grim and merciless in their memories as those of Europe. To them came men in the full tide of youth and hope and inspiration. There they staked their all; fought the sage-brush and alkali, the indifference of politicians, the hunger of poverty, and the bitter remorse of failure. Generation after generation they moved westward from the fecund East. Wave after wave lost and passed away. Stalwart men had their hopes turn to mock them; faithful wives watched their children grow up in poverty and denial. But as the defeated ones dropped out, others took their places. Neither disappointment, nor failure, nor hardship deterred them. Prolific nature threw new lives into the battle and gradually the fight was won. The desert has disappeared. Nothing of it remains but the tawny, golden sunshine—the regal, desert sunshine.

Thus there sprang up in the State a second tradition, quite different from that of the placer gold at first glance, but singularly like it in its implications. It was a tradition of hard work, of visionary plans made true, of impossible obstacles overcome. It added further proof of the rewards that come to the man who takes a chance; but it hardened the muscles of the gambler. This second epoch of the State was the development of irrigation. Irritation farming, they call it in more favored localities; but the irritation of the early settlers, wearily waiting for the water that seems never to come, is soon forgotten once the project is completed.

Today, the man with a vision points to the rolling hills of volcanic dust, rich in phosphates, but dun gray with sage and greasewood, streaked with alkali in the sinks, and smoldering under a summer sun that dries up every vestige of water, and exclaims: "All it needs is good men and water!" And the doubting Thomas, voicing all the weight of conservative caution and disinclination for personal discomfort, drawls: "Like hell!" But in ten years, the good men and water are there; the land is transformed; a new city is budding forth; and a thousand families or more have been raised to a new prosperity.

This is still a story of sudden fortunes within the reach of the man who will take a chance and of sudden shiftings of personal position. Such a history, such traditions, especially when compacted within the short span of sixty years, make for democracy. Such a history cannot help but leave its impress upon the citizens of the State: they are individualists and their creed is self-reliance. Another influence as potent in molding public character as the traditions of placer gold and irrigation is the topography of the State. The scenery of Idaho is wonderfully picturesque and diversified. There are endless forests and boundless sage-brush flats; precipitous, serrated mountain ranges and great desert plains; clear lakes encased in granite walls and desolate lava fields; gigantic waterfalls and burning, arid volcanic areas, pitted with dead craters; rich irrigated valleys and rolling hills incapable of cultivation.

This ever-present environment inevitably creeps into the blood and spirit of the men and women of the State, and because of its extreme diversity makes for restlessness "Habit," says William James, "is the great fly-wheel of society." If it is, then restlessness must be the driving-rod. It is the force that tempts civilization into new experiments. Habit has never had much opportunity to be developed in Idaho, nor the social stratas much chance to become solidified. The State has been constantly plunging forward into new activities during all of its brief history.

Thus we have in Idaho the curious anomaly of a community of nearly half a million citizens still animated by the simple and individualistic tradition of the pioneer, when the remainder of the nation has progressed into a class-conscious, conservative, and cynical age. Of course the lines are not clearly defined. Idaho is still a pioneer State but it is only an expurgated edition of the old West. Its citizens still possess a subdued gambling instinct but all lawlessness and excess have disappeared under the mollifying influence of the schools.

To the casual observer the State seems to be absorbed in the cultivation of prunes, politics, and potatoes, to the exclusion of all else. As a State it has taken the lowly potato and the prune of ill-repute and elevated them to the rank of semi-luxuries, and it is the home of William E. Borah. In spite of the fact, however, that the State produces 75 per cent of the green prunes marketed in the United States, or that it is the source of the huge baked potatoes for which the railroad dining-cars ask such fabulous prices, or that it possesses the highest dam in the world, the Arrowrock, that impounds the water to irrigate 234,000 acres of land, a large portion of its area is still virgin territory. However restless its citizens may be, they find plenty of opportunity to express themselves in overcoming the immediate problems of nature. However prosaic their ordinary daily activities may appear, back of them there is the knowledge that over the hill or beyond the valley lie the wilderness and the romance of the unknown.

In the mind of most persons the name of Idaho connotes just one thing—Senator William E. Borah. And yet, notwithstanding the political prominence of her most noted son, Idaho is not very much interested in politics. The presence in Washington of a most ardent and fearless liberal as representation of the State would lead the observer to expect the existence of an active and articulate liberal element in the State. But it is doubtful if Idaho is honestly in sympathy with Senator Borah's liberalism, although it is in downright sympathy with his personality. The pioneer likes a fighter and a man of action. It is not so much what a man stands for but how he stands that appeals to Idaho. Senator Borah has a disconcerting ability to do things and the State applauds if it does not approve.

It may be difficult for the citizens of other States to understand Idaho's continued support of William E. Borah if it is true that the State as a whole does not uphold his policies. The explanation of this seeming inconsistency lies in an understanding of the pioneer temperament. There is no one so quick to give homage to merit as the pioneer. To Idaho, William E. Borah is a national figure, not a State representative. He has made his mark by his own efforts and ability. His reputation for fearless integrity and sincerity is nation-wide. Idahoans feel that he deserves the State's support in recognition of these achievements, and that the State can find plenty of other men to work in Washington for its sheep or lumber or mining industries. The absence of class solidarity is a marked characteristic of Idahoans. As a whole they are very intolerant of any class or geographical moves, but they are more than tolerant of individuals.

Senator Borah, like his fellow-citizens, is an individualist. He is not afraid to express his opinions even though "the entire nation of all Idaho" disagree. Some communities might accept such an attitude as a challenge and immediately prepare to send a man to the national Capitol who would echo the wishes of his constituency, or at least, the articulate portion of it; but your true pioneer is more tolerant and has a keener sense of humor. He may not think very much of the recognition of Russia, and he may not be very much interested in the continued presence of United States troops in Caribbean countries—in fact, he may have a marked imperialistic strain in his mental make-up—but he never thinks that that is sufficient reason for him to try to silence every man who disagrees with him.

All of which shows, perhaps, that Idaho does not take its politics very seriously. Toward the end of the Civil War there was an influx from the Southern States of such proportions that it came to be known locally as "the left wing of Price's army." Due to this disturbing factor political rivalry for a time was very keen and followed with deep interest by the average citizen. Of late years it has ceased more and more to be an important element in the life of the State. Idaho accepts the periodic outpourings of puritanical paternalism, or of culture, or of radical philosophy, from the East, not with disinterest, but with good-natured tolerance. Such things do not reach home in Idaho; but if the majority of the nation wants them they are accepted placidly. Like all pioneers, Idahoans are materialists. They are impressed by results, by concrete actions, more than by abstract theories, and on all topics that do not touch them directly they are strict conformists.

This is admirably illustrated by the schools, which possess no radical improvements but which excel in all those branches approved by modern practice. Just what it has meant to Idaho to bring its schools to this point of perfection is best understood by consulting the 1920 census tabulations. Idaho has a population of 5.2 per square mile, whereas the ratio for the entire United States is 35.5. This means that every individual in Idaho has to aid in the maintenance of the State government, roads, and schools to an extent practically seven times as great as the average citizen in the United States. Last year the maintenance and operation of State schools cost $18.87 for every citizen of the State. The fact that the percentage of illiteracy is only 1.5 per cent, and that all foreigners and Indians who cannot read and write the English language are included in that percentage, is sufficient proof that Idahoans have not made their sacrifices to no purpose. Of late there has been some tendency to attempt to curb the growing burden of taxation in the State. It speaks well for the citizens of Idaho that there has been no reduction or curtailment of the activities of the State schools in spite of the fact that they received the burden of criticism.

Once or twice in the past the State has been shocked by some concrete evidence of the development within its borders of problems which had never been considered very seriously. The most notable of these cases was the murder of Governor Steunenburg. Then followed, after sundry involved actions, the Moyer, Haywood, and Pettibone trial. Idaho suddenly found itself playing a part in the great social drama of the nation and in contact with some of the most brilliant minds of the country. Clarence Darrow was there, remembered in Boise for his characteristic remark that he was a lawyer by ear and not by note. Several of the brilliant men of the State found in this brief flash of the spotlight their opportunity. Borah and Nugent both emerged from obscurity to national prominence and have not suffered by the publicity they received.[1]

There were labor troubles in the Coeur d'Alenes, in which the I.W.W. was the main disturbing element, and only recently Kate Richards O'Hare was forcibly ejected from Twin Falls—a complicated affair involving socialistic and pacifistic angles.[2] The sympathy of the State in all of these cases was decidedly on the

[1] In 1907 the State of Idaho, with the aid of Pinkerton detectives, brought Charles Moyer, William Haywood, and George Pettibone, officials of the Western Federation of Miners, to the state from Colorado without extradition warrants to stand trial for the murder of Frank Steunenberg. John F. Nugent, later senator, was part of the defense team; William E. Borah was the special prosecutor. [D. H. B.]

[2] Kate Richards O'Hare, socialist lecturer and organizer, was editor and publisher of *Socialist Revolution*. [D. H. B.]

side of conformity. The Nonpartisan League had but a short life in the State. When the leaders of the sheep industry tried to corral a large slice of the public domain, they were very promptly jeered out of court, although the action involved some prominent names. The true Idahoan is daring and original enough as an individual but he is not interested in class movements.

And now, lest we have drawn too idyllic a picture of our Western mountaineer, steeped in the romance of the past, let us take a look at the outward man, the Idahoan the casual observer sees from the transcontinental train. Well, for one thing he has changed his one-time miner's garb for the conventional straw hat and blue overalls of the farmer. He insists on having electric lights in his ranch house, and the very latest improvements in farm implements or mining equipment. In some parts of the State he even heats his house with electricity while his wife cooks the meals for the hungry hay-hands on an electric stove. He likes to have his children attend the best schools in the land and does not oppose any educational frills provided they are cut along practical lines—vocational training, agricultural short courses, and so forth. He likes to have the latest model of his favorite automobile, and he believes in having a frequent vacation. He and the family and as many friends as the car can hold may be seen every day of the season sliding over the rough mountain roads to some camping ground where the fishing is good. He does not read on an average a book a year, but contents himself with the daily paper and a farm journal. Lacking any information on which to base a diverse opinion, he accepts all of the newspaper headings at their own valuation and does not know that he is being robbed.

He likes to see things undertaken on a big scale and put through with snap and go. Back to his every-day task he is dreaming of some big project of his own—a mine to be developed, an irrigation project to be undertaken, a factory to be built. Whatever his position in life may be, he does not feel that it is the slightest handicap to him in achieving any of the bold plans he has secretly developed. He has too many fine projects of his own to be very much interested in the sins or sorrows of other persons. Art and literature are all very well but he considers them dull things, indeed, when there is a fortune to be made in the next day or so.

The point that our Idahoan misses, as do all pioneers, is that a great many persons, due to their very numbers, are forever denied the pleasures and responsibilities of prosperity, no matter how hard they may work or strive or how nobly they may plan. The percentage of opportunities for material success is still so favorable in Idaho that it is difficult for a citizen of that State to realize how tight the shoe pinches in less-favored localities. Consequently, he is selfish, and since he can secure all he wants without upsetting any of the existing customs and laws of the land, he is not interested in any discussion of changing the established order. His mental attitude toward the reforms of the hour is best illustrated by the expression: "Set the clock of progress ahead if you want to, but human nature will still be behind time." Time, he considers, with its slow methodical evolution, will solve all the perplexing social problems of the present moment.

Our Idahoan, immersed in the gigantic task of remaking a desert, or isolated in the rocky gorges of the State's central mountains, unearthing their rich minerals, makes the same mistake as does his Eastern brother, ensnared in the roaring mechanism of modern business. He carries his specialism too far. It is not that he overestimates the importance of his practical problems, but that he devotes all of his time to them at the expense of his cultural interests. This disregard for the finer, kindlier, abstract things of life in preference for more spectacular action represents a weakness not restricted to Idaho, although, perhaps more noticeable in the pioneer than in anyone else. It is a common trait. A brass band on the street will gain more votes for a political candidate than the scholarly treatise by his opponent resting in the bookshop window—whether in Boise or Washington, D.C.

The lack of the critical sense is an all too human characteristic, and the tendency toward conformity due to this cause would be quite as monotonous and deadening in Idaho as it is elsewhere were it not relieved by the gambling spirit. This willingness to take a chance, this sympathy for restlessness, this understanding of the lure of the unexpected, makes Idahoans surprisingly and delightfully tolerant of each other. They are as susceptible as other good Americans when they hear the tom-toms of mob appeal, but they are rarely carried off their feet on local issues or personalities. They are not reformers, crusaders, or whiners. Bigotry and egoism are very rare. They are first and last individualists, zealous of the rights of their neighbors lest their own freedom be infringed; proud of their self-reliance, but not domineering over those associated with them. These are the traits and tendencies that cannot help but have tremendous influence on the future of their State.

ILLINOIS

First Province of the Middle Kingdom

HOWARD VINCENT O'BRIEN

AUGUST 22, 1923

THE STATE OF ILLINOIS "in tres partes divisa est": (a) Chicago; (b) "down State"; (c) the circulation of the Chicago *Tribune*—a domain of resentful serfs who pay their tributary coppers even beyond the Mississippi. The distillation of such complexity into the compass of a few thousand words presents difficulties, because, though the three parts have a semblance of geographic and political identity, they are really in no way related. Chicago is a part of Illinois only as Rome was a part of the Italian peninsula; and the "World's Greatest Newspaper," as it modestly calls itself, belongs only to its owners.

If one write of Illinois, with subordinate consideration of Chicago and the County of Cook, the citizenry of the metropolis will rise as one man to point out that he has rather absurdly discussed the dog's tail, with only incidental mention of the dog. On the other hand, if he set forth Chicago, with Illinois as the side dish, he offers insult to half the population of a sovereign State. Nor can he straddle: to be neutral is to enjoy the unhappy ignominy of one in Dublin who is neither green nor orange. It is, indeed, a dilemma!

To personalize the situation, one may picture a farmer, white and native born, who can read and write, but doesn't—much—with a son who ran away and more or less accidentally got very rich. Relations between parent and offspring are a trifle strained, son being somewhat contemptuous of dad, and dad in a constant state of irritation with son, because the latter appears to think he's going to run the whole gosh-blamed farm. There were other children, of greater filial piety, some of whom went into manufacturing, and have done very well, such as Rockford and Moline and Joliet. There was also Peoria, a dubious source of pride, which took to distilling, and until the advent of a statesman of Scandinavian descent, from Minnesota, was one of the most prosperous of the family.

But to characterize Illinois as a farmer is only in part accurate. True, it ranks second in the production of corn and in the south is a land of *dolce far niente,* a low, hot region, with extraordinarily fertile soil, known, for various reasons, as "Egypt." One of the reasons is the name of its principal city, which is Cairo.

It would be impolitic to specify the other reasons. But as one proceeds north-ward, though the semblance is beautiful to the agricultural eye, the beauty is quite literally "skin deep," for immediately below the green and smiling prairie lies a vast bed of bituminous coal, and the pick becomes almost as symbolical of the State as is the hoe.

Statistics are dreadful things. But they are as inseparable from a statement of Illinois as figures are from a bank. A European or a New Englander would con-sider Illinois as very sparsely populated. But the relative handful of people who inhabit it are extremely busy. With a population of six million odd, and a size less than the average of the Union—56,000 square miles—it ranks among the first three in manufacturing, savings-bank deposits, soft coal, pig iron, and corn. And in the *value* of its agricultural produce, as distinguished from mere quan-tity, it ranks first.

Contrary to Eastern notions of the Middle West, merely material distinctions are held of less moment than those which must be measured on finer scales. Illinois is proud of its rating in dollars and tonnage, but it is very much prouder of the fact that, although the density of its population is about three times that of the average of the country as a whole, its percentage of illiteracy is only 4.2 per cent, as opposed to 10.7 per cent in the country at large.

The farmers, the miners, the artisans, and the shopkeepers of Illinois share an obsession with education. Scratch the average citizen, and you find an individ-ual who has, or has had, or is about to have, a son or daughter in the University of Illinois. Eastern eyebrows may elevate at mention of this provincial seat of learning, the Eastern lips may curl at sheepskins awarded for excellence in hip-pology and Ph.D.'s in animal husbandry, and Eastern skin may creep at the spec-tacle of uncouth youths roaming what should be cloistered solitudes in sweaters. But the citizen of Illinois is placid. He knows the opulence his university enjoys, as a consequence of the provisions for education in the establishment of the Western Reserve. Through his legislature he is ever ready to supplement that wealth. And when legal methods are too slow, he is quick to dig down into his blue-jeans for what may be needed. At the moment, it is a stadium—an enor-mous affair, costing millions, and every penny provided by private subscription.

In Winnetka, a suburb of Chicago, when the school problem became acute and the bonding capacity of the village was exhausted, the citizens, led by a lawyer who was serving as the head of the school board, stepped in and built a magnificent *public school*. The principal contributor was a wealthy Jewish cloth-ing manufacturer: the others were Tom, Dick, and Harry.

The man of Illinois is a practical man, and he knows that money talks. It en-ables him to provide his university with better buildings and more of them than any seaboard seat of learning can boast, and it enables him to offer financial inducements to professional skill that are beyond resisting. To an Eastern ob-server there is something appalling in the positive enormity of everything at the University of Illinois. After seeing the armory, an edifice large enough to house the old Yale campus, he is too numbed for comment when he hears that the student band alone is almost half the size of the entire Princeton undergraduate body. A bell rings, and from a huge building come a swarm of girls and boys, like ants from a burning log. Ten thousand students, he mutters, and when he is told that the bass drum, used by the aforementioned student band, is of such magnitude that it requires a special flat car for its transport, he shivers and flees from further Brobdingnagian data.

Illinois has a placid exterior. But there is turbulence within its bosom. It can run to extremes. It can, for instance, run a temperature as high as 107 degrees, and in a few weeks or hours—it is done by *minutes* in Chicago—drop to 24 below. This mercuric climate may, perhaps, be held accountable for Illinois's rather distinguished record for violence. Excluding minor lynchings, which, after all, are of importance chiefly to the individual concerned, Illinois has attained the front page of the yellower journals, and the editorial columns of the fireside press, several times of late years. There were, several years ago, the Springfield riots, of a racial character, with fire, murder, and rapine flourishing in the very shadow of the State Capitol. There was, later, the outburst in Chicago, in which black men were murdered somewhat more atrociously than white men usually murder white men, and during which, in the heart of the city where the Great Emancipator was nominated, it was unsafe for a man of color to show himself on the street. And, most recently, there was the Herrin "massacre" in which the ever-present emotional dynamite of the coal fields was bloodily detonated.[1]

The real feature of this last affair, in which murder was followed by mutilations worthy of Armenia, was the lineage of the malefactors. As in the great railway strike, the devilment was not the work of alien "reds," but of more or less direct descendants of Mayflower stock. Much editorial comment damned the atrocities at Herrin as "un-American," whereas, like the anarchy which ruled the streets of Chicago in the summer of 1894,[2] it was as thoroughly American as the Declaration of Independence. The people of Herrin are singularly free from any consciousness of sin. They recently reelected to office, by an overwhelming majority, a local official admittedly involved in the affair. This gave great pain to Chicago, which, having forgotten the race riots of 1919, refers piously to the Herrin incident as a blot on the State's escutcheon.

Chicago is old enough to have forgotten a number of things. One of them is its origin. Everyone knows that Chicago is the greatest railway center in the world. But no one can really explain why. The fact is that Chicago is an accident. It did not begin, as most cities do, as an answer to the needs of commerce. Its nucleus was not a trading-post, but a military one—Fort Dearborn—situate

---

[1]On June 21, 1922, a strike of miners in southern Illinois turned violent after a company guard allegedly shot a striker. Enraged strikers hired a plane, dropped dynamite on company property, and killed nineteen strikebreakers and company officials. [D. H. B.]

[2]In 1894 a strike by employees of the Pullman Rail Car Company was joined by the American Railroad Union and shut down all rail traffic through Chicago, the nation's hub. Only when federal troops pushed the mail through did the strike end. [D. H. B.]

State Street, Chicago (circa 1915). At the time this stereograph was made, the city was the fourth largest in the world. "One does not stroll in Chicago. Neither does one contemplate. One goes and one does—at the greatest possible speed."

(the military methods of the period apparently not differing from those now current) in a peculiarly disagreeable and unhealthful swamp, beside a wretched little river, the Indian name of which was Wild Onion.

One likes to picture the pioneers, those sparks from Plymouth Rock, as foreseeing the greatness of Chicago. But unfortunately some of them made the mistake of committing their views to paper. One, for instance, came to the little hamlet, tarried a while, and then, when he had satisfied himself, moved on to a village in the neighboring Fox River valley, where he settled. That village, he said, was destined to be the metropolis of the Western Reserve. The Fox River still flows, and the village is still there—no larger than when he found it! Another, owning a lot on what is today Michigan Avenue, Chicago's principal boulevard, allowed it to be sold for taxes, and moved his family to Milwaukee, a city which had a "future."

The Chicago city seal is graced by a somewhat portly female of Grecian origin, whose motto is "I will." The words are better than the picture. There is nothing feminine or Hellenic about Chicago. A better personalization of it would be the type so familiar in the recent era of high prices and labor scarcity—hands rough and a little soiled, wearing a silk shirt and diamonds, who ordered two pianos at a time, stripping bills from the "wad" extracted from his "pants" to pay for them.

It is, in short, a gross lout of a city, long on health and vigor and ruthlessness and imagination and money, and with less sign of sprouting what is known as "culture" than a cement sidewalk shows of sprouting grass. H. G. Wells called it a "lapse from civilization." An Oriental undoubtedly had it in mind when he spoke of America as being inhabited by the flattest-minded people on the globe. And for anyone whose interest in babies, prohibition, and the stock market is tepid, dining out is a weary business.

And yet—there is a population of some four hundred thousand Jews. Where there are Jews, the cultural spark is never quite extinguished. Under the glossy concrete shell of commercialism there is evidence of a warm lush soil in which good seed will one day flourish. There are pianos. The fathers bought them for decorative purposes: signs are not wanting that sons and daughters are learning to play them. The bluff scorn of the pioneers for effete things like opera has softened. Opera has had the accolade of "civic" accorded it, and the plain people are beginning to give it the respect they give the Cubs and the Stock Yards and the Municipal Pier. It has lost something of its mere social significance, and the gallery sells out before the boxes. The Symphony Orchestra—still referred to by ladies of the old school as the Thomas orchestra—and Ravinia, that extraordinary outdoor temple to the muse, on the North Shore—nothing like it this side of Germany—are known wherever music matters. Not long ago, a fountain by a famous sculptor was unveiled on a city thoroughfare. Every city, of course, has fountains by famous sculptors. But the significant thing about this one was the fact that it was paid for from a fund bequeathed by an utter unknown—a man of the people who had amassed riches out of lumber, a Maecenas of the democratic order. Near the river, on the West Side, is a grim pile of red brick—a monument to that refinement of modernism, the mail-order business. It is quintessential of merchandising and turnover and distribution and profit. And in the Art Institute, held worthy of place on walls with Corot and Van Dyke, are canvases painted by the active head of that mail-order business. Nor is his case isolated. There is an active and not inconsiderable group of business men who paint pictures—many of the members being highly successful business men, who paint extremely well.

In Chicago hospitality has retained its small-town quality. Unlike the New Yorker, the Chicagoan does not dine his outlander friend at a restaurant and take him to a theater—he takes him home. That is one of the reasons why the visitor does not see the "night life" of Chicago. The other reason is that there isn't any. Nightfall sees the streets deserted, save on what the newspapers call the Rialto, ordinarily known as Randolph Street, where one may see some of the New York shows, acted by the kind of actor that doesn't mind traveling. There are also several places for circumspect dancing, after twelve. And at Huyler's, if you go early enough, you can secure excellent soda water.

The lake front is an evidence of the profound foresight the city's forefathers did not have. One wonders what was in their minds—or in their pockets—when they allowed the Illinois Central Railroad to lay its tracks in the municipal front yard, quite literally under their very noses. This civic Helgoland was, until recently, both in figure and in fact, nothing more than a dump. But as time passed it became evident that rubbish is objectionable only when there is not enough of it; for the dreadful litter of dirt and garbage and tin cans presently became a considerable area of new land. The water was driven back, and beyond the railroad tracks lies the broad expanse of Grant Park.

The only building ever raised on the lake side of Michigan Avenue was the Art Institute. But some years ago all the realtors of the city, as if moved by a common impulse, suddenly announced their intention of putting up new, large, incomparably magnificent edifices to flank the institute. There was great jubilation. "Boosting" attained the proportions of a delirium. The Avenue, which about this time became the Boulevard, or as B.L.T.[3] dubbed it, the Boul Mich, was, in the familiar American hyperbole, to be the finest in the world. But into this iridescent dream stepped the unpleasant reality of one Montgomery Ward, another man who had made a success of the mail-order business. His weapons were law-suits and injunctions: his purpose to keep the far side of the Boulevard forever free of buildings. The litigation was endless, and to a cheated and outraged public the name of Ward became anathema. But the Watch Dog of the Lake Front never let go, and the city can still see the blue waters of the lake. And today there is a widespread contention that Grant Park ought to be Ward Park. The beautification of the land which this obstinate old man preserved for the people against their will continues steadily. The Illinois Central is to be put under ground and electrified. There are to be flowers, plashing fountains, gondolas on the silver bosom of a lake tamed into lagoons, a stadium, museums, and what not—all for the pleasure and edification of the common people.

The quality of paradox in the composition of Chicago reached its climax in the person of its erstwhile mayor, Mr. William Hale Thompson, who gained international fame for quite accurately, but with poor judgment, characterizing the place he governed as the "sixth German city of the world."

Chicago, like other American cities, has always enjoyed varying degrees of bad government. But several years ago the "better element" was roused to reform. It was time, they said, to take the city out of politics. So, very carefully, they picked a man with no political affiliations, of independent means, and of good, sound American stock, to raise the banner of civic virtue. Their candidate was duly elected. Whereupon he put a sombrero on his head and became "Big Bill"—prince of demagogues. Before the ink was dry on the felicitations of press and pulpit, Chicago was in the grip of a political machine that made the efforts of such men as Tweed seem bungling and experimental.

Thompson has now passed from the scene. But what may be called Thompsonism remains. It is a kind of bond between Chicago and Illinois, because it rules both. The governor of the State, Len Small, yields fealty to the "organization." Not long ago he was tried for the unromantic crime of embezzlement—and acquitted. Now, those who acquitted him are about to be tried. When members of the Chicago school board were under a similar indictment the case

---

[3]The signature of Bert Liston Taylor, whose column in the Chicago *Tribune*, "A Line o' Type or Two," was a city favorite. [D. H. B.]

could not be brought to trial because the attorney general of the State lacked the funds necessary to prosecute it. And he lacked them because the governor had vetoed the necessary appropriations. No, this is not a scene from *The Mikado*— it is just Illinois politics.

Thompsonism has many friends and apologists. But their loyalty is for the most part negative—inspired by their dislike of the *Tribune,* which is bitterly hostile to Thompsonism. But why is it so hostile and so bitter? Well, dear children, that goes back to its feud with Senator Lorimer, who, not a little from its efforts, was chased out of the United States Senate. Mr. Lorimer was, in a way, the progenitor of Thompsonism, and a little verse which appeared in the "Line o' Type" summarizes the whole matter:

> You may ventilate, fumigate, douche if you will,
> But the odor of Lorimer will cling to you still!

The *Tribune* is vindictive, clever, and irreconcilable. It is rich beyond computation, and enormously powerful. It is as personal and unstable as a country weekly—which is natural, since its owners are also its active editors. It is less popular than prohibition. A great many people hate it violently. Those who have anything like affection for it are negligible. And yet one out of every five families, in five States, subscribes to it. The people of Illinois have no enthusiasm for Thompsonism, and less for the *Tribune.* But they vote for the one, and buy the other. They would shed no tears at the downfall of either. But the fact remains that the *Tribune,* if not the world's greatest newspaper, certainly is one of them, and Thompsonism does build roads and bridges and supply fetes, even if they cost more than they should.

Youthful and masculine is Chicago—generous, impulsive, and somewhat skeptical of "dog." It takes a person of great hardihood to stroll down the Boulevard carrying a cane. Though that skepticism is more for the stroll than the stick. One does not stroll in Chicago. Neither does one contemplate. One *goes* and one *does*—at the greatest possible speed. The Frenchman, sipping his *sirop grenadine* and discussing Balkan politics, and the German, with his beer, listening to Wagner, are alike beyond the comprehension of Chicago. The Chicagoan does not discuss politics—he takes sides; and he would rather dance to music than listen to it. And he regards his watch more highly than his imagination.

And yet, he has a boundless imagination. His dreams have magnitude, if not intensity, and he has the energy to bring great plans to fruition. His city is all compact of the yea and nay which is in him. It is tolerant of graft, and prudish about art. It is liberal as regards business ethics, and bigoted as regards social ethics. It is polyglot and conservative. It welcomes new people, and mistrusts new ideas. And though, unlike other great cities, it has no leisure class, and the sons of wealth are obliged by the pressure of public opinion to toil as sweatily as their grandfathers did, there is a certain unmistakable wistfulness for the things which set human life apart from the beasts of the field, and make the human economy something more than a digestive tube.

Chicago has the feeling for Illinois that the dweller within gates has always had for the outlander; and Illinois fears and dislikes Chicago because it is "foreign." But under the surface of mutual distrust, of vainglorious pride, of crude commercialism on the one hand and smug ruralism on the other, lies a questioning and hopeful pessimism. It is like the coal beds under the fields of smiling corn—latent fire. Illinois, by the record, has done well in all the ways of the flesh. To the historian, if not the prophet, it is clear that she will presently flower into achievement in the things of the spirit.

INDIANA

Her Soil and Light

THEODORE DREISER

OCTOBER 3, 1923

T HERE IS ABOUT IT a charm which I shall not be able to express, I know, but which is of its soil and sky and water—those bucolic streams and lakes which so charm those who see them. And where else will one find such beech and sugar groves, so stately and still and serene—the seeming abodes of spirits and elves that are both friendly and content? Rains come infrequently and then only in deluging showers. Corn and wheat and hay and melons flourish throughout the State. Spring comes early. Autumn lingers pleasingly into November. The winters are not, in the main, severe. Yet deep, delicious snows fall. And a dry cold in the northern portion makes sleighing and skating a delight. The many lakes and streams afford ample opportunity for house-boats, lakeside cottages, and bungalows as well as canoeing and fishing and idling and dreaming. In the beech and sugar groves are many turtle doves. The bluejay and the scarlet tanager flash and cry. Hawks and buzzards and even eagles, betimes, soar high in the air. Under the eaves of your cottage are sure to be wrens and bluebirds. Your chimneys are certain to shelter a covey of martins. And to your porches will cling the trumpet vine, purple clematis, and wistaria. From the orchard and woodlot of your farm will sound the rusty squeak of the guinea hen and the more pleasing cry of the peacock, "calling for rain."

One should not conclude from this, of course, that the State is without manufacture, or that, size for size, its cities and towns are not as interesting as those of other States. To me they are more so. There is something in the very air that sustains them that is of the substance of charm. What it is I cannot say. You will find it suggested in the poems of Riley and the stories of Tarkington, a kind of wistfulness that is the natural accompaniment of the dreams of unsophistication. To be sure the State is lacking in urban centers of great size which somehow, regardless of character, manage to focus the interest of the outside world. Apart from Indianapolis, a city of three hundred thousand, there is no other of even a third of its size within its borders. Evansville, on the Ohio, and at the extreme southwest corner of the State, has possibly eighty thousand. Ft. Wayne, in the northern portion of the State, the same. Terre Haute, the most forthright of its several manufacturing centers, had, until recently at least, a population of seventy thousand. And because of the character of its manufactories which relate to steel and coal it is looked upon by many who are not a part of it as grimy. Its smaller cities such as Gary, Hammond, South Bend, Kokomo, Richmond, Muncie, and several others literally resound with manufacture, being centers for steel, packing, automobiles, engineering supplies, farm machinery, and so forth. Yet contrasted with the neighboring States of Ohio, Michigan, and Illinois—in particular the latter's northern portion—it pales as a center of manufacture. Ohio can boast quite ten centers to its one. In passing from any of these States into Indiana one is reminded of the difference between Holland and Germany or France, the one with its canals, its windmills, and level fields, dotted with simple homes, the other with its plethora of cities and factories and, in the old days, its ever-present army. The one is idyllic, the other almost disturbingly real and irritatingly energetic.

Yet to my way of thinking the State is to be congratulated rather than not upon this limited commercial equipment. Not all of our national domain need to be commercial, I trust, however much we may wish it. A few such pastoral areas might prove an advantage. Besides, as I have indicated, there is running through the mood of the State something which those who are most intimate with it are pleased to denominate "homey" or "folksy"—a general geniality and sociability. And with this I agree. The automobile and the phonograph, plus the dancing which the latter inspires, have added so much to the color of the small town and the farm in these days. Or, if it be the lone cottage, far from any town, with neither automobile nor phonograph, then the harmonica and the accordion are found to be in service. And one may sing and dance to those. It is the light, or the soil, or what?

In this connection the church life of Indiana, as well as its moral taboos, have always interested me. Morality, one might well assume by now, as well as all important social regulations, is best and most understandingly based upon and regulated by the Golden Rule. Beyond that, among the intelligent, restrictions and compulsions are few. Neither theory nor dogma nor ritual nor custom nor creed is disturbingly binding. Yet in my native State, and despite the steady growth in scientific knowledge, devotion to denominational liturgy and dogma appears to be unmodified. Go where you will, into any city or town you choose, and there will be not one but four or five or six or more churches of the ultra-sectarian type and each with a lusty and *convinced* following. Nowhere, considering the sizes of the various cities and towns and hamlets, will you see larger or more attractive edifices of this character. And not infrequently the Bible school attachments or additions are almost as impressive as the churches themselves. In short, sectarian religion appears to flourish mightily. It is the most vigorous and binding of all local social activities. The affairs of the church are not only spiritually but socially of the utmost importance. Nearly everyone belongs to one or another of the various denominations and the rivalry between the several sects is not infrequently keen, especially in the smaller places. And in the main, and despite all science, they are still imperialistic in their claim to revelation and devotion. Religious innovations are taboo. Even modern liberalizing theologic tendencies, though sanctioned by a stray soul here and there, are not in the main either understood or approved of. To this day in many orthodox quarters the youths of the hour are still discouraged from attending the State or any other university on the ground that they are "hotbeds of infidelity and irreligion." And the local press, running true to form, as it does everywhere, editorially sustains this contention.

And yet, as the world knows, Indiana has its "genius belt," geographically deliminated even, as "south of a line running east and west through Crawfordsville." And, locally at least, and until recently, there was no hesitation in stamping the decidedly successful literary and art products of the State as the effusions of genius. Well, there's neither good nor ill but thinking makes it so. Certainly the State may well be proud of George Ade and Booth Tarkington and William M. Chase, the artist, to say nothing of those distinguished elders James Whitcomb Riley and General Lew Wallace, the author of *Ben Hur*. Whether as much may be said for some others still remains to be seen. Certainly from the point of view of current popularity they have nothing to complain of. And as for posterity, well, posterity pays no grocer's bills. There are many aspiring writers who would gladly change place with George Bar McCutcheon or Charles Major, who wrote *When Knighthood Was in Flower*.

Yet apart from these the State is not without a few personalities whose names will awaken responsive and other than literary thought beyond its borders— William Henry Harrison, the "Indian fighter" and quondam President, for instance, and Thomas B. Hendricks, once a Vice-President. Also Oliver P. Morton, an efficient early governor; John Hay, diplomat, author, and cabinet officer of his day; and John Clark Ridpath, the historian. As a true and loyal Hoosier I suppose I should add that James B. Eads, the distinguished engineer, once lived in Brookville, Indiana, that Robert Owen founded his human brotherhood experiment at New Harmony, in Posey County, that Henry Ward Beecher was once pastor of the Second Presbyterian Church of Indianapolis, and that Abraham Lincoln is supposed to have studied those few books and caught that elusive something that later gave character and beauty to his utterances somewhere in a log cabin in Spencer County.

But beyond these, what? Well, beyond an agreeable and respectable and kindly social world in which to be and pass one's brief and changeful days, what more is needed? Trusts? There are several in active operation, ye tin-plate and ye steel trust, for instance; the former organized at Kokomo, Indiana, the latter in full and dictatorial swing at Gary and Hammond, where only so recently as July, 1919, a number of very respectable employees on strike were promptly and in true liberty fashion shot to death upon the streets of Hammond, their crime being, apparently, opposition to insufficient wages and certain (as they seem to have assumed) unsatisfactory piece-work conditions. The moral entanglements resulting from this method of adjusting labor difficulties are before the courts of Indiana at this very time. Large industries? Indianapolis, Kokomo, and South Bend are assumed to be automobile manufacturing centers of the greatest import, nationally and internationally speaking. The steel interests of Gary, Hammond, and Terre Haute are assumed, not only locally but nationally, to be second to none in America. Indianapolis has not one but several enormous packing plants. The underlying coal-beds of southwestern Indiana—especially about Terre Haute—are listed as among the important resources of the Central West. The melon- and fruit-bearing powers of the climate and soil of that same area have brought about not only specialization and intensive cultivation but a trademark which is of the greatest value. In addition the State has scenic wonders such as the caves about Wyandotte and such natural scenery and curative springs as have given rise to French Lick, West Baden, Mud Lavia, The Glades, and all the delightful lake life that characterizes its northern half.

But perhaps, after all, this is not the type of thing that should be registered of Indiana. Despite a long and happy intimacy with it, it is entirely possible that I have not even suggested or have entirely missed its truer spiritual significance, as we are wont to say of so much that is but deeply human. Going south through Indiana once with a friend and fellow Hoosier, we two fell into a solemn and almost esoteric, I might say, discussion of the State and its significance, intellectually, emotionally, and otherwise. Previous to what I am about to set down I had been pointing out a number of things—not only those that have always appealed to me, the poetic and folksy charm of the State and its inhabitants— but also a number of other things that rather irritated me, its social devotion to dogmatic religion, for one thing, its rather pharisaical restfulness in its assumed enlightenment and knowledge of what is true and important to the world at large, its political somnolence as suggested by its profound and unchanging devotion to the two ancient and utterly platitudinous parties. With all of this he most solemnly agreed. Then, having done so, entered not so much upon a defense as an interpretation of the State which I will here set down as best I can.

"You should go sometime to an automobile speed contest such as is held annually at the Speedway at Indianapolis, as I have often, year after year; in fact, since it was first built. There, just when the first real summer days begin to take on that wonderful light that characterizes them out here—a kind of luminous silence that suggests growing corn and ripening wheat and quails whistling in the meadows over by the woods, you will find assembled thousands from this and other countries, with their cars and at times their foreign tongues, individuals interested in speed or fame or the development of the automobile. And this might cause you to feel, as it has me, that as rural as it all is, at times Indiana is quite as much of a center and more so even than places which, by reason of larger populations, set themselves up as such. As I say, I have been there often, and getting a bit tried of watching the cars have gone over into the woods inside the course and lain down on the grass on my back.

"There, about me, would be the same familiar things I have always known and loved since I was a boy here, but that getting out into the world for a time had made me think that I had forgotten, though I hadn't—the sugar and hickory and beech trees, the little cool breezes that come up in the middle of the day and cool the face and hands for a moment, and rustle the leaves—the same fine blue sky that I used to look up into when a boy. But circling around me continuously, just the same, to the south and the north and the east and the west, where were the banks of the track beyond the woods, were these scores of cars from all parts of the world, with their thunder and dust, the thunder and dust of an international conflict. Then I would get up and look to the south along the immense grandstand that was there and would see, flying in this Indiana sunlight, the flags of all the great nations, Italy and England, France and Belgium, Holland and Germany, Austria and Spain. And it came to me then that the spirit that had been instrumental for some reason in distinguishing this particular State from its sister States, as it unquestionably has been distinguished, was and still is, I think, effective. It has won for Indiana a freedom from isolation and mere locality which is worldwide. It has accomplished here, on this quiet Hoosier soil, a very vital contact with universal thought."

"Universal thought is a pretty large thing to connect up with F——," I contended genially. "And this is all very flattering to dear old Indiana, but do you really believe yourself? It seems to me that, if anything, the State is a little bit sluggish, intellectually and otherwise. Or, if it isn't that, exactly, then certainly there is an element of self-complacency that permits the largest percentage of its population to rest content in the most retarding forms of political, religious, and social fol de rol. They are all, or nearly all, out here, good and unregenerate Democrats or Republicans, as they have been for, lo! these seventy years, now— come next Wednesday. Nearly all belong to one or another of the twenty-seven sure-cure sects of Protestantism. And they are nearly all most heartily responsive to any -ism which is advertised to solve all the troubles of the world, including those of our own dear nation. I call your attention to the history of the Millerites of southeast Indiana, with their certain date for the ending of the world and their serious and complete preparation for the same; the Spiritualists and free lovers who fixed themselves in northwestern Indiana, about Valparaiso, if I am not mistaken, and Mormon fashion ruled all others out; the something of soil magnetism which drew Robert Owen from Scotland to New Harmony and there produced that other attempt at solving all the ills to which the flesh is heir. Don't forget that the Dunkards—that curious variation of Mennonism—took root out here and flourished mightily for years, and exists to this day, as you know. Also the reformed Quakers. And now I hear that Christian Science and a Christianized form of Spiritualism are almost topmost in the matter of growth and the enthusiasm of their followers. I have no quarrel with any faith as a means to private mental blessedness. But you were speaking of universal and creative thought. Just how do you explain this?"

Indiana farm life. The bucolic and placid nature of Indiana farm life stimulated the nostalgic musings of Hoosier poets and novelists. It was such soil and light that Theodore Dreiser regarded as the essential source of the state's unique character.

"Well, I can and I can't," was his rather enigmatic reply. "This is a most peculiar State. It may not be so dynamic nor yet so creative, sociologically, as it is fecund of things which relate to the spirit—or perhaps I had better say to poetry and the interpretative arts. How else do you explain William M. Chase, born here in Brookville, I believe, General Lew Wallace, James Whitcomb Riley, Edward Eggleston and his *Hoosier Schoolmaster,* Booth Tarkington, George Ade, John Clark Ridpath, Roswell Smith, who founded the *Century Magazine,* and then Lincoln studying and dreaming down in Spencer County? All accidents? I wonder. In fact I am inclined to think that there is much more to soil and light in so far as temperament and genius are concerned than we have any idea of as yet. There may be, and personally I am inclined to think there is, a magnetic and also generative something appertaining to soil and light which is not unrelated to the electro-magnetic field of science in which so much takes place. I look upon them as potent and psycho-genetic even, capable of producing and actually productive of new and strange and valuable things in the way of human temperament. Take little Holland, for instance, and its amazing school of great painters. And Greece, with its unrivaled burst of genius. Or Italy, with its understanding of the arts. Or England, with its genius for governing. There is something about the soil and light of certain regions that makes for individuality not only in the land but in the people of the land."

"For instance," he continued, "I insist that the Hoosier is different mentally and spiritually to the average American. He is softer, less sophisticated, more poetic and romantic. He dreams a lot. He likes to play in simple ways. He is not as grasping as some other Americans and some other nationalities. That may be due to the fact that he is not as practical, being as poetic and good natured as he is. If he be poor and uneducated he likes to fish and play an accordion or sing. If he is better schooled he likes to read, write verse, maybe, or books, and dream. In a crude way, perhaps, he has the temperament of the artist, and so I still look to Indiana, or its children, at least, to do great things, artistically. And all this I lay to the soil and light. Why? I don't know. I just guess that they have something to do with it.

"Nothing else explains to me Edward Eggleston and his turning to letters at that early time and in the region from which he hailed—the extreme southeastern part of Indiana. Or General Lew Wallace writing *Ben Hur* there in Crawfordsville, under a beech tree. Neither will anything else explain to me why the first automobile this side of France was built right here at Kokomo, and almost at the same time that the first one was perfected in France. Nor why the first automobile course, after Brooklands, England, was built here at Indianapolis—not near New York or Chicago, as one might have expected, perhaps. Or why an adventurer like La Salle should come canoeing up the Maumee and the St. Joseph into this particular region. The French, who first had this territory, chose to fortify at Terre Haute and Vincennes. Why? They might just as well have fortified at other points beyond the present State borders.

"What I am trying to get at is this: Via such a soil and such light as is here cooperating you have a temperament more sensitive to the resource above mentioned. In the case of those who wandered in here, like La Salle and Lincoln, you have sensitives affected by the conditions here. Their dreams or aspirations were here strengthened. This is a region not unlike those which produce gold or fleet horses or oranges or adventurers. There are such regions. They are different. And I look upon Indiana as one such."

"Bravo!" I applauded. "Very flattering to dear old Indiana, to say the least, and as an honest native, and moved by self-interest, I hereby subscribe. But—" And then I went back to the churches, the hard-headed conventionalities, the fact that the "inventor" of the first automobile here was accused of robbing the French of their patents, that Robert Owen was a canny Scot who saw to it that he never lost a dollar in his idealistic enterprise but held the whole town of New Harmony and all that thereunto appertained in fee simple, so that when the idea proved groundless he was able to shoo all his assembled theorists off the place and sell it for what it would bring. But my friend was not in the least abashed. He reproached me with being incurably materialistic and clung to his soil and light theory, which, I may as well admit, appeals to me very much. His final rebuke to materialism was that human nature in toto is nothing but a manifestation of forces which unavoidably assume opposite phases, which same we label good or evil, but which really are found to be supplementing each other in any manifestation which can be labeled life. So you may see how far Indiana, with its temperament, carried us.

But admiring and even revering the State as my native heath I am perfectly willing to admit all of his claims and even more of such as may be in its favor.

IOWA

A Mortgaged Eldorado

JOHAN J. SMERTENKO

DECEMBER 13, 1922

I<small>T</small> <small>IS</small> <small>THE</small> <small>BOAST</small> of Iowans that one cannot cross the State's boundaries at any point without realizing that here is a land of plenty as different from its neighbors as the plains of Canaan differed from the fields of Gomorrah. Everywhere within these borders is fecundity, wealth, and solidity. The stranger is at first amazed and eventually bored by the unrelieved regularity of bumper crops, trim wire fences, pure-bred and well-fed live stock, huge barns and silos, smug and freshly painted homes. And if he is surprised at the country, he must indeed marvel at cities and towns which have no slums, no ramshackle outbuildings, and no decaying genteel quarters. Virtually the only signs of the poverty that one habitually associates with urban life are the red, superannuated freight cars which house the Mexican road-builders. Farm and factory, church and dwelling, school and library partake of the heavy, formidable air of prosperity which is Iowa.

Statistics—and Iowa "boosters" revel in statistics—bear out this impression of general well-being. According to the latest United States census report Iowa leads the nation in the value of her horses and hogs, of pure-bred live stock, of farm machinery and farm property per farm; she has the greatest number of poultry, of pure-bred hogs and cattle, of autos per capita—one to 5.5 persons—and of telephones on farms; she excels in the production of eggs, corn, and oats. Her road system, railroad facilities, her dairy products and packing industry are among the first in the country. She has coal, water-power, and lead mines, foundries and lumber mills; she produces enormous quantities of cereals and canned goods, cement and bricks. In short, Iowa is self-sufficient in most of the necessaries of life and is creditor of all other States in many of them.

Still, today the farmer groans. When he is articulate, he reviles the railroads, the bankers, the commission merchants, and all the other agents that stand between him and the consumer. He seems to be the only Iowan who is not convinced by statistics. In his nightmares the corpulent cow which is Iowa to the passengers of the through train looks as lean as the kine of Pharaoh. And at the end of each year he experiences a mirage: his fields, his farm, his crops, and his cattle fade to a blank page on the credit side of the ledger. His computations lead him into blind alleys and his remedial legislation does not remedy. Then he curses again his pet enemies and also the land which is a deception to the eye, even as the fair body that hides a cancer.

But this contradiction is a recent experience. Twenty years ago it was unknown and before that inconceivable. The first settlers found a land which waited but the turn of a plow to uncover its golden riches. Their reports of the "strike" sped eastward, and soon the farmers who had used up the shallow soil of New England, the pioneers of the Middle Atlantic States who had found the cheap lands of the Northwest Territory equally unproductive, and the poor whites who had been forced out of the South by slave labor fell like locusts upon the virgin prairie, clean and level as a playful ocean and just as inexhaustible. Thus for thirty years after the first permanent settlement all roads west seemed to lead to Iowa. From the mountains of Kentucky and Tennessee, from the forests of Michigan, from the clay of Virginia and the sands of Ohio, from the mines of Pennsylvania, the orchards of New York, and the coast of New England came the seekers of a farmer's Eldorado. At the end of this period, 1870, Iowa's 1,194,752 inhabitants exceeded the population of Michigan, which had been settled 150 years before. The numbers of burrowers in black loam had doubled, trebled, or quadrupled within each decade.

There are certain features of this million which cannot be overlooked by those who would know contemporary Iowa. Chief of these is the fact that no Northern State has ever had so great a proportion of original settlers from the South. Though there is a general impression that New Englanders settled Iowa, the earliest census shows that there were as many immigrants from Tennessee as from all of New England; there were more from Virginia than from Tennessee, and more Kentuckians than Virginians. Even as late as 1850 the Iowans from Southern States outnumbered the immigrants from New England almost six to one. By 1860 the influx of Yankees had changed this proportion to a little more than two to one in favor of the South but the Southerners still held most of the political offices, dominated State and local legislation, threw the State's sympathy to pro-slavery views, and generally fought all "Yankee notions and for'ard movements." And during the Civil War they were strong enough to attack companies of Northern soldiers training in the State. How much they contributed to the making of Iowa is a mooted question of doubtful importance. Both important and certain, however, is the fact that the Iowan of today is in the fullest sense an American; in his veins is mingled the blood of practically every Colonial. On the other hand, there is probably less foreign blood in the Iowan than in any other native of the Middle West. Few States in America have been settled with as small a percentage of foreign-born. For so uniformly rich was the soil that nothing remained here for the land-starved European who in other Middle-Western States was permitted to take the leavings of the natives.

And finally, it is vital to record that the settlers were of a definite and uniform character. Though the three streams of our westward movement conjoined in this

State, the amibitious, the adventurous, and the lawless elements passed on. By virtue of her protected frontiers and peaceful Indian settlement, her monotonous and heavy tasks, her stable and rising wealth, Iowa appealed more than any other State to the cautious, prosaic, industrious, and mediocre. Here, at last, is the synthesis of an American agrarian type like the yeomanry of England and the peasantry of Russia. Here, too, is the answer to that rebellious song,

> When Adam delved and Eve span,
> Who was then the gentleman?

For cultural tradition and leisure are necessary to the making of gentlemen. The first Iowans do not possess; neither can they develop it, inasmuch as the second is contrary to all their standards of right living. He who has met the pathetic, puttering creatures known as retired Iowa farmers, or retired Iowa anything, with their tool sheds and truck gardens, their bees and their Fords, their incompleted real-estate deals and their worthless auction bargains, will thereafter find cosmic disturbance in the flutter of a leaf and universal significance in the movements of an ant. Yet this is all the leisure they know in "Ioway," and even this is reserved by public opinion for those who are on the grayer side of sixty.

The result has been justly called a dull, gray monotone. With the exceptions of a thinly disguised immorality and a spiritless church affiliation, rural Iowa— more than a million souls—has no interests beyond bread and butter. The movie and the pool room, the church social and the high-school entertainment are the amusements of town life. And the sophisticated city has its stock-company comedies, its lodges, its card parties, and its dances. There is really no community life in the State—neither folk-gatherings by the lowly nor common enterprises by the élite. And no one has been able to rouse this people to a participation in any creative expression of the commonwealth.

"But," cries the indignant Iowan, "look at some statistics. Man alive, just examine a few unbiased census reports! We have 'the highest percentage of literacy, 98.9, of any State in the Union or of any equal area in the world.' We have more schools, urban, rural, and consolidated, and a better school attendance than most anybody. We have libraries and museums that can accommodate thousands more people than use them. There are women's clubs that study lite'ture, poetry, music, and furniture, and all that sort of stuff. We get lectures and concerts and readings galore. We're among the first in city planning, in State music contests, and in community dramatics. And there's no State west of the Mississippi that can show more culture than we've got—that's a fact!"

All of which is perfectly true. And so, out of their own mouths are they confounded. They confuse literacy with education—witness their extensive primary-school system and their privately endowed, undernourished, and mendicant academies styled colleges. They mistake the social activities of a few liberated housewives for the cultural expression of a people—thus they visualize art as a half-dozen much-mispronounced, expensive, and authenticated masters; they understand poetry in terms of syndicated "people's bards" and leather-bound sets of undying and uncomprehended "classics"; they make the acquaintance of music in an annual enthusiastic meeting with an operatic banality. Their best theater is a child of the drama league of Chicago; their folk-songs are creations of Broadway; their epic theme is a misguided cyclone.

Descendants of New England stock, proudly conscious of what is expected from their heritage, are frankly perturbed about this condition. They plead the State's youth and they blame the South. "What can be expected of a State that has barely outlived her first hodge-podge and irrelevant laws, that is still unmindful of the work of her historical society?" they ask. Again they say: "The preponderance of Southerners in our early days formed the deadweight which still holds Iowa's eagle close to the ground." The South—autocratic county management which supplanted the intimate, democratic township system of New England; implacable opposition to the growth of governmental power through the fear of taxation and of encroachments on personal liberty; vigorous resistance to education at public expense, which is still reflected in the dearth of significant institutions of collegiate rank; and, above all, impenetrable indifference toward civic and social questions, which has been a most effective barrier to progressive legislation—the South, then, and all the backwardness that the word connotes is held responsible for the Iowaness of Iowa. And undoubtedly a good deal of energy has been wasted in combating Southern lethargy which might have been used in furthering New England ideals. But we need not look farther than Kansas to see what Iowa might have been with less dominant Southern influences—instead of the mulct law, outright prohibition; instead of a hopeless, languorous sanity, a militant puritanism.

Despite their comfort in flattering figures the Iowans manifest an unmistakable inferiority complex. Their jealous watch on the *Who's Who* for a proper representation of State celebrities, their far-fetched and persistent claims on the nation's great ones in the fields of art and literature, politics and finance, their furtive emulation of other States in publicity-giving enterprises, good, bad, or indifferent, are obvious signs. During the war it was this sense of inferiority rather than praiseworthy zeal which was responsible for an unabashed and militant system of extortion in liberty-loan drives. At the head of this violent effort for glory was, appropriately enough, the father of Hanford MacNider, the American Legion commander who has so violently demanded a bonus.

It is a curious coincidence that the fleeting observation-car impressions of the traveler and an equally superficial perusal of statistics should lead to the same conclusions. And thus Iowa's well-being is in danger of becoming a truism. Not one in a thousand sees that the goodly apple is rotten at the heart or suspects that Iowa's troubles are caused by something other than periods of national depression. As elsewhere, there is constant talk of a greater prosperity toward which Iowa is supposed to be moving as inevitably as the Mississippi flows to the Gulf.

In their slight knowledge of both, the orators of popular causes are fond of comparing the river and the State. They seem equally placid, equally slow-moving, equally intent on one direction.

There is an analogy, to be sure, but a totally different one. For he who has plunged beneath the surface of the river knows there are countless currents, springs, and whirlpools that pull up-stream and to either side in obedience to hidden forces which can stem even the downward flow of waters. So it is with Iowa. There is the old, broad current pulling to the West, depositing its rich burden of superannuated farmers at "Loss Anjelees." There is the phenomenon of former feeders now either dry or drawing sustenance from the main stream— pioneer trails, again peopled, but the people headed in opposite directions. There is a boisterous rapid in the *Iowa Homestead,* an agricultural weekly which is the source of liberal power in the State. There is a cool, clear spring, the Des Moines *Register,* one of the most honest, thoughtful, and fearless dailies in the country. There is a Pierian spring at Grinnell whither flock the thirsty after knowledge. There is the vicious, seething whirlpool of a Greater Iowa Association that every so often sucks down some weak or foolish victim. And there are fine, deep, quiet backwaters—these peaceful colonies of Quakers at Oskaloosa, of Hollanders at Pella, and of religious communists at Amana.

All this is to be seen in the stream of Iowa life. And close observation discloses more—discloses that the seven times seven years of plenty are past, and that the lean years have come upon the land. We see that one of the purest land-holding communities in the world has been transformed during the past thirty years into as bad a tenant-farmer State as any north of the Mason and Dixon's line. Even the statistics that are so dear to the Iowan heart support this view, though one must glance beneath the surface of census columns.

The first signs of this momentous change are evident in a study of population. In the decade of the sixties Iowa's numbers increased 96.9 per cent while the whole of the United States showed a growth of 26.6 per cent. During the following decade the State's population rose 36 per cent as against 26 gained by the nation. By 1880, however, the peak of Iowa's growth had been reached. Her most desirable land was taken up. She no longer showered welcomes on the immigrant. In the next ten years her numbers mounted 17 per cent; the country at large increased 25.5 per cent. And thereafter Iowa falls farther and farther behind the national expansion, until, in 1910, a period of unparalleled prosperity in the State, there is an absolute as well as a relative decline in population, a loss of 0.3 per cent. In the last decade there has been a gain but still 6.8 per cent below the national average.

Again, as early as 1890, began the exodus of enriched farmers to southern California. (Few have realized the extent of this migration; some idea may be obtained from the fact that at the annual picnic in 1920 more than 40,000 Iowans gathered at Los Angeles.) In the main, these farmers sold their land before leaving, but on terms which eventually proved worse for the buyer than any form of rental. It is then that Iowa achieved the distinction of having the most valuable farm land in the country—a reputation which did much to bring about a greater increase in land values than that of any other State. Speculation, with its consequent overvaluation, was inevitable, and the ridiculous prices of three, four, and five hundred dollars per acre were paid in the feverish anxiety to plant a stake in this Eldorado. The pioneers or their descendants, on the other hand, could not resist the temptation of selling. They found a hysterical mob of bidders who were convinced that Iowa land would be worth any price they chose to set on it and who were incapable of realizing at the moment that even the richest soil has a definite limit of production. The land was sold. Then came the reckoning.

Now this land-boom phenomenon has been recurrent. The last, started by the war and ended by the recent industrial depression, was the most intense, the most vivid, and the farthest-reaching in its results. The reckoning came quicker and is therefore more apparent. When the process of deflation set in, it was found that a majority of the transactions were "paper sales," bought with a minimum of cash payment and a maximum of mortgage, the interest on which—much less the principal—could never be gleaned from the land. By and large, the sellers were content, for this interest was greater than any income obtainable from rentals; but the purchasers quickly came to realize that they had become debtors in perpetuity.

What wonder that they grin sardonically today when the Iowa Chamber of Commerce proudly publishes the fact that there are 124,375 farm owners on the two hundred thousand odd farms in the State! The figures are meaningless; true to the records, yet false to the actual conditions. But these very figures, taken in sufficient detail, further reveal the situation. They show that the two counties which have the highest percentage of farm owners stand fifth and sixth from the bottom in a table of land values, whereas O'Brien and Lyon which have the greatest percentage of tenants rank twelfth and thirteenth among the ninety-six counties in the value of their farm lands. This corroborates the suspicion that only the poorer soil is still tilled by the so-called owners; the more expensive farms are rapidly reverting to the original possessors and are being worked by tenant labor. Thus mortgaged owner and broken tenant sweat to pay the increased bills of Iowans in southern California.

Important as this is in the life of Iowa, it gains still greater significance as a presage of national development. With the exploitation of our virgin resources goes the loss of individual independence and the growth of economic slavery. Elsewhere this exploitation has meant stripping of forests, impoverishing the soil, exhausting the mines, and draining of oil wells. In Iowa it is summed up in the one word, mortgage. Her resources are almost intact but the fruit of that land and the labor of her people are eaten by strangers.

"Go West, young man, go West," said Horace Greeley to a poor theological student. And the young man settled in Iowa, founded a town, helped build a college, and accumulated a modest fortune. Today if he made his way there, he could not supply the pettiest pulpit at starvation wages. Today it is more likely that the Iowa farmer's son will seek a church or shop or field in the East or

Iowa corn. The commodity best associated with the state, corn accounted for more than half of Iowa's gross product. Doggerel in the New York *Tribune* in 1922 read as follows: "Flat as a pancake, fertile as can be / All the way from Keokuk to Calliope / Corn that kisses the cloudlets when its tassels wave / Land that laughs a harvest when the reapers slave."

farther West in an effort to pay off the mortgage, to stave off the day when another "owner" must turn tenant. Perhaps a dramatist will one day portray the tragedy of this act, the poignant sorrow of those who relinquish this yellow slip of paper, empty symbol of ownership, and return to till the soil on shares.

This tragedy is being enacted everywhere in the State. The attempts to forestall it are now political history—a history of transformation. Standpatter Senator Kenyon turned leader of the agricultural bloc and passed measures of relief that shocked the "interests." The boss-ridden Republican Party of the State turned out its regular candidates and elected in Kenyon's place Colonel Smith W. Brookhart, friend of the *Iowa Homestead* and avowed liberal, who is characteristically described by the small-town press—and not a few of the "college" presidents—as a "socialistic and anarchistic Bolshevik." The people turned a deaf ear to the radical-baiting of the Greater Iowa Association, and flocked to the meetings of the Nonpartisan League which a few years ago was unable to gain a foothold in the State. Local measures passed recently are in harmony with the new spirit, and students in college economics classes no longer vote unanimously to have Marx's *Communist Manifesto* barred from the shelves of the public libraries. Everyone demands reforms. Reactionary Iowa is insisting on measures as drastic as the Interstate Commerce Commission which its Senators brought into being during an earlier crisis.

Lest those who think that radicalism and idealism go hand in hand should grow unduly optimistic about the "soul of Iowa," let me state at once that there is no spiritual background, no generous purpose in this reform movement. The appeal to black, or rather, red magic for relief is hardly an omen of better days. Never was Ellis Parker Butler's motto for his State,

> Three millions yearly for manure,
> But not one cent for literature,

more pat. Seldom has a people been less interested in spiritual self-expression and more concerned with hog nutrition.

Nevertheless, neither the increased materialism, nor the astonishing new-found radicalism, nor the bounty of nature can avail much in the present situation. The luxuriant Iowa scene will remain as little changed, as deceptive as ever, but the aspect of the future is bleak indeed. What might have been a landed gentry must now become a burdened peasantry. Another land flowing with milk and honey must now feel the yoke of iron. Another set of prophets must sound lamentations. Perhaps a new spiritual life lies in this bleakness; perhaps the Mississippi will find its folk-songs more kin to the minors of the Volga than to the empty clangor of Broadway. Perhaps the farmer of Iowa will be first to follow the peasant of Russia in freeing his land from the yoke. Is not his sententious motto: "Our liberties we prize and our rights we will maintain"?

KANSAS

A Puritan Survival

WILLIAM ALLEN WHITE

APRIL 19, 1922

IT IS CURIOUS how State lines mark differences in Americans. There are no climatic differences between Kansas and Missouri, and small climatic differences between Kansas and Nebraska; yet the three States hold populations in which are marked differences—differences at least which Americans may distinguish. Doubtless to Chinamen all Americans look alike! But Americans know the differences between Americans North, East, South, and West, and dwellers in a section know minor differences between persons living in neighboring States in the same section of the United States. The larger sectional differences in Americans may be somewhat the result of climatic influences. But the distinguishing points between a Kansan and a Missourian, between a New Yorker and a citizen of Vermont, between a Georgian and a Virginian or a Louisianian, or between an Oregonian and a Southern Californian arise from the changes in men made by social and political institutions.

Kansans are marked by Puritanism. "Kansas," said our greatest statesman, John J. Ingalls, nearly forty years ago, "is the child of Plymouth Rock." In the beginning of the settlement of Kansas, the State was invaded by immigrants from New England or sons and daughters of New Englanders, who came to Kansas to make this a Free State. Congress left the question of slavery to the voters of the new State. A fair fight in an open field ensued; the abolitionists crowded out the proslavery people, outvoted them, and captured Kansas. The first Kansans, therefore, were crusaders, intellectual and social pioneers, covenanters of various sorts; which, if you like to live comfortably upon your soft yesterdays, means that Kansas was full of cranks. Slavery being abolished, your Kansan had to begin abolishing something else. Abolitionism was more than a conviction; it was a temperamental habit. It is a good or a bad habit according as you feel that you are your brother's keeper or that the devil should take the hindermost. Soldiers from the great war for the Union flooded into Kansas attracted by the free homesteads. But only Union soldiers could get free land, so Kansas was settled in the seventies and eighties almost exclusively by Northerners—partisans, bitterly controversial and biologically marked by a blue stripe under the waistcoat; Yankees and children of Yankees. Something had to happen to Kansas with such a population. It happened. It was prohibition, adopted forty years ago. Curiously enough the Republican Party in Kansas always indorsed prohibition in its State platforms and through its candidates, while the Democratic Party, representing the feeble protest of the easy-going citizenship that had come in to Kansas in the fifties and sixties bringing slaves, opposed prohibition. But the Democratic minority was negligible and the prohibitionists took away the liquor of their less scrupulous neighbors as their slaves had been taken. For two decades the prohibition problem engaged Kansas. It was a hard fight, but it never wavered. The Puritan won. The Law and Order League in every town and county worked day and night, and to make the victory surer, five years after prohibition came in, the State allowed women to vote in municipal matters, and women having the ballot in the towns where liquor was sold never stopped until prohibition succeeded. It required laws which permitted search and seizure, which prohibited doctors prescribing liquor, and druggists from keeping it in stock, laws which permitted the confiscation of liquor-running automobiles, and which made the second offense of the liquor seller a felony, sending him to the penitentiary for it—but in the end, prohibition won. Your Puritan is no slouch; he is thorough at all costs; thorough and fairly consistent.

For then came Populism. Populism had its genesis in the South probably; and it ran a mild course in the Dakotas and Colorado and Nebraska, States all more or less like Kansas in climate, in economic status, and in blood and breed. But because of the blood and breed, because of the Puritan inheritance of Kansas, the dour deadly desire to fight what was deemed wrong for the sheer sake of obliterating wrong, Kansas took Populism much more seriously than her sister States. Kansas produced most of the leadership of Populism. And long after Populism was defeated and forgotten Kansas clung to it, adopted its creed, and forced a dilution of Populism upon an unwilling nation. The insurgence of insurgency, the progressiveness of the Bull Moose, was the restless spirit of Kansas trying to realize the dream of Populism. Murdock, Bristow, Stubbs, Allen, and Capper in the uprising of the first two decades of the century gave to the national movement a certain blind crusader's enthusiasm. It was with a ghoulish grin that Victor Murdock met a fellow Kansan the morning when Roosevelt threw his hat into the ring in 1912.

"Well—he's finally in," said the Kansan.

"And it's a fine joke on him," says Victor.

"Why?" says the Kansan.

"Because he thinks it's '60 and it's only '48," chuckled the Puritan, delighted that a great man was to aid a good cause and go to defeat in it, even if the great man did not dream what was ahead of him.

That was the Kansas of it. Murdock had no remote thought of hesitating because he saw the inevitable defeat. Defeat was his meat and drink. But he had his sneaking doubts about the Puritan zeal of Roosevelt, who was practical Dutch, doughty, and gorgeously militant; but with a sly sweet tooth for victory and its fruits. Your Puritan regards any sweet tooth as a weakness bordering upon sin! So Kansas has delighted in causes rather than conquests.

After prohibition succeeded and Populism passed, the pioneer spirit of Kansas engaged itself in several social and political experiments, most revolutionary then; but now they have become sane and commonplace attitudes in the ordinary way of life. The theory, for instance, that the State has a right to interfere in the individual's habits on behalf of the better health of the people of the State. Under the State Board of Health which had unusual police powers Kansas abolished the common drinking cup and the roller towel from public places, took over the distribution of various toxins against contagious diseases, inspected hotels and food stores, and closed them up when they were unsanitary. The State also guaranteed bank deposits and restricted the sale of stocks and bonds to projects that had State approval; established a State hospital where crippled children may be cured at State expense; printed its own school textbooks and distributed the books at cost; tightened its grip on public utilities operating in the State; passed a law which virtually socializes all Kansas industry except agriculture, and passed the long line of legislation, once referred to as socialistic and now merely sneered at as laws of Meddlesome Mattie, but accepted by most of the progressive States of the Union and loudly bewailed by those who believe in the laissez-faire theory of morals and economics.

Kansas delighted in being among the first to pass all of these and actually the first to enact many of them. Again it was the Puritan spirit cropping out. Prohibition had kept out of Kansas hundreds of thousands of Germans and Scandinavians and Bohemians who flooded Nebraska and the Dakotas in the eighties and nineties, and the New England strains of blood continued to dominate the life of the State. Nearly 77 per cent of our population is of American-born parents. The Puritan blood even now is the strongest current—almost the only current directing our thought in Kansas. We censor the movies and prohibit them on Sundays. We forbid race-track gambling—indeed, gambling of all kinds is illegal; stop the sale of cigarettes—or try to. We permit Sunday baseball, but only because it is amateur sport and is not commercialized. We prohibited the thing called white slavery before the passage of the Mann Act, and commercialized prostitution has been stopped in Kansas, as entirely as commercialized horse-stealing or commercialized arson or commercialized larceny of any kind. All these inhibitions against the natural tendency of depraved man cut loose from the apron-strings we are pleased to call moral restrictions. We make the questions moral issues arising before and after the passage of our restrictive laws. We go to the churches and schools for our political majorities. The politician who tries to assemble a majority without the churches and schools, without the women, and without what is known as the best influences in the community always finds himself leading a minority. He rails at the long-haired men and short-haired women; he rages at the Pecksniffian attitude of life. But it is deeply ingrained in the Kansas character. It seems so infernally pious; so hypocritical to those who oppose these causes. Yet at base these questions—abolition, prohibition, health, stability of savings, cigarettes, prostitution, gambling, and social and industrial justice—are not moral but economic in their value to society. Slavery would not work in a modern world; neither does the saloon; cigarettes and common drinking cups and prostitutes and roller towels and impure foods and long working hours cut down the producing power of men, cripple their economic efficiency; so puritanism which is always keen about the main chance makes a cause out of abolishing them, sings hymns—as, for instance, ''Onward, Christian Soldiers,'' or ''Where Is My Wandering Boy Tonight,'' or ''The Slave's Lament''—and quotes texts and holds prayer meetings to gild the main chance with the golden glow of piety. But after all it is the main chance the Puritan is after. He is an idealist planning a great democratic civilization; but one wherein a dollar will travel further, work harder, and bring in more of the fruits of civilization than any other dollar in the world. The waste of slavery, the social expense of the saloon, the venereal disease, the crooked stock seller, the purveyor of expensive schoolbooks or impure food, or the dishonest banker—each immediately becomes a check to the Puritan scheme of things and automatically is invested with evil! Meddlesome Mattie is the machinist operator who is forever listening into the works to hear a knock or a bur-r-r; and hearing it, jabs her monkey wrench into a lot of fun for some one, not because it is fun, but because it costs too much to maintain the bad adjustment.

So much for the institutions of Kansas—for her society and politics. Now for the life of Kansas, for which she has instituted her laws and social standards and upon which they rest. What manner of people are these Puritans who sing hymns and quote texts and glorify moral issues to cover the main chance, who glorify God to grease their busy dollars? As a pragmatic proposition does their civilization work? Is it worth while? Are people freer, happier, more prosperous, more comfortable and wise under this order of things than they are under the scheme of things which shrugs its Latin shoulders and says it does not care; says to waste is human, to enjoy divine? First let us look at the material side. As to wealth, for instance. Ten years ago the figures indicated that the county in the United States with the largest assessed valuation was Marion County, Kansas, a county in central Kansas, not materially different from any other county; Marion County happened to have a larger per capita of bank deposits than any other American county. Its average of per capita wealth and per capita bank deposits was not much higher than the Kansas average. Yet no man in Marion County was then rated as a millionaire, but the jails and poorhouses were practically empty. The great per capita of wealth was actually distributed among the people who earned it. They were sober, so they saved; they were healthy, so they worked. They were well schooled, so they worked to purpose and with direction and made money. They were clear-brained, well-bred, cold-blooded Yankees, who knew exactly what they wanted, how to get it, and where to put it. That is your Kansan. Typically he lives either upon an eighty-acre farm or in a detached house within a fifty-foot lot, near a schoolhouse, with an automobile in the garage, whether farmer or town dweller; if a farmer he lives upon a rural free-delivery route along which the postman brings to him at least one daily paper, one weekly paper, and one monthly; if a town dweller he lives upon a paved street, a sewer line, a telephone wire, an electric light and power conduit and a gas main. In the county wherein these lines are written, an ordinary Kansas county, the number of telephones exceeds the number of families, the daily newspaper prints as many copies as there are heads of families, and in the towns the number of electric light connections is more than the number of residences. Water and gas are common, and the bank deposits for the town and county are $6,260,000 and the number of depositors 21,500 in a county with a total population of 26,496 people. Ninety per cent of the families are within five miles of a high school in this county, and 25 per cent of the children of high-school age attend the high school. The county contains two colleges, and the attendance from the county in the colleges is 623! A farm agent who receives $2,200 a year advises the farmers about crops, helps them to overcome bugs and pests, and organizes them for marketing. The county is spending a quarter of a million upon its own hospital and no citizen of the county is in jail. Twenty-five miles of hard-surfaced roads are under construction and as much more ordered in. It cost less than $2,000 last year to try all the criminals that infest the courts, and a preacher is police judge of the county-seat town. He commits less than a dozen men a year to jail—and this in a town of 12,000 surrounded by a county of 26,496.

This is a Kansas average, and there is your ideal Puritan civilization: a prosperous people, neither burdened by an idle and luxurious class who are rich, nor taxed to support a sodden and footless class verging upon pauperism. A sober people practically without a criminal class, an intelligent people in so far as intelligence covers a knowledge of getting an honest living, saving an occasional penny, and living in a rather high degree of common comfort; a moral people in so far as morals consist in obedience to the legally expressed will of the majority with no very great patience for the vagaries of protesting minorities. A just and righteous people in so far as justice concerns the equitable distribution of material things, and righteousness requires men to live at peace among men of good-will. A free people in so far as freedom allows men and women to have and hold all that they earn, and makes them earn all that they get. But a people neighbor minded in the Golden Rule, a people neighbor bound by ties of duty, by a sense of obligation, by a belief in the social compact, in the value of the herd, in the destiny of the race. All these social totems are concentrated in the idea of God in the Kansas heart. We are a deeply religious people. Time was when they used to say in Kansas that the Republican Party and the Methodist church were the spiritual forces that controlled the State. "Ad astra per aspera," to the stars by hard ways, is the State motto, and kindly note the "hard ways." Ours is no easy approach to grace, no royal road to happiness, no backstairs to beneficence. There is no earthly trail paralleling the primrose path in which one can avoid the wrath of God and the lady next door. Life and liberty are indeed highly esteemed in Kansas; but the pursuit of happiness only upon conditions set forth in the Ten Commandments, the Golden Rule, and their interpretation by the Kansas statutes.

Still we are not a joyless people. We laugh easily, and for the most part kindly. But we often approve the things we laugh at; we laugh one way and vote another. Our sense of humor saves us, but not entirely whole; we have never laughed ourselves out of our essential Puritanism. Laughter as a solvent has been tried—the anti-prohibitionists tried it, the opponents of Populism tried it, the defenders of Cannon and Aldrich and conservation tried it. But they all failed as flatly as the Missourians and the gay Southerners failed who tried to laugh at the abolition rifles by dubbing them "Beecher's Bibles." Deep in our hearts is the obsessed fanaticism of John Brown. Joy is an incident, not the business of life. Justice as it works out under a Christian civilization is the chief end of man in Kansas.

But alas, this is begging the question. For who can say that the establishment of justice is the chief end of a state? Indeed who can say even what justice is? Is it just that every man should earn what he gets and get what he earns? Or is it just that those who see and feel and aspire to do great things—to make life beautiful for themselves and others—should be pared down to the norm in their relations with mankind? Is it justice to establish a state where the weak may thrive easily and the strong shall be fettered irrevocably in their most earnest endeavors? Should a state brag of the fact that it distributes its wealth equitably—almost evenly—when it has produced no great poet, no great painter, no great musician, no great writer or philosopher? Surely the dead level of economic and political democracy is futile if out of it something worthy—something eternally worthy—does not come. The tree shall be known by its fruit. What is the fruit of Kansas? Is happiness for the many worth striving for? What is the chief end of a civilization? What is the highest justice?

What we lack most keenly is a sense of beauty and the love of it. Nothing is more gorgeous in color and form than a Kansas sunset; yet it is hidden from us. The Kansas prairies are as mysterious and moody as the sea in their loveliness, yet we graze them and plow them and mark them with roads and do not see them. The wind in the cottonwoods lisps songs as full of meaning as those the tides sing, and we are deaf. The meadow lark, the red bird, the quail live with us and pipe to us all through the year, but our musicians have not returned the song. The wide skies at night present the age-old mystery of life, in splendor and baffling magnificence, yet only one Kansas poet, Eugene Ware, has ever worn Arcturus as a bosom pin. The human spirit—whatever it is in God's creation— here under these winds and droughts and wintry blasts, here under these drear and gloomy circumstances of life, has battled with ruthless fate as bravely and as tragically as Laocoön; yet the story is untold, and life no richer for the nobility that has passed untitled in marble or in bronze or in prose. Surely the righteousness which exalts a nation does not also blind its eyes and cramp its hands and make it dumb that beauty may slip past unscathed. Surely all joy, all happiness, all permanent delight that restores the soul of man does not come from the wine, women, and song which Kansas frowns upon.

Yet why—why is the golden bowl broken, the pitcher at the fountain broken, and in our art the wheel at the cistern still? This question is not peculiarly a Kansas question. It is tremendously American.

KENTUCKY

Where Men Die Standing

BEN LUCIEN BURMAN

JULY 25, 1923

T HE LIMITED, Boston bound, roared over the flat Ohio farms. The melancholy New Englander in the seat opposite us, a boy returning East for a first year in Harvard, shook his head. "Kentucky," he repeated, gloomily. "No. Not as my home. All the people there are savages. Aren't they?" We spent an earnest ten minutes in proving the falsity of this belief. At the end of which time, optimistically, we rested our case. The grave youth thought a moment, then again shook his Mayflower head. "Well, anyway," he said, "it isn't a Christian country." A remark which was probably prompted by thoughts of the well-known but mythical old lady of the Cumberlands whose acquaintance with religious figures was limited to a certain mysterious God, familiar only through his last name, "Dam." The doleful New Englander's indictment was pronounced before the Darwinian tempest swept down the Blue Grass; now a serious sophomore, the youth probably condemns the State as too Christian. Belief in its savagery, however, he will undoubtedly hold until his death. For to a diminished degree his verdict is the verdict of the nation. Is not Kentucky the land of grizzled feudists and defiant moonshiners; of soft-hatted politicians who recite poetry and tote pistols; is it not the land of dashing Night Riders and tobacco-chewing Methuselahs; is it not Wild West on Main Street? It is. All of these. But it is not savage: merely romantic. Therefore let a mechanized world be grateful.

The mountaineer who—if he can draw the faster—slays on sight a cousin in war over a pig three generations dead is not a fiction: he is a fact. Yet he is the same mountaineer who to a weary, hungry stranger will give all his rickety bed and more than half his scanty corn pone. He is hospitable, kind, noble, even at the starvation point. His violence arises from the single passion which masters his existence—he must not be trod upon, he must be free. His cousin's kin, he argues, cheated his kin; they are trespassers upon his family's, and thus his own, kingdom of self; they must be annihilated. By no means is Kentucky all mountainous, nor all its dwellers mountaineers, yet from the misty heights of Pine Mountain on the east to the mud-lapping Mississippi on the west, the creed is

143

one: I will be myself. The laws that please me I will obey; the laws that suit me not be damned. "A Kentuckian kneels only to his God," declaimed Crittenden, doomed for aiding the Cuban insurgents, as he faced the rifles of his Spanish executioners.

Alas that the Kentuckian forgets that the doctrine of "You let me alone" connotes "Then I'll let you alone"; certain of his own righteousness, he is not content until he is transfigured into an exalted crusader, off for the battle. Willynilly, he would then ram baptism by sprinkling, baptism by immersion, or whatever the momentary credo down his townsman's throat, with revolver as ramrod. Intense, passionate, pious, his emotions are easily stirred, and the unschooled evangelistic parson, with his jeremiads of literal blood, fire, and brimstone, can whip him into acts, if not of violence, of ridiculous stupidity. Such are the black-frocked clerics who would make of Kentucky a virgin gold-field for the Ku Klux Klan with nuggets lying beside every tobacco plant—were it not for one fact: a Kentuckian revels in a fight, but it must be a fair fight.

One glossy laurel these rustic churchmen almost won: the law to prohibit the teaching of evolution—a law the bare mention of which should cause the giant pine trees, whose ancestors heard the Kentuckian bitterly assail the repressive Alien and Sedition Acts, to turn their spiny tops from the sun. The history of the Darwin episode is illuminating. A veteran Kentucky legislator's daughter enrolled at the State University. The time arrived when she returned home. One afternoon parent and child were conversing. "Father," the girl announced, "what you and mother taught me is wrong. All wrong. I've studied science in college. There isn't any God." And the father wept. But mere weeping is vain, he knew. He decided to act, and deliver the youth of Kentucky from these lethal educators who taught that men were no better than monkeys or dogs, with the same hope of heaven. The battalions of the pulpit rallied at his jousting cry. Bryan entered the capital. He addressed the legislature. The Nebraska breath was fire; the silver tongue scattered vitriol. The lower house heeded, with ears acute, and minds on the little church back home, thronged with voters. Enough votes were pledged for a victory. When at the last dramatic moment the thrice-blessed figure of independence and free-thinking rose from the corner where it had been pushed and sat upon: the bill was defeated by one vote. In the Senate, had it not been smothered in committee, the measure would have passed. A fact we confess with shame.

With shame, because the law would have violated every tradition that has brought the State glory. The tradition, for example, of the Kentucky which when still an unweaned, unprotected infant, surrounded by Indians, many times verged on a break from the Union because of Federalist autocracy; the tradition of the Kentucky governor who at the outbreak of the Civil War, when commanded by the Union's military chief to send troops, telegraphed the haughty officer a courteous "Go to," and sent the same valiant message to the Confederates; the tradition of the Kentucky militiamen who in the early conflicts of the nation, disgusted with the campaigns' conduct, told the chiefs their opinions, packed up their kits, and went back to the Blue Grass; the tradition of a Kentucky which, when the decision of the State's highest court did not satisfy the people, abolished the court. After all the anti-Darwin bill *was* defeated and tradition saved. Let hosannas ring!

High up in the Cumberlands where men live in the log houses their forefathers chopped from the shadowy forests, where there are no doctors in a county, no automobiles, no railroads, no telephones, there reigns liberty unfettered—and systematic scorn for law. It is moonshiners' paradise. Back from the creek bottom serving as a highway sits Steve Miracle, rifle at his side. In his pigmy clearing, deserted except for a hissing rattler, or a "blowin' " viper, he watches stoically as the mountain "dew" drips from the rusted still into the jug below. Maybe, if Steve isn't conscientious, he adds a bit of alkali. Certainly the gun is there. Kept handy, too. Et's his liquor, ain't et? His corn, his still, by God, it's all his'n. What right's them folks up in Frankfort or way out East to say he cain't make liquor ef he wants to? Let a dam revenuer come aroun'! He'll show 'em, by God.

The Kentucky mountaineer shoots first and thinks afterward. In a county whose voting population was eleven hundred, three years saw twenty fatal shootings and sixteen woundings. No conviction followed. Amazingly trivial are the causes of this deadly gun play. A farmer kicks his neighbor's dog. A father gives his intoxicated son an unwelcome order—orders are not popular in the mountains. One ingenious highland merchant after a quarrel, knowing his life to be in danger, constructed a stockade the entire distance from his house to his store. He died from a bullet nevertheless. The statute-books denounce gun-toting: the law is futile as a sun parlor in Mammoth Cave. In this year of grace nineteen hundred twenty three, of subways, radio, and chewing gum, every man taking the oath of office in Kentucky must swear he has neither as principal nor second participated in a duel! When the last constitutional convention assembled in 1890 obsolete enactments came up for repeal. The dueling law was retained; the legislators believed revocation would be dangerous. More than once has a judge rendered a decision and afterwards affirmed it with his life. The vigorous breath of this warning in the columns of an old newspaper still blows up the Licking. "I . . . thus publicly give notice to all sheriffs, constables, bailiffs, marshals, and their deputies, that if they do serve any precept on me preparatory to coercion that I will . . . put a period to their earthly career. . . . "

Withal, the Kentuckian is kind, devoted, lovable. Though his only books be the Bible and the Sears Roebuck catalogue, he is never uncouth. He is always the gentleman. Woman, beautiful, black haired or golden haired, flashing eyed, soft of form and soft of voice, here dwells in the age of chivalry. Upon her pedestal she is enthroned, for stranger, lover, husband to worship. In the Blue Grass the mannish-collared college girl would be a sight so bizarre that her walk upon the streets would signal a parade of gaping ragamuffins and grinning piccaninnies. When Kentucky was still an eighteenth-century wilderness of forest, Indian, and trapper, a dancing-master established a school for pirouettes in the blockhouse of Lexington. Nor did he starve. Kentucky is the land where woman must be woman; her castle her home. True, the State did at length ratify the suffrage amendment; why, is a mystery. At a document-strewn desk a prominent Kentuckian, pounding with his fist as though each blow annihilated one of the guilty, scathingly harangued to us why the law was the most calamitous act in all the nation's history.

How ran the old song the school boys chorused when no teacher was nearby? Something after this fashion:

> In Kentucky. In Kentucky.
> Where the horses are the fairest,
> Where the women are the fastest,
> And the politics the damndest:
> In Kentucky.

Let the sleek horses graze quietly in their velvet pastures; bid farewell to the Kentucky maiden—though verily she merits far more than a glance—and muse instead upon ballots and balloteers. The writer of the song's closing line was a man of truth. Politics are the damndest in Kentucky. The reason? Again it is individuality, exalted, bringing with it strange contradictions. Whether classroom novice, farmer, lawyer, clerk, or tobacco picker, every male is a politician. Asked whence came the principles he cherishes, his proud reply would be "Myself": almost certainly these principles were handed down by his father, and by his father's father, slightly changed in the passage of time. Yet, stubborn partisan as he is, should the interpretations of other fathers' sons, clashing with his own, be made the dominant creed of the party, instanter he bolts. A party split is as regular and expected as frogs after a Visalia rain. The schisms sometimes prove fatal. For politics in Kentucky are never impersonal. Wrote one statesman to a rival: "I will not call you liar, villain, or scoundrel; but with all the politeness imaginable, I could prove you so."

The office-seeker is delightfully ingenuous. Thus advertises one highland candidate: "I am out of a job for some time. My wife and six children need my support. Think it over, friend, and let me have your vote for clerk." A poster with the honest rustic smiling out blazons these cryptic sentences: "All my life I lived in this county. My father and grandfather, too. Not one of us ever asked for a political office. I think it's about time they got one, don't you?" "A dog for every man in the mountains," promises a son of Clay County, wistful for the legislature. While what more could be asked of man than this: "I will make the people of our county a good, sober sheriff"?

Along the river valleys, where time is marked by the coming of the showboat, or on the rolling plains where the clock is the county fair, the buying of ballots is a commerce probably far rarer than in the Northern States stretching up from the clayey Ohio, with their Cincinnatis, their Terre Hautes, their Chicagos. In the Republican mountains, however, where there are few to see and none to tell, the ballot merchant—so say the Democrats—disdains retail barter, and opens his shop for the wholesale trade. The clientele is that benumbed caste, supposedly the progeny of criminals who fled from England; their slogan, "A vote for a dollar." In a plateau county, so insistent became the cry for greenbacks a few days before election, the tiny bank serving the community was drained, and compelled to telegraph the Sub-Treasury for a new supply.

In the Goebel assassination mountain political fury attained its height; the case is a twentieth-century tragedy of two cities begun with death in a duel and ended with murder. . . . William Goebel is State Senator from Covington in the lowlands. The commoner hails him as a liberator; corporations denounce him as a self-seeking despot. . . . The Senator writes a political article attacking Colonel John Sandford, an officer of a Covington bank. . . . The two men meet at the bank's entrance. . . . Both draw, both fire. . . . Sandford falls, mortally wounded. . . . Goebel is never indicted. . . . Four years pass. . . . The Senator is now Democratic candidate for governor. . . . The returns show the Republicans to be elected by 2,383 votes. . . . The verdict is accepted, then contested on a charge of intimidation and fraud in the mountains. . . . The legislative committee assembles at Frankfort to hear the contest. . . . Feeling is intense. . . . Nine hundred and sixty armed mountaineers invade the capital "to see justice done." . . . The decision of the contest is about to be announced, in Goebel's favor. . . . When Goebel, entering the capitol grounds, is shot to death by a bullet fired from a window in the Secretary of State's private office. . . . Repubican leaders are accused, among them the governor whose office Goebel was contesting. . . . It is testified that mountain feudists had agreed "to kill off enough Democrats to make a Republican majority in the legislature." . . . One confesses, some are convicted: to be pardoned later when a Republican chief executive comes into power. . . . One is repeatedly sent as a mountain representative to Congress. . . . In a single aspect the grim episode is not typical; Goebel was slain by an assassin, not by an enemy face to face—Kentuckians abhor cowards who shoot from behind. Another fatal drama, so recent that the trial may not yet be ended, is the "Bloody Election" of Clayhole. In this hamlet, where political control vacillated, gunmen entered the polls, shot promiscuously and mortally, riddled the ballot boxes with bullets, and dumped them into the river nearby.

On the same stage as these tragedies of blood are rightly, in comic relief, enacted high political comedy and farce. The legislature, less corrupt perhaps than in many other commonwealths, naturally could not exist without its lobbies for drollery and divertissement. Here the jovial entertainers are the Three Musketeers—the coal lobby, the railroad lobby, and the race-track lobby; appearing in their sportive interlude:

> All for one. One for all.
> Dare he strike one, three on him fall.

No bribes, says Mr. Legislator. Away, Satan, with your bribe! But a drink of whiskey from a friend in a dry country—that's different. So the soft-coal lobbyist must stock his hotel chambers with the mellowest of Scotland's pride, and keep open house for the men who make the laws. There's work to be done! The influence thus exerted is said to be tremendous.

Out of England to the Indian-haunted forests lumbered the caravans of the Kentucky settlers. The wilderness did its work, and the traits of the newcomers identifying them as Englishmen vanished. Except one: the Englishman's love of a horse race. From the days when "scalping" was a dread fact of the moment, not a dim tradition, the bronzed inhabitants of each little settlement gathered to watch shining steed vie with shining steed. Today the sport, commercialized, has aggrandized until it is imperial; the daily health bulletins of its Morviches, its Silver Kings, are flashed about the world as though they told of a god upon whose well-being hung the universe; millions are won and lost when the favored Derbyite stumbles and breaks a leg.

It is the race-track lobby, fighting the church lobby for its life, whose methods are unique. This is the procedure laid down by the race-track political Book of Etiquette. About the busy paddocks are a myriad hangers-on, watchmen, machine-tenders, ticket-takers, all well paid. Be you envious of such an easy livelihood, or out of employment, call upon the king of horses and jockeys, and petition for a place. "Go," commands the monarch, "and seek out the political chieftain of your province. Worthiest of all, let it be a legislator. Ask him to inscribe for you an indorsement. Return to me then, and the post is yours. If ye gain no such indorsement, return not, for we are busy, and life is brief."

Thus, indirectly, the politician goes deep into the race-king's debt: and debts it is not etiquette for a politician to forget. As another effective expedient, the sovereign places the legislator upon his regal pay roll, at a stipend of fifteen dollars a day with no onerous labor demanded of him.

One unsophisticated, conscientious legislator, apprised of this boon, so goes the story, besought of the king to know his duties. "You see that concrete wall over there?" growled the monarch. "Yep," returned the anxious inquirer. "Well, you're the wall guard," sniffed His Highness. "Keep your eye wide open to see that it doesn't walk away."

Always a paradox is the Kentuckian; an ultra-conservative in making laws, he becomes a passionate radical in breaking them. The tenant tobacco farmers, "hill billies" who were ever in debt to the grocer and at the mercy of a tobacco trust which paid as the mind of its buyer varied, decided something must be done. Failing to consult Blackstone, they banded together, agreeing to retain the crops until a life-supporting price was offered. If a neighbor more prosperous, or preferring to play his football game alone, insisted on selling at any figure tendered, he received three or four warnings. If the warnings went unheeded, upon a cloudy night a troop of cavalrymen dashed through his fields, and a few moments later tobacco barn and its black leaves were in flames. These incendiaries, haters of trusts, were, and are, the "Night Riders." Similarly, when toll-gates along the ragged highways in Campbell County harassed the travelers, and negotiations for purchase appeared never to end, rustic cavaliers galloped down: when the toll-keeper appeared after dawn to collect his levy from every voyager he found the gates hacked into splinters. The sale was consummated at once.

Kentucky, the Kingdom of Self. It is a land which has borne or fostered many of the famous: Daniel Boone, Simon Kenton, Henry Clay, Henry Watterson, Jefferson Davis and Abraham Lincoln, the President of the Confederacy and the President of the Union; but always the greatness is of the individual, never of the reflected group. It is the Land Where Anything Might Happen; where judges spit tobacco with grandiloquent attorneys, and one judge opens court with hymns; where school teachers kill wild-cats by lying upon them; where schoolboys whip pedagogues because no holiday is granted to honor the visiting elephant; where a newspaper-contest promoter addressing circular letters in the conventional "My Dear Mrs. Bowlsey" is invited upon the street to fight numerous irate husbands for flirting with their wives; where the casual wayfarer is introduced to the college president by the driver of the mail hack. It is a land where love of liberty compensates for grievous imperfections; a land of the lotus which the Kentuckian may leave, but never abandons. This is the State's sin: life is too cheap. Let the Kentuckian barter his revolver for a book, and die in bed.

Lest the Blue Grass–inclined vacationer be frightened from his pilgrimage, to the sorrow of commerce chambers, we hasten to add that there are policemen in Kentucky, and spots where the stranger might dwell five years without hearing the sound of a gun.

LOUISIANA

(*Madame de la Louisiane*)

BASIL THOMPSON

NOVEMBER 15, 1922

A CLEAR AND UNIMPASSIONED VISUALIZATION of so unique a commonwealth as Louisiana becomes a complex and disquieting performance, especially when your raconteur is a native son not wholly lacking in sentiment toward his delightfully volatile soil-mother. Native-born Louisianians, Kentuckians, and Virginians, unlike native-born Georgians, Arkansans, and West Virginians, must of necessity retain some sly regard for the romantic, historic, and traditional foibles of their several *terrae matres.*

Madame de la Louisiane fairly screams romance. At once piquant, naïve, effete, blasé, and bumptious, she presents to her sister commonwealths more or less the same aspect that Mam'selle Nouvelle-Orléans, her capricious daughter, exhibits to her staider cosmopolitan brethren. Though her glitter, her arrogance, her superficiality, her little minauderies are beyond question, beneath the veneer one glimpses her true personality—elusive, coy, droll, if you will, but very real, quaint, colorful.

Madame de la Louisiane is woman and mother. Regard her thus. Only as woman and mother may one detect her authentic gesture—her history, sentiment, tradition, her odd little quirks of character. She is, moreover, "a woman with a past." But she is, too, a mother humoring the whims of her favorite child, Mam'selle Nouvelle-Orléans. Her whole life whirls about this elder daughter, whose manner and insouciance are inimitable; whose fame and dark beauty have gone the world around; who is not, despite all her extravagance, ever anything but herself. Let us consider her *en fête, en costume de bal,* arrayed at her best— as one should always consider lovely woman.

It is February. The air is crisp, clean, invigorating. You have just had an absinthe in the "Assassins' Den" of the Old Absinthe House. Monsieur Cazenave, on learning you are down for the Mardi Gras from Hoboken, Kansas City, or the Yukon, unbends graciously. He concocts for you an absinthe, cool, milky, satisfying. Your gullet titilates deliciously. You have another, this one frappéd by way of change. For the nonce, Mr. Volstead is relegated to the limbo of the unborn. You sip your drink dreamily, reminiscently. Shades of Paul Verlaine and Jean Lafitte! Where are you? Parnassus, Paris, or Nouvelle-Orléans? The last indubitably.

The hoot of horns, the cries of masqueraders intrude from the street below. It is Mardi Gras in New Orleans in the year 1922. There must be some mistake. You are dreaming. You are drunk. "L'addition, M'sieu?" Your reverie is disturbed. The bill settled, Félix, the garçon, offers you hat and top coat. You are out in the street—Bourbon Street at the intersection of Bienville. You walk toward Canal, surrounded by a riot of color and sound. The deliciously treacherous absinthe seeps into your brain. The day is rich, glorious; the air, tonic; the people, mad, young, wanton. . . .

A masked girl in cotton tights bumps into you. "Pardon, M'sieu," she laughs and is away. A ten-year gamin, in Charlie Chaplin make-up, notes your abstraction—"Hey, Mister, come out of it! Git in the push." He supplies the push. You are aroused. You look about eagerly, excitedly. You nudge your friend. You ply him with innumerable questions. "Rex" is making down Canal Street. Bands are playing. Club galleries gleam with pretty frocks and faces. A storm of confetti bursts upon you. The Carnival colors are everywhere. Buildings, windows, galleries, signs, banners, the people themselves blaze with color. It is a vital, an electric pageant, veritably charged with passion, imagination, beauty, madness. . . .

A slight picture. Ineffectual, if you will, but where else in all America may you glimpse it? And Mardi Gras Day is but one day in the year, and New Orleans but one section of Louisiana. None the less it is this carnival spirit that pervades New Orleans, and it is this New Orleans spirit that pervades Louisiana. Louisiana is New Orleans and, by the same token, New Orleans Louisiana. This despite great sugar and cotton plantations, the rice and sulphur industries, the oil fields, the timberlands, the salt islands, the big game preserves, the State capital at Baton Rouge, the "city" of Shreveport, the insane asylum at Jackson, and the protestations of upstaters.

Perhaps it were not amiss to rehearse here somewhat of the history of this *soi-distant grande dame* among States. Parenthetically one begs your indulgence a space wherein Madame's past is, one trusts, tactfully if not entertainingly reviewed. In speaking of a lady's past, however, it seems not gallant to become personal lest, by the token, one also becomes odious. Thus shall be given over, for the time, Madame's femininity as such and her origins sketched in the broad, impersonal, though be it confessed lack-luster manner of historiographers.

Aboriginally *locus* la Louisiane was a body of water, a geological sea. More late, a prehistoric dwelling-place for amphibious brutes, where primitive peoples built shell mounds to climb upon in high-water time. These mounds excavated today betray a certain native art, evidenced in rude bowls, earthen vases, stone implements. Later the Indians: some indigenous, like the Attakapas; some nomadic, probably from Mexico, like the sun-worshiping Natchez tribe; in all five or six groups, living each a community life.

The early roads of la Louisiane were waterways. The pirogue, a sort of canoe built for four, was means of transit from bayou to river and river to bayou. Wild fowl and buffalo served to victual the winter season. Fish and local crustaceans sufficed the summer. Fruit and nuts, notably the pecan, were plentiful. Corn was planted. Rice grew naturally. With nothing to do, with no need to go anywhere, with labor done by the women (days that are no more!) it was usually too warm or too rainy deliberately to make war, so even fighting, a pastime in the "Canetuckie" country, could not cajole these pre-Caucasian Louisianians out of their native indolence.

But the forest stillness of the swamp country, just below the mouth of Red River, was soon broken by the clanking armor of Hernando de Soto's men. Moscoso buried De Soto in the waters of the Mississippi, and with the remnant of his conquistadores floated on a raft down past the site of Nòuvelle-Orléans, putting out upon the Gulf of Mexico. The Spanish were not then seriously impressed with the somber, mossgrown wilderness of this future American commonwealth, and so did not formally include it except as an extension of Florida.

A century or so passed before Père Marquette and the merchant Joliet, followed by Robert, Cavalier de La Salle and Tonty of the Iron Hand, came down the river from Canada. The Fleur-de-lys was raised at the mouth of the Mississippi. The country, the entire valley from the Alleghenies to the Rockies of the West, was, with much ceremony, named la Louisiane, after *le grand monarque* Louis Quatorze and his Queen-Mother, Anne of Austria. Thenceforward, we have recorded the familiar story of Louisiana.

After pioneering discoveries by La Salle came settlement by Iberville at Biloxi. The French King sent over ships and soldiers. Hardy men and women followed to hew wood, draw water, and procreate. In and about were the omnipresent Jesuits, lending first aid to the sordid lives of a people whose very existences depended on daily exertion and innumerable hardships. The story of the province of Louisiana—a French colony five months' sail from France; barely known to exist by the people of Europe; moving slowly onward; filling its requirements to the best of its abilities; taking lessons from its Indian neighbors in fishing and providing food; waiting ever for encouragement from the King— this chapter in the history of Louisiana was but one of desperate effort to survive flood, fever, and famine. Yet stout hearts prevailed and another generation was gradually born—the Creole, so dubbed in France. Here upsprang this new American breed, scarcely aware of the Fleur-de-lys, breathing the air of "freedom" and "liberty" along with their brethren—bird, bear, and Indian.

A ship came over in 1766 bringing from Europe a new Governor and a new flag. The King of France had handed over to his cousin, the King of Spain, the colony nominally cared for since the days of John Law. After the Mississippi Bubble had burst, the Province de la Louisiane ceased longer to interest the

Court of Paris.[1] The Creole at last had something to break monotony. He revolted. Cutting the hawser that held the Governor's ship to the levee, he sent word by the same ship as it floated to the gulf that, "We, the people, if no longer subjects of France, elect to be subject only to ourselves." Strange that a declaration arrived at in Mecklenburg and Lexington some years later should have been born down in the forests of the delta, still born, if you will, for the revolting group was executed in 1769.

Cession of Louisiana to the United States in 1803 affixed to the young republic more territory than all it had until this time possessed. From a chain of States on the Atlantic seaboard, whose farthest west was then the Ohio country, Oregon, Texas, and California alone remained to complete the vast bulk that forms the United States today.

If the condiments that go to make up the type now known as American depend on quantity and proportion of Caucasian blood, this Latin strain as diffused through the French and Spanish Creole forms a nice balance to the Swede and German of the West, and the New England and Virginia strains of Anglo-Saxon. Most persons should know, by this, that the Creole is Latin-American, a white man, and not, as sometimes vulgarly believed, *café au lait* French mulatto. In Louisiana the Creole is white. He is the direct descendant of the Spanish and French pioneer. The term in its original connotation implied a colonial Frenchman, one born in the colonies. But there are four distinct varieties of Frenchmen in Louisiana: the Frenchman, born in France, the Creole native of French descent, the San Domingan Creole, and the Nova Scotian Acadian or Cajan.

This Cajan is worth a word. In the Teche country—southern Louisiana—he preponderates, speaking a peculiar dialect or patois quite at variance with that of the Creole. In the towns of St. Martinsville and New Iberia this emasculated lingo is almost the common tongue, certainly *la langue de famille*. It is estimated that some fifteen hundred Cajans of those expelled from Nova Scotia settled in Louisiana. They now number one hundred and fifty thousand or thereabouts and for the most part adhere to their native speech. Of course, the Cajan and the Creole must not be mentioned in the same breath. The Creole is, in his kind, a cultured though somewhat decadent type; the Cajan, in his, a crude, ingenuous one. An interesting fact in connection with the French-speaking people of Louisiana is the publication, at the present time, of several purely French papers scattered over the State, and in New Orleans of two weeklies: *L'Abeille,* the earliest existing journal pirnted in the Mississippi Valley, and *La Guêpe.* These titles are not without significance but one cannot help but feel their sting has gone.

But I digress. When Louisiana came under American dominion in 1803 it included a great variety of new citizens, the majority French speaking, but all

---

[1] John Law, a Scot who settled in France, reformed French state fiscal policy and established its first national bank. When Law's Company of the Occident, which was designed to colonize Louisiana, could not meet its obligations in 1720, the "Mississippi Bubble" burst and the company's vastly inflated stock prices sank overnight to near zero. [D. H. B.]

apparently eager to gain identity and cut away from European traditions. The battle of New Orleans proved an excellent baptism. From that time on until the Civil War a gradual Americanization took place. The Confederacy failing, Louisiana was to be born again. This time the process included the customary "sackcloth and ashes." Reconstruction, slavery abolished, brought the individual white man into action as an entity. He, of course, has remade himself, and recently, when our latest American army assembled, looking down the line there seemed but one composite face. Gray veterans of previous wars would indeed have had a difficult job to pick out the grandson of Johnny Reb—Cajan, Creole, cowboy, cracker Hoosier, and New Englander, all looked alike.

Louisiana today! One pauses and ponders, withal a bit ruefully, Louisiana today! "Mais où sont les neiges d'antan?" Master Villon's cry, sounding down the ages, bemouthed and hackneyed as it is, was not more pat in his application than it is to the subject in hand. Where are the leaves of yesteryear? Where are the Louisianians of the past? The buccaneers, pirates, filibusters, scented quadroons, gentlemen duelists, starched Creole ladies, lordly planters, sugar barons, and impeccable barristers—the odd fish, the aristocracy of pre–Civil War days? Where are the clubs, the cotillions, the liqueurs, the fine old customs and courtesies of the past? What has become of Madame Macarty and Dominique You; Maspero's Exchange and the Théâtre d'Orléans; the Baron and Baronesa de Pontalba; the Carondelets? Where are the haunts of Lafitte, Humbert, Pêpe Llula, Croghan the Sandusky hero, Lopez, Walker, Walt Whitman, and Lafcadio Hearn?

What remains? A deal. The life, the spirit, the essence of Louisiana, what are they but heritage of the past? Louisiana is a Catholic State and New Orleans is a Catholic city. When we say Catholic we mean none of your invading, upstart, alien populations. The Catholic church is part of Louisiana, bone of her bone, moss of her oaks. Bigotry, that so afflicts some of our Southern and perhaps some of our New England States, is little known here, unless perhaps in the extreme north where pioneer "red necks" from South and North Carolina, Tennessee, and Georgia came in to settle. In southern Louisiana and New Orleans there is little intolerance, but an intense spirit of rivalry between the Catholic and Protestant elements, the rivalry of each trying to out-distance the other in the social, economic, and educational race. This last accounts perhaps for the recent gratifying reduction in Louisiana's illiteracy. By government census of 1910 she was rated the most illiterate State of the Union with 23.9 per cent of her population unable to read or write; but the census of 1920 shows a reduction of 7.1 per cent as against 1.7 for the whole country.

That Louisiana has produced little or nothing in the creative arts is a fact that can't be blinked. In poetry (quite amusingly) Adah Isaacs Menken—burlesque queen, "intimate" of Dickens, Swinburne, the elder Dumas, and Gautier; wife of Heenan the prize-fighter, "Orpheus C. Kerr" the humorist, and a brace of less noted husbands—despite her obvious extravagance and lack of technique for sheer dramatic interest tops the list. The Menken legend is certainly the most delightful in the literary and theatrical history of the State. In music the older heads cry up L. M. Gottschalk—a composer of ante-bellum days. In fiction George W. Cable, who has treated of the Creole in satirical vein, is as yet unchallenged. The Cable novels certainly rank first in the old-guard fictional output of our State. Then we have Grace King, not so much novelist as raconteur, charming in her kind. And then Professor Brander Matthews, who according to a native "has forsworn his birthplace after acquiring honors at Columbia University and environs." Our historians are sturdier. To Charles Gayarré goes the crown. His *History of Louisiana* has almost attained the distinction of a classic. The late Dr. Alcée Fortier ranks perhaps second, though François Xavier Martin is conceded the sounder student.

Still, in the creative arts Loiusiana has produced little or nothing. True, Walt Whitman, Lafcadio Hearn, Eugene Field, Degas the painter, and others sojourned, found inspiration for and accomplished some of their finest work in New Orleans. Yet where is our poet? and where our painter? and where our novelist? excepting the early Cable. And this in one of the most inspirational atmospheres in America. Sherwood Anderson, writing in a Southern magazine, says: "I proclaim New Orleans from my own angle, from the angle of the Modern. Perhaps the city will not thank me, but anyway it is a truly beautiful city. Perhaps if I can bring more artists here they will turn out a ragtag enough crew. Lafcadio Hearn wasn't such a desirable citizen while he lived in the 'Vieux Carré' . . . I am in New Orleans and I am trying to proclaim something I have found here that I think America wants and needs."

"There is something left in this people here that makes them like one another, that leads to constant outbursts of the spirit of play, that keeps them from being too confoundedly serious about death and the ballot and reform and other less important things in life."

The nomenclature of Louisiana, too, tells its story. The place names of New Orleans, the names of the parishes, rivers, bayous, towns, plantations, evince an imagination not perceptible in less Latin sections of the country. The old Spanish and French Creoles, men of sentiment and invention, named their thoroughfares and their mansions with the same feeling as they did their sons and daughters. Instance some of the place names of New Orleans—Elysian Fields Street, Madmen Street, the Rue des Bons Enfants, Mystery Street, Music Street, the Rue d'Amour, Virtue Street, Pleasure Street. There are streets named for the nine muses; for the great poets, musicians, philosohers; oddly named streets such as Craps (which pastime, by the by, had its incipiency in New Orleans), Bagatelle, Tchoupitoulas, Prytania, Lotus, Ophir; streets after saints, battles, generals, heathen gods and goddesses—streets with *names*, not numbers or commonplace associations!

And the nomenclature of the rivers and the beauty of these rivers—the dark glamor of the Tchefuncta, the misty languor of the Bogue Falaya, the Ouachita, the Atchafalaya, the Vermilion. . . . And the mysterious bayous—Goula, La Fourche, Teche, Barataria. . . . Here I pause. The uncanny remoteness, the quiet, the peace, the sort of primal witchery of this little "no man's water" just out of New Orleans stings the blood like Veuve Cliquot or malaria, as you will—poisons you into forgetfulness. And the parishes! (Not "county" as in all the other States.) Here are some: Acadia, Concordia, Tangipahoa, Avoyelles, Terre Bonne, Lafourche, Calcasieu, Plaquemines, Rapides, Natchitoches, and many others as odd and sonorous.

Some years ago New Orleans earned for herself the metronym "Paris of America." As Louisiana has been dubbed the Pelican State, the Arm-chair State (not out of tenor with the whilom proverbial lassitude of its people), the Boot State, etcetera; so New Orleans has been termed the Crescent City, the Pageant City, etcetera; but "Paris of America" sticks and will so long as American "liberty" and that child-like, festive, emotional temper of its citizenry permit. We are, those of us who are acclimatized, an emotional love-loving people. Though we are not by one-third or one-fourth of French descent, we have nevertheless subconsciously taken on habit and attitude of the Continental.

Thus New Orleans supported a legalized tenderloin long after the custom was taboo everywhere else. The restaurants, cafés, and cabarets of "befo' de war" (the recentest fracas, of course) exhibited an atmosphere distinctly un-American in every respect. Garçons were garçons and not waiters. The proprietor, Madame or M'sieu, cooked the meal. Politeness itself was smiled upon. Men grew tipsy in a perfunctory sort of a way that annoyed no one, not even themselves. An evening at the cabaret followed the burlesque show or the opera and the local cabaret lights sometimes seemed to outdo the imported performers. "Storyville," so named in honor of Councilman Story who arranged the matter, bloomed, boomed, and wassailed. Even "the dollar women" smirking from their "cribs" seemed not unhappy—in the old days. Row upon row of them in bright colored shifts ogling, leering, wheedling: "Come in bébé . . . be a nice boy . . . " The larger "houses"—Arlington's Palace, Piazza's, Lulu's, and the rest—loomed disdainfully above these lesser fry. One pictured as he passed the great mirrored salons; the old "madam," white haired, powdered, spotless (in the laundry allusion), the paint-smeared, puffy-eyed girls, and the "professor." Tom Anderson's at the one corner, Toro's at the next, the Tuxedo a block in, and so on—in the old days. A filthy mess perhaps, a dunghill of disease and immorality, but have we entirely done away with it? Driven it out? Can we? One wonders. Stamp it out in one place, it pushes up in another. Legislation is all very well and good, but legislation is—legislation.

What else? A state, viewed as the bird flies, very like any other State; fertile, well-tilled; combed with farms and factories; quick with gross, bustling, active humanity—typical one hundred per cent Americans, dulled by commerce and competition, deadened to romance and tradition, alive, apparently, but to covet and profit: hardy, stupid spawn, molelike, ferreting out existence. All of course according to one's slant. But what differentiates Louisiana, say, from Georgia? History, traditions, romance—the past.

Though Louisiana as a State today is very like any other State, New Orleans as a city today is very unlike any other city. For New Orleans, despite the recent ravages wrought by post-war propaganda, the Eighteenth Amendment, blue-sky laws, and modern office buildings, came through almost unscathed. Her identity, her individuality, her cap-and-bells quality seem as droll and native as ever. In fact, a sort of renaissance is now transpiring in her heart. The "old town" or French Quarter is being renovated, represerved to its former uniquity. Buildings toppling in ruins are being touched up much in the manner of Leonardo's *Last Supper* with sometimes, alas, like results. But the spirit remains, the old buoyant spirit of pristine times, and the Place d'Armes flanked by the Pontalba buildings, the Cabildo and Cathedral with its Presbytère still remain to memorialize the Vieux Carré of the *ancien régime*.

Where in America will you find cheek by jowl examples of architecture that include the best traditions of the French Renaissance, the Spanish—Moorish and Colonial—as interpreted by a ship carpenter, and a pot-pourri of gaudy exotics, stemming from God knows what countries and eras? The rhythmic arts—music and the dance—have always had a home in this "Venice of the Gulf." The opera was here in 1796, before the birth of Chicago and San Francisco. And when New York had but a paltry two hundred thousand population, Nouvelle-Orléans was a sophisticated city with cabarets, coffee houses, bathing parties, dueling bouts, gallantry, and sportsmanship. The horse race, "two forty on the shell road," originated on the old driveway past Metairie to Lake Pontchartrain.

If present-day Louisiana has any claim to an individuality, a color, a note of her own, it is lodged unmistakably in this sport-loving, sun-loving, unquenchable spirit which was and is New Orleans. Mistress of chivalry, cuisine, and the dance; cosmopolis of legend, caprice, and motley; the Columbine of the cities—New Orleans!

THE STATE OF MAINE
—*"Down East"*

ROBERT HERRICK

AUGUST 23, 1922

IN MY BOYHOOD about Boston they called that part of the United States which lies between the White Mountains and the Canadian province of New Brunswick, with two hundred and more miles of fretted sea-coast from Eastport to Portsmouth—"Down East." It has been "the State of Maine" for only a hundred years, previously having been attached more or less uncertainly to the Commonwealth of Massachusetts, and it was not until 1850 that Massachusetts finally relinquished her undivided half interest in all the Maine State lands. With its 33,000 square miles of territory (still mostly in forest), 5,000 odd streams of sufficient size to be mapped, 1,500 large lakes, 400 sea-coast islands of over a thousand acres each, and several respectable mountains—about half of all this being still in "unorganized townships," "plantations," and "ranges" without names—the State of Maine is a considerable province, almost as extensive as the remaining five States of the New England group, with but three-quarters of a million people in it. In character Maine always was and still is a province by itself, distinctive from its neighboring States. The coastwise steamers, which still ply much as they did in my youth between its river ports and Boston, bring with the salt fish, lobsters, lumber, hay, and potatoes a special breed of rugged, ungainly, stalwart New Englander. For a half century and more "Down East" has been famous as a vacation land of romantic variety, with its roadless forests, rivers and inland lakes, Indians and moccasins, deep bays dotted with rocky, spruce-covered islands. The tail of the province running south from Portland to the Piscataqua has never been wholly characteristic, but to wake in the early morning as the Bangor boat rounded Owl's Head Light into Rockland, to see looming through the fog dim outlines of rocky coast and wooded islands, to smell the brine of cold sea water rolling clean against granite ledges was to realize that one had reached a far country, altogether different from well-tamed Massachusetts. It was much the same, if one descended from the exotic Pullman almost anywhere within the borders of the State to smell the pungent odor of fresh sawdust and cut lumber, with blueberries lying purple on the burnt pine

158

barrens and raspberries hanging from roadside bushes. There was always, in my memory, something strong, wholesome, rugged, untamed, and romantic about the Maine of those days, and more than most parts of the modern world Maine has kept its native quality, moral and physical. Indeed, whatever may be left of that famous old New England, sometime Puritan and always Protestant, will be found today more purely and abundantly here in Maine than elsewhere. The types of faces, the habits, and the ideas are much like those I remember in the Massachusetts of thirty years ago. It is the last stronghold of the Puritan.

Of Maine's three-quarters of a million of inhabitants today, five-sevenths are of native-born white stock, less than one-seventh of foreign parentage (mainly French Canadians), with only a thousand Negroes and less than a thousand Indians. Where else in the United States can be found an equal homogeneity of Anglo-Saxon blood? And in spite of the annual influx of a half million of strangers, who have discovered the beauty and the freedom of Maine, in spite of the estimated thirty million dollars which they pay for their summer vacations, except for a thin fringe of parasitic "resorts," with their corruptions, mainly along the southern sea-coast, this great province has never turned itself into a summer boarding-house like New Hampshire. Within its ample borders, along its lakes and rivers and sea-coast, it can absorb such an enormous transient population without noticeable interference with its own proper activities. These are many, and all basic. Wood pulp, lumber, hay, potatoes, apples, blueberries, sweet corn, building stone, lime, fish—these are the characteristic products of this northern land—and one must not forget ships and sailors! Maine is prosperous. Out of its many farms and inexhaustible forests much wealth has been taken. There are few cities and none of sufficient size to have become a plague spot. Here and there are textile mills, mostly scattered in small towns, so that the industrial population has never become massed, nor a preponderant element in any community. In short, in spite of its many resources, not least an abundant water power, Maine is not developed industrially to the maximum—and may that day never come! Such wealth as it has has largely been taken out of the soil and the sea and is pretty widely distributed. Even after the Great War and its eruptive profiteering there are, I suspect, few millionaires in Maine, and there are few miserably poor or unemployed. Rarely even in the back country does one come across a squalid farm, and I know of no slum street in its few cities. Thus as a whole in Maine there is a stable condition of comfort, self-reliance, non-parasitic occupation common in the New England of a previous generation, which makes for sturdiness, individualism, and conservatism. Maine is not so much reactionary as stationary.

That, I suppose, is why Maine has been found so often in the Republican ranks at national elections. Its people learned their political faith in the Civil War and have found no reason to abandon it, all the more as Republican tariffs look closely after Canadian competition and its long sea-coast provides ample opportunity for Federal "recognition" of one sort or another. For they still believe in high tariffs in Maine and in strictly partisan government. The State has

sent to Washington such men as Blaine, Dingley, Reed, and Hale, typical perhaps of the Republican Party ideal of statesmanship not merely in Maine. But
except for the fact that Maine votes in September and is therefore the subject of
much earnest party solicitude, to see that her citizens continue to set a good
example to other States, I do not feel that national politics play a large part in
the life of Maine. (The two matters which are most negligible in the psychology
of the true American are his religion and his politics.) In State and local politics
Maine well illustrates the theory that the less government the better for those
governed, for the State legislature with an admirable self-restraint meets but
once in two years and then only for a three months' session, chiefly concerned
with game laws and road building. For the rest the famous town-meeting still
flourishes in Maine, once a year at least, and the actual administration of its
large, rambling townships (often fifty square miles and more in area) is left to
the selectmen, who presumably give their communities as much good government as they will pay for. In a word Maine is the least-governed and therefore the
best-governed American State that I know. Fortunately the prizes are not rich
enough to attract heavy grafters, and there are many leisurely eyes and ears to
supervise the activities of public servants.

Maine, it must not be forgotten, is an intensely individualistic community. A
few of its more advanced thinkers may regret that the State disposed of all its
forest lands, a precious heritage, for as little as twelve cents the acre to private
exploiters, lumber companies, and pulp manufacturers, but no doubt if the question recurred today the folly would be sanctioned by popular vote, notwithstanding the fact that the income derived from these forest tracts might have made
Maine a very rich State, with good bridges and roads and a modernized school
system, all without cost to its citizens. But like good Americans everywhere
Maine prefers to give away its natural wealth to greedy individuals and issue
bonds for its public needs. The story of the looting of the pine woods is monot-
onously the same from the Penobscot to Michigan, to Wisconsin, and now in
Washington and Oregon.

If politically and economically Maine is simple, "stalwart" American, it
should not be overlooked that the State was "advanced" in the matter of
prohibition. It went "dry" two generations before the nation passed the
amendment. Not quite dry! There were always zones of dryness from the well-
saturated border towns to the more arid interior about the State House at Augusta. For Maine administered its prohibition temperately and intermittently,
like prudent New Englanders: those who wanted to remain dry could do so without much temptation, and those who wished to drink might do so with circum-
spection. But the act had the support of the people of the State. It is
characteristic of Maine that it believed in prohibition and tried to get it long
before other States in the Union strove for this ideal. Something of the puritan
tradition of discipline has lingered here into these relaxed days. . . .

The backwoods, the wilderness and the frontier, also a stern ocean, have
never been far from man's consciousness in this easterly province. It is not

Logging, Aroostook County, Maine. Wrestling with nature has long characterized the state. Known primarily for its potatoes, Aroostook County was once a lumbering center as well.

surprising, then, that the lighter, the more suave growths of civilization are not much in evidence. Architecturally, except for a few handsome examples of old colonial to be found in coast towns like Wiscasset, Gardiner, and Portland, Maine is bleaker than its more southerly neighbors, where there has been greater wealth, ease, and ready intercourse. The usual Maine farmhouse is a strong plain affair, too steep in the roof (to stand heavy snowfalls), too heavy and angular, perched on big granite blocks, connected by a long shed with an even larger barn, equally homely. Even in the older inland towns size and substantiality count for much more than grace of line and proportion. Timber is cheap, winters long and rude, and the Maine man is not given to adornment, to prettiness. Yet perched on the hills—and I think that Maine farmhouses are more frequently placed on high ground than in other New England States as if to survey the approach of possibly hostile strangers—with a broad fall of plowed land and pasture and backed by heavy "dark growth," these rude white buildings have a solidity and abidingness about them which make them part of the rugged landscape. One realizes that each fertile farm is the result of a long struggle with an unyielding nature, to which generations of tenacious, strong men have given themselves. The fishermen's houses along the coast and on the many islands are smaller than the inland farmhouses, equally white and graceless, and dotted with a pleasant irregularity about the waterfront, their faces turned often to the open sea, quite negligent of the road, because from the sea comes the struggle and the livelihood. All these outer aspects of old Maine are, of course, undergoing change, being gradually overlaid with new and cheaper growths, as automobiles increase and the number of miles of passable roads. But Maine yields more slowly to new ways than other parts of the country, and it will be many a year before the "ranges" and "plantations" of the north have become tamed to the bungalow and garden hose. Meanwhile there are many "unspoiled" towns and villages, where except for the new garage the outer aspect of things is much what it was fifty years ago.

What the inner aspect is of the life in these towns and villages it would be more difficult to pronounce. Culturally Maine is proud of its old New England college, Bowdoin, of its State musical festival, of its newer schools, but culturally these days American seems too much of a muchness to be discriminating about. The trains run daily from the great cities of Boston and New York, and the *Saturday Evening Post*, the Hearst newspapers, the cinema reels, and the Hart Schaffner and Marx clothes penetrate, one and all, to the northernmost and easternmost corners of the province. What Maine has "done in literature" may be read of elsewhere. Maine is not primarily concerned with aesthetics. I think it never will be. That comes like the summer visitor superficially into men's and women's minds. I doubt if many inhabitants of the State are aware today that our most considerable American poet was born and has lived many years among them.[1]

Maine is a great example of the prodigal beauty and richness of our America. From one of its innumerable hilltops you may look across whole counties of pine and fir and hemlock, dotted with farms and lakes, across to other ranges of blue hills, and to still other far-away misty mountain tops, or to the ledgy reefs and dark salt water of its broken coast. There is a sense of space and variety and wildness in Maine not to be felt elsewhere in the United States east of the Rocky Mountains. The old province is not yet tamed and crowded. One can realize how those early adventurers felt when they sailed up to its coast out of the Atlantic— the Sieur de Monts, the Jesuit colonists, Captain John Smith, and all the others. The same fir-covered islands stand sentinel before the deep bays, the same fog hangs over the cold deep waters, the same vista of hills and wide upland rises from the coast, still wild, still pungent with many mingled scents of sea and land. There is still the sense of wide, free space. There is still the wilderness for background. So life remains "Down East" a little more like what it was in the days of the forefathers, when men came to this unknown Western world to be free, to win their right to survive by struggle with nature rather than with their fellow-men.

[1] Henry W. Longfellow was born in Portland in 1807. [D. H. B.]

MARYLAND

Apex of Normalcy

H. L. MENCKEN

MAY 3, 1922

IN ALL TABLES of statistics Maryland seems to gravitate toward a safe middle place, neither alarming nor depressing. The colony was settled after Massachusetts and Virginia, but before Pennsylvania and the Carolinas; the State lies today about half-way down the list of American commonwealths, in population, in the value of its manufactures, and in its production of natural wealth. I thumb all sorts of strange volumes of figures and find this median quality holding out. The percentage of native-born whites of native parentage in the country as a whole is somewhere between 55 and 60; in Maryland it is also between 55 and 60; below lie the very low percentages of such States as New York, and above lie the very high percentages of such States as Arkansas. In the whole United States the percentage of illiteracy is 7.7; in Maryland it is 7.2. In the whole country the blind number 62.3 in every 100,000 of population; in Maryland they number 61.9. Ranging the States in the order of the average salary paid to a high-school principal, Maryland is twenty-third among the 48; ranging them in the order of automobile licenses issued it is twenty-ninth; ranging them in the order of the ratio of Roman Catholics to all Christian communicants it is twenty-second. The chief city of Maryland, Baltimore, lies half-way down the list of great American cities; the State's average temperature, winter and summer, is half-way between the American maximum and minimum. It is in the middle of the road in its annual average of murders, suicides, and divorces, in the average date of its first killing frost, in the number of its moving-picture parlors per 100,000 of population, in the circulation of its newspapers, in the ratio between its street railway mileage and its population, in the number of its people converted annually at religious revivals, and in the percentage of its lawyers sent to prison yearly for felony.

Popular opinion holds the Mason and Dixon line to be the division between the North and the South; this is untrue geographically, culturally, and historically. The real frontier leaps out of the West Virginia wilderness somewhere near Harpers Ferry, runs down the Potomac to Washington, and then proceeds irregularly eastward, cutting off three counties of the Maryland Western Shore and four of the Eastern Shore. Washington is as much a Northern town as Buffalo, despite the summer temperature and the swarms of Negroes; Alexandria, Va., across the river, is as thoroughly Southern as Macon, Ga. In Maryland the division is just as noticeable. The vegetation changes, the mode of life changes, the very people change. A Marylander from St. Mary's County or from the lower reaches of the Eastern Shore is as much a stranger to a Marylander from along the Pennsylvania boundary, or even from Baltimore, as he would be to a man from Maine or Wisconsin. He thinks differently; he has different prejudices, superstitions, and enthusiasms; he actually looks different. During the Civil War the State was even more sharply divided than Kentucky or Missouri, and that division still persists. It results in constant compromises—an almost Swiss need to reconcile divergent traditions and instincts. Virginia to the southward is always Democratic and Pennsylvania to the northward is always Republican, but Maryland is sometimes one and sometimes the other, and when Baltimore is one the counties are commonly the other. The influence of this single big city, housing nearly half the population of the State, is thrown toward maintaining the balance. It has *nearly* half the population, but not *quite* half; thus the rural Marylanders must always pay heed to it, but need never submit to it slavishly. The result is a curious moderation in politics. Maryland is liberal and swiftly punishes political corruption, but it is suspicious of all the new surecures that come out of the South and Middle West—the recall of judges, the city manager system, prohibition, the initiative, government ownership, and so on. That moderation extends to all the social and economic relationships. Though there are large minorities of Negroes in every political division, there is seldom any trouble between the races, and even in the darkest counties every well-behaved Negro is now allowed to vote. Though Baltimore, in some parts, is alive with foreigners, they are not harassed and persecuted by the usual 100 per cent poltroons, and even during the war and at the height of the ensuing alarm about radicals they were reasonably protected in their rights. And though the typical Marylander, once a farmer, is now a hand in a factory, industrial disputes of any seriousness are relatively rare, and even the Maryland miner, though his brothers to both sides, in Pennsylvania and West Virginia, are constantly in difficulties, is but seldom butchered by the State militia.

In brief, Maryland bulges with normalcy. Freed, by the providence of God, from the droughts and dervishes, the cyclones and circular insanities of the Middle West, and from the moldering doctrinairism and appalling bugaboos of the South, and from the biological decay of New England, and from the incurable corruption and menacing unrest of the other industrial States, it represents, in a sense, the ideal toward which the rest of the Republic is striving. It is safe, fat, and unconcerned. It can feed itself, and have plenty to spare. It drives a good trade, foreign and domestic; makes a good profit; banks a fair share of it. It seldom freezes in winter, and it stops short of actual roasting in summer. It is bathed in a singular and various beauty, from the stately estuaries of the Chesapeake to the peaks of the Blue Ridge. It is unthreatened by floods, Tulsa riots, Nonpartisan Leagues, Bolshevism, or Ku Klux Klans. It is bare of Len Smalls, Mayor Thompsons, Lusks, Hylans, A. Mitchell Palmers, Bryans, Vardamans, Volsteads, Upton Sinclairs, Parkhursts, Margaret Sangers, Mrs. Carrie Chapman Catts, Monk Eastmans, Debses, Hearsts, Mrs. Kate O'Hares, Prof. Scott Nearings, John D. Rockefellers, Stillmans, Harry Thaws, Jack Johnsons, La Follettes, Affinity Earles, Judge Cohalans, W. E. Burghardt Du Boises, Percy Stickney Grants, Dreisers, Cabells, Amy Lowells, Mrs. Eddys, Ornsteins, General Woods, William Z. Fosters, Theodore Roosevelt, Jrs., Cal Coolidges. Its Federal judge believes in and upholds the Constitution. Its Governor is the handsomest man in public life west of Cherbourg. The Mayor of its chief city is a former Grand Supreme Dictator of the Loyal Order of Moose. It has its own national hymn, and a flag older than the Stars and Stripes. It is the home of the oyster, of the deviled crab, of hog and hominy, of fried chicken *à la* Maryland. It has never gone dry.

I depict, you may say, Utopia, Elysium, the New Jerusalem. My own words, in fact, make me reel with State pride; another *Lis'l* of that capital moonshine Löwenbräu, and I'll mount the keg and begin bawling Maryland, My Maryland. Here, it appears, is the dream paradise of every true Americano, the heaven imagined by the Rotary Club, the Knights of Pythias, and the American Legion. Here is the goal whither all the rest of the Republic is striving and pining to drift. Here, as I have said, is normalcy made real and visible. Well, what is life like in arcadian Maryland? How does it feel to live amid scenes so idyllic, among a people so virtuous and so happy, on the hooks of statistics so magnificently meridional? I answer frankly and firstly: it is dull. I answer secondly: it is depressing. I answer thirdly: it steadily grows worse. Everywhere in the United States, indeed, there is that encroaching shadow of gloom. Regimentation in morals, in political theory, in every department of thought has brought with it a stiffening, almost a deadening in manners, so that the old goatishness of the free democrat—how all the English authors of American travel-books denounced it two or three generations ago!—has got itself exchanged for a timorous reserve, a curious psychical flabbiness, an almost complete incapacity for innocent joy. To be happy takes on the character of the illicit: it is jazz, spooning on the back seat, the Follies, dancing without corsets, wood alcohol. It tends to be an adventure reserved for special castes of antinomians, or, at all events, for special occasions. On all ordinary days, for all ordinary Americans, the standard carnality has come to be going into a silent and stuffy hall, and there, in the dark, gaping stupidly at idiotic pictures in monochrome. No light, no color, no sound!

So everywhere in the Republic, from Oregon's icy mountains to Florida's coral strand. But in Maryland there is a special darkening, due to an historical contrast. Save only Louisiana, and, for very brief spaces, Kentucky and California, Maryland is the only American State that ever had a name for gaiety. Even in the earliest days it knew nothing of the religious bigotry that racked New England, nor of the Indian wars that ravaged Georgia and New York, nor of the class conflicts that menaced Virginia. Established on the shores of its incomparably rich waters, its early planters led a life of peace, tolerance, and ease, and out of their happy estate there grew a civilization that, in its best days, must have been even more charming than that of Virginia. That civilization was aristocratic in character, and under it the bonds of all classes were loose. Even the slaves had easy work, and plenty of time for jamborees when work was done, and perhaps a good deal more to eat than was good for them. The upper classes founded their life upon that of the English country gentry, but they had more money, and, I incline to think, showed a better average of intelligence. They developed their lands to a superb productiveness, they opened mines and built wharves, they lined the Chesapeake with stately mansions—and in the hours of their leisure they chased the fox, fished the rivers, visited their neighbors, danced, flirted, ate, and drank. It was then that the foundation of Maryland's fame as a gastronomical paradise was laid; it was those ancients who penetrated to the last secrets of the oyster, the crab, and the barnyard fowl. Nor were they mere guzzlers and tipplers. Annapolis, down to Washington's presidency, was perhaps the most civilized town in America. It had the best theater, it had the best inns, and it also had the best society. To this day a faint trace of its old charm survives; it is sleepy, but it is lovely.

What overturned the squirearchy, of course, and with it Maryland civilization, was the rise of the industrial system. It shifted the center of gravity from the great estates to the rushing, pushing, dirty, and, after awhile, turbulent and hoggish town of Baltimore, and so, bit by bit, the old social organization fell to pieces, and the very landscape itself began to lose its old beauty. Wherever there was a manor house along the Bay in the eighteenth century there is now a squalid town, and wherever there is a town there is a stinking cannery, or an even more odoriferous factory for making fish guano. For years there was a more or less fair and equal struggle between town and country. Baltimore grew and grew, but the old landed gentry hung on to their immemorial leadership, in politics if not in trade. Even so recently as a generation ago, half of the counties were still dominated by their old land-owning families; out of them came the supply of judges, State senators, governors, congressmen. Even into our own day they retain tenaciously a disproportionate share of seats in the State Assembly. But it was a losing fight, and as year followed year the advantages of the new industrial magnates grew more visible. As in so many other States, it was a railroad—the Baltimore & Ohio—that gave mere money the final victory over race. The Baltimore & Ohio, for more than fifty years steadily debauched the State. Then it was overthrown, and the political system that it had created went with it, but by that time it was too late to revive the aristocratic system of a more spacious day. Today the State is run by the men who pay the wages of its people. They do it, it must be said for them, with reasonable decency, but they do it absolutely without imagination, and all links with the past are broken forever. Maryland was once a state of mind; now it is a machine.

The tightening of the screws goes on unbrokenly; the end, I suppose, as everywhere else in These States, will be a complete obliteration of distinction, a wiping out of all the old traditions, a massive triumph of regimentation. It is curious to note some of the current symptoms of the process. There is, for example, the Fordization of the Johns Hopkins University. The Johns Hopkins was founded upon a plan that was quite novel in the United States: it was to be, not a mere college for the propagation of the humanities among the upper classes, but a genuine university in the Continental sense, devoted almost wholly to research. To that end it set up shop in a few plain buildings in a back street—and within twenty years its fame was world-wide, and its influence upon all other American universities of the first rank was marked. It had no campus, no dormitories, no clubs of college snobs, no college yells, but if you go through the roster of its students during its first two or three decades you will go through a roster of the principal American scholars and men of science of today. The death of Daniel Coit Gilman was a calamity to the university, and following it came demoralization. Today the Johns Hopkins is reorganized, but upon a new plan. It has a large and beautiful campus; its buildings begin to rise in huge groups; it challenges Harvard and Princeton. Interiorly it turns to the new efficiency, the multitudinous manufacture of sharp, competent, $10,000 a year men. There is a summer-school for country schoolmarms eager for six weeks of applied psychology, official history, and folk-singing. There is instruction for young men eager to be managers of street railways, automobile engineers, and city editors of newspapers. There is patriotic drilling on the campus. There is a growing college spirit. Gifts and endowments increase. Everything is booming. But the old Johns Hopkins is dead.

Turn now to Baltimore society. In the old days it was extraordinarily exclusive—not in the sense of stupid snobbishness, but in the sense of prudent reserve. The aristocracy of the State was a sound one, for it was firmly rooted in the land, and it looked with proper misgivings upon all newcomers who lacked that foundation. It had friendly relations with the aristocracy of Virginia, but with the industrial magnates of the North and their wives and daughters it was inclined to be a bit stand-offish. When it gave a party in Baltimore or in one of the county towns, the display of clothes was perhaps not startling, but there was at least a show of very pretty girls, and their pa's and ma's were indubitably gentlemen and ladies. I am still almost too young, as the saying is, to know my own mind, but I well remember the scandal that arose when the first millionaire bounders tried to horn in by *force majeure*. Even the proletariat was against them, as it would have been against a corporation lawyer who presumed to climb upon the bench with the judge. But today—God save the mark! The old landed aristocracy, put beside the new magnates and their women, seems shabby and unimportant; it has lost its old social leadership, and it has even begun to lose its land, its traditions, and its *amour propre*. The munitions millionaires of the war years entered to the tune of loud wind music; a fashionable ball today is an

Baltimore Harbor. It was scenes such as this one that led H. L. Mencken to regard the city as a "rushing," "pushing," "dirty," "turbulent, and hoggish town."

amazing collection of gilded nobodies; all eyes are turned, not toward the South, but toward New York. There are leaders of fashion in Baltimore today whose mothers were far from unfamiliar with the washtub; there are others whose grandmothers could not speak English. The whole show descends to a fatuous and tedious burlesque. It has the brilliance of a circus parade, and the cultural significance of an annual convention of the Elks.

The decay of the Johns Hopkins is accompanied by a general eclipse of intellectualism. Music becomes a mere fashionable diversion; it is good medicine for pushers to go to opera and symphony concert and suffer there for an hour or two. As for intellectual society, it simply doesn't exist. If some archaic bluestocking were to set up a *salon*, it would be mistaken for a saloon, and raided by some snouting cleric. In Baltimore lives Lizette Woodworth Reese, perhaps the finest poet of her generation yet alive in America. Some time ago a waggish newspaper man there had the thought to find out how Baltimore itself regarded her. Accordingly, he called up all of the town magnificoes, from the President of the Johns Hopkins down to the presidents of the principal women's clubs. He found that more than half of the persons he thus disturbed had never so much as heard of Miss Reese, and that all save two or three of the remainder had never read a line of her poetry! Edgar Allan Poe is buried in the town, in the yard of a decrepit Presbyterian church, on the edge of the old red-light district. It took sixteen years to raise enough money to pay for a modest tombstone to his memory; it took seventy-two years to provide even an inadequate monument. During that time Baltimore has erected elaborate memorials to two founders of tin-pot fraternal orders, to a former Mayor whose long service left the city in the physical state of a hog-pen, and to the president of an obscure and bankrupt railroad. These memorials are on main streets. That to Poe is hidden in a park that half the people of Baltimore have never so much as visited. And on the pedestal there is a thumping misquotation from his poetry!

Such is Maryland in this hundred-and-forty-sixth year of the Republic—a great, a rich, and a puissant State, but somehow flabby underneath, somehow dead-looking in the eyes. It has all the great boons and usufructs of current American civilization: steel-works along the bay, movies in every town, schools to teach the young how to read and write, high-schools to ground them in a safe and sane Americanism, colleges for their final training, jails to keep them in order, a State police, a judiciary not wholly imbecile, great newspapers, good roads. It has vice crusaders, charity operators, drive managers, chambers of commerce, policewomen, Y.M.C.A.'s, women's clubs, Chautauquas, Carnegie libraries, laws against barking dogs, the budget system, an active clergy, uplifters of all models and gauges. It is orderly, industrious, virtuous, normal, free from Bolshevism and atheism. . . . Still, there is something wrong. At the moment, thousands seem to be out of work. Wages fall. Men are ironed out. Ideas are suspect. No one appears to be happy. Life is dull.

MASSACHUSETTS

A Roman Conquest

JOHN MACY

DECEMBER 27, 1922

IT WAS AT commencement in Cambridge, more than twenty years ago. A multitude of us loyal alumni was lifting its voice in "Fair Harvard." Beside me stood a handsome young man in the garb of a priest, whose clear Irish baritone struck pleasantly upon my ear through the mass of noise.

Till the stock of the Puritans die.

My neighbor was psalming with unconscious heartiness and representing in his own comely person a new era in the oldest intellectual stronghold of the old Bay State. The Puritan was beginning to die. He is not dead yet in Massachusetts and he survives vigorously in the new New England, the Western States. But a generation ago he was losing grip and his hymn was coming true in a way that the author had not intended nor foreseen. A boy with an Irish name was captain of the football team. There had been scandalous and rebellious talk about the hold of boys from Back Bay families and saintly schools upon the crew and the baseball team. At about this time Dr. Eliot, then president of fair Harvard, observed, in one of his frequent shrewd moments, that Massachusetts is a Roman Catholic commonwealth. The stock of our forefathers was visibly losing power. It was losing in religion, in politics, in education, in business.

I hold no brief for any race, creed, party, or other condition of servitude, but merely note facts, especially changes and developments. When Dr. Eliot observed that the codfish commonwealth is dominantly Roman Catholic, he made the observation, we may be sure, with a bland freedom from prejudice. The fact is there. Let us consider it. The most potent clergyman in Massachusetts is William Cardinal O'Connell. But there is no sign of a successor to Edward Everett Hale or Phillips Brooks. Add together the "orthodox" Congregational churches, which are the traditional godly center of all Massachusetts towns, the right and left wings of the Episcopalians, housed in The Advent and Phillips Brooks's Trinity, the Unitarians of old King's Chapel, where once worshiped the intellectual aristocracy of Boston, and all the other Protestant, nonconformist sects, such as Methodists, Baptists, and the rest. The Catholic Cathedral dwarfs them all—that is, as a spiritual institution. I once heard a member of the Clover Club, composed of Irish Roman Catholics, many of them brilliant and delightful, and probably prolific, say that the time was near when a Baptist parade would be impossible in the streets of Boston, partly on account of lack of material and partly on account of interference. The Clover Club thrives. The Papyrus Club is dead. And the Saturday Club of the elder New England wits and poets died so long ago that one has to think of it in terms not of decades but of generations. If it existed today there would not be anybody to belong to it.

Roman Catholic does not mean Irish, in Massachusetts or anywhere else, even in Ireland. But if the two terms do not register exactly, if in Boston and the surrounding mill cities is a large population of Italians, Canadian-French, Portuguese, Poles, who are spiritually subject to the Celtic-American cardinal, nevertheless Irish and Catholic are roughly synonymous in the Bay State. And non–Roman Catholic does not, in an age of slackening interest in religion and of wavering demarcations of faith, mean either Puritan stock or any one brand of nonconformity. The Protestant forces are scattered, lukewarm, and blurred. Consider that the First Church of Christ Scientist is about half way between Brimstone Corner and the Harvard Medical School. If you want to start a sect, start it in Massachusetts. Other States will take it up later. Any dark-skinned individual with straight hair can initiate a new creed in the Back Bay with no other equipment than the dermatological—with pleasure for all concerned and profit to himself. But alone among all diverse groups Irish Catholicism marches triumphantly on.

Politically Massachusetts still plays an important part among her forty-seven sisters, and she has acute private troubles. Nothing can be proved but much can be suggested by contemplating three of her sons who represent her wisdom in the national government. We shall not argue about the party politics of any of them but shall view them as expressions and examples of interesting social conditions. First there is the senior Senator. Mr. Lodge is an aristocrat by birth and training. Perhaps he has never had a great thought. Without question he is neither a Sumner nor a Hoar, but at least he has not for fifty years written or spoken a bad sentence. If he had not given up to politics what was meant for mankind he might have been a distinguished historian and writer of essays. His introduction to the autobiographical "Education" of Henry Adams is a neat bit of writing, worthy of Adams himself. He carries on the traditions of a State which in times past has sent men of letters to all the capital cities of the world, including Washington.

The junior Senator is David Ignatius Walsh, a graduate not of Mr. Lodge's fair Harvard but of Holy Cross, a member not of the Massachusetts Historical Society but of the Irish Historical Society of America. He was a small-town lawyer and seems to have no literary ambitions. For two years he was Governor of the State. He does not belong to the Boston political rings, and his public life has

State House, Boston. John Macy may have taken the lack of activity around the State House as confirmation of his assertion that Boston was "uninspired and static," but one could just as easily admire the human scale.

been clean. However that may be, it is safe to predict that he will be succeeded by many of his own race and kind. There will be no more Lodges. That breed is passing.

Above these two learned gentlemen from Massachusetts sits Calvin Coolidge, Vice-President of the United States, Calvin Coolidge of Northampton, born in Vermont and not, distinctly not, of the Boston Coolidges. They are on the boards of directors of great trust companies. The highest fiduciary position attained by Mr. Coolidge was that of president of the Nonatuck Savings Bank of Northampton. How he got to be Governor of the State and Vice-President of these United States is one of the inexplicable jokes of politics. The three men, the two Senators and the Vice-President, may be easily placed. Mr. Lodge is the aristocrat, well bred, well educated, with literary talent. Mr. Walsh is the successful small-town Irish lawyer, inclined to progressive ideas, not brilliant but with sufficient command of words not to make a fool of himself, inherently a democrat, and growing with his public experience. Mr. Coolidge is the yokel, neither of the blue-blooded aristocracy nor of the red-blooded invasion. He neither represents staid tradition nor brings insurgent progress. I have lived among New England farmers and I have read or heard many specimens of what is supposed to be the Yankee manner of speech from Hosea Biglow to *The Old Homestead* and *Shore Acres*. Mr. Coolidge's diction outdoes caricature and parody but has no trace of the shrewd humor of the soil. It must grate on Mr. Lodge's exquisite Boston ear.

There are two men in the political-legal life of the nation of whom the more enlightened citizens of Massachusetts may be proud. How often you find in the dissenting minority of the United States Supreme Court Justices Holmes and Brandeis! Were ever two men of such different origins and traditions linked in the interests of liberalism and humane interpretations of law? The one is an aristocrat with blood as blue as the bluest vein in the fine hand of the senior Senator (it was, I think, Judge Holmes's father who first applied the term "Brahmin" to the Boston swell); and the other is a Jew, whose appointment to the supreme Court made members of clubs writher in their leather chairs, not because he is a Jew—he had been accepted socially—but because he had dared to attack State Street and the New York, New Haven and Hartford Railroad. These two men are almost always together on the same side, the minority, the beaten, the right side. And both are citizens of a State which is assumed to be the heart of conservatism, of reaction, of the safe and sane. There is matter for reflection in this pair of colleagues. They are in a sense the living survivals of the best New England tradition, of independence, of intellectual courage, of *noblesse oblige* applied to public service—an indication in their disparate origins that the blood-stream is not the channel through which the faith is perpetuated.

The legal profession of Massachusetts has always had a reputation for wisdom and integrity. I once heard a Boston judge say that the decisions of the Massachusetts courts carry weight in England as compared with the decisions of the courts of other States or even of the United States courts, and I think he quoted Pollock as his authority. I am not sure. I merely noted the judge's remark as showing the pride which exists in Massachusetts, and probably in all Atlantic States, in having the approval of Englishmen, and also as showing the great respect, no doubt deserved, in which judges and lawyers are held.

Not long ago the legal profession of Massachusetts, or rather a small part of it, was under fire. Long-standing and well-intrenched corruption in the district attorney's office in Suffolk County, and an infection therefrom in the neighboring Middlesex, was at last brought to the bar of judgment.[1] An elaborate system of extortion and blackmail was revealed and the offending district attorneys were removed from office and disbarred. Now this state of affairs had long been current and generally known in the State. But inextricably bound up in it were the threads of religious and racial antagonism and prejudices. The central figure, the district attorney of Suffolk County, was the "Supreme Advocate" of the Knights of Columbus and hence probably the most conspicuous Catholic layman in the State. This had played no small part in the immunity generally credited to him and his ring. His safety was axiomatic in the whispering galleries of non-Catholic Massachusetts. That he was found guilty by a unanimous Supreme Court of which two members were of his own faith calls for no encomiums, but

---

[1]Joseph Pelletier, the Democratic district attorney for Suffolk County (Boston), had engaged with two others in a lucrative scheme of frame-ups, blackmail, and suppressed prosecutions. They were indicted and convicted in early 1921. [D. H. B.]

merely a solid satisfaction that the prophets of peril were again proved wrong. On the other hand the conviction was apotheosized into a religious martyrdom by a group of his friends and a very considerable Catholic following—despite the two Catholic judges, his replacement as district attorney by another Knight, and the Protestantism of his fellow-malefactor in Cambridge. The Catholic following was sufficiently strong to secure for Pelletier the Democratic nomination for the office of district attorney from which he had been removed; and the Democratic nominee for Senator, Mr. W. A. Gaston, a former president of Boston's leading bank, did not repudiate his fellow-candidate. But the voters in this overwhelmingly Democratic district did and so ended a nauseating episode.

The tinder-box is ready for the irresponsible match-thrower. The burning of a convent in the fifties is still street-corner campaign material. The use of public funds for parochial schools is a constantly recurring issue. That they have not been voted in 80 to 90 per cent Catholic Boston would indicate that this religious group is not more than any other politically a unit, nor, as is charged, clay in the hands of its hierarchy. Of course State support may come and will, if the resident "Prince of the Church" has his way. The political cleavage is, generally speaking, along religious lines. Protestant Democrats are for the most part isolate iconoclasts, individualist dissenters, whose part in the State's party politics is wholly disproportionate to their numbers. Social cleavage is even more marked though it is diminishing. But there are still many business firms which exclude typists and office boys because they are Catholic, and owners of estates to whom their gardener's faith is more important than his work. This is of course resented by the Catholics, whose most effective response is their steady increase.

The signs of this increase are obvious in the daily press, which in no other metropolitan city so extensively chronicles the four-corners gossip and the personal item. The County Kerry Associates are holding their annual ball—with the Mayor, or perchance even the Governor, leading the grand march. The St. Joseph's or Sacred Heart parish is busy with its whist or other entertainment. The Cardinal has dedicated a new church or chapel with Celtic monsignori in attendance, filling specialized sacerdotal and, to the native, exotic-sounding functions. The Irish are everywhere. "Take for granted in talking with anyone that he is a Catholic unless you definitely know the contrary" was the advice given by a Boston newspaper editor to one of his reporters. Boston is filled today with O'Brien and Fitzgerald and Murphy "Squares" named after the boys who fell overseas—and the square which once bore the name of Edgar Allan Poe now bears the name of Matthew Emmet Ryan. And many communities, like South Boston or Dorchester, the summer resorts around Nantasket, or Brant Rock further south, are as homogeneous as the villages of Tipperary. If they are more slovenly they are perhaps more joyous than the habitats of the inbred Bakers and Davises on the Cape, of the Litchfields and Turners of Plymouth County, of the Lanes and Pooles of Cape Ann. If these more recent Americans sometimes mistakenly and stupidly abuse their new-found strength in applying their Index Expurgatorius code to debar from public libraries works on the Spanish Inquisition or the novels of Zola, theirs is but a slight transformation of Puritan zealotry. When the trustees of the public library of Brookline, stronghold of the elder respectability, exclude Professor Chafee's scholarly *Freedom of Speech* on the ground of "radicalism," what consistent grounds of protest against newer forms of obscurantism remain for these suppressors?

I have referred to the Boston newspapers, which deserve one more word. In the scandal involving District Attorney Pelletier and others the editors began unctuously rubbing their editorial palms and congratulating Boston and the commonwealth on the house-cleaning—after it was all over. For years every cub reporter had known that all was not well, and many of them with the crusading enthusiasm of youth and decency burned to bring out the facts. Boston editors, if they stay Boston editors, are not made that way. At least not since the days of the late Edward Hazen Clement who despite restrictions and his inhibitory environment gave the *Transcript* much of the quality which made it the best-known Boston newspaper in the country at large. The rest of the press, unless we except the *Monitor*, which is national rather than local, exhibits the dress and cultivation of a boom mining-town. Of it no less an expert than Jason Rogers, publisher of the New York *Globe*, says in his book *Newspaper Building*:

> I don't recollect whether the *Post* is responsible for leading nearly all the other Boston newspapers into big black type on the front pages and the playing up of really trifling items beyond news of world-wide interest or not, but I think so. . . . The fact that some small preacher in Lynn slipped from the straight and narrow path is bigger news from the Boston newspaper standpoint than almost any ordinary first-page news in other newspapers throughout the country. Likewise the Boston papers of large circulation follow the erring village pastor and erring mill-worker clear up into Maine or New Hampshire. On the surface of things it would seem that there was a fine opportunity for a first-class, honest-to-God morning newspaper in Boston. . . .

There is such a fine opportunity for real newspaper in Boston, but there will not be one if we concede the truth of Chester S. Lord's dictum that a newspaper cannot be greater than its editor. A newspaper need not be a moral crusader, and its chief business may not be to reform a naughty world, but, in the face of long-continued social blood poisoning those papers did nothing, did not even call for the facts. It was the Attorney General, assisted by respectable and indignant members of the bar, who took the lid off the unsavory Pelletier mess. But no newspapers in America—and the standard is not high anywhere—do less than those of Boston to encourage common ordinary decency in public affairs. They start nothing, but live in timid subserviency not only to the greater economic and denominational powers but to the pettiest wire-pullers, to the cheapest advertising bullies. The editor of the *Herald*, which pretends to be the organ of the cultured—in the jargon, "the quality medium"—once remarked that the modern newspaper was essentially an advertisers' broadside, and its editors were merely hired to fill in the chinks between the advertisements. But even under this conception which dominates Boston journalism the possibility for improving the filling is immeasurable. To find a paper which tries, or in times past tried, to work for the good of its local community, the State, the nation, and the universe, one has to go to Springfiled, the home of the *Republican*, an individual and beautiful community, notably free form political scandal, with a fine and justified civic pride.

This suggests that Boston is not the whole of Massachusetts. It is both more than the State and less. It is more than the State because it is the business capital of all New England and it is a national financial center second only to New York and equal to Philadelphia and Chicago. It is the citadel of "protection" and privilege. In the capitalization of the West, the building of railroads, the exploitation of mines, the developing of the textile industries, Boston money was, and is, potent. Boston has no Rockefeller, no Carnegie. But the aggregate wealth in the stockings both of old families and of modern upstarts is tremendous. Nor should we omit mention here of the considerable and fruitful profession of trusteeship—the handling of the estates of defunct industrial pioneers, which nowhere has been more firmly established. That the third and fourth generations are frequently unable to take care of the copper deposits, paper or spinning mills developed by their energetic forbears; that they ride the hounds, or live abroad, or sometimes form innocuous connections with bond houses, indicates that the older stock has not merely been driven out by more fecund newcomers. The old race has of itself been petering, and not a few of its occasional atavistic scions sensing its atmosphere of dry-rot have of late gone elsewhere to seek fortunes founded on their own abilities. Even the children and grandchildren of the recent Abolitionists have faded into complaisant and insignificant conformism. That last and greatest chapter of the contribution of Massachusetts to America has melted into past history. The Union Club still has the tradition of its founding—otherwise it is scarcely distinguishable from the slightly more effete Somerset. Uninspired and static—that is Boston today. Who can adduce tangible or visible evidence to the contrary?

Boston is less than the State because the smaller cities and towns, especially those of the western part of the State, have a character or characters of their own. The eastern cities are Boston, even though they preserve their municipal entities. The region from Lowell to Fall River may be considered as a vast industrial city, interspersed with lovely bits of country, which are rapidly becoming a vast suburban garden. To the west there is something different. The difference may be slight and I do not know how to express it. There is all too little difference between small American cities. But as William James's friend the farmer said: "There's mighty little difference between one man and another, but what little there is is mighty important." If you consider that Massachusetts is so small that measured on the map it would look like a mere county of a Western State, and that in an age of communication the distinctions between neighboring communities are being obliterated and State lines are artificial, then you will expect to find the diversities between the eastern and western portions of the little commonwealth faint and hard to define. Yet they are mighty important, if you can capture them. I think of Massachusetts as jammed in between her neighbors, separating them and sharing their natures. Lowell and Lawrence, although near Boston, are like New Hampshire's industrial cities, like Nashua on the same Merrimac. Brockton, Fall River, and New Bedford resemble Pawtucket and Woonsocket in Rhode Island. If I suggest that Pittsfield is like up-State New York, it is not wholly because the General Electric Company has also a plant in Schenectady. It has one in Lynn. Yet Pittsfield is liker to what lies across the line than she is to her sister who lives on the Atlantic coast. Is it not said in this community, where county pride exceeds State pride, regional affection, and patriotism, that "the best thing about Berkshire County is the chain of mountains to the east which shuts it off from the rest of the State"?

Perhaps we put too much emphasis on cities. But Massachusetts is, for America, thickly populated, and the passage from town to town by train or motor is almost imperceptible. The rural life is changing, it is changing character and changing hands. It is changing character because the old village is becoming a small manufacturing town or suburb of a manufacturing town, and the smoke of the mill blows over the files. I have known many old Yankee farmers but few young ones. Those who turn the sod now and make market gardens in the east and tobacco fields in the Connecticut Valley are foreigners who know how to work and make things grow. The native has not been entirely supplanted, but the tendency is that way. The Yankee farmer is disappearing in Massachusetts, going into business—or getting to be Vice-President of the United States. The most beautiful farms are the playthings of gentlemen who live in Massachusetts or who come to Massachusetts in summer. And Tony or François does the work.

In the villages and small towns you see a State road, sometimes in need of repair but usually good. It runs past a pretty common. Facing the common are stores, bank, church, movie theater, and a few old houses, some of which are run down, some of which have been spruced up by new owners or by heirs who live somewhere else but take a pride in the old place; in some of them the heirs, as pathetic as Hawthorne's Hepzibah, are trying to make a living by a tea-room where tourists are fed nothing for a big price. A factory district. A splendid estate, either the old house made over a new not altogether successful Italian villa. One of the stores is still owned by Ezra Chapin, who has been town clerk for thirty years, but he is being put out of business by the Greek or Italian grocer on the other corner. The post office is dingy, the church is good, thanks to Wren and a defunct race of carpenters who built both churches and ships, the "libery" is not offensive, the soldiers' monument is a fright, the trees on the trim common are gorgeous unless the beetles or the moths have completely routed the local tree warden and the State commission.

And so to the next town, which is much the same. But it is not always the same. There is diversity within the compass of this tiny commonwealth. If you happen to have been under the delusion that Boston is Massachusetts and that

Harvard and Bunker Hill are intellectual and historical Boston, you may be disabused of that idea at odd turns of the road; by the thrill that follows one's glimpse of the gentle dignity and beauty of Williamstown and its college; of Greenfield, of Leicester, of old Salem, of Sudbury, or the quaint charm of Deerfield, of Ipswich, of Marblehead, of Duxbury, of Provincetown, of Newburyport. None of us knew until recently, because it is a recent structure, the beauty of that excellent building which Boston College has erected on the hill overlooking the city. The State is full of learning, at least of visible signs of the effort to learn, Amherst, Williams, Tufts, Wellesley, Smith, Clark, Holy Cross, Boston College, Boston University, Technology, Mt. Holyoke, Wheaton, and others. No State has more conspicuous educational institutions. And every small town provides in its own high school, or by arrangement with a neighboring town, free instruction in preparation for any college. Colleges and college education as they are today need not be taken too seriously, but I insist on the number and variety of the colleges in Massachusetts, because while the other States were developing their own institutions, perhaps greater and better, they always looked to Massachusetts for education, common and preferred.

Then, with all this equipment, is Massachusetts intellectually decadent? In some ways she is, but decadent from the standards which her own people set. Boston is, as Mr. Herford said, the abandoned farm of literature. But not in literature alone. In all the arts, in all intellectual matters Boston, once the Athens of America, is stagnant, moribund. The *Atlantic Monthly* is the sole heritage of the vanished Pericleans.

One reason is that young people of talent follow a tendency, already cited, which is both social and commercial, to move to New York, much as Englishmen seek London and Frenchmen seek Paris. The migration does not greatly matter for it makes little difference where a man of talent lives. And it seems that the intellectual life of Massachusetts is not quite exhausted by departing sons and the declining vigor of the native stock. For note this, making due allowance for the fact that there is immigration as well as emigration and for the general fallibility of statistics: in the Geographical Index of the latest *Who's Who* New York occupies twenty-seven pages, Massachusetts is second with ten, Pennsylvania and Illinois are third with eight each. And the rest are also-rans. If I have seemed a bit severe at times with the Massachusetts that I have known and loved a generation, it is, I repeat, in relation to values of her own erecting, to ideals of her own creation, to the visions and hopes and aspirations she herself has inspired. It is not by the standards of Mississippi or Arkansas that one judges Massachusetts. Come back to her from afar and there is a clean orderliness, a wholesome stability, a familiarity with the coinage of culture—in short, a civilization, which is as a high plateau to Middle Western flats and Dixie swamps.

The intellect of a community is its great interest, its human value. But God, the God of the Puritans, was active long before the Puritans, or the Indians, or the Irish, or the Italians. He happened to lay out, not as a commonwealth but as a landscape, one of the loveliest corners of His footstool in the small strip of land which is now by man called Massachusetts—the North Shore with its rocks, the South Shore with its sand, the Berkshires on the west, the Connecticut Valley, and all the tumbling hills and gentle smiling little corners in between. It is not so rugged and vivid as the more mountainous and still wild States to the north. Connecticut is a bit softer. The Bay State, most of which is not on the bay, lies between, the heart of New England. God made it so, and man has not yet unmade it.

MICHIGAN

The Fordizing of a Pleasant Peninsula

LEONARD LANSON CLINE

NOVEMBER 1, 1922

ON THE GREAT SEAL of the State of Michigan, under the woodsy emblems of elk and moose and sunrise over the water, is the legend "Si quaeris peninsulam amoenam, circumspice." If you seek a pleasant peninsula, look about you. There is something pastoral, Arcadian, daisy-and-cress about it. It chimes a gentle angelus. It smells of warm milk in the pail, of new hay in the loft. And one can fairly see the Michigander, sturdy and kindly rustic, standing bareheaded at his hospitable threshold, gazing with a smile of pure and simple content at the hills and flashing lakes and meadows brimming with toadflax and browneyed-Susans.

Actually, it is with quite different sentiments that the Michigander looks about him. If he is a farmer he glooms at his fields, wondering why the devil his son, who has gone to Detroit to work in the factory, doesn't write, and where in hell he can get help for the harvest. If he is a salesman he grins with glee at the billboards stuck up in front of pleasant views wherever paved highways lead; and, then, driving on, he ponders whether to go to Yellowstone for his vacation or to Atlantic City. If he is a mechanic he never looks about him at all unless he is on his back under the hood of the car.

Some day some convention of salesmen will agree to a much more appropriate coat-of-arms for the new Michigan. It will picture the lean cheeks and the death's-head smile of Henry Ford, in the halo of a spare tire, flanked by chimneys and flivvers on a ground of soot. Underneath, in place of the stately Latin, will be inscribed the more salesmanlike legend: Always in the Lead.

And yet, Michigan is a pleasant peninsula, or peninsulas, for there are two of them—the only State of the Union boasting a spare part. It is a land of undulating hills, spendthrift in wild-flowers. Save for desolate stretches of cut-over timber land trees abound. On the east lies Huron, on the west Michigan with its yellow dunes, and on the north Superior—blue waters, cold and beautiful. Inland along the courses of many streams are little lakes and ponds estimated at from five thousand to fifteen thousand in number. The older residents love Michigan for these things, but the new find reinforced concrete more gratifying to their eyes; and the new constitute the State.

Before them, in the latter part of the last century, Michigan stood for nothing. It was at the end of its frontier period, with the first impulse wasted and animation low. In 1820 there were less than nine thousand persons in the State. Timber in the Lower Peninsula, copper and iron in the Upper, started an avalanche of immigration. When the forests soon gave out, those with transportation in their pockets departed, leaving a dozen cretinoid towns huddling around the ruins of their mills, gaping dully at the stumps and naked hills. In 1900 Michigan had a population of 2,420,982, of which more than one-fifth was of alien birth, including large settlements of Poles, Scandinavians, Finns, Germans, Dutch, French, and Italians—in short, a typically American mid-Western State in respect to its foreign-born. The Michiganders were a people without identity, without community of purpose or past, without tradition.

Then Ford.

In twenty years the population swelled to 3,668,412, the increase being almost wholly in the southern cities. Detroit became four times as large as it had been, Lansing four times, Flint eight times. And Michigan is coming to stand for something: mechanics, factory methods, salesmanship, in life as in business, for the two are one.

The Fordizing of the State is not yet complete. Toward the north there is a great deal of bitterness, not unmingled with envy, at the growing domination of Detroit. Nevertheless the thrill of new vigor shoots into every flaccid limb of Michigan. Highways poke like scalpels into the moribund towns of the timber district, and leave garages like new thyroids to give alacrity and bustle. As you come south the cities more and more take on an air of newness, of hardness, of thin varnish, faking up what passes for prettiness, lending themselves to the salesman's glib rehearsal of modern improvements. In Detroit at last you find the consummation of the salesman's ideal.

In the residence districts there are block after block of two-and four-family flats, as alike, as cheap, as ephemeral, as quantitatively produced as the Ford to which they owe their presence. Each has its skimping lawn in front, its backyard with clothes-lines strung from the stoop of the house to the bleak little flivver-sized garage on the alley. Each is shinily decorated, equipped with laundry chutes, toilet extras, French doors, glued-on ceiling beams in the dining-rooms, gaudily painted glass chandeliers suspended by brass or nickel chains, and built-in bookcases that serve as depositories for anything but books. These dwellings satisfy Detroiters because their desire is not to find something different, but something just like So-and-So's. And what difference does it make that in the winter a stiff gust may blow the carpets from the floors, or that in summer a drenching rain may loosen the ceiling, or that the prepossessing big brick hearth won't draw, or has been built without any means of removing ashes? In the spring one sells one's house and buys another. These places are built not to be lived in, but to be sold. Good salesmanlike dwellings.

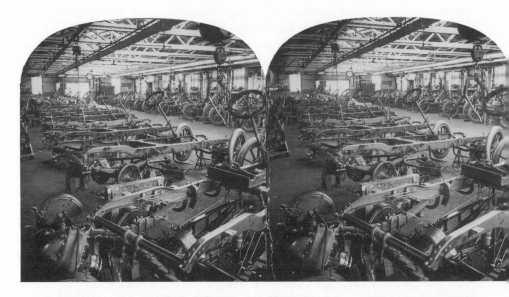

Cadillac chassis assembly room, Detroit. The shells of the machine that dramatically
changed the nation's habits during the decade await assembly.

In matters of government modern factory methods have been applied generally. The new Detroit quickly adopted a new charter. It replaced the old 42-man
council with one of nine members. The old council had at least a sense of humor.
The new is grim, sacrosanct, with a Sunday-school tidiness in its habits, but not
appreciably more honest or more efficient. The Detroit Citizens' League brought
in a crew of energetic young men who have been several years now modernizing
the city departments. In spite of a display of innocent political energy closely
modeled after Henry's own, the millennium is still bashful.

A new municipal court has been created, and deals rapidly and severely with
such miscreants as the excellently organized police can catch. The juries here are
no longer random affairs; the panels are chosen from a select list of the ministers, the leading salesmen, the eminent figures of the community. Detroit is
proud of the long sentences given its criminals and the proportion of convictions
in the total number of arrests. Yet in spite of so many ways to discourage it,
banditry slugs its dozen a day, at noon or at midnight. Banditry is particularly
bold in Detroit. Naturally the salesmanship ideals here gleam most splendidly
and lure one most temptingly to steal. One must wear silk stockings and drive a
big car; one must build one's chimneys as high as Ford's, whether for patented
roller-bearings or blackjacks; one must satisfy that craving which originates in
the habit-forming narcotic of fifty miles an hour.

While the noonday bandits are hunting down paymasters and shooting bank
clerks, the dining-rooms in the hotels are serving cheap collations to the rotary
clubs, the lion clubs, the exchange clubs, the conventions and confraternities of

salesmen that serve Detroit's noblest purposes. The Elks are gathering in their imposing new home for the business men's lunch, gobbled between snappy rehearsals of new tricks to catch prospects. And the workmen in an enormous pit are laying the foundations of the new Masonic temple, to be built at the cost of millions of dollars, probably the most grandiose temple of the bib-and-tucker brotherhood in the world.

No doubt about it, Detroit is coming to be a city sweet to the eye and satisfying to the intelligence of the salesmen and mechanics who inhabit it. Sublimated peddlers, "get-it-across" advertising men, and other hundredpercenters look on their work with a smile of perfect admiration. Proper credit is also due the real-estate agent swaggering in the glory of his new title of realtor, proud of the miles of pleasant woodland he has turned into "subdivisions" with sidewalks and lamp posts but no water, trees, or houses. Salesmanship it is that makes the prospect visualize a "home" in this "development" for so much down and so much a month.

And if one of these boosters is selling you his city, he may ask you, after dinner, whether you like music. "Don't think our city hasn't got anything but factories," he says. "If you're a highbrow you can find lots in your line. We got the best orchestra in the world, with this . . . now . . . Gabrilosky for conductor. We got an art museum owned by the city. We got the most beautiful public library in the world. Say, let's take in a concert!" And with a guffaw and a clump on the back he hauls you off to Orchestra Hall.

Detroit really has a remarkable collection of paintings, old masters as well as new, and ground for an imposing museum is being broken on a site across Woodward Avenue from the Library. Its Orchestra has its own auditorium, one of the most charming in the country. But these things are the outward and visible sign of an inward and spiritual salesmanship. They are a gesture, like the carnation on Mother's day in the buttonhole of the man who has not written home for twelve years. The Art Museum and the bulk of its collections were given to the city. A few thousand dollars are appropriated every year for acquisitions. But in order to get the money it is necessary to argue that pictures increase in value and are most profitable investments. The Orchestra has a deficit every year, and the public is asked to subscribe because as the jazz-adoring salesman tells you it will be a wonderful advertisement for the city. It is a fact that if Gabrilówitsch played the music his patrons beseech him to play his programs would be choked with Tostigoodbyes.

As for the Library—the luxurious new building is displayed to visitors—but its staff so far hasn't had much success in selling a taste for books to the natives. Detroit is the worst book market among all our cities of anywhere near its size. Good publishers will not advertise in the local papers because they sell no books. Detroit reads Eddie Guest.

Eddie Guest, the great intellectual product of the new Michigan! No doubt about the sincerity of that acclaim. He is extolled again every week as poet laureate of the State. His poems are taught in the public schools seriously as

literature. He has proved his salesmanship by collecting the leavings of the bon-
bon bacchanalia of Eugene Field and peddling them. Detroit loves him not only
for his sentimentalism for his success and the way he can turn off four or five
stanzas every day of his life. Henry Ford, too, stands as one of the great philo-
sophic forces of the new Michigan. After the disaster of the peace ship this
homme-dieu got him a new Rosinante in the *Dearborn Independent*, and tilts
weekly at wind-mills, routs flocks of sheep, and otherwise advances the cause of
salesmanship. "It's like Bryan's *Commoner*," sighed a melancholy dissident;
"only commoner."

After them come the diplomats : the Ambassador to Japan, who has served as
Republican sales manager in Michigan and enjoyed some success; the Secretary
of the Navy, a lay figure; the junior Senator, Mr. Newberry who, demonstrated
his salesmanship recently in a most convincing way. [1]

There is another prophet in Michigan whom the community has come to regard all the more highly since a sixteen-story building bearing his name was put
up. He is a five-and-ten-cent-store magnate, and naturally a violent prohibitionist; Commissioner Haynes named him as national head of the league for spy service in the homes of friends. Not long since the papers printed a little story
touching upon this man. Some unfortunate had been arrested for shoplifting in
his five-and-ten-cent store. It turned out he had swiped some whiskey glasses.
This was eminently good salesmanship. It was about as good as that of the other
leading Michigander who generously volunteered to lend some of his mummi-
chog underlings to swell the numbers in an august patriotic parade, to make the
parade bigger. He supplied them with banners advertising not the serious matter
being commemorated but his own private business. Just what the occasion was
has slipped my mind; I think now it was in token of respect for Michigan's dead
in the war. But the memory of those dairy ads is as clear as yesterday.

The nearest thing to the sublime in Michigan is the Ford factory. See it at dusk
some October afternoon, from a distance away, a vast squat looming monster,
glinting a shrill blue light from its windows into the shadows, jibbering, omi-
nous. Out of the tall chimneys drifts black smoke. It smuts one's nose and collar,
and the soot of it cakes over one's imagination and is too heavy for wings.

In its glooms and glares the young Michigander labors and plays. He plays
hard, and drinks his whiskey without a chaser. The national prohibition commissioner has declared Detroit one of the driest cities in the country. That shows
only what a good salesman of prohibition he is; for Detroit is saturated. Or perhaps he has been deceived by the seeming of sobriety in the new Michiganders.
They go to church dutifully, and listen to panting harangues against rum, by
salesmanlike ministers who have carried out the Coney Island idea in religious
advertising to remarkable perfection, adorning the house of the Lord with illuminated revolving crosses and other kewpie bangles. Once, when an Episcopa-

---

[1]Truman Newberry was convicted in 1919 of violating the Corrupt Practices Act by extorting
campaign funds for personal use. [D. H. B.]

lian minister ventured to express a belief that wine was not entirely evil, his brothers of the cloth were permitted to heap on him the vilest abuse, with hardly a single voice lifted in his defense. After church, however, the new Detroit goes home to bottle its last brew. It has given numerous members to the society against the prohibition amendment, but not one of the wealthier topers has been willing to let his name be used as local head of it. In New York and Philadelphia there were men courageous enough to be leaders. The big men of Detroit have been quite candid in their refusals. It would hurt their business. It would be bad salesmanship.

Anything for a sale. Success is indicated in the one maxim, Never let go of a prospect. The young business man is the most agreeable person in the world, in your company. Though your hobby be Sanskrit, philately, billiards, whiskey, or venery—the demijohn or the demijane—he will learn it. He defers to your opinion with unctuous eagerness, and offers himself to do valet service for your spinster cousins. You find him in your church Sundays, seeking the prominence of the front seat and bawling his hosannas. One of them boasted to me that it took over a year once to land a sale. But he cheerfully wallowed in the dirt his prospect was soaked in, and put the deal across. Then he was ready to change his religion, with conscience serene, to that of another.

Sunday afternoons Detroit gets in its car and goes riding. The car whenever possible is not a Ford. That would not be big enough for the salesman. His idea is to sell Fords and ride in a Packard. And on his Sabbath outings he drives fast, taking the same straight, flat roads week after week, the roads everybody else takes. When he gets home he squints at the speedometer to see if he has had a good time; how many miles has he traveled?

The population of Michigan has doubled in the past twenty-five years, but you perceive little difference in the beautiful northern lake districts, the wooded shores of Lake Huron, the solitudes of the dune country along Lake Michigan, with its living pictures exquisite as the most sensitive Japanese print. It was my pleasure to spend seven summers on Portage Lake, and in that time the only new cottages were put up by visitors from Illinois, Wisconsin, Ohio, even New York City. Yet the Long Island shores hardly offer more than does Portage Lake. Railroad communications with these northern places are little more developed than they were before the boom. Recently the Detroit & Cleveland Navigation Company announced the suspension of its summer steamship to historic old Mackinaw Island, at the head of Lake Michigan. I am not sure that the line actually was suspended, but certainly it has not prospered. And yet twenty years ago there was plenty of traffic on these boats, northbound from Detroit. The pleasantness of Michigan is virtually ignored today. But what can one expect? When the salesman goes vacationing he wants a boardwalk, a dance hall, a rollercoaster, and a brass band, something big, loud, and gaudy.

From a high place—from the colossal new General Motors Building, an Acropolis of salesmanship; from one of the towering structures that are beginning to loom up from the ruins of old mansions above the trees of Washington

Avenue and Grand Circus Park—one can almost see Ann Arbor, thirty-five miles away. The Blackman of the new Michigan, that jigs in the wind every morning on the top of Henry Ford's chimney, looks about him and sees it. Sometimes he points that way, with an empty gesture.

Here Michigan plays its sweetest charms. The little city basks on its hills, under its elms and oaks. The Huron River, most gracious stream, curves past, slipping through a park-like country for miles. There is no Niagara here, nothing to make one gasp, but a delicacy and intimacy and loveliness that one returns to always with a gentle exaltation and thrill of release. Here stands the University of Michigan.

The State has not been ungenerous with its appropriations. The last legislature set aside several millions for the expansion and improvement of an already excellently equipped institution. Some big men are on the faculty. But the liberal minds of Michigan are subject to nightmares. If the Blackman sees what they are up to, they get fired. For the university, controlled largely by the same interests that put Truman Newberry in the Senate, is administered by an elected board of regents who are therefore the jumping jacks of triumphant Republicanism. Salesmanship reigns. Courses in business administration are being built up at the expense of courses in intelligence and feeling. One learns at Ann Arbor to judge one's aspirations by the way they jingle.

Not many years ago the editor of the campus paper prepared a series of stories showing unsanitary conditions in the water supply. These the authorities would not permit him to print. Their argument was, as he reported it, that the stories might scare prospective students away from the university. They might hurt sales.

Only from time to time a few of the young people in this great university bolt their classes in economics and salesmanship and learn greater verities out in the pleasant hills of Michigan. They are scolded in the classroom and sneered at on the campus. They are not invited to Detroit as guests of the alumni club, which brings in football coaches and players to make speeches, and undertakes as its principal object to get good high-school half-backs to matriculate at Ann Arbor. They are not enough to give the University of Michigan any tradition at all of literature or art or idealism, or anything but salesmanship and business ability.

In the past the university won fame by her football team and her College of Dentistry. For the present, as is quite appropriate in the university of the new Michigan, she seems content to produce more mechanics and salesmen.

The bachelors and masters of arts from Ann Arbor will sell other people things they themselves would not use. They will get rich, and build big houses which they will decorate with dried starfish and souvenir gewgaws from summer excursions. They will continue to thrill over the *Saturday Evening Post*, and believe the sumach a weed, beauty a pinwheel. And whenever they pass the Jim Scott Memorial Fountain they will pause to admire.

This, the most costly, most magnificent, most prominently situated memorial in Michigan, is being slowly constructed at the foot of Belle Isle, that beautiful park lying in the middle of the Detroit River. Seventy-five acres is being reclaimed from the stream. There will be a great basin 1,200 feet in length, filled with leaping jets of water. Over it will soar a white shaft, dominating all the waterfront of Detroit, saluting every ship that enters the harbor.

And who was Jim Scott? A man who made some money, and died, bequeathing to Detroit the sum of $500,000 on condition that it be used to erect a monument to his memory. A few voices shrieked in protest, crying that Jim Scott had never done anything people wanted to remember, that he knew perhaps too well the distinction between a straight flush and two pairs, that beside this Jim Scott project camembert would have no odor but a faint fragrance of lilies. But Michigan, the new Michigan, was staggered by the bigness of $500,000. It accepted the bequest.

Jim Scott never bothered about his fellow-men when he was alive. On his deathbed he thought it was time. And he sold himself to them. Around his monument for years and years to come the Sabaoth of Michiganders will shuffle, gawking, and they will ponder here the great lesson of salesmanship.

MINNESOTA

The Norse State

SINCLAIR LEWIS

MAY 30, 1923

ON MAY 9, 1922, Mr. Henry Lorenz of Pleasantdale, Saskatchewan, milked the cows and fed the horses and received the calls of his next farm neighbors. Obviously he was still young and lively, though it did happen that on May 9 he was one hundred and seventeen years old. When St. Paul, Mendota, and Marine, the first towns in Minnesota, were established, Henry was a man in his mid-thirties—yes, and President Eliot was seven and Uncle Joe Cannon was five. As for Minneapolis, now a city of four hundred thousand people, seventy-five years ago it consisted of one cabin. Before 1837, there were less than three hundred whites and mixed breeds in all this Minnesotan domain of eighty thousand square miles—the size of England and Scotland put together.

It is so incredibly new; it has grown so dizzyingly. Here is a man still under forty, born in a Minnesota village. Twenty-two years before he was born, the village was a stockade with two or three log stores and a company of infantry, a refuge for the settlers when the Sioux came raiding. During a raid in 1863, a settler was scalped within sight of the stockade. Yet so greatly had the State changed in those twenty-three years that not till he was sixteen did the man himself ever see an Indian. That Indian was on a train, bound East to continue the study of Latin which he had begun on the reservation.

On the spot where the settler was scalped in 1863 is a bungalow farmhouse now, with leaded casement windows, with radio and phonograph, and electric lights in house and garage and barns. A hundred blooded cows are milked there by machinery. The farmer goes into town for Kiwanis Club meetings, and last year he drove his Buick to Los Angeles. He is, or was, too prosperous to belong to the Nonpartisan League or to vote the Farmer-Labor ticket.[1]

Minnesota is unknown to the average Easterner, say to a Hartford insurance man or to a New York garment-worker, not so much because it is new as because

---

[1]The Minnesota Farmer-Labor party was created in the early 1920s from the remnants of the Nonpartisan League, which originated in North Dakota but spread to Minnesota. [D.H.B.]

it is neither definitely Western and violent, nor Eastern and crystallized. Factories and shore hotels are inevitably associated with New Jersey, cowpunchers and buttes with Montana; California is apparent and Florida and Maine. But Minnesota is unplaced. I have heard a Yale junior speculate: "Now you take those Minnesota cities—say take Milwaukee, for instance. Why, it must have a couple of hundred thousand population, hasn't it?"

This would be a composite Eastern impression of Minnesota: a vastness of wind-beaten prairie, flat as a parade ground, wholly given up to wheat-growing save for a fringe of pines at the north and a few market-towns at the south; these steppes inhabited by a few splendid Yankees—one's own sort of people—and by Swedes who always begin sentences with "Vell, Aye tank," who are farmhands, kitchen-maids, and ice-men, and who are invariably humorous.

This popular outline bears examination as well as most popular beliefs; quite as well as the concept that Negroes born in Chicago are less courteous than those born in Alabama. Minnesota is not flat. It is far less flat than the province of Quebec. Most of it is prairie, but the prairie rolls and dips and curves; it lures the motorist like the English roads of Broad Highway fiction. Along the skyline the cumulus clouds forever belly and, with our dry air, nothing is more spectacular than the crimson chaos of our sunsets. But our most obvious beauty is the lakes. There are thousands of them—nine or ten thousand—brilliant among suave grain fields or masked by cool birch and maples. On the dozen-mile-wide lakes of the north are summer cottages of the prosperous from Missouri, Illinois, even Texas.

Leagues of the prairie are utterly treeless, except for artificial windbreaks of willows and cottonwoods encircling the farmhouses. Here the German Catholic spire can be seen a dozen miles off, and the smoke of the Soo Line freight two stations away. But from this plains country you come into a northern pine wilderness, "the Big Woods," a land of lumber camps and reservation Indians and lonely tote-roads, kingdom of Paul Bunyan, the mythical hero of the lumberjacks.

The second error is to suppose that Minnesota is entirely a wheat State. It was, at one time, and the Minneapolis flour-mills are still the largest in the world. Not even Castoria is hymned by more billboards than is Minneapolis flour. But today it is Montana and Saskatchewan and the Dakotas which produce most of the wheat for our mills, while the Minnesota farmers, building tall red silos which adorn their barns like the turrets of Picardy, turn increasingly to dairying. We ship beef to London, butter to Philadelphia. The iron from our Mesaba mines is in Alaskan rails and South African bridges, and as to manufacturing, our refrigerators and heat-regulators comfort Park Avenue apartment-houses, while our chief underwear factory would satisfy a Massachusetts Brahmin or even a Chicago advertising-man.

Greatest error of all is to believe that Minnesota is entirely Yankee and Scandinavian, and that the Swedes are helots and somehow ludicrous.

A school principal in New Duluth analyzed his three hundred and thirty children as Slovene, 49; Italian, 47; Serbian, 39; American, 37; Polish, 30; Austrian and Swedish, 22 each; Croatian, 20; colored, 9 (it is instructive to note that he did not include them among the "Americans"); Finnish, 7; Scotch, 6; Slav unspecified, 5; German, French, Bohemian, and Jewish, 4 each; Rumanian, Norwegian, and Canadian, 3 each; Scandinavian unspecified; Lithuanian, Irish, Ukrainian, and Greek, 2 each; Russian and English, 1 each—60 per cent of them from Southern and Eastern Europe!

Such a Slavification would, of course, be true only of an industrial or mining community, but it does indicate that the whole Mid-Western population may alter as much as has the East. In most of the State there is a predomination of Yankees, Germans, Irish, and all branches of Scandinavians—Icelanders and Danes as well as Swedes and Norwegians. And among all racial misconceptions none is more vigorously absurd than the belief that the Minnesota Scandinavians are, no matter how long they remain here, like the characters of that estimable old stock-company play *Yon Yonson*—a tribe humorous, inferior, and unassimilable. To generalize, any popular generalization about Scandinavians in America is completely and ingeniously and always wrong.

In Minnesota itself one does not hear (from the superior Yankees whom one questions about that sort of thing) that the Scandinavians are a comic people, but rather that they are surly, that they are Socialistic, that they "won't Americanize." Manufacturers and employing lumbermen speak of their Swedish employees precisely as wealthy Seattleites speak of the Japs, Bostonians of the Irish, Southwesterners of the Mexicans, New Yorkers of the Jews, marine officers of the Haitians, and Mr. Rudyard Kipling of nationalist Hindus—or nationalist Americans. Unconsciously, all of them give away the Inferior Race Theory, which is this: An inferior race is one whose members work for me. They are treacherous, ungrateful, ignorant, lazy, and agitator-ridden, because they ask for higher wages and thus seek to rob me of the dollars which I desire for my wife's frocks and for the charities which glorify me. This inferiority is inherent. Never can they become Good Americans (or English Gentlemen, or Highwellborn Prussians). I know that this is so, because all my university classmates and bridge-partners agree with me.

The truth is that the Scandinavians Americanize only too quickly. They Americanize much more quickly than Americans. For generation after generation there is a remnant of stubborn American abolitionist stock which either supports forlorn causes and in jail sings low ballads in a Harvard accent, or else upholds, like Lodge, an Adams tradition which is as poisonous as communism to a joy in brotherly boosting. So thorough are the Scandinavians about it that in 1963 we shall be hearing Norwegian Trygavasons and Icelandic Gislasons saying of the Montenegrins and Letts: "They're reg'lar hogs about wages but the worst is, they simply won't Americanize. They won't vote either the Rotary or the Ku Klux ticket. They keep hollering about wanting some kind of a doggone Third Party."

Scandinavians take to American commerce and schooling and journalism as do Scotsmen or Cockneys. Particularly they take to American politics, the good old politics of Harrison and McKinley and Charley Murphy. Usually, they bring nothing new from their own experimental countries. They permit their traditions to be snatched away. True, many of them have labored for the Nonpartisan League, for woman suffrage, for cooperative societies. The late Governor John Johnson of Minnesota seems to have been a man of destiny; had he lived he would probably have been President, and possibly a President of power and originality. But again—there was Senator Knute Nelson, who made McCumber look like a left-wing syndicalist and Judge Gary like François Villon. There is Congressman Steenerson of Minnesota, chairman of the House postal committee. Mr. Steenerson once produced, out of a rich talent matured by a quarter of a century in the House, an immortal sentence. He had been complaining at lunch that the Nonpartisan League had introduced the obscene writings of "this Russian woman, Ellen Key"[2] into the innocent public schools. Some one hinted to the Swedish Mr. Steenerson, "But I thought she was a Swede."

He answered: *"No, the Key woman comes from Finland and the rest of Red Russia, where they nationalize the women."*

Good and bad, the Scandinavians monopolize Minnesota politics. Of the last nine governors of the State, six have been Scandinavians. So is Dr. Shipstead, who defeated Senator Kellogg in the 1922 election; so is Harold Knutson, Republican whip of the House. Scandinavians make up a large proportion of the Minnesota State Legislature, and while in Santa Fe the Mexican legislators speak Spanish, while in Quebec the representatives still debate in French, though for generations they have been citizens of a British dominion, in Minnesota the politicians who were born abroad are zealous to speak nothing but Americanese. So is it in business and the home. Though a man may not have left Scandinavia till he was twenty, his sons will use the same English, good and bad, as the sons of settlers from Maine, and his daughters will go into music clubs or into cocktail sets, into college or into factories, with the same prejudices and ideals and intonations as girls named Smith and Brewster.

The curious newness of Minnesota has been suggested, but the really astonishing thing is not the newness—it is the oldness, the solid, traditionalized, cotton-wrapped oldness. A study of it would be damaging to the Free and Fluid Young America theory. While parts of the State are still so raw that the villages among the furrows or the dusty pines are but frontier camps, in the cites and in a few of the towns there is as firm a financial oligarchy and almost as definite a social system as London, and this power is behind all "sound" politics, in direct or indirect control of all business. It has its Old Families, who tend to marry only with their own set. Anywhere in the world, an Old Family is one which has had wealth for at least thirty years longer than average families of the same neighborhood. In England, it takes (at most) five generations to absorb "parvenus" and "profiteers" into the gentry, whether they were steel profiteers

---

[2]Ellen Key was a Swedish feminist whose writings extolling the innate nurturing powers of women enjoyed a vogue in the 1910s and 1920s. [D. H. B.]

in the Great War or yet untitled land profiteers under William the Conqueror. In New York it takes three generations—often. In the Middle West it takes one and a half.

No fable is more bracing, or more absurd, than that all the sons and grandsons of the pioneers, in Minnesota or in California, in Arizona or Nebraska, are racy and breezy, unmannerly but intoxicatingly free. The grandchildren of the men who in 1862 fought the Minnesota Indians, who dogtrotted a hundred miles over swamp-blurred trails to bear the alarm to the nearest troops—some of them are still clearing the land, but some of them are complaining of the un-English quality of the Orange Pekoe in dainty painty city tea-rooms which stand where three generations ago the Red River fur-carts rested; their chauffeurs await them in Pierce Arrow limousines (special bodies by Kimball, silver fittings from Tiffany); they present Schnitzler and St. John Ervine at their Little Theaters; between rehearsals they chatter of meeting James Joyce in Paris; and always in high-pitched Mayfair laughter they ridicule the Scandinavians and Finns who are trying to shoulder into their sacred, ancient Yankee caste. A good many of their names are German.

Naturally, beneath this Junker class there is a useful, sophisticated, and growing company of doctors, teachers, newspapermen, liberal lawyers, musicians who have given up Munich and Milan for the interest of developing orchestras in the new land. There is a scientific body of farmers. The agricultural school of the huge University of Minnesota is sound and creative. And still more naturally, between Labor and Aristocracy there is an army of the peppy, poker-playing, sales-hustling He-men who are our most characteristic Americans. But even the He-men are not so obvious as they seem. What their future is, no man knows—and no woman dares believe. It is conceivable that, instead of being a menace, in their naive boosting and their fear of the unusual, they may pass only too soon; it is possible that their standardized bathrooms and Overlands will change to an equally standardized and formula-bound culture—yearning Culture, arty Art. We have been hurled from tobacco-chewing to tea-drinking with gasping speed; we may as quickly dash from boosting to a beautiful and languorous death. If it is necessary to be Fabian in politics, to keep the reformers (left wing or rigid right) from making us perfect too rapidly, it is yet more necessary to be a little doubtful about the ardent souls who would sell Culture; and if the Tired Business Man is unlovely and a little dull, at least he is real, and we shall build only on reality.

The nimbler among our pioneering grandfathers appropriated to their private uses some thousands of square miles in northern Minnesota, and cut off—or cheerfully lost by forest fire—certain billions of feet of such lumber as will never be seen again. When the lumber was gone, the land seemed worthless. It was good for nothing but agriculture, which is an unromantic occupation, incapable of making millionaires in one generation. Suddenly, on parts of this scraggly land, iron was discovered, iron in preposterous quantities, to be mined in the open pit, as easily as hauling out gravel. Here is the chief supply of the Gary and

South Chicago mills. The owners of the land do not mine the ore. They have gracefully leased it—though we are but Westerners, we have our subsidiary of the United States Steel Company. The landowners themselves have only to go abroad and sit in beauty like a flower, and every time a steam shovel dips into the ore, a quarter drops into the owner's pocket.

This article is intended to be a secret but flagrant boost. It is meant to increase civic pride and the value of Minnesota real estate. Yet the writer wonders if he will completely satisfy his chambers of commerce. There is a chance that they would prefer a statement of the value of our dairy products, the number of our admirable new school-buildings, the number of motor tourists visiting our lakes, and an account of Senator Nelson's encouraging progress from poverty to magnificence. But a skilled press agent knows that this would not be a boost; it would be an admission of commerce-ruled barrenness. The interesting thing in Minnesota is the swift evolution of a complex social system and, since in two generations we have changed from wilderness to country clubs, the question is what the next two generations will produce. It defies certain answer; it demands a scrupulous speculation free equally from the bland certitudes of chambers of commerce and the sardonic impatience of professional radicals. To a realistic philosopher, the existence of an aristocracy is not (since it does exist) a thing to be bewailed, but to be examined as a fact.

There is one merit not of Minnesota alone but of all the Middle West which must be considered. The rulers of our new land may to the eye seem altogether like the rulers of the East—of New England, New York, Pennsylvania. Both groups are chiefly reverent toward banking, sound Republicanism, the playing of golf and bridge, and the possession of large motors. But whereas the Easterner is content with these symbols and smugly desires nothing else, the Westerner, however golfocentric he may be, is not altogether satisfied; and raucously though he may snortle at his wife's "fool suffrage ideas" and "all this highbrow junk the lecture-hounds spring on you," yet secretly, wistfully he desires a beauty that he does not understand.

As a pendant, to hint that our society has become somewhat involved in the few years since Mr. Henry Lorenz of Saskatchewan was seventy, let me illogically lump a few personal observations of Minnesota:

Here is an ex-professor of history in the State University, an excellent scholar who, retiring after many years of service, cheerfully grows potatoes in a backwoods farm among the northern Minnesota pines, and builds up cooperative selling for all the farmers of his district.

Here is the head of a Minneapolis school for kindergartners, a woman who is summoned all over the country to address teachers' associations. She will not admit candidates for matriculation until she is sure that they have a gift for teaching. She does something of the work of a Montessori, with none of the trumpeting and anguish.

Here is the greatest, or certainly the largest, medical clinic in the world—the Mayo clinic, with over a hundred medical specialists besides the clerks and nurses. It is the supreme court of diagnosis. Though it is situated in a small town, off the through rail routes, yet it is besieged by patients from Utah and Ontario and New York as much as Minnesotans. When the famous European doctors come to America, they may look at the Rockefeller Institute, they may stop at Harvard and Rush and Johns Hopkins and the headquarters of the American Medical Association, but certainly they will go on to Rochester. The names of "Charley" and "Will" have something of the familiarity of "R. L. S." and "T. R."

Here is a Chippewa as silent and swart as his grandfather, an active person whom the cavalry used to hunt every open season. The grandson conducts a garage, and he actually understands ignition. His farm among the lowering Norway pines he plows with a tractor.

Here is a new bookshop which is publishing the first English translation of the autobiography of Abelard.

Here are really glorious buildings: the Minneapolis Art Institute, the State Capitol, the St. Paul Public Library, and Ralph Adams Cram's loveliest church. Here, on the shore of Lake of the Isles, is an Italian palace built by a wheat speculator. Here where five years ago were muddy ruts are perfect cement roads.

Here is a small town, a "typical prairie town," which has just constructed a competent golf course. From this town came an ambassador to Siam and a professor of history in Columbia.

And here are certain Minnesota authors. You know what Mid-Western authors are—rough fellows but vigorous, ignorant of the classics and of Burgundy, yet close to the heart of humanity. They write about farmyards and wear flannel shirts. Let us confirm this portrait by a sketch of nine Minnesota authors, eight of them born in the State:

Charles Flandrau, author of *Harvard Episodes* and *Viva Mexico,* one-time Harvard instructor, now wandering in Spain. Agnes Repplier has called him the swiftest blade among American essayists. Scott Fitzgerald, very much a Minnesotan, yet the father of the Long Island flapper, the prophet of the Ritz, the idol of every Junior League. Alice Ames Winter, president of the General Federation of Women's Clubs. Claude Washburn, author of *The Lonely Warrior* and several other novels which, though they are laid in America, imply a European background. He has lived for years now in France and Italy. Margaret Banning, author of *Spellbinders.* Woodward Boyd, whose first novel, *The Love Legend,* is a raid on the domestic sentimentalists. Carlton Miles, a dramatic critic who gives his Minnesota readers the latest news of the continental stage. He is just back from a European year spent with such men as Shaw, Drinkwater, and the director of La Scala. Brenda Ueland, who lives in Greenwich Village and writes for the *Atlantic Monthly.* Sinclair Lewis, known publicly as a scolding corn-belt realist, but actually (as betrayed by the samite-yclad, Tennyson-and-water verse which he wrote when he was in college) a yearner over what he would doubtless call "quaint ivied cottages."

Seventy-five years ago—a Chippewa-haunted wilderness. Today—a complex civilization with a future which, stirring or dismayed or both, is altogether unknowable. To understand America, it is merely necessary to understand Minnesota. But to understand Minnesota you must be an historian, an ethnologist, a poet, a cynic, and a graduate prophet all in one.

MISSISSIPPI

Heart of Dixie

BEULAH AMIDON RATLIFF

MAY 17, 1922

IT IS HARD, perhaps impossible, for a Northerner to understand Mississippi; that is, to realize its past, to accept its social and economic present, to feel at home living according to its standards, to face its future with hope and assurance. Though Mississippi has grown neurotic over its "war-time anguish," there is no doubt that the State suffered cruelly during the war and reconstruction. Except Virginia, no other State was the scene of so much actual fighting.

At the end of the war, the State debt, according to Attorney General Harris, was over $16,300,000. Prices rivaled the staggering quotations from Vienna and Moscow today: men's boots sold at $200 a pair at Natchez; a coat was priced at $350; flour, $50 a barrel; salt, $4 a pound; soap, 75 cents a cake. The State finances were hopelessly involved after several issues of railroad scrip, treasury notes, and State bonds. The repudiation of the huge debt incurred "in aid of the rebellion" complicated instead of simplifying the financial tangle. The fields had not been tilled for four years. The stock had died or been driven off to feed the armies. Buildings and fences had fallen into decay. Railroads and such highways as once existed had deteriorated till they were almost useless. Levees had been cut by both Union and Confederate armies and thousands of acres were flooded. According to the United States census of 1860 and the State census of 1866 the population had decreased 66,585; the decrease of the white population being 10,499, of the black population 56,146. (Famine and disease took such toll among the Negroes during the war and reconstruction that Governor Sharkey stated in 1866 that half the Negroes of the State had perished, and the race seemed doomed to early extinction.) Such schools as the State had possessed were utterly destroyed, and the printing presses had not fared much better. The economic system, in use since Colonial days, was scrapped, and the laborers wandered about the country, refusing to work under the belief that "Marse Linkum gwine gib ebry niggah fo'ty acres an' a mule ob his own." The State leaders who had survived the war were humiliated and uncertain.

History fails to record an instance of a victorious people dealing mercifully and patiently with their late enemies. The Federal Government made harsh and stupid blunders in meeting the problems of reconstruction. Both the presidential and the congressional reconstruction policies were hastily formed and tactlessly administered. Beaten, impoverished, weary, confused, the State was in no temper to accept calmly and judge on their merits the startling innovations of the victorious Northerners. To people reared in a society based on human slavery, and accepting that institution as the just and necessary foundation of economic life, it was sufficiently revolutionary to have their late property suddenly snatched away, without compensation, by an arbitrary law in the making of which they had had no voice. But in addition to this they were expected to accept their former slaves as voters, office-holders, and court witnesses—in short, to have their cattle transformed overnight into citizens.

Carpet-baggers, sufficiently clever and unscrupulous to exploit to the limit the disorganized condition of the State and the childish ignorance and egotism of the Negroes, made their disgraceful contribution to the misery of the situation. From the paralysis of utter panic, the Mississippians passed to a state of resentment, which culminated in the well-organized "Revolt of 1875." The carpet-baggers were driven out. Negro office-holders were unseated. White franchise was established. Mississippi had made a successful beginning in blotting out the odious Thirteenth, Fourteenth, and Fifteenth amendments from the life of the State.

The Mississippi of today bases its activity and its ideals on the rosy tradition of "befo' de wah." The "Revolt of '75" destroyed, as far as Mississippi was concerned, the fruits of the war: emancipation and Negro citizenship. Since then the effort has been to go on as though there had been no war. Slavery, of course, could not exist in name, but as far as possible the institution has been preserved in fact. Naturally, this effort has been more successful in remote country places than in the towns. Today there is a marked difference between "field niggers" and "town niggers."

Practically all plantations are divided into small farms of five to twenty-five acres, which are "let" to a Negro family for a "season" on the "tenant-farmer" plan. That is, the Negro and his family work the land, using the stock and tools of the landowner, pick the cotton and sell it, either to a cotton buyer, to a gin, or to the planter himself. The planter furnishes food and kerosene to his hands on credit, and advances small sums of money till the crop is sold. Then there is a "settlement," when the accumulated debt of the tenant is set off against the value of his crop (minus the rent for his land) and the cash balance due him is paid the tenant. Often the end of the season finds the Negro possessed of a debt instead of a balance. Then he must remain another season, to "work off his debt," or the planter may "sell" him to another planter, who pays the amount of the debt, in which case the Negro is bound to his new "boss" for the amount of the "purchase price."

Cotton picking, Greenwood, Mississippi. Although this stereograph was probably made in the 1910s, it does depict both the working conditions and the racial oppression of plantation life that still prevailed in the 1920s.

The planter has numerous opportunities to profit under the "tenant-farmer" system:

1. The planter divides up his land to suit himself. The farm he "lets" as 20 acres may contain 20 acres, or it may contain 15 or 16 acres. Most planters "let" at least a fifth more land than they own.

2. Supplies are furnished the Negroes from the commissary, the plantation store. The planter fixes his own prices, does his own book-keeping, and adds 20 per cent to all accounts "for carrying."

3. The tenant must accept the planter's figures for the settlement. There is no tribunal to which he can appeal if he considers the settlement unjust. I heard a planter tell, with roars of laughter, that "Jeff done sued me fo' seven hunder' dollars after the settlement," elaborating on the tenant's "fine book-keeping," and "the smart Aleck lawyer" he got to file the suit. I inquired when the case would be tried. I was met with a stare of blank amazement, and then the indignant question: "Do you think there's a co't in Mississippi gwine entertain a nigger's suit against a white man? That there suit was throwed out o' co't mos' afore it got in."

4. Classing cotton takes a high degree of skill and intelligence. No plantation Negro is trained to class his own cotton. A planter, therefore, can buy the tenant's cotton at many grades below its real worth, selling it at its true value, and realizing a handsome profit on every bale.

Contracts for the coming season are made the first of each January. After a Negro has made his "contract" he is bound to his "boss" as completely as in slavery days. He cannot purchase supplies except at the commissary. He must not change employers or leave the plantation. If a Negro "runs away" the planter may pursue him, bring him back by force, punish him with a whipping, and stand over him with a gun to prevent another runaway. Various Southern writers have vehemently denied that planters ever whip their Negroes. I can only testify to what I have seen and heard. A Negro woman was once whipped in my hearing for quarreling with another Negress. "As crazy as a nigger woman getting a lickin' " was the simile used by a leading Greenville lawyer in my hearing. A neighbor asked a planter, in my presence, what had become of a certain Negro. The reply was:

He run away. I never did figger out how. Lit out one night. I went after him and come up with him at R——'s. Owed me close to $400. I brought him back and whipped him till he couldn't stand up. Thought that would hold him a while. But the next morning he was gone. Never got a trace of him. I'd sure like to know how he got off. He couldn't stand up when I got through with him.

A friend once telephoned me: "We can't get in to play cards tonight. S—— had to give a nigger a whippin' today and it always makes him so nervous he can't do nothin' but go to bed."

The jovial, singing, courteous Negro of Southern plantations has passed away from Mississippi, if he ever existed outside fiction. Field-hands of the present are unbelievably slow and stupid. "Jes' sense enough to hold a plow and yell at a mule," a planter once described them to me, and the characterization is apt.

Their speech is so thick and mumbled it scarcely seems like human articulation. They are dull and surly, apparently without ambition or human affection. Nine field Negroes out of ten cannot tell you how old they are, where they were born, whether their parents are living, how often they have been married, or how many children they have. Their sex life is utterly bestial. Ask a piccaninny whose child he is, and he will reply, "Norah's boy" or "Kate's boy." Neither the child nor his mother could state his paternity.

In many country districts there are no schools for colored children. In the more progressive counties, like Warren, there is a term of five months for colored children, and in many of the schools, thanks to the Jeanes Fund, some form of industrial training has been introduced. Other counties have terms of ninety days a year for the Negro children. In all counties the country schools for blacks are wretchedly equipped—drafty little sheds, with plank benches, a chair or stool for the teacher, a few tattered, out-of-date books, a few cracked slates, no blackboards, no desks, no pens, pencils, or paper, no pictures, no music, and a teacher scarcely less illiterate than his scholars.

From the age of five or six the children go into the fields, "chopping" cotton with a hoe, or picking cotton. Cornbread, biscuits, molasses, rice, and salt pork form the diet of plantation Negroes of all ages. Ninety-nine out of a hundred families lack the energy to raise vegetables or chickens to vary the coarse fare, though around every cabin there is plenty of space for a "garden patch."

The life of the Mississippi plantation Negro is toil, ignorance, hopelessness, animal stupidity and bestiality. He is a filthy, stolid, unloved and unloving creature, as far from the "merry, singing hoehand" of fiction as is the dirty, diseased, reservation Indian from Cooper's "noble redman."

The patience with which a Mississippi planter deals with his dull, irresponsible labor is almost unbelievable to a Northerner. If he is harsh in punishing a "runaway," too shrewd in his contracts, quick to take advantage of all his opportunities to exploit, the planter is also the long-suffering guardian of these difficult children. If a hand falls sick, the planter's physician is called. The planter purchases the necessary medicines, and he or his wife watches through the night beside the sick person, for no plantation Negro can be depended upon to administer medicine regularly or in the prescribed dose. Family or community quarrels are patiently heard and decided. Many planters give an annual barbecue, when all the plantation hands are invited to a feast and merrymaking. A Negro cheated by another Negro or by a white man can count on his "boss" to safeguard his rights. The planter protects his Negroes from the countless "agents" who are always trying to sell the ignorant hands some trifle at an exorbitant price. The average planter looks on his hands as responsibilities to be fed, clothed, guarded, and cared for in sickness or disaster. At the same time he is unalterably opposed to anything that would help these "children" grow up. As a civic duty he would assist in tarring and feathering any "interfering Yankee" who urged the Negroes to obtain an education, buy a farm, learn a trade, leave the land, or, most heinous crime of all, organize. As far as he can achieve it, the Mississippi planter will keep the Negroes slaves, overworked, mal-nourished, terrorized into submission by corporal punishment, lacking initiative or ambition, dull, landless.

The "town Negroes" are markedly different. In Vicksburg I know of Negroes acting successfully as ministers, teachers, physicians, and dentists to their own race, and to both races as trained nurses, cooks, nursemaids, plumbers, carpenters, plasterers, dressmakers, store clerks, mail carriers, chauffeurs, mechanics, painters and paperhangers, brick masons, and truck drivers. "Town Negroes" are, of course, in closer touch with the white race and with the white man's way of living than the field hands. They try, and with startling success, to arrange their houses, prepare their food, and dress "like white folks."

One of my cooks was an interesting example of the difference between "field Negroes" and "town Negroes." Effie had been born on a plantation, but at the age of six she was taken to Vicksburg by the daughter of the planter for whom her mother worked, and brought up as the playmate of a little white girl. This meant that she was kept seasonally and neatly dressed, shared the meals of her little charge, played with the same toys, learned to read and write at the same time, had attention paid to her speech and manners, and for ten years was exposed to all the influences of a refined and pleasant home. I sometimes saw Effie's mother and sisters when they trudged in from the country, typical, dull, awkward, ugly, slovenly field Negroes. But Effie was immaculate in her person and clothing, dainty and attractive in appearance and carriage, intelligent, courteous, able to read simple books, and to write and spell fully as well as the average ten-year-old public-school child, an advanced degree of erudition for a Mississippi Negro. The difference in environment and training made Effie seem of another race from her "cornfield relations."

The Negro school buildings and equipment in Vicksburg (and in other large towns, I was told) compare favorably with the white schools. The teachers were graduates of colored high schools and colleges in many cases. There are pictures, playgrounds, and even a few victrolas, "visiting days" with very creditable programs, and a little industrial training. But there is neither incentive nor opportunity for progress beyond the grades, and most colored children drop out of school at the age of ten or twelve.

The "color line" in Mississippi is a devious thing for Northerners to trace. There are, of course, "Jim Crow" cars on the trains, "Jim Crow" waiting-rooms, theater galleries, and street-car sections. The school systems are entirely separate, as are the churches. But Negroes patronize "white stores," and are at liberty to try on any hat, garment, or pair of shoes they fancy. I have often seen Negresses "trying out" expensive dresses which were hung back on the racks and later tried on and purchased by white customers. "Town Negroes" use the banks and stand in line beside "white folks," though they could not do so in a street-car aisle. Doctors and dentists minister to white and colored alike, though there are separate wards in the hospitals, with colored nurses for the colored wards, working under the direction of white nurses. White children of the well-to-do classes are left almost entirely to colored nurses. Incidentally, "the charming Southern accent" and "the delightful Southern drawl" are to be traced to this fact, for the little children in learning to talk from their nurses, pick up also the slovenly Negro articulation and the Negro's whining intonation, and later training, while it corrects in a measure the Negro grammar and diction of early childhood, leaves the "accent" and the "drawl."

There are numerous colored prostitutes, and "kept women" are as apt to be colored as white. There are two remarkable statements I have heard again and again from Mississippians, in the same breath in which they protested "By God, there'll never be social equality or mingling of the races in this State": "There isn't a full-blooded nigger in the State of Mississippi" and "there's not a virgin Negress over fourteen years old in this State."

"Town Negroes" take and leave employment as they choose. They appear in court as witnesses, and I recollect a case in Warren County where a white man was hanged on the testimony of a Negro. I never heard of a suit brought by a Negro against a white man in Vicksburg, but I feel sure that such a suit would not be summarily "thrown out of court" there, or in any of the other large towns. Communications from colored people on matters of general interest are printed in the Vicksburg papers, and such matters as colored school programs, the death of respected colored citizens, colored Red Cross activities and charities are fully reported.

But even in Vicksburg, where the relations between the two races are particularly good, the Negroes are "kept in their place." They are not citizens. They neither vote nor hold office, though they pay taxes. A crime against a Negro is not punished as is a crime against a white person. For example, during the war Mississippians held that everyone able to work must work. Various patriots appointed themselves to enforce this rule. Four such patriots (white, of course) in Vicksburg went to the home of a Negro woman who was not working, seized her by force, whipped her, and tarred and feathered her. She was pregnant and lost her child, almost losing her own life, as the result of the experience. Nearly two years later the four patriots were tried on a minor charge ("assault," I believe) and sentenced to six months in jail, but the sentence was not served. Though I asked many Mississippians about it, I never heard of a Negro voting or attempting to vote in Mississippi. A prominent man from the north of the State told me: "They don't come to the polls in our part of the State. None of our niggers are crazy to commit suicide."

Mob rule and "lynch law" are sometimes resorted to in punishing Negro criminals or those suspected of crime. While I was living in Mississippi I knew of Negroes being killed for the following causes: attacking a white woman, 1; trying to enter a movie theater on the "white side," 1; trying to enter a "white restaurant," 1; house-breaking, 1; helping a Negro murderer to escape, 1; killing a white man, 1; shooting a white man, 4; drawing a gun on a white man, 1. In the case of the Negro helping the murderer to escape the victim was tortured before being hanged. The Negro lynched for attacking a white woman was burned alive, after horrible tortures. The victim of the attack, who was uninjured, failed to identify him as her assailant, once stating definitely that he was not the man. The Negro who tried to enter the theater with "white folks" and the one who wanted to eat in the "white restaurant" were both ex-service men in uniform, recently returned from France. This is not a complete list of the lynchings that occurred during the two and a half years I lived in the State. It is, merely, a list of those of which I heard the details from reliable sources. I also know of two cases in which a Negro who killed a white man was legally tried and executed.

Mississippi is undeniably a backward State. It has fewer hospitals than any other State in the Union. Its educational appropriation is $7.49 per "educable child," the second lowest in the country, a seventh of the amount appropriated in Middle Western States. Because of the inadequate schools, and the lack of compulsory education laws, illiteracy among whites as well as among blacks is not uncommon. Most of the roads are impassable during the rains. There are no child-labor laws, no compulsory-education laws for either white or colored children, no first-class colleges, few and impoverished libraries; there is unchecked malaria, hookworm, and pellagra. Such folderols as juvenile courts, pure food, public kindergartens, city sanitation, public health clinics are generally unknown and undesired.

Mississippians admit, many of them regretfully, the backwardness of their State. They speak with pathetic apology of "the horrors of war"; the "reconstruction debts" which still oppress the leading towns; "the flower of the State dead in battle only one generation ago"; the financial burden of the Confederate pensions; "the poverty following the war"; "more than half our population ignorant blacks"—all of which are, doubtless, contributing factors. But I believe that the cause of Mississippi's backwardness is something more fundamental than the aftermath of war or the color of the population.

Human slavery is an outworn and discarded institution. That, at least, humanity has left behind. A society based upon an institution tested, found basically wrong, and cast aside cannot itself be sound and capable of normal growth. Mississippi has made every effort to keep her Negro population slaves in fact, if not in name. To oppress an inferior race is not so degrading to the oppressed as to the oppressors. In attempting to retard the normal development of the Negroes the whites have retarded and perverted their own development.

Mississippi does not want "damyankee notions upsetting the niggers," so Mississippi has shut itself off from the North as completely as possible. Northern ideas of business, education, agriculture, road-building, and finance have been stubbornly excluded. Federal aid has been refused—"damyankee meddling." The hostile attitude of the State toward the attempted pellagra investigation last fall is typical. "The good old days" have been the ideal, and so Mississippi has scorned the community efforts that have developed in other sections, clinging to the intense individualism of sixty years ago. The bad schools and the isolation from the rest of the country have naturally resulted in a smug, impenetrable provincialism that is appalling. "We do it so in Mississippi" or "We don't do it so in Mississippi" permits or forbids anything.

Criticism of anything Mississippian is hotly resented, particularly criticism of the existing order. Anyone, but especially a Northerner, comments on the "Negro problem" at his peril. Even a calm and impartial description of actual conditions is resented. "It's our business"; "It's something no Yankee can understand"; "We don't want our affairs written up in no damyankee paper."

And yet Mississippi and Mississippians have such splendid possibilities! There are a few Mississippi women whose charm and humor and loveliness of spirit and person I have not seen equaled in this country. They are, of course, of the "aristocracy," widely traveled, and fairly well read. If they had had the education and the horizon of Northern college women they would be among the leaders of American womanhood.

The climate of Mississippi, with malaria controlled and good roads and decent hotels built, would make it a tourist paradise. It has the softness of Florida and the invigorating air of the West blended into what is, seven months of the year, "the perfect atmosphere." In addition Mississippi has the lavish, openhanded beauty of a mild climate, blessed with plenty of rain. Anything will grow and blossom with half a chance—roses and fruit trees and children and flowers. The land is rich and, if scientifically farmed, it would yield enormous wealth. Experiments like the truck gardens around Crystal Springs have shown what production the State is capable of, when dragged away from "cotton an' co'n" to twentieth-century crop rotation.

Whenever I read of "missionary movements" I wonder why China and Africa and India are preferred to fields so much nearer home. Missionaries to Mississippi—now, there's a real need! Educational missionaries, to bring both white and colored schools up to modern standards; medical missionaries, to teach hygiene and sanitation, and establish country clinics where the sick can obtain something more scientific that "a dose of calomel an' a dose of quinine," administered by a self-made "doctor"; agricultural missionaries, to teach modern methods of farming; and evangelical missionaries, who, neglecting the favorite Mississippi doctrines of "hellfire and damnation," would preach the Golden Rule and the preciousness of little children.

It would take a sturdy breed of missionaries, ready to accept ridicule, misunderstanding, and ostracism; unafraid of the whipping post, the tar kettle, or the inglorious martyrdom of a midnight lynching bee. Yes, a difficult and a dangerous field; but any unselfish, stout-hearted American, eager to see the light of civilization penetrate the uttermost parts of his own country, will do well to go to Mississippi, "the glorious heart of Dixie."

MISSOURI

Doesn't Want to Be Shown

MANLEY O. HUDSON

OCTOBER 17, 1923

NOTHING IS SIMPLER than to throw a few millions of human beings into a hopper and ascribe to all of them qualities which not one of the individuals may possess. For a generation now four millions of Missourians have been herded under the music-hall slogan, "I'm from Missouri and you've got to show me." And as a consequence they have gained the reputation for being a cautious and inquiring people.

Now few things might be said about Missourians which would be further from the truth. In the large—by which I mean that I cannot produce statistics for what I am about to say—in the large, they deserve no credit for such skepticism. You do not have to show the Missourian. He knows already. And he is quite content to let it go at that. Missouri doesn't care to be shown!

> Every time I come to town
> Th' boys keep kickin' my dog aroun';
> Makes no diff'rence if he is a houn',
> You' gotta quit kickin' my dog aroun'.

This Ozark doggerel is not merely the original of Senator Vest's famous eulogy. It breathes also the sentiments with which the Missourian looks at the world. His dog may be a hound, but it is his and he proposes that others shall take it at his valuation. Missouri may not be the greatest State in the Union. Illinois may have a richer soil and a more prosperous people; Iowa may have a better organized community life; and Kansas, a quicker sense of civic responsibility and political opportunity. But Missouri doesn't care to hear about it. Missourians are satisfied with her, and she is satisfied with herself. Besides, who can say that Arkansas excels her in anything?

For Missouri—we who are to the manner born call her "Mizzourah" with no apology for rolling the r—Missouri is not merely a geographers' diagram. It is not simply a place. It is a state of digestion. It is a set of conventions. It is a slant on life. In brief, it is a civilization.

205

An effete Easterner whose travels in America are bounded by Baltimore on the south, by Buffalo on the west, and by Bar Harbor on the north may wonder that the straight lines remembered from his school geography as the boundaries of Missouri could so clearly mark out the personality of a people. I have met Americans on the Atlantic coast to whom Missouri was no more than a name for a river or a waltz or a compromise. Judging by the date-lines not many editors know today that Kansas City does not vote in Kansas. And perhaps few New Yorkers will be able to understand why it is that we resent their placing Missouri in that trans-Allegheny vastness which they call "the Middle West." Our query is, "West of what?" It all depends on where you start. We don't find Missouri west of where we begin to measure the continent. To us it is difficult to see why the rest of the country does not call it "the center." The nerve controls may be elsewhere. And we're willing to use Chicago as a sort of aorta through which to supply the rest of the country. But Missouri is the heart of America!

What other State was so favored by the geographers? The eight bordering States give Missouri a contact with the Great Lakes, the Alleghenies, all of Dixieland, the Gulf, and the Rockies. They make her the friend of the North and the South, the common ground of the East and the West, without identifying her with any section.

As a place, Missouri is not quite coterminous with the map-makers' shuffle. The two broad portals which she opens so generously to the outer world are for most purposes not part of Missouri herself. We must exclude St. Louis first of all. For that sprawling city lops over into Illinois and takes its cue from the screeching factories and glaring furnaces of other lands. It serves Missouri chiefly as a sieve for Eastern money and Eastern manners. It is a huge railroad terminal—the only American city besides Chicago where passengers always change. No train ever passes through St. Louis. It is an island of Germanic culture in a sea of American indifference. It once had a Fair which made it great, and the laurel has been borne in slumber these twenty years since. Only this year a bond issue seems to have waked it up; it was no mean thing to vote eighty-seven million dollars for improvements on the crest of a high tide of taxes. But except for Forest Park and its unique open-air theater, St. Louis sets no pace. It forms no part of Missouri. Even the postal clerks know it as St. Louis, U.S.A.

At the opposite end of Missouri's corridor, Kansas City stands as an outpost flung out by the great Southwest in its reach for Chicago. Busy, boasting, and Babbitt-ful, Kansas City holds a key position in the American system of inter-state commerce. It is a way-station for the country's hogs and corn and oil. It is a warehouse for Montgomery Ward & Co. It has life but it lacks character. It once got bold enough to experiment with a Board of Public Welfare, but the courage faded when Jacob Billikopf went East. It lacks history, too, though a few of us can still recall the days when we bought our trousers from the Grand Pants Co. for "$1.75 a leg, seats free." Those were the good old days! Then as now Kansas City was like New York—all of its people come from somewhere else and many of them are still in transit. Like New York, it is a part of no State. It is interstate. It does not wear Missouri yarn, and its face is turned toward Kansas.

These exclusions leave to Missouri a territory larger than all New England, with a population almost as large as that of the Irish Free State. They leave the farmers who cultivate each year a half a million acres of wheat and oats and corn and hay. They leave the miners who produce a large part of America's zinc and lead and coal and iron. They leave a host of small villages, each consisting of a few houses clustered around a combined post-office-and-general-store which handles postage-stamps, prunes, and potatoes, all in the bulk. They leave St. Joseph, Kirksville, Hannibal, Columbia, Jefferson City, Sedalia, Springfield, Joplin, Carthage, Cape Girardeau—each with a niche in our national history, each with a Main Street all its own.

For its population, Missouri was originally indebted to three things—the bad land in Virginia, the failure of the potato crop in Ireland in 1847, and the revolution in Germany in 1848. From Virginia came a yeoman stock of purely English blood, urged by the hard times of the twenties to seek their fortunes in the promised land across the plains. Some of them stopped en route in Kentucky—in Madison County, Sir! A few of them brought their slaves along. But with the climate inhospitable to both cotton and tobacco, slavery got no firm hold in the State. An abolitionist conference at Lexington in the late twenties attracted little attention, and if Missouri was a bone of contention it was not due to her own defense of slavery. One-twentieth of the people are still black or mulatto, but we have no Jim Crow cars and a lynching or two a year is regarded enough to "make the Negro keep his place."

This Virginia immigration gave to Missouri society a Southern tinge which many communities still retain. They built their court-houses on the best Virginia models of the time, and where the court-house square exists today, with the town built around it—in Liberty, in Marshall, in Mexico, in Springfield—the architecture remains unsurpassed by any of the styles borrowed from Chicago or Cleveland suburbs. A Southern family tradition lingers, too, where the invading Yankees have not smothered it, and helps Missouri to resist change. I recall entering a farmhouse "in the kingdom of Callaway" a few years ago on a cold winter day, to find a glowing fire cracking out its welcome. As I held out my hands, I exclaimed to my host about his fire. "It ought to be good," he parried, "it's been burning long enough." I asked when it had been started. "In 1832. My father brought it out from Virginia when he came across the prairie in a wagon, and it's been burning ever since."

It was a very different strain that came from Ireland and from Germany. The Irish soon mixed, for here they never limited themselves to politics and the police force. But the Germans held aloof, and they still live in *enclaves,* secure from the ravages of puritanism. In the early days they captured South St. Louis, whence they've ministered since to many a thirst. They proved themselves superior agriculturists, and in the eastern counties they gradually crowded the

Virginians out of the better bottom lands. With their militant ideas of freedom, they opposed the extension of slavery, they kept Missouri from seceding, they sent Carl Schurz to the Senate. More recently they held back the Volstead onslaught until the general capitulation. They began as Republicans in 1860, and they've voted straight ever since—until the combination of the war and prohibition led them to reelect Senator Reed.[1] Content with what they have escaped in Europe and what they have found in America, they add no ferment to Missouri's society. They help to keep her satisfied.

The Atlantic seaboard is too far away for a large European immigration—there are some Greeks in St. Louis and a few Italians in Kansas City. But if some explorer sent out by peasants of Southeastern Europe should ever rediscover Missouri, and if a 3 per cent limit would not bar it, the Ozark wilderness might be transformed into another Switzerland!

A traveler who journeys from Kansas City to St. Louis on the Wabash or the C. & A. or the Missouri Pacific or the Rock Island—all of our railroads seem to run east and west—may wonder about Missouri's prosperity. For in a land of teeming plenty, poverty still lifts its ugly head. But if we take as a test the existence of a favorable trade balance, there can be no doubt about it. Not that she depends on her foreign trade; if she chose to do so, Missouri could probably live more comfortably on her own resources than any other State in the Union. She could produce almost everything she needs except coffee and rubber, and doubtless the agricultural experiment stations would soon find substitutes for those luxuries.

But what community would care to be self-contained with such wares to spread its fame? There is, for instance, the corn-cob pipe on which Missouri holds a world-wide monopoly. Wherever a few smokers gather together, a hymn of thanksgiving can be heard for the Missouri meerschaum! Then there is the Missouri mule. He it was who won the war. Indeed he has won all the modern wars. He opened up Cuba for our bankers, he stilled the Boer's insolence, he elevated Japan to the international peerage, he waded through blood in the Balkans, and now he has made the world safe for Poincaré and Mussolini to play in. But he never gets a decoration. He was the only part of the A.E.F. that got left behind in Europe. And a few days ago I saw him trying to win the peace in Haute-Savoie.

We take our religion very seriously—that is, we insist that every man must profess it and on all red-letter days we bow to its authority. We shouldn't think a marriage were valid unless a preacher tied the knot. And any renegade is entitled to a funeral from a church. But on ordinary week-days we don't allow ourselves to be greatly hampered by our faiths. On Sundays the Irish to go mass, the Germans gather in the Lutheran Church, and the rest of us are exhorted from

---

[1]James Reed was elected to the Senate in 1910 as a Wilson Democrat. Frightened of concentration of power in the government, he turned against Wilson's plan to centralize power over the economy and all other reform measures. [D. H. B.]

the Baptist or South Methodist or Presbyterian or Campbellite pulpits. A small Virginian aristocracy is Episcopalian, and Christian Science was growing in power until its recent difficulties. The Latter-Day Saints have won a prescriptive right to their center in Independence. But for other queer peoples we have no time and no toleration. We don't care to be shown that our beliefs are not the only true beliefs. I once heard it whispered that a Baptist minister had gone over to Unitarianism, but the rumor was too awful to follow up. Since the war, we feel the citadels of our faith attacked by a newly strengthened modernism. William Jewell College recently dismissed a professor who had yielded to the temptations of the "higher criticism." Until the final victory is won, we must all be fighting fundamentalists.

As to our politics, they don't much matter. We like the game. A few men— and latterly women—play it and are much admired. A few more spectate. But Missouri was never a "sovereign independent State," and we look upon our State government as merely a local division under a government which has its seat in a far-off Washington. Bill Stone was far more interesting to us when he ruled the bosses at Jefferson City than when he was chairman of the Foreign Affairs Committee of the United States Senate. We pointed with pride when three of our politicians—Clark and Folk and Hadley, not one of them native sons—were ranked among the presidential possibilities in a single electoral year. One reason for the toleration of Reed is the feeling that he wants what he wants when he wants it. In the ordinary campaign the inherited categories of Democrat and Republican are quite enough for us. The Prohibitionists have disappeared. As for being a Socialist, it isn't done. Our farmers were cold to Townley.[2] On the whole, it is men not measures that matter. We endured an obsolete taxation system and an antiquated constitution for a whole generation. We didn't propose to take any newfangled notions from Oklahoma or Wisconsin.

We keep a store of patriotism always ready, and on the war Missouri was ready to follow the lead of the East by going in or by staying out. Once in, it was necessary to have a certain measure of forced taxation in behalf of the Y.M.C.A. and the Red Cross, to prove that we were united. We held in readiness for any pacifist who might appear the same medicine that was administered to Lovejoy in 1836. We insisted that it was not enough for one to say that he was against the Kaiser and for the war—he had also to believe that the Kaiser was a mad dog loose in the world and that the war was a heaven-blessed righteous crusade or we questioned his Americanism. When it came to the peace, we were all for the League of Nations until our politicians got so nervous about it, and now—we wait for a lead from Washington.

Education is a necessity in Missouri, but only for those who are growing up. It ends with the close of the last spring term. A week of Chautauqua each

[2]Arthur Townley, a former Socialist, founded the Nonpartisan League in North Dakota in 1915. [D. H. B.]

summer and three Lyceum evenings during the winter are enough to keep the adults alive to an outside culture. I asked a Baptist home missionary what books he found in the homes he visited. Just two, he said, the Bible and the Sears-Roebuck catalogue. But in the towns, the parlor tables exhibit Wells's *Outline* and the latest Hutchinson novel—Sinclair Lewis would be resented. The State maintains a circulating library, and will send out a case of "standard authors" on proper demand, but the supply is quite equal to the demand.

But Missouri does not read books—she reads magazines and newspapers. Any up-to-date person will know the progress of the latest serial in the *Saturday Evening Post*. We once had a great magazine of our own, great because it introduced America to Spoon River; but his *Mirror* and Reedy were buried in the same grave. The new *Point of View*, published in Kansas City, "for all who are interested in Travel, Art, Architecture, Music and Drama," has yet to make its mark. And once, in Colonel Nelson's lifetime, we had a great newspaper—the paper that introduced daylight saving to America; but today, in spite of its wide territorial influence, the Kansas City *Star* takes no precedence over thirty other dull American dailies. In St. Louis, the *Post-Dispatch* still crusades in an intrepid and intelligent way for an old-fashioned brand of Pulitzer righteousness; and the *Globe-Democrat*, since killing off its hoary rival, the *Republic*, justifies its morning monopoly only by the excellence of its editorial page. But the leadership of the metropolitan dailies is fast waning. Missouri editors have gone to school to Walter Williams and their annual Journalism Week at Columbia is beginning to show results. The smaller cites are developing a press of their own, with United Press service, and the publication of a daily paper is coming to be one of the earmarks of urban respectability.

Another challenge to Missouri's self-satisfaction is bringing learning to the land. The farmers have begun to read government bulletins. The time was, not so many years ago, when the farmers and the homemakers knew more about their jobs than any bureau chief could tell them. But now they have capitulated to hard times and to the craze for modern babies. The farmer kills his hogs, fills his silos, and rotates his crops, and the homemaker cans her cherries, sets her hens, and nurses her baby according to the latest bulletin from the State University.

For the University of Missouri is bringing a revolution in lower as well as in higher education. Thirty years ago, in the pre-country-club period of American college education, it was a sleepy recruiting ground for the learned professions. The first shift came when athletics and highly colored sweaters captured the enthusiasm of the small town high-school boys and girls. The university began to standardize the high schools throughout the State, and that in turn drew it into the job of training the teachers to man them, or more accurately to woman them. The curse of too many colleges has been met by creating the rank of Junior College and by fitting the professional courses at the university onto the sophomore college year. The regimentation of the schools is now all but universal, with a few outstanding exceptions such as the original School of Osteopathy at Kirksville.

And now the College of Agriculture is regimenting the farmers. There are first the clubs to which the boys and girls at home go to spurt themselves in farm endeavor. Then the "short-horn course" at Columbia for the older ones who can be spared from home only during the slack winter months; four months in each of two winters makes a boy into a farmer who will never be a peasant. Then the regular four-year course which is training the farm leaders of the next generation—the county agents, the experiment-station experts, the teachers of agriculture, and the "gentlemen farmers." But most important is the Farmers' Week in January when even the genuine dirt farmers gather at Columbia to listen to lectures, to watch demonstrations, and to civilize up generally. There they courted favor with "Chief Josephine" while still she held the record as the world's largest-producing milch cow. They heard David Lubin once, and when he scolded them for not organizing and controlling their markets they took it sitting down. During the war they entertained an English lord.

It is a revolution which promises freedom from many a tyranny. The chinch-bugs and the chiggers have had their day. The menace of the grasshopper is gone. The weather man has lost his spell. The "hill-billies" are passing. Missouri has begun to be shown—by herself.

The millstone today is bad roads. The Missouri farmer was imprisoned until Henry Ford broke his chains. For fully a third of the year he is still mired in the mud. Recently the members of an automobile club, motoring from the Pacific coast to the automobile show in New York, had to take the train at Kansas City and ship their cars to St. Louis. But the reluctance to learn from road-buliding elsewhere is now yielding, and the Santa Fe Trail and the Jefferson Highway are promising beginnings. A sixty-million-dollar bond issue, a non-partisan highway commission, and a project for primary and secondary roads for the entire State are the progress registered in a single year.

In spite of the mud, or because of it, each new generation seems to find its way out. Many towns seem to be peopled with old men. To Oklahoma, to Idaho, to California the boys go off. And though they never cease to be Missourians, they never come back. Many of them become famous, and a few deserve fame. There are Harlow Shapley, the astronomer at Harvard; Walter Stewart, the teacher at Amherst when Amherst valued teaching; Glenn Frank, the editor of the *Century;* Charles G. Ross, the Washington correspondent; Fred Deering, the Minister to Portugal—to mention only a few who are under forty. Every State has its great men; in Missouri we grow them for the rest of the country. And let it not be forgotten, we gave Mark Twain and Jesse James to the world!

The girls roam less and have a shorter range of opportunity. Everywhere they are teachers. We still have a notion that business is not their sphere. Journalism is opening up to them, and medicine and other social work. Domestic service, being the preserve of the colored folk, is not respectable for the whites. But most of the girls are drawn down that vista of dreariness which we refer to as "Just staying at home." And though we have always had fewer women than men, we count them lucky if the last call for the dining-car does not pass them by. Home means hard work for them, and often valiant sacrifice. But it is a world in which nothing happens.

I chanced to meet one of these stay-at-homes on a train out of St. Louis last Christmas Eve. She was tall, shapely, thin-skinned, with small ankles and small wrists but large feet and large-knuckled hands, and she still nestled up to twenty-five. The crowded condition of the car led to conversation, and I asked where she lived and what she did and what the prospects were. She lived in Warren County; though an artist by temperament, having once had a few lessons with Fannie Bloomfield Zeisler, she was now a farmer; and the prospects were horrible. I dilated on the glories of a life out-of-doors. "You talk like a novel," she replied. "You haven't sat on a plow from sunrise to sundown for fifteen days straight running." "Well, don't you make money?" "We're supposed to be partners—father, mother, and I. But I never see any money."

I asked her how she spent her leisure. She read a bit—she liked Browning's poems and Barrie's plays. But there wasn't a library within forty miles and books were so hard to get. "But for Father Donovan's lending me books and giving me ideas, I'd go mad. Life gets so awfully dull. I get to a point now and then where I feel I can't stand it any longer." I inquired what her escape was. "I have to have a fling. There's no other way out." "Are you returning from a fling now?" "Yes. At breakfast two months ago I told my parents I couldn't go on another day; that I was going away. They asked where, and I said I didn't know. Away! They refused to drive me to the station, so I carried my suit-case and walked the eight miles. Fortunately I had saved a little money from the music class I used to have in Jackson County. I took the first train that came along and went to St. Louis. There I found a hotel, and went out to the theater. Next day I got a job as governess through the Y.W.C.A. The children had been unmanageable, but after a week I got the household straightened out. And tonight I did so hate to leave them. But then—that's not the way I want to live my life."

"And what now?" I asked. "I'm going home. The family want me to marry. But there's no chance to meet anybody except the farmer boys in the neighborhood, and they wouldn't understand why I have to have my fling. Tomorrow I'll feed the pigs, and I guess we'll soon be getting ready to put in the crop." When I had watched her greet her father at the station in Jonesburg, I spent the rest of my journey searching for the secret of a civilization which could produce such a human being.

Perhaps Missouri herself has been a stay-at-home too long. Saddled with the monotony and drudgery of plowing the fields, her life has lacked color. For too long she had no desire to see how the rest of the world was living, not even how it was doing its plowing. She did not want to be shown. But a new era is breaking. Missouri too must have her fling. And she is now beginning to look for it, in a flivver.

MONTANA

Land of the Copper Collar

ARTHUR FISHER

SEPTEMBER 19, 1923

SIX MONTHS is the longest one may live in Montana without making the decision whether one is "for the Company" or "against the Company." Even some members of that ever-growing stream of automobile pilgrims which enters our hot sage-brush plains from North Dakota's prairies and threads its way westward through the irrigated valley of the Yellowstone are frequently to be found enlisted in one camp or the other before they have zigzagged down from some pass over the Rockies and crept along a narrow ledge above a roaring stream through the canyon into Idaho. The all-pervading and unrelenting nature of the struggle admits of no neutrals. Since the territory's admission to statehood in 1889 the struggle has continued. On the one hand, firmly intrenched, stand the ramifying and interlinked corporate interests centering in the copper industry, now under the leadership of the Anaconda Copper Mining Company. On the other stands the rest of the population which feels it has no stake in the Company's prosperity but suffers from the Company's exploitation of every natural resource and profitable privilege, its avoidance of taxation, and its dominance of the political and educational life of the State. The latter side has the largest potential manpower, although the forces of the Company, including all officers, henchmen, agents, sub-agents, employees who feel their livelihood is dependent upon their public attitude, unaffiliated business interests who sell to the Company and its subsidiaries or who must secure banking credits, and professional men to whom business can be thrown and who desire to rise in the social world—all these total a considerable number. But the opposition is only partially united by farmer and labor organizations led by intermittent crusaders for the democratic idea, frequently by men not entirely devoid of personal political ambition, although even for these the risks and the sacrifices are by no means small. But the Company is led by a single united command of professional soldiers designated in Montana by the term "on the pay roll." The local field office in Butte is popularly known as "The Fourth Floor of the Hennesey Building"—awe-inspiring title. Of the general headquarters back of the lines, ultimate source of all authority, Montanans are never reminded by the local press except when a short news item announces that the private car of Mr. John D. Ryan or Mr. Con Kelly arrived on the Missoula or Great Falls or Butte siding last night—from New York City.

This important event usually occurs just prior to the breaking out of one of the big engagements, the biennial election, when the heavy guns are brought up and the very heavens are torn by the thunder of the campaign artillery and illumined by the fireworks of the press. Money is poured out like water; and men fall by the hundred before the temptations of the bribe-giver or the promise of future preferment, and the fear of the consequences if they do not yield. Frequently the atmosphere is charged to such a point that neighbor hardly dares speak to neighbor, and entire communities are rent in two by passion and fear.

Between the major campaigns ceaseless guerrilla warfare is waged, now and then breaking out in the form of a labor battle in the mining camps, the ambushing of a teacher in the State University, or the shooting in the back of some small business man who talked too independently. In addition a continuous flood of propaganda is poured out by the Company press, which includes nearly every daily paper and most of the weeklies, to maintain morale and win new recruits. Every newcomer to the State is approached through suggestion and advice, through business pressure and social temptation, until the day when he expresses some sentiment which henceforth throws him definitely into one camp or the other. Thereafter he is fair game for the side which he has slighted. And there are no closed seasons. The struggle of the Company to maintain its rule and its privileges against the people's attempts to subject it to democratic control is an economic and political conflict in which the entire social development of the State is inextricably interwoven. But the conflict is more than that. It is the leading sporting event in Montana life.

What the Harvard-Yale game is to intercollegiate football, what the Davis Cup matches are to international tennis, what the Grand National is to the English racing world, the World's Series to baseball, the Mardi Gras to New Orleans, or the Rose Festival to Portland, what a good county court-house trial used to be before the days of the movie, all this and more the battles with the Company are to Montana. They form Montana's epic; an epic told through ten thousand newspaper editorials, ten thousand stump speeches, ten thousand unwritten anecdotes. The universal topic of conversation, it serves as a common interest to unite the people of the State even as at the same time it separates them into two warring camps.

Just now the key to every major operation in the conflict is a short clause in the State constitution, adopted when Montana entered the Union with the purpose of encouraging the mining industry to develop the State, and remaining unchanged since then. This clause provides that mineral lands shall not be assessed for purposes of taxation at a higher value than the price at which the lands were acquired from the Federal Government. As in no case did this amount exceed $5 an acre, and as today many of these holdings in "the richest hill in the world,'' as Butte proudly boasts, are worth many hundreds of thousands of dollars, it is not difficult to understand why the Company considers expenditure of unmeasured sums for the purpose of winning an election or for "publicity and education" justified by the strictest business considerations.

Just at present the severe agricultural depression through which the State is passing has brought all tax issues to the front and has united the forces demanding a revision of the constitutional provision, so that the Company has succeeded in blocking reform only by the narrowest of margins. Prosperity may disunite the people before the change is effected. But some day, perhaps in five years, perhaps in twenty, this peculiarly crude and obviously discriminatory constitutional privilege is certain to be remedied. It is by no means as certain, however, that this will end the struggle between the people and the Company. The situation in Montana is not the same or as simple as that which formerly existed in most of the Middle Western States in the old days of railway rule. In Montana the railways have long since yielded first place to the Company. They still, of course, employ expert lobbyists, but they attempt no wholesale winning of elections nor purchase of legislatures. In a State with only half a million population, which it takes as long to cross by limited train as it does to go from Chicago to New York, the influence of three transcontinental railway systems is by no means slight. And although there is considerable talk of taking the public into the railways' confidence, there is good reason for suspicion that the bonds of unity of interest reaching out from higher banking circles lead the railways to take the Company more often into its confidence than the public—and to find reasons for siding with the Company in its hottest battles.

These battles will not end so long as the Company remains a combination of all the really profitable privileges and large-scale undertakings in the State. Copper is only the core. Surrounding this core are the largest lumber interests in the State; and the untouched timber resources in the jumble of mountain ranges which cross Montana, reaching their highest point in the Continental Divide, are extensive and are controlled by the Anaconda Company. So also are the principal banks, the largest water-power company, the smelters, coal companies, land companies, public utilities, newspapers, mercantile concerns. Where there is not outright ownership by the Company there is identity of interest and an affiliation which reaches the same end of harmonious and united action. All this is the Company; and the Company is more than this; for it controls in Connecticut the largest American brass company and domestic user of copper, and controls extensive ore deposits in South America and other parts of the world. When the constitutional mining-tax clause is a thing of the past, the struggle will still go on, widened, more complex, more difficult to dramatize, but no less vital to the success of the democratic ideal in our third largest State.

Unlike the situation in some other States, such as Delaware, where the power of the Du Ponts is perhaps even more complete and no less ramifying and carefully protected by every outwork and fortification of control of education and public opinion, the Montana fight is characterized by its openness and the vigor

of the champions on either side. There is no supine admission of the hopelessness of the struggle, no silent submission to an insidious all-embracing octopus.
In Montana the copper collar shines brazenly forth for all to see. Davids go
bravely forth to the blare of trumpets to battle with Goliath. And their whitening
bones strew the wayside like the skulls of the bison which once in countless
thousands roamed Montana's plains.

The tradition of the open fight began in Montana in the days before the copper
industry had been brought under one single dominant control as it is today. The
mining interests worked together against the live-stock men and the rest of the
State, but within their own ranks there were vigorous clashes in which Irish labor followed Irish mine owner against opposing operators with the traditional
loyalty and fighting spirit of the old country clans. The occasion for these sanguinary battles between companies has passed and the Irish blood has been
largely replaced by immigrants from Southern Europe but the fighting spirit and
much of the Irish leadership lives on. Nor has the fighting spirit failed to draw
some sustenance in blood and traditions from districts removed from the mining
camps. Montana cherishes her traditions and has developed a form of ancestor
worship of which hardly less is heard than in Massachusetts Bay itself—albeit
the canvas of Montana's Mayflowers was nailed down on the hoops topping
heavy prairie schooners, and her pilgrim fathers bear the locally revered title of
"the pioneers." These traditions speak much of vigilantes, of posses, of hangings after quick trials, of cattle wars against homesteaders and sheep men, of
Indian wars and Custer's last stand.

The hand-to-hand engagements of most of the battles of today occur in or
about the trenches of the Butte hill—that city in size and downtown appearance,
perched on a gashed and torn foothill of the Rockies, shafts and drifts and tunnels and ore dumps cropping up between skyscrapers and prosperous downtown
clubs and churches, a city, yet no more than "the biggest mining camp in the
world." Seen from a distance at night as the limited train starts crawling down
from the crest of the Continental Divide it is not unbeautiful, a hill of sparkling
lights under a cloudless heaven of stars. At noon with a hot sun beating down
from that same cloudless sky upon a jumble of tall buildings and shacks, not a
spear of grass or other vegetation in sight, clouds of dust swirling through the
streets filled with miners idle through a lay-off, the blacklist, or a preference for
bumming to going back into the deep hot mines, it is as forbidding a town as any
in the United States. Either in the heat of summer or in the severe cold of the
winter it is a town where the thin air of the high altitude stimulates men's nerves
and their appetites for the night life of the mining camp; and readily turns the
hard-faced restless crowd full of injured, limbless, and diseased men into a mob.

These physical conditions and the nature of the occupation have had none of
their raw edges smoothed by the labor policies of the Company. The temperature
in the mines is commonly above 100 degrees, and the men's lungs are eaten by
the dust and their skin by the drip of the copper-impregnated water on bare,
stooping backs. Following periods of tremendous profits, such as that enjoyed

Smelter at Butte. Located in the heart of the largest copper-producing region in the world, Butte was the industrial headquarters of the Anaconda Copper Mining Company. Known in the state simply as "The Company," the corporation dominated state politics and culture.

during the war, the mines and smelters have been closed without the slightest provision for the mass of the employees or their families. It is not strange that few men undertake the burden of a family which must almost of necessity trans-form them into abject slaves of the Company. The intemperance, instability, and violence of the Butte labor movement and its publications—foremost of these the sometimes brilliant and always radical Butte *Bulletin*—are the natural result of conditions in Butte and of the labor policies of the Anaconda Copper Mining Company and the personnel of local managers selected by absentee ownership.

But Butte is not Montana, nor are even the smelter towns of Anaconda and Great Falls and other lesser mining districts Montana in any other sense than that they caricature the ultimate product of the Montana conflict, the symbol of which is the body of the union organizer Frank Little hanging from a railway trestle, or the office of the Butte *Daily Bulletin* in an abandoned church guarded by a "red guard" of rifles through a night of battle, a night, be it said, not en-tirely unwelcomed by the members of that "red guard," the fiery writers of the *Bulletin,* and the officers of the local O.B.U. and I.W.W.

Up to the outbreak of the World War, and even for a year or so thereafter, almost anyone in Montana would have risked the prophecy that another decade would see agriculture the dominant interest of the State. It seemed certain that a new weight was to be thrown into the scales of battle and that the Company would soon have to yield to the new battalions arriving by the trainload, lured by the vivid recruiting literature and enticements of the railroads and the State immigration service—lawyers, mechanics, teachers, factory hands, clerks, doctors, farmers from the Middle West, none familiar with the peculiar problems either of dry-farming or irrigation, all hoping to find their Eldorado. For a few years those who first turned the sparse desert sod in this new migration prospered. They enjoyed better than normal rainfall and better than normal prices for wheat. Then followed four years in which the rainfall dropped from the 16-inch average to 8 inches, and the price of wheat was cut more than in half. Many a dry-land home miles from water or tree knew actual hunger, and all knew privation, disappointment, and misery as they saw green fields wither and die before the hot winds. And even the irrigated districts saw all profits disappear before low prices, high transportation rates, and burdensome charges for water.

So today these acres on the margin of profitable cultivation which are Montana—on the margin both because of scanty rainfall and the cost of placing water on the land—are being foreclosed and abandoned wholesale. In some dry counties of Montana 80 per cent of the farm lands have reverted to the State for failure to pay taxes, and bank after bank has closed its doors. Pressure of population is almost certain to make the irrigated districts ultimately profitable for those who can hang on, or for their successors. In the meantime the Federal irrigation service will have to wait for repayment of its expenditure and even for interest on the money. But whether the great dry-land area of Montana will ever be more than a siren temptress to the uninformed—one good crop year and two failures—remains to be seen. The possibilities of science in soil culture and in plant breeding are beyond prediction; western Nebraska and Kansas, with hardly more rainfall than eastern Montana's average, were once abandoned by the first disillusioned victims of the railway settlers' bureaus. Science in marketing methods and cooperative distributing may also do much. But in the meantime the once-tilled lands of dry Montana are going back to the cattle range, a range scarred and ruined for years to come by the turning of the natural sod.

"Montana's real trouble," said an old rancher to me, "is that her graveyards aren't big enough." He explained that he was not advocating a general resort to the hangings of vigilante days, nor even waiting until a new generation came on the scene, but that more Montanans must come to look upon the State as their permanent home and final resting place. From the first pioneers who washed their fortunes out of the gold placers, with hydraulic pressure turning pleasant hillsides into desolate wastes of boulders, nearly all who have come to Montana have looked forward to the day when they would have accumulated sufficient funds to permit them to live out the remainder of their days in southern California, Florida, or New York. Now and then a big brown stone house is erected on the hilly streets of Helena as a monument to financial success; but the owners are usually found living elsewhere. And the mansion of Montana's richest citizen, who still keeps his local legal residence (whether out of sentiment or to avoid income and inheritance taxes is not known), stands on Fifth Avenue, New York City—the "home" of ex-Senator W. A. Clark.

Unlike such a State as Colorado, where the tourist population almost exceeds the resident population and is one of the State's leading industries, Montana has done little to promote tourist traffic. Glacier Park is the advertising product of one railway and the plaything of the son of a great railway pioneer who opened up northern Montana, James J. Hill. It has hardly yet repaid interest on the investment, though its striking beauty may before long do so. Other sections of Montana's mountains are hardly less attractive; yet they have not been capitalized to the extent even of the establishment of the "dude ranches" of Wyoming. Nevertheless every Montana rancher feels he has neglected his family if he is unable to find some period between planting or irrigating or harvesting or fall plowing when he can pack them all into a car or wagon, leaving the stock in charge of relatives or neighbors, and take a camping, fishing, or hunting trip in the hills.

Indeed, a symbol of Montana second only to the copper collar itself is that of a fisherman whipping a trout stream. No single subject in the legislature evokes the statewide attention, the enthusiasm, or the intelligent interest of a debate on the biennial revision of the fish and game laws. But even in this fact the coils of the Anaconda may be seen. Native Montanans who can sell nothing directly to the tourist trade are not enthusiastic about poachers on their fishing preserves; and it is expensive to build roads which will stand up under the wheels of the endless chain of cars which goes trekking across the State piled high and bulging sidewise with tents, extra cans of oil and gas, blanket rolls, and every sort of paraphernalia, the dust hardly given time to settle before it is stirred up by the Ford behind. Although rain may turn this duct into a quagmire of mud—the famous gumbo—in the course of a few moments' shower, and all automobile traffic of whatever nature be forced to suspend, no trip or family picnic is ever spoiled for a native Montanan by rain. In the midst of the hardest downpour or the most prolonged drizzle, whether in town or country, he greets everyone he meets with a broad smile.

"Fine weather, isn't it?" he beams.

"Another million-dollar shower," is the response.

"If we get one more like this the crop is made."

Doubtless even the officials of the Company welcome a real Montana soaker, and watch with satisfaction the official rain gauge creep upwards, in the critical time of year, above the 8-inch minimum to the 16-inch average, even though they never find time to say so in the midst of their praises of the benefits to the State of A.C.M. development and their denunciations as dangerous radicals of every member of farmer organization, labor union, or independent political group. For in a personal way the Company's officialdom and subordinates are for the most part "good fellows" who have risen from the ranks; something of the free and easy ways of the mining camp or the open range still clinging to them; and Montana is still too young and too near to the frontier to have yet produced that worst of human products, snobbery and the glowering resentment of a long-submerged people. In Montana one may still speak to a man as a man—before drilling him or his business or his reputation full of holes.

NEBRASKA

The End of the First Cycle

WILLA SIBERT CATHER

SEPTEMBER 5, 1923

THE STATE OF NEBRASKA is part of the great plain which stretches west of the Missouri River, gradually rising until it reaches the Rocky Mountains. The character of all this country between the river and the mountains is essentially the same throughout its extent: a rolling, alluvial plain, growing gradually more sandy toward the west, until it breaks into the white sand-hills of western Nebraska and Kansas and eastern Colorado. From east to west this plain measures something over five hundred miles; in appearance it resembles the wheat lands of Russia, which fed the continent of Europe for so many years. Like Little Russia it is watered by slow-flowing, muddy rivers, which run full in the spring, often cutting into the farm lands along their banks; but by midsummer they lie low and shrunken, their current split by glistening white sand-bars half overgrown with scrub willows.

The climate, with its extremes of temperature, gives to this plateau the variety which, to the casual eye at least, it lacks. There we have short, bitter winters; windy, flower-laden springs; long, hot summers; triumphant autumns that last until Christmas—a season of perpetual sunlight, blazing blue skies, and frosty nights. In this newest part of the New World autumn is the season of beauty and sentiment, as spring is in the Old World.

Nebraska is a newer State than Kansas. It was a State before there were people in it. Its social history falls easily within a period of sixty years, and the first stable settlements of white men were made within the memory of old folk now living. The earliest of these settlements—Bellevue, Omaha, Brownville, Nebraska City—were founded along the Missouri River, which was at that time a pathway for small steamers. In 1855–60 these four towns were straggling groups of log houses, hidden away along the wooded river banks.

Before 1860 civilization did no more than nibble at the eastern edge of the State, along the river bluffs. Lincoln, the present capital, was open prairie; and the whole of the great plain to the westward was still a sunny wilderness, where the tall red grass and the buffalo and the Indian hunter were undisturbed. Fre-

220

mont, with Kit Carson, the famous scout, had gone across Nebraska in 1842, exploring the valley of the Platte. In the days of the Mormon persecution fifteen thousand Mormons camped for two years, 1845–46, six miles north of Omaha, while their exploring parties went farther west, searching for fertile land outside of government jurisdiction. In 1847 the entire Mormon sect, under the leadership of Brigham Young, went with their wagons through Nebraska and on to that desert beside the salty sea which they have made so fruitful.

In forty-nine and the early fifties, gold hunters, bound for California, crossed the State in thousands, always following the old Indian trail along the Platte valley. The State was a highway for dreamers and adventurers; men who were in quest of gold or grace, freedom or romance. With all these people the road led out, but never back again.

While Nebraska was a camping-ground for seekers outward bound, the wooden settlements along the Missouri were growing into something permanent. The settlers broke the ground and began to plant the fine orchards which have ever since been the pride of Otoe and Nemaha counties. It was at Brownville that the first telegraph wire was brought across the Missouri River. When I was a child I heard ex-Governor Furness relate how he stood with other pioneers in the log cabin where the Morse instrument had been installed, and how, when it began to click, the men took off their hats as if they were in church. The first message flashed across the river into Nebraska was not a market report, but a line of poetry: "Westward the course of empire takes its way." The Old West was like that.

The first back-and-forth travel through the State was by way of the Overland Mail, a monthly passenger-and-mail-stage service across the plains from Independence to the newly founded colony at Salt Lake—a distance of twelve hundred miles.

When silver ore was discovered in the mountains of Colorado near Cherry Creek—afterward Camp Denver and later the city of Denver—a picturesque form of commerce developed across the great plain of Nebraska: the transporting of food and merchandise from the Missouri to the Colorado mining camps, and on to the Mormon settlement at Salt Lake. One of the largest freighting companies, operating out of Nebraska City, in the six summer months of 1860 carried nearly three million pounds of freight across Nebraska, employing 515 wagons, 5,687 oxen, and 600 drivers.

The freighting began in the early spring, usually about the middle of April, and continued all summer and through the long, warm autumns. The oxen made from ten to twenty miles a day. I have heard the old freighters say that, after embarking on their six-hundred mile trail, they lost count of the days of the week and the days of the month. While they were out in that sea of waving grass, one day was like another; and, if one can trust the memory of these old men, all the days were glorious. The buffalo trails still ran north and south then; deep, dusty paths the bison wore when, single file, they came north in the spring for the summer grass, and went south again in the autumn. Along these trails were the buffalo "wallows"—shallow depressions where the rain water gathered when it ran off the tough prairie sod. These wallows the big beasts wore deeper and packed hard when they rolled about and bathed in the pools, so that they held water like a cement bottom. The freighters lived on game and shot the buffalo for their hides. The grass was full of quail and prairie chickens, and flocks of wild ducks swam about on the lagoons. These lagoons have long since disappeared, but they were beautiful things in their time; long stretches where the rain water gathered and lay clear on a grassy bottom without mud. From the lagoons the first settlers hauled water to their homesteads, before they had dug their wells. The freighters could recognize the lagoons from afar by the clouds of golden coreopsis which grew up out of the water and waved delicately above its surface. Among the pioneers the coreopsis was known simply as "the lagoon flower."

As the railroads came in, the freighting business died out. Many a freight-driver settled down upon some spot he had come to like on his journeys to and fro, homesteaded it, and wandered no more. The Union Pacific, the first transcontinental railroad, was completed in 1869. The Burlington entered Nebraska in the same year, at Platsmouth, and began construction westward. It finally reached Denver by an indirect route, and went on extending and ramifying through the State. With the railroads came the home-seeking people from overseas.

When the first courageous settlers came straggling out through the waste with their oxen and covered wagons, they found open range all the way from Lincoln to Denver; a continuous, undulating plateau, covered with long, red, shaggy grass. The prairie was green only where it had been burned off in the spring by the new settlers or by the Indians, and toward autumn even the new grass became a coppery brown. This sod, which had never been broken by the plow, was so tough and strong with the knotted grass roots of many years, that the home-seekers were able to peel it off the earth like peat, cut it up into bricks, and make of it warm, comfortable, durable houses. Some of these sod houses lingered on until the open range was gone and the grass was gone, and the whole face of the country had been changed.

Even as late as 1885 the central part of the State, and everything to the westward, was, in the main, raw prairie. The cultivated fields and broken land seemed mere scratches in the brown, running steppe that never stopped until it broke against the foothills of the Rockies. The dugouts and sod farm-houses were three or four miles apart, and the only means of communication was the heavy farm wagon, drawn by heavy work horses. The early population of Nebraska was largely transatlantic. The county in which I grew up, in the south-central part of the State, was typical. On Sunday we could drive to a Norwegian church and listen to a sermon in that language, or to a Danish or a Swedish church. We could go to the French Catholic settlement in the next county and hear a sermon in French, or into the Bohemian township and hear one in Czech, or we could go to church with the German Lutherans. There were, of course, American congregations also.

There is a Prague in Nebraska as well as in Bohemia. Many of our Czech immigrants were people of a very superior type. The political emigration resulting from the revolutionary disturbances of 1848 was distinctly different from the emigration resulting from economic causes, and brought to the United States brilliant young men both from Germany and Bohemia. In Nebraska our Czech settlements were large and very prosperous. I have walked about the streets of Wilber, the county seat of Saline County, for a whole day without hearing a word of English spoken. In Wilber, in the old days, behind the big, friendly brick saloon—it was not a "saloon," properly speaking, but a beer garden, where the farmers ate their lunch when they came to town—there was a pleasant little theater where the boys and girls were trained to give the masterpieces of Czech drama in the Czech language. "Americanization" has doubtless done away with all this. Our lawmakers have a rooted conviction that a boy can be a better American if he speaks only one language than if he speaks two. I could name a dozen Bohemian towns in Nebraska where one used to be able to go into a bakery and buy better pastry than is to be had anywhere except in the best pastry shops of Prague or Vienna. The American lard pie never corrupted the Czech.

Cultivated, restless young men from Europe made incongruous figures among the hard-handed breakers of the soil. Frederick Amiel's nephew lived for many years and finally died among the Nebraska farmers. Amiel's letters to his kinsman were published in the *Atlantic Monthly* of March, 1921, under the title "Amiel in Nebraska." Camille Saint-Saëns's cousin lived just over the line, in Kansas. Knut Hamsun, the Norwegian writer who was awarded the Nobel Prize for 1920, was a "hired hand" on a Dakota farm to the north of us. Colonies of European people, Slavonic, Germanic, Scandinavian, Latin, spread across our bronze prairies like the daubs of color on a painter's palette. They brought with them something that this neutral new world needed even more than the immigrants needed land.

Unfortunately, their American neighbors were seldom open-minded enough to understand the Europeans, or to profit by their older traditions. Our settlers from New England, cautious and convinced of their own superiority, kept themselves insulated as much as possible from foreign influences. The incomers from the South—from Missouri, Kentucky, the two Virginias—were provincial and utterly without curiosity. They were kind neighbors—lent a hand to help a Swede when he was sick or in trouble. But I am quite sure that Knut Hamsun might have worked a year for any one of our Southern farmers, and his employer would never have discovered that there was anything unusual about the Norwegian. A New England settler might have noticed that his chore-boy had a kind of intelligence, but he would have distrusted and stonily disregarded it. If the daughter of a shiftless West Virginia mountaineer married the nephew of a professor at the University of Upsala, the native family felt disgraced by such an alliance.

Nevertheless, the thrift and intelligence of its preponderant European population have been potent factors in bringing about the present prosperity of the State. The census of 1910 showed that there were then 228,648 foreign-born and native-born Germans living in Nebraska; 103,503 Scandinavians; 50,680 Czechs. The total foreign population of the State was then 900,571, while the entire population was 1,192,214. That is, in round numbers, there were about nine hundred thousand foreign Americans in the State, to three hundred thousand native stock. With such a majority of foreign stock, nine to three, it would be absurd to say that the influence of the European does not cross the boundary of his own acres, and has had nothing to do with shaping the social ideals of the commonwealth.

When I stop at one of the graveyards in my own county, and see on the headstones the names of fine old men I used to know: *"Eric Ericson, born Bergen, Norway . . . died Nebraska," "Anton Pucelik, born Prague, Bohemia . . . died Nebraska,"* I have always the hope that something went into the ground with those pioneers that will one day come out again. Something that will come out not only in sturdy traits of character, but in elasticity of mind, in an honest attitude toward the realities of life, in certain qualities of feeling and imagination. Some years ago a professor at the University of Nebraska happened to tell me about a boy in one of his Greek classes who had a very unusual taste for the classics—intuitions and perceptions in literature. This puzzled him, he said, as the boy's parents had no interest in such things. I knew what the professor did not: that, though this boy had an American name, his grandfather was a Norwegian, a musician of high attainment, a fellow-student and life-long friend of Edvard Grieg. It is in that great cosmopolitan country known as the Middle West that we may hope to see the hard molds of American provincialism broken up; that we may hope to find young talent which will challenge the pale proprieties, the insincere, conventional optimism of our art and thought.

The rapid industrial development of Nebraska, which began in the latter eighties, was arrested in the years 1893–97 by a succession of crop failures and by the financial depression which spread over the whole country at that time—the depression which produced the People's Party and the Free Silver agitation. These years of trial, as everyone now realizes, had a salutary effect upon the new State. They winnowed out the settlers with a purpose from the drifting malcontents who are ever seeking a land where man does not live by the sweat of his brow. The slack farmer moved on. Superfluous banks failed, and many lenders who drove hard bargains with desperate men came to grief. The strongest stock survived, and within ten years those who had weathered the storm came into their reward. What that reward is, you can see for yourself in you motor through the State from Omaha to the Colorado line. The country has no secrets; it is as open as an honest human face.

The old, isolated farms have come together. They rub shoulders. The whole State is a farm. Now it is the pasture lands that look little and lonely, crowded in among so much wheat and corn. It is scarcely an exaggeration to say that every farmer owns an automobile. I believe the last estimate showed that there is one motor car for every six inhabitants in Nebraska. The great grain fields are plowed by tractors. The old farm houses are rapidly being replaced by more cheerful dwellings, with bathrooms and hardwood floors, heated by furnaces or hot-water plants. Many of them are lighted by electricity, and every farm house has its telephone. The country towns are clean and well kept. On Saturday night the main street is a long black line of parked motor cars; the farmers have brought their families to town to see the moving-picture show. When the school bell rings on Monday morning, crowds of happy looking children, well nourished—for the most part well mannered, too—flock along the shady streets. They wear cheerful, modern clothes, and the girls, like the boys, are elastic and vigorous in their movements. These thousands and thousands of children—in the little towns and in the country schools—these, of course, ten years from now, will be the State.

In this time of prosperity any farmer boy who wishes to study at the State University can do so. A New York lawyer who went out to Lincoln to assist in training the university students for military service in war time exclaimed when he came back: "What splendid young men! I would not have believed that any school in the world could get together so many boys physically fit, and so few unfit."

Of course, there is the other side of the medal, stamped with the ugly crest of materialism, which has set it seal upon all of our most productive commonwealths. Too much prosperity, too many moving-picture shows, too much gaudy fiction have colored the taste and manners of so many of these Nebraskans of the future. There, as elsewhere, one finds the frenzy to be showy; farmer boys who wish to be spenders before they are earners, girls who try to look like the heroines of the cinema screen; a coming generation which tries to cheat its aesthetic sense by buying things instead of making anything. There is even danger that that fine institution, the University of Nebraska, may become a gigantic trade school. The men who control its destiny, the regents and the lawmakers, wish their sons and daughters to study machines, mercantile processes, "the principles of business"; everything that has to do with the game of getting on in the world—and nothing else. The classics, the humanities, are having their dark hour. They are in eclipse. Studies that develop taste and enrich personality are not encouraged. But the "Classics" have a way of revenging themselves. One may venture to hope that the children, or the grandchildren, of a generation that goes to a university to select only the most utilitarian subjects in the course of study—among them, salesmanship and dressmaking—will revolt against all the heaped-up, machine-made materialism about them. They will go back to the old sources of culture and wisdom—not as a duty, but with burning desire.

In Nebraska, as in so many other States, we must face the fact that the splendid story of the pioneers is finished, and that no new story worthy to take its place has yet begun. The generation that subdued the wild land and broke up the virgin prairie is passing, but it is still there, a group of rugged figures in the background which inspire respect, compel admiration. With these old men and women the attainment of material prosperity was a moral victory, because it was wrung from hard conditions, was the result of a struggle that tested character.

They can look out over those broad stretches of fertility and say: "We made this, with our backs and hands." The sons, the generation now in middle life, were reared amid hardships, and it is perhaps natural that they should be very much interested in material comfort, in buying whatever is expensive and ugly. Their fathers came into a wilderness and had to make everything, had to be as ingenious as shipwrecked sailors. The generation now in the driver's seat hates to make anything, wants to live and die in an automobile, scudding past those acres where the old men used to follow the long corn-rows up and down. They want to buy everything ready-made: clothes, food, education, music, pleasure. Will the third generation—the full-blooded, joyous one just coming over the hill— will it be fooled? Will it believe that to live easily is to live happily?

The wave of generous idealism, of noble seriousness, which swept over the State of Nebraska in 1917 and 1918, demonstrated how fluid and flexible is any living, growing, expanding society. If such "conversions" do not last, they at least show of what men and women are capable. Surely the materialism and showy extravagance of this hour are a passing phase! They will mean no more in half a century from now than will the "hard times" of twenty-five years ago— which are already forgotten. The population is as clean and full of vigor as the soil; there are no old grudges, no heritages of disease or hate. The belief that snug success and easy money are the real aims of human life has settled down over our prairies, but it has not yet hardened into molds and crusts. The people are warm, mercurial, impressionable, restless, over-fond of novelty and change. These are not the qualities which make the dull chapters of history.

NEVADA

Beautiful Desert of Buried Hopes

ANNE MARTIN

JULY 26, 1922

NEVADA to most Easterners suggest divorces, or gambling in mining shares of doubtful value on the New York or Philadelphia stock exchange. Some, more informed, have heard of our "big bonanza" mines which produced nearly a billion dollars in silver after the Civil War, thus helping to restore national credit, and incidentally producing a crop of millionaires and adventurers, some of whom have won seats in the United States Senate. The wild and woolly" character of the pioneer mining State fixed on her by Mark Twain in *Roughing It* still clings in the popular mind and is confirmed by most of the news that seeps through the press. Few outsiders have ever heard of her agriculture or any constructive activities, and no one with eyes can see her as anything but a vast, exploited, undeveloped State with a meager and boss-ridden population. Those who wish more information will find in reference books that Nevada began well. She was admitted into the Union in 1864 as the "battle-born State," to give President Lincoln additional support in the Senate, and with her vast domain and natural resources gave great promise. Almost as old as Kansas, Minnesota, and West Virginia, and older than Nebraska, Colorado, the Dakotas, Montana, and all other Far Western States except California and Oregon, "youth" cannot explain away her backwardness and vagaries, her bizarre history, her position as the ugly duckling, the disappointment, the neglected step-child, the weakling in the family of States, despite her charm and beauty and great natural advantages.

The casual railway traveler who has crossed Nevada remembers with wonder or weariness, according to temperament, her twelve hours of "desert" plain, her endless chain of sunny sage-brush valleys surrounded by opalescent mountains, all fertile land but valueless without water, and all without sign of water or habitation, excepting a few railroad tanks and straggling towns, or the drying bed of a river. Reformers know her as perhaps the most "wide-open" State of the West, where prize-fighting, gambling, and saloons have been encouraged greatly to flourish, and where the six-months' divorce still reigns, backed by legal and business interests of Reno. They remember her as the last Western

State to adopt woman suffrage, and one of the last to accept State prohibition. She is the despair not only of reformers but of case-hardened lawyers, who must be agile indeed to keep pace with the rapid and contradictory changes in laws made every two years by servile legislatures, at the command of the selfish interests which elected them. To national political leaders she is known as a "doubtful State, a "pocket-borough," which can be swung more easily than any other into the Republican or Democratic column, according to the amount of money used by either side. (She should therefore not be called "doubtful," but *sure*.) She is known as a State where politicians, irrespective of party, cynically combine every campaign to elect congressmen and legislatures pleasing to the "interests." These legislatures so chosen are largely migratory. Some members have been known to leave the State, pockets bulging, by the midnight train after adjournment. I recall the difficulty experienced by a former governor in securing a quorum for a special session, as many of our itinerant legislators were already far afield in other States, or in Mexico, Alaska, South America, and South Africa.

It must be admitted there are other Western States which differ only in degree. But what makes Nevada an extreme example? Why has she a larger proportionate number of migratory laborers (as of legislators), of homeless men, than any of her neighbors? Why is she the most "male" State in the Union, with more than twice as many men as women, and the smallest proportionate number of women and children? Why has she the smallest and sparsest population of any State, and why has it decreased since 1910? Why has she a peripatetic male electorate nearly half of which has vanished by the next election, with new voters taking their places who will themselves soon vanish? Why is she perhaps the most backward State in precautions against the spread of venereal diseases, the most shameless in her flaunting of prostitution and red-light districts, surrounded by high board fences, to the children of the towns? With no large cities and a largely rural population, why has she a greater percentage in her jails and prison, her almshouses and insane asylum than certain of her neighbors? How can we account for these extreme peculiarities of her industrial, political, and social life?

The migratory character of mining and railway labor has some influence, but the fundamental cause of every one of these conditions undoubtedly lies in the monopoly by the live-stock industry of the water, the watered lands, and the public range lands of the State. At first blush this may sound like saying that sun-spots cause insanity, or that there is an epidemic of pellagra in the South, of small-pox in China, or of cholera in Russia because Wall Street governs us in Washington. But the relation of cause and effect in Nevada is clear. Some may insist that her backwardness is due to her exploitation from the very beginning by the railroads; others, that the mining interests have picked the vitals from her, have taken everything out and given nothing back: witness San Francisco's and even some of New York's finest structures built largely with bullion from her "ghost cities," the Postal Telegraph and Cable system which girdles the globe by means of the Mackay millions[1] taken from the quickly gutted Comstock lode, the Guggenheim and other similar interests still picking the bones for all that is left! True; but mere exploitation by railroads and mine owners does not account for the condition in which we find her today. Other Western States with comparable natural resources have been similarly exploited, and are not a "notorious bad example" of political, economic, and social degeneration.

The live-stock industry, established as a monopoly in Nevada under very extraordinary conditions, is responsible. It has prevented the development of small farms, of family life, of a stable agricultural population, and has produced instead an excessive proportion of migratory laborers and of homeless men, larger than any State in the Union. The 1910 census figures give 220 men to every 100 women. The number of married women in the State is about one-third the number of men. The number of children from six to fourteen years is less than two-fifths of the usual average in other States. Utah, for example, with natural resources not much larger than Nevada, has more than eight times as many school children. (The 1920 census figures so far received show an improvement in these proportions more apparent than real, due chiefly to the reduction of the homeless male population since 1910 by the migration of thousands from dying mining camps.) It appears that practically one-half the men of Nevada, or nearly 20,000 out of our total population of nearly 80,000, are living under bad social conditions outside the home environment, as cowboys, sheep-herders, hay-hands, miners, and railwaymen, sleeping in company bunk-houses or on the range, and dependent for their few pleasures and social contacts on the frontier towns the traveler sees from the train window. These afford a movie, perhaps, certainly a gambling house with bootleg whiskey, and a "restricted district" behind a stockade, in which the women are "medically inspected" (for a price) while the men are not.

A characteristic Nevada sight, and to those who know its significance one of the most pathetic, is the large groups of roughly dressed men aimlessly wandering about the streets or standing on the street corners of Reno, Lovelock, Winnemucca, Battle Mountain, Elko, Wells, Ely, Tonopah, Goldfield, and other towns, every day in the year. They are in from the ranches and mines for a holiday with hard-earned money, and the only place they have to spend it is in the numerous men's lodging houses, gambling dens, or brothels. In our suffrage campaign in 1914 and in later campaigns we found it always possible to gather these men into a quick, responsive, and generous street audience. But a large proportion of them are wanderers, and are, of course, prevented from voting by the election laws. Of those who can vote many have most naturally no sense of civic responsibility and are easily corrupted by the political machine. If instead of the land and water monopoly by the live-stock interests for the almost exclusive production of hay, cattle, and sheep, this same land with water, now

[1]John Mackay was founder of the Commercial Cable Company (1883) and the Postal Telegraph Company (1886), which broke Jay Gould's communications monopoly. [D. H. B.]

Silver mining town, Nevada. In the early years of settlement, the state was dotted with such towns, in which civic services were minimal. Note the parallel streets connected only by wooden walkways and the rudimentary water-supply system.

manned chiefly by "ranch-hands" and in the hay-making season by a large influx of migratory hay-hands, were subdivided into small farms for diversified and intensive agriculture, Nevada would soon have many new homes with women and children in them, she would soon have a large and growing farm population, larger towns and community centers, and greater social stability, instead of languishing on as an exhausted weakling in the sisterhood of States. But the strangle-hold of the live-stock interests continues as the cause of the mortal illness from which she is suffering, and to grasp the case we must consider some physical features.

Nevada's area is 110,000 square miles, more than twice as large as New York or Pennsylvania. Her population is 77,000, or about one person to every one and one-half square miles. Her *land* area is more than 70,000,000 acres, of which nearly 90 per cent is still owned by the National Government. The remainder is chiefly land granted by the Government to the railroad, with the exception of a little more than 3 per cent, or about 2,300,000 acres, which are reported in privately owned farms in 1920. Of this amount nearly 600,000 acres, or less than 1 per cent of the total land area, are under irrigation. The water for this purpose is supplied chiefly by Nevada's four rivers, the Truckee, Carson, and Walker which rise in the Sierra Nevada Mountains, and the Humboldt, which rises in the northeast. The snow-fall in the mountain ranges which traverse the State north and south produces in addition a few small springs and streams. These water part of the valley lands. It has been estimated that the State has enough water, if carefully conserved and used, to irrigate 2,000,000 acres, or about 3 per cent of her area. But owing to the great cost of constructing the necessary dams and reservoirs for the storage of flood waters, and the dams and ditches for its distribution, and because of waste of water by many users, the irrigated area is not increasing. According to the 1920 census it has decreased. The vital fact is that about 97 per cent of the State's enormous area has no agricultural value except as grazing land for cattle and sheep (unless water can be developed from new sources such as artesian wells), and that the National Government owns nearly all this grazing land. Uncle Sam owns it, but a few live-stock companies monopolize its use for their herds. This is made possible by the fact that the law under which government grants of school lands to Nevada were administered enabled certain stockmen to select practically all the land with water, so as to control all water available for irrigation and drinking purposes for live stock. Unlike other States, the Nevada law controlling the sale of the millions of acres granted by the Government enabled a stockman to pick out only the forty-acre tracts with water on them. He could buy 640 acres directly, and get as much more as he wanted by using the names of relatives and employees— "dummies." The price of the land was $1.25 an acre, but only 25 cents had to be paid down, with long time for the balance. So a man with $5,000 could buy 25,000 acres, carefully selected in forty-acre tracts along the banks of rivers and streams, and through this water monopoly he could secure the exclusive control of a million acres of public range land as free pasture for his herds. In other States the government land grants consisted of numbered sections according to United States surveys, and buyers could not pick out exclusively the areas with water. (The bill granting 7,000,000 acres of government land to Nevada, which passed the United States Senate in 1916 through the efforts of Senator Pittman, was drawn on similarly vicious lines. It would have increased the hold of the land and water monopolists and large-scale live-stock producers on the people.)

Thus was fixed the strangle-hold of the live-stock interests on Nevada. A few families and corporations control nearly all her many million acres of range land (97 per cent of the State's area) through their control of the water, and own most of the watered land. Trespassers are kept off by the laws of nature, as they cannot use the pasture unless they have drinking water, or if necessary, by the "law of the range," as shown by many past conflicts of stockmen with their small competitors. With rare exceptions like the Newlands irrigation project at Fallon, Truckee Meadows, and a few other valleys early settled in small and fertile farms by the pioneers, this monopoly has made Nevada practically one large and desolate live-stock ranch. But deliberately or unconsciously its population of homeless workers has taken its revenge, as told by Nevada's overflowing jails and prison, her almshouses and insane asylum, by her lack of political, economic, and social stability, by the most backward position of all the States. No society can allow its natural resources to be monopolized and neglect its workers without paying a heavy price. As Professor Romanzo Adams points out, in no other State is there such concentration of land ownership in a few families, or are there so few farmers. In no other State is the average size of farms, and the average number of cattle or sheep on each farm, so large. And in no other State are there so many migratory farm workers in proportion to the number of farms. "Nevada has from two to six times as large a percentage in prison, jails, alms-houses, and hospital for the insane as certain neighboring States where farms and farm homes are numerous and migratory workers few."[2] Paupers, insane, and prisoners are largely recruited from the migratory workers. But the sorry population of her institutions does not tell the full story of damage done. Thousands more must have been maimed in body and soul, and roam free to spread the social canker, while the State continues to decrease in population and to deteriorate in nearly all that increases human welfare.

What is the remedy? Will the live-stock interests subdivide their holdings? Will pigs fly? The stockman's motto is "What I have I hold," down to the last drop of water. I have seen large quantities of it overflowing the ditches and running to waste on the fields and roads of company ranches, producing a rich crop of willows and tules after irrigating the wild hay lands. Across the road were the scattered "dug-outs" and cabins of settlers who under great difficulties had cleared a few acres of sage-brush land. They were struggling to "prove up" and sustain life for their families and themselves on a "dry" farm, as their entire water supply was from a well. Staring at us through the sage-brush or clinging to their mother's skirts were two or three eerie little children, timid as jack-rabbits, growing up without school or toys, in ignorance even of children's games. Sooner or later these settlers are starved out, as Nevada is literally the "driest" State in the Union (as regards rainfall), and dry-farming is hopeless. These failures please the large owners; they do not want homesteaders "fussing about," fencing the land on their own government range, and breaking the continuity of their holdings. I know intrepid settlers who have hoarded trickles from mountain streams and seepage that would otherwise be wasted, and used it to water crops on their homesteads, into which they had put years of work and all their meager capital. But they were enjoined at the behest of the neighboring live-stock company from using the hoarded water, on the ground of "prior rights." I have seen them denied its use and lose everything in court. Only their cabin home and the parched land with its withered crops were left them. The manager of this company replied to my protest: "This is *our* country, and we don't want any damned squatters and water stealers around interfering with our water and range and settling it up. We'd *run* them out if we couldn't get rid of them any other way!" However, it is generally not necessary "to run them out," as under our big-business system of government, national and State, the natural resource monopolists, the banks, and the courts are of course in cahoots, and the verdict is to the strong.

[2]Romanzo Adams, "Public Range Lands—A New Policy Needed," *American Journal of Sociology,* November 1916.

We have in Nevada some laws that automatically keep water away from the land and the settler. On one of my campaigns I met a sturdy young fellow climbing out of a tungsten mine in the Humboldt Mountains, who told me with pride of his wife's work as school-teacher to help them in his struggle for a farm and home for their children. "This is no sort of life for a man to lead," he admitted, wiping the yellow dust from his face, and gazing off at the desert. "I've got to live on top of this mountain in a company bunk-house (and pay $40 a month extra for board) instead of having a home. We can't have it until I get water on my land. The water's there in the Humboldt River, but I can't get it." He had filed on 320 acres under the Desert Land Act, "proved up on it" by making the necessary improvements and payments, cleared the land of sage-brush, dug ditches, secured a water right to certain river waters from the State engineer, and put in a crop of wheat which sprouted well but died, because he was not allowed to run water to his ditches. Instead of the profit of $2,000 he was counting on to pay his debts and build a house, he lost several hundred dollars and all his work, and was now struggling as a miner for a fresh start. He took from his pocket a letter from the agent of a land and live-stock company owning adjoining land. It curtly refused his request for a ditch right of way over its land to his. Another company had filed a protest in the State engineer's office against granting his water right because the company "believed" a dam built at the point of diversion of his ditch from the river would back up the water and flood its land, and because his ditches would have to cross numerous company ditches and thereby prevent it "from enjoying the free use of its vested water and ditch rights." Only by winning lawsuits against neighboring land owners—and both cards and courts were stacked against him—could he fill his ditches. "And with water running to waste in the Humboldt Sink!" he said bitterly. "We fellows haven't a man's chance, and all we want is a fair show to live by our own work." He held out his large, muscular, calloused hands. "And with the Government wasting billions on airplanes and shipyards and railroads and foreign loans! We're doing some thinking for ourselves!" The tungsten mine has since shut down and he has joined the army of homeless men looking for work, while one of the neighboring land companies has filed on his water right, on the ground that he never put it to beneficial use by raising crops.

I have seen families stoically enduring life in little hot cabins in the heart of a burning desert. A well, a few scraggly chickens, a cow perhaps, and a sparse and parched field of rye or wheat were their only visible means of subsistence. The father of one of these families confessed almost apologetically: "I ain't one of these dry farmers, ma'am. I've got some good wells located and could grow fine crops if I could only get a few hundred dollars for a pump." Throughout the State I found it: on the one hand, men and women who had shown energy and hardihood and a pioneer spirit in their struggle against nature for a meager existence, asking only for water; on the other hand the Government, national and State, indifferent to the crying need for farms, homes, and jobs, doing nothing.

The settlers struggle on until they lose everything, the land remains barren and unproductive for lack of "a few hundred dollars for a pump," while underground rivers flow beneath the floor of Nevada's driest looking valleys, and undeveloped artesian water abounds. (Senator Pittman's underground waters bill, recently enacted, reserving the right to any citizen or "association of citizens" to drill for water for two years on land areas of 2,560 acres, thus securing a patent on 640 acres if water is developed, does not help the settler; as a director in one of these water-drilling corporations recently told me: "Only big companies can afford to drill and get land and water on these terms." Several companies have already done so, thus increasing monopoly in the hands of a few.)

I have seen rivers flooding their banks on their way through barren valleys which in the language of congressmen would "blossom as the rose" with the storage and distribution of this water. The Humboldt River spreads out into a lake at one point, owing to a bad channel, and loses 300,000 acre feet in a few miles, due to evaporation and absorption. This is enough to irrigate 200,000 acres through the season, and provide homes for 2,000 families. Fertile sagebrush lands, but waterless, spread on both sides of the river for miles to the foot of distant mountains, waiting for the homemakers.

Utah has shown our bosses both in Washington and Nevada how to manage large land and water holdings for the public good. It was the policy of the Mormon church to divide good land into small farms. And Utah, with nearly equal agricultural resources, has a much larger population and greater economic and social stability than her neighbor. The Mormon church carried out this policy in Nevada, when a large cattle ranch of several thousand acres in the eastern part of the State accidentally came into its possession. It planned at once to divide it into a large number of small farms. The Mormon bishop there tells me the church was warned that the colonists would starve, as "the ranch was only fit for cattle." But the colonists came, and the land today supports two villages of more than one hundred families, which are producing diversified crops under sound social conditions, instead of wild hay for cattle at great social cost to a lot of homeless men and to the State.

What is the solution of Nevada's problem? Undoubtedly the Government should end its long neglect of its vast public domain and administer these lands as it recently began the administration of its forest reserves, but in the interest of the small settler. The Government should extend its irrigation projects, providing credits and other necessary aid to settlers during the first difficult years, and, even more important, in cooperation with the State, should buy from the large stockmen tracts of land which control water for live stock. It should manage land, water, and public range with the definite purpose of increasing the number of small farms, of small stockmen, and range users. As Professor Adams suggests, it should also reduce the number of animals pastured on the public range by the large owners, which would of course reduce their yearly production and profit and thus lessen the value of their watered lands. Thus the natural operation of economic laws would lead to the subdivision of their holdings. But this will never be done until the people make their bosses see that government, national and State, if it is to endure, must develop natural resources for the good of all, instead of gutting them for the enrichment of a few, to the ultimate injury of all. Until it is done, Nevada's stable population cannot increase, despite the efforts of boosters' clubs and chambers of commerce. She will continue to lie, inert and helpless, like an exhausted Titan in the sun—a beautiful desert of homeseekers' buried hopes.

NEW HAMPSHIRE

Not Yet Abandoned

RALPH D. PAINE

AUGUST 20, 1924

T HE LITERARY TRADITION of a rural New England consisting of abandoned farms, queer, flat-chested spinsters, and faded wives who go insane because of solitude and Puritan complexes has found its focus, to a large extent, in rock-ribbed New Hampshire. Contending with a hard climate has made us a patient folk, unemotionally enduring the buffets of fortune, but we grow a little weary of a certain condescension among outsiders. It is quite the fashion to ask what's the matter with New Hampshire and then start another survey or investigation.

During the brief summer thousands of motor tourists stream over our highways to visit the White Mountains. They come from regions as remote as the Pacific coast. It is a flamboyant invasion that scatters millions of dollars among hotels, camps, tea houses, garages, and small-town merchants. New Hampshire piously thanks God for this bountiful source of revenue, but reserves comment. Of this multitude of transients some are decent people who deserve to be at large. They have manners and intelligence. Many others, however, offend the landscape which they have not eyes to see while they step on the gas in order to arrive somewhere else for no particular purpose. And as they go tearing through noble gorges and verdant valleys or past lakes whose ripples brightly beckon they glance with pity at the natives of New Hampshire.

In their opinion we are the ultimate hicks. Poor stupid clods who have never learned to put pep into life and jazz it up! Slaves to a plain white farmhouse on a windy hill, and a hundred acres of tillage, woodland, and meadow, with a thousand a year cash income as the measure of material comfort. Always struggling to pay off the mortgage on the old homestead, so it is alleged, speaking a curious Yankee dialect, counting a journey as far away as Boston as the event of a lifetime.

Do we envy these birds of passage? Well, not enough to say so. Your New Hampshire farmer is not easily fooled by the buncombe and bluff which the city dweller accepts as a doctrine of existence. He is not sufficiently up to date to live beyond his income and be satisfied with keeping one jump ahead of his creditors.

As one result, the tenant farming which has blighted the Middle West is a negligible factor. Ninety-three per cent of our farmers own their land. Only 37 per cent of the farms are mortgaged, the literary tradition notwithstanding.

The rural position is steadily decreasing, no doubt of that—12 per cent since 1900, or 22,000 fewer sturdy men, women, and children on the soil of their ancestors, but the total valuation of the farming lands of the State has increased considerably during this time. The picture has its melancholy aspects, but it is not so dark as the sentimental fictionist delights to paint it. It was sagacious to abandon a great many of these farms. They belonged to the pioneering era of American history. Changing economic conditions have made it impossible to wrest a livelihood from them. They are too small, isolated, and sterile. It is better to let them grow up in timber for the benefit of posterity. The pathetic cellar hole by the roadside or the weather-beaten set of buildings given over to decay are often mute memorials of an obsolete social fabric, like the sod house of the prairie or the log hut of the Kentucky frontier. They may invoke the tribute of a sigh, but their day is done excepting as they attract the pilgrim in search of a summer home.

But wherever in New Hampshire there is mellow soil and convenient access to markets you will still find modest prosperity and contentment. Few good farms are being abandoned. The older generation is able to make both ends meet and a little more. New Hampshire was almost untouched by the adverse conditions which have put the Western farmer flat on his back in recent years. Never affluent and with little to lose, it steers a course that avoids the rocks and manages to pinch through. The State University is sending its agricultural experts into every rural nook and corner to teach better methods of farming. Other agencies are working in the same direction. New Hampshire will not surrender without a stiff battle. It does not have to be told that its one asset beyond price is the people of its farms and villages and the things they stand for.

The drift to the industrial cities is slowly devitalizing the old stock with its rugged virtues of industry, thrift, stubborn independence, and respect for law. This is the profound tragedy of it. If the salt have lost his savor, wherewith shall it be salted? Certainly not in the polyglot mill communities of Manchester, Berlin, or Dover. These are in no wise typical of New Hampshire. Their rotary clubs or chambers of commerce shout the get-together, booster jargon of Seattle or Dallas. Their politicians are as fat-witted, selfish, and inefficient as elsewhere. Their backgrounds of dignity and tradition have been obliterated by the rising tide of French Canadians, Irish, Greeks, and Slavs. Massachusetts is ever so much worse off. Vermont has almost escaped the curse. Maine has preserved much of its native integrity because it is still a vast wilderness province.

New Hampshire is a small State of 450,000 people who reflect, to an intimate degree, the prevailing currents of an American life which had its rise in the very beginnings of the nation. Past and present rub elbows. Industrialism is a canker and the summer tourist has been both a bane and a blessing. The countryside has been infected with shabby ideals, a vulgar code of behavior, and a slangy, slipshod dialect from New York and Chicago that is spoiling the English speech, pure and undefiled, which New Hampshire received as a heritage from its fore-bears. The younger generation imitates these invaders and refuses to be buried alive on a farm. It prefers the bondage of a white-collar job with small hope of advancement. For an eloquent comment, the average age of the owner of a New Hampshire farm is fifty-three years. One-fifth of them are sixty-five or over. They have grown old behind the plow. And yet it heartens one to find a certain number of educated, upstanding young men returning to the acres that their childhood knew. With their practical knowledge and wider point of view they are the hope of rural New Hampshire. One of them, a neighbor of mine, started a poultry farm and cleared $10,000 in the third year of operation.

There is an automobile in almost every country dooryard and few of them are bought on the installment plan. The next time you are driving through New Hampshire, please note how trim, well-painted, and comfortable most of these farmhouses are. Grinding poverty is not reflected from such homes as these. Miracles of economy are performed. It is in the blood. There has never been enough money to go round. But what percentage of city folks are as well off at the end of the year?

More than half the population is still rural, living on farms or in the villages whose characteristics have survived the changes of the modern scene. This is the real New Hampshire, when you sift it from the urban rubbish. Nowhere can it be observed to such advantage as in the State legislature, which meets every two years. This assemblage has made New Hampshire famous, like Mount Washington and Lake Winnepesaukee. We have long boasted of it as the largest legislative body in the world, with 419 members in the lower house. It supplied Winston Churchill with excellent material for novels written after the fact. Gone is the epoch, however, when the Boston and Maine Railroad was said to purchase New Hampshire patriots in carload lots and a Jethro Bass could deliver the goods in the room of the Pelican Hotel, renowned for its red plush furniture. The legislature has become honest and unromantic. There are no more leaders, good or bad. Politically New Hampshire is as unproductive as an abandoned farm. It once sired a Daniel Webster. Now it sends a George H. Moses to the United States Senate.

A novelist would find poor pickings under the State House dome at Concord. The lobbyist is branded as a suspicious character who has to watch his step. Several years ago the writer served a term as a member of the Appropriations Committee. The chairman was the last of the old guard which had carried New Hampshire in its breeches pockets. A patriarchal person, white-bearded, soft-spoken, he maintained the ancient rites, a secluded room in the Eagle Hotel, whispered conferences, confidential bargains.

But a progressive Speaker of the House, young and unterrified, defied this "Uncle Jim," mocked his dynasty, and figuratively stood him upon his ancient head. He was outvoted in the very committee which he had hand-picked and dominated for a generation. The State finances were snatched from under his thumb. He became no more than a ghostly reminder of a time when New Hampshire politics had been intensely practical. He was no better and no worse than the other leaders of his day. A zealous watchdog of the treasury, he opposed every modern scheme of welfare for the common good.

Shorn of the glamour of that picaresque era, the New Hampshire Legislature is a social club for the plain people, a biennial party for getting acquainted in a leisurely manner. In this respect it is worth all its costs. Numerous bills are passed, most of which are superfluous and inconsequential. They are never extravagant. The rural members see to that. Every dollar appropriated is squeezed until its shrieks echo along the Merrimac Valley. The pleasant familiarity of a session whose weeks stretch into months is seldom disturbed by a Governor with brains or gumption enough to make himself seriously annoying. If an able man happens to hold the chair, it is the exception to prove the rule. The average type is a rather elderly banker or lawyer who desires the honor for the sake of his progeny and is willing to foot the bills. The salary of $2,500 is not apt to attract younger men of parts who have to make their way in the world.

The Senate, of twenty-four members, is cut more or less from the same cloth for the reason that its electoral districts are divided according to taxable wealth, and not population. This makes the worthy senators view with alarm any departure from things as they are. Their chief pastime is killing what may be called popular legislation as passed by the lower house. Membership in a State senate of this description means boredom to tears unless one happens to be built that way.

The teeming House of Representatives is the place to study and enjoy mankind. As a body it mills about with a vast deal of waste motion because of its unwieldy size. It grinds a small amount of grist for the number of hands employed. Every attempt to decrease its numbers by the enactment of a constitutional amendment has been pugnaciously defeated. The men from the farms and villages refuse to be robbed of the prize of going to the legislature. It is an honor which custom decrees should pass in rotation from one substantial citizen to another. As a rule it shows a greedy spirit to expect more than one term at Concord. The emoluments consist of $200 for a term of perhaps three months and railroad transportation. It is to the credit of some of these incredibly thrifty legislators that they save a few dollars of this impressive salary after paying their living expenses in Concord. A population of 600 entitles a village to send a representative regularly. A village of three hundred people rates a member every other session, or one-half member per session, to work it out arithmetically. Above the 600 mark the community acquires another representative for every increase of 1,200 souls. As a consequence, Manchester sends 68 representatives, Nashua 23, and Concord 18. This is absurd. It might be inferred that the few cities, with such topheavy delegations, could control legislation for their own ends. It doesn't work out that way.

The Manchester contingent, composed largely of French Canadians and Irish ward politicians, is usually rent by internal dissension and too ignorant to achieve results. The balance of power is held by the canny men from the rural districts. The brains and common sense of New Hampshire still come from close to the soil or from the simple environment of the small town. A refreshing, interesting lot of men they are. In a benighted age of standardization they have maintained an individualism which refuses to be card-indexed. They cannot be led unless they know precisely where they are going. Many of them were isolated from neighbors until the "flivver" banished the barriers of poor roads, intervening hills and mountains, and sparsely settled regions. They have had unhurried rainy days in the barn or long winter evenings by the fireside to think and talk. They are self-taught in the best sense of the word.

The wives and daughters, no longer shut in and deprived of stimulating contacts, are more energetic and ambitious than the menfolk. Nowhere will you find groups of women more genuinely cultivated and alive to modern trends and values than among the clubs of the little New Hampshire towns. They do not belong on Sinclair Lewis's Main Street nor are their husbands Babbitts. It was Waldo Frank whose lively fancy depicted the wretched New Hampshire housewife as gazing from her kitchen window only to pick out a tree from which to hang herself. This was not meant to be humorous. It was in line with the accepted legend.

And so our farmer comes to Concord with a pretty keen desire to make himself useful, realizing that his women will prod him on and scrutinize his legislative record with great care. He is mostly interested in keeping taxes down and diverting the available funds toward good roads and better schools. It is appealing, in a way, to find how heavily this question of taxation weighs upon him. In the districts where rural depopulation is going on the burden falls more heavily each year upon those who are left behind. And the chief fiscal problem of the household is gathering together enough cash to pay the tax bill.

However, when a new educational law was passed in 1918 whose purpose was to reorganize the public-school system of New Hampshire and raise it to a par with far richer States, these legislators from the farms and hamlets supported it earnestly. They were willing to pay the price as soon as they felt they would receive their money's worth. It signified that they hoped, more than anything else, to make their children contented at home and to give them some of the advantages of the city-bred youngster. For once rural New Hampshire was pulling together.

The writer was appointed a member of the State Board of Education, which had the task of putting this new system in operation. He made a speech at a meeting of the State Grange to an audience of a thousand farmers and their wives. Flattering himself that he had put the argument across, he sat down with that specious glow of satisfaction that sometimes rewards the amateur spellbinder. Later a competent-looking woman with a piercing eye cornered him in the hallway and spoke as follows: "I have had to attend a lot of meetings this year, Mr. Paine, as president of our woman's club. And it does seem as if 'most everywhere I go I have to listen to you make a speech. Of course that can't be helped. But I must say I do get sick and tired of hearing you say this new Board of Education serves without any salary. Now, you know as well as I do that if you were wuth anything the State would pay you for it.''

There you have the genuine New Hampshire flavor. This admirably candid woman wasted no breath in weasel words but went straight to the point. Alas, she was quick to suspect the other person's motives and wonder what there was in it for him. This is a flaw in a catalogue of splendid native qualities. It has thwarted most of the efforts to bring about cooperation in government, in improving the conditions of agriculture, in reducing the cost of living. It is found in rural communities elsewhere, but New Hampshire has been a soil peculiarly congenial.

Some of these legislators come from the North Country, beyond the White Mountains, where little towns exist twenty to forty miles from a railroad with great stretches of forest between them. This is a stalwart, clannish breed, with force of character above the average. The north countrymen have always been conspicuous in New Hampshire affairs. One may fitly call them the Highlanders of this old New England commonwealth.

Others come from the southeastern border, where the sea pounds the reefs and forelands of a granite coast. They recall the stately mansions of Portsmouth, built by shipping merchants and captains whose topsails gleamed in ports exotic and far distant, or Paul Jones and the *Ranger* fitting out for a famous cruise in the English Channel. New Hampshire wrote its pages in the briny chronicle of Yankee ships and sailors that won maritime supremacy for this nation in its infancy. Now Portsmouth is awakened from its drowsy peace by the crews of the gray war-ships at the Navy Yard and the wealthy cottagers of Rye Beach, whose motors fill the old square in July and August.

To Concord also come the men from the western counties of the Connecticut Valley, whose farms are fertile and never abandoned unless for a goodly sum per acre. They ask no sympathy and are doing very well, thank you. The White Mountains sends its hotel-keepers and merchants to the legislature, dapper, worldly persons who have learned how to capitalize scenery for all the traffic will bear.

Most worth while are the farmers from the hills, slow-spoken, round-shouldered, who strive tenaciously to keep their places going with a few cows, a gnarled orchard, some hay to sell, an acre or two of potatoes. Their social center at home is often the little red schoolhouse. They look askance at new-fangled ideas. They are cast in the mold of their ancestors, who marched from Nottingham Square and Durham to the battle of Bunker Hill.

These are the folks for whom a term in the legislature is a memorable experience. It is inaccurate to call them taciturn. They are not given to incessant chatter, but they love to sit and talk. And it is good talk; shrewd, seasoned, meaty. The outside world has accepted Calvin Coolidge as the typical Vermonter, compared with whom a clam is fairly garrulous. The New Hampshire folks are not like that, the Lord be praised. There is blood in their veins and not ice-water. And in other respects they are quite human and likable. Their so-called reserve is merely a habit of having something to say before they say it.

New Hampshire is very much in transition between the old and new, somewhat fettered to the past, but by no means blind to the future. Its textile mills, which are the sinews of its industrial life, are seriously menaced by Southern competition. It is not impossible that the cities may be sapped of their strength by an economic revolution of this kind, and the conditions of former days more or less restored. This would mean various industries fostered among the smaller towns, employing native labor amid wholesome surroundings. The undeveloped or abandoned water-power of a hundred little rivers is waiting to be utilized. Meanwhile tired business men buy New Hampshire farms and the campers flock to every wooded lake.

On the whole, New Hampshire is not yet bound over the hill to the poorhouse nor is its vigorous native stock submerged beyond rescue. It utters no loud cries for help and intends to work out its own salvation. Robert Frost has said it very well in these lines:

> The glorious bards of Massachusetts seem
> To want to make New Hampshire people over.
> They taunt the lofty land with little men.
> I don't know what to say about the people.
> For art's sake one could almost wish them worse.
> Rather than better. How are we to write
> The Russian novel in America
> As long as life goes so unterribly?
> There is the pinch from which our only outcry
> In literature is heard to come.
> We get what little misery we can
> Out of not having cause for misery.

NEW JERSEY

The Slave of Two Cities

EDMUND WILSON, JR.

JUNE 14, 1922

F ROM THE FIRST FRINGE of houses that one leaves on emerging from the Pennsylvania Tunnel and that litters the slope of the hill like the scum of a receding sea, from the yellowed and foundering marshes and the rusty back-yards of factories, from the tangled grooves of railroad tracks and the greasy black of Newark Bay, one finds oneself immersed in an atmosphere of tarnishment and mess. The cities are indifferent and dingy; the people are seedy and dull; a kind of sloppiness and mediocrity seems to have fallen on the fields themselves, as if Nature herself had turned slattern and could no longer keep herself dressed. The chances are that you merely pass through, on your way to Pennsylvania or the South, and that New Jersey seems to you essentially a region that one traverses to go somewhere else, a kind of suburb and No Man's Land between New York and Philadelphia. It has the look of a dreary dumping-ground for odds and ends not wanted in the cities, a scrap-heap of ignoble manufactures and uninteresting amusements, that manages to cheapen even the silence of its southern pines. And in this first unflattering impression you would not be far wrong. It is precisely its suburban function which gives New Jersey such character as it has. It is precisely a place where people do not live to develop a society of their own but where they merely pass or sojourn on their way to do something else. Its distinction among Eastern States is that it has attained no independent life, that it is the door-mat, the servant, and the picnic-ground of the social organisms which drain it.

Almost every characteristic phase of New Jersey takes its function from the nearness of the cities. This is largely what prevents its minor cities from rising above their flatness and drabness. They are content to leave to New York and Philadelphia ambition, liveliness, and brilliance. Where a small Western city, however barren and crude, may command attention through the violence of its energy and the freshness of its enthusiasm, a similar place in New Jersey is likely to lapse into a leaden sleep scarcely distinguishable from death. For the Western town, isolated, thrown in on its own resources, and without a base already laid in the past to support the activities of the present, is obliged to be a success or it is nothing at all; it depends on the efforts of the present generation to make it a going concern; whereas the New Jersey town exists very largely either as a sleeping-place for commuters, who have their business, their amusements, and their associates in New York, or as a mere blackened stump of a town, from which all the more enterprising people have departed, leaving only the feebler to nest in the trunk which their ancestors have planted. The commuters, in their less fashionable phases, are the pure type of American suburbans—lawn-mowing, baseball-watching, Sunday-paper-reading merchants or business men: they live in new concrete houses and own Buicks and Red Seal Victrola records. But the remnants left behind of the original local society decay drearily in great box-like houses which they seem gradually to have ceased to paint, dwelling languidly amid family photographs and shabby Victorian furniture, asking nothing of the commerce of the town but what the grocer and the drug-store can supply, breathing the stale tepid air of an atmosphere where even gossip has lost some of its virulence. They keep not even the charm of social ideals which are admirable even in decay—such as one finds in the South or New England; such taste and manners as there have been have long since emigrated or worn off; nor is there enough energy left behind to launch the town on a vulgar career of booming. Only Newark, so far as I remember, has ever tried anything of this kind and that was more of a special centenary than a prolonged campaign of boost. The best they could do for a slogan was "Newark Knows How" and their mean and dingy imaginations rose no higher than mean and dingy boasts. "History shows us that when poets appear," ran the legend on one of the gala arches, "civilization has begun to decay. Newark has produced no poets."

But the smarter communities come even further from fostering an independent local life. It is either a question of well-to-do commuters who are fundamentally New Yorkers and who never really identify themselves with New Jersey as citizens of that State or of people with country houses who merely come down to New Jersey for a few months in the summer. And they do not even carry smartness to a particularly brilliant point. Rich brokers and powder manufacturers build houses like huge hotels, where their families go about the familiar business of motor and country club. There are the regular tennis, golf, and polo, and, occasionally, a half-hearted fox-hunt. Scattered fragments of a local squirearchy live in the country all the year 'round, accustomed to the society of their horses and dogs and not greatly missing any other. The children of both these elements, rather unusually stupid flappers and youths, pursue a monotonous round of recreation of which they never seem to tire. They are neither very sprightly nor very wild and between the beach club, the tennis club, and the country club attain a sun-baked, untroubled comeliness of healthy solid young animals. They have not even much of a heritage of snobbery to give them the distinction of a point of view.

As for the vulgar resorts that strew the coast culminating in Atlantic City, they have even less charm than the fashionable ones. Here on sticky summer evenings the inland horde swarms like flies. They plunge shrieking on roller-coasters, explore the amorous tunnels of the Old Mill, and listen to phonograph records of Al Jolson on musical slot-machines; they have their pictures taken on buttons, consult negroid gypsy fortune-tellers, bid for bogus *objets d'art* at elegantly conducted auctions, eat pop-corn and salt-water taffy, win fans at Japanese ball-rolling games, shout with laughter at the Magic Mirrors, look on at sand-sculptors modeling President Harding, and squeal with glee as they grab each other's legs in the squirming eel-pot of the surf.

No, New Jersey can boast no Cannes nor even any Provincetown. Here the ancient loud-murmuring sea that breaks so grandly on the coast of New England, that laps the soft smooth sands of Long Island with its little crystal waves—affronted by nightmare villas, pricked by endless piers and casinos, befouled with the droppings of picnics, garbage-pailfuls of egg-shells and orange-skins, balked abruptly of its long sweep of shore by the encroachments of bulkheads and beach clubs—chafes dully against its curb, bleaching out the flimsy summer cottages and in the winter gnawing sullen chunks from the bathing pavilions and boardwalks. Only at such comparatively remote and unpopular refuges as Mantoloking does one find the open yellow sands free for men and children to play on, where, unencumbered by boardwalks and beach clubs, you may sprawl as naked as you please, turning orange at the pressure of the sun among the dark green garlands of the seaweed, while the sea softly worries the shore like a friendly and playful dog. For the rest, the turbid surf made stale with a million hired bathing-suits, the bleak private beaches where cottages lodge like the sea-dried mummies of fish.

Even the countryside of New Jersey has largely lost its local flavor. Where fifty years ago a tranquil race not unlike that of New England went about the work of farm and village in faithful allegiance to the church, which formed the center of a genuine community with a civilized society of its own, there is nothing today but great truck-gardens to feed the straining populations of the city and towns which have been gored by the motor roads and are losing their identity as gasoline stations. I take as symbol an amiable old lady inhabiting a low white house, built close against the road but screened off with yellow rambler and clematis; in the dining-room are smooth mahogany and some fine thin old silver; in the book-case are Shakespeare, Milton, Dickens, and Frank Stockton. The road, now become a State highway, buries the rambler and the clematis in dust; the old lady dies of lacerated nerves from the shrieking of joy-rides to the shore; the mahogany is bought up at auction by the wife of a gasket manufacturer.

Only three kinds of life in New Jersey are really free of subservience to the cities and these do not contribute much that is vivid to the stagnant society of the State. There are, first, the industrial centers, like Paterson, Newark, and Trenton, which do their share to blacken the landscape and spread desolation on man. They are as grimy and as dismal as possible, but it is characteristic of New Jersey that not even the horrible here attains really heroic proportions. In the plumbing and rubber goods of Trenton, the sewing-machines of Elizabeth, the silk mills of Paterson, and the petroleum of Bayonne, and in the jungle of diversified industries which gives Newark a sort of grim richness: the Agatine Shoe Hooks, the Metal Buttons and Novelties, the Jigs, Fixtures, and Dies, the Grey Iron Castings, the Washers and Steam Discs, the Milling Cutters and Reamers, the Celluloid, Varnish, and Corsets, the Artificial Leather Products, and the Electric Hoisting Machinery—you get the blank brick walls, the leaden streets, and the cramped smudgy life of industry without the epic sky-blasting monsters that one finds in the steel-mills of Pittsburgh. But here life reaches what is almost the only intensity it ever attains in New Jersey: the grinding and bitter conflicts which make an industrial ulcer of Paterson.

Another element of New Jersey society which exists independently of the cities is the settlement of poor white trash or "pine rats" which infests the southern pines. Below Lakewood one enters an arid tropics of pine-needles and sand. The air is like molten flannel; the streams dry up to green streaks. To whole tracts of this desolate wilderness there has never come anyone but the surveyor, and the very landmarks have been branded with such sinister names as Mount Misery. But scattered about the edges of this desert are found rudimentary communities of men who manage to live in a perpetual state of indolence and destitution. Without lawyer, doctor, or clergy, in the crudest of timber shacks, devoured daily by fleas, mosquitoes, sand-ticks, and gigantic flies, they ask nothing of the world but to be allowed to deteriorate in peace. They have practically nothing except gin that civilization can supply. They are interrupted only by sociologists who find them a useful laboratory of degeneracy. I remember that the last thing I saw as I was leaving one of these settlements one summer was a huge snake being assaulted by two half-naked little girls who savagely did it to death with large tree-branches for bludgeons. These are perhaps the only autochthonous and autonomous Jerseymen.

But it cannot be altogether the suburbs which give New Jersey its tarnished quality. There is something in the very climate which seems to blur life out of clearness. The sticky winds from the sea, and the miasmal vapors from the marshes, the muggy suffocating summers, and the long dissolution of the fall spread a haze and a kind of blowziness upon the human life of the State. Does the flatness of the country itself tend to flatten the lives of the inhabitants? Is it for this reason that when I think of New Jersey it tends to appear to me as a set of phenomena so uniformly blighted with a lack of stature or distinction? I see the dusty and smelly ailanthus trees of the dog-eared public park in Newark, the crazy husks of summer hotels deserted and collapsing on the shore, sparse groves slowly turning to junk-heaps with accretions of cans and old shoes, wooden houses turned abjectly into billboards for long extinct brands of Liver Pills, a man in a furry green hat wrangling rancidly with his wife in a country club, a puncture in a soft red road at the edge of a settlement of Negroes, an imitation of the Villa d'Este (with overtones of the Hanging Gardens of Babylon) by a Jewish theatrical manager, "Souvenir of Atlantic City," root-beer booths beside the road, three actors catching sallygrowlers on an hilarious out-ing in a row-boat, women reading the *Ladies' Home Journal* by blue and green-glass soda-fountain reading-lamps, a State Senator bribed in a lavatory, a Sunday-school excursion to Ocean Grove, the public library of a large town which never gets the works of H. G. Wells, oyster-openers at Keyport striking because the Board of Health had perforated their buckets and thus, allowing the juice to escape, had made it necessary for them to open more oysters, girls in the Passaic handkerchief factories trying to bring down the price of the thread which, though an essential material of their work, they are forced to buy from their masters.

Yet, on the other hand, one should not blame too harshly the landscape and the climate. After all, our unhappy State must once have had its charm like another. When Colonial standards still prevailed, New Jersey must have been nearly as attractive as the South or New England. It is true that this earlier civilization seems to have been more completely obliterated than elsewhere: the old towns, like Perth Amboy or Elizabeth, with beautiful or distinguished names, have become now the most hideous of all. Perth Amboy is a scrofulous common glared upon by ghastly corpse-like houses; Elizabeth's ancient church is wedged tight between dry-goods stores and banks; at New Brunswick the fine sweep of the Raritan is begrudged by a huddle of factories. But here and there, none the less, one finds a relic of the old quality. At Princeton, most of all, is it possible to guess what life must once have been. Here, at last, whatever tone New Jersey has may be seen at its best; for Yale and Harvard are not more of New England than is Princeton of New Jersey. Here where clear windows and polished knockers are still bright on Colonial houses, where Nassau Hall, in dry grace of proportion, still wears the dignity of the eighteenth century, the eternal lowland haze becomes charming, the languor a kind of freedom. Here, as elsewhere in New Jersey, it is as if life were on the point of stopping, turning no face to the future, not caring if the future ever comes; so careless, so untroubled by the tides of life are the gestures and voices of its men that our visitors from New England universities have been known to rail at Princeton for idleness, for drifting gaily through delightful days in a backwater of the world, as the other inhabitants of New Jersey may be supposed to drift dully through shoddy ones. One seems at last to have reached a place where no one cares what is happening in New York. . . . An old Negro in a rickety hack rattles listlessly along Nassau Street . . . men in white hats and white flannels lounge gently toward the tennis-courts . . . cries flung from the playing-fields are lost in the wide flat silence of the countryside . . . on the canal a lock-keeper and his wife live for ever in a small white lock-house and the white ducks bob and float on the green surface of the canal . . . crows hawk in the low wet woods where the lady-slipper lifts her pink . . . the tame locomotive that runs lazily between the town and the junction pants and shuffles vaguely in the distance like a comfortable pet. . . . And at night from the campus rise fragments of song, friendly names tossed at open windows, spray of music splashed lightly from casements to dissolve in the quiet air—half-meant, half-heard, half-finished, thrown careless to the careless night. . . . But by as much as Princeton is moribund from the point of view of the cities by so much does she suit herself better to be a place of reflection and play. The flowers of poetry and of learning scarcely open in our crowded air. There are too many interruptions and too little patience to tend them. But at Princeton it is possible, at least, for men to find their forebears again and to practice the arts which they cherished in an atmosphere not different from their own. If the tempo of life is indolent, why indolence nourishes poetry; if the outlines of things are blurred, why one is so much less beset by the real. Here at least New Jersey the slattern may lift nobly the head of a Muse. . . .

Yes: one must not fall into the error of making Nature a scapegoat for everything: she might be dignified and charming enough even in the mild fields of New Jersey if the beings who insist upon infesting her did not murder those qualities with their own.

NEW MEXICO

A Relic of Ancient America

ELIZABETH SHEPLEY SERGEANT

NOVEMBER 21, 1923

NEW MEXICO has an austere and planetary look that daunts and challenges the soul. In the East and the Middle West, the honors are nowadays relatively even between man and nature. In much of the West and the Southwest they are not, and in New Mexico the game is still so heavily loaded on nature's side that the life of the citizen is profoundly affected. Although the fourth of our States in area—three-fifths the size of France, with single counties as big as Wales or Scotland—New Mexico has a population smaller than that of many an American city. Evenly distributed, there would be about three persons to the square mile. In contrast to chill snow peaks, and mesas that drop starkly to rivers running naked in their canyons, the few little clusters of human habitations which the flowing mountain ranges have secreted at their bases seem as negligible as the burrows of the prairie dogs.

For all that, the State has fabricated out of soil, and climate, and racial stock a special brand of civilization, an individual pattern for life to run in that is of peculiar interest in the record of American States. The newest in the Union, it boasts two cultures as ancient as anything on our continent, as little modified by centuries and circumstance. It is still without the machinery of modern industrialism except in the depths of mines. Flocks and herds and agricultural crops support the greater part of its economic life. But many of the Indians and Spanish Americans, and even the now dominant fair-skinned settlers still live, in their vast colored solitude, as pioneers in space and time, more closely huddled together than New Englanders outside of big cities. The Pueblos are sheltered like monks in their walled villages and terraced community houses of sun-dried brick. The "Mexicans," in their intramontane valleys, which are often mere rock crevices with a mountain stream in the middle and the width of a fertile field of wheat on either side, set their little dice-like ranch houses end to end. Where their dwellings have space to be wider spreading, as in their Palestinian villages, they have a semi-fortified look; the same flat roof covers three or four generations, which cling together patriarchally. The old Spanish towns of importance, as one may discover in Santa Fe, were drawn tight about plazas and streets edged with colonnaded sidewalks, and their many religious and conventual buildings, which lift slated mansards to the blue sky, are as secretly inclosed as in France or Spain. Bernalillo, on old Spanish town, built on the side of an Indian pueblo where the army of Coronado made its first winter quarters, has an air of being religiously set in walls and gardens against the assaults of a dangerous universe. The genuinely frontier towns, like Gallup, near the Arizona line, important as trading centers for sheep or mining or Indian country, are no more than a raw street or two on the edge of infinity. Even Albuquerque, the only bustling modern city of any size, gives no effect of proud assertion: Sandia Mountain, floating above, carries off all the magnificence.

In an hour or two on horseback one may pass from the desert, with its dusty evanescent lights and pale lunar convulsions, through the rich green of an irrigated valley filled to the rim of its sandy pink foothills with corn or alfalfa, where mint and cottonwoods grow thick along the running ditches, and up into the virgin pine forest of the mountains, a place of blue-black shadow. Two or three more hours, and the high sheep range opens its vistas, fabulously vast, yet green and smooth and soft as an English park. Even in the desert, the purple vetches and petunias of early summer, the scented sheets of yellow that mark August and September, the gray-green sagey growths give color and fragrance to aridity. Owing to the altitude, nowhere less than 2,500 or 3,000 feet, tropical vegetation such as one finds in Arizona is lacking. Even the extreme south, along the Mexican border, is a land of perpetual summer. In the more northerly counties, like Taos and Santa Fe—the State capital is built at some 7,000 feet under the Sangre de Cristos, which rise to a jagged 14,000—snow may fall at any time between September and June, and spring winds blast the fruit blossoms; while summer sends to the ripening crops anything from torrential rains and cloudbursts to the most blasting drought. But somehow there is always enough hot sun and golden weather (there is the South of it) and enough zest in the brilliant air (there is the West of it) to keep the soul of the agricultural land alive, and brace men's hearts for new struggles.

Climatic adversity and violent human conflict have always been the lot of the natives, one learns from history and from the fascinating records of vanished races that lie on the scarred surface of the land—or just below. Besides the few that have been studied by the archaeologists in the last quarter-century, thousands of unexcavated cave and cliff ruins loom over the New Mexico canyons, giving the transplanted Kansas farmer or the grocer of the Kiwanis Club an upsetting vision of human destiny. The Spanish records name many aboriginal populations which have wholly vanished today. When the florid Conquistadores—the bulk of them, the historians tell us, the younger sons of Spanish noblemen, sent out to make their fortunes—arrived in this country, about a century before the sober Pilgrims were landing on the gray New England rocks, the red man was, of course, in sole possession. The Conquistadores' chief objective was, unlike the Pilgrims', frankly materialistic: treasure, first the supposed treasure of the Seven Cities of Cibola, from which the present pueblo of Zuni, in the western part of the State, descends. But these adventurers were genuine explorers, and the province claimed as New Mexico, in the name of the Spanish Crown and the Holy Catholic faith, by the strong arms of the generals and the determined devotion of the Franciscan friars, included, in 1700, what are now Arizona and Utah, most of Colorado, and parts of Kansas and Texas. The official figures of the population, in 1799, were 23,000 Spaniards and 10,000 Indians, living in missions.

Modern New Mexico history begins about 1821, when the province passed from Spain to Mexico, and the opening of the romantic overland route to the United States gave a region that had lived chiefly by its southern connections a trade outlet to the East. This was the moment when the names of Otero, Luna, Baca, Romero, Ortiz, and others famous in territorial history—some still to be reckoned with in State politics—came to the fore. The Mexican government made large grants of land to leading individuals. These reinforced the older Spanish grants, and the Spanish Catholic gentlemen, established, some of them by many previous generations, in their great ranch houses, with their patriarchal families, their great flocks and herds, their practically peon labor of their own racial stock, and their Indian "slaves," were, if not kings, at least barons in their own right. That picturesque and privileged and quasifeudal system in land tenure, stock farming, government, which has carried over into the present social and political system of New Mexico, goes straight back to these gentry.

The American era, following the military occupation of General Kearney in 1846, and the treaty of Guadalupe Hidalgo, by which the territory passed to the United States, initiated a new struggle: the Spaniards, like the Indians before them—but with a much more bitter reluctance—had to yield moral and commercial sovereignty to a race backed with more money and resources than they could now put forward. It was a slow and gradual and subtle process. The country was wide and undeveloped beyond all avarice and exploitation. But as the pioneers of the Santa Fe trail, traders, miners, sheep ranchers, and the rest—quite as arrogant and unscrupulous and ready with the six-shooter as the Spanish settlers—filtered in, and later the building of the railroads introduced new elements of progress and competition, including "wild catting" in mines, the old Spanish families began to lose their supremacy and their land. The ones who did not must have been those in whom the sensitiveness of the Southern aristocrat had been thoroughly tempered by Western air and sun; who were not only tough enough to endure the competition of a race that esteemed itself superior, and adaptable enough to Americanize themselves, but shrewd enough to use their old prerogatives over the inarticulate mass of their own race to secure for themselves a new sort of political hegemony.

The fate of Arizona was joined to that of New Mexico till 1863, when the former became a separate territory, and both were admitted to statehood by the Enabling Act of 1910—New Mexico in 1912. But Arizona's greater pioneer remoteness from the capital of Santa Fe and the older Spanish settlements made her formative history rather different, and her burning modern problems are more involved with the mining industry than with the ancient prides, grudges, and traditions noted above. The superficial observer, savoring in New Mexico something more closely resembling European "atmosphere" than he finds elsewhere in this country, does not at first realize the degree to which what may be called the Spanish complex influences the conscious and unconscious mind of the State. He will be surprised to discover that Spanish is more often heard than English in many country districts, and that he cannot bargain for a horse or a beautiful old hand-woven blanket or a night's lodging without the mediation of a child who has learned English at school. The State constitution provides that for twenty years after it goes into effect laws shall be published in both Spanish and English, and·that no citizen shall be deprived of the right to vote or sit on juries or hold office because of his inability to write or speak English or Spanish. As a matter of fact, until very recently sessions of the legislature—in the memory of many opened with six-shooters—have been conducted in Spanish or bilingually, through a Spanish interpreter, and the interpreter is an important figure in the courts, where, though the judges are usually "American," the juries are preponderantly "Mexican." The Republicans attribute much of their success with the women voters to the fact that they send out Spanish-speaking women canvassers. Twenty counties are more than half Spanish in population, a few almost 100 per cent. Even the Pueblos, with five root languages of their own, and no love for the "Mexicanos," use the Spanish tongue commonly for inter-tribal communication.

That only the Indians are spiritually free in New Mexico is one of the paradoxes in which the State abounds. For of course they are at the bottom of the social scale. The man from Main Street (Santa Fe) loves to tell the Eastern tenderfoot that these lazy Indians own much land which sure ought to be in the hands of white men. As a matter of fact they own, or occupy on reservations, four million acres out of seventy-eight millions, while the private land grants, so useful to the cattle interests, validated by the Court of Private Land Claims, amount to six millions. There are some 20,000 Indians all told—the least of the tribes in numbers and importance being the once fearful Apaches, some of them the descendants of Geronimo, living on two reservations, the Jicarilla in the north and the Mescalero in the south central part of the State, which ex-Secretary Fall tried last year unsuccessfully by a venture of his own called in New Mexico "the spotted park bill" to transform into a National Park. In the northwestern corner of the State live the Navajos, 9,000 of them—there are 25,000 Navajos on the entire reservation but only one corner of it lies in New Mexico—a race of nomadic sheep farmers speaking a language quite as difficult as ancient Greek, and so protected by canyons and sand that nobody had bothered much about them but the traders who make a profit from their wool and their fine blankets, and the white sheepmen who carried on a sort of border warfare over grazing rights till oil began to gleam like a jewel in their foreheads. The other large Indian unit, the Pueblos, have from a long time past been jealously

Pueblos, Taos. "The Pueblos have never lost their poise in the universe of being. In the midst of these contending dominant races which they have watched this long while with appraising eyes, their balanced communal life, their beautiful handicrafts go on."

regarded, through their ownership of rich agricultural grants scattered through the Rio Grande valley. They have suffered many encroachments upon both land and water from white and especially Spanish-American settlers; and by a deal put through by Fall and Bursum, through which the voters would greatly have profited, they would last year have lost forever but for the national uprising against the Bursum bill all the disputed portions of their territory. The New Mexico politicians still attribute their defeat to "paid propaganda." Meanwhile the Pueblos have never lost their poise in the universe of being. In the midst of these contending dominant races which they have watched this long while with appraising eyes, their balanced communal life, their beautiful primitive handicrafts go on. And their extraordinarily decorative dances and religious ceremonies, carried on in the sun-baked plazas against the Gauguinesque background of the mountains, seem to release from the tensions of altitude and climate the inner mystery and sensuous harmony of the immemorial earth.

The simple Spanish folk whom the Kansas colonist misprizes are also charming to look upon, with cherished and curious traditions dating far into the past. Winnowing their grain in baskets, weaving gay blankets on hand looms, dancing old folk dances, and singing old Spanish tunes to the tinkle of guitars, they look in their mountain villages, under the shadow of their great mission churches, as if they had just emerged from a peasant pastoral like their own Our Lady of Guadalupe; a miracle play given at Christmas in the dark-ceiled, whitewashed interiors. Hard working, or as much so as sun and *poco tiempo* will allow, seriously undernourished on a diet of beans and chile, honest and law-abiding and proudly independent on their ranches, they are harder to account for through the years and centuries, with the ascetic ardors of their Penitente rites and the black shawls on their heads, than the Spanish-American aristocrat. Though they probably have a dash, acquired perhaps some time since, of Indian blood, they are in no way to be confounded with the peon Indian-Mexican of Old Mexico— nothing insults them so much as to be called anything less than the good Americans that they are. But the little wrinkled Don Quixotic person who smiles at one from his blue door, the señorita, so powdered in her hours of ease, who haunts the Santa Fe plaza, consider themselves bound by ties of true kinship to Nina Otero Warren, descendant of the Conquistadores, sister of the powerful Eduardo, high in Republican councils; herself the first New Mexico woman to run for Congress. And Nina Otero talks of them and loves them as "my people."

Ten years ago it was customary, in a certain valley—so the "white" farmers tell me—for the "native" voters to receive their ballots neatly marked and wrapped in a two-dollar bill, as they mounted the hill to the schoolhouse. Last year on the election day which gave the Democrats their unexpected landslide, the representative of a certain candidate was walking up and down in this schoolhouse, among husky farmers and black shawls, grumbling loudly: "What's the matter with these women? They've all had their five dollars—" After this somebody carried out the ballot-box and somebody else made a row. A stranger to New Mexico might misunderstand this little scene. He would be wrong. The Spanish-American usually votes as his father advises over the morning cigarette. And his father advises what the local Don advises, on the advice of his cousin in Santa Fe. The control of the Spanish-American vote by the Republican Party, which has usually held the balance of power, has been worked out through an elaborate "padrone" system in the counties and a strong Spanish-American leadership at the top, with men of the Bursum and Fall variety pulling the strings in the background. There is no saying that a greenback passes more often here than in New York City or that one party is more simon-pure than the other in this regard. As with Tammany, a job may be a return for a tribute of loyalty, given by those who for so many centuries took their orders from the patriarchal master of the hot heart and strong hand.

Surely much of what happens in New Mexico may be attributed to overweening nature. Mountains may set you free, like a Chinese sage, in the contemplation of Everlasting Truth, or they may merely project your giddy egotism into the empyrean, and then hurl it back into the timid harness of the taboos and privileges and prohibitions of a clan. New Mexico communities, in spite of the many benignant gifts of God, are dominated by spectral fears from which those who rub elbows under the shadow of skyscrapers are liberated. Free speech is undoubtedly less flourishing here than in Boston. Public opinion is likely to get snarled up in private personalities and "small-town stuff." Opposite factions do not sit down at the same table and discuss their differences. An Indian claim has never had a fair deal in the lower New Mexico courts. A gentleman of the Republican persuasion may be asked by his clan to renounce friendship with a sister turned Democrat. The real reason why the "artist" who now figures as a definite element in the social grouping is so resented by a certain type of average citizen is that he is an iconoclast who does not live according to Hoyle—who hesitates, perhaps (it is not so sure), to steal his neighbor's water, as ranchers habitually do, who likes, actually *likes* as human beings these Indians and Spanish people, and wants them to continue in their benighted ways; and gazes upon the purple land and breathes the crystalline air with no feeling but of sensuous enjoyment and spiritual liberation.

The nearest problem of the State is to assimilate the racial stocks without sacrificing their worth, to become progressive without cheapness. If the picturesque features, like Indian villages and Spanish missions, become as in California merely tourist attractions played up by hotelkeepers and chambers of commerce, the last fate of the Indian will be worse than his first and the rare distinction of the State will vanish away. And there is no telling what future developments in the rich and largely unexploited mining and oil fields will do to the civilization and the landscape. The archaeological possibilities of this region, where a pottery jar as fine as any in Crete can be had for the digging, have as yet scarcely been suggested. One can conceive of future schools of art and decoration, music and the theater, based on native strains, which would produce in pupils of Indian or Spanish or long-established American-Southwestern provenance a flowering of creative American expression of a totally new sort. The colonist artist or writer of today, struggling to present the violent images registered on brain or retina, can point the way: no more. Before the ceremonial dance paintings of the young Pueblo painters which come straight out of instincts fundamental as the earth, they must bow their heads in reverence and say—here, classic still and luminous, is the pastoral of ancient America.

NEW YORK: I.

The City—Work of Man

ERNEST H. GRUENING

NOVEMBER 29, 1922

CERTAIN BROAD FACTS about New York are obvious. It has become the metropolis of our planet. London, by virtue of the steady inclusion of adjoining districts, still surpasses Greater New York's population of 5,802,638. And while other European capitals retain vestiges of their power and glory—Paris is still by a dwindling margin the leader in feminine fashion and the pleasure capital of mankind—New York surpasses them all. Its high finance settles the fate of nations. Its shops display the rarest and costliest of the earth's goods. It assembles the brains and talent in business, invention, and the arts. It is the lodestone for ambition, the ultimate of human gregariousness, the culmination of twentieth-century civilization. Here nature has been pushed back to the vanishing-point to make way for a house built by human hands, a great synthetic monolith of steel and cement and stone, an ordered macrocosm to house man and his works.

It is a farther cry, a more quaintly grotesque contrast than even our land of great change can show elsewhere, from the island which the Dutch traders settled in 1613 to the Manhattan of today. They found, the historian tells us, "its lower end made up of wooded hills and grassy valleys, rich in wild fruits and flowers, and its middle portion covered in part by a chain of swamps and marshes and a deep pond, with a tiny island in the middle, while to the northward it rose into high rocky ground, covered by a dense forest, which was filled with abundance of game. Smaller ponds dotted the island in various places, and these with a score of brooks and rivulets swarmed with fish." For nearly two centuries man remained little more than a furtive intruder, an inconsequential guest among the hills and dales of Manhattan. A genial settlement at its lower tip expanded into a town and here and there amid the wilderness of its upper reaches sparse hamlets nestled. Hardly more than a century and a quarter ago Mrs. John Adams wrote from her residence in Lispenard's meadows—south of Greenwich Village: "The venerable oaks and broken ground, covered with wild shrubs, which surround me, give a natural beauty to the spot which is truly enchanting. A lovely variety of birds serenade me morning and evening, rejoicing in their liberty and security, for I have, as much as possible, prohibited the grounds from invasion, and sometimes also wished for game-laws when my orders have not been regarded. The partridge, the woodcock, and the pigeon are too great temptations for the sportsman to withstand.''

And then in 1811—eight years after the City Hall had been faced with red sandstone on the north (while the other three façades were of marble) because "few citizens would ever reside on that side"—the brain of man shaped the destiny of New York and made it what it is today. The "city plan," laid out with what many decried as reckless fantasy the city that might some day be. It is related that the three commissioners, while examining the ground one fine day, stopped to discuss the problem near a pit where workmen were screening gravel. In illustration of his ideas one of the trio began to trace with his cane a rough map of the island. As he finished the outline and was about to sketch his proposed system of streets the sun, emerging from behind a passing cloud, shone through the screen throwing its criss-cross shadow upon the map. "There is the plan," exclaimed another; and immediately it was adopted. The authenticity of this story may be dubious, but certain it is that for all time the shadow of that gravel screen will darken the Island of Manhattan. From then on the rigid lines of this plan seared their way through the rolling, smiling woods and fields, disregarding topography, leveling hills, smothering brooks and rivulets, crushing nature into a man-made mold, as artificially as a Chinese woman's foot. The assumption that the lines of traffic would always be from river to river instead of north and south was wrong, of course. But for a century, instead of attempting to rectify the mistake, New York proceeded to suppress all traces of its heritage, to will nature to conform to its error. Relentlessly it has tunneled through rock, buried rods beneath the surface of the rebelling springs and streams it could not annihilate, flattening every undulation, straightening every variation, squeezing itself into endless rows of rectangles, as impersonal as pig iron.

Was not here for the first time cast and forecast the regimentation that is America?

The prescription which patterned the body of Manhattan likewise gripped its soul. Impersonal, a vast amorphy of stereotypes, its complex formlessness, its decentralization have given it a myriad-faceted character all its own. Of the countless generalizations leveled at New York few are wholly true, few wholly false. There are a thousand New Yorks, overlapping, disparate, visible, hidden, obvious, obscure, material, spiritual, forming the gamut of human experience. Yet each of these microcosms pay toll to the surrounding larger entity, subject to its environment, to its dangers, to its drifts, like a protozoon in a teeming sea.

Of the generalizations there is, first, that no New Yorkers know New York and that few love it. It has become too vast and too heterogeneous for either intimate acquaintance or deep affection. Within its immensity a New Yorker may know his neighborhood, his beat, his district. He may love his home, his set, his club, but only vaguely if at all does he relate this fondness to the civic background.

Aerial view, lower Manhattan. Prominent in the foreground are the corporate headquarters of Manhattan Life, Bankers' Trust, Equitable Life, Singer Sewing Machine, and Woolworth. In this "lodestone for ambition, the ultimate of human gregariousness, the culmination of twentieth-century civilization . . . nature has been pushed back to the vanishing-point to make way for a house built by human hands, a great synthetic monolith of steel and cement and stone, an ordered macrocosm to house man and his works."

Devotion to his section of the city is wholly lacking. As for the cosmopolis, he ignores its history, its traditions, its most elementary topography, its unparalleled resources, intellectual and material. Nor is this average of ignorance wrought through the presence of its vast number of foreigners and native strangers. The indigenous know and care about as little and apparently have always been as indifferent. A spiritual heritage more glorious than any in the land is as spurned by neglect as are nature's lavish gifts all about.

In his author's apology to the Knickerbocker History of New York, Washington Irving wrote that he "was surprised to find how few of my fellow-citizens were aware that New York had ever been called New Amsterdam . . . or cared a straw about their ancient Dutch progenitors." How many New Yorkers today know that their city was once called New Orange? How many can name the villages which were obliterated by the Juggernauting city plan? Greenwich Village, uniquely revived, and Murray Hill, the only eminence below Morningside which did not wholly yield to the general leveling, and Harlem, but a generation ago a separate entity, survive as place names and localities. But who can locate Yorkville, Chelsea, Bull's Head Village, Bloomingdale, Richmond Hill, Odellville, Carmansville, Mount Pleasant? The city plan has blotted them out, except where here and there the slightest trace of irregularity, a jog in the sidewalk, a slightly curving alley, betrays to the curious antiquarian a sentimental remnant of the past.

But it is not in a relatively unimportant assimilation of sterile facts that the New Yorker lags behind his brother Philadelphian or Bostonian. In those historic cities no "city plan" artificially erased ancient landmarks and frontiers; instead the old settlements have fused gradually, preserving their ancient contours, evolving naturally to modernity. It is only in a slight degree pertinent that these cities are smaller. When Boston reaches New York's present size, the Back Bay, Charlestown, Chelsea, the North, West, and South Ends will persist, individual and colorful, woven into their greater city as the figures in an Oriental rug—unlike the linoleum carpet of New York.

Nor is it merely in the physiographic that New York has submerged its component parts. Long before the city achieved its metropolitan bulk, when it was still "little old New York," it appeared careless of its localism, indifferent to its civic entity. It was as if the city had been aware somehow of a national, a cosmic role, which made local concerns, local pride mere provincialism. The Massachusetts tradition has permeated the land, sanctified at the source, wafted abroad with the blessing of each succeeding generation, its relics carefully treasured and displayed. New England has captured American history. It has made 1620 the great date, the *Mayflower* the great argosy. It has striven manfully and successfully in most quarters in making Puritanism our great cult. It has unblinkingly exalted as sheer ruggedness the intolerance, the harshness, the bigotry inextricably mingled with the brave pioneering of its founders. It has almost succeeded in making its own paternity the national fatherhood.

Yet nearly a century before, an Italian—a Florentine sailing for a French king—had discovered New York. Dutchmen were comfortably settled on Manhattan when the first boatload scrambled ashore on Plymouth Rock. And where the Puritans who had dared greatly for freedom of worship persecuted the slightest forms of dissent, and practiced wanton deviltries on helpless women in the name of the Lord, the Dutch colony welcomed their exiles. Roger Williams and Anne Hutchinson both found refuge in New Amsterdam, where the mother country's traditional policy of religious toleration prevailed. In consequence colonists of every faith, Waldenses from Piedmont, Huguenots, Swedish and German Lutherans, Scotch Presbyterians, English Independents, Moravians, Anabaptists, and Jews gathered there. Some eighteen languages were spoken in New Amsterdam about 1650. Indeed the "polyglot boarding-house," derided in our time as a latter-day plague, is of ancient lineage, while the most inherently American doctrines of religious toleration, of personal freedom are our Netherlandish, our New Amsterdam, our Manhattan heritage. The Puritans who have appropriated it honored it only in the breach except as applied to themselves.

Revolutionary history repeats the abnegation. The Boston Massacre has been popularly credited with the first bloodshed for the principles of our War of Independence. Yet, six weeks before a two days' skirmish between the King's soldiers and the Sons of Liberty was fought around what is now City Hall Park, and the unhonored and unsung sailor lad who there received a mortal thrust from a British bayonet was the first to sacrifice his life in the cause of freedom. Where Boston has erected a monument to Crispus Attucks and his fellows on Boston Common, an obscure tablet in the dingy post-office building alone records the Battle of Golden Hill. And so on. How many New Yorkers know that New York was for six years the national capital? Faneuil Hall in Boston and Independence Hall in Philadelphia and other less important settings of great incidents are preserved and cherished, and in their shadows the atmosphere of olden time lingers pleasingly, hardly dispelled by the encroachment of the modern city all around. Who can walk across the Common in the heart of Boston without a reminiscent thrill? Yet in lower New York Washington walked, and Hamilton, and Jefferson, and Adams—here our nation struggled in its infancy—and not a trace remains. Federal Hall, where Congress first assembled, vanished over a century ago. Cherry Street, where Washington and Hancock lived—one of the beautiful residential streets of its day—long ago passed into a filthy slum. St. Paul's, where the first President worshiped—surrounded by the graveyard where not a few of his time are buried—is miraculously preserved, its dark slender spire seemingly as accidental in its survival among the towering polyhedra of business as a violet emerging between the flagstones of lower Broadway. St. Paul's and Fraunces's Tavern, where Washington bade farewell to his officers, are virtually the only links that connect what was the old New York with the era of the founding fathers.

Recently the *Globe*, New York's oldest paper, printed a series of articles on "things as old as the *Globe*"; that is, which were extant in the closing years of the eighteenth century. The remnants of old New York were countable on the fingers of two hands. The two structures above mentioned, an ancient residence on Cherry Street scarce recognizable as a tenement, a beautiful mansion on State Street, its architecture happily preserved in its present function as a Catholic home for immigrant girls, parts of the Church of St. Mark's-in-the-Bouwerie, and a small piece of the old Jewish burying-ground in the new Bowery, consecrated in 1656—these six remain. The outlying sections of the present, but not the old, city are more fortunate. In upper New York the Dyckman House, the Van Cortlandt and Jumel mansions, and a bare score of houses in Brooklyn and on Staten Island have, thanks to a few public-spirited citizens, escaped the utilitarian pressure of the day—and with the awakening to a sense of their values, let us hope, permanently. Indeed, when we speak of what remains of old New York the term is wholly relative. Here and there bits of yesterday's charm still linger—North Washington Square, still almost intact; the London Terrace in West Twenty-third, Stuyvesant Place, Front Street—a fading remnant making a brief but valiant stand against the onrushing day. The city as no other on earth is constantly destroying and replacing itself—only the pattern persists, mortmain of the city plan. Scarcely a section has been preserved to the uses of its beginning for a full lifetime. Every epoch thus far has been a transient phase. Throughout most of lower Manhattan one can observe from a given spot the varying architectures of ten successive decades. The abstract thing—New York—the city itself, alone has remained, demonstrating ruthlessly its dominance over all its parts. No place, no period, no personality have been spared. A very few New Yorkers may still be living who recollect the canal in Canal Street, charmingly lined with brass-knockered residences, but the grandsires of the oldest were still unborn when the Broad Street canal placidly reflected the gabled houses bordering it. Every New Yorker recalls the Fifth Avenue Hotel, whose history is so inextricably woven into the political life of the nation. Fewer remember the Astor House's greatness, and very few indeed the heyday of the City Hotel, New York's leading hostelry in the first half of the last century. The City Arms and the Province Arms of Colonial days are forgotten. There are many New Yorkers who remember Tiffany's on Union Square, but few who recall it on Broome Street; many who clearly recall the joys of the Eden Musée with its chamber of horrors and Ajeeb, the chess automaton, but to whom the greater wonders and freaks of John Scudder's American Museum and the rival establishment of Reuben Peale, both later acquired by Phineas T. Barnum, are unknown. Many of Columbia's living graduates spent their constricted college lives around the old brick buildings of Forty-ninth Street, and recently the university bestowed an honorary degree on a centenarian whose undergraduate days were lived on Murray Street. But nowhere is the past so quickly buried as in New York.

"Everything in New York is a nine days' wonder." These were the words of Tammany's present Chief Sachem in disparaging a political flurry that was distasteful to him. Tammany has always known its New York, where no sensation survives the day. In Chicago the Great Fire, the World's Fair, the Iroquois Theater holocaust, the Eastland disaster are still constantly recurring topics. New York had her great fire, and for a time the year of its occurrence was so labeled, a disaster of sufficient dimensions to precipitate a national financial panic; more recently New York has had her Triangle holocaust, her General Slocum disaster, her Wall Street explosion, but they are swept into the oblivion of the past. New York has no monuments for her dead. She alone survives.

Neither has she thrones for her living. A contemporary Julius Caesar would never aspire to more than second place in our metropolis. There are no firsts in New York, scarcely any seconds or thirds. In the great cities of other lands which are also political capitals, kings, presidents, premiers with their satellites dominate, at least for the period of their brief authority. In those cities the social structure is concentric. Whatever their size is, or may be, their human pinnacles are as outstanding as the castle towers in a medieval town. Other American cities have their first families, their founders, their big business dominators. But who is first or even second in New York? Not the mayor of the city, not the president of the university, not the senior senator, not the editor of one of its great dailies, not the president of its leading banking institution, not the archbishop or bishop, nor the richest man in the world, nor the greatest tenor of the ages. Satraps in their own little circles, they are at best captains and majors in

New York's army of humanity. Even the social oligarchy, the category of snobbery, in New York is but a pale phantasm in the city's imagination. The vast public which gleans some vicarious satisfaction from reading of the activities of "Society" either through the social columns or through the occasional effervescence of some scandal or tragedy in the magazine section of the yellow journals is dimly acquainted with the name of a few "great" families. The "four hundred" remains, a pleasing if attenuated fetich. But the individuals here as always in New York are lost in the shuffle. There are Vanderbilts and Astors, but there is no Vanderbilt and no Astor, and their names have become largely symbols, of which the frequent parodic combination in one name affords evidence. Their world is not in New York the pinnacle of a structure toward which the millions climb, but merely a unit, a cell, a sphere, one of many in the vast whole.

What then is New York? And whose is New York? It is not the New York of those whose houses are carefully boarded and electrically protected from May to November—the New York of which Edith Wharton writes so well. It is not the New York of the politicians, either of enduring Tammany or ephemeral Fusion. Indeed it is essentially characteristic of democracy's metropolis that nowhere is the governmental structure of less import in the life of its citizens. Not one New Yorker in ten knows the name of his Congressman, and not one in a hundred the name of his State senator, assemblyman, alderman, or the number of the congressional and assembly districts in which he lives and can vote. It is not the New York of banking and great business—the city of the twentieth-story luncheon clubs. It is not the New York of the cloak-and-suit trade—a world that supports its own daily newspapers. It is not the New York of the theater or of music. It is not the New York of the swarming ghettos—Lower or Upper East Side, Bronx or Brownsville, the vast domain of Yiddish newspapers and a thousand synagogues. It is not the Negro New York of Harlem or the San Juan Hill district. It is not the great Italy south of Washington Square, not the little Syria of Hudson Street, nor the Athens of Pearl Street, nor the Sparta of the Tenderloin, nor any of the exotic worlds lodged in our midst, representing almost every land and sect on earth. It is not the Bohemia or pseudo-Bohemia of Greenwich Village. It is not the New York of the countless restaurants, paneled grills, and coffee houses. All these New Yorks have had their chronicles, many of them faithful and brilliant. The Wall Street of Edwin Lefevre, the New York of crime portrayed by Arthur Train and Arthur Stringer, the Jewish New York of Abraham Cahan, James Oppenheim, Bruno Lessing. There is the New York of the current types—Chimmie Fadden, Van Bibber, Potash and Perlmutter. There is the unspecialized New York—the New York of a million comedies and tragedies of everyday life, recorded among others by Harris Merton Lyon, Gouverneur Morris in his earlier stories, and of course by O. Henry, whose stories about the city come closer to being its epic than anything in our literature—each story a chapter in the book, a flash in the great moving picture, a novel indeed of apparently unrelated fragments in which the great central theme, the central figure—it can scarcely be called hero or heroine—is New York. There has never been the "great New York novel" just as there has never been the "great American novel," and we are as little likely to get one as the other.

What, indeed, is New York? In vain may one seek to capture its spirit, to define its catholicity. Throughout the land it is the target for the scorn, suspicion, and antipathy of villager or provincial. At the same time it is his pride and boast, the goal of ever-projected pilgrimages of pleasure or profit, and with or without his cognizance the arbiter of his manners and thoughts. It designs his clothes, it supplies his music, in large part his books and magazines—even his newspaper has New York's imprimatur on all but the local news. He may berate it as the temple of Mammon, as a hotbed of vice and iniquity, as foreign, continental, un-American. But he projects his local hotel on the model of its great caravanseries. Its Woolworth and Flatiron buildings are national monuments to him. Its Broadway is reproduced in the "gay white way" of his town. Its business axioms become his own, its speed, its "pep," its magnificence, its idolatry of success his constant admiration and inspiration.

"A fine city to visit, a poor city to live in." How many times has it been said! And despite its triteness it voices in varying degree the individual's fear of insignificance in the great mass. But the tribute exacted goes beyond personal submergence. In New York, despite its transcendent opportunities, one confronts also as nowhere else in the world the frustrations of modern material civilization. New York is its masterpiece, its *magnum opus*. And New Yorkers pay the price. Throughout their childhood and through their lives millions are denied horizontal vision. Their outlook is eternally on stone or brick walls. Even the sky is circumscribed, shrouded in dust, its vault gouged by great cornices. There is limitation not only for the eye, but for every sense. Nowhere has constriction been carried further. In the poorest sections the population reaches a density not approached elsewhere on earth. To the great apartment-renting middle class, space—or rather lack of it—becomes an ever-intruding factor. The very word kitchenette began as a New York colloquialism, and the problem of a room more or less, or even of the size or number of closets, often profoundly affects the habits and life of the entire family. On Fifth Avenue one still sees the palaces of the very rich, Gothic and Renaissance chateaux flush with the street. The demolition of ten-story buildings to substitute others a few stories higher is a common phenomenon. The rearrangement of business interiors, the erection of partitions, the frantic attempts to re-deal space are as characteristic of New York as trail-blazing of the wilderness. Nowhere can the New Yorker stand off to gaze at a beautiful edifice—his church, his theater are mortised into the city's blocks, troweled into indistinguishable conformity like the bricks of adjacent walls. And whatever adornment the sculptor may have wrought on façade or cornice is hopelessly skied in the narrow corridors of New York's thoroughfares.

The constriction is clearly more than a physical difficulty. It lays its hands on the soul. It robs New York children of childhood's natural heritage. Their choice of playground is the street, the backyard, or the fire escape. The street, with its pathetic games inevitably adapted to environment, "area"—hide-and-seek, a *rubber* ball, thrown against the house, street shinny—games constantly shattered by the passing automobile, the surveillant policeman, or the disappearance of the ball through a window, or down the sewer. Or the backyard—four walls enclosing a few feet of caked dirt in which only the smelly ailanthus can live. Or the precarious fire-escape, when there is not even a backyard. Smut, tension, peril, restriction. . . . There are so-called parks—but the city plan made allowance for none, and the spacelets of Washington, Union, and Madison squares and Bryant Park owe their existence to the accident of having served in the city's earlier history as Potter's fields. (There is a slight debt, it would appear, to the unknown civilian!) So that in the great city—Manhattan below Fifty-ninth Street, virtually all that was New York two generations ago, a city that houses a million and half human beings—there is neither park nor waterfront. The half-dozen tiny spaces labeled parks in this great district denote merely absence of buildings. The trees, shadowed by great structures, their leaves withered by the noxious exhalations of the city, are dying. From what little patches of grass manage to break through the crusted earth the public is warned away, confined to a few slender circling bands of concrete between the dust-dejected verdure. Neither refuge nor seclusion from the din or dirt of the city is furnished in appreciable degree. And miles of magnificent waterfront which should have been the people's inalienable heritage, as it is in European and South American cities, are, save for the sliver of Battery Park, walled off for the nation's and the world's commercial use.

Above Fifty-ninth Street, where the per capita wealth increases and the congestion is somewhat less, the relief is also greater. Central Park, belatedly purchased at great cost, is in itself a typically New York marvel of compression, and Riverside Drive, despite the intrusion of the railroad tracks, has preserved a rarely beautiful stretch of the Hudson's shore. But even here nature is steadily losing her fight with the creature of the twentieth-century Frankenstein. The great elms which adorned the Mall a generation ago are dead. A tree forty feet high in the lower half of Central Park is a rarity. Everywhere the forces of nature are shriveling, perishing before the relentless advance of stone and steel and poison gas. In Park Avenue we see today an amazing admission in the shape of imitation trees—wire frameworks overtrained with ivy! There are other and still beautiful parks—Bronx, Van Cortlandt, Pelham Bay, where nature is not yet stultified, where the illusion of the primitive still persists—but the way to them for the New York that needs them is through miles of subway, crowded, stifling, pungent with the dust of concrete, iron, and sweat.

The frustration and constriction, we have said, grips the human soul. The rush hour when New Yorkers acquiesce in a bodily compression, engage in competitive physical struggle to wedge themselves into subway trains, is merely a burlesque epitome of New York life. In the contiguity of the great city, as in the enforced contacts of the subway, there is little room but for repulsions. New York is hard, cynical, ruthless, even beyond other cities. From their early repression its children emerge sophisticated, both stunted and overdeveloped, perverted, premature, forced by the artificiality of their environment. There is exaction too of time. The two eternal verities, time and space, alone are restricted amid the city's abundance. Where leisure has become exotic, the supreme experiences— love, friendship, and human contacts—are harassed and trammeled. Courtship in New York is of necessity hurried, furtive, interrupted, irrationally exposed or confined. The streets, offering at best the stoop or a bench, the crowded parlor, the dance, even the taxicab and the roof are substitutes for the free spaces, or the seclusion of a real home. Friendship in New York is hindered by its distances, its haste, its proprieties, its irresistible propulsion. As for casual contacts, the city's philosophy is everyone for himself—and the devil take the hindmost. Where the competitive urge has reached the highest notch, where each man is out to rise upon the bones of his fellows, suspicion and introversion are constant. One speaks of course of generic New York. But however wide the individual varia- tion, however great the individual human impulses, they all are subordinated to the custom of a city in which with more people living closer together than any- where else on earth, neighborliness is reduced to a minimum. In New York one rarely seeks acquaintance with one's neighbor; it would be unusual, suspect. One never leaves a robe or any other portable object in a parked automobile— even for five minutes; it would be gone on one's return. These may be but tri- fling incidents, but they are the symptoms of the New York complex. If in New York the milk of human kindness is not wholly dried up or turned to gall at least it is pasteurized. Something remotely analogous to what war does to human be- ings, some modification of the precept "If you don't know, you get killed" is New York's imprint on its denizens. And, like war, the New York Moloch de- mands and gets its victims. Countless moths and butterflies are singed at its flame, countless brave swimmers dragged down into its maelstrom, sunk with- out trace.

Nowhere in the world has the process of subduing nature progressed farther, become more highly developed. The skyscraper, in part a response to the irre- fragable horizontal straitjacketing of the city plan, was conceived in constric- tion, sired by aspiration. Drilled a hundred feet into solid gneiss, built on a base that defies all laws of equilibration, rearing itself on high as a challenge to the stress of wind and gravity, it is essentially a symbol of man's conquest. Tunneled into the earth is a great system of subways, of corridors under river and through bedrock, of conduits, of pipes, of wires, like the alimentary and respiratory tracts, blood vessels and nerves of the human body—linking the vast amorphous structure into one coordinating, functioning whole. Here man has been not merely in conflict with nature. Here nature has not been merely checked, tamed, and converted to his service. Here nature has been fully conquered and is now being destroyed. Here civilization is creating its own code and manners, its lan- guage variations, new ways of life, new diseases, a new human species. New forms of beauty, too. These canyons, these pinnacles and spires, these airy wire- hung bridges over which multitudes thunder daily, this skyline—these million lights, blinking massed and scattered through the city's vast night—these achieve a poignant beauty of line and atmosphere which stirs the emotions deeply and has in it something almost spiritual. Will this spiritual quality, now merely subjective, ever become a reality? Will man learn to use his great powers for the good of mankind? Or will he become increasingly the slave of his machine, his own creation? This is the unsolved riddle of civilization. New York, where the integration of man's energies has gone farthest, will first furnish an answer.

NEW YORK: II.

State of Unwilling Progress

CHARLES W. WOOD

APRIL 23, 1924

NOBODY KNOWS NEW YORK STATE. Very few, if any, have traveled through it. Konrad Bercovici discovers a different New York almost every time he turns around, but he hasn't yet got outside the New York City limits. Socially, psychologically, and physically the whole State contains about everything there is and lots of it. It is mountainous. It is flat. It seems to touch the sea only in one little corner, but it manages to have hundreds of miles of seashore just the same. It is agricultural. It is industrial. Great areas are so deserted that they seem like desert. Also it has its mining camps. And much of the State—very much of it—is physically, socially, and psychologically just plain backwoods.

People from "up-State," by the way, do not like to be taken for New Yorkers. A man from Santa Barbara is sure to let you know that he is a Californian, but the man from Syracuse is just from Syracuse. This holds all over the State. You have to get down below Poughkeepsie to discover any willingness on the part of the population to be mistaken for residents of the world's metropolis.

New York City contains something of almost all the world. The rest of the State contains something of almost all America. It is not from New York City that the most startling stories of modern miracles come. It is more apt to be from the laboratories of Schenectady. It was there that man first made and hurled the thunderbolt. It is there that radio is reaching its highest development. It was there that the dream of superpower originated. Nevertheless, one need travel but a few hours from Schenectady to find oneself in a civilization to which all progress is anathema and whose favorite term of opprobrium is "new-fangled."

Occasionally in some Catskill cabin or in the back counties of the Adirondack region the State police discover a nest of seemingly human animals described, for the purposes of journalism, as a "destitute family in a deplorable condition." Sometimes they are starving. Sometimes they are freezing. Usually, they are 100 per cent American but inbred to the point of intellectual extinction. Usually also they are Christians, with their fundamentalist theology preserved intact, but without spiritual force enough to go to church or to take part in any

267

religious exercises excepting funerals. In one case a mother-pervert reigned over the nest, keeping her grown sons, thirty and thirty-five years of age, in bed for life by the exercise of her fierce animal will. In another a father and a gaunt crew of pregnant daughters constituted the "family." I do not mean that these are typical instances of life in the backward sections of the Empire State. They are extreme cases, no doubt, but they are significant.

One is inclined to associate the backwoods with the pioneer spirit. One might as well associate the Daughters of the American Revolution with revolutionary thought. These folk are not early settlers. They are the descendants of early settlers. The early settlers had spirit and initiative and daring. That is, until they got settled. The more adventurous of their offspring, of course, refused to stay settled. They ran away from the settlement and built cities and towns. But the timid remained. They stayed settled, in body, mind, and soul.

Resistance to change is their most sacred principle. Modern conveniences appear as signs of degeneracy to them; and the boy who leaves home to go to the city is still their most popular theme of tragedy. The girl who marries the "city chap" is looked upon as disloyal: for in a community where everybody is pretty much everybody else's cousin, such unions seem to partake of the nature of miscegenation. "Who knows," sighs Uncle Amos, as he hopes for the worse, "who knows but what he's got a wife already?" This is the cue for Aunt Mary Jane to reply, "Beats me why folks want to be so stuck up."

This is not the language of the American farmer. It is the language of inbred descendants of farmers who have largely abandoned agriculture. They may still grow potatoes and beans and corn for their own use. They may still keep a pig and a cow. But the land is worn out, the barns are falling in, the more adventurous of the young people have left home, while the old folks and all the young ones who can be induced to oppose change in any form stick miraculously. They manage to get a living some way. They manage to marry. They manage to breed. They are a hardy tribe, enduring much tribulation and proud of their endurance; and there is a certain shrewdness about them which passes for intelligence. They are economical in money matters, also in ideas and in speech. They use few words and indulge in few facial expressions. They do not open their lips to talk, but blow their syllables through a very narrow aperture.

Numerically, this backwoods element of New York State life may not be very great. But socially, politically, and spiritually they have a throttle-hold upon the State. They furnish the traditions to which the natives think they should be loyal, even though they have physically run away. New York State is notoriously "conservative." This is generally attributed by outsiders to the influence of Wall Street. It is more probably due to the traditions of the "Old Home." The native up-Stater is seldom able to free himself from the attitude of fear and suspicion which was a most important part of his bringing up. Actually he may be having his bathroom tiled, or be looking around for an eight-cylinder car; but theoretically, he is still prejudiced against new-fangled notions.

The pressure of modern life may not permit him to act upon these theories in his everyday pursuits. But he can act upon them on Sunday; and large areas of New York State are as conservative, religiously, as the Middle West or South. He can also act upon them at Albany, and "new-fangled notions" have slim chance of getting through the legislature.

The State lags, for instance, in prison reform. It is not as bad as Florida, to be sure; but in this as in most progressive legislation, the State which should in all logic march in the vanguard of American culture is anything but up to date. This is likewise true of the problem of the feeble-minded, which New York psychiatrists agree is almost desperate. Those who knew the situation placed the terrible facts before the legislature, year in and year out; but it took a scandalous fire in one of the institutions known to be antiquated and unsafe to get any considerable number of people interested.

The richest and most populous State in the Union was slow to accept the automobile. New York State fruit-growers, with the finest apples in the world, surrendered their natural markets to California and Oregon three thousand miles away because the folk from "York State" could not bestir themselves to evolve new methods of marketing. The beautiful city of Syracuse, with nearly two hundred thousand population, still has the New York Central Railroad running through its business center at grade, for no other reason, apparently, than that it always did run that way; and it has a great and highly endowed university whose chief pride has been that it has never once shown a sign of hospitality toward a new idea.

I don't mean, understand, that Syracuse University is scandalously behind the times. It has striven faithfully to keep nearly up to date. But not once has it gone ahead of the times. Not once has it taken a position of leadership. Professor John R. Commons is the only nationally known leader of thought I can think of now who was ever connected with Syracuse; and he was ousted for his economic heresies so early in his career that the incident attracted almost no attention. Since the death of Chancellor Day, Syracuse seems to be recovering from this chronic dread of the new; and recently its faculty permitted a public discussion of birth control. This is hopeful. Discussing the problem of over-population may not seem radical elsewhere, but it was decidedly radical for Syracuse. The Syracuse Common Council, in fact, had just passed an ordinance forbidding any public reference to the problem. The ordinance was vetoed by the mayor and barely failed of passage over his veto.

I have lived in a dozen different sections of New York State and have found them all dissimilar. There's a reason. There is no State pride and no common historic tradition.

New York, Pennsylvania, and New Jersey are the only States I know of which do not fall naturally into some particular group. Maine and Connecticut, no matter how different they are, look upon themselves and are uniformly looked upon as New England. Florida and Tennessee are South. From Ohio to Kansas is a long jump, but the jumper is still in the Middle West. The geographies used to put New York and Pennsylvania into a theoretical bunch known as Middle or Middle Atlantic States, but this classification never had any psychological meaning. In Pennsylvania the tradition of William Penn is still held in reverence; but the story of the Dutch settlers who bought Manhattan Island from the Indians for $24 is an item of foreign history as far as the school-children of New York State are concerned. They know nothing whatever about the Duke of York. He isn't even an item.

There is no song which these people sing which is in any way connected with the glorification, charm, or historic significance of the State. "The Sidewalks of New York" is the nearest attempt at such a song, and that couldn't possibly have any meaning outside the city limits. Ocean navigation was made possible here, but it is difficult to hymn the praises of a man named Robert Fulton or a boat called the *Clermont*. Finally, and most discouragingly, if one were to celebrate the event which really made New York State, one would have to write a hymn to the Erie Canal. Even that might have been done, I suppose, if the Erie Canal had made the State and then resigned with proper dignity, as the Prairie Schooner did after it had fulfilled its mission. But the Erie Canal evolved into a Barge Canal with a lot of Barge Canal scandals and nothing whatever in the way of either barges or canal that anyone has ever felt proud about.

New York State has glories aplenty, but they don't belong to the whole State and it is difficult to strike a common note in celebration of them. There's Binghamton, for instance. Probably no city in the modern world has had such an influence upon modern civilization. It was from Binghamton that Patent Medicines came. It was due to the enterprise of Binghamton that one hundred million people, naturally leaning toward total abstinence, suddenly rose as one man and began to rid themselves of all human ills at only one dollar per bottle. They not only began but they kept it up. Cure called for cure: the ills were often obstinate but the cures didn't feel bad; also one could be a prohibitionist and a convalescent at the same time. Eventually, after a chapter of newspaper corruption hardly equaled in history, the business of doping the gullible became somewhat restricted by law. Theoretically, at least, the patent medicines which can be purchased freely at all druggists are now non-alcoholic, and they are not supposed to contain any habit-forming drugs. But Binghamton is still great. The rewards of her enterprise have been harvested. The big, patent-medicine fortunes are intact, and there is no limit to the opportunities for philanthropy and bootlegging which the future holds in store.

Then there's Rochester. Rochester is the Art Center of the United States. No one can deny this. Rochester admits it freely. All over the world, in any discussion of art, you will be told that American art is photographic, and Rochester is the home of the Kodak industry. Rochester glories in this, and not without reason; but she never thinks of it as a New York State achievement. Rochester is Rochester. She has her own culture, her own ideals, and her own distinct sense

Cemetery, Sleepy Hollow, New York. The quiet of this cemetery suggests the traditional rhythms of upstate life. On its outskirts, however, is the Rockefeller estate in Tarrytown, built from the proceeds of one of the most powerful modern corporate organizations in the world.

of superiority. She knows exactly how people ought to live, and she is seeing to it that Rochester children are trained in the way that they should go.

Buffalo is different. One could write a song about Buffalo. In fact, one did. It was "Put me off at Buffalo." I could never be sure in Buffalo just where I did get off. It seems like Chicago, in a way, with a suggestion of arrested development. It reminds one at once of wharves and grain elevators and "Fingy" Conners. Steve Brody took a chance in Buffalo—and got away with it. He ran a "music hall" in which he himself was the main attraction; and his fame was built solely on the fact that he had jumped off the Brooklyn Bridge. Buffalo used to be like that. On each succeeding visit the thing that impresses me most about Buffalo is that it is so much as it used to be. Year by year it gets farther from the top of the list of America's greatest cities; but it manages, nevertheless, to be as big as it ever was.

The rural sections of New York are as varied as its cities. The dairy region in the vicinity of Binghamton, the peach belt between Buffalo and Rochester, the grape belt out near Dunkirk—each has a character of its own. The last is peculiarly interesting. Prohibition gave a decided boost to the grape industry. The grape-growers no longer have to sort out their grapes or pack them carefully for the market. They just jam them into barrels and express them to New York. They can't send them by freight or they would ferment and explode in transit; but they can express them, and do; and the Italian buyer simply puts the barrel in his cellar and takes off the head. Then he lets nature take its course. The ultimate mess may then be sold for "red ink," but no one in the grape belt has violated the law.

Saratoga is still in New York State—much greater, in fact, and far more beautiful than in the days when it was reckoned great. The automobile is supposed to have put the horse out of business, but it brings thousands to the horse races who could never have attended them before. It is still a "watering place," and the water is good, even if the word has lost the grand meaning it once held. Saratoga has lost nothing much except its exclusiveness, and it has gained a State park.

The "summer resort" business hasn't fared as well in other sections. The automobile has brought everybody into the country, but the country isn't the same kind of treat that it used to be. Mammoth wooden hotels, equipped according to the standards of elegance that obtained during the seventies and eighties, are not even places of interest any longer. They are not gay and they are not profitable. There aren't as many of them as there were ten years ago. Many have mysteriously burned down, and the insurance money has been put into other enterprises.

New York State may not be pushing ahead, but it is being pulled ahead quite noticeably. I have lived in rural New York when ox-teams were common. The folks preferred oxen in many cases to the more expeditious horse because, when the road was washed away (as it usually was in spring), the oxen would pull the rigs out with a steadier pull and with less danger of breaking expensive harness. The automobile and motor-truck have now supplanted them; and with the automobile came concrete highways, electric lights, telephones, and a thousand conveniences never dreamed of before. An external hand has been laid upon these people, dragging them almost against their will into a bigger world. In that world, thanks to the automobile, their children are going to real schools and are getting acquainted with all sorts of different people; and instead of looking upon these new acquaintances as queer and foreign, they have come to find them charming. They are having real adventures, real courtships, and real marriages now; and the eugenists tell us that they are having a smaller percentage of deformed and idiotic children. But still you can go into any number of these communities today and be told by the bearded sages thereof that "the ruination of this here kentry is this automobile." These people are giving voice to the inhibition from which New York State suffers most. It is our infant fixation. It isn't strong enough, let us hope, to forbid progress, but it is strong enough to keep us from being genuinely progressive.

It is commonly assumed that the beauties of nature have a refining influence upon human life. What can one expect, it is asked, of a child born in a tenement or in the man-made environment of a factory town? Well—New York State is altogether beautiful, wherever the landscape has not been so defiled by man. It hasn't the terrifying beauty of the Rockies, nor the languorous beauty of the South; nor is there anything in New York scenery or climate which beckons to adventure or lulls to calm. But the physical charm of the State simply cannot be shaken off. This is especially true of northern New York, where the sharp frosts of early autumn work like magic on the oaks and maples and produce a thousand gorgeous hues unknown in the southern section of the State. The crystal frosts of spring are equally intoxicating. One whose eyes have fed in childhood upon Lake George with its mountain background can almost be excused in later life if he refuses to thrill at the masterpieces of nature in other sections of the world. The prairies will be pretty sure to bore such a person. The wide open spaces will produce in him nothing much but uneasiness. The sea will seem too uncertain, the desert too empty, and southern California altogether too artificial and tame.

Lake George is only one of a hundred perfectly satisfying bits of homeland in New York State. The Adirondack wilderness is still a wilderness over wide stretches and still beautiful despite the invasion of "hard roads" and hitch hikers. The great range of mountains around Marcy is accessible only to persons who are willing to climb all day and sleep in the open at night; its chains of lakes can be traversed only by canoe and carry. Lake Ontario with its thousand inlets, and each of the little lakes, north, east, and west, has a color and a fascination of its own. There is no blue on earth like Skaneateles blue.

The casual traveler through the State may think of Herkimer as a tank station, Auburn as a place of punishment, and Geneva as nothing at all. But get off the train at any of these places, take to the open highway, and you'll get an eyeful. The splendors of the Mohawk Valley can not be appreciated from a car window, and you see practicall nothing of the western chain of lakes. Did you ever hear, for instance of Coneśus? One of its charms is that you never did. The motorist in western New York has the privilege of discovering for himself ever so many beauty spots that are not famous at all. The local inhabitants, to be sure, will point them out with pride. But it won't be pride in New York. New York means nothing to them. A dreadful city chuck full of foreigners has monopolized that term. New York, to the up-Stater, exists primarily for the purpose of paying the State's taxes. No one from Utica or Elmira or Mechanicville would want you to suppose that he would live in a place like that.

Then, there is Long Island. One tip of it is metropolitan and one borough on this tip contains a population greater than Manhattan's. But the other tip lives a life of its own, less disturbed by visitors perhaps than any other section of the State, a stretch given over to moors and lakes and sharp sand cliffs dropping into the sea. In between is an area given over largely to great private estates, with palaces lying so far back in the forests that the passing motorist does not see them. Westchester County and the Catskills are equally magnificent. All that wealth can add to nature is added here, not to build up or to develop the territory but to keep it as excluded and unvisited as possible. It is customary to indict American millionaires for their lack of refinement and discrimination. I can't join in this indictment. It seems to me, whenever I visit these estates, that they have done well. They may muss up the scenery which the rest of us have got to look at; but they keep their own premises free from billboards and noise and smoke.

And while I am at it, I want to give voice to one more heresy. It is a popular sport among intellectuals to sneer at mere industrial advance. Its main contribution to society, it would seem, is to smear the landscape and turn our natural beauties into piles of filthy lucre. The despoiling of Niagara Falls is their classical example. One-twentieth of the water has already been diverted into mere channels of usefulness. Too bad—perhaps. But the discovery that Niagara can be enslaved is producing a dream of human freedom which is mightily affecting New York State today. Syracuse, Rochester, and Buffalo are sharing in this dream of superpower. (Although Rochester, to be sure, prefers its own superb falls.) A hundred smaller cities and villages are beginning to thrill to it. Niagara may be doomed: but on the other side of the ledger millions of people are breaking from the past.

It is too much to expect that they will become suddenly progressive. Only recently New York established a moving-picture censorship for fear their young folks might get some suggestion out of harmony with the permanent and fixed morality of "back home." Strenuous efforts are being made to extend this censorship to books and publications. Laws forbidding this and that are as common in New York as they are in Kansas. Free speech does not exist. It is still a crime to make public those discoveries of modern science which make it possible for women to bear children when children are wanted. The notorious Lusk laws, which made it a crime for school-teachers to teach, have been repealed; but this only after a hard fight in the legislature and because of the insistence of a Tammany Hall governor rather than because of any awakened public opinion throughout the State.

Still, New York State is changing. It is becoming American, due very largely to the influx of so many foreigners. New pioneers are supplanting the descendants of pioneers and are keeping the pioneer spirit alive. There is nothing much doing in politics, but electricity is marching on and leading New York State into a different civilization. The "halls of learning" in Syracuse and elsewhere may still echo and reecho the dogmas of the past; but in the laboratories of Schenectady there is no intellectual inbreeding. Foreigners, even Socialists like the late Dr. Steinmetz, may seem to be in charge; but what they discover leaves no room for argument; New York State will have to use it; and having used it, cannot be what it was before.

NORTH CAROLINA

A Militant Mediocracy

ROBERT WATSON WINSTON

FEBRUARY 21, 1923

W HEN BANCROFT wrote that North Carolina was the freest of the free he might have added "the slowest of the slow." She got into the Union too late to vote for George Washington, she got out too late to vote for Jefferson Davis. Until recently she was provincial and proud of it. Lying between Virginia and South Carolina, it amused and pleased her to be called a valley of humility between two mountains of conceit. No F.F.V.'s for her! Her early settlers were plain people, neither rich nor aristocratic. "Esse quam videri" her motto, the old Tar Heel State would fight, but she would not brag about it, Sir. She wanted no archives, no Historical Associations, no written history. What good was State pride, anyhow? She began life as a tail to Thomas Jefferson's kite, and was quite willing to do the work and let Virginia have the glory.

This is the way that we North Carolinians have been wont to put it. One does not fail to detect a note of aggressiveness in these declarations of modesty. A citizen of a neighboring commonwealth once said, in the course of a good-humored dispute with a Tar Heel: "The trouble with you fellows, is that you're so d——d proud of your humility." But, anyway, the self-abasement is a thing of the past now. The former valley is becoming a pretty good mountain itself when it comes to telling the world. No longer does there take place this sort of colloquy, which one could hear at Virginia Springs back in the days when there were no North Carolina resorts:

"Oh, you are a Virginian, of course?"

[Apologetically] "No, Madam; but I was born quite near the Virginia line."

The late Governor Aycock summed up the educational status in these words: "Thank God for South Carolina! She keeps North Carolina from the foot of the column of illiteracy." The press made no contribution to the problem. The task of Josephus Daniels's daily paper, for instance, was to turn everything to political advantage, in its own words to "save the State." The two following citations are illustrative: "Who discovered the North Pole? Dr. Cook, of course, and it's the usual Republican trick to take the glory from Cook because he is

275

a Democrat, and give it to Peary, a Republican." The efforts of the Rockefeller Foundation to eradicate hook-worm with its deadly consequences Mr. Daniels declared to be nothing less than a reflection upon the State whose people were the healthiest on earth and had no such disease as hook-worm—the whole thing being another illustration of meddling Northern philanthropy.

The best philosophy the State could boast for a long time was that of Nathaniel Macon, Speaker of the National House in the early days of the Republic. "Bury me," he said, "in the rockiest spot of my plantation, cover me over with white flint rocks, and do not mark my grave." And among his wise saws were: "Hold elections every year," "Don't live near enough to your neighbor to hear his dog bark," "Poor land is the best neighbor," "Pay as you go—that is the philosopher's stone." Governor Vance followed with the wisdom that "When a man left the farm for the factory he ceased to be a free man and became a slave."

How could there be outstanding men or commerce in these circumstances? And great cities, such as Atlanta, Georgia; Richmond, Virginia; or Charleston, South Carolina, would be a menace to liberty and not to be thought of for a moment. North Carolina hasn't them today—uniquely among Southern States.

This is a far cry indeed from today, when we find Virginia and South Carolina and Georgia newspapers asking, almost plaintively, why North Carolina goes ahead so much faster than her Southern sisters in education, good roads, industrial development. I shall not encumber this discussion with statistics. The facts are easily ascertainable from Federal census reports and other official documents. Suffice it to set down a few of the most important evidences of the remarkable awakening, merely to show the contrast between old era and new.

In the first ten months of 1922 North Carolina communities voted $11,000,000 for school buildings, more than Virginia, South Carolina, Georgia, Alabama, and Tennessee combined. In the last two years she has voted $50,000,000 for good roads and is preparing to vote $15,000,000 more, a total that promises nearly to equal the combined outlay for roads in all the other Southern States south of the Potomac and east of the Mississippi. She leads all Southern States in cotton and tobacco manufacturing, and in textile manufacturing is second in the nation to Massachusetts. In twenty years industrial wages have increased from 14 to 137 millions of dollars, and capital employed from 68 to 669 millions. The State has been conspicuously generous, in comparison with other States in the same section of the country, in supporting institutions of higher education, notably the University, the College for Women, and the College of Agriculture and Engineering.

Turning to the dark side of the picture, we are faced with the living and working conditions of a great part of North Carolina's agricultural population. Tens of thousands of small farmers are owned body and soul by the landowner and the money-lender. Their crop is mortgaged before it sprouts, and if cotton and tobacco prices reach a low level, which happens many years, not only is there no margin over and above the debt, but a deficit which leaves the farmers deeper in the mire than ever. It is these Americans sunk in poverty of whom Walter Hines

Page wrote in "The Forgotten Man." Competent observers have estimated that between two and three hundred thousand of these tenant farmers—"croppers," as they are called—and their families are not possessed of the wherewithal for even the simplest sort of decent life.

Another condition of which North Carolina has no cause to be proud is the low state of culture reflected both in the creation and in the appreciation of literature, painting, sculpture, and music. True, there is a cultured class around the colleges and in some of the cities, with scattered points of light in the villages and the country, but it is a deplorably insignificant showing. A recent report upon the small number of books bought, and borrowed from public libraries, brought forth avowals of mortification and vehement self-criticism from the State's organs of news and opinion.

The saving factor, as regards both tenant farmer and the neglect of literature and the arts, is that North Carolina is working to remove both these reproaches. It is decreasingly trying to distract attention or blind its own eyes by rhapsodic allusions to its Mecklenburg Declaration of Independence in 1775 and the gallant deeds of '61 to '65. The leaders of the State's thought are zealously striving to remedy its weaknesses, and they are supported by an active forward-looking element the absence of which thirty-five or forty years ago was so vividly recorded by Mr. Page. A State literary and historical association, an active library association, and an organization at the university to develop dramatic talent are leading manifestations of the will-to-progress in one direction. In the other direction, the farm-tenancy evil is being attacked by experts in rural sociology, a public-welfare department, farm-demonstration agents, and of course through the steady expansion of the schools.

In our history a few incidents, now forgotten by most folks, deserve to be recalled because of their important consequences; and a half dozen or so men have had an influence, far more profound than is commonly realized, upon North Carolina life and policies in the last twoscore years. Less than a generation ago in the river bottoms of the far South ague and fever were universal. The remedy was quinine in solution with its bitter taste. Now a certain Dr. Grove from Tennessee discovered a way of concealing the unpleasant taste and produced a remedy, real or alleged, which netted him a fortune. He chanced to pass through the Land of the Sky. The chateau of George W. Vanderbilt and its magnificent grounds attracted his attention. He investigated the Thermal Belt, well-nigh immune to frost and especially adapted to the growth of choice apples. He traveled over the Yonnalasee highway, skirting the Grandfather Mountain, with its great cascades tumbling through rhododendron and mountain laurel; his eyes dwelt on Mt. Mitchell, 6,800 feet above sea level, with a hundred sister peaks of more than 5,000 feet each; he caught rainbow trout in the Oconolufty, the Cataloochee, the Tuckasegee. He found, notably at Tryon and Flat Rock, cultivated families from Chicago, Charleston, New Orleans, and remoter sections, writers, authors, scholars, Army and Navy men, seeking an all-the-year climate and finding it. He compared western North Carolina, with its dry climate and gorgeous scenery, with New England or the playgrounds of the Old World. To his appraising eye the Blue Ridge and the Craggies seemed superior to the White Mountains or the Green, the Adirondacks or the Berkshires; the sylvan Wye and the gentle Afton inferior to the rippling French Broad, the picturesque Swannanoa, the romantic Nantahala, dashing over pebbly bottoms. His mind was made up—Asheville would be his headquarters. And at Asheville he constructed the costliest resort hotel in the world. To Grove's Tasteless Chill Tonic let us rise and sing! Last year 300,000 people visited the Asheville region with its long stretches of hard-surfaced roads. Nearby the Government has two hospitals for soldiers; and Black Mountain, Hendersonville, Montreat, and Junaluska are assembly grounds for religious bodies of all kinds. Two boys' schools, one with patronage extending from South Carolina to Texas; the other filled with the picked youth of New England, Chicago, and the West, are the pride of this metropolis of the mountains. Camps for boy and girl scouts are plentiful. Through the newly created Pisgah National Forest and Game Reserve runs the national highway to Pisgah, 5,700 feet above the sea, furnishing a panorama of mountain scenery of marvelous beauty and grandeur. Perhaps the greatest playground for the people east of the Mississippi has come into being.

Just after the Civil War a sturdy man, living in the hill country, drove a covered wagon loaded with tobacco, which he had manufactured by hand, to the Capehart herring fishery on the Albemarle Sound. The two mules required the better part of a week for the journey to and fro, for the roads were muddy and rough. The venture was a success; his tobacco had been bartered for corned herring and the herring in turn had been traded for fresh pork, which the merchants in Raleigh bought at good prices. Out of his double profit our small tobacco manufacturer could afford to be generous, even lavish, so he laid out a dollar in brown sugar, bought a tin bucket, a dozen shiny pewter spoons, and, on reaching home, proudly bade his three sons pitch in and eat all they wanted. In about half an hour the second lad called out: "Daddy, they've cheated you on this sugar, the bottom isn't half as good as the top." This red-headed lad was James Buchanan Duke, today the richest man in all Dixie.

While he was eating his first sugar another lad, somewhat older and of gentle birth, lately returned from Lee's army, was sitting on the generous veranda of his ancestral home regretting the fate which brought him into the world too late to have been a major general, and asking himself "What next?" This was Walter Clark, a Confederate colonel at 17, now, and for the last third of a century, Chief Justice of the Supreme Court of North Carolina, the most talked-of man in the State's history.

These two men, Clark and Duke, differing *toto coelo*, have taught the State to think in terms of millions. Before the coming of Duke and Clark "Pay as you go" was the fixed policy of the State, good roads or bad roads, education or no education. Macon had promulgated it, Vance advocated it, Aycock got roundly abused for violating it in the cause of universal education, Daniels's paper frightened legislature after legislature into following it. But "Pay as you go" is no more. Dead are the old leaders—and eight years in Washington have educated Josephus Daniels. It should be set down in his favor that for a long time now he has been a consistent champion of progress. No longer does he fight bond issues on behalf of great enterprises; and at this time, cities, counties, and the State, released from the dead hand of the past, are marketing bonds by the millions, for roads and schools, for water-works and other public necessities.

All this pleases the Chief Justice immensely. It dwarfs the individual and magnifies the State. "Give the people all comforts, all conveniences," says Clark. When Circuit Judge, his standing orders in a hundred counties were: "Remove those uncomfortable chairs from the jury box, replace them with the latest revolving chairs; tear up that ill-smelling carpet; put a clock on the wall; bring the county law library into the courtroom; transact public business in a business way." In one county, where the commissioners refused to obey, he called the matter to the attention of an admiring grand jury with satisfactory results. Asked what will become of our grandchildren, burdened with the weight of debt, he smiles and says: "Don't you worry about the grandchildren, they will take care of themselves, much better than you or I did."

When the late Bishop Kilgo, then president of Trinity College, praised Washington Duke for a large gift to the college, Clark, a trustee, took offense, spurned the money, sought to expel Kilgo from the faculty, and in a ringing article parodied President Kilgo's speech of acceptance: "My Lord Duke, give us money; thou art the greatest man in this our Southland; thy little finger is thicker than the loins of the law; money, money, all else is but as dust in the balance." After these plain words the atmosphere of Clark's city church, its stewards being also Trinity trustees, grew decidedly cold. The fight got into the courts and threatened to disrupt the Methodist church. Clark suggested that to the Trinity College motto "Eruditio et Religio" should be added "et Tobacco." Following hard on this episode, Brother Kilgo was made Methodist bishop, while Brother Clark continued to do business as usual.

Chief Justice Taft recently declared that he would not trust Judge Clark with the Constitution overnight, and it is said that when a writ of error was recently demanded of the previous Chief Justice the following conversation took place:

Railroad Attorney: "We are asking a writ of error to the Supreme Court of North Carolina, Mr. Chief Justice."

Chief Justice White: "What is the nature of the action, and who wrote the opinion?"

Railroad Attorney: "The action is against a railroad for damages for personal injury and the opinion was written by Chief Justice Clark."

Chief Justice White: "You need not trouble to read the record. I will sign your writ."

The corporation papers often charge that Clark is trailing the judicial ermine in the dust. He likes this. It calls the people's attention sharply to the fact that corporations dislike him. Tireless years has Clark labored to improve sanitary conditions in factories, protect the health and life of the wage-earner, throw safeguards about women and children, bring about woman's suffrage, and explode an opinion, in Hoke *vs.* Henderson, that a public office is a contract. "The people gave, the people can take away," said Clark, Chief Justice. To Walter Clark the Constitution of the United States is but a buffer to protect the rich in their ill-gotten gains. Washington, Henry, Marshall, Adams, Franklin were land-grabbers, time-servers. Jefferson was the honest man of the Revolution. The greatest usurpation in judicial history was Marshall's declaring an Act of Congress unconstitutional. Whatever the people say is the law. He admires fighters like La Follette and Tom Johnson. As for the trusts, they are snakes which must be killed, not scotched. Shall a handful of Rockefellers and Dukes be suffered to possess the wealth which, of right, belongs to one hundred and twenty million free men? The people will never get their dues until the government acquires all natural resources, coal, iron, and oil fields, the means of transportation and of disseminating news, all railroads, steamboats, telegraphs and telephones, and the like. Squeeze every drop of water out of this stock, issue millions of bonds if necessary, and purchase those properties at prime cost, restoring them to the people. Perhaps you inquire why the Chief Justice is so busy about these matters; why is he not solemn and dignified and like other wearers of the ermine? He is not made that way. He wants these changes to take place in his lifetime, and he verily believes that they will be. If in the pursuit of them he become lonesome, unsocial, cut off from companionship with his class, run out of the aristocratic city church to the little Methodist chapel in the outskirts, a man without party, friends, pleasures, or vices—what of it? That way duty and destiny lie.

And "Buck" Duke? He does not know that Judge Clark is after him. He started life with nothing, and if he is the most powerful capitalist in the South he achieved it all himself. Before he organized the tobacco trust and put cigarettes in the mouths of the Chinese and Japanese, the tobacco crop of North Carolina was a pitiful sixty million pounds—today it is four hundred million pounds, for which he pays the farmer the tidy sum of two hundred and fifty million dollars annually. It was he, he contends, who gave the State a standing in the financial world. From his brain and energy have sprung mill-towns and cities and great wealth for thousands of North Carolina associates, and into State and national coffers millions upon millions of taxes have been poured, so that all property in North Carolina today is exempt from taxation for State purposes. Before he built his cotton mills many a poor family in mountain cove or in the valley was eking out a living, rearing children pale and underfed. Today the same family has some money in the bank, ample food and clothing, and the blessings of schooled offspring.

Not long ago Duke's imagination was aroused by the hydro-electric possibilities of his State and he formulated plans for the Southern Power Company. "I shall develop," said he recently, "millions of horse-power, sufficient to heat and light the State; and our people will no longer pay tribute to the coal barons. Of

Textile mill near Raleigh. Once known as the "valley of humility between two mountains of conceit," North Carolina rose to prominence in the New South on the strength of its textile manufacturing. As the cotton growing up to the factory walls indicates, manufacturers devoted nearly every available square inch of land to their modernization project.

Piedmont, Carolina, I shall make a garden spot where there will be ample work for all; and agriculture shall be brought out of its long bondage. Trinity College, founded by my father, shall become the most heavily endowed college in America. Do you see that hydro-electric plant there?'' pointing to his Catawba development. "It has cost me eighty million dollars."

"What do you expect to get out of it, Mr. Duke?" he was asked.

"Nothing. I was born in North Carolina. It is about time I was beginning to think of a monument. I want to leave something in the State that five hundred years from now people can look at and say 'Duke did that.' Everyone owes something to the State he was born in, and this is what I want to leave to North Carolina. Do I look like a dangerous man to be let loose in the State?" he concluded. In this fierce fight between Clark and Duke, which will win? Shall it be Clark's "Dream of John Ball," or the dream of Buck Duke? In either case there will be progress.

In the nineties a native of the Pine Barrens of Central North Carolina, where land went begging at 50 cents an acre, was sitting in his cabin door when a stranger, driving over roads hub-deep in sand, halted near him. The stranger was Leonard Tufts, a soda-water manufacturer of Boston. He called:

"Hello, friend! Are you the owner of this entire farm?"

"That's what they say."

"Well, I can only say that I am truly sorry for you."

"Well now, stranger, don't you go wasting any of your sympathy on me, I don't own as much of this land as you think I do."

Today the Sand Hill Red-Skinned Peach Association, the Page family, and other peach growers own great tracts in this region which are hard to get at $100 an acre, and from Cameron to Hamlet are flourishing orchards of peaches, grapes, dewberries, and blackberries.

This transformation came about because of Leonard Tufts's visit in search of a winter climate to his taste, and Pinehurst and Southern Pines, in consequence of his work, are better known than the State itself. And what a stimulus they have been to the State, with their herds of blooded Berkshires and Ayrshires and their community fairs! But, true to the "esse quam videri" motto of the State, these good people have not made it known that they are raising a peach more luscious and more costly than the Georgia peach and that they shipped this season nearly a million crates, together with hundreds of thousands of crates of berries.

And yet all the material development in North Carolina would have been in vain but for an incident which be writ large in State history.

A barefoot boy in his humble home is practicing writing these words: "Now is the time for all good men to come to the aid of the party." His father has just sold a little piece of land and the County Squire has come to take the signature of the little boy's mother. "You sign on the second line, Madam, just under your husband, please." "I cannot write my name, I will have to make my mark"; and the boy is listening to the conversation. Not boastingly, but just to show the impelling power which made him pledge his life to the cause of education, Governor Charles B. Aycock, North Carolina's "educational Governor," once related this story, and added—"I then and there made a vow that every man and woman in North Carolina should have a chance to read and write."

The new amendment to the Constitution required that white boys and black boys alike, after January, 1908, possess certain educational qualifications as a prerequisite to the ballot. It was then that the voice of Aycock, like the crack of a new saddle, arouse the people as never before, bringing compulsory education, a six-months' school term, and farm-life schools throughout the State: "I tell you men that from this good hour opposition to the cause of education must be regarded as treason to the State. People charge me with spending great sums of money in the cause of education. I admit it; I am going to keep on doing it, and if I don't spend more it will be because I haven't got any more to spend."

McIver, laboring for the education of women, himself a college-mate of Aycock, declared: "When you educate a man, you educate one person; when you educate a woman, you educate an entire family." These men died young, died with their boots on, died spurring their hobby-horses—and these galloped on.

To the outsider the question at once occurs—what has made this State different from the rest, what explains its going ahead more rapidly than other Southern States in education and industrial development and road-building?

Now, let us not take too much credit to ourselves, but give some of it to Providence. The State of North Carolina is so placed that it escapes the rigors of severe cold and yet is free from the oppression that prolonged intense heat visits upon mind and body. Soil, the seasons, the temperature, and the distribution of rainfall enable us to grow every important crop grown in the United States. North Carolina alone in the Union is both a big cotton and a big tobacco-growing State. In cotton it stands with South Carolina, Georgia, Alabama, Mississippi, in tobacco with Virginia and Kentucky. This circumstance in itself would explain the millions by which its agricultural products exceed in value those of other States of about the same area.

Another natural advantage of capital importance to industrial expansion is water power, in which North Carolina leads all other States east of the Mississippi, excepting only New York with its Niagara. Hundreds of thousands of horse-power are already used for mills and public utilities, and a great deal more await development. In manufacturing North Carolina would never have been able to forge ahead as she has without rivers tumbling down from the heights of the Appalachian chain. Here is wealth in inexhaustible form. Coal is burned up, and even the fishes of the sea are numbered, but water keeps on coming out of the clouds.

So much for the help of Nature. But that is not the whole story. The other great cause has to do with men. North Carolina's development is the triumph of a vigorous middle class. The State never had the aristocratic tradition of either Virginia or South Carolina. To be sure, it had its planter class, the members of which cherished their escutcheons and family trees as the Virginia and South Carolina grandees cherished theirs; but this favored company never established itself so firmly in a holy of holies as its blood brethren to the north or south. It was closer to the ground, and when the big smash came the aura which had surrounded it was dissipated more quickly.

The more complete dominance of an upper class in Virginia had its advantages. It was favorable to leisure for a privileged few, and that leisure in turn was favorable to the growth of culture. No unbiased observer of the life of these two neighbors, no student of their history, can fail to find that North Carolina has been behind Virginia in polish, in the amenities of intercourse, in devotion to things literary and artistic.

The lesser gap between high and low in North Carolina in ante-bellum days has been reflected in a greater readiness to welcome new ideas, a lack of reverence for old allegiances and preconceptions. True, the dead hand of the past seemed to have as firm a grip here as elsewhere in the first quarter of a century after Appomattox, but more recent events have proved that this was not so.

There are those who will say: "Not so; there is no difference between the mass of the people in Virginia, North Carolina, South Carolina, and Georgia. They are from the same stock. Your faster march is due to your luck in having the right leaders at the right time." A good deal may be said for that view. While South Carolina and Georgia have been worshiping at the altars of such gods as Blease and Tom Watson, North Carolina has been heeding the advice of Aycock and McIver and Alderman and others with a passion for real democracy and democratic education. Whatever the reason there arose in the nineties a few leaders who answered miraculously to the need of the hour. They had to combat a vast ignorance—the heritage of slavery, war, and subsequent dire poverty—as well as sectarian prejudices fanned by persons who knew better. They attacked inertia and reaction with the fervor of crusaders. Their fight is being won although we still have far to go before we attain their ideals.

NORTH DAKOTA

A Twentieth-Century Valley Forge

ROBERT GEORGE PATERSON

AUGUST 8, 1923

T HE DRAMA OF North Dakota has been one of the great American epics. Scene of a gigantic struggle for independence, fought almost as fiercely and tenaciously as the Colonists' revolt in 1776, its far-stretching prairies have been a continuous battlefield since the bloody days of Custer. There is a sparkle in the piercing northern air "out in those vast spaces where men are men" that prompts the clash of dominating spirits. Regarded by the sedate East as America's *enfant terrible,* its numerous reforms have made its name a synonym for radicalism, for amazing governmental ventures that have startled the conservative world, shivering its spine with the latest spectacle of the Nonpartisan League, whose daring shadow has broadened across the whole Western horizon. There has been real romance in the story of its forceful *dramatis personae,* stalwart builders who visualized empires, political chieftains who slapped each other's faces, earnest home-makers converting the great plains into a chrome-yellow sea of ripening grain, strong men bold enough to strike out for ideals and break the invisible chains of unseen rulers exacting tribute from afar.

Aside from the war, North Dakota's revolt has been one of the century's outstanding political events in America. It has had as many interpretations as it has had observers. Many passively noted it as one of those freakish experiments in which in the name of progress certain Western States occasionally have indulged themselves, a temporary obsession to be viewed with no more concern than a city changing to the commission form of government. To some it has seemed the heroic effort of the second generation of a pioneer people to conquer political chiefs, economic overlordship, and the forces industrial civilization has erected, as their fathers subdued Indian chiefs and the forces of nature. Others saw it as a conflagration fired by the incendiary bombs of demagogues whose personal destruction offered the only hope for its extinction. Still others have fancied it everything from the first American foothold of the foreboding International to a revolt of the tenantry. Ample evidence may exist for these contentions. It certainly was not a revolution without its Jacobins, its carpet-bagging exploiters

285

Threshing wheat, North Dakota. The Nonpartisan League, which dominated state politics from 1915 until the middle of the 1920s, gathered much strength from the complaints of the state's farmers that they did not share in the wealth that their labor and skill had created.

suddenly swooping down upon it to direct its generals from behind the scenes, its feverish mob howling for the political decapitation of all survivors of the old regime. Nor was it all without its Dantons sincerely seeking the economic classes from a system that ground them into vassalage while they produced the world's daily bread.

Yet none of these estimates is wholly correct. North Dakota has been greatly misunderstood, for it is not a State of Marxian idealists. Prior to the Nonpartisan League's appearance it had but a straggling Socialist element scarcely able to muster two thousand votes on election day. Unlike its neighbors of South Dakota and Iowa to the south, it never had any land tenantry worth mentioning. It has not been bothered by labor disturbances, as it has no laboring class except its floating farm helpers who come and go with the spring and autumn. While in 1913 there was a brief I.W.W. flurry at Minot, the rioters were not North Dakotans but the typical Western rovers who frequent the trans-Mississippi region during the harvest season together with a boisterous handful of Butte's mining element who had strayed eastward out of Montana. Of all the States North Dakota is one of the freest from poverty. Nearly all of its half million people are landowners. A country of magnificent distances, its mighty expanse adapted itself to the acquisition of enormous tracts. The "bonanza farm," covering thousands of acres, sprang into vogue. Inconsequential indeed was the farmer possessing less than a section—640 acres—of land. The forty- or eighty-acre

farm of the Eastern or Middle States is inconceivable to the average North Dakotan. The majority of the 30 per cent of its people that are not Scandinavian are
keen-faced Yankees who migrated from Iowa, Illinois, and western New York to
get rich quick in the early land boom, but on seeing the country's possibilities
decided to stay. The years have dealt generously with them, and though North
Dakota boasts only a few millionaires nearly every one is well to do. Virtually
every farmer has his car, some three and four. A few years ago the tremendous
business of the Ford plant at Fargo ranked it near the top of that company's
branches throughout the country.

North Dakota's revolt came as the direct result of its complete subjection to
outside domination. Hunger, poverty, class distinctions, religious oppression,
political graft and chicanery all prompt rebellion. But nothing is more certain to
provoke it than the attempt of one people to govern another.

Nominally a sovereign State, in reality North Dakota has experienced few of
the thrills of sovereignty. From the hour of statehood it has been merely the
"flickertail" of the Minnesota gopher. Albeit Bismarck is the capital where the
Governor resides and the legislature convenes, the actual seat of the State government always has been in St. Paul and Minneapolis, homes of the overlords
who played with its destinies. At the outset James J. Hill became its acknowledged patron saint and colonized it with Norwegians as Minnesota already had
been settled by their Swedish cousins. Throughout his years his excellent paternal care well entitled him to the fond sobriquet of "Father of North Dakota."
From St. Paul he watched over its interests—so closely interwoven with his
own—with the same anxious eye a keen guardian displays for a wealthy ward.
From a carefully guarded chamber in the West Hotel in Minneapolis its political
wires were manipulated with rare dexterity by that most astute of all the Northwest's political chiefs, the frequently mentioned but infrequently seen "Alec"
McKenzie of Klondike fame—fame suggested, if not exactly extolled, by Rex
Beach in *The Spoilers*. Perchance because of the proprietary concern exhibited
in the State by these two gentlemen, the financiers, merchants, and millers of
Minnesota's chief centers assumed that North Dakota was their private preserve.
And few moves in North Dakota became possible without their sanction, as its
legislators, bankers, and grain growers soon came to understand.

Whenever a North Dakota politician aspired to public office in North Dakota
it was first necessary to run down to Minneapolis and see McKenzie. Whenever
a new general business policy was promulgated for the State its announcement
usually followed the return of some prominent North Dakotan from the Twin
Cities. When Fargo wanted a new chief of police it sent to Duluth, and as a new
Commercial Club secretary it selected one discarded by St. Paul. When Fargo
was chosen as the site for the French Government's gift to the Norwegians of the
United States of a statue of Rollo—the Norseman who invaded France ten centuries ago—the Hill interests managed, despite Fargo's spacious parks, to have
it placed on the tiny greensward of their Great Northern railroad station where
it has an uninspiring background in a yellow brick wall. When Minnesota's

big-business interests learned that the North Dakota farmer no longer was producing enough to meet the advancing cost of their operations they launched a "Better Farming Association" in North Dakota to scrutinize his efforts and to make him produce more, sending up an energetic young man from Minnesota to run it. And upon discovery that, instead of ever becoming self-supporting, the "association" would always be a drain on their purses, they calmly tried to unload it on North Dakota's State Agricultural College and replace the college president with the energetic young man. Never has North Dakota been free from the supervision of its eastern neighbor. Its first submitted constitution, indignantly rejected as "a piece of unwarranted outside intermeddling," was drafted by James Bradley Thayer of the Harvard law faculty on request of the Northern Pacific Railroad's president, Henry Villard. There is no doubt that Mr. Villard was actuated by the best of motives in his desire to assist the new State's admission into the Union. But that he was not a North Dakotan militated against the acceptance of his good offices. Even the turbulent upheaval which finally overthrew the yoke of alien domination failed to restore to North Dakota's soil the seat of its government. The shrewd Loftus, the Robespierre of its revolution, and the autocratic Townley, grabbing the tempest with Napoleonic opportunism, both directed their annihilating campaigns from St. Paul.

Sporadic outbursts from the beginning revealed North Dakota's unconscious groping for self-determination. Queer things, impulsive and incoherent, were done in this battle for independence, but all revealed the underlying aim. At its second election it chose a Populist governor. The experiment did not last. The next uprising in 1906 had more enduring effect and made North Dakota a vital contributor to the subsequent Republican schism. For six years a Democratic governor and an "Insurgent" Republican legislature fought the McKenzie "Stalwarts" for control. In that time they enacted into law nearly every suggestion that promised hope of deliverance from outside political and financial influence. The statutes bristled in their defiance of the railroads and all outside business operating within the State. They affected nearly every commodity used, inasmuch as North Dakota is wholly agricultural and manufactures practically nothing for its own consumption. The rigidity of the State's pure-food laws for a number of years barred entrance to the products of several concerns of national prominence.

These caprices disturbed distant campaign managers, not because of North Dakota's power in national conventions, but on account of the misleading impression its unexpected treatment of their chosen candidates might give the electorate at large. It inaugurated several disquieting political novelties. It was the first State to hold a Presidential primary, and in it forsook the magnetic leadership of its once widely boasted foster son, Roosevelt, for the progressivism of La Follette. Later, in the effort to rid itself of Nonpartisan rule, it established another disconcerting precedent as the first State to recall its governor—the inoffensive Nonpartisan figurehead, Frazier—whom it subsequently elected to the Senate in place of the veteran conservative, McCumber. Its great organized protest followed in natural sequence to this list of reforms. It was but another, more emphatic, more defiant step toward independence. The protest subsided gradually, partially due to the overwhelming outside financial pressure marshaled to kill it; but chiefly because the Nonpartisan League as conducted proved it was not wholly an agrarian nor a cooperative movement. As distasteful in its dictatorial methods as any previous experiment, it failed in its five years of virtual State power to fulfill its chief promise to the North Dakota farmers for whose express benefit it was supposed to exist.

Farming on a huge scale, the ills of the North Dakotan lie in marketing. His crop is wheat and small grains. He is dependent on the railroads to move it and on the grain commission men of the Minneapolis Chamber of Commerce to sell it. Between the two he early found himself a helpless victim of strange price fluctuations and freight tariffs that more frequently favored the big elevator, milling, and railroad interests than himself. The chief Twin City millers and elevator magnates controlled the Chamber of Commerce, and the trading privileges of its floor were largely restricted to their representatives. As they were in position to buy grain virtually at their own grading, the North Dakota farmer felt himself at their mercy.

Amelioration of this condition was sought through a railroad commission empowered to adjust shipping disputes, through elevator commissions created to sit in Duluth and Minneapolis and seek fairer grading. Finally came a proposal for the construction of North Dakota State-owned and State-managed terminal elevators at Duluth and the Twin Cities. This caught the popular fancy and gradually edged its way into the political platforms. But owing to that happy lapse of memory with which politicians seem blessed after election, the cherished projects always found a waiting grave in legislative committees.

Meanwhile a Farmers' Equity Society sprang into being to market the crop independently, and opened a Cooperative Selling Exchange in St. Paul. Immediately it became the target of the Minneapolis Chamber of Commerce. Both were located in Minnesota's Twin Cities, but as North Dakota furnished the crop it became the battleground of the conflict. The North Dakotans welcomed it, for they always relish a fight and are ever ready to take sides. Loftus, president of the Equity Exchange, a spectacular figure with a keen knowledge of crowd psychology, staged his skirmishes in Fargo every January when it was filled with farmers attending its annual grain growers' convention. His bizarre appeals and escapades stirred the State. He rented auditoriums, threw men out bodily, and applied for the removal of that police chief who dared refuse him protection. Townley sat in his audiences, an obscure but studious observer. When Loftus had keyed the farmers to open revolt and marched them on to Bismarck, while the legislature sat, to demand the long-promised State-owned elevator, Townley cleverly stepped in and wrested away the leadership for himself. He steered the Equity's membership into an organization of his own. Until that moment this new king, suddenly rising over this Egypt which knew not Joseph, had never been heard of even throughout his own country, the "slope country," on the western edge of the State. Dynamic, resorting to all the bombastic tricks of Loftus, he swept North Dakota like a Billy Sunday whirlwind. Staking his fortunes on this spirit of revolt, at its height he toured the State in an automobile and secured the signed pledges of the farmers to support the child of his brain—the Nonpartisan League—which was to make him North Dakota's dictator for the next half decade.[1]

Ostensibly the Nonpartisan League began as an association of North Dakota farmers formed to run their own State. But it gathered its leaders from the earth's four corners. While Townley was its czar, he was not so unwise as to conduct it without advisers. One came from far-away Australia and New Zealand, another from Colorado and Washington, some from New York, several from Minnesota, but few from North Dakota. Some of these special importations had been prominent I.W.W. attorneys, and nearly every one of them had a record in several States as a candidate for some exalted office on the Socialist ticket.

Under League rule North Dakota launched energetically into numerous enterprises and sought to become its own financier. It opened a State bank. It started a home-building scheme. It attempted coal-mine seizures. It enacted legislation to seize necessary industries either in peace or war. It created an appointed State sheriff to whom all elected county sheriffs were made answerable. It subverted its public educational system to propagandize the League in all the public educational institutions. It attempted its own immigration commission to determine who should enter the State from Canada. That one tribunal expected to be the exemplar of law and order, its Supreme Court, indulged itself in a travesty of all order which might have gone well in opera-bouffe but was hardly expected in a serious government. Three newly elected League justices appeared at the capital and demanded their seats a month before their predecessors' terms expired. One of the court's League justices, evidently of journalistic bent, found a unique pastime in penning for the press a weekly letter which commented freely on his associates and discussed important cases up on appeal before they were decided. The League taught North Dakotans some new tricks about how to perpetuate a State administration's power. It legally supplied the voter with advisers to help him prepare his ballot correctly. It then granted him the ingenious supplemental privilege of re-marking it at the polls upon discovery that he might have checked the wrong candidates.

It would be difficult to imagine a tranquil hour in North Dakota. Born in strife, it has been seething ever since. Long before the battle of the bottle made the American flag its champion and attacked the freedom of the seas, North Dakota wrestled single-handed with the demon rum. With its twin to the south it was the first State to write prohibition into its constitution when framed.

[1]The League was founded in 1915 and eventually had branches in thirteen farm states. Its greatest successes came in 1916, when it elected a governor, and 1919, when the League-controlled legislature set up a state elevator and state bank. Attacked for Bolshevism and disloyalty (its members were largely of German and Scandinavian origin), the League declined in the early 1920s. [D. H. B.]

North Dakotans love their State with an admirable devotion. Their language describing it is rich with superlatives. They call Fargo the "biggest little city in the world" and don't relish having it belittled. They like to think of the Red River valley as the "world's bread basket" and to compare it to the Nile. Fargo assumes importance because it is the State's cultural, financial, and political clearing-house, but in more densely settled sections it wouldn't pass for a town of secondary consequence. Quite usual, Eastern in tone, similar to towns of 30,000 in Ohio or any Middle Atlantic State, it has a couple of bishops, plenty of churches, good public schools, an enterprising daily press, some handsome homes and streets, and an "exclusive set." There is considerable civic spirit in the State and nearly every hamlet has its "white way."

Yet with all its boasted State pride, notwithstanding its readiness to spend money on futile impeachment trials, on all sorts of elections and primaries, on new governmental experiments, North Dakota never has found the energy or wherewithal to build a decent State capitol. The nondescript hulk it calls a capitol unblushingly is shown to Bismarck visitors as one of the sights. And it is one. Although its location is superb on an ideal spot overlooking the town and the bald hills beyond the Missouri, it is a ramshackle, pieced-together arrangement, constructed in three sections, each of a different kind and color of brick— the front dark red, the middle wing vivid yellow, and the rear white. On all sides handsome new State capitols have been erected but North Dakota makes no effort to replace this architectural monstrosity. On its sloping grounds are the log cabin Roosevelt occupied during his three years at Medora, and a bronze statue the North Dakota women have reared to the Indian "bird woman" who guided Lewis and Clark across the Rockies.

Educationally North Dakota is quite abreast of other States. Its percentage of illiteracy is surprisingly small. Except for a meritorious but unknown epic drama of its famous Indian massacre by Aaron McGuffy Beede, an old Episcopal missionary among the Sioux, so far it hasn't figured much in literature and produced no distinctive literary geniuses of national renown—unless the monthly preambles of Sam Clark in his *Jim Jam Jems* could possible rank him as a littérateur.

To live North Dakota's life is thrilling. It has a bleak, white winter when the mercury occasionally plays around forty degrees below and the railroad rails snap in the crispness. But there is a mighty call in its summer with its nine o'clock sunset and lingering twilight. And it has an irresistible autumn when the prairie chicken and wild-duck hunting is unequaled. From the picturesque undulations that pocket Minnesota's myriad sparkling lakes the country flattens out into the broad surfaces of North Dakota's smooth, fertile prairie which stretches away in a vast sweep to where the Bad Lands' jagged cliffs trace their lonely outline against the leafless Western sky. North Dakota possesses some strange germ that enters the blood and makes whoever leaves it want to go back.

OHIO

I'll Say We've Done Well

SHERWOOD ANDERSON

AUGUST 9, 1922

I AM COMPELLED TO write of the State of Ohio reminiscently and from flashing impressions I got during these last ten years, although I was born there, my young manhood was spent within its borders, and later I went back and spent another five or six years as a manufacturer in the State. And so I have always thought of myself as an Ohioan and no doubt shall always remain, inside myself, an Ohioan.

Very well, then, it is my State and there are a thousand things within it I love and as many things I do not like much at all. And I dare say I might have some difficulty setting down just the things about Ohio that I most dislike were it not for the fact that what I am to write is to appear in *The Nation,* and *The Nation,* being, well anyway what they call broad-minded, cannot well refuse room to my particular form of broadening out, as it were.

Ohio is a big state. It is strong. It is the State of Harding and McKinley. I am told that my own father once played in the Silver Cornet Band at Caledonia, Ohio. Warren G. may remember him as Teddy, sometimes called Major Anderson. He ran a small harness shop at Caledonia. Just why he was called Major I never knew. Perhaps because his people came from the South. Anyway, I ought to have a job at Washington. Everyone else from that county has one.

And now Ohio has got very big and very strong and its Youngstown, Cincinnati, Akron, Cleveland, Toledo, and perhaps a dozen other prosperous industrial cities can put themselves forward as being as ugly, as noisy, as dirty, and as mean in their civic spirit as any American industrial cities anywhere. "Come you men of 'these States,' " as old Walt Whitman was so fond of saying, in his windier moods, trot out your cities. Have you a city that smells worse than Akron, that is a worse junk-heap of ugliness than Youngstown, that is more smugly self-satisfied than Cleveland, or that has missed as unbelievably great an opportunity to be one of the lovely cities of the world as has the city of Cincinnati? I'll warrant you have not. In this modern pushing American civilization of ours

292

you other States have nothing on our Ohio. Credit where credit is due, citizens.
I claim that we Ohio men have taken as lovely a land as ever lay outdoors
and that we have, in our towns and cities, put the old stamp of ourselves on
it for keeps.

Of course, you understand, that to do this we have had to work. Take for example a city like Cincinnati. There it sits on its hills, the lovely southern Ohio
and northern Kentucky hills, and a poet coming there might have gone into the
neighboring hills and looked down on the site of the great city; well, what I say
is that such a poet might have dreamed of a white and golden city, nestling there
with the beautiful Ohio at its feet. And that city might, you understand, have
crept off into the green hills, that the poet might have compared to the breasts of
goddesses, and in the morning when the sun came out and the men, women, and
children of the city came out of their houses and looking abroad over their sweet
land of Ohio—

But pshaw, let's cut that bunk.

We Ohioans tackled the job and we put the kibosh on that poet tribe for
keeps. If you don't believe it, go down and look at our city of Cincinnati now.
We have done something against great odds down there. First we had to lick
the poet out of our own hearts and then we had to lick nature herself, but we did
it. Today our river front in Cincinnati is as mean-looking a place as the lake
front in Chicago or Cleveland, and you please bear in mind that down there in
Cincinnati we had less money to work with than they did up in Chicago or even
in Cleveland.

Well, we did it. We have ripped up those hills and cut out all that breasts-
of-goddesses stuff and we've got a whanging big Rotary Club and a couple of
years ago we won the World Series, or bought it, and we've got some nice rotten
old boats in the river and some old sheds on the waterfront where, but for us,
there might not have been anything but water.

And now let's move about the State a little while I point out to you a few more
things we have done. Of course, we haven't any Henry Ford over there, but just
bear in mind that John D. Rockefeller and Mark Hanna and Harvey Firestone
and Willys up at Toledo and a lot of other live ones are Ohio men and what I
claim is—they have done well.

Look at what we had to buck up against. You go back into American history
a little and you'll see for yourself what I mean. Do you remember when La Salle
was working his way westward, up there in Canada, and he kept hearing about
a country to the south and a river called the Ohio? The rest of his crowd didn't
want to go down that way and so, being a modest man and not wanting to set
himself up against public opinion, he pretended to be down of a bad sickness. So
the rest of the bunch, priests and Indians and others, went on out west and he just
took a couple of years off and cut out southward alone, with a few Indians. And
even afoot and through the thick woods a man can cover quite a considerable
amount of territory in two years. My notion is he probably saw it all.

I remember that an old man I knew when I was a boy told me about seeing the Ohio River in the early days, when the rolling hills along its banks were still covered with great trees, and what he said I can't remember exactly, but anyway, he gave me the impression of a sweet, clear, and majestic stream, in which one could swim and see the sand of the bottom far below, through the sparkling water. The impression I got from the old man was of boys swimming on their backs, and white clouds floating overhead, and the hills running away, and the branches of trees tossed by the wind like the waves of a vast green sea.

It may be that La Salle went there and did that. It wouldn't surprise me if some such scandal should creep out about him. And then, maybe, after he got down to where Louisville, Kentucky, now stands, and he found he couldn't get any further with his boats because of the falls in the river—or pretended he couldn't because he was so stuck on the fine Ohio country up above—it may be, I say, that he turned back and went northward along eastern Ohio and into a land of even more majestic hills and finer forests and got finally into that country of soft stepping little hills, up there facing Lake Erie.

I say maybe he did and I have my own reasons. You see this fellow La Salle wasn't much of a one to talk. He didn't advertise very well. What I mean is he was an uncommunicative man. But you go look him up in the books and you will see that later he was always being condemned, after that trip, and that he was always afterward accused of being a visionary and a dreamer.

From all I've ever been able to hear about Ohio, as it was before we white men and New Englanders got in there and went to work, the land might have done that to La Salle, and for that matter to our own sons, too, if we, God-fearing men, hadn't got in there just when we did, and rolled up our sleeves, and got right down to the business of making a good, up-and-coming, Middle-Western, American State out of it. And, thank goodness, we had the old pep in us to do it. We original northern Ohio men were mostly New Englanders and we came out of cold stony New England and over the rocky hills of northern New York State to get into Ohio.

I suppose the hardship we endured before we got to Ohio was what helped us to bang right ahead and cut down trees and build railroads and whang the Indians over the heads with our picks and shovels and put up churches and later start the anti-saloon league and all the other splendid things we have done. I'll tell you that the country makes no mistake when it comes to our State for Presidents. We train our sons up right over there.

Why, I can remember myself, when I was a boy, and how I once got out of a job and went one fall with a string of race horses all over our State. I found out then what La Salle was up against when our State was what you might call new, in a way of speaking. Why, I got as dreamy and mopy, drifting along through the beautiful Ohio country that fall, as any no-account you ever saw. I fooled along until I got fired. That's how I came out.

Then of course I had to go into the cities and get a job in a factory and the better way of life got in its chance at me, so that for years I had as good a bringing up and knew as much about hustling and pushing myself forward and advertising and not getting dreamy or visionary as any American there is. What I mean is that if I have slipped any since I do not blame the modern Ohio people for it. It's my own fault. You can't blame a town like Toledo or Cleveland or Akron or any of our up-and-coming Ohio cities if a man turns out to be a bum American and doesn't care about driving a motor at fifty miles an hour or doesn't go to the movies much evenings.

What I mean to say is that this business of writing up the States in the pages of *The Nation* is, I'll bet anything, going to turn out just as I expected. There'll be a lot of knocking, that's what I'll bet. But I'm not going to do that. I live in Chicago now and our motto out here is, "Put away your hammer and get out your horn." Mayor Thompson of Chicago got that up. And, anyway, I think it is pretty much all silliness, this knocking and this carping criticism of everything American and splendid I hear going on nowadays. I'm that way myself sometimes and I'm ashamed of it.

The trouble with me is that I once had a perfectly good little factory over in Ohio, and there was a nice ash-heap in a vacant lot beside it, and it was on a nice stream, and I dumped stuff out of my factory and killed the fish in it and spoiled it just splendid for a while. What I think now is that I would have been all right and a good man, too, but on summer afternoons I got to moping about the Ohio hills alone, instead of going over to the Elks Club and playing pool where I might have got in with some of the boys and picked up some good points. There were a lot of good bang-up Ohio pushers over in that Ohio town I had my factory in and I neglected them. So of course I went broke and I'll admit I've been rather a sorehead ever since. But when I come down to admit the honest truth I'll have to say it wasn't Ohio's fault at all.

Why, do you know, I've had times when I thought I'd like to see that strip of country we call Ohio, just as that Frenchman La Salle must have seen it. What I mean is with nothing over there but the dear, green hills and the clear, sweet rivers and nobody around but a few Indians and all the whites and the splendid modern cities all gone to—I won't say where, because it's a thought I don't have very often and I'm ashamed of it.

What I suppose gets me yet is what got me when I stayed away from the Elks Club and went walking in the hills when I was trying to be a manufacturer, and what got me fired when I was a race-track swipe. I get to thinking of what that darned old man once told me. I'll bet he was a Bolshevik. What he told me set me dreaming about swimming in clear streams, and seeing white cities sitting on hills, and of other cities up along the northern end of my State, facing Lake Erie, where in the evening canoes and maybe even gondolas would drift in and out of the lake and among the stone houses, whose color was slowly changing and growing richer with the passage of time.

But, as I say, that's all poet stuff and bunk. Having such pipe dreams is just what put the old kibosh on my factory, I'll bet anything. What I think is that a man should be glad it's getting harder and harder for any of our sons to make the

Small Ore Loaders, Conneaut, Ohio. Ohio industrialization has rarely been aesthetically pleasing. The massive size of machines, Sherwood Anderson argues, blots out more intangible concerns.

same mistakes I did. For, as I figure it out, things are going just splendidly over in Ohio now. Why, nearly every town is a factory town now and some of them have got streets in them that would make New York or London or Chicago sit up and take notice. What I mean is, almost as many people to every square foot of ground and just as jammed up and dirty and smoky.

To be sure, the job isn't all done yet. There are lots of places where you can still see the green hills and every once in a while a citizen of a city like Cleveland, for example, gets a kind of accidental glimpse at the lake, but even in a big town like Chicago, where they have a lot of money and a large police force, a thing like that will happen now and then. You can't do everything all at once. But things are getting better all the time. A little more push, a little more old zip and go, and a man over in Ohio can lead a decent life.

He can get up in the morning and go through a street where all the houses are nicely blacked up with coal soot, and into a factory where all he has to do all day long is to drill a hole in a piece of iron. It's fine the way Ford and Willys and all such fellows have made factory work so nice. Nowadays all you have to do, if you live in an up-to-date Ohio town, is to make, say, twenty-three million holes in pieces of iron, all just alike, in a lifetime. Isn't that fine? And at night a fellow can go home thanking God, and he can walk right past the finest cinder piles and places where they dump old tin cans and everything without paying a cent.

And so I don't see why what such cities as Cleveland and Cincinnati have done to knock dreaminess and natural beauty of scene galley-west can't be done also by all the smaller towns and cities pretty fast now. What I'm sure is they can do it if the Old New England stock hasn't worn out and if they keep out foreign influences all they can. And even the farmers can make their places out in the country look more modern and like the slums of a good live city like Chicago or Cleveland if they'll only pep up and work a little harder this fall when the crops are laid by.

And so, as far as I see, what I say is, Ohio is O.K.

OKLAHOMA

Low Jacks and the Crooked Game

BURTON RASCOE

JULY 11, 1923

P OLITICS IN OKLAHOMA are, if anything, not much more corrupt than they are, say, for instance, in the city of Boston. The economic parity in Oklahoma is, if anything, not much more out of balance than it is, say, for instance, in the city of New York. The averages of literacy and intelligence in Oklahoma are little lower than they are, say, for instance, in the city of Chicago. The difference is that whereas in these great urban communities one may easily live in comfortable ignorance of the socio-economic condition that sustains one, there is in the State of Oklahoma no city large enough to conceal the hideous aspect of its fundamental organization. The sinister and discomforting skeleton is not only devoid of all the draperies, rouge, rice powder, and mascara of civilization; it is not even presentably filled out with the fat and tissue of human illusions.

It is not that Oklahomans are men and women set aside as an especially enigmatic exhibit in the mysterious way God moves His wonders to perform. They only seem so. That is because the State is so young and unpopulous as never to have acquired a social fabric with a nap of culture: it is a haphazard homespun every thread of whose woof is visible. An Oklahoman knows, if he keeps his eyes open at all, everything that is going on about him and he knows that it is not conducive to respect and solicitude for his fellow-men. It is the worst possible place for an idealist and, since most people of normal intelligence and decent instincts are weighted in adolescence with the impedimenta of illusions, they either shed their burden and become Oklahomans or shake the State's dust from their feet at the first opportunity. As a result the Oklahoma towns and cities are constantly being drained of their young and vigorous blood, blood which might redeem them from the mental, moral, and spiritual torpor into which, since statehood, they have fallen. Even in the larger towns such as Tulsa, Oklahoma City, Muskogee, Okmulgee, and Shawnee, the population, on the whole, is transient. People come and go in them with such rapidity that it is often difficult for one to discover a familiar face in the streets after a few years' absence. Only those who are anchored by real estate and resignation remain.

The reason is fairly obvious. Oklahoma has been, from the first, a boomer State, even before it was a State—when old Oklahoma Territory was first thrown open to settlers. It was peopled largely by land gamblers instead of home seekers. Like other boomer States, since the days of the California and through the Alaska gold rushes, Oklahoma was, when it first attracted attention, the goal not of people who wished to till the land, build homes, and develop a commonwealth on secure foundations, but of people who wanted to get rich suddenly and with as little effort as possible. That was the situation before oil was discovered in the State and that discovery intensified rather than diminished preexisting conditions. The State's cattle and agricultural resources are hardly more than self-sustaining, much less exploitable; but this fact did not prevent the land gamblers from inflating prices out of all proportion to the value of the land's increment. Towns, like Lawton, sprang up overnight with populations of 15,000 or more, on absolutely arid land, unfit even for grazing. They died out, of course, when the inhabitants discovered they could not live solely by trading real estate among themselves. In other towns, like Oklahoma City, more advantageously situated, on intersecting railway main lines and in reasonably productive districts, the boomer spirit was equally disastrous. Such towns were not permitted to grow normally. Their population figures were distorted into an aspect of metropolitanism and the optimistic real-estate boomers set about making the towns live up to these false figures. They sold bonds and erected skyscrapers for which they had no use, and these buildings sometimes remained vacant for years. They sold stock and erected great meat-packing, canning, tanning, and other industries which seldom got farther than buildings and equipment when bankruptcy revealed the enterprises as plain financial swindles, fostered often enough by local chambers of commerce to attract immigrants and sell them real estate. One naturally asks how it was that plain, common foresight did not tell the business men in communities where such things were going on that crashes and depression were bound to follow; but the answer is that there were almost never in these communities any business men in any acceptable use of that term, no business men mindful of the credit system, contented with a legitimate margin of profit, careful of future security; they were boomers, eager to make their immediate pile even at the cost of their established residences, stores, and reputations, and skip elsewhere. They took chances, that is all; they gambled, because the State has been from the first one vast roulette wheel played by adventurers from other States.

True enough, it has its farmers who bear the burden of producing the food, its manual laborers, small shopkeepers, clerks, and other accretions of industrialism which give some semblance of a permanently organized society; but behind them all is the gambling spirit producing probably the vulgarest low comedy offered anywhere under the name of democratic government. Where else is afforded a spectacle similar to this: The theft by night of the State papers from the Capitol in Guthrie by automobile bandits from Oklahoma City who sped back and established the State capital in the Lee-Huckins hotel; the indictment of a governor and a State bank examiner for graft arising from false statements of solvency of banks under State supervision; the emptying of the State prison overnight by a lieutenant governor who held the reins of government for a few hours in the absence of the governor and issued pardons at so much a head; all the important State officials selected by a lawyer for a great oil corporation, to whom they are in debt for campaign expenses incidental to their jobs and for whose laws and political wishes they are merely the agents and office boys; graft so prevalent and inalienable a feature of State government that the only citizens who are not partaking of it are the stupid or unlucky?

Let us consider for a moment the history of a State in which such a spectacle is possible. When the western part of the territory which the United States Government had reserved as a haven for the Indians who had been driven out of the other States was thrown open to land grabbers, certain portions were designated as Indian reservations and as school land. The remainder, up to a stated number of acres, was his who first staked it out as a claim. The west and southwest were suitable only for cattle raising; the northern and northeastern sections were soon a rich grain-producing region, yielding wheat, oats, barley, corn, alfalfa, and milo maize. The central, eastern, and southern sections of the territory were given over to cotton, corn, alfalfa, and potatoes. There was coal to be mined near El Reno, Oklahoma City, and Guthrie. At first, except in the extremely fertile district, there were extensive ranches and cattle ranges, acquired by the enterprising, and these were in due time fenced off and converted into small farms. Settlers out of the bleak hills and rocks of Arkansas, the dry prairies of Kansas and Texas, the swamps of Louisiana, and the barren lands of southern Missouri came through in covered wagons, prepared to establish homes. They found that the better portions of the land had already got into the hands of people who were holding them for speculation—town residents, bankers, real-estate operators. To acquire land one had either to pay a whopping price for it or marry an Indian woman. This latter method was a favorite one with a great many who were not already burdened with a family. Each adult Indian woman had 160 acres in her own right, as a government land grant, and for each child she should have there would be additional grants for 160 acres. At first there was also a government allotment of money to full-blooded Indians and to such children as they bore. This proved an allurement not only to a great many white men but to Negros as well, and as a consequence black and white squaw men and their progeny came into possession of such desirable lands as had not already fallen into the clutches of speculators and land operators.

There was established then almost from the first an agricultural caste system, divided into landowners, tenant farmers, and share-croppers. Less than 30 per cent of the farmers of the State own the land they work. The landowners rarely live on the land they own. They rent it to tenant farmers or leave its yield to the industry and intelligence of the share-croppers. A tenant farmer has his own teams and implements, cows, hogs, and chickens; he undertakes to till the land, pay for the extra farm labor, and market the crops. If he does not rent outright he pays over to the landlord a stated share of the gross proceeds on the farm for the year. The share-cropper is among the most pitiable of human beings. He owns nothing whatever except the clothes on his back. He usually has a wife and numerous children. These, and his own bodily strength, are his assets. The landlord provides him with a house in which to live, teams and implements with which to work, and, often enough, an advance of money for food while he is laying in the crops. He and his wife and children perform the labor in the fields and get in return a fraction of the yield of the crops.

The only way he knows of meeting the situation is that of voting the straight Democratic ticket if the Republicans happen to be in office, or of electing Republicans if the administration is Democratic. Mankind, to him, has three constituents: Democrats, Republicans, and the others, roughly classified as Reds. Without differentiation he includes among the Reds: socialists, anarchists, syndicalists, I.W.W.'s, Catholics, Jews, pacifists, labor unionists, atheists, and what not. If he is a Republican it is conceivable to him that a man may be a Democrat without being a menace to the community, or if he is a Democrat he will concede that a man may be a Republican and still be only misinformed politically; but it is not conceivable to him that a man may be neither a Democrat or a Republican and still hold a shred of honor. The most persistently and mercilessly exploited human being in the country, he is the most zealous and intractable upholder of the politico-economic system that exploits him. Let him hear that some other share-cropper as illiterate as himself has been converted to socialist doctrines and he will help his fellow Ku Klux Klanners that night give the poor wretch a tar bath and a coat of chicken feathers. He will not suffer for a moment anything that threatens his privilege of being mulcted.

Although the State has the most rigid banking laws, bringing all banks under State or Federal supervision, most banks in all but the larger cities are not banks at all; they are the offices of a group of men whose principal business is real-estate speculation, horse-trading, and mortgage foreclosing. Their depositors are not farmers; they have nothing to deposit. The bank officials are their own depositors who lend their money out at usurious rates. The State usury law limits the interest rate to 7 per cent. But this is the way it works. Farmer Brown has a span of mules worth in the market $650 and farm implements worth a couple of hundred dollars more. He needs $200 for food and for the salary of farm hands to tide him over until he has finished bringing in his crop. Early in the season he has already mortgaged his crop at the bank for the money necessary to live on while he is planting his crop. He applies for a loan of $200, giving as security a mortgage on his mules and implements. He receives $175 in cash and is obliged to sign a note promising to pay back $200 at 7 per cent. In other words, $25 in interest is collected from him before he gets his money. The amount subtracted from the original loan varies according to the pressure of the farmer's need and the negotiability of his securities. Sometimes the amount deducted from a loan of $100 is as much as $30. If he invokes the usury law (as some poor devils have done) he is blacklisted by every bank in the State and thereafter cannot borrow a cent, no matter what security he has to offer. If his crops fail or if the market place for his produce does not enable him to pay off his note or notes at the bank and he is unable to dig up more security, the mortgage is foreclosed.

A generous national government reserved the most fertile sections of the country for those Indians which it had hopes of making over into good and industrious citizens. It had been unable to tame the Apaches, Comanches, and Arapahoes, so it permitted them to die out of boredom in great numbers, under the armed surveillance of Federal troops in the arid regions of the southwest part of the State. The Osages, heirs to fertile broadlands in the north-central section, and good farmers by inclination and training, became, proverbially, the richest nation, per capita, on the face of the globe. Discovery of oil upon their lands and upon the lands of many of the Creeks and Cherokees (who had been granted nice rocky hills to roam around in) made millionaires of many of these original citizens of the country. The Seminoles and Creeks intermarried freely with the Negroes; and the Pottawottomies, Shawnees, Sacs and Foxes, and Cherokees intermarried equally freely with the whites. The Cherokees had a language and even a literature of their own; but with rare exceptions the Indians have not taken cordially to the blessings of the civilization which has been offered them. The Apaches, Comanches, and Arapahoes actively resented it as long as they were numerous, and even after they were shut up in stockades they occasionally broke out and scalped a few settlers. The Osages and the mixed breed Seminoles, Pottawottomies, Cherokees, Shawnees, and Creeks tilled their land, or had it tilled for them, and complied in some degree to the customs of the whites; but the full-blooded Indians, even of the younger generation, have consistently refused to embrace white culture. They live in tribal communities; they wear their beads, moccasins, and blankets; they hold such ceremonial dances as the government will permit them (they are denied the privilege of the war dance); and they allow themselves to be cheated out of their land by the enterprising whites. Under the Federal law, an Indian may dispose of his inherited land, but not of his original allotment, when he has reached the age of twenty-one. Knowing this, in every county seat in the State, land sharks literally sit around on the doorsteps of the county buildings waiting for old Indians to die and young ones to come to the age of twenty-one. These sharks know how much land each Indian can dispose of, what it is worth at the current land valuation, the date of the Indian's birth, his guardian, and his personal disposition.

Here is a typical instance of what goes on every month in a dozen different counties. The two leading bankers, which is to say the leading land sharks, in rival towns had their eye on the property of an Indian who had 800 acres of bottom land, worth at the lowest estimate $300 an acre as prices go. Two weeks before the youth's birthday one of them stole a march on the other, invited the boy on a trip, took him to Chihuahua, Mexico, got him drunk, showed him a riotous time in the redlight district, crossed the border back into the State on his birthday, had the deeds drawn up for him to sign, giving him $8,000 in cash for

Burning Oil Tanks, Jenks, Oklahoma. Wildcat drilling accounted for great success stories but also carried great risks.

$240,000 worth of property, got his signature, and rushed the deed through the probate court the next day.

So much, in sketch, for the productive complexion of the State exclusive of its bonanza of gas, oil, and coal—a comparatively recent discovery, and already, according to many expert estimates, a source of wealth that is rapidly being exhausted. The general features attending the discovery of oil in the Tulsa-Sapulpa and Ada-Ardmore districts do not differ in essentials from the turn of events such a discovery brings about in every State. There was, of course, the rush of adventurers, oil promoters, highjackers (an oil-region term for murderous robbers), laborers, and camp followers. Until Tulsa amassed a wealth in its local banks which compared favorably with that of St. Louis and Kansas City it was, like most of the smaller oil towns now, a gay and lawless community, with gambling houses running wide open, a redlight district in full blaze, moonshine whiskey readily obtainable throughout the periods of senatorial, State, and national dryness, and the frenzied excitement prevailing which is always a concomitant of sudden visions of wealth. Millionaires were made overnight, and men and women who had until yesterday toiled barefooted in the fields trying to wrest a meager living from the sandy and rocky soil suddenly found themselves in possession of incomes from oil leases amounting to thousands of dollars a week.

This sudden acquisition of unexpected wealth on the part of illiterate white settlers had its comic aspect: they knew but two or three ways of spending it— buying high-priced and luxurious automobiles and tearing them up on the rocky roads, only to buy new ones; chartering special cars for a trip to Niagara Falls

or to Washington; and buying diamonds. They tell of a wealthy Osage who inspected the cars for sale in Oklahoma City and found nothing to please him until
he chanced upon a white hearse, which he purchased forthwith. This vision and
fact of sudden, immense wealth has also its tragic side. The farmers, the normal
producers of the State, live buoyed up by the hope that some day oil will be
discovered on their land. Meanwhile they persist in the most backward agricultural methods obtaining in any State in the Union, and market their produce
through the most inefficient and wasteful channels of middlemen and profiteers
it is possible to imagine.

Within the last year the Oklahoma Cotton Growers' Association, a sort of
farmers' union, has been perfecting a cooperative scheme for marketing and
warehousing which may check some of the losses the farmer ordinarily sustains
in the disposal of his cotton. Another part of the plan of the association is to
limit the acreage in cotton to prevent overproduction. I was privy to one such
agreement by the assembled farmers of one country. The following spring every
single one of them increased his cotton acreage by at least a third, on the theory
that every one else would decrease his acreage, the price of cotton would go up,
and he would be the gainer. There was an excess of cotton produced throughout
the country that year; the price slumped, and these men who had solemnly
agreed to cut their production and raise corn for their stock and potatoes and
other vegetables for themselves all but starved.

After such a demonstration of stupidity and covetousness, such a general indifference to the common weal, one grows skeptical of any profound change for
the better in the source of wealth, the land; and this skepticism is deepened by
the knowledge that, so long as reports come from time to time that another well
has been sunk by oil-stock promoters, hope will spring eternal in the farmer's
breast that he will not have to plant either cotton or corn; so he sinks back in
sloth and squalor, living principally upon cornbread, salt pork, and sorghum
molasses—a diet so preponderatingly of corn that pellagra epidemics spread
through the State every year and children, who by all rules of hygiene should
wax strong in the fresh quiet and pure food of the farm, are emaciated, rickety,
weak, and sallow, easy preys to malaria, tuberculosis, and pneumonia. This because the mass of the farmers are at once so poor and so greedy that they do not
keep cows, and the bulk of such eggs and chickens as they raise they sell in the
town markets. There are plenty of schools, good schools for these children to go
to; belief in education amounts in Oklahoma to a superstition. The State is
heavily burdened with school taxes; a great portion of the land of the State is
reserved as a source of income for the maintenance of schools; and there is in
force a modification of the Indiana school system which offers probably as fine
a public means of education as to be found in any State. But the physique and
minds of the bulk of the farmers' children are stunted by malnutrition; and education in the towns and cities only leads the young men and women to a disenchantment and disgust with a social-political and economic scene from which
they are glad enough to escape.

OREGON

A Slighted Beauty

CHARLES H. CHAPMAN

FEBRUARY 7, 1923

WHEN IT FIRST occurred to Oregon some years ago to put up her charms for sale, she found the market monopolized by a more sumptuous beauty in the south. Competition was risky and the advertising it seemed to demand was expensive. One may possess beauty enough for an adored wife and mother without quite coming up to the mark of a reigning belle. The Creator slighted Oregon when he bestowed Mt. Hood, Crater Lake, and Neahkahnie upon her by scattering those picturesque assets too widely. It is a long journey from each to the next one and the intervening stretches fall regrettably short of heavenliness. When the tourist at last reaches the marvel toward which he has been straining through monotonous sage-brush or the still more monotonous Willamette Valley and compares it with the Grand Canyon or Rainier Park or the Yellowstone he can seldom suppress a sigh. It is not a sigh of disappointment precisely but rather one of melancholy that anything so lovely should, by a hair's breadth, miss being of the loveliest.

The Emerald State put more than common dependence upon the sale of her beauty because it was about all she had received from nature that seemed to promise quick returns without much work. A little coal, a little gold, a little quicksilver had been strewn here and there in her wide territory but not enough to make a spread over. The forests could not be shipped to market as they grew. Wheat, apples, prunes, and live stock hardly yielded more wealth in the long run than human hands and brains sunk in them.

When it came to sea-going commerce the Creator had slighted her again. He had given her but one harbor and that not his best sample. Ships can sail up the Columbia to Portland if not too big, after they once surmount the obstacles at the river's mouth, but if they are too big they must sail away to some other port; if they are wrecked crossing the bar, that finishes them so far as trade is concerned. Portland, therefore, is obliged to seek the consolations of philosophy when she contemplates the vessels in her harbor.

It takes as much philosophy, perhaps more, to bear the slight the railroads have put upon the city and State. They sheer off to the north and south, perversely aiming at the deep waters of the Sound and the Golden Gate as if conspiring to keep Oregon forever blushing unseen in her continuous woods and deserts, a wallflower at the commercial dance where richly married sisters of the north and south disport themselves.

The immigrants of the days before the railroads played the same trick upon her. They strayed away from the Oregon Trail to California seeking gold and left only the weary and second rate to drift down the Columbia into the Willamette Valley. It would be inaccurate to say that the State was born tired, for the earliest of the immigrants, the primeval Jason Lees and the later Applegates, had vim enough for any enterprise. It was Oregon's hard luck to have that tired feeling thrust upon her by the cracker infusion of the years to follow. But the State never has been positively overwhelmed by a flood of immigrants either good or bad. The population has grown slowly like her business. Lured by deep water and railroads, Portland's business kings are apt to have more of a stake in Seattle than at home. Lured by the climate of paradise, they hope to die in California.

Oregon's climate is not bad enough to make anybody curse it nor good enough to make anybody love it. The winter rains just barely fail of being execrable. The summers would be divine if it were not for the smoky haze which hangs over the landscape and hides nature's miracles. What thanks does Oregon owe the Lord for giving her Mount Hood when it blots it out with a veil of smoke in summer and a veil of mist in winter? The smoke is the unkindest cut of all, for after obscuring everything all summer long it clears away in the fall when the tourist season is over and leaves the scenery in crystalline glory with nobody to pay for looking at it. Mt. Hood is a veiled idol ten months in the year but Portland adores it for its potential vendability and dreams passionately of a day to come when tourists will flock to see it as they do to the Jungfrau. Doubtless they will when the mists have cleared away. Meanwhile they swing off to the Yellowstone, the Grand Canyon, the Yosemite, and leave Oregon to theorize with empty pockets over their neglect.

She has framed an hypothesis to account for it. There is a conspiracy between man and nature to slight her. Nobody can stay long in the State without catching on to the prevalent sense of slight and the resentment against it. The resentment is only half articulate. It is a good deal like those suppressed reactions in the brain of an unappreciated youth who has stayed too long in his home town which work out finally in an inferiority complex. The poor fellow comes to believe that there is neither fame nor fortune in doing what he was born to do and tries to succeed by imitating gifts alien to his nature.

If Oregon would work out her native qualities in her life she might make herself a world's delight and wonder. Blooming as she does on a mossy bank in the shelter of the mountains under the shade of the evergreen forests, she might be the sweetest violet ever seen, but she pines to be a sunflower. She has every chance and allurement to sow and harvest a unique civilization. Her geographical situation means exactly that, and so do her mental and material resources. If she chooses to imitate the cheap and tawdry on the outside it is not for want of fine possibilities at home nor of men who understand how to make the most of them. Oregon has always had men, from the first of the pioneers, who comprehended her vocation to original beauty and greatness, but the call of the sham has put them out of business before they got very far.

The first thing the primeval pioneers of the Jason Lee stamp did when they reached the Willamette Valley after their trek across the continent was to found schools. Every settlers' camp had one—the Methodists at Salem, the Congregationalists at Forest Grove, the Presbyterians at Albany, the Baptists at McMinnville, the Wesleyan Methodists at Corvallis, the Quakers at Newberg, the Campbellites at Monmouth, strung along the Willamette River for a hundred miles or so. The schools went by all sorts of names—academies, institutes, colleges. They had no money, no buildings, no football teams, no booster presidents—nothing but consecrated teachers, ambitious students, and the divine fire.

In those days Harvey W. Scott, a wild and woolly young man, footed it down from the Sound to Forest Grove with his blankets on his back and entered the college there. He turned out, as it happened, to be Oregon's one big man. Whether his Alma Mater made him so or not, at any rate the good creature did not spoil him. During the forty years and more that Scott edited the *Oregonian* newspaper at Portland he put his college into his editorials. He wrote crisp, bold, positive English. He whaled away at every religious superstition in sight even when it cost his paper money, and between elections at least he railed at the sacred Republican tariff, although the *Oregonian* was a Republican organ. In the afternoon, when his editorial was written for the day, he read Ovid for recreation. He could recite from memory page after page of *Paradise Lost*. He modeled his style on the English Bible and his political philosophy on Burke. Cant and humbug he hated and said so in print. Free thought and free speech he preached and practiced. Now Scott is dead and the *Oregonian* has flatted down to the pitch of the New York *Times*. There is less free intelligence in Portland than there was thirty years ago when he was in his prime. The little college where he got his fine education does not produce any more like him, but it has an enviable football record.

The Campbellite academy at Monmouth, small and hungry as it was, sent out a group of men to whom must be attributed an altogether disproportionate share of whatever nobility Oregon's life and politics can show. This mother of men with high brows and big souls has been transfigured into a State normal school which makes over farm girls into schoolma'ams without changing anything about them but their handwriting and the way they do up their hair. When I visited it two or three years ago the president was feeling jubilant over a new building he had just squeezed out of the overtaxed public. I remembered the boys who had sat under great teaching there long ago in a little shed and asked him what he was doing along that line. He did not know or did not care. He could talk of nothing but his new building. He died soon afterward and went to heaven, and when Peter examined him at the gate he found that new building tattooed on his presidential heart. The inferiority complex has got in its work on every last Alma Mater of that Willamette bevy. They are out for cash and buildings with football teams and booster presidents. Their first love is forgotten.

It has never been much the fashion among Portland's millionaires to bequeath money for public purposes. When the city was young its frugal proprietors pinched it up along streets too narrow for anything but camel traffic and the same thrifty spirit has animated their real-estate deals and commercial policy ever since. But with all their vigilant husbandry of pennies few of them have been comforted at death with the assurance that they had saved more than enough to provide for their own families. The shining, or prodigal, exception to their strictly Biblical death-bed policy was Amanda Reed, who bequeathed some three million dollars to found what she supposed would be a technical school but what has turned out, oddly enough, to be a college of arts, letters, and football.

Amanda Reed's bequest was Portland's opportunity to work out something new and big in education. The city lies so far away from current academic idiocies that there was nothing to hinder, except its fear of being original. The first president of Reed College, W. T. Foster, a young man of brains and ideas, saw the possibilities in the situation and set out to realize them. He chose for himself the maxim that "college students were there to study" but the studies he dealt out were of the free, noble sort that youth thrives on. Foster's plan was to connect the college with the city's intellectual resources, making it a central ganglion for the civic body. With the courage of a very young president he shut his doors in the face of intercollegiate athletics. Well, President Foster got just so far with these big notions of his and then the inferiority complex closed down on him and extinguished him. Portland did not want any grand, original experiments in education. It wanted an obsequious imitation of the commonplace football colleges in the East, and that is what it has got out of Amanda Reed's bequest.

W. S. U'Ren is another adventurous soul who has tried to make Oregon travel the road on which the pioneers started her, the Pacific highway of free thought and original experiment. He saw what a chance she had to become the world's political laboratory in those remote mountain solitudes unpestered by big business and big cities. The pioneers themselves had been practical anarchists. They had no political government, needed none, and perhaps never would have had any but for a wrangle with the British Hudson's Bay Company which infected them with the disease of patriotism and in due course erupted in a written constitution. Up to that time schools and churches had sufficed to keep the settlers straight, but the first act of their new government was, characteristically, to build a jail and then to fill it. With this grand political start Oregon outsped some of her sisters on the downward way. When U'Ren came on the stage in the 1890's politics was flowing in a sticky, malodorous stream bearing along the usual stuff of sewers.

U'Ren was a student, a thinker, and a man of constructive imagination. He knew the dreams the sages have dreamed of a perfect democracy and by what a close shave the pioneers had failed of realizing them. Perhaps it was not too late to recall Oregon from her paddling in the political sewer. An accidental eddy in the current enabled him to launch his "Oregon System." The State legislature had, in literal fact, so clogged itself with its own offal that it could not stir hand nor foot. It had ceased to function. The people were out of all patience with it and sick to death of the bosses. The time seemed ripe for something bold and big and U'Ren rose to the occasion with the Initiative, Referendum, and Recall.

It was Oregon's chance to move in one leap from foul politics to the golden prime of democracy, but the chance was not taken. His system was adopted formally and that was the end of it. It has not been worked to see what there was in it. The novel scheme scared the politicians into fits at first. They expected that the people would use it to buck them off their backs and run the State government for their own benefit, but the people did nothing of the sort. The inferiority complex busted them as deftly as a cowboy does a broncho by warning them how unsafe it was to set out on a political experiment so bold and unprecedented. Of course it was gloriously alluring but think how outside statesmen would talk. Oregon would get a bad name. She would be called the fool of the family. By the time the flurry was over, the politicians had patched the Oregon System so neatly into the seat of their old overalls that they could sit on it and graft as comfortably as if U'Ren had never been born.

In spite of the frugality of her founding fathers Portland has one wide and beautiful street downtown. It runs about halfway through the city from south to north and all of a sudden it stops. The Arlington clubhouse has been built squarely across it and bars its course to the logical terminus. "Thus far and no farther" is the edict of the brick walls and the street peters out into shanties. That rich men's clubhouse, standing where it does, is the concrete embodiment of Oregon's inferiority complex which sooner or later has blocked every move toward beauty and greatness. The wonder is that the fine ideal survives in spite of all the times it has been killed. It is an invincible spark of heavenly flame, the significant thing in Oregon's life. No sooner is one idealist flattened out than another jumps up waving the torch. It extenuates many sins, even the Rose Festival.

There is enough in the experience of Portland and the Willamette Valley to work up into an incomparable annual pageant. This could be done without trenching on the territory of romance preempted by Pendleton in the Inland Empire and the cow country. The Indians, the missionaries, the pioneers, the mountains, and the Columbia are waiting for their poet and there must be some young genius at Reed College bursting to answer their call if he could get the chance, but he does not get it. The pageant he would build, with all its living beauty, might not pay at the outset and Portland, true to the spirit of the men who laid out her Oriental streets, wants quick returns. So she wastes herself competing in a display or roses with cities to the south where roses bloom like weeds. When the perverse June weather blights the home supply she imports a few carloads. The inferiority complex entices her from what she could do supremely well into a competition where at best she can only be second or third rate. The situation is about the same as if Cinderella had been tempted by the slights of her step-mother to despise her native beauty and had painted her face for the King's ball.

Pendleton's Round Up is in the same boat. This has become a settled yearly event and might have a world-wide charm. For Pendleton lies in the rich bosom of the wheat country, at the door of the cowboys' home, with the Indian tribe which murdered Marcus Whitman still at hand, the sage-brush aromatic on the hills, and the keen air bright with the sunshine that never was anywhere else on land or sea. Pilgrims would come from the world over to smile and weep at the vanished range life she could evoke, its romance, its hardship, its invincible gaiety, its sleight of hand and horsemanship, and its fidelity to everyday work. But she does not evoke the vanished life. She calls instead from the vasty deep a commercialized substitute which is supposed to pay better. Half the cowboys are cowgirls, incredible monsters that never rode the range, and the other half are roped out of dime novels. They travel the country from show to show exhibiting their unreality for a livelihood. Round Ups are now as common as flies and Pendleton has frittered away the chance of a thousand years.

Oregon prides herself on her literary eminence almost as much as she fears the Pope. The tradition of letters runs down unbroken from the Protestant missionaries who wrote polemics against the Jesuits for their imagined complicity in killing Marcus Whitman to Mrs. Dye, who offers an agreeable home brew of fiction and history in *The Conquest* and other books. Frank Norris is counted among Oregon's authors because he once worked on an Astoria newspaper and Joaquin Miller because he is said to have held up a man east of the mountains in the placer mines. H. W. Scott's editorials have a good deal of the flavor of genuine literature. His family has published them in two gigantic volumes. I do not know that anybody reads this formidable collection but it is far less a waste of money than most tombstones. Some of the lads who work on the newspapers have written verses of promise as a matter of course, but Oregon's truly great poet was Sam Simpson, who courted the muse in the days when an apple from California sold for two bits in the Willamette Valley and everything else, including poetry, was priced on the same scale. Whether his local fame needs deflation or not the curious may say for themselves after reading his poems, which are on the market under the title of *Songs from the Golden West*.

Thus far the inferiority complex has been too much for Oregon's idealists. Some of them it has killed outright with the deadly sickness of hope deferred, some have wearied of the everlasting fight and compromised with the second rate for the sake of peace and a living, some go to San Francisco and New York for a breath of the keen air of freedom, but there are some, too, who will not die and will not run away from the tournament. A newspaper published in Rome must be Roman or else perish of inanition, but the *Journal,* of Portland, lives and makes money in spite of flashes from the eternal light that sometimes streak like chain-lightning down its columns. Around the *Journal,* for example, is a group of Oregonians to whom politics is something more than graft and life a little better than penny-pinching. Their ideals hark back to the pioneers and the brave old academies strung out along the Willamette. They are pioneering yet, out on the old trail, following the stars. I have seen U'Ren with a mob of supporters cheering him on and I have seen him plodding forward all by himself, but I have never seen him discouraged or afraid.

This loyalty to the ideal has been the saving factor in Oregon's life so far. Who knows how soon it may become the dominant factor? The faith in Oregon's unique vocation to a great destiny is a living faith. It is not dead yet and it will never die. I could name men in Portland and Salem and Pendleton who understand that her geographical situation, her resources and climate, and the prepotent genius of the pioneers have destined the State not to be an imitator of the sham and shoddy in outside civilization, but to create a civilization of her own for outsiders to imitate if they know when they are well off. And there are enough of those men to keep the pioneering ideal alive and to pass it on. By and by the idealists will win. They will frame another Oregon System and not leave it mummied between the covers of a statute book but work it out in life. Then we shall see something in the Willamette Valley and the wheat and the cow country that it will be worth a trip across the continent to look at.

PENNSYLVANIA

Still a Keystone

REGINALD WRIGHT KAUFFMAN

MARCH 7, 1923

GIVEN A CHANCE or making it—but particularly making it—the Indianian proclaims himself a Hoosier, the San Franciscan announces his Californian birth. That Southerner whose father came from Naples yells when the band plays "Dixie," and the New Yorker is ostentatious in his ignorance of anything west of Riverside Drive. Why is Pennsylvania diffident?

In a world so mixed as this of 1923, metaphors cannot escape the general *mélange*. We Pennsylvanians—and the politico-economic "we" means, of course, the controlling majority—used to speak of our commonwealth as the Keystone State. It is still that; but we don't say so. We don't say anything about it, and our silence is a symptom of our disease; nevertheless, we hope that ours will become the Keynote State, and therein lies our chance of cure. For we are suffering from over-immunization against the present epidemic of radicalism, and so soon as we are convinced that the plague has run its course, or that at least we are safe, we shall recover from our reaction. We trust that the orchestra of the Union will tune its instruments to ours; but *we* are going to be right, anyway.

"It seems to me," wrote *The Nation's* managing editor, "that you might effectively give Pennsylvania her place as the keystone of the American industrial edifice. Leaving out New York, it cannot be questioned that Pennsylvania is the most important State in the Union. One can well imagine any other withdrawn without affecting our national life. Upon the steel and coal of Pennsylvania has been built our vast economic structre—indeed, Wall Street is but the retail office of the power that comes from Pennsylvania."

The truth, but not the whole truth. He might have added that Lancaster County is agriculturally the richest land of its extent in the world, and that Chester and Berks and Bucks are not far behind. Nowhere is there a valley like our Donegal, scarcely anywhere such food as comes thence: the fat sausages, the gray pork puddings, the mush, the sauerkraut, the scrapple, proud capon and mighty beeves, cream cheese and cottage, meat-jellies, and apple-butter boiled in vast cauldrons over veritable conflagrations—we live well and grow fat on them among things good to look upon. Our lowlands are yellow with the grain or green with the tobacco; the Alleghenies, the Tuscaroras, the Blue Ridge—to learn them is to lose your taste for the ruder Rockies; our Susquehanna is as beautiful as the Rhine and more beautiful than the Hudson.

Out of the beauty that is ours and the wealth, we have, indeed, extracted what the journalist just quoted precisely describes as "the very essence of American feudalism, imperialism, materialism." But not all at once. In production, the State has held its own; my thirty-five years' old school geography adequately describes the Pennsylvania of today. As to mental and moral changes, most that was written of us in the eighties would still apply: our thinking people, and those wise enough to know that they don't think, have not, thank God, gone far in the direction that those who think they think call "forward." But socially we used to be paternalistic, whereas, though we need not, we have become indeed imperial and, consequently, material. We have stepped too far aside to avoid modernism, when, really, it is less annoying to stand quiet, or to go back, until this year of grace shall have become "one with yesterday's sev'n thousand years."

A pugilist that I know puts it: "Pennsylvania's lost her pep." The protest against industrialism has sorely wounded our enthusiasm. Now we can manufacture everything save that. Lately, we have produced only Woolworth and the five-and-ten-cent store, which, in turn, gave New York the biggest building in the world. Repeat the name of Keith to our average citizen; you will evoke no mention of Sir William, the first royal governor to espouse the popular cause: what you will evoke is a reference to that enterprising person who brought "refined vaudeville" to the Quaker City.

"Where," inquired a French friend of mine, "is Independence Hall?"

And a native Philadelphian answered: "Downtown, near the Curtis Publishing Company Building."

"For unknown geological reasons," says Lesley, "Pennsylvania is peculiar for exhibiting the Paleozoic system in its maximum development." For clearly discernible historical reasons, Pennsylvania's natural state was long paternalistic. Not only did the 1681 grant of Charles II give William Penn the patriarchal powers conferred by most royal grants; its recipient wisely, for all his immediate erection of popular suffrage, proceeded to administer his powers paternally. One of the greatest of advertising geniuses, he saw that his immigration prospectuses went to a list that, enormous as it was, was carefully "selective." He made his "holy experiment" upon people chosen for its success: in bestowing liberty of conscience, it is well to be sure that the freedmen are a sort whose ideas of liberty will not conflict with one's own. The land that had been given by the King had to be taken from the Indians: the English Quakers only sometimes cheated them; the Scotch-Irish Presbyterians only sometimes massacred them; the French Huguenots left them alone; the Swiss and German Quietists made friends with them. Then all these elements patterned their microcosms after the Proprietor's Manor.

An Englishman's house might be his castle: a Pennsylvanian's land was his kingdom. He held it in fief to an emperor vaguely personified in the Commonwealth, to whom he paid certain taxes and to whose general laws he was amenable; but he was its liege lord. Notwithstanding its religious precepts, the Society of Friends was composed of feudal-minded individuals, and the Friends' neighbors were their political brothers.

When, in the Maryland Border War, unarmed John Wright met the raiders alone, he was protecting that which was John Wright's, and, although his reading of the riot act was performed in his character of royal magistrate, it was his sermon as a Quaker owner that induced the invaders to down arms and help him with his harvest. Lord Hardwick's decision in chancery and Mason and Dixon's subsequent survey did divide the North and South, but they also "confirmed the original claims of Penn" and protected the border dependencies of his dependents. Even the Revolution respected the paternalistic point of view; the annulment of the old charter in 1778 carried a payment of £130,000 in satisfaction of the Penn demands.

Until time within living memory, there was no substantial change in the Pennsylvanian attitude. The French and Indian alliance compelled a synthesis between non-resistance and self-protection; the balance swung toward self-protection in the Revolution, and self-protection became patriotism. The State's war records are among its proudest; but even its defense of the Underground Railway was in part a defense by individuals maintaining the sanctity of their own bits of earth. Until twenty-five years ago, we Pennsylvania-Dutch always referred to a large landholder as *König* So-and-So.

And, in the old days, the administration of those little kingdoms was beneficient. First on the farm, then at the mill, and finally in the mine, it was a point of honor and a badge of pride that one's employees should be contented. We had our "coal families" that owned the fuel-veins, our iron and steel families that worked the ore-banks and ran the furnaces; one clan possessed a little mountain-range and kept its hold on the lumber until the great rafts had escaped rock and rapids as far south as Peach Bottom or Port Deposit. Homestead is a red blot, but, excepting that and a few minor outbreaks in abolition days, there have been, even to this date, only four bloody internal disturbances: the Whiskey Rebellion, the affair of the Molly Maguires, and a couple of sanguinary railway strikes. My Marxian friends to the contrary notwithstanding, the workers were better educated than now—knew just as well what was good for them and yet were satisfied: they had no chains to lose and, consequently, no ambition to gain a world.

Later immigration was slow to affect the old order. The Germans that came to us in the nineteenth century were largely law-abiding Western Catholics; so were the Irish, and so have been most of the Italians that followed these. Our later Hungarians and Poles stand in the same faith, and our Russian and Serb miners, our Greek confectioners and bootblacks, and our Syrian merchants are Eastern Orthodox: they obey the catechism of Platon of Moscow.

The confluence of the Allegheny and the Monongahela Rivers, Pittsburgh. This strategic intersection of rivers catapulted Pittsburgh to industrial prominence in the late nineteenth century. By 1920, the city's role as industrial keystone was waning.

It was the employers themselves that made the change. Not even a manifestation of economic determinism did it. The feudal holdings of life's necessities were so large a proportion of the whole nation's store that the holders could have maintained their position. They simply didn't want to.

We still boast an entire town making chocolate under family rule: it is a survival. Most of us went corporation-mad. The Pennsylvania Railroad became the best railway in America, and it was too much for us industrially; John Wanamaker happened into the Bon Marché, and our retail system, though bettered in twenty particulars, could never be the same again. We opened our gates to the new movement; the mountains were "lumbered" above until naked; they were mined below until city streets caved in: for years the story of Pennsylvania was that of any other business State. Many a mine-owner lost his badge; combinations of capital produced combinations of labor. Then we discovered that among other guests whom we have invited was the radical. It was the reaction of our paternalistic inheritance to this discovery that produced our present plight.

The process pursued in our economics had to be pursued in our politics. There has been a deal of nonsense talked about them: representative government is still on trial; our sort has not been the best imaginable, but we considered it plenty good enough for us and long perpetuated it. Mark Sullivan, in the *Atlantic Monthly,* once blamed our Quietists: he said they wouldn't interfere to set up their own ideals. He was wrong. Our Quietists do not interfere for the excellent reason that their ideals have been set up. When their ideals are endangered, they go to the polls.

The Amishman is the standard type of our non-voter, yet he was the silent cause of the abnormally large Republican vote cast in Pennsylvania at the Congressional elections of 1918. After them, an Amishman came to Columbia—which, as Wright's Ferry, escaped from being Washington by one vote in the Continental Congress—to attend the funeral of a brother who had "turned Methodist." Another brother, turned member of the Church of God, sat beside the coffin. During the services, the Amishman plucked this one's sleeve.

"Well," he said, "we done it, ain't?"

"Done what?" asked the backslider to the Church of God.

"Woted," explained the Quietest. "Sink o' this here Wilson tellin' us a Democrat Conkress had ought to be elected: him sendin' word to us yet, orderin' us how to wote—*we woted!*"

No, we Pennsylvanians were the satisfied subjects of paternalism: Stevens died on a Tuesday in the August of 1868; the Lancaster County Republican primaries for the nomination of a Congressman had been set for that Saturday; no candidates would present themselves while the body of the representative whom the people loved remained above ground; the voters knew that he was dead, yet, when the ballots were counted, it was found that every one had been deposited for Thaddeus Stevens.

The Cameron Dynasty, father and son, ruled us to our taste. Quay was their heir; even his factional rivals like now to think that no other State has produced so great a master of political strategy. Then Penrose came, Harvard *magna cum laude,* holder of the bequeathed power *magna cum laude,* too. But at his death there was the fear of the radical. Heretical *tirailleurs* were advancing toward the electoral field of the coming gubernatorial contest, and, at the primaries, there were the schismatic Vares from Philadelphia. Being conservatives, the paternalists followed a well-worn recipe: they chose as their candidate a man that the onward-lookers believed to be a vessel of Progressivism, but a vessel that the Organization believed to be by no means full of that liquor. Far from being the triumph for reform that it was heralded as being, Pinchot's nomination was due to the 5,000 votes given him by Buck Devlin, the Penrose boss of the Eighth Philadelphia Ward—Penrose's own.

Over-immunization. The Pittsburgher journeying into Canada puts a full flask in his suit-case. If that Act which Miss Laura Volstead so ably drafted for her father depended upon the majority of our Pennsylvania voters, it would not be invalidated: it would be decapitated. We are not for things as they are; certainly not for things as they threaten to be elsewhere; we are so much for things as they were with us that we are a bit rough-handed.

Our conservatism best exhibits itself socially, our over-immunization in education, science, and the arts. The Lincolns of Berks County, who sound their second *l,* were not asked to Reading charity balls just because their kinsman became President; the clan that forbade a marriage with the young Carnegie because he was "in business" would not have changed its mind when he became the man that could not die poor; Market Street is still a dead-line in Philadelphia, and the Dunker farmer knows the Christian name of the least important of his great-great-grandfather's brothers-in-law.

"Mom," asked Joe Ritner's children, after their father's election in 1835, "are we *all* governors now?"

"No," answered the Governor's wife: "only me an' pop."

That concept of family remains among us, and with it the old concept of chivalry. If you are a woman, Pennsylvania is a good State in which to kill your husband; in substituting barbarous electrocution for dignified hanging, we have not extended our acceptance of woman's rights to her right to death when she has taken up the sword; but if you are a man, you had better do all your murders in New Jersey.

Of course, at least in the countryside and the small towns, we have remained a friendly folk and tolerant. The Quakers are passing, but the Mennonites in their shovel-hats, the Amish—the "Beardy Men"—in the brown homespun that bears hooks-and-eyes instead of buttons, because "buttons is a wanity": they reap by turn, for each helps his neighbor bring the harvest in. Does the girl cashier in the county town embezzle a little money? She was underpaid: we raise her salary, and she makes restitution on the instalment plan. We have little drifting labor, and our jails are seldom full.

Nevertheless, we are answering our radicals with more of what they object to. It is denied that Bryn Mawr uses an expurgated *Iliad* or bans *Othello* because of that dark warrior's love for a white lady; but the University of Pennsylvania's Wharton School of Finance cannot be concealed, and our "business colleges" are a contradiction in terms the most thorough in the world. We have more kinds of religion than any other State, but our most popular preacher's most popular sermon is called "Acres of Diamonds." James M. Beck is in Washington; John G. Johnson is dead, and the world-wide proverb about a Philadelphia lawyer with him. The Da Costas, the Solis-Cohens, De Schweinitz, and Keen did not graduate from our medical schools yesterday; it is a long time since Henri, Sloan, Parrish, and Scofield left our Academy of the Fine Arts. The Philadelphia Orchestra flourishes, but many a Pennsylvania town has 12,000 population and no library. Out of such hands as Wister's the literary tradition has passed into those of Mr. Joseph Hergesheimer.

Is all this a mere lament for "the good old times?" It is. But it must not end in a dirge: it must rise to a fanfare. For Pennsylvania is that State of life unto which it has pleased God to call me, and I love it; in its kindly earth lie the bones of all my people for the past two hundred years and more: my own bones will lie easily nowhere else. Again, then, the truth, but not the whole truth: I have tried to tell what Pennsylvania peculiarly is; what she will be is another matter. Economically there will be little change for long, radical or other. But spirit is more important than economics, and stronger: already there are signs of a return to former ways.

Charles M. Schwab wanted to move a house; in the route stood a tree that his mother loved: he had the house lifted over the tree. There is something more than materialism in our capitalists.

In that something-more in everything about us waits our salvation. Even now our farmers have ceased buying gold-mine stock. The black smoke is not symbolic of Pittsburgh; Philadelphia holds promise of deserving again the priceless epithet of "slow." In Scranton, Altoona, Columbia, York, Lancaster, and Bethlehem men and women are getting drunk once more, and drunkenness is one of the commonest, if most misdirected, expressions of divine discontent.

We procure our beer, though we must drink it quietly. Our people don't want to marry either above or beneath them. Welfare-work and the pension-system are softening the Pharoah-heart of Labor. In our Episcopalianism the Highs have it; Bishop Darlington is friendly with the Eastern Orthodox; Western Catholicism gains converts; Zionism has returned hundreds of Pennsylvania Jews to their fathers' faith; our Lutherans are beginning to think of what they call their Orders; Methodists have "vested choirs." The day may yet dawn when we shall recover form in the arts, and when the rich man of a small town will again support it rather than exploit it. After all, the Republican Organization is still in power: our next Governor after Pinchot will not even seem to be a Progressive.

Over-autonomic-immunization against certain specific disease-tendencies: S. Solis-Cohen, who belled that cat, has given it a beautiful name—vaso-motor-ataxia. It is significant that he is himself a Pennsylvanian; his disease, as I have said, is Pennsylvania's trouble. But Cohen, in his contribution to the Osler Seventieth Birthday volume, bears hope:

"The writer has felt justified in reassuring patients who—presenting marked autonomic disorders, and aware of tendencies to tuberculosis or carcinoma in their families—have expressed a fear of developing cancer or consumption, by telling them that they are protected; that they are, in all probability, suffering from an 'excess of protection.' Thus far, the assurance of immunity, the prediction of safety, has not proved false in any known instance."

With us Pennsylvanians, the malady is only mental. When our subconcsiousness have been convinced of our immunity, we shall resume the paternalistic attitude in everything possible; we shall return to—*normalcy.*

RHODE ISLAND

A Lively Experiment

ROBERT CLOUTMAN DEXTER

FEBRUARY 27, 1924

Her People and her politics are the distinguishing features of Rhode Island. Deeply chiseled over the granite portal of the magnificent State Capitol in Providence are these words, taken from the charter of 1663: "to hold forth a livelie experiment that a most flourishing civill state may stand . . . with a full liberty in religious concernments." The experiment began as a rebellion against the religious intolerance of a Puritan theocracy, but it has continued to furnish a lively experiment of one kind or another ever since. Not that the smallest State in the Union is barren of other distinctions. Rhode Island clam chowders have been imitated, but never equaled; and the white cornmeal of the South County surpasses in texture, flavor, and color the commoner yellow meal of Dixie. Despite these contributions to our national cuisine, however, the significance of Rhode Island lies in its social developments.

Geographically, Rhode Island can scarcely be called independent. Massachusetts on the east and north and Connecticut on the west have both felt that this upstart with its peculiar ideas and its desirable waterfront ought to belong to them. When, to quote a local ballad,

> In sixteen hundred thirty-six
> Roger Williams got into a fix
> By saucing the governor of Massachusetts
> And skedaddled away to Rhode Island

Roger and his followers had no rights which the Chosen of Massachusetts were bound to respect. It took all the faith and courage of Williams, all his well-deserved popularity with the Indians, and all his political sagacity to maintain his foothold. Even after Rhode Island had a royal charter, Massachusetts and Connecticut did not hesitate to exercise jurisdiction whenever possible.

Well-grounded fear of her more powerful neighbors, and the resulting jealousy to preserve her own rights and privileges as a sovereign State, have colored all Rhode Island's development. Rhode Island is separatism personified. Separatism in religion, separatism in politics, separatism in personal life: these have been the key-notes of her history. Her daring formulation of Williams's doctrine of soul liberty in the face of bitter opposition from without and lack of unity within transmitted this strong emphasis on individualism. It is hardly an accident that until quite recently Rhode Island, the smallest State in the Union, was the only one which had two capitals. The tradition of separatism explains, also, why each of the thirty-nine towns in the State has one State senator, so that West Greenwich, with 367 inhabitants, is as potent in the upper house as Providence, with a population of 237,595. This rotten-borough system has been one of the factors in the half-century of political degradation from which Rhode Island is now trying to emerge. The old-line Rhode Islander will cite with justice the national Senate as analogous to his local situation; but neither Nevada nor New Shoreham (another of the Rhode Island pocket boroughs) has legislative records that prove the wisdom of this particularistic democracy.

Of greater importance even than its historical separatism, for an understanding of present-day Rhode Island, is its preeminent industrialization. Politics and people both are quite literally the "fruit of the loom." It is true that the rotten boroughs furnish the possibility for corrupt politics, but it has been the manufacturers of Rhode Island who have taken advantages of these possibilities.

It is the mill-owners, also, who for their own purposes have diluted the colonial stock of the original settlers, first with English mill-hands, later with Irish, and then with French-Canadians, Poles, Italians, and Portuguese (black and white), until a Saturday afternoon stroll along Westminster Street, Providence, leaves one with the conviction that Rhode Island is not one of "these United States" at all. One looks in vain for "tall, blond Nordics." Main Street, Pawtucket, speaks every language but English, while in Woonsocket the writer spent an hour recently in the City Hall without hearing a word of English spoken, by visitors or officials, except that addressed to him. Rhode Island is not only the most densely populated State in the Union; it is also the first in the proportion of foreign-born. Largely because of this immigration Rhode Island holds the lowest position regarding illiteracy of any Northeastern State.

We of the North are apt to think that the harrowing tales of child labor belong wholly to the past, or at least to the far-away South. Rhode Island, however, has met Southern competition during the last decade by augmenting the number of her laboring children, while every other State in the Union, even North Carolina, the bete noire of industrial reformers, has shown a decrease. Child labor in the United States during the last decade fell off 47 per cent; in Rhode Island it increased 6 per cent. Thirteen and four-tenths per cent of all the children in the State between ten and fifteen years of age are gainfully employed. Whàt is to be this "fruit of the loom"? What of the future citizens of Woonsocket, with the highest percentage of child labor—18.7 per cent—of any city in the United States, or of Pawtucket, with 17.3 per cent? In the South, at least, only about half the employed children are cooped up in mills and factories; in Rhode Island, four-fifths of the 8,569 working children spend their days in the damp, hot, lint-saturated atmosphere of the spinning-room. Furthermore, Rhode Island has the unenviable distinction not only of having the highest percentage of employed girls between the ages of sixteen and twenty-one of any State in the Union, but also of employing over two thousand women nightly in its mills. Is it strange that there was opposition at the State Capitol last year strong enough to defeat a forty-eight-hour law; or that bills abolishing night work do not pass? The legislature, if not controlled directly, is frequently intimidated by the mill-owners' threat to go South, where they can do as they like—and consequently they do as they like in Rhode Island.

The heart of Rhode Island is not Providence; Providence is simply its marketplace. Rhode Island owes its prosperity to two rivers, the brawling Blackstone, which turns more spindles than any river in the world, and the winding Pawtuxet. It is along these rivers that the mills are located, and along these rivers that the mill operatives live. In these days of the motor-car, the owner lives in Providence on the East Side, or, in more and more cases, in New York or Boston. What have the mills given the workers for homes? The ordinary mill village presents little that is attractive. The mill is the center of the picture. Around it are grouped the mill tenements huddled together along one or two streets. Frequently these tenements are white, freshly painted, with well-kept palings in front. There is none of the hideous ugliness of the coal or iron town; the chief aesthetic defect of the mill town is its uniformity and its lack of space. The houses are built in long rows closely adjoining one another like city blocks, while all around are the undulating hillsides, winding rivers, and shining lakes. The town turns its back on these, however, and faces its master, the mill. In addition to the mill and the mill houses there are a store and a church—sometimes two churches, the larger and more pretentious topped by a gilded cross, and the smaller, generally a mere chapel, weather-beaten and in need of repairs. The latter too often supports only a visiting minister; the former is served by one or two priests, usually conducts its services in an alien tongue, and is frequently flanked on the one side by a parochial school, partly financed by company donations, and on the other by the tightly shuttered residence of the teaching sisterhood. Almost a hundred such villages exist in Rhode Island, utterly independent of town or county lines, and consequently having no political unity.

Jewelry is another potent industry in Rhode Island affairs. Providence is the largest jewelry center in the United States if not in the entire world; everything from Gorham's silver to Woolworth's hair ornaments comes from the city of Roger Williams. The jewelry industry contributes to the child-labor problem a unique element. During the brief time in which the federal child-labor law was in operation the Department of Labor discovered a system of home-work for children which has been in existence from the earliest days of the industry in the State. The Federal Department, in contrast to State departments, was shocked at the extent of child employment, and made a study of the problem in the three cities of Providence, Pawtucket, and Central Falls. Its report, recently published showed 4,933 children, or 7.6 per cent of all school children examined, doing "home work." Such work consisted of carding snaps, stringing tags, setting stones in various types of jewelry, and wiring and stringing rosary beads. What a commentary on our commercialization, even of religion, that the very rosaries on which the faithful count their prayers in the name of Him who loved little children should be made by these little ones in poorly lighted tenements in the long evenings after school hours! The federal investigation revealed the fact that in some of these homes in which the rosaries which were to be kissed by the faithful were being made, members of the family were afflicted with tuberculosis, influenza, and even more loathsome diseases. Two-fifths of the child "home workers" were of Italian parentage and one-fifth French-Canadian.

The industrial picture that Rhode Island presents is not encouraging. True, it produces excellent textiles, first-class tires, admirable lathes, as well as mountains of ten-cent-store brilliants, but its industries and its politics alike have been managed with little consideration for the human element. Unstinted immigration from Europe so long as that was possible, supplemented now by "habitants"from Quebec; long hours of labor for men, women, and children under conditions detrimental to health and happiness; the exploitation of children; the grouping of foreigners in mill villages barren of genuine American influences in either education or recreation—these are not the most hopeful ingredients out of which to make a commonwealth.

Fortunately there are more promising aspects of present-day Rhode Island. The power in the Pawtuxet Valley prior to 1919 had been the B. B. & R Knight Company, a family concern, which had commenced with the Pontiac Mills in the eighteen-forties and gradually grown until it controlled over a score of mills. The Knights were notoriously unprogressive; in their own offices a typewriter was a rarity; oil lamps had been sufficient for lighting when they took over the mills: they were sufficient when they finally relinquished them. A Knight mill tenement had a reputation that was unsavory in more senses than one. Despite their antiquated methods they managed to secure maximum profits. In 1919 Robert Knight's sons sold their mills at boom prices to a New York corporation. But the company soon found that conditions in 1921 were not the same as in the years 1916–1919, and in order to pay dividends on their excess capitalization they ordered a 20 per cent reduction in wages with a continuation of the fifty-four-hour schedule. The result was an immediate and complete tie-up of every mill in the valley. Not only did the workers strike, but they organized for a protracted resistance. Local men at first headed the strike, but soon the leaders of the Amalgamated Textile Workers were called in, and thorough and complete organization was effected. The food supply was arranged for, dietitians and nurses were employed by the *strikers,* food kitchens were opened, and sufficient funds secured to *fight it out if it took all summer.* And fight it out they did from January until the autumn, when the wage cut was rescinded and the strikers went back to the mills victorious. There was little violence in the valley, although deputies and State troops were stationed there, and the result of the strike has been an immediate and definite change in attitude on the part of both workers and owners. Both sides admit that the workers are now in control, and while this presents difficulty to the owners, especially in view of their attempt to pay dividends on an overcapitalized investment, it is distinctly a sign of a better day. And finally, the children were found better nourished and healthier at the end of the strike than at its beginning. The day of feudal overlordship in the Pawtuxet Valley has disappeared; in its place we have corporate responsibility on the one side and well-organized labor on the other.

Lincoln Steffens wrote an article in *McClure's Magazine* in 1905—Rhode Island, a State for Sale—in which he proved beyond doubt his initial thesis that "the political situation of Rhode Island is notorious, acknowledged, and shameful." Then Nelson W. Aldrich was "the boss of the United States Senate" and at the same time the head and fount of Rhode Island's political corruption. Aldrich and his associates exercised their power through General Brayton, the famous blind boss of Rhode Island. So absolute was Brayton's power that the story is told that coming into his office one morning he inquired for a certain State senator. Being informed that he was in the Senate, Brayton replied, "Bring him here; I want him to lead me out to (let us say for politeness' sake) get a drink." Brayton was "of counsel" for the New Haven Road, and Aldrich was especially interested in the Rhode Island Company. The New Haven as a factor in New England politics has passed away, and the poor Rhode Island Company is still struggling to pay off the indebtedness which Aldrich, Brayton, et al. fastened on its stockholders. Aldrich, Brayton, and their associates died politically intestate. The Republican Party machine in Rhode Island is now "in commission," and a weak commission at that. This decadence of the bosses is one of the most auspicious omens on the political horizon of the State. The Democratic Party has always been a party of the disinherited and discontented, and it has been particularly lacking in unity. A Rhode Islander was asked a few years ago which party he was going to support in the forthcoming election; he replied "I don't know; I feel like a jackass between two bales of excelsior." Twenty years ago the Republican Party was known to be corrupt but powerful; the Democrats were less corrupt but impotent. A change has come about in Democratic policy. No one conversant with Rhode Island politics will maintain that the Democrats are a unit, but at any rate they are more united than they were, and they still are the party of the disinherited and consequently of the progressives. I say disinherited, despite the fact that they hold the governor's chair, one of the two United States senators, and the presiding officer of the State Senate. But they are still of the disinherited; they do not represent the textile interests, or the metal trades, or the jewelry manufacturers. The Democrats have leaders: Flynn, the Governor; Toupin, the erratic Lieutenant Governor; and George Hurley, the present assistant attorney general and former chairman of the State Committee. Hurley is easily the most interesting figure in Rhode Island today: a Providence boy of Irish extraction, a brilliant student at Brown, a Rhodes scholar of distinction, an able young lawyer, and a resourceful politician. Hurley has always stood for cleanness in politics and in public and private life, and at his own request was given the position of assistant attorney general because he wanted to clean up the gambling-hells at Narragansett Pier, Johnston, Cranston, North Providence, and elsewhere that for years past had made Rhode Island a Mecca for sporting gentry and had furnished an easy living for politicians and local officials. Clean them up he did. The story of Hurley's fight single-handed is too long for this article, but it should be written. Quiet, gentle-mannered, with a pleasant Irish smile, and an altogether juvenile expression, he has cleaned up practically every gambling house in Rhode Island within the last year. He made no distinction between high and low. A few months since he summoned into court a philanthropic Rhode Island millionaire and eight or ten social leaders from New York to tell the grand jury what they were doing at a certain Pier resort. They told. The consequence was that the resort is closed, and some local politicians are now working for a living.

With the Republicans disorganized, the textile workers conscious of the value of organization and the ballot, and the Democratic Party in the hands of men like Hurley, it can be said with truth that Rhode Island is no longer a State for sale.

Rhode Island cannot be dismissed without mention of Brown University, which dominates the intellectual life of the State to a much greater extent than do either Harvard or Yale their respective commonwealths. Under E. Benjamin Andrews, Brown gathered to itself some of the brightest minds in America, and many of the political leaders of the younger generation are practicing the precepts taught in Brunonia's halls. But "Benny" offended the industrial magnates in Providence by daring to have an opinion on political issues, and was dismissed. Andrews left to his successor some splendid youngish men, but one by one the Meiklejohns, the George Grafton Wilsons, and their kind have slipped away to positions of influence elsewhere. Brown is the poorer by their loss.

A typical Rhode Island institution is the Dexter Donation—six thousand feet of wall which incloses many acres of the best residential part of the city of Providence for an aristocratic poor farm—a poor farm with a property qualification. A century ago Ebenezer Knight Dexter left his native town sixty thousand dollars to ameliorate the condition of the poor, and he picked out the best site in the town for his benefaction. He requested that "a good permanent stone wall at least three feet thick at the bottom and at least eight feet high . . . and sunk two feet in the ground" be placed around his farm. There it stands today, despite efforts to have the land sold and the proceeds used to erect a more modern institution elsewhere. It affords care only for residents of Providence whose fathers or grandfathers have owned property; and it has no waiting list. The institution at Cranston for the poor who were not so fortunate is generally overcrowded.

In the face of such solid conservatism it is difficult to be optimistic. However, Rhode Island has been despaired of many times, particularly by her neighbors. Whether it is the protecting shade of Roger Williams or the healing waters of the Bay, the "lively experiment" still continues, and slowly, but nevertheless surely, changes come. Rhode Island was excluded from the New England Confederation, whose self-righteous members referred to their neighbor as "that sewer," principally because she consistently refused to exclude the sectaries persecuted by the "lord brethren." Her conduct during the period of paper money was scandalous, and yet it was during that same agitation that in Trevett *vs.* Weeden the dictum was established that the courts were competent to find illegal acts of the legislature contrary to the common law. Rhode Island's privateering was little short of piracy, and yet it is on this basis that the American merchant marine of the early nineteenth century developed. Rhode Island was the first to declare her freedom from Great Britain, but the last to adopt the Constitution. It took an armed rebellion in 1848 to establish manhood suffrage, but the rebellion came. Twenty years ago Rhode Island was literally and absolutely controlled by its feudal mill-owners and their political henchmen; now that situation has changed. Although Roger Williams would find it difficult to make his way about the Providence Union Station built where in his time was a shallow cove, and would stare aghast at the new Biltmore, we can be sure that the stirring aspirations of the mill-workers, the movements for the abolition of child labor the striving of the disinherited for political power and freedom, the demands of the modernists in the church and state would enlist the sympathy of this first and greatest of American radicals. He kept his faith in the lively experiment in the face of adverse circumstances; may we not believe that enough of his spirit remains in the Commonwealth he founded at least to justify its motto, "Hope"?

SOUTH CAROLINA

A Lingering Fragrance

Ludwig Lewisohn

July 12, 1922

A TINY TONGUE OF LAND extending from Broad Street in Charleston to the beautiful bay formed by the confluence of the Ashley and the Cooper rivers is all of South Carolina that has counted in the past; the memories that cling to the little peninsula are all that count today. More than thirty years have passed since Ben Tillman led the revolt of the agrarians, the "poor white trash," the "wool-hats" of the "upper country" against the old Charlestonian aristocracy. He won. The time-spirit was with him. The new men control the State; they control the State University; they will not send their sons to the College of Charleston; they have industrialized the "upper country" and made it hum with spindles and prosperity and their particular brand of righteousness. Spartanburg is both a more progressive and a more moral city than Charleston. It even indulges in cultural gestures and is visited by a symphony orchestra once a year. It is the headquarters of the cotton-mill men and of the Methodists; it is the seat of Wofford College where they cultivate Christian prosperity and the tradition of the sainted Bishop Duncan: "In my time I used to read Shakespeare and Scott and all those writers. But nowadays I read nothing but the Bible because I know it is the word of my God. . . ."

The new men brought neither freedom nor enlightenment. They oppress and bedevil the Negro without the old gentry's vivid and human even if strictly feudal sympathy with his character and needs; they sentimentalize in political speeches and commencement orations about the Old South. Of its genuine qualities, as these were represented in old Charleston, they know nothing. It was, indeed, in mute deference to them that the president of the College of Charleston ceased, long before the days of prohibition, to serve wine at his receptions and permitted engineering courses to be added to the undergraduate curriculum. In this atmosphere the sons of the Charleston gentry who until a few years ago studied Greek as a matter of course have sunk into that appalling and intolerant ignorance and meanness of spirit that mark the cultural vacuum known as the New South. They no longer study in Europe or found periodicals or issue shy

Hoeing rice, South Carolina. Although the state witnessed a commercial influx that resulted in the eclipse of the old aristocracy, agriculture continued to be labor intensive.

volumes of verse or cultivate a perfectly genuine though somewhat pseudo-Roman and oratorical spirit of service to the State and nation. They are letting their civilization perish without resistance.

They are, of course, vastly outnumbered and energy died out of the stock long before they were born. They are mere descendants and cling to the husks. In the early years of the present century one of the last of the Pinckneys wrote a *Life of Calhoun* in which he defended the doctrine of nullification as fundamentally necessary to the structure of American government. Then he went mad. At the reunions of Confederate Veterans the contemporaries of this gentleman spoke with tears of the glories of the Old South. They did not mean the spirit of true civilization which, somehow, old Charleston had possessed; they meant the "peculiar institution of slavery" and the oligarchical rule of the planters of the sea-board counties. Yet at that very time faint remnants of the Old Charleston spirit could be observed. The Master in Equity, a *novus homo,* but long accepted through association and marriage into, let us say, the South Carolina Society and the St. Cecilia Society, desired to publish in a volume the poems he had written in the course of a lifetime beautifully though rather ineffectually dedicated to literature and learning. A group of his friends—colleagues of the Charleston bar—made up a purse for him and the book was duly brought out by a New York firm noted for its sharp business practice and its long association with American literature. That was a last flicker of the life of old Charleston. . . .

I seem to be detailing gossip. But these anecdotes are significant and they are, at least, authentic. They should be corrected in the impression they convey by others. The old Charleston group had its darker side. William Gilmore Sims was treated shabbily, though I am willing to believe that he was a man of rude manners and unprintable speech; Henry Timrod, the best of their poets, was treated abominably. He was, in the first place, the son of a German tradesman and poor and a tutor in planters' families. More sinister in its meaning is the bit of gossip which floated down the years that he or the young woman to whom he was betrothed had "a touch of the tar-brush." This thing—interesting and picturesque if true of the poet himself—was whispered to me in a kind of murderous secrecy as a sufficient excuse for whatever need, misery, humiliation poor Timrod was permitted to endure. The old Charlestonians, in brief, loved letters and learning and romance. They were often capable of a fine and gallant and even intellectual gesture; they bore themselves not without distinction. Under that cultivation and distinction, as under the cultivation and distinction of the eighteenth-century type everywhere, lurked cruelty, violent intolerances, stealthy and relentless lusts. . . .

It is hard to realize that today. Quiet has stolen into the old houses of the lower city; scarcely a breath seems to ruffle the wistaria vines in spring! In such a spring Mr. Owen Wister visited shady drawing-rooms—and talked to exquisite old ladies and wrote *Lady Baltimore*. Henry James communed with such frail figures during his last stay in this country. He saw a long disused harp, a lovely colonial cabinet, autograph letters of Hayne, and was told that Mr. Thackeray, when he lectured here, took tea in this very room. And it caressed his ear when old ladies with delicate shadows amid their porcelain-like wrinkles sounded the vowels of English as he knew, from the rhymes, Pope must have sounded them, but as he never expected to hear them upon mortal lips. These "values" pleased him amid the violent and raw distractions of the American scene. They are soothing. I, too, have lingered among them and savored them. But they do not tell the complete story of the civilization from which they derived.

That tight and peculiar Charleston culture was created by settlers partly of English, partly of French descent. Names, put down almost at random, will help to convey its quality and atmosphere. Among the English names are Wragg, Middleton, Pinckney, Gadsden, Drayton, Hayne, Trescott, Bull; among the French are Manigault, Gaillard, Huger, Simon, Legaré, Porcher, de Saussure, Jervey (Gervais). The Ravanels were probably Marranos; the French settlers were Huguenots and though many of them, under the political and cultural domination of Britain, went to augment the Anglican parishes of St. Michael and St. Philip, enough clung to their ancestral faith to make the only Huguenot church in America a quaint and agreeable Charleston landmark to this day. There were dissenters from other countries, like the Dutch Mazycks; there was, from a very early period on, a small colony of Sephardic Jews—Lopez, De Leon, Moise, Ottolengui. All the names I have mentioned exist in Charleston today. Of the immediate youngsters I cannot speak. The bearers of these names who are now approaching middle age all, or nearly all, preserved within them something of the spirit of their ancestral civilization.

They were not Puritans in the fierce, vulgar, persecuting and self-persecuting sense. Their theological and moralistic assents were social gestures; they had, themselves, large mental reservations and though in their own persons they considered it rather bad form to parade those reservations, they were not intolerant of the type of conscience that held silence to be hypocritical. They were snobs to the marrow, but a few of them, at least, were capable of contemplating that fact consciously and a little sorrowfully. A Charleston gentleman, almost of the ancient regime, was heard to say to a friend of his; "I don't blame you at all for leaving a city where your social standing will never be quite what you deserve. It is a pity; Charleston needs you. But I should do the same in your place. . . ." Yes, they were snobs and facile assenters who made the free life more difficult. But they had a real respect for the arts, for the things of the mind, for the critical spirit they could never quite share. They were and are, when every deduction has been made, among the most civilized of Americans. They had, in addition, grace, ease, personal charm. When I think of the people who are pressing them hard—the horse-dealer from central Georgia, some hustler from the Middle West—I am inclined to lend them an almost legendary worth. I must, at all events, set down this fact: the present descendants of most of the old Charleston families are poor. The men are still members of the learned professions, as their fathers were. They still consider them learned professions—even the law. The handsome new houses in Charleston are the houses of new people. Many a beautiful and time-mellowed mansion on Legaré Street is in a state of gradual decay.

The history of the old Charleston group is, of course, like the history of other such urban and patrician groups in other parts of the world. It can be matched in Mantua and in Lübeck. The pathos of its downfall lies in the fact that it has gone down not before the authentic spirit of the modern world, but before the mean barbarism of sharp business men and Ku Klux Klanners. Its enemies and conquerors would consider the personalities it produced at its best moments— Hugh Swinton Legaré, Paul Hamilton Hayne, William Henry Trescott—very much as a Tulsa or Winesburg hundred percenter would consider, if he could consider them at all, Nietzsche or Verlaine or Bertrand Russell. For what Legaré and Trescott had was the critical and distinguishing mind, the culture of the intellect. Legaré, a diplomat, a scholar, a brilliant and romantic personality, a writer like the Edinburgh reviewers of the early days, hastened home from Brussels to protest against secession; Trescott, a statesman who cultivated quietly a gift for extraordinarily limpid and expressive prose, wrote, soon after the Civil War, reflections that blended human warmth with philosophical detachment.

These men and Robert Hayne and Calhoun were, however, less intimately characteristic of the Charleston culture that projects feebly into the present than the minors—the shy spiritual and literary adventurers found in almost every family. In the very early days they were bolder, like Washington Allston, the poet and painter and friend of Coleridge. Later their efforts were more tentative and hushed, like the verses of the Simon brothers, or the really admirable poems of the almost legendary James Mathew Legaré, or the Crashaw-like outpourings of Caroline Poyas. Often they sought anonymity and printed verse and prose in the Charleston periodicals which succeeded each other from before the Revolution to the founding of the *Nineteenth Century* in 1870. And when one considers that the contents of these magazines were all written in Charleston and that Charleston, which has fewer than seventy thousand inhabitants today, was a very small town indeed, one gains a high notion of the pervasiveness of the literary culture and spiritual aliveness that existed in the city between the Revolution and the Civil War. Much of this writing was, of course, feeble and jejune. There is scarcely an original note. The Byronic lyric succeeds the couplet and the didacticism of the late eighteenth century; the emergence of Keats can be noted almost to a day; later that of Tennyson. But behind this imitative expression there was an extraordinary number of cultivated, impassioned, vivid personalities. Everybody wrote—men of public affairs like William Crafts; merchants like Isaac Harby. One Manigault published anonymous novels, another was a really able scientist who brought home a great collection of natural history that is still to be seen. Still others expressed themselves through exotic adventure like Joel R. Poinsett, who found in Mexico the decorative flower that bears his name. I am deliberately jumbling periods. The spirit of the civilization of old Charleston was, while it lasted, one. From Alexander Garden—discoverer of the Gardenia—before the Revolution to Dr. Dixon Bruns of the Civil War period and to Professor Yates Snowden today, one of the marks of the gentleman and the eminent citizen has been to turn out an elegant or a stirring copy of verses at will. But the last or almost the last has been written. Only the descendants of the Sephardic Jews have shown a queer kind of vitality and have produced in the last generation and in this two writers of the shabbily popular variety—Rodriguez Ottolengui and Octavus Roy Cohen.

From Charleston "neck" to the Piedmont region there may well come the indignant question: Is Charleston gossip an adequate account of the great, proud State of South Carolina? It is. Or shall one record the labor conditions in the cotton mills or the antics of former Governor Blease or expatiate on the lynching statistics? I once traveled with Blease from Charleston to Cincinnati. He was going to a national meeting of the Elks. He was, with a touch of consciousness, almost of staginess, the typical leader of the democracy of the New South—ostentatiously large wool hat, dark rather fierce eyes, heavy black mustache, gaudy insignia on a heavy watch-chain, a man who radiated or wanted to radiate a constant ferocity against the irreligious, the impure, "Nigger-lovers," aristocrats, "pap-suckers," Yankees, intellectuals, a son of the soil and of the mob with a chip on his shoulder. His conversation had a steady note of the belligerent and the self-righteous. A noisy, astute yet hectic obscurantist. He might have been from Georgia or Mississippi. He despised Charleston with a touch of inverted envy. A South Carolinian quite merged in a larger and lower unity and without any relation to the specific character of the State. Finally shall one make much of the fact that though, whether through the influence of race or climate, the demands of the senses are rather exorbitant in South Carolina, the State has the amusing distinction of being the only commonwealth in the civilized world that will tolerate no provision for divorce on its statute books? In Charleston, at least, there has never been a lynching and her citizens have, at need, disregarded their Draconian lawgivers. Also, they and their ancestors have created a beautiful thing—the old city that clings to the bay. Linger in these streets and lanes and gardens and enter a few shadowy interiors beyond the deep verandas that turn to the South. A race lived here that loved dignity without ostentation, books and wine and human distinction. Its sins, which were many, fade into the past. They were always less vulgar and ugly than the sins of those who have come after.

SOUTH DAKOTA

State without End

HAYDEN CARRUTH

JANUARY 24, 1923

Our Rivers slip down from the North, our Rivers sneak in from the West,
They roll along in the Spring, but most of the year they rest;
For they list to the lure of the Wind, the Sun's beguiling song,
And our Wind is a thirsty Wind, and the kiss of our Sun is long.
The Cannon Ball filters through from where the Indians come
Who draw their Government beef and swap it away for Rum;
The Big Sioux creeps through the Prairie, a mile in a day with luck,
The Jim is un-nav-i-gay-ble for even a light-draught duck.

But the Old Missouri, the Old Big Muddy, that rises God knows where,
Comes down from the North, and in from the West, then passes out Down There;
It makes one bite of Robinson's ranch, and goes on its waggish way,
But dumps it down in Doyle's corral, so everything is O.K.!
                                    "Mess-Room Song" (Fort Lookout, 1879)

T HE WAY of a serpent upon a rock seems broad and distinct compared with a parallel of latitude or longitude. I remember some years ago a friend showed me that every time I went to the post office I crossed latitude forty-five north. I had not been aware of it. He pointed out the exact place, by a tree, and ever afterward I found myself stepping high when I passed over it, bound not to trip. But a State that must depend on these artificial map decorations for its boundaries is unfortunate. How shall it know itself? How develop individuality? Perhaps it can, but it will take time. Of course I am thinking of South Dakota, which, except for a few miles in two corners, exists only because it is a certain distance north of the Equator and west from Greenwich; and the Equator is imaginary, and I have my doubts about Greenwich. Enter it from north, south, east or west; nothing from the sky, or the soil, or the people, or their houses will call to you that *this* is South Dakota. Over endless prairie you come. Over endless prairie—you go on.

332

Let me pretend I am living in South Dakota, as once upon a time, and may be addressed: Journeys End, Rose Bud Prairie, Near the Bijou Hills, Sentinel Butte, S.D. But though feigning of residence is easy, the assumption of birth in South Dakota may scarcely be. No, not here; but in southern Minnesota; between the same imaginary latitudinal lines and of a longitude not so much nearer Greenwich, with the same Indians, and the same blue sky and wild flowers, and the same weather.

There was a map; it was truly of a size, and half covered one wall. It was large, it still covered These United States only so far as one hundred and four degrees and a few odd minutes of longitude; so the scale was ample. It was printed on extraordinarily heavy paper, of a rich yellow-brown tone; one-third of the counties were of a soft pink-red, and another third of a mild blue-green, leaving the last third to the mellow parchment of the paper. That is, the older States bore this embellishment of county, but Kansas and Nebraska, the latter probably and the former perhaps still Territories, had only a few square counties heaped up in the eastern parts, as a child would make a block pile; but the Indian Territory and Dacotah (as the map had it) showed no counties at all. I found more pleasure in Dacotah than in anything else on the map; it was near enough to be not unattainable; there I traveled, fascinated by a vast region three hundred miles long and fifty miles wide edged with map-makers' mountain fringe, called Table Land; another half as large with the enticing name of Coteaux des Prairies; with the names of different Indian tribes scattered carelessly here and there, and above all else, to the northwest, a great region of Unexplored Country. When this map of maps was made I know not; probably before the Civil War or early in the conflict.

I went to Dakota (came, I mean) in the early eighties, while it was a Territory, and still one, the North and the South, but hostile. Many changes had occurred from the old map. The Rivière au Jacques had become, by way of the James, the Jim. The beautiful Table Land had been found not worth putting on the newer maps, the Coteaux des Prairies had suffered the same fate. Where were Spirit Hill, Butte de Sable, Dead Colt Hillock, Hole-in-the-Wall Mountain, and, above all, The Lightning's Nest? Many enticing names had gone, but a few others had been acquired, as Charles Mix and Bon Homme for two adjoining counties, and, in the Black Hills, Deadwood, beloved of the authors of the dime novel, by recent analysis shown to be our only true American literature. You enter the picturesque Black Hills region through Buffalo Gap, and leave it by way of the Cheyenne River, Grindstone Butte, the Bad River, and Fort Pierre; at least I did—on horseback. But Old Harry's, Blue Blanket Island, Dog's Ears Butte, October Cache, and Bear-in-the-Lodge Butte are gone.

Perhaps without further delay I should confess that I shall not give many statistics, so dearly beloved of our State, such as that if all the cows in South Dakota were placed end to end they would reach to the moon, and leave one to jump over. But who would believe this, cold, provable fact that it is, allowing the modest estimate of seven feet and four inches to each cow? Nobody. So with a thousand other facts about our glorious State, which I with painstaking care have collected. Who would believe what I could tell our production of wheat and corn, of cattle and hogs, of butter and eggs; of gold? The facts are too tremendous for human consumption; the simple, smiling truth becomes a figure of fright. I shall pass it all over in detached silence. You, of course, saw recently in the newspapers that South Dakota stood next to the top in the percentage of drafted men found acceptable by the medical examiners in the late war. It is not my fault that this fact was made public. Only Kansas was ahead of us. But I shall make no triumphant references to our products, our resources, our intellectual achievements, or our virtue.

But there is one thing of which I must speak pridefully, perhaps boastingly. I do so the more boldly because it is never mentioned in praise of this or any other region. On it the Boosters are silent. Along our rivers, about our lakes, among the mountains of our southwest corner, there is much beautiful scenery of the conventional type, which receives due praise; but all States have the regulation scenery. We have the Prairie. We have it to a greater extent and in more beautiful guise than any other State. The Prairie, level or gently rolling, is the earth we inhabit brought to its highest point of perfection; it is the world ordered, arranged, settled; the world at peace; the world kind, thoughtful, brooding; the world passed beyond the treachery of the sea, the clamor and savagery of the mountains; the earth with its other half, the sky, above us and about; the world open, frank, constant, giving man to look about him and to know his littleness or to exult as a god; the Prairie is the world in its calm, serene, beautiful old age, meditative, unhurried, unafraid; approaching Nirvana. To know the Prairie friendly-wise, above all to know it as mother, is to feel ''the exceeding beauty of the earth.''

There is no other place where so fully may be realized the immensity of the earth as in the midst of the Prairie. There we know our earth for what it is, and turn our faces to our sky, and know that we are part of all. The Prairie is clothed by the universal grass, and beautified by the flowers that are fitted to it, the pasque flower of spring, the wild rose of summer, the goldenrod and wild sunflower of autumn; the sky is a deeper blue, the clouds a more glowing white than anywhere else; at night there are the stars. Every spot on the Prairie is a High Place whereon may be offered sacrifices to Truth and Beauty. The Prairie is but the desert watered, and, as hath been said, ''The desert is of God, and in the desert no man may deny Him.''

And with the prairie there is what may be called an attribute even more important for the progress of mankind: the Wind. Above, ''Messer Sun'' of the hymn of Saint Francis of Assisi; below, and part of it, ''Brother Wind.'' The prairie is static, the Wind dynamic. The prairie nourishes thought—the Wind demands action. The Wind of the prairie is a long, long Wind. It comes not by fits and starts, but as steadily as the sun moves across the sky; it is the eternal calmness of the prairie in motion. There are no gusts, no pauses; if you are without you cannot hide from it; you can breast it, overcome it, but you cannot avoid it. And there is no sleep like that companioned by strains "rung by the running fingers of the wind."

It cannot be denied that our Wind on occasion momentarily oversteps the bounds. It is as a test at the end of the school term. Even then it is beneficial, with its lesson in forethought, resourcefulness, mind against matter. Great Pan stamps his foot in the Lightning's Nest and the prudent citizen retires to his cyclone cellar.

But we who are at school in the great Academy of the Wind have our vacations. In October, usually, the winds are hushed; the sun floats big and red in the hazy sky, the land is a cloth of gold and purple, gossamer streams lazily on the wandering airs, and alone, on a little uprolling of the Immensity, you may catch the faint tones of far-off fairy music—"tired bells chiming in their sleep"—Pan again, I dare say, in gentler mood, perhaps this time at Spirit Hill with his pipe and the little animals, his friends, about him.

What is the effect of all this beauty upon the dweller in South Dakota? No effect is discernible. There are our sunsets—for they are beyond compare, a prairie sky being the only canvas adequate for this daily miracle, making it the marriage of heaven and earth, celebrated with a mighty harmony on Nature's color-organ; well, there it is—what about it? When the farmer sits down to milk his cow of a summer evening he turns his back to the sunset. . . . But the cow sees it. Maybe through her milk a little of the sunset may somehow touch the youthful members of the family. Certainly in time the effect will come, since no man may escape nature. Our "intimate contact with wind and sky" must touch our physical nature first. Our world has been too new, we have had too much to do. Before were were settled and had things put to rights the distracting recent inventions jumped at us. We brought the bicycle with us, "high," perhaps, but still a "wheel." Candles we never knew; electric lights were ours before we harvested the second crop. We lisped in telephones, for the telephones came. Then ensued the motor-car, and we had no solid tradition of ox-teams to help us withstand the shock. We saw that they were created for our benefit. We have yet to discover that a man may not own a motor-car and still be respectable. But it cannot be denied that to be able to call the doctor twenty miles away over the telephone, and have him dump himself at your door from his car within an hour, is a privilege not to be surrendered. The way of a motor-car on the prairie is one of swiftness. In time past distressing stories have been told in this country of life on the great central plains; especially for women; of its drabness, of resulting depression, insanity. The holy anchoret would probably find a telephone in his cell an affliction, with tradesmen calling up about the overdue payment on his last hair shirt; but it has brought needed companionship to the plains woman. And now there is radio.

South Dakota is the heart of the prairie region of North America. Take a pair of compasses and on your map set the legs to cover six hundred miles. Plant one in the middle of South Dakota and swing the other around, and in your great circle, twelve hundred miles in diameter, you will have the prairie, nipping the Rocky Mountains a bit, to be sure, and missing some plains to the north in Manitoba and Saskatchewan and to the south in Oklahoma and Texas; but mostly you'll have your prairie inclosed in your imaginary line—as good as anybody's imaginary line. And South Dakota in the exact middle of this great plain of the world should be its very heart and soul, and is. It finds itself the essence of prairieism. Perhaps, after all, there are more negative than positive qualities in a great plain, and if the State exhibits the same qualities the reason may be geographical. The nature of the State is subdued to what it lives in.

On the old map there were three towns, Yankton, Vermilion, and Sioux Falls. When, in the experimental eighties, I came, there must have been several score— or hundred. Now there must be twice—or ten times—as many. The railroads came and made them. The railroads did not have to be coaxed to South Dakota; there was something to come for: wheat. Everywhere wheat. Number one hard. While they were building the station, and before the trains began to run, the settlers would bring it in and pile it up. It grew, and still grows, as if indigenous to the soil. Number one hard. There was, and is, no other wheat like ours.

Still, though the railroads were eager to come, I believe a benevolent government at Washington did present some of the roads with every other section of the good rich land, though by chance, I think, this all occurred in the northern half of the Territory. With the man who wanted to acquire a farm and home, the dear thing, our government, was less open-handed. "Root, hog, or die, for you, old man!" it said to him. And he truly had to, or he did; built his house of sod, twisted wild hay for his fuel, greeted the uprising sun from the field, and plowed two furrows after this luminary had set; and his wife had a harder time than he. But if he didn't die, and became the "following-named settler"—I quote from the notice he had to put in the local paper, and pay for—when the gentle powers finally gave him a patent to his land—if he didn't die, I say, and if the local money-lender (equipped with extra rows of teeth) didn't get him, he has now, I am assured, an immense barn, a big house, a telephone, a phonograph, a radio set, a motor-car. I hope he has; and I hope, too, he has the same wife.

And of these original settlers who came into South Dakota from thirty to fifty years ago, there are still many thousands, grown a bit sedater, it is true, and less inclined to make merry of nights with barber poles and other movable objects. This may be understood when you remember that we Originals on our advent were usually in age somewhere between eighteen and twenty-four; with a few graybeards verging on thirty. We were young, but we didn't know it. It was before Youth was looked upon as a career in itself. There were a few middle-aged men with families; and if one of the families chanced to include a growing-up daughter, he was the most deferred-to man in town, and was immediately elected Justice of the Peace. As for the girl, marriageable age was desirable, but not necessary; age sufficient for the purpose of courtship would do—say fourteen. The really marriageable girl had to keep a card index of her young men. The sexes are now more, evenly balanced, though still with the emphasis on the male, and it might pay any young woman in the East who is beginning to feel the least bit anxious to drop in casually. Of course our best men are already married; but that is the case everywhere.

In the old days prairie fires illuminated the night, coming winking over the tops of the little hills, zigzagging down their sides, and rushing literally on the wings of the wind with the ranker grasses of the lower land. The old days were, too, the heroic age of the tumble weed. I am tempted to boast of their speed. They suggest another fast-moving object, the county court-house of the early days. In a county each town aspired to be the county seat, and most of them were, sooner or later. I lived in a town, new-planted by the railroad authorities; two miles away on the open prairie stood the county capital, two buildings, a farmhouse and a small structure containing a safe for the records. A bright legal mind in our town showed us how we could incorporate the town, with a shoe-string gerrymander to include this county building, and thus become the county seat. We warmed to the thought, and took up a collection to pay the fees at Bismarck, the capital of the Territory. Alas! "That very night the Romans landed on our coast," coming in the guise of practical men and mule teams from the rival town, and took away the county building on wheels. We never saw it again. The bright legal mind refused to return the collection.

Taking into consideration the proportion of our people still living who came here to virgin soil, I sometimes think that South Dakota is the youngest State in the Union, though of course in this respect it must stand beside its northern twin. The other Western States, it seems to me, with the possible exception of Oklahoma, were settled more gradually. The Territory of Dakota was settled with a bang. Since practically everybody is either an Original or but once removed, how can the State have developed much individuality? The fact is, it hasn't. Our people are still "from" some place. Even though you were born and brought up here, if your father and mother were from Indiana, and they talked Indiana, and got letters and newspapers from Indiana, and visited Indiana years when the crops were good, you find yourself a good deal of a Hoosier. South Dakota was settled chiefly by people from Minnesota—from Minnesota and Iowa and Wisconsin. But even these States, especially Minnesota, were so young that their people were "from." Thus, though people directly from New England, New York, or Pennsylvania, for example, were not numerous, these regions were well represented among our settlers either by real natives who had tarried a while in the newer and nearer States or by the second generation. Even the Scandinavians, who seem to liquify at such a low temperature in the melting-pot, usually reached our prairies from some neighboring State.

These Scandinavians of whom we have so many—though our northern neighbor is much ahead of us in this respect—have made a good record in the State. At least, they readily become Americanized, which may be a desirable thing if you are going to stay in America. They take kindly to our politics and our cooking, which in another generation or two will probably have a baleful effect on the honesty and clearness of their blue eyes. A long way after the Scandinavians in number come the Germans, and I know of nothing that can be said against the way in which they have comported themselves. Our percentage of foreign-born population is somewhat smaller than that of the average of the neighboring States. In the matter of Indians, the statistical tables give South Dakota third place, Oklahoma standing first and Arizona second. One wonders where they keep themselves. Still, there are reservations, and there it is fair to assume they stay, except for neighborhood excursions. In a newspaper printed close to one of these reservations there appeared recently an account of how Frank Bear Running, Charles Kills First, and John Brown Wolf came to town and stole a— there, gentle reader—I've caught you! You've guessed that they stole a Ford car. You're wrong! They had a Ford car. They came to town in it. What they did, while Jim Eddy, a ranchman, was getting a noonday snack at the hotel, was to steal the engine out of his new Ford car, transfer it to their own car, and "light out across the country like greased lightning," as the local paper expressed it. "Sheriff Bender," the paper adds, "started in hot pursuit in his Pierce-Arrow." But can a Pierce-Arrow overtake a Ford where buffalo wallows and prairie-dog towns abound? I think not.

It will be seen from this that our Indians are also becoming Americanized—if an Indian may do so. These Indians I think are mainly natives of this State, or the immediate region. Their fathers and grandfathers must have seen the exploration parties of Captain Sully. Lieutenant Warren, and Governor Medary marked on the old map as occurring in the 'fifties. Think of the talk these hurried and rattling military passings must have made around the Indian campfires. Too, perhaps, a little examination of arrow points, and plans for trips down the Missouri to trading posts where peltries might be exchanged for that emblem of civilization, the powder-and-ball gun. The savage has a most contemptible habit of taking a hint. Especially when, after having been shot at by a flock of Christians, he finds another flock anxious to sell him arms with which to shoot back. Showing, it must be confessed, a sporting spirit on the part of the Christians.

Still, none shall deny us the beginnings of State personality, even if that personality consists of having next to none. Our northern twin is given to political experiments. Our southern neighbor has brought forth Mr. Bryan, contains Omaha, shares a boundary with Kansas. And why need dwell on the varied distinctiveness of our two eastern and two western sisters? Now what is there about South Dakota to put one's finger on, to point to with pride?

Once we had a Senator at Washington named Pettigrew, R. F. Pettigrew, the only man of distinction we ever had at Washington in any capacity. But we did not keep him there. He tells why in his latest book. No doubt there is another side to the story, but that doesn't matter. I wish every voter in the State could read the book. There are three or four Senators from other States who are troublesome, sometimes wrong-headed, often cantankerous, who are not understood by their constituents, and who represent the universe rather than their State. Still their States keep them in the Senate. If South Dakota had done the same with

Pettigrew it would have been a good thing for South Dakota, the Senate, and the country. Who ever hears of South Dakota's Senators today?

I have been mentally struggling to think of something to say that will reveal the Soul of Our People, but I shall have to give it up. Barring the mining in one corner, where the Black Hills beckon to their parent Rockies, we are an agricultural folk, caring more for sufficient rain and warmth in June than for Mr. Einstein's ingenious theory, Mr. Hardy's most recent book of poems, the movement for freedom in India, or even the probable state of our own souls. The price of wheat in Chicago comes home to our business and bosoms. "How a good yoke of bullocks at Stamford fair?" How, indeed! And freight rates too high. And what is that feller we sent to Washington doing about it all? Yes, we are an agricultural folk, and pluck the bright dollar (silver—weighing a pound, more or less) from the reluctant earth. We have no large cities, or a prospect of any. Perhaps there is nothing to make them.

Our only navigable river has ceased to be so. I wish the Missouri could be dredged out and the delightful old steamboats restored. But perhaps the water would have to be strained first—I am no engineer. Besides, I may be prejudiced about the Western river steamboat; I love the various noise it makes. To me a steamboat always comes round the bend with "a nigger squat on her safety-valve, and her furnace crammed, rosin and pine."

This lack of large cities may be only what should be expected in an agricultural State, not admitted to the Union till 1889, but the absence of any towns of distinction may be less easy to explain. Stop a man on the street in New York or San Francisco and ask him to name a town in South Dakota. "Why-er-yes," says your man. "Yes—Sioux City!" "But Sioux City is in Iowa." "Why, to be sure—yes—good day!" If your man is elderly he may answer your question with Yankton, because time was when it was the capital of Dakota Territory, and the only town. If he is middle-aged or younger he may say, "When I was a boy I read a bully story about Deadwood Dick—Deadwood, of course—it's in South Dakota—or is it Wyoming?" Pierre boasts (boasts is a figure of speech) of being the smallest State capital in the union, always excepting Carson City. Our largest town, Sioux Falls, had only a few over 25,000 people in 1920. There were but eight towns of above five thousand population—but two above ten thousand. Still the population of the State was over 636,500. We are country dwellers; we live on our prairies.

As a people we are liberal financially toward education. Of course we don't know what education is; but what State does? We seem to have our fair share of the regulatory spirit, perhaps derived from our New England blood, or perhaps not. We took up with Prohibition before the country did. My recollections of observed effects of strong drink in the early days seem scanty. I do recall an immense Scandinavian who would come to town driving a yoke of oxen. On occasion he indulged too freely, and then invariably sought the grocery store, bought a package of soda crackers, begged a soap box, and repaired to where his patient oxen stood in the streeet. Standing the box in front of them he would sit down on it and proceed to feed the crackers to the oxen, a single biscuit at a time, alternating between the two animals. It was a scene of tranquillity and loving-kindness calculated to touch the heart of the most callous. On another occasion a visiting clergyman, mistaking, presumably, the potency of the cup before him, ventured too far, and later, making his way across town in the dark of a moonless June night, fell into a new cellar. Unable to deliver himself therefrom, he became so singularly vocal that the reverberations have come down with me through the years, haunting my ears when other sounds are momentarily hushed.

What if Christ came to South Dakota? Absurd; such things only happen far off in time and space. But if He did come it is hoped that He would get a quarter-section of our superior land and, through diversified farming, acquire the point of view of our leading people. Any funny notions put into the heads of our hired men with regard to hours or wages—quite unthinkable! If a miracle were really required—impossible things, of course—but if there *must* be one, say a good soaking rain, without clouds, in the latter part of May. Great for the Wheat. Naturally, no turning of portions of this rain water into any other liquid. The authorities—and so forth.

So runs the world away; but even after all these years I sometimes wonder if it was best that the old Territory was divided into two States and given names which, when their handles are considered, are not impressive. In those old days Congress was slow, and State conventions before there was any State were common. These were always held by but half of the Territory. Some of us, contrary-minded children of the Opposition, thought the Territory should become one State, and called by its own truly beautiful name of Dakota; and we talked of how it would be the second in size in the Union, surpassed only by Texas, a grand, imperial State, striking terror into the other States. We accused the two-staters of being a hungry generation, anxious to make more offices. They called us impractical, visionaries, unmindful of the need in the Senate of four more members of the True Party; finally they threw us out. But after upward of forty years outside the hall on the sidewalk I still say I think we were right.

And yet—if they hadn't! Dakota might have been a turbulent, a strong, a virile State, a leader, a maker of movements, a State to shatter precedents, a State of destiny. But it is not well that one, just one, of These United States should keep, should be, the spirit of the great plains—unending, unchanging, calm? South Dakota . . . the prairie. . . .

TENNESSEE

Three-Quarters of Bewilderment

E. E. MILLER

SEPTEMBER 20, 1922

N o TENNESSEE ORATOR feels he has done his full duty until he has expatiated on the State's diversity of soil and climate and its variety of scenery and re-source: "A mightly empire in itself, stretching from the cloud-crowned summits of the Great Smokies to the sun-kissed banks of the mighty Father of Waters, an empire capable of yielding every product to temperate climes and dowered with every natural resource necessary to the well-being of man"—every one of us who grew up in the State has heard it time and again.

It is largely true. Nature has done her part. In the east balsam-clad mountains with the flora of New York and New England; in the west cotton fields with their billowy whiteness. Cranberries grow in the mountain bogs; muscadines and figs ripen in the lower valleys.

The population is as diversified as the topography. Back in the mountains dwell the living types and characters of Charles Egbert Craddock and John Fox. In secluded cabin settlements men and women of scant "book larnin" but of keen native sense tend little patches of ground in pioneer fashion, sometimes hauling the crops on sleds from fields too steep for a wagon. Here survive the old-time hand industries—spinning, weaving, basket-making. The roads still wind up the creek beds and the ridges are crossed by foot-beaten trails. The coves are searched for "sang," and the squirrel rifle not only helps supply the mountineers' larder, but serves at times to settle—or to perpetuate—inherited family disputes or to speed inquisitive "revenooers" back to the lowlands. With an individuality and a picturesqueness of life that should be preserved, the hill country has also a poverty that often makes life squalid and an ignorance that in many cases blurs the mental vision and stunts the soul. The problem of the mountains is how to preserve the individuality of mountain life and thought while bringing to the more backward districts the opportunity for better educa-tional development and more profitable work.

In the old days the current of slavery flowed around the southern hill country and hemmed the mountaineers in a little continent of their own. Poor, untaught, but independent and self-assertive, they saw in the rich slave owner of the cotton country or the bluegrass lands a "furriner" with whom they had neither tastes nor interests in common. They came to hate slavery and the wealth and culture it produced. The feeling persists in the more remote districts, and to this day the mountain people have to some extent remained cut off from the rest of the world, while an ingrained conservatism has held them to the manners of life and modes of thought of seventy-five or a hundred years ago. Though closely related by blood to the dweller in the lowlands, the hill man has been kept so distinct by environment and economic heritage as often to be thought a race apart. To be sure, the mountain traditions are gradually giving way, and the hill country is not all ignorance and poverty, feudists and moonshiners. Uninformed people in Boston and New York sometimes seem to think so, and then good Tennesseeans tear their hair and speak evil words.

In the center of the State, in the Bluegrass, are the remains of an ante-bellum aristocracy, a country-dwelling gentry, prosperous farmers who once raised speedy trotters and showy saddle horses. The love of them has not yet departed from the land, even though Jerseys and Shorthorns and Southdowns now graze on the rolling pastures and motor cars on the hard, white limestone roads outnumber the trotting horse a hundred to one. The Bluegrass is one of nature's beauty spots, and is loved of all who see it. Its inhabitants are not always so loved. They have a certain sense of superiority that cannot always conceal itself, and that is sometimes galling to the people of other parts of the State.

Beyond the Bluegrass lies a stretch of poorer country—the Highland Rim—and then comes the true cotton belt of tenant farming and supply stores and many Negroes, which differs widely from the Bluegrass in appearance, in its people, its habits of life and thought, and more closely resembles Mississippi or Georgia. With the mountain country of the Unakas or the Cumberlands it has as little in common as with Pennsylvania or Illinois.

In one Tennessee county that last census showed but eleven Negroes. In another there were three blacks to every white. In some sections the man who votes the Democratic ticket is looked upon with suspicion by his neighbors, in others a few lost and lonely Republicans look to the game laws for protection.

This diversity of country and population offers fine oratorical opportunities and gives the basis for a certain kind of pride, but it holds for us distinct disadvantages. For one thing, it has made smaller the unit of our provincialism; it has made us think in terms of our section rather than of our State. "East Tennessee," "Middle Tennessee," "West Tennessee" are not only fixed phrases in our vocabulary, but actual divisions recognized in our law-making. Members of our State Railway Commission, Board of Education, and Tax Commission are parceled out by legislation among the "three Grand Divisions of the State." When we established a State training school for teachers we had to establish three of them so that all sections could be taken care of. Other State institutions are similarly distributed, except the Penitentiary, which is generously conceded to the capital.

Our diversity of environment has also done much to prevent our having any definite State ideal or any State-wide enthusiasm. We have had no real State hero since the pioneer days. The list began with John Sevier and ended with Andrew Jackson.[1] We have not had any great State figures largely because we have not had State ideals, and we have not had State ideals largely because we have not known or cared much about the very different people at the other end of the State. We inherited from the Civil War not merely a sharp political cleavage between east and west; the economic cleavage is as great. The farming in the Valley of East Tennessee is essentially different from that of West Tennessee. Certain larger problems are common, but the home-owning, self-supporting farmer in a land of mixed farming has neither the same methods, nor the same needs, nor the same outlook as the farmer of a sale-crop, tenant-farmed section. Our cities vary as much as our country districts. Memphis is the commercial center of a great agricultural region; it prospers or suffers with the prosperity or adversity of a hundred thousand cotton farms in Tennessee, Mississippi, and Arkansas. Chattanooga is a manufacturing town, looking outside the State for a market for most of its products. Nashville is the trading headquarters of a grain and live-stock farming section. There is no real State center of industry, of interest, or of thought.

We have been from the first essentially a political people. The men who laid the foundations of the State—Sevier, Jackson, Crockett—were equally ready to fight or to run for office, and what genius the State has so far displayed has been in these directions. So many Tennesseans went to the early wars that Tennessee soon became known as the Volunteer State. Every normal Tennesseean since the first settlers crossed the Smokies has been a potential, if not an active, politician, and early in its history Tennessee became a doubtful and pivotal State in national elections. From Monroe to Lincoln it was largely what Ohio has been since the Civil War—a State which might decide presidential campaigns and which kept ready to run for President a supply of safe and sane mediocrities. Andrew Jackson, of course, was not considered exactly safe and sane by the "best minds" of his time. Neither was he a mediocrity. Nor was Hugh Lawson White, whom Jackson kept out of the Presidency, but the colorless James Knox Polk was the perfect prophecy of a succession of Ohio presidential candidates, successful and otherwise. The estimable John Bell—the choice of his own and two other States for President when Lincoln was elected—carried on the tradition of eminent mediocrity and closed his political career trying to reconcile the irreconcilable and to hold together the North and the South by keeping one foot on either side of the chasm that was widening between them.

The war brought a new type of leader. Isham G. Harris, greatest of "rebel" war governors, succeeded in dragging the State out of the Union after it had voted to stay in. When the Federal forces were closing in on Nashville he took

[1]John Sevier (1745–1815) was a pioneer in eastern Tennessee and became the first governor of the state in 1796. [D. H. B.]

the State funds and fled to Mexico. Soon Andrew Johnson, the anti-slavery, anti-secession Democrat—rude, untaught, ungenerous, but with an ability and a love of country not yet generally appreciated—became military governor, to be succeeded when he became Vice-President by the erratic and odiferous "Parson" Brownlow. Brownlow was a pro-slavery but anti-secession Whig— preacher, politician, journalist, something of a genius and a good deal of a blackguard. A reward of $5,000 was offered for the capture and return of the fiery Harris, but he stayed away until a general amnesty was proclaimed. Then he returned, bringing the State money with him and soon finding his way to the United States Senate, where he served until his death many years later. These three picturesque figures form the State's latest contribution to the nation's gallery of political notables. Even they were scarcely of national stature, but since we have had only politicians of the common run. And in no other field—save for such capable and showy fighters as Sam Houston, David Glasgow Farragut, Nathan Bedford Forrest, and Alvin York—has the State ever had a citizen for whom it could even claim high rank. In art, literature, science, invention, business achievement the proudest name Tennessee can boast is far down among the minors. Our present is as our past. We have not today a writer, a musician, a painter, an educator, a scientist, an editor, a captain of industry, a lawyer, or an orator even who may be numbered among the country's best.

The little groups of our people who are really interested in literature and art and intellectual attainment and the higher things of life are lost in the mass to whom these matters are of small account. Our cities are not concerned to be beautiful; our country towns find amazing ways of achieving ugliness and squalor; our farmers seem to doubt, if indeed they ever think on this subject, that good taste and good business can live together. If we had among us a great prophet or poet or sculptor or architect most of us would care nothing about him. We do without the dreamers and idealists and do not miss them. We can manage to get along with the things we have. They fail, it is true, to satisfy us; but this is at best an unsatisfactory world.

But what is it we have that is distinctively and typically Tennesseeans? Let us take stock:

We have—so much do we value our present-day crop of politicians—a fat, friendly, fiddling, fox-chasing Governor of 73, a genial soul who was a defeated candidate for the same office in 1886.

We have—so profound are our political convictions—two United States Senators, elected by the same party and largely by the same voters, voting against each other on nearly everything from the League of Nations to free seeds, yet both claiming to be true and representative Democrats, and both standing a chance of "getting by with it."

We have a deep-seated faith in our ability to elect every two years the worst of all possible legislatures, and we have, on this account, a grudge against Kentucky for beating us to a near-acceptance of the educational theories of Mr. Bryan and his fellow-scientists.

We have fifth place from the bottom of the list of States in illiteracy.

We have thousands of country children who have a chance to go to school for only five months each year.

We have county officials—mere court clerks with duties purely clerical—who receive $10,000 or $20,000 or $30,000 a year, and this despite the enactment of two anti-fee laws and an unprecedented clamor against the taxes we pay.

We have a State constitution fifty years old, which has so far protected these fee-grabbers, which prevents our getting the tax relief we clamor for, which with one voice we admit to be "antediluvian and full of grasshoppers," but which we are afraid to try to change lest worse befall us.

These are our main claims to distinction. We have more than the average number of homicides, but we compensate by having fewer than the average number of convictions. Of illicit stills, bootleggers, and law-breaking prohibition officers we have plenty, but probably no more than our quota.

We have, in short, some little difficulty in getting statistics to bear out the proudest claim we now dare seriously make—that of being a typical and average American State. Statistics not only tell us that we are a bit below the average in most things, but that every now and then we drop a notch or two in this category or that. They are so discouraging at times that we feel inclined to cry out against them as did old man Jenkins up in the hills.

Jenkins could not read or write. He owed the local storekeeper and sold him some hogs. The storekeeper figured their price, deducted the amount of his bill, and told Jenkins how much was coming to him. It was not more than half what the old man was expecting and he protested. The merchant went over the figures again, checking them off with the trite assertion: "Figures can't lie, you know, Mr. Jenkins," "Mebbe not," said old Jenkins, as he stuffed the money into his pocket, "I aint sayin' nothing agin' figures, but I've allus tuck notice that liars has to figger more'n anybody else, an' I wouldn't trust no feller that I seed a-figgerin' all the time."

Tennesseeans sometimes feel like suggesting to the statistician that "liars have to figger more'n anybody else": but even so the figures only confirm our own conviction that something is wrong with Tennessee. For thirty years the State has been losing rank in population, in wealth, in agricultural and industrial development, in educational advancement, in political enlightenment. Neighboring States have passed us or gained upon us in one after another of these things. We are not living up to our possibilities and we know it. Our politicians, our newspapers, our religionists, our "successful business men" give us their same old platitudes over and over. They no longer satisfy us. We realize that they give no help, but we do not know what we need or where to look for it. So we spend most of our time milling about in circles, doubtful, mistrustful, bewildered. Our discontent with what we are is the most promising thing about us, and it as yet remains unfruitful.

Take our politics. We turn this year to our favorite election game, but we turn to it with little enthusiasm or hope. With all our plethora of politicians there is no constructive program of State improvement or State betterment offered us. We know they are trying most of all to say the things we wish to hear, that they are not striving to guide our thought to any great accomplishment, but merely seeking to capitalize our discontent and our uncertainty to their own advantage. There is with them no vision, for us no real leadership.

Here we are—a once great State that has become in every sense a very ordinary State. In 1920 one out of every eight of our citizens of voting age was recorded as an illiterate. This must mean that at least an equal number had only the most elementary education. Perhaps we do well to doubt ourselves, to fear our own political ineptitude; but surely, facing these facts, we cannot much longer fail to see what it is that keeps us on the downward grade in the scale of States.

We are an ignorant people and we are paying the penalty of ignorance. Only half a dozen States have school systems of less efficiency. In some of the poorer counties our rural schools are merely excuses for schools. Attendance laws are often poorly enforced and thousands of boys and girls have quit school barely able to read and write, some absolutely illiterate. Poorly trained teachers and low salaries are the rule. And some of our politicians are proposing to reform the schools system and help educate our children by cutting down appropriations for the State University and the teacher training schools!

Up on the Cumberland Plateau lie five thousand square miles of undeveloped farming land—it lies undeveloped because it was not suited to the farming methods of earlier days and because the scattered population on it today lacks the technical knowledge to make it the great fruit and garden region it will some day become. Down the sides of the Appalachians flow, unutilized, streams that could turn every wheel of industry in the State and put light and running water in every East Tennessee farmhouse. They flow unutilized because the people who live beside them have neither the knowledge nor the capital to put them to work. A thousand hillsides that should have remained forest forever have been stripped and the soil allowed to wash away because no practical system of agricultural and forest management has been worked out for our mountain regions. Out in the western lowlands tortuous creeks wind through brush-grown fields given up by the cultivator because neither he nor the community understood the technique or the advantages of drainage.

Every year malaria, typhoid, and hookworm take their toll, women die in childbirth, and little children give up their lives to the general lack of health knowledge and public hygiene. So are our boasted natural resources wasted and our hopes for the future set at naught while we wonder what it is we need to do. "My people are destroyed for lack of knowledge."

The heart of the State is sound, but its head is muddled. A romantic history remains without any adequate telling. Daring deeds and noble lives that should have been embodied in song and story to grow into beautiful legend and inspiring tradition remain unwritten and unsung. They, too, are part of our children's wasted heritage, and the future will be the poorer for our neglect of them. Material resource or historical wealth, the failure is the same. We lack the understanding to profit by what is ours. We do not see clearly the goal we would have the State attain, nor can we bring ourselves to follow the long, hard road of endeavor and sacrifice which all who would reach golden goals must tread. The perception of the Tennessee that should be and might be is not yet in our minds: the inspiration that quickens the heart and strengthens the thews for great accomplishment has not yet come to us.

TEXAS

The Big Southwestern Specimen

GEORGE CLIFTON EDWARDS

MARCH 21, 1923

T EXAS, it should be observed by a native anxious to begin on the right note, is great. It is great in size. As it shows on the map it is as large as New York, Pennsylvania, Massachusetts, Illinois, Ohio, and Wisconsin, all in one. It is larger than France; larger than Germany; and, in products, more abundant. We produce more cotton than any other State; more oil, both cotton-seed and Standard; more cattle and sweet potatoes; more peanuts and mules; more brass-bound Democrats and Democratic officeholders; more Ku Klux Klansmen, killings, and lynchings. We sent to the Baltimore Convention a group of shock troops that came away shouting that they won the nomination for Woodrow Wilson. Mr. Wilson must have believed this, for he allowed Texas to contribute to our country's welfare the slave-driving Burleson, who used the post office to abolish freedom of the press; T. W. Gregory, who developed a spy system vaster than the Czar's; and Colonel House, who abolished secrecy in diplomacy. But size and raw products are not our only grounds for complacency. We are proud of our history; and we boast of our business.

Our career "Under Six Flags," French, Spanish, Mexican, Republic of Texas, Confederate, Union; the heroism of our pioneers: Houston, Crockett, Bowie; the massacre at the Alamo, the victory at San Jacinto—these are topics our school-books and our orators glow about. Texas is now fully within the American industrial machine; but we had vivid and varied experiences getting there.

This history left some marks. It left us with a tendency to act first, and later to think, if ever; and it left us with a scant regard for human life when feelings are stirred. Of the early French there are few traces. Spanish influence has not been obliterated, however. Thousands of Mexicans have remained, unchanged and unassimilated. Texas law contains many Spanish survivals, particularly concerning land, the family, and the rights of married women. Franciscan missions, combinations of fort and church, the Alamo, San Fernando, Concepción, and San José, still stand, relics of Spanish architectural grace and of Spanish devotion to the Indians whose souls the friars sought to save. Physically this vast State is far from uniform. In the southeast, about Beaumont, are forests, swamps, and rice fields; and in Democratic war days, shipyards. It is low, moist, warm, and busy. About San Angelo it is bare, high and dry and drowsy, except, as it seems to a visitor, for the evidences of the fight against tuberculosis at the State Sanatorium, where the principles Trudeau developed at Saranac are admirable carried out in this more genial climate. Water is all the Angelo country needs. Where they can irrigate, they manufacture garden truck at will. To the south, in the lower Rio Grande valley, it never freezes, and irrigation produces even more bountifully, with oranges and grape fruit. Half a thousand miles northwest and four thousand feet higher, the Panhandle country knows winters piercingly cold, with northers, the ranchers say, straight from the Pole, broken only by barbed-wire fences. Sometimes it snows in the Panhandle as late as May; but the May snows quickly vanish and in a few days the plains are an endless exquisite green. On the eastern side of the State are dense pine forests. On the western edge, near El Paso, the Guggenheims operate one of their largest smelters, and the United States holds its army crouched for the spring on Mexican oil fields.

But these extremes do not express the spirit of present-day Texas as does the middle: the cities to which the rich "black waxy" land counties and the oil counties are tributary, where the population is dense, the tenant farms numerous, the banks powerful and interlocked. Here are no arid plains, no wind-swept plateaus, no forests, rice fields, no cowboys. The rich little city of Waco has one twenty-story skyscraper sticking up like a totem pole among the Baptists. Houston has more skyscrapers; Dallas more and higher; all modern machine made, as much like the north as may be; crammed with offices, bankers, lawyers, oil men, "realtors"—effective Texas of today. For landscape and Old World atmosphere, history and heroes do not occupy our thoughts much. The substantial characteristics of Texas are suggested not by the flower glowing prairies under gorgeous skies or the mellow Spanish missions, but by the ubiquitous oil tanks and the electric power lines.

To be sure, the masses of Texans are not business men and do not make much money; they are hardworking people, and just get along; they do not starve, and rarely suffer from cold—except in the winter. Few farmers make anything above a living unless by some rise in land values; farm laborers live as wretchedly as tenant farmers, who are not much better off than serfs. But we are easily taken in by the business men and the newspapers. The larger our city, the larger our capacity for being fooled: cities are the habitat of the corporations and their lawyers, pleasant, facile sophists, with all the ancient and modern skill in making the worse appear the better part. In Dallas, for example, from the time it first became a paying field for franchise-holders, every city government has been dominated by business and the public-service interests. Some administrations have been more eager than others, but all, without exception, have served the interests primarily.

The telephone company has just hired off the bench the chief justice of the Supreme Court of Texas. The man who was lately supposed to exercise, for the people, the highest impartiality in deciding fundamental law questions is now running hither and yon, before courts, city governments, and commissions, for the telephone monopoly and against the people. The president of the most powerful street railway in Texas, a system owned by absentee capitalists, is a former mayor of Dallas, a lawyer with no knowledge of railways but with a commanding ability to fool the people by his pose as a good citizen of the home town. This man was, with possibly one exception, the most subservient mayor the interests have ever had, and they have had them all. In 1918 the mayor, specially elected by the street railway company, and the commissioners allowed the street railway company to add to its capital account an item of $100,000 expended by the company in "promoting the franchise." Which, being interpreted, meant in electing that mayor and getting for nothing a franchise worth millions. Dallas is paying and will continue to pay dividends on this $100,000, spent not to buy cars or to lay tracks, but to debauch an election. This is one reason for the six-cent fare in Dallas, established during war prices as an emergency and continued now after deflation as graft. Against this domination of the city by the utilities there is scarcely any citizen's protest, and no newspaper protest whatever. The rewarding, after the fact, of men chosen to serve the people who instead served the corporations is regarded as good business. Modern Texas considers it the proper thing for such officials to be on the make, so long as they pay virtue the proper tribute of canting talk and are "good men."

In State politics the situation is the same. Politicians and business men tell us, and we swallow, huge and solemn lies. In 1919 a start was made toward a minimum-wage law for women and minors. It had some teeth. As soon as the employers found this out they had it repealed, which the legislature did on the ground that it was impracticable "without doing serious injury to the female and minor employees"! Our child-labor law, city home-rule law, and workmen's compensation law, viewed from the theoretical purpose of the laws, are about as bona fide as the anti-trust law: which last is as much a joke in its ultimate effectiveness as the Sherman law. Once the Standard Oil Company was fined a million dollars, which we, the consumers, paid, and was driven from the State, but after walking through dry places for a while, it came back with seven, or more, other spirits, and we are now worse off than before. We have an "Open Port Law," so named because it was designed, it was said, to keep "open" the port of Galveston. The day before election our young Baptist Governor would not use it, seeking union votes. He got them, and the day after election, it was put into effect to break the railroad strike at Denison four hundred miles from any port. He estimated rightly our capacity for being fooled.

With the modern business spirit, the killing industry has changed somewhat. Rarely do we now have a killing like that in which an early Dallas mayor and a brother lawyer were looking for each other in the court-house. They drew on sight, but the lawyer drew first. The death of Brann, the "Iconoclast," our Waco literary light, was old fashioned. He had quarreled with the Baptists—and many others—and a fellow-citizen shot him, mortally, from behind; but Brann braced himself against a telephone pole, turned, and killed his killer. This is not the modern style. It is not businesslike and involves some risk.

The best preventive against conviction in a Texas murder case is money. The best trial defenses are the "unwritten law" and the "hip-pocket move," both, generally, based on pretense and perjury. The "unwritten law" is large and liberal as the all-embracing air of rumor. It is, as it works out, that any person who can allege that a man has committed adultery with, or insulted, or "talked about" a female relative (marriage, blood, step) can kill that man on sight, shooting from front, side, or back, without word or warning. Recently a young man was accused of having had a sexual adventure with a young woman. The father of the young woman and her stepfather, that is, the present husband of her mother, got the young man into a hotel room, by himself, unarmed, and killed him, shooting him nine times. These killers were, for a long time, not indicted; it was doubtful whether they would ever be indicted; and it will be a waste of time to try them in a Ku Klux court, now that they are indicted. After the preliminary hearing on bonds, the Ku Klux lawyer stated that he was greatly surprised that the prosecuting attorney would not agree to a low bond for "these Christian men." Yet no one should get the notion that the men of Texas are Miltonic in the practice of chastity. They are much as other men; but it is the custom of the country to talk as did that Ku Klux lawyer.

The Texas "hip-pocket move" is pleaded against a person who after death by shooting is shown to have had nothing in his hip-pocket. It is quite distinct from the effort to draw a weapon, a movement where the person killed has a gun. Three recent Texas cases typical of the "hip-pocket move" reveal a man killed with a cigar in his mouth; one standing talking at a wall telephone; another, sitting at his desk, with a fountain pen in his hand.

The open-shop movement in Texas is active; and it exhibits the frauds we are gulled by, in purest form. In theory, the open shoppers are animated by devotion to abstract justice and make no distinction between union and non-union men, loving them equally. In practice, the open shop means the scab shop. Its most liberal supporters are those corporations, in particular the utility corporations, that as matter of principle fire every employee who joins a union. Yet day after day, in letters, speeches, circulars, and newspapers, the statement is repeated that the open shop is not fighting the unions. Every one of its speakers, and every informed man, knows this is a brazen falsehood, but the open shoppers know our Texas public. They know it is not informed and that it loves the process of being fooled.

Morality—the compulsion upon others of the ideas of the old men of the various religious groups—we talk a great deal about; but we have little interest in scientific, or indeed in any sort of knowledge, from books, unless immediately merchantable. We are not hostile after a matter has become a commonplace of the newspapers and the *Saturday Evening Post,* which we buy by the ton. Before it has been thus diluted and denatured, we will have none of it. It is hard to believe that a large, rich, technically and mechanically efficient newspaper can fill its editorial page, eight long columns, 365 days year without indicating somewhere in it that sometime some editor has read a book. But the Dallas *News,* our greatest Texas daily, achieves this. About the only book ever named is the Revised Statutes, and the only one ever reflected is *Science and Health,* this reflection appearing every Sunday in a column of editorial bathos. Sometimes the hostility to a new idea is quite frank. The editor of another Texas daily printed a characteristically violent attack on the Plumb Plan.[1] Shortly after, in his office, he kindly hunted up a little book on the Plumb Plan to give me. "No," he said genially, "I haven't read it and I don't want to. I can lambaste it better if I don't." At the top of this paper's editorial column, the editor prints a classic quotation from the well-known Mr. Bartlett; and he has thereby a great popular reputation as a reading man. Just equally interested in books is the Dallas Scripps paper, our representative of liberal thought; but it is strong for morals. It modestly admits in 12-point black on the front page, editorially, that it is "run on the Golden Rule." And few laugh in its face.

The most prominent and "eloquent" preachers in Texas expound doctrines as primitive as those of the Salem witch hangers. They are as certain as Bryan and Billy Sunday that there is nothing to evolution save a slander on humanity; they call it "monkeyism." They believe in and teach the actual physical resurrection of the body, and the actual physical flame and burning of hell. Toward which well-deserved fate, of course, freethinkers and Unitarians are moving directly. The preachers are vastly patriotic. They still talk about "Hunnishness" and about the "war for democracy," though it must be admitted that they do not claim now that the war ended war. In the cities the preachers are apt to be good business men. The active young Episcopal bishop of Dallas was one of the organizing committee from the Chamber of Commerce, to establish the open shop. The most lurid of our Texas Baptists is generally believed to have set fire to his own church as an advertising stunt. This man is very successful in Texas.

It is a matter of pride to us in Texas that our early statesmen, preoccupied as they were with the violence and the difficulties of their times, did plan for a good educational system. The public schools and the State University were bountifully endowed with gifts of land; but these have not been well managed. Our country schools are poor, and the teachers miserably paid. In the cities the schools are far better, and the teachers fairly well paid; but it is made clear to them that they are to stick in the rut, must not be too much interested in learning or books, and shall be strictly conventional if they desire to get on. City school boards repeatedly refuse to "reelect" (the teachers hold by one-year tenure and are "reported on" regularly) teachers who show any signs of thinking and speaking independently. What is wanted in schools and colleges is the industri-

---

[1]The Plumb Plan was a union-based plan that would have transferred ownership and operation of the railroads to the federal government. [D. H. B.]

ous type that will not do or say, or be caught thinking, anything except what is approved by those factory directors, the trustees. Some men have been let out of the University of Texas for matters of opinion purely; but mostly this censorship intimidates in advance. Teachers very frankly admit that they cannot teach what they think or follow to conclusion lines of thought constantly reached in classes. They either decline to speak or they evade issues; their jobs depend on it. The Damoclean sword of "investigation" hangs over all, save the machine-minded and the time-servers. A Texas legislator recently charged that the University was teaching Socialism, and cited the catalogue, where in plain black print it was set out that there were classes in and teachers of *Sociology*. Rice Institute, a millionaire-endowed college at Houston, discharged a teacher for his opinions, expressed outside of the college, in reference to justice to the Bolsheviki. Baylor University, a large and rich college, but Baptist, "investigated" and discharged a teacher who wrote a very conventional textbook on sociology that aroused the Baptist ministerial hatred of science and evolution.

The Southern Methodist University at Dallas was established to take the place of Vanderbilt University, which had fallen from grace and its Methodist swaddling bands. Dr. John A. Rice, one of the teachers, published a book on the Old Testament. There was nothing startling in the book unless one excepts some of his personal testimony on the extremes to which Southern Methodist literal belief can go. But as soon as the echoes of this book (the book itself they would not read) reached the Methodist preachers of the State they went after Dr. Rice's scalp. And there was no lack of frankness. He was fired for cause, and the cause stated. An incident showing the connection between business and intolerance in the schools developed shortly thereafter. In one of the student publications a writer took a fling at the president, charging him with "playing politics" in the Rice case. The president called a meeting of the students, demanded the passage of a resolution stating that the article was false, and made this argument: "There are three men who have put in their wills big endowments to the university who will withdraw these endowments if the student body does not support the faculty in this matter." Plainly the president regarded his action toward Dr. Rice, if not politics, at least good business. The resolution was passed. The three endowments are safe. The president has since been made a bishop.

The intolerance that depresses our schools and intimidates the teachers exists nearly everywhere. The lunch clubs defend all existing means of exploitation, boost public utility schemes, afford publicity to attacks on unions and strikers, entirely refusing to hear the other side. One club denounced the Plumb Plan at a time when most of the lunchers thought it is a new method for fruit raisers. The only speech that I ever heard in Dallas openly advocating violence was at a lunch club. At a Rotary Club luncheon a very rich and prominent corporation lawyer advocated summary shooting for all I.W.W.'s, agitators, and soreheads against the government generally, the method of identification not being specified or regarded as important.

But there are no I.W.W.'s in Texas. The unions are pure and simple after Gomper's own heart.[2] The labor leaders are conventional, generally ignorant of the labor movement outside of their personal experience in their own craft. Often the leader is subject to purchase or pressure because there is neither idealism nor principle in his equipment. His office means to him merely a steady job to collect at least the full wage scale assured by keeping in line a majority of his local or council. The labor press is venal, paid for in advertising. Dallas is the head of the open-shop movement in Texas; and the Dallas official labor paper carries constantly large well-paying advertisments from the utility interests that are the brain, backbone, and treasury of the open shop. Though this is the frankest sort of bribery, resentment by the simple union men is lacking.

The unions last year, however, under the leadership of the Farm Labor Union, joined a nonpartisan political conference, and tried in the Democratic Party to emulate North Dakota's success in the Republican. The farmer-labor nominee was not successful in the primary, but more union men than ever before voted for a man they themselves, with the farmers, had selected. There is hope in this showing, even though the platform and the candidate both evaded the Ku Klux issue and the use of troops and rangers against the strikers. What political progressive activity there is in Texas has its origin among the farmers, for the union men are befooled by the daily papers and hoodwinked by the Gompers type of labor leader.

All of our present-day characteristics—our fondness for being fooled, our intolerance, our hatred, our preference for violent action, our prejudices against the Negro—have flowered in the Ku Klux Klan. Dallas, the city most thoroughly dominated by the utility interests, is the Klan stronghold. There is no complete record available to "aliens" of its achievements; but no less than sixty mobbing episodes took place in Dallas before the anti-Klan elements began to organize last spring. A Negro, with his back lashed and his forehead branded K.K.K. with acid, was thrust into the Adolphus, the showy, leading hotel of Dallas. Then we learned that before we had waked, at a special election in the preceding summer, the Ku Klux had elected a State Senator. Other mobbings took place, of Negroes and whites, and finally a reputable business man was taken from his home, dragged from the presence of his daughters, one of whom was knocked down by the chivalrous knights, taken to the river bottom and terribly beaten. Not once did police or sheriff find any of the mobbers. The only two men arrested charged with offenses were police officers, and both were promptly acquitted. The Dallas sheriff and the Dallas city police commissioner are leaders in the Klan. At the great Dallas Ku Klux parade the electric company kindly cut off all the downtown lights and let the masked men march in their desired darkness.

[2]In contrast to his more theoretical opponents within the labor movement, Samuel Gompers, president of the American Federation of Labor, favored "pure and simple" trade unionism organized around hours and wages. [D. H. B.]

The Ku Klux Klan came into Texas with a selling organization that beats the instalment furniture collectors in effective personal work. Its paid organizers made money as the snowball grew. They took in the small church people who wanted to vent their virtue on others. The head of the Dallas Klan now is a Christian preacher, an oil speculator, and an Elk. The most wholesale approval of the Ku Klux was expressed in a Dallas speech by the man whom the Methodists have just elected head of the church in North Texas. While he made a little lip protestation of belief in law and order, he promptly added that "not one person had been attacked by the Ku Klux who had not got what he deserved." The very officials, police, sheriff, judges, prosecutors, who are charged with responsibility for law enforcement, were solicited and with few exceptions taken in. A newspaper man friendly to, if not a member of, the Klan told me in answer to my question about the men guilty of one flogging: "Why, it's the police. But they can't prove it on them. They ought to have killed the damn Jew." "It's a fine grandstand play the mayor is making over that Jew, ain't it?" I heard one plain-clothes officer say to another. "It's all bluff. He's one of them himself." This is the Dallas feeling about the Ku Klux, the church, and the officials.

The women of the churches were not taken in directly, but effectively annexed in a capacity that the "alien" world thought a joke when it was first announced—namely as "rumor spreaders," who charged opposition candidates and officials with being Catholics, or having Catholic wives, or with being about to be Catholics. True to our Texas practice, the dentist Evans, now the Imperial Wizard, announced that the "Klan is not a political organization." This buncombe was carried on by Earle B. Mayfield, who was on the Ku Klux ticket last election, but refused to answer any question about it or to discuss it "because it was not an issue." Not until he had won the nomination for the United States Senate did he admit that he had been a member; then he asserted that he had resigned, but he continued to attend the Klan meetings. This combination of officials, fanatics, preachers, and politicians has finally gone into partnership with the great utility corporations. The campaign manager of the Klan in Dallas was the law partner of the ex-mayor of Dallas who is the president of the Dallas street railway company. This union of fanaticism and finance has swept Dallas and the State.

The Governor, the House of Representatives certainly, and the Senate probably, most of the trial judges, sheriffs, and the police—practically all are Klansmen in membership or in spirit. In Dallas the entire county government, prosecuting attorney, sheriff, judges, all the clerical officers, were elected by the Klan. Now they are openly planning to take possession of the city government, get the offices for themselves, and furnish the electric interests with an enthusiastically, not a grudgingly, subservient administration. They will probably be successful. The electric interests are powerful and will take much other business along with them in their raid on the city hall. They will, however, probably soft pedal the mobbing industry in Dallas. In fact this has already been done. There has not been a case of mobbing in Dallas since the fight on the Klan began last

May: the leaders have been too intent on offices to let the mobbers act. The more hopeful of us think that as the Klan gets better known and its connection with the utilities is exposed, it will lose some of its power. This is not likely to happen in the smaller towns. There the mob spirit and the church fanaticism will bear bloodier fruit. Catholic priests have been, and will be, taken out and whipped for "pro-Germanism" at this late day. One woman was mobbed, beaten, her hair cut off, and brought back to the little town half naked. There is no measure that can be given of the cruelty this movement has brought to bear on the Negroes. The Ku Klux has, of course, simply exaggerated the feeling that is common in the South and in Texas. Here men will discuss the weather, a lawsuit, a grocery bill, or a building scheme and use their best intellect; let them touch the Negro question and they are no longer demonstrated by their thinking—they become a mass of feeling and flaming prejudice. And this is truest of those who are themselves almost as poor and wretched as the Negro, economically. And while thousands do not believe in any sort of mob law, do not desire to oppress the Negro, and realize that religious intolerance is a pure curse, they are not in an effective majority now.

The regulation question in Texas as elsewhere in the United States, addressed to one not properly commendatory of the herd's ways, is "Why don't you go back to where you came from if you don't like it here?" My answer satisifies me at least. I was born in Dallas, and I am not a workingman or a farmer. The Texas climate is good and the utilities do not yet own it. It is true that we have a difficult social situation, but few other States are in a position to throw stones at us. Little as can be said for Texas justice, it has no Mooney case, nor such anti-thought laws as California. We cannot match Ludlow; nor the Chicago riots and East St. Louis riots; nor the cold infamy of the mine owners of West Virginia; and if we have no Socialist legislators, we have not thrown any out, as has New York. Our school intolerance is due to ignorance and is not crystallized into Lusk laws. While we have the worst case of the Ku Klux, Georgia invented it. Texas lynches, mutilates, and burns Negroes; but, except for this, the Ku Klux year, other Southern States rank ahead of us in this pastime—they have more Negroes to lynch. Still, the mass of Texans, in varying degrees, are suffering and will suffer from the reactionary Democratic Party, oppression of the Negro, corporation domination, church fanaticism, and the perfect embodiment of them all, the Ku Klux Klan, just as the whole South suffered from slavery. These things are a denial of civilization, and a lover of civilization cannot be comfortable here. Why any workingman or farmer, or any person who expects to live by honest toil, should come to Texas, or, if he is foot-loose, should stay here, is hard to see—except that there are few better places to go. It is a good State for exploiters to profit by credulity and fanaticism, by defrauding and oppressing the weak. But, after all, is it not really just the big Southwestern specimen of American capitalism?

UTAH

Apocalypse of the Desert

MURRAY E. KING

JUNE 28, 1922

MORE THAN three-fourths of the people of Utah are Mormons. Stretching away from Salt Lake City, from Ogden, from the smelter towns and mining camps, which are half Gentile and indistinguishable from similar centers in other parts of the West, is a rural hinterland almost wholly Mormon. Here one sees the Utahan in his native setting. Here life is uniquely organized, and here is rooted the power that dominates the State religiously, socially, and politically.

A sight of the Mormon conference crowd in Salt Lake City every April and October should dispel impressions of the Mormons that have grown out of stories of polygamous escapades, Danites,[1] and Avenging Angels. It is Mormon Utah assembled. From a tenth to an eighth of the State's half million inhabitants gather semi-annually at the call of the church for a general spiritual refilling. The multitude on the Tabernacle grounds looks much like any predominantly rural crowd anywhere between Duluth and Dallas. It differs neither in dress nor in physiognomy. It is not less good natured and sturdy. Certain backwoods, puritanical, and patriarchal touches impart a picturesque effect, but its only striking peculiarity is that the older generation is an unusual patchwork of nationalities. Many blond, sun-burned, raw-boned, and stolid Norsemen, largely peasant types, from all parts of the State and from counties almost solidly Scandinavian contrast with groups of dark, stocky Welshmen and women talking excitedly with hands and tongues. These are largely from exclusively Welsh rural settlements and coal-mining camps. English folk are much in evidence—under-sized factory workers, Cockneys, stolid Yorkshire farmers—Icelanders from Spanish Fork, Hawaiians from bleak Skull Valley, and a sprinkling of Germans, Dutch, Scotch. Notwithstanding physical divergencies, this crowd is noticeably homogeneous. A common spirit imparts a clearly collective character. One senses a self-conscious, optimistic, literal, and provincial mind brimming over with local

---

[1]The Danites were members of a Mormon secret society, believed to have been pledged to destroy their enemies by violence. [D. H. B.]

357

pride and conceit. It is Mormonism manifesting itself through varying types. This religion and its outworkings distinguishes the people of Utah.

The Mormon religion is so simple and literal; it appeals so strongly to the love of the spectacular, dramatic, and miraculous; it promises such large and quick results; it is so directly and solidly authoritarian that it has a peculiar hold on primitive minds. The whole spiritual universe is explained in materialistic terms and analogies. God is a perfected human being with "body, parts, and passions." He is a good Mormon with many wives and is literally the father, his wives the mothers, of our spirits. He placed us on earth to test us and to educate us in a school of experience. After the resurrection we will have immortalized bodies and will eat, drink, and enjoy physical existence and beget children forever. Believers will attain different degrees of glory according to their merits. The highest glory, the celestial, can be attained only through the practice of plural marriage. The polygamist Mormon will become a god and will beget children and construct solar systems for his descendants "out in space" forever, while his monogamic or bachelor brother will continue to exist as a mere angel.

Mormonism keeps its adherents in a perpetual state of spiritual enthusiasm by promising everything to the present generation. It is a "last days" preparation for a "winding-up scene" always a decade or two away. Hence the Mormon is a Latter-Day Saint who expects to live to see dreadful, spectacular, and glorious events that are to accompany the gathering of Israel to the region of Utah, the destruction of all the wicked who refuse to accept the Gospel, the return of the Lost Tribes of Israel from the region of the North Pole, the founding of the city of Zion at Independence, Jackson County, Missouri, the second coming of Christ, the first resurrection,[2] the translation into immortal beings of all good Saints then living, the beginning of the millennium. Before 1891, that date was set by thousands of Latter-Day Saints as the year of the second coming of Christ. The belief was based upon a passage in the *Doctrine and Covenants,* the Mormon book of revelations, in which God informs Joseph Smith, the founder of the church, that if he lives until he is eighty-five years old he will "see the face of the coming of the Son of Man." Mormons now explain that Joseph Smith did not live until he was eighty-five. These abnormal expectations have culminated from time to time in periods of religious excitement and miracles when whole communities have been rebaptized and have started life anew. Such occurrences have become less and less frequent, but today there are thousands of aged persons in Utah who are happy in the belief that they will see the "winding-up scene" and will become immortal beings without having to die.

The main Mormon arguments for polygamy are: the exemplary and approved personages in the Bible practiced it; it supplies human bodies more rapidly than

[2]When the Mormons speak of the first resurrection they ignore the accepted resurrection of Christ nineteen centuries ago and refer to a supposed general resurrection of the righteous, which they say will take place at a comparatively early date. Long after this will come the second resurrection, which will consist of the resurrection of the wicked after they have been purged sufficiently of their sins.

monogamy for the hosts of waiting spirits who must be "born under the covenant" before the end of the world; it is necessary for the purification of women by earthly trial. In practice it broke or crushed women or drove them into ungovernable rebellion. Children of polygamist parents turned upon their fathers and demanded the abolition of the practice. Caught between a young Mormon element and the Government, the authorities promulgated a revelation in 1891 suspending the practice. At that time, it is said, 7 per cent of Utah families were polygamic. Secret plural marriages developed later and the church authorities were compelled by public opinion to excommunicate the offenders. Cases of this kind have not come to light for about ten years, but relics of the institution still survive. Old men quietly cling to their former wives and support them. But despite the passing of polygamy, Mormons continue to live that part of their religion which requires the rearing of large families. A Provo, Utah, school teacher recently asked her geography class, "What are the principal means of transportation in Utah?" A small boy promptly answered, "Baby carriages."

Celestial marriages have taken the place of plural marriages. A celestial marriage is a secret Temple rite wherein men have dead women "sealed" to them as their wives for eternity, and unattached women are sealed to dead husbands. There is no evidence that the ghost has any choice in the matter. These harmless ceremonies open the gates to the celestial glory temporarily closed by the revelation of 1891. An unsuccessful bachelor may collect the names of decedent old maids or wives of other men not married "under the covenant." At the Temple after the "sealing ordinance" he is given a record of the heavenly names of these celestial wives. Only by repeating these names at the gates of heaven can he get them inside. This explains what a grief-stricken Mormon bachelor in Salt Lake City several years ago meant when he sobbed, "I have lost my wives: the mice have eaten them up!"

A Latter-Day Saint will tell you that the distinguishing principle of his religion is "continued revelation." He means that his church is ruled and guided from heaven through the constituted authorities here. All good saints may receive "testimonies," see visions, or perform miracles for themselves in accordance with church authority, but only one man, the president, prophet, seer, and revelator of the church, may receive revelations from God for the guidance of the church or any part of it. Many devout Mormons accept this doctrine without qualification. It confers upon the Mormon hierarchy a potential political power that may well be a challenge to democratic institutions. Many Mormons, however, accept it with reservations, or ignore it. This, combined with the caution and cunning of the leaders, prevents it from being pushed to extreme lengths. The practice of promulgating revelations has declined to such an extent that no authorized revelations have appeared in Utah for years. On the other hand, the authorities have been greatly embarrassed by the competition of self-constituted prophets. Not many years ago an aspiring John the Baptist in southern Utah paved the way for the advent of a certain son in a certain family who would be "the chosen one" to lead the saints back to Jackson County, Missouri. As the natal day approached the excitement grew among the followers of the unborn Messiah. Suddenly the whole movement miraculously collapsed and the church was saved. The expected boy turned out to be a girl.

The average Mormon is a composite product of this religion, the desert, the mountain land with which he blends, and a modern American world which pushes in upon him and changes him in spite of himself. Stop at his home and one of the first questions he asks is, "Do you belong to the church?" If you do, he will reveal himself as an enthusiast very much enamored with the visions of miraculous things about to transpire. If you do not, he will discover to you a practical, common-sense, shrewd, fairly human and neighborly individual interested in a great many worldly, materialistic, and modern things. Despite his belief in polygamy he has a rigid code of sex morality. There is not an unusual amount of immorality or illegitimacy in Mormon communities. Notwithstanding his belief in "continued revelation," his head is full of canny and stubborn reservations which save him from being the priest-ridden creature one might expect to find. Assertions of independence often come with quaint effect from stern old believers, as in the case of a Welsh brother who, having been pressed a little too hard for church contributions, shouted in church: " I tell 'oo the church do look after itself furst. I hereby serve notice that henceforth I will look out for David Evans furst, and the church after." An old Danish peasant in Ferron compromised between his spirit of independence and religious fears by declaring to the congregation: "Ay tank yet dis is de church of God, but Ay tank no longah you ah de Lord's people."

To hear whole Mormon congregations in village meeting houses on Sundays shouting their hymns to the mountains is to realize the love of this people for the country they dwell in.

> O ye mountains high, where the clear blue sky
> Arches over the vales of the sea,

they shout. Or they sing,

> O Babylon, O Babylon, we bid thee farewell;
> We are going to the mountains of Ephraim to dwell,

or thunder,

> For the strength of the hills we bless Thee,
> Our God, our fathers' God.

The preachers lovingly refer to Utah as "the Valleys of the Mountains," or "Desert." The natural ties that unite the people and country are augmented by religious and historical bonds. The Mormons came from Missouri and Illinois, a hunted people, and found valleys that were places of refuge and mountains that were walls of defense. The deserts, valleys rivers, and salt lakes realized the visions of the wilderness, of the Jordan and Dead Sea of ancient Palestine, and stamped the country as the new Land of Promise. Here the somber and apocalyptic imagination of a modern Israel finds its home.

Picture a wild tumble of forest-splashed mountain ranges flung in a great semi-circle from the middle of the northern boundary of the State to the southwest corner. To the west and north of this a vast, gray desert—wide, flat valleys, far, lone hills, low, sun-burned ranges, salt-rimmed lakes, glistening alkaline flats, blinding-white salt deserts—all spreading with increasing desolation to Nevada and beyond. To the east and south an immense red sandstone desert beats in tumultuous rock waves from the edge of the State to the base of the mountains—a mesa land, abysmally gorged, savagely painted, weirdly weathered and sculptured, and touched with a thorny, subtropical vegetation. This is Utah in outline. Its inhabitants cling tenaciously to the central crescent of mountains. They huddle along the edges of the red and the gray deserts. But only rarely and timidly do they follow the river valleys out into these wastes.

If this is a forbidding picture, you have not learned the lure and deception of Utah. Through the heart of the mountains for three hundred miles north and south runs a single connected chain of watered valleys, green in the north among the jumbled, snow-capped peaks of the Wasatches, gray among the naked, forest-fringed mountains of the south, except where the little settlements have spread their rugs of green—Cache Valley, Ogden Valley, Salt Lake Valley, Provo Valley, Indianola Valley, San Pete Valley, Sevier Valley, Circle Valley, Panguitch Valley, Grass Valley. Here along torrents emerging from canyons, or on the banks of valley rivers, in cozy towns and villages girdled by green fields and smothered in orchards and shade trees, dwell more than half the rural folk in Utah.

Not less picturesquely placed are the towns on the edge of the gray desert at the mouths of the canyons of the Pavant and Tushar mountains. From each of these green deltas, which look down upon the wide desert fading to purple and azure in the distance, rises a green lane beside torrential waters through ragged gorges to a cool upland of lakes, woods, and meadows. But strangest of all are the settlements on the edge of the red desert in Utah's Dixie. The gorges of the painted desert head in little, funnel-shaped canyons at the base of the mountains. Canyon torrents drop sheer to these through zones of fir, white pine, long-leaf pine, cottonwood, squaw bush, chapparal, cactus and Joshua trees, and are diverted by the settlers to the hot, sandy soil. The canyon floors and the mesas above become bowers of subtropical foliage, flower, and fruit in the midst of gaunt desolation.

The farming communities in this setting embody what is basic in Utah. The location of more than three-fourths of them at the mouths of canyons is most propitious for delightful contrasts of climate and scenery and communal self-sufficiency. The canyon is a boulevard and a summer resort; the canyon stream an exclusive community possession for turning the industries and conquering the desert and transforming it into a fruitful Eden; the mountains a great, free timber reserve and summer pasture; the valley an empire of land in process of conquest; the desert a winter range. These communities are compact and self-sufficient, and are separated by respectable distances of field or desert space from neighboring towns. Around them are zones of green or russet fields gradually advancing upon the desert as methods of irrigation improve. This zone is quite without houses and outbuildings. The owners of its fenced plots live in the town and fare forth daily during the busy season to cultivate the land and haul in the crops. The church, the desert, and the canyon stream have conspired to produce this village concentration. The church has created so many religious activities and so monopolizes social activities that it cannot carry out its program except in organized communities. There is little isolated rural living in Utah. The man who cultivates the soil is the main pillar of a highly structured town life, a life that is indeed tinged with communism. Many towns have cooperative stores, creameries, cheese factories, and canneries. The irrigation system is owned and administered cooperatively. Milch cows and work horses graze placidly on a common pasture. The church has a communal provision against indigence. Part of the "tithing," Relief Society, and a fast-day "offerings" is used to provide for those who are unable to provide for themselves. The result of all these conditions is an unusual diffusion of comfort and absence of extreme poverty. The 1920 census shows that only 10.9 per cent of Utah farmers are tenants, as against 38.1 per cent of the farmers of the remainder of the United States.

The town is a regular arrangement of substantial brick homes. Each house stands in an orchard and garden plot of about an acre, with barn and corrals in the opposite corner of the lot. The square, fenced blocks are like wicker baskets bursting with fruits and flowers. The sidewalks are bordered by running water and smothered under shade trees. The meeting-house, tithing office, and other church buildings are great bulks of red brick. Schoolhouses are plentiful. Utah ranks fourth among the States in secular education; but the church administers an immediate antidote in the shape of the most complete system of religious education in the United States.

Quaint and various are the religious manifestations. A venerable patriarch, with flowing beard, solemnly blesses awed young boys and girls, reveals the tribes of Israel from which they have descended, and foretells their futures. Elders cast out devils, lay hands on the sick, anoint them with olive oil, and pray for their recovery. Dances are opened and closed by prayer, and religious instructors teach proper "round dancing." Everybody fasts once a month and turns the equivalent of the meals saved to the church for the poor. Young and old assemble at the meeting-house fast day for "testimony meetings." These are Pentacostal affairs where all who feel "moved by the spirit" arise, confess their faults, ask forgiveness, and bear their testimonies. These consist of the narration of miraculous incidents in the course of which the emotions of the assemblage are often loosed and some of the speakers become incoherent. Young ward teachers visit all the families each month and question the members about their

Salt Lake City (circa 1920). Gentile influences notwithstanding, the dominant position of the Church of Latter-Day Saints continued during the 1920s. This panorama of the city, with the Mormon temple on the right and the information center on the left, reveals that authority. The building in the background is the state capitol.

religious and moral conduct and condition of faith and report back to the bishop, who is the "temporal" head of the community. The women of the Relief Society have sewing bees for the benefit of the poor and a granary stored with wheat against the predicted famines of the "last days." Life is one continual round of meetings—Sunday schools and religion classes for the children, the Young Men's and Young Women's M. I. A., deacons' and teachers' meetings for youth, Relief Society meetings for women, priesthood meetings of all orders of the priesthood for men, general meetings of all kinds for everybody.

The church utilizes every resource of organization, education, and spiritual hope to erect its formidable power and counteract Gentile and modern influences. Every male member over ten or twelve is required to join the priesthood. The ascending orders of the priesthood are: deacons, teachers, priests, elders, high priests, seventies, the Twelve Apostles, the first presidency, consisting of the president and his two councilors. In addition to its enormous educational activities in each community the church has a system of academies and colleges. Its Temple work of "sealing," "ordinances," "endowments," vicarious baptisms grips the Mormon imagination powerfully. Its missionary work requires every young man to leave Utah and proselyte among the Gentiles several years. Of all methods calculated to produce an ingrained Mormonism, this is the most effective.

Out of all this has developed a political power potentially incalculable. Devout Mormons deny this, notwithstanding the bitter political fight between Gentiles and independent Mormons on one side and the church and its devoted followers on the other, which has torn the State asunder for a generation. The political purpose of the church has been to keep Utah as much as possible in the camp of the dominant political party in order to obtain for Mormonism an advantageous and influential position in the nation. In the course of the long fight the church has swung around from the position of a power that fought the United States army under Johnston to one that teaches patriotism and proclaims the Constitution a divinely inspired instrument. The visible method used to swing the State politically is to drop gentle hints at public meetings as to what "would be best for Zion at this time." There have always been enough church members who literally accept the divine authority of the dignitaries and put the interests of the church above everything else to constitute a comfortable balance of power in the hands of the authorities. But the independent Mormon element has been growing steadily and the practice of such methods has developed scandals within the church resulting in "trials" of overzealous members. They end usually in the overzealous brother receiving solemn censure from an Apostle who mayhap also winked the other eye. The church has gradually become more cautious in its methods and the conflict less direct and bitter, until today external peace prevails in the State.

Perhaps the most sinister development of the church is its gigantic material power. It bases its strength increasingly on the acquisition of property. This control has been secured with funds created out of a system of taxes and levies probably without parallel. Every member is required to pay annually one-tenth of his or her gross income as "tithing." In addition there are fast offerings, Relief Society offerings, missionary contributions, and donations of all sorts for building and other purposes. For many years the church has been investing part of these funds in various financial and industrial enterprises. It now owns or controls several shoe and overall factories, several publications and printing and publishing houses, great funds for the aid of reservoir and irrigation projects, the Deseret National Bank, Zion's Savings and Trust Company, Zion's Cooperative Mercantile Institution, Hotel Utah, the Utah-Idaho Sugar Company, with nineteen plants in Utah, large ranches upon which it has colonized members, much real estate, and sugar plantations in Hawaii. It employs church members and deducts its tithing from their pay checks. Unions are not tolerated by this gigantic employer. There is mutual and bitter hostility between the labor unions and the Mormon church. Encouraged by public statements of church authorities in the Tabernacle, sons of Mormon farmers "scab" on union strikers in the mining camps. The late Mormon President, Joseph F. Smith, once offered as principal justification for opposing labor unions that they were secret societies! It is said in Salt Lake City business circles that the church authorities are enriching themselves from these investments; but of vastly greater consequence is the capital and the investment fund that remain the property of the church. Fed from the pockets of hundreds of thousands of members, these expand abnormally, threatening the whole State with a form of dominance intolerable to contemplate.·

Yet in spite of this highly mobilized religion and church, the Mormon—and Utah—are responding rapidly to Gentile and modern influences. Originally the church was so determined to develop a separate and peculiar people that the Utah settlements were made as self-sustaining, interdependent, and cooperative as circumstances would allow. These efforts·culminated in the establishment at Kingston, Orderville, and other places in the early eighties of communistic colonies. These efforts developed a spirit that made it possible to keep the Mormons out of the gold rush to California, and later when the surrounding States were filled with prospectors all that was necessary to keep the saints for several decades out of the great mining movement was a warning from the church that the opening up of mineral riches in Utah would cause Zion to be submerged by inrushing hordes of Gentiles. In those days the Mormon religion was a terrific reality. Life in Utah was a continuous riot of miracles and visions. The steady trickle into the Great Basin of Gentile cattlemen, prospectors, and merchants was bitterly resented. Church authorities thundered constantly in the meetings against association or intermarriage with these intruders. The feelings aroused resulted in acts of persecution and violence against Gentiles culminating in the Mountain Meadow massacre.

Remembering these former intensities, the grip of Mormonism and the organized power of the church, one may well be amazed over present conditions in Utah. The Mormon, with some exceptions, is a greatly changed and modernized person. The Gentile is everywhere. Scarcely a town or village is free from his presence. He finds his way into Mormon circles and homes. He is still treated with a lingering aloofness and clannishness, but with increasing courtesy. There are intermarriages. Where a considerable number of Mormons and Gentiles dwell in the same community, and the Gentile church looks superciliously across the street upon the Mormon meeting-house, society tends toward two exclusive social divisions, but the feeling of aloofness and superiority is as much on one side as on the other.

Two things have struck Mormon isolation and exclusiveness staggering blows. America has closed in on the Mormon with an infiltrating intellectual environment of current ideas, opinions, phrases, news, literature, which in the long run affect him more than his *Book of Mormon* or *Doctrine and Covenants,* which he hardly ever reads any more, or his *Deseret Evening News,* and church magazines, which he does read. Utah Gentilery has released ponderous industrial and commercial forces that are changing his incentives, habits, and social organization. It is boasted locally that Salt Lake City is the greatest smelter center in the world. Utah is already one of the leading mining States. In the feverish industrial foci of the State the struggle for trade advantage makes the major claim on life. Here Gentile and Mormon business men mingle closely and approximate despite themselves the mentality and standards of life that belong to this environment. Here Mormon and Gentile workers rub elbows and the Mormons, drawn into labor organizations in spite of the church, develop interests, motives, and views that blend them with the great mass of American toilers. Here the Mormon church becomes a competing sect among sects and must conform to certain standards of religious competition. Here the Mormon comes gradually to ignore those religious doctrines that fail to square with this material and intellectual environment. Often he remains a Mormon only in name, or according to his own interpretations of Mormonism, because he does not wish to disconnect himself from a people he still regards as his own.

VERMONT

Our Rich Little Poor State

DOROTHY CANFIELD FISHER

MAY 31, 1922

EVERYBODY KNOWS that New York State is a glowing, queenly creature, with a gold crown on her head and a flowing purple velvet cloak. The face of Louisiana is as familiar—dark eyed, fascinating, temperamental. Virginia is a white-haired, dignified *grande dame* with ancient, well-mended fine lace and thin old silver spoons. Massachusetts is a man, a serious, middle-aged man, with a hard conscientious intelligent face, and hair thinned by intellectual application. And if I am not mistaken, Pennsylvania is a man too, a well-dressed business man, with plenty of money in his pockets and the consciousness of his prosperity written large on his smooth indoor face and in his kindly calculating eyes.

These State countenances are familiar to all of us, and many more; but back of this throng of affluent, thriving personalities, quite conscious of their own importance in the world, stands one, known to fewer Americans, lean, rather gaunt compared to the well-fed curves of the others, anything but fine, aristocratic, or picturesque. Yet the little group of mountaineers who know the physiognomy of Vermont from having grown up with it have the most crabbed, obstinate affection and respect for their State, which they see as a tall, powerful man, with thick gray hair, rough out-door clothes, a sinewy ax-man's hand and arm, a humorous, candid, shrewd mouth and a weather-beaten face from which look out the most quietly fearless eyes ever set in any man's head. They know there is little money in the pockets of that woodman's coat, but there is strength in the long, corded arm, an unhurried sense of fun lies behind the ironic glint in the eyes, and the life animating all the quaint, strong, unspoiled personality is tinctured to its last fiber by an unenvious satisfaction with plain ways which is quite literally worth a million dollars to any possessor. Not to envy other people is an inheritance rich enough; but Vermont adds to that treasure the greater one of not being afraid. It seems incredible, in our modern world, so tormented with fears about its safety, that a whole Stateful of people have no ground for apprehension; but it is true. The Vermonter is so used to the moral freedom of not

Dorothy Canfield Fisher

dreading anything that he is hardly conscious of it. It is the breath he draws, this lack of fear, it is the marrow of his bones. Why should he be afraid of anybody or anything?

What are some of the things that other people fear? Well, most of them are afraid of being poor. This fear, rather more than love, is what makes the modern world go round. The Vermonter is not afraid of being poor because he is poor already and has been for a hundred and fifty years, and it hasn't hurt him a bit. To trade for money this lack of fear of poverty would seem to him the most idiotic of bargains, and if there is one thing on which he prides himself it is on not making poor bargains. This quality makes him by no means a favorite with people who try to organize the world along what they call "strictly business lines of industrial efficiency." Most of their operations are based on their certainty that people are afraid to be poor. We Vermonters often notice a considerable heat of exasperation in such devotees of industrialism when they encounter the natives of our State. We make no comment on this at the time, taking them in with the silent attentive observation which they furiously dub "bucolic stolidity"; but after they have gone back to the city we laugh to ourselves, and some old fellow among us hits on just the droll, ironic phrase to describe the encounter. For years afterwards, we quote this to the mystification of the outsider.

Another well-known and much-described fear is that of not keeping up with the social procession, of being obliged to step down a rung on the social ladder. This is another fear which stops short before it gets into Vermont. That small section of the country has never kept up with other people's processions and has found it no hardship to walk along at its own gait. And as for social ladders, any glimpse of a social ladder or of purely social distinctions moves a Vermonter to the unaffected, pitying, perhaps rather coarsely hearty mirth which white people feel at the sight of the complicated taboo of savage tribes. Of course, the Vermonter pays for his high-handed scoffing at sacred social distinctions by a rough plainness, not to say abruptness, of speech and manner which people from outside do not relish and which they describe in far from complimentary terms. This is a pity. But I daresay you can't have something for nothing morally, any more than materially, and perhaps it is not too high a price to pay for the total absence in our world of any sort of servility or overbearing arrogance or any sort of pretentiousness. Every man to his taste. We like it better the way we have it.

Another fear, perhaps the most corroding one in our world of possessors of material wealth, is the panic alarm at any glimpse of possible changes in the social fabric which may make things uncomfortable for possessors. The Latin poet who many years ago described the light-hearted stride of a poor man across a dark plain infested with robbers described the care-free gait at which Vermont moves through the uncertain and troubled modern world. Vermont, like some of the remote valleys in the Pyrenees, has always been too far out of the furiously swirling current of modern industrial life to be much affected by it or to dread its vagaries. For generations now, when times get hard and manufacturers are flat and deflated and the mills in the industrial States around us are shut down,

Vermont farmhouse. This typical Vermont farm scene pictures the state's modest standard of living and confirms Dorothy Canfield Fisher's contention that the people of the state hewed to the ethic of self-reliance. The long barn allowed farmers to store supplies for the entire winter and to house livestock without having to brave the elements.

and the newspapers are talking about bankruptcies and bread-lines, the Vermont family, exactly as rich and exactly as poor as it ever was, remarks with a kindliness tinged with pride: "Well, we'd better ask Lem's folks up to stay a spell, till times get better. I guess it's pretty hard sledding for them." And when times get better and Lem's family leave the poor little frame farm-house which has been their refuge, and drive off down the steep stony road which is the first stage of their journey back to wages and movies, the Vermont family stand looking after them, still with friendliness.

They realize shrewdly that already they seem countrified to their mill-town, factory-hand guests, but this does not worry them: rather it makes an ironic quirk come into the corner of their mouths, as at the transparent absurdity of a child. They continue to stand and wave their hands with undiminished kindliness, this time tinged by an amused humor which would be distinctly unpalatable to the others if they could understand it. I am afraid there is an element of sinful pride in the granite-like comfort they take in the security given them by their plain tastes and ability to deal with life at first hand. No dependence on employers for them!

Another problem of which we read occasionally as bothering serious-minded folks in other parts is what to do with accumulated wealth. It bothers us as little as how to fight cobras. For the most part, society in Vermont is organized along the most obviously solid and natural lines, primitive and elemental. Everybody is working. Yes, working, you jeering step-lively outsiders, although Vermonters may not hit up the hectic pace of factory hands and although some leisure for talking things over and reading the papers and cracking jokes about life and going hunting and nutting is a necessity for Vermonters even if they are obliged to pay for it by the forgoing of sacred dollars. Almost everybody is working, and at the plainest, most visible, most understandable jobs, to raise food, or grind corn, or make shoes, or put houses together, or repair Fords, or teach children. It is very rare when anybody in Vermont fails to secure a fair amount of shelter and clothing and food and education; and it is equally rare when anybody secures very much more than that. There are, so to speak, no accumulated possessions at all.

But perhaps what Vermont is least afraid of and what other people fear and hate most is politics. You know as well as I do that most Americans are low in their minds about politics. They feel that politics are really beyond them, that they never will be able to get what they want through their political action. The "fatalism of the multitude" weighs like lead upon their hearts. When there are so many, what can one man do? Well, you see in Vermont there aren't so many. There isn't any multitude. Self-government may not be perfection there, any more than anywhere else, but it bears the closest, realest relationship to the citizens, and is not at all given over to professional politicians who are always below the level of the best voters. Vermonters see nothing in self-government (especially local self-government) inherently more complicated than keeping your bank-book balanced. Perhaps this is because Vermont puts up as little as possible with that lazy substitute for self-government known as the "representative system," under which you tell somebody else to do the governing for you and not to bother you about it lest your money-making be disturbed. There is so little money to make in Vermont that few people are absorbed in making it. Nearly everybody has sufficient strength and time left over, and more than sufficient interest, to give to self-government. The Town Meeting is self-government, direct, articulate, personal. It is the annual assemblage not of the representatives of the governed, but of every one of the governed themselves. Anybody—you who are governed by a non-existing entity called "the country" cannot understand this, but it is true—anybody at all who does not like the way things are going in his town can stand up and say so, and propose a cure, as pungently as his command of his native tongue will allow. And Czar Public Opinion not only lets him do this, but rather admires a man who has something to say for his own point of view.

Every question concerning the welfare of the town, to the last forgotten valley in the mountains, is brought up at this open meeting and decided after loud and open discussion. When it is over and the teams and Fords and lean wiry men stream away from the Town Hall over the rutted roads in the sharp March air, they are all tingling with that wonderfully stimulating experience, having spoken their minds out freely on what concerns them. They step heavily in their great shoes through the mud, which on March-meeting Day is awful beyond belief, but they hold up their heads. They have settled their own affairs. The physical atmosphere of town-meeting is rather strong with tobacco and sawdust and close air, but the moral atmosphere is like that on a mountain-peak compared to any political life I ever saw elsewhere, either in France or in other American States. There is none of that stultifying, bored, cynical, disillusioned conviction that the rogues will beat the honest men again this time, as always. Not on your life! The honest men are on the job, with remarkably big and knotty fists, their dander ready to rise if somebody tries to put something over on them. And although they might not be able to cope with specially adroit political rogues, there is blessedly so little money involved in most Vermont operations that it is hardly worth the while of specially adroit rogues to frequent town-meetings. The Vermonter has for a century and a half found self-government not so very daunting, and often the highest form of entertainment.

This tradition of looking the world in the eye and asking no odds of it probably seems to the rest of you a rather curious tradition for a small, poor, rustic State with hardly a millionaire to its name, no political pull of any sort, and nothing to distinguish it in the eyes of the outside world. But all Vermonters know where it comes from, straight down from our forefathers who did look the world in the eye and made the world back down. With nothing on their side but their fearlessness and a sense of human rights as against property rights, they held out stoutly and successfully against oppression and injustice, though dressed up in all the fine names of ''legality'' and ''loyalty to the organization of society.''

Not many people outside Vermont know the dramatic story of the State's early life, but everybody inside the State does. There are fewer people in the whole State of Vermont than in the city of Buffalo, which is not at all huge as cities go now. But even at that, there are a good many men, women, and children in the State, over three hundred thousand. There is hardly one of this number who does not know about the history of the New Hampshire Grants, and how our great-grandfathers stood up against all the then existing British state for their naked human rights; and won the fight.

I know you are vague on this point, though you probably had it as a lesson one day in high school; so I will give you a sketch of it, compressed to a brevity which ought not to bore you too much. After the end of the French and Indian War, Vermont was safe ground for American settlers and the bolder spirits began to come in from New Hampshire and Connecticut. They settled, went through the terribly wearing toil of pioneers, felled trees, reclaimed land, drained swamps, built houses and mills, braved isolation, poverty, danger, health-breaking labor, and made Vermont a region of homes. They had learned to love it as we love it now, silently, undramatically, steadfastly, detesting any florid, high-flown talk about it, burying our love in our hearts and pretending to outsiders that it is not there. Vermonters are not sentimental, articulate Celts, but hermetically sealed Yankees. But they live on this love for their homes and they have shown themselves quite ready to die for it.

Back there in the eighteenth century, just when the settlers had definitely proved that they could make homes out of the wilderness, they were informed that by a legal technicality the grants by which they held their land were not valid; and that the King of England authorized New York lawyers to send officers of the law to take the Vermont land away from the men who had reclaimed it. It was then to be given to soft-handed, well-to-do men, with political influence who had no more rightful connection with that land than did the inhabitants of Peking. The Vermont settlers did not pretend to understand the law of that day. They only knew in their hearts that the land they had so painfully reclaimed, worked over, brought up their children on, was theirs, if anything ever belonged to anybody. A shout went up from Vermont to the New York officers of the law: "Just come and take it away, if you dare!" And they got down their long rifles, ran some bullets, and dried their powder.

The hated "York State men" tried to do this, ventured into the Vermont settlements, were roughly treated, and sent home. They were afraid to try it again and retreated to the Albany courts of law, which summoned the Vermonters to submit the matter to trial. With nothing but their inherent human rights back of them, the Vermonters went down to Albany (no true Vermonter can abide the name of Albany since then!) and there went through the solemn twaddle of a law-trial, where the standards were not those of human rightness and fair-dealing, but were drawn from yellow parchments. Of course the parchments won. That is their habit in law-courts.

Ethan Allen was in Albany through this trial, to help the Vermonters. After the decision was rendered, he walked out of the law-court, on his way home, surrounded by a mocking crowd of York State men. The whole history is so familiar to us Vermonters that any one of us would know just what is coming next in this episode. When, in speaking to a Vermont audience, you begin this story, you can see people lay down their umbrellas and handbags to have their hands free to applaud, and you can see every backbone straighten as you go on in the phrases consecrated by time, "They shouted jeeringly at Allen 'Now, do you know you're beaten? Now will you lie down and give up?' Ethan Allen drew himself to the full height of his magnificent manhood" (we never use any less fine a phrase than this) "and cried out in a ringing voice 'The gods of the mountains are not the gods of the plains,' and strode away leaving them silenced." (Here is where the speaker always has to wait for people to get through clapping.) He strode back to Vermont and organized a resistance. Was there ever a more absurd, pitiable, pretentious attempt? A handful of rough ignorant mountaineers, without a legal leg to stand on, to try and defend themselves against the British law! And their only pretext, the preposterous one that they had earned what they held!

Well, to make a long and complicated story short, the rough handful of ignorant men did continue to hold the land they had earned, and we, their descendants, are living on it now. They did more. For fourteen years after that, those men, our great-grandfathers, ruled Vermont, free of any sovereignty, an independent republic on the continent of North America. You never heard that quaint and colorful fact about our little State, did you? Yes, for fourteen years they stood straight and strong on their own feet, owing allegiance to nothing in creation but their own consciences. They stood steady in a whirling shifting world, and proved to their own satisfaction that to stand steady is not an impossible task.

Down to this day, down to the last corner of our green, wooded, mountain-bedecked State, we all stand steadier because of that memory back of us. Every foot of the land on which we live was held for us by the courage, almost absurd in its simple-heartedness, of our tall, ironic grandfathers, and by their candid faith in the inherent strength of a just cause. They risked their fortunes and their lives on their faith in this principle: that those who work and create have certain sacred rights, no matter what laws may be, more than those who do nothing. With that principle as our main inheritance, we Vermonters can cock our feet up on the railing of the porch and with a tranquil heart read the news of the modern world and the frightened guessing of other folks at what is coming next!

VIRGINIA

A Gentle Dominion

DOUGLAS FREEMAN

JULY 16, 1924

V IRGINIA BURIED her beloved at Appomattox, as her sons stood by, very ragged. All that she was, all that she hoped, all in which she had taken pride she told herself she had interred there. But it was spring for her sons, plowing-season, and they were hungry. They tramped back home and fortunately found in the reclamation of stumpy fields and neglected meadows an outlet for their grief. They thought of the past as seldom as they might and talked of it scarcely at all. It was five years before they had the farm in order, ten before they had any leisure, twenty before they possessed any money, thirty before they were measurably prosperous as their fathers had been in 1860. After the Spanish-American war—they never knew why—they could paint the house and buy a new surrey and take the wife to town for her shopping twice a year. By 1905 they began to argue whether it would not be possible to send the girl as well as the boy to college.

Since then there has been plenty. The village no longer looks as though its solitary street were a streamer of crape on the door of the landscape. The countryside is not quite trim, as yet, but has brightened immeasurably. The "Eastern Shore"—which comprises the two counties between the Chesapeake and the ocean—has become one of the richest agriculture communities in the United States. The Shenandoah Valley is white with apple blossoms almost as soon as the snow is gone. The section beyond the New River, "the gre-e-at Southwest," as its residents proudly style it, finds double wealth in its coal mines and in its export cattle, fattened on a very luxuriant blue grass. The people of the "South-side" counties, between the James River and the North Carolina line, are improving yearly the quality of their tobacco, and if they succeed in raising the early cotton they have planted experimentally they will rival the Carolina farmers, whom they now envy. Cooperative marketing is slowly taking hold, though eyed doubtfully by some bankers and vigorously fought by rich warehousemen. The breeding of stock has improved so much that the scrub Pennyroyal bull now belongs with the bear that has disappeared from the mountains and the deer that has been killed in the swamps. Enough has been done to furnish abundant themes for the writers of booster-literature and to pile up statistics that sprain the backs of the graphs official bureaus delight to draw. Virginia's sons and their sons after them have done a brave, clean job since Appomattox.

The Mother herself, Virginia, went straight from Appomattox to the old house that typified the civilization that had perished. She climbed to the second-story bedroom; she pulled down the blinds and through the darkness of reconstruction sat in her mourning. She would put out the Southern flag on May 30 and go down to the porch when the veterans passed by on the way to reunions; she never missed a session of the U. D. C.[1] and tended a booth in the old-fashioned bazaar that was held to raise money for another Confederate monument. She went to church and sat very quietly in the ancestral pew, though perhaps she could not bring herself to say Amen at the end of the prayer for the President of the United States and all others in authority. Sometimes she walked in the garden. But her thoughts were still of the war between the States. She could not forget and she had no desire to forget its triumphs and its agony. Her face has been turned to the past. Without pose or ostentation (those who are noisy have simply married into the family and do not understand), without making a fetish of her veil or a spectacle of her tears, Virginia has been "in deep mourning."

While the Widow has been lamenting in the front chamber upstairs, her daughters have been receiving new callers in the drawing-room and her sons have been paying court in strange parlors. Society has changed vastly during the great lady's widowhood—has changed so much, in fact, that she is beginning to doubt herself ever so little when daily she replies to a daughter's mention of a visitor's name with emphatic, "Why, my dear child, I never heard of him; who was his grandfather?"

Names and blood still count in Virginia, but lack of them handicaps a man less in acquiring social position than possession of them aids him in preserving it. A few who have ancestry and no money keep their place; many who have money and no ancestry make their place. Even in Richmond, where the doors of the Monday German once were unlocked only for those who had as many quarterings as an officer in the bodyguard of a Bourbon, the daughter of the rich newcomer always is invited after two or three years and, a little later, her mother and father. "He's rich" is now an apologia for many shortcomings. Now and again there is scandalized squawking when a nobody wins the heart of an old aristocrat's daughter; but the girl seldom loses caste and the boy may gain. Where a great lady rules, why should not there be matriarchy? Nothing better illustrates the slow effacing of the old hard lines than that unless a union is hopeless the station of man and wife in a few years becomes that of the more distinguished of the two, be it that of the man or that of the woman. The old mercantile aristocracy of the cities died with the industrial era to which it belonged. Not one name in ten that appear in the list of those who entertained

---

[1]United Daughters of the Confederacy. [D. H. B.]

Mount Vernon. Veneration of the First Families still dominated the cultural life of the commonwealth. As early as 1853, the Mount Vernon Ladies Association endeavored to preserve Washington's home not only as a national monument but as a reminder of the glory of the gentry.

Lafayette, or were the familiars of John Marshall, or even of those on whom Jefferson Davis called when visiting in Virginia cities after the war is heard now at social functions. Many of the greatest lines are near extinction. General Robert E. Lee had three sons and four daughters. There survive only one grandson, two granddaughters, one great-granddaughter, and one great-grandson. This is characteristic. Cynics have affirmed that if two or three families of great planters had not been inexhaustibly prolific and had not intermarried early and widely, genealogists would have to despair of proving descent from early colonial times, except, of course, for the goodly host of those who possess, or think they possess, some of the blood of Pocahontas.

In rural Virginia the old aristocracy still clings to a few of its ancient seats, such as Shirley on the James and Mount Airy on the Rappahannock, but elsewhere it has perished or migrated and has had no successor. Nowhere in the South is the passing of the old order more manifest than in certain of the older counties, lower Hanover or King William, for example. Some of the old mansions remain, though fire has claimed more; but these often are habited by people ignorant of the history of the houses in which they dwell. One gets almost the impression that plague or an approaching army had driven the natives before it and that after years of decay another race has moved in.

With the lesser aristocracy and the middle classes the change has not been so great. Where the family was numerous it often happened that some of the sons went to the cities while the others remained at the "home place." Twenty years ago fully half the urban population in this way had kin in the country. Now the ties have been broken—one reason, this, for the sharpened legislative antagonisms between town and country. In the social life of the farmers much depends on the extent to which the old families have held on. There still are districts where some of the planters do not call on neighbors who are as prosperous as themselves but do not have a like background. Elsewhere the rural church has worked for democracy in the leveling of the old barriers. Even the aliens who occasionally settle in the counties gradually are made welcome in the homes of the neighborhood if they are well-behaved. Usually, however, there is one generation of something very much like probation: after that the son goes where the father might not. Conditions in the country on the whole are destructive of the aristocratic tradition. It is hard to be socially exclusive where neighbors are few and solitude wears down pride as well as nerves.

An element fast increasing in some parts of rural Virginia is that of the city-dweller, the son or grandson of a planter, who buys himself a country home which he uses part of the year. In northern Virginia, around Leesburg and Middleburg particularly, and in the beautiful foothills between the homes of Jefferson and Madison, are numerous colonies of these reformed burghers who spend on the land the money they make in trade. Sometimes these men attempt to figure in the political life of the county, but more frequently they consort with their kind. They are welcomed by the small farmer, who sells them his produce or his labor at prices well above the market, but they are jealously eyed by the larger planter, whose sun they dim and whose colored farmhands they hire at prices the "practical" farmer cannot pay. Not infrequently some wealthy man from the North or from the West, with a liking for the historical and with a desire to found a family, will purchase one of the large and famous estates and will make a theatrical attempt to lead the life of which he has read in a levant-bound life of Washington. Where taste and tact are sustained by patience and a purse some of these efforts to recreate the spacious style of the eighteenth century do not fail altogether of their purpose. Where any of the essentials is lacking the outcome is comical.

The last of the great social raconteurs, Captain W. Gordon McCabe, is dead. The great foil for his wit, Major Robert W. Hunter, preceded him a full ten years. The "old Virginia gentleman" is very rarely seen. Even his conscious imitators are no longer numerous. Not often does one hear, as at old court days, the orator who climbs vocally skyward, after the fashion of the preacher reading the hymn in Tom Sawyer, and then suddenly drops to the lower register with an inflection for which there is no better name than the colloquial "curling." The old-time lawyer, the fabled country doctor, the kindly old "mammies," the dignified house-servants live now only in the stories of Thomas Nelson Page and his school.

One type there is that still links the great Widow with her past. It is a type seen often in Virginia cities and every Sunday in the country. On Franklin Street in Richmond, of a Monday afternoon, one may observe a dozen exemplars. They are the little old ladies, dressed inconspicuously in black, who trip to the Women's Club, hear a program, sip their tea, and then, grasping their handbags tightly, trot home again. Some are widows, but most of them are the unmarried daughters of well-to-do business men of the last generation. They grew to womanhood in the seventies. Men were scarce then. Thousands of the young Virginians who should have been wooing them were moldering bones on the battlefields of the war between the States, or else, if spared, had given up hope in the Old Dominion and had sought a livelihood where cities were not in ashes and farmers' fields were not burrowed with trenches. Many of the young women of that day married men not worthy of them. Many others had no lovers. They stayed on in their fathers' houses until their parents died and then they went to reside with kinspeople or had a spinster cousin of like temperament come to live with them. They use the old furniture and read the old books and adhere to the old fashions and think the old thoughts. They are given to charity, they write regularly to all their relatives, and they know what is happening in the homes of all their friends. To sit for an hour with one of these women and to hear her talk of "Pa"and of "Ma"—for they cling to the eighteenth-century pronunciation— is to agree that the women are the great social conservators. Virginia society in its distinctive sense would have breathed its last long ago for the little old ladies.

Numerous as the changes in society have been during Virginia's widowhood, the essential quality of social life, which is the fundamental characteristic of the people, remains precisely what it was when General Lee was its incarnation. That quality is consideration for the feelings of other people. A man may be fairly sure in Virginia of a courteous answer to his inquiries and of a friendly reply to his greeting. Whether a mountaineer on the side of a wretched little clearing or the inheritor of a great name chatting over his first editions, the average Virginian displays an inherited thoughtfulness for the sensibilities of another. He dislikes to say unpleasant things or to touch a sore spot, and he is equally anxious not to have his own bruises handled or his own feelings hurt. All this sounds very much like boasting that lacks the very quality it describes; yet there is no understanding Virginia, and her people's courtesy, their reserve, and their sense of values unless one realizes that an atmosphere of good-will and friendliness is prized above industrial advance or agricultural progress.

Consideration is certainly one of several explanations of the comparative amity between employer and employee in Virginia. Their relationship rests on the first law of the South—that a white man is a white man and must be treated as such regardless of his station. A certain deference, a noticeable restraint in manner, is to be observed in the bearing of the manager to the workers. There is little swearing or shouting and, more often than not, the deliberate use of "Mister" when the operative is addressed. Carelessness in these matters or neglect of the consideration the employee demands as a white man would cause him to quit his job instantly and would lead to a strike as readily as any difference over wages or hours would.

Consideration enters into the treatment of the Negro to an extent that may not be credited by some readers. The Virginia Negro is the blue-blood of his race and has behind him nearly a century more of life on the continent than have most colored people of the cotton belt. Many Virginia Negroes are the descendants of seventeenth-century slaves; perhaps the majority date their American "line" from around 1750. After that date Virginia did not willingly import any blacks. From 1800 onward there was a rather steady southward movement of slaves. The manner, the bearing, and the intelligence of the Negroes of Virginia so definitely exhibit the benefits of their longer residence in America that it is surprising no ethnologist has studied them. They have advanced splendidly in many ways. Stephen Graham found them, as Olmstead had sixty-five years before, indisputably the most prosperous of their race in the South. They have their social strata, their clubs, their fraternal organizations, their vigorous churches, their stores, their doctors and dentists, and even their banks, though these last, it must be admitted sorrowfully, are entirely too prone to fail. In education they are zealous and persistent. They have not yet been allowed in the rural districts properly trained teachers, suitable school-buildings, or a session of decent length; but in the cities they have all these and have made the most of them. In one Virginia town, not long ago, it was discovered that a larger percentage of beginner-pupils among colored girls than among white boys was continuing through to graduation from the high school. But the colored people have more than physical aids to self-help. They have the moral support of nearly all the whites; and though the point of contact is of course the point of friction, they understand and are understood far better than is generally believed in the North. It is commonly said in Virginia that if the State were free alike from the racial involvements of the North and from the troubles of the Gulf States the two races could live side by side through the centuries and have no strife. Lynchings are rare and are a humiliation to the white people. Justice at the law is meted out to the colored man—justice with consideration.

In politics, too, there is consideration, perhaps too much of it, in fact, but less justice. The State has been unswervingly Democratic since the Civil War, though prior to that time it was often contested hotly by the Whigs. The disfranchisement of the Negro under the constitution of 1902 has not led many white men to change their politics. A few manufacturers and bankers have concluded that their economic interest lies with the Republicans. An occasional seeker after place and an infrequent tuft-hunter goes over. Now and again protestants abstain from voting or even support a Republican candidate when the Democratic nominee is notoriously feeble. In the southwestern counties, where slavery was never seated and where few Negroes have settled, the Republicans are in the majority and are fought with weapons of many forgings. Many State offices go to the exacting and hungry Democrats of this district, the Ninth, to strengthen them in their warfare with the "heathen." Elsewhere in Virginia men accept the Democratic Party as they do their religious affiliation—chiefly by inheritance. Perhaps unjust tax laws may force a political uprising. Otherwise it seems probable that for the next ten years whatever is done for progress in Virginia must be begun within the Democratic ranks. The primary must take the place of the general election. The equivalent of the bi-partisan system must be sought, as far as may be, between the factions of the Democratic Party.

These factions follow the world-round cleavage, so old that it might be called geologically political, of conservative and liberal. In the factional war the peculiar quality of the people, that same good-natured consideration, makes it difficult for liberals to get results. The conservatives, who form the State Democratic "machine," are generaled by those who want office and will work for it. The liberals suffer from a lack of leadership because those who are qualified for office do not as a rule desire it and will not bestir themselves to win it. Then, too, the conservatives have a disconcerting way of conquering their conquerors. With the single exception of former Governor Westmoreland Davis, father of the very excellent Virginia budget law, every liberal who has defeated the machine in recent years has been won over to the conservatives or else has been silenced by the consideration they have shown him. The directors of the machine, furthermore, are cautious. The Juggernaut car is not used for political joy-riding. They seldom attack unless they are assailed or find their political structure endangered. Their success is usually not difficult, for nine times in ten it involves nothing more than defeating the bills the liberals introduce.

Besides, when it is hard put, the machine can mobilize most effectively for government of the cities by the counties, through the courthouse "rings." Every county in Virginia has a clerk of its court, a sheriff, a treasurer, and one or more commissioners of the revenue, the officers who assess taxes. These are all elective. They work together. They are sociable and friendly as a rule; they know virtually everyone in the county. They lend money and give advice. They are almost the only officials in the county who are permanently employed, and they are well paid by a vicious system of fees that liberals vainly have sought to destroy. Naturally the county "ring" has a community of interest. As the members of the "ring" or their deputies are moving about constantly, and as politics is as much their sport as it is their business, they are always recruiting their ranks, reclaiming deserters, and disciplining the unruly. With their kinsfolk, their debtors, their friends, and their henchmen these engaging gentlemen muster a vote definitely ponderable in a State where the franchise is the privilege of the few and is not exercised by all of them.

Here is the skeleton in the great Widow's closet. In order to exclude the Negro from the polls the framers of the present constitution of Virginia set *chevaux de frise* of qualifications in the voter's way. He must reside in the State two years, in the county or city one year, in the precinct thirty days; he must apply for registration in his own handwriting and must be able to explain a section of the constitution if asked to do so; he must pay a poll tax of $1.50 six months in advance of the election in which he wishes to participate. This last requirement is the stake on which the slow-footed are impaled. Nobody ever seems to remember from year to year when the six months begin or end. The newspapers diligently print "boxes" and occasionally "streamers" of warning. Organizations remind their members. The unions suspend those who do not qualify. But the indifferent citizen is negligent, pays his tax too late, and if he goes to the polls in resentment of some political outrage is told he is not on the book. There must be hundreds in Virginia who have not had a voice in choosing a candidate since the constitution of 1902—a curious sunset document of another age—became operative. Thousands who are able to vote may reason that the candidates are all decent men or that it is no use wasting one's time in voting against the machine's favorite, who is certain to win. Personalities in campaigns are barred by unwritten law. Consideration shows itself in a sharp reaction to the side of a man who is too vigorously assailed, either by his opponent or by the newspapers. The result is that a State of 2,300,000 does not poll in the average Democratic primary more than 150,000 votes. In the general election the number will not exceed from 200,000 to 230,000. The counties rule even as they are ruled by the county "rings." The "green terror" of which Joseph Caillaux writes so speciously in France does not fall very far short of reality in Virginia. It is all a political curiosity—a people too considerate of office-holders to overcome the phalanx office-holders are careful to muster. Of course, consideration is not all. Qualification is a barrier. Indifference is a killing obstacle in the way. Pride in the past, a belief that a State which has been well governed heretofore will be governed equally well in the future—this enters largely.

What does the future hold? The Widow will not take off her weeds until all those who have memory of the war between the States, even as children, have gone with the elders. As long as there are a dozen Confederate veterans in Virginia they will meet in annual reunion. Their daughters will erect more monuments. Their sons will read Confederate history and will teach it to their children. Their grandsons in their first school-speeches will call the roll of great Virginians. The influence of General Lee will remain in splendid potency. All this is certain. But for the rest, is Virginia ever to be "great again," in General Lee's own words? Great in agriculture she can be, though never among the first dozen States. Great in commerce she may be, if the Hampton Roads are utilized by American shippers. Whether she is great in achievement, great in the bearing of intellectual leaders, great in service to the country as one of the few States that remain predominantly of British stock—whether she ever is great again in this fullest sense depends on her ability to make her superb history dynamic through the new educational movement that is the hope of every progressive Virginian. In 1860 Virginia had the most adequate system of colleges in the United States, with the largest attendance per 1,000 of population. She must have for the future a system not inferior to the best. Her public schools must be in kind. Her history must be for inspiration rather than for contemplation. It is not enough to say: "We have Abraham to our father."

WASHINGTON

The Dawn of a Tomorrow

ROBERT WHITAKER

DECEMBER 19, 1923

$\mathbf{M}$Y PREDECESSOR in the pastorate at Seattle thirty-five years ago, a typical Titan of the frontier, was never weary of demonstrating that the Puget Sound country is not the Northwest corner of the United States. Seattle, he insisted, is considerably nearer New York City on the east than to the farthest extension of Alaska on the west. Washington State is the doorway, and the only doorway to more than one-sixth of the total continental area of the United States.

One can hardly say of Alaska now what might have been said truthfully thirty-five years ago, it hasn't been scratched yet. It has been scratched, and with wonderful results. What those results have been in Alaska and in the world at large does not concern us here. What they were for the State of Washington would take many paragraphs to tell. It is enough to say that Washington's hour of greatest advance followed hard upon the golden dawn of Alaska's Klondike discovery. It was but a dawn, with a bit of dull gray morning following. But the day of Alaska has yet to come, and that day must mean more to Washington than any flurry of such ephemeral prosperity as a gold rush brings.

The doorway to Alaska, and to all the coast of North America which lies between Puget Sound and Alaska, that is the State of Washington. What is of more consequence to Washington's future is that Puget Sound is the doorway to Asia as well. Asia, indeed, confronts our whole West Coast. But it is characteristic of the land mass on both sides of the Pacific that the shores approach each other toward the north, and recede rapidly from each other on the south. This, with the shorter arc of earth curvature as one goes northward, brings the ports on Puget Sound several days' sailing nearer those of China and Japan than are the ports of California. The volume of commerce which passes now from Puget Sound to the Orient is many times in excess of that of all our harbors which lie further south combined.

It was Theodore Roosevelt who said, with dramatic conciseness: ''The Mediterranean Era died with the discovery of America; the Atlantic Era has reached the height of its development; the Pacific Era, destined to be the greatest, is just at its dawn." One need not agree with the negative phases of this epitome of world history to appreciate the promise of the Pacific. And Puget Sound is the most remarkable of its inland seas. In area and contour, accessibility and security at all seasons of the year, scenic variety and beauty, in the healthfulness and invigorating quality of its climate, and the wealth of sea food to be found in it and adjacent to it, Puget Sound will bear comparison with any inland sea on the earth. It is no idle dream that its shores will some day be the dwelling-place of many millions of people.

The State of Washington might claim much of promise from the world carriers to tomorrow if it had no wealth of its own to offer. But of such wealth, present and prospective, there is no lack. Consider what we may call primeval wealth, that which was there before man ever saw the land, the treasure of the great woods and the treasure of the great waters. There is no need to conjecture what only yesterday were those primitive conditions, nor to waste tears on man's extravagant misuse of the resources he found. Sickening as is the desolation of the forests where immediate profit has dominated the white man's devastation of them, the area of Washington State still exhibits a wealth of standing timber which cannot be stated in terms easily grasped. Half the timber of the United States today is on the slopes of the Cascades, the Coast Range, and the Olympics of Oregon and Washington, the Bitterroots and Rockies of Idaho, Montana, and Wyoming. Washington itself is exceeded only by Oregon in its share of this vast bounty of nature, and today leads all other States in lumber production. Five and a half billion board feet of lumber a year are the product of her three hundred logging camps and eight hundred sawmills. Four hundred thousand houses a year in the United States have but a few months previous been standing timber in Washington.

Fishing in the Pacific Northwest is an industry with an output of eighty-five million dollars a year. The business exceeds that of the east coast of the British Islands and New England combined. Washington handles not only her own great product, but the vast volume of fish which comes down from the north. This wealth of wood and water, which man did nothing to create until very recently and which he has most miserably failed to conserve, would in and of itself give Washington a considerable place in the commerce of the world.

But there is the potential wealth of the State to be considered, in particular the magic "white coal," which is to transform the earth, is transforming it today. One thinks of Niagara naturally with the mention of hydro-electric power. The potential capacity of the Niagara Basin is said to be six million horse-power. The Colorado Basin surpasses this expectancy by a million horse-power. On the authority of Eastern experts the potential hydro-electric power of the Columbia River Basin, which lies largely within Washington, is twenty-one million horse-power.

And besides this primeval and potential endowment lavished on the land there is what we may call the provisional wealth, the grains, live stock, and fruits upon which man has so learned to depend. You may travel for hundreds of miles within the State far from the haunts of the salmon, throughout what is fittingly known as The Inland Empire, where the all but treeless land is an ocean of billowy grain at harvest time. Even the eye accustomed to the vast wheat fields of the Mississippi Valley marvels at the illimitable vista of soft-hued grain. The dairying interests are especially favored over large areas of the State by a rainfall that does not fail them in summer. Poultry raising prospers peculiarly in that climate and is carried on with a scientific efficiency and success to that of no other portion of the land. Washington is the greatest apple-raising section of the earth, is made for berries as naturally as its streams are made for fish, and under right economic conditions could produce fruit enough to feed a continent.

A healthful climate is everywhere recognized today as a prime factor in the building up of a country's population. So also we are beginning to understand the value of scenic beauty. Let another free from the habitant's bias speak of what Washington offers the seeker after health and natural loveliness. In *The Conquest of Consumption,* Dr. Woods Hutchinson writes:

> When once we cross the summit of the Cascades we enter a totally different climate, an air which is mild, gentle, and moist, but never depressing; a country of green mountains, dazzling snow-tipped peaks, of grass, of moss and fern, which knows neither the barrenness of winter nor the brownness of summer, a land which has all the best and most invigorating qualities of the cradle of our Teutonic race, with none of its extremes. From one end to the other it is the land of tall trees and tall men, of the apple, the peach, the prune, and the pine; the land of the green valley and the rushing river. The rosy pink of its orchards every spring is equaled only by the sunset glow upon its peaks of eternal snow. It is the charmed land of the American continent, where a temperate sun, a mild climate, and a fertile soil give man the stimulus of the green and rain-swept North, with the luxurious returns for moderate effort of the teeming tropics. . . . If you have never seen Oregon, Washington, or British Columbia in summer, you lack important qualifications for imagining what the climate of heaven may be like.

That world traveler and generous commentator on America, the late Viscount Bryce, has written:

> Neither Europe nor Asia nor South America has a prospect in which sea and woods and snow mountains are so united in a landscape as in the view from Puget Sound of the great peaks that rise like white towers above the dark green forests of the Cascades.

If these testimonies seem to stress unduly the region of Puget Sound, it is not for lack of loveliness to praise in other sections of the State. For mingled grandeur and beauty I have seen nothing on the Pacific Coast which surpasses the view one gets under favorable conditions in going up the canyon of the Columbia River, from the fords fifty miles below Wenatchee to the hills and gorges north of that city. The somber severity of the lower canyon, with its bald, massive cliffs all but bare of vegetation, is in striking contrast with the wealth of apple orchards and vine-clad hillsides where the valley broadens at the confluence of the Wenatchee with the greater Columbia. The mountains are there also, towering to greater heights by far, with their sharply silhouetted crests melting into the sunset skies till lost in a golden haze where cloud and crest are indistinguishable. And there are other sections and scenes a plenty of which one might write with no less enthusiasm.

Yet with all this Washington State is neither truly prosperous nor contented. In common with all the agricultural States Washington is hard hit at present by the general paralysis of the producers' markets. It avails Washington little that her grain yield is so generous when the price for grain is so inadequate. She fares better perhaps with her live-stock and subsidiary interests, but the same general condition prevails. Her precedence as the foremost apple-producing section of the world is but a mockery to the men who ship great cargoes of the finest fruit to the market, only to find themselves actually out of pocket when the freight charges are paid. Her very plenty is her poverty when that plenty lies rotting upon the ground because it is the day of the profiteer and the parasite in America just now instead of the day of the producer.

Likewise the very magnitude of her potential wealth, her undeveloped water-power, makes for her difficulty in realizing upon it. If it were less, the private corporation might be sufficient for it, or the State itself might assume the burden of bringing the water to the magic wheels. But so vast is the undertaking that we shall have learned a much larger measure of cooperation than anything we have yet realized before the stupendous task is done. Washington's history shows an unusual degree of devotion to the cooperative ideal. Her experiments have been many on this line, and the spirit of solidarity has wrought to more effect there in the Northwest than most of the people can either believe or understand. The things which have been reckoned her calamity and disgrace are really large with promise. But meanwhile there are vast areas of desolation where there should be enjoyment and fruitfulness because in common with all America Washington waits for the practical values of brotherhood among the masses of mankind to make themselves understood.

Within half a dozen years Washington State has seen two massacres in connection with her lumber industry. Amid the eternal grandeur of the snow-clad giants the spruces stand, tall, cool, and silent. But the tension of the fevered pigmies at their feet is ever at the fighting-point.

Seven men were shot to death on a beautiful Sunday morning in November, 1916, when a company of two hundred and fifty I.W.W. went from Seattle to Everett to the help of their comrades who were waging a free-speech fight there. It is possible that the fatalities were more, some bodies being swept overboard from the ship *Verona* in the terrible fusillade which was directed against it by those who had said that the workers should not land. Many others were sorely wounded. High-handed measures had been used against the workers for months, and barbarities endured by them which were provocative to the last degree. The men who represented property there and who were responsible for the unlawful interference with the right of the workers and their comrades to land were not officially molested for the part they had in the massacre. On the other hand the workers, who had suffered by far the heavier mortality and the more serious injuries, were swept wholesale into jail and every effort was made to hold them there for life, or hang them as the aggressors in the affair. The trial, carried on at length in Seattle with the financial backing of the lumber interests against the accused, resulted in the complete acquittal of the workers.

In Centralia on Armistice Day in 1919 there was likewise loss of life on both sides, and if the heavier loss on this occasion fell upon the champions of law and order, they made the balance more than even in the unspeakable barbarity of their vengeance following. This time a conviction was secured of part of the workers placed under arrest, the arrests being again altogether from the ranks of the workers. The judge who tried the case had already made public oration against the workers. The evidence to prove prior conspiracy upon the part of the accusers he ruled out of court. Soldiers surrounded the courtroom and paraded their uniforms before the jurors. Intimidation was there to the fullest possible measure short of open violence or formal demand for a verdict of guilty on the part of an armed force. Nevertheless only a part of those under trial were condemned, the verdict, second-degree murder, being absurdly inconsistent with the circumstances of the massacre if the accused or their comrades were the aggressors. Even this compromise verdict was accompanied by an appeal from the jury to the judge for clemency, and since that time no less than five of the twelve jurors have made open affidavit that the verdict was not according to the evidence but was wrung from the jury through fear. Add to this that an extra-legal jury composed of representative labor men sent there by conservative labor bodies unanimously acquitted all the accused in their verdict. Four years later men who are serving terms at Walla Walla, their requests for a new trial refused without show of reason or right, may think themselves forgotten, but their fate is a constant fertilizer of the ever-thickening growth of labor solidarity.

One need not resort to labor pamphlets to discover what the deeper rootage of this labor solidarity is. Here is a passage from an eminently respectable and conservative journal of California, *Sunset* magazine, under date of February, 1917:

> Shingle-weaving is not a trade, it is a battle. For ten hours a day the sawyer faces two teethed steel disks whirling around two hundred times a minute. To the one on the left he feeds the heavy blocks of cedar, reaching over with his left hand to remove the heavy shingles it rips off. . . . Hour after hour the shingle-weaver's hands and arms, plain, unarmored flesh and blood, are staked against the screeching steel that cares not what it severs. Hour after hour the steel sings its crescendo note as it bites into the wood, the sawdust thickens, the wet sponge under the sawyer's nose fills with fine particles. If "cedar asthma," the shingle-weaver's occupational disease, does not get him, the steel will. Sooner or later he reaches over a little too far, the whirling blade tosses drops of deep red into the air, a finger, a hand, or part of an arm comes sliding down the slick chute.

Seattle, Second Avenue viewed from Yester Way. The city came to prominence in the 1890s as the outfitting center for the Klondike gold rush. It maintained its position through its financial control of the state's natural wealth. Along these streets some of the vivid confrontations of the general strike of 1919 were staged.

To this vivid presentation of the price at which the lumber profits in Washington have been made should be added at least mention of the revolting, body- and soul-destroying conditions which prevailed in the lumber camps till the I.W.W. forced some decency there. Out of such travail was born the militant solidarity of the shingle-weavers' union and later the compact and effective resistance of the Washington I.W.W.

It was a new-found sense of union that brought about that surprising coordination of the working forces of Seattle which produced what is still known as the Seattle Revolution. A "revolution" in the sense of intending any bodily harm to anybody it was not. The actual conduct of it was as orderly as a Quaker Quarterly Meeting. It was revolutionary only in the sense that it revealed to a startled public, including the workers themselves, the unrealized dependence of a modern community upon the least and poorest of the workers, and showed what the economic power of the workers means once they move and act with a common purpose.

The origin of the Seattle general strike at the beginning of 1919, otherwise described as the Seattle Revolution, was simple enough. Workers' solidarity had been necessary during the period of the war, had been profitable to the employers, and had been encouraged by them. Consequently the labor unions grew extraordinarily in numbers and power. Then came the cessation of hostilities, the beginnings of "retrenchment" with the "deflation" of the wages of the ship-yard workers, the interference of red tape at Washington D.C., which it is claimed stalled successful settlement of the matter in Seattle, and then the walk-out of the workers of the city in common protest. The like of it had never hap-pened in America before, and is not likely to happen again soon. It was as when the son of an overbearing father learns for the first time that he can throw his father, and fears to use his new-found power until he is ready to go his own way. Seattle labor was not ready to cut loose from the capitalist organization of society, had not dreamed of it, and had not the remotest thought of challenging the State. It has no such dream today. Spirit there is in Washington labor, and unity beyond that which is common. The Northwest has been made by men who have had to stand up to nature, and therefore are not afraid to stand up to each other. More dirt has been moved in the making of Seattle itself than anywhere else on the American continent except at the Panama Canal. They know how to resist there. But resistance is not revolution. The workers of Seattle were over-whelmed with confusion at their own success, but made an orderly retreat back to their jobs.

It was the supreme opportunity of the owning and governing classes in Amer-ica if they had possessed either the intelligence or public spirit to meet it. As it was, they made a god of one of the cheapest demagogues who has ever disgraced the mayoralty of a great city, a man who had fawned and cringed to the workers until the logic of their own success compelled them to draw back and he could rush in and make great ado about the suppressing of a revolution which had never been. But the weakness and the disgrace of it, as the hurt of it, was more theirs, the responsible leaders of business and culture in Seattle, that they could avail themselves of such paltry subterfuge and display. If there is any possibility of understanding between labor and capital it was theirs then, and they might have done the capitalists of all America a service. Instead there were pyrotech-nics in the press and on the platform, and a vengeance upon a foe which had voluntarily dispersed scared of its own strength, such vengeance as reacted quickly to the undoing of their own interests and particularly to the punishment of the small business man.

The emphatic quality of Washington State is its adaptability to the purposes of creative labor. The climate is a worker's, not an idler's climate. The land is no parasite's paradise; it is a treasure house that waits upon free, untrammeled la-bor to bring forth its resources. "The summer playground of the American con-tinent" it may deserve to be. But its summer is short, and its merits are not of the few weeks only in which men rest and play, but rather of the whole working year. The dawn of a tomorrow is upon the woods and the waters, the fruit-fields and the grain-fields of Washington, a tomorrow which can only come to the great commonwealth of the Northwest with that better social order in which the workers shall enter into their own.

WEST VIRGINIA

A Mine-Field Melodrama

JAMES M. CAIN

JUNE 27, 1923

ROUGH MOUNTAINS rise all about, beautiful in their bleak ugliness. They are hard and barren, save for a scrubby, whiskery growth of trees that only half conceal the hard rock beneath. Yet they have their moods. On gray days they lie heavy and sullen, but on sunny mornings they are dizzy with color: flat canvases painted in gaudy hues; here and there tiny soft black pines showing against a cool, blue sky. At night, if the moon shines through a haze, they hang far above you, dim outlines of smoke; you could throw a stone right through them. They are gashed everywhere with water courses, roaring rivers, and bubbling creeks. Along these you plod, a crawling midge, while ever the towering mountains shut you in. Now and then you top a ridge and look about. Miles and miles of billowing peaks, miles and miles of color softly melting into color. Bright yellows and reds give way to greens and misty grays, until they all fade into faint lavender and horizon blue. . . . A setting for a Nibelungen epic, revealing instead a sordid melodrama.

A melodrama where men carry pistols, often in leather holsters, and wear big black felt hats of the kind affected by the late William Frederick Cody. Where they give each other three-fingered handshakes, and slips of paper pass from palm to palm. Where hoarsely whispered plots are met by counterplots, and detective agencies flourish. Where personal differences are settled by guns, and letters taken from bodies designate persons by initials and numbers. Where the most casual visitor is a myster'us stranger. Where murder, dynamiting, arson, and insurrection are the usual order of the day and night. In brief, where life is a silly hodge-podge of two-gun heroes, find-the-papers villains, and sweaty mysteries—a peanut-and-hisses melodrama of coal.

For it is coal that has brought about this state of affairs. In West Virginia it is the staff of life. The State is a huge layer cake, hacked into grotesque slices by the elements; the slices are the mountains, the layers are rock, and the filling is coal. Coal, coal, coal; everywhere coal. On one side of the creek, away up the slope, you see the blue-black streak; on the other side, the same distance up, you

389

see the same streak. The seams run for miles, jumping across rivers and creeks, now broken by some convulsion an eternity ago, now tilted at crazy angles, but for the most part flat, thick, regular, and rich. Railroads, indispensable adjunct of mining, run beside every creek. A grimy structure of steel, a ribbon of shining rails right up the mountain side, a smudge of black dust, a monotonous grinding and clanking, and you are at a tipple. It is coal on which a third of the population depends directly for its living; it is coal on which probably another third depends indirectly. It is coal that has converted the State into one great pock-work of mines.

The coal development, however, is relatively recent. Only in the two closing decades of the last century was it of much importance; the richest fields of all are scarcely twenty years old. Before that, the State was a sort of wilderness, carved out of the backwoods of Virginia in the turmoil of the Civil War. Indigenous to it was a unique type of human being, the mountaineer. Here and there he survives today, and in spite of his baffling idiosyncrasies, is a most lovable person. If you have won his regard, he will take you into his home and seat you before his rude fireplace as the guest of honor. He will listen with respect to your discourse, and entertain you with homely comment of his own. He speaks a quaint language. It recalls an America that is fast passing, the America of the cross-roads schoolhouse and the cabin in the hills—with echoes of James Fenimore Cooper, and a forgotten generation of leather-shirted woodsmen. It uses "ary" and "nary," "cayn't" for "can't," "hayn't" for "hasn't"; "done" and "done been" with verbs, instead of "have" and "had"; it has odd words peculiar to itself: "swag" for a small marsh; and retains words long discarded in other parts of the world: "poke" for bag; a "panther" is still a "paynter." It is spoken with a plaintive drawl, gentle and unassertive. A language arresting and attractive, pathetically and insistently American. That, probably, is because this mountaineer who speaks it is one of the oldest and purest American types extant. He drifted westward with the migration of the eighteenth and nineteenth centuries, and finding habitable creek bottoms, loitered by the wayside, while his more energetic brethren pushed on to the Ohio River and the West. For a century he stayed here, and raised a few hogs, and corn for hominy, and carried on a small traffic in illicit whiskey. He was his own law, and his rifle was his last court of appeal. As time went on he and his kind interbred, the strain grew weaker and weaker, and he developed unusual ideas and customs. Personal grudges obsessed him. He nursed them for years, and prosecuted them with his rifle, until the outside world began to hear of strange feuds, such as the one between the Hatfields and the McCoys, that arose from trivial and incomprehensible causes. Whole families were exterminated in these feuds, and the rifle came forward with more and more sinister prominence in the West Virginia scheme of things.

About all this was the flavor of a queer, half-savage code, a *cavalleria montagnola* that was at least picturesque. Then came coal and the ever-advancing railroads. Mining companies bought the hillside cabin and dispossessed its lodger. The gaunt mountaineer, waiting for days, rifle on knees, eyes starry with hate, until his enemy should come up the creek bottom, was forced inevitably to enter the coal bank and toil for his living. Moreover, his new masters took leaves out of his own book and used them against him. They adopted the law of the rifle themselves. They hired armed gentry to watch him and police him and curtail his liberties. They told him where to go to church and where to send his children to school. They told him what he must take for his labor, how much he must pay for his food, and where he must buy it. Lastly, they told him what organizations he might join, and those that he must not join; prominent among the latter were labor unions. In vain he arose in his wrath. He oiled his rifle, but there was no dignity in it. He swore his vendettas against the mine guards, but the old heroic venom was gone. He killed his man, and it was a blowsy murder. He had brought all his former stage trappings, and they had become tawdry overnight. He was degraded, a serf: the Last of the Mohicans turned tourists' cook.

This was the condition of the mountaineer-miner when the United Mine Workers of America undertook to strike off his shackles. In this valiant enterprise the union was also strengthening its own position, for by the early years of the present century its pristine security in the Central Competitive Field was being threatened seriously by the growth on all sides of large non-union fields, and the largest of these was West Virginia. So it set about organizing the State. It was repulsed with medieval ferocity by the operators, who could make more money if they didn't have to pay the union scale. But it kept on, and eventually gained a membership of a few thousand. And to the occasional whisperings and shootings in the mining camp there was added a new and bigger kind of plotting. The union soon saw that the mine-guard system was the main bar to its organization; if the guards persistently ejected union organizers, there wasn't much hope of getting very far. So the mine guards quickly became anathema to all union miners; they were dubbed thugs, and took their places as permanent members of the cast, upstage, right, striding scowlishly about slapping their holsters while the trembling miner signed the open-shop agreement. . . . The first phase of the union's fight came to an end in 1912 and 1913, with strikes on Paint and Cabin Creeks, and three hundred guards imported by the companies, some of whom didn't get out alive. In all, nearly two score men lost their lives in those strikes, and people began to take gunplay and dynamiting for granted.

In 1918, the union, through a political deal, was allowed to organize the Fairmont field. By securing this territory and consolidating in the central part of the State, it pushed its membership to some fifty thousand. But ever the coal frontier receded past the horizon, and now southern West Virginia was mining enough coal to undermine the union power—to render any national strike largely ineffective. The southern part of the State was a big non-union stronghold, with the mine-guard system functioning perfectly. It embraced Mingo, Logan, McDowell, Raleigh, Mercer, and Wyoming counties. The union tackled Logan first—in 1919.

As usual, it met with armed resistance. Here was a mine-guard system, paid by coal operators, its main duty to eject union organizers. Its guards were invested with all the majesty of the law; they were deputy sheriffs of the county, duly sworn in under the Logan high sheriff, Don Chafin, who directed their activities and paid them out of a pool assessed against the operators. Mr. Chafin's deputies did their work thoroughly, and soon a wail drifted down the stage, over the Guyon Ridge: "They're a-murderin' the women an' children!" This is a very important line in the West Virginia libretto. It is always the cue for the big scene, of which more in a moment. So far as I know the deputies have never murdered any women or children, but art is art, and it is a good line. Why sacrifice it? Taking their cue, the union miners to the north assembled at a place called Marmet, within a dozen miles of Charleston, the State capital, and marched about a thousand strong on Logan. Then ensued the spectacle of the Governor of the State, John J. Cornwell, hoisting the gubernatorial robes aboard a wagon, beseeching the miners to go home, promising an investigation, and finally threatening troops. The miners went home, and their effort was abortive. But the West Virginian, a regular attendant at Western feature films and a diligent student of the *Pluck and Luck* series, had noted the possibilities of the scene.

So all energies were bent toward a successful staging of the great drama. The operators hired extra guards and howled defiance at the union. The union girded its loins, counted its money, and swore loudly that might should not conquer right. It sent its organizers into Mingo. A number of camps were organized. The union demanded recognition; the operators refused it. The union called its men out on strike; the operators evicted the strikers. As fast as the operators evicted them the union put them in tents. Guerrilla warfare broke out. There were massacres, ten men being killed in a battle at Matewan. The operators set spies to watch the miners and the miners pot-shotted the operators' witnesses. Plots were hatched by the dozen and card indices were needed to keep track of vendetta oaths. Federal troops were called in twice. The new Governor, E. F. Morgan, declared martial law, and the military commandant began clapping union men in jail. Finally, two union sympathizers, Sid Hatfield and Ed Chambers, as the result of a quasi-official feud, were shot down at Welch, and this, with heavy mutterings and threatenings sounding to the north, rang down the curtain on Act I—in August, 1921.

When Act II opened, two weeks later, union miners were assembling again at Marmet for another march. They gnashed their teeth and gritted they would redress their wrongs and stop further outrages. This time the plan was to march through Logan, kill Don Chafin on the way, continue to Mingo, liberate prisoners in its jail, nullify martial law, and proclaim liberty and justice once more in the land. For days they gathered and the press of the country screamed their purpose far and wide. Then they started, and as they swung down the road to Racine they sang:

Hang Don Chafin to the sour-apple tree,
Hang Don Chafin to the sour-apple tree,
Hang Don Chafin to the sour-apple tree,
As we go marching on!

They were halted once when their president addressed them at Madison. They threatened to hang him to a baseball grandstand, but they went home—at least, most of them did. Some of them stayed, commandeered a train and played with that—and waited. They didn't wait in vain. Down at Sharples, in Logan County, there came a clash between union miners and a party of Logan deputies and State police, coming, 250 strong, to serve warrants—at midnight (*sh! sh! sh!*). Two miners were killed. Then came the long-delayed cue that had been holding up the show: "They're a-murderin' the women and children!" The miners reassembled, eight thousand strong. They flung out battle lines and donned red brassards. They gave out a password.

"Who's there?" whispered the sentries.

"I come creepin'," replied the miners, *misterioso*.

"Pass," said the sentries.

They drilled around the schoolhouse at Blair, while coal-company officials, powerless for the moment, snooped faithfully and took notes in memorandum books. Meanwhile the miners were bringing in truck-loads of food, rifles, machine-guns, and ammunition, and presently preparations were complete for the grand offensive.

On the other side of the ridge all was buzzing action too. Don Chafin issued a call for volunteers, and several thousand sprang forward ready to die for Logan County. He imported four airplanes. Then arrived a lord defender of the realm, appointed in this emergency by the Governor. He came, he saw, he took command. He addressed his troops and told them to advance not on these misguided miners, but to retreat not a single step. In the stilly night he had trenches dug. He filled the airplanes with bombs. All now being in readiness, both sides entered their positions and shot at each other for three days. The airplanes zoomed and dropped bombs on the rocks. The machine guns went *put, put, put;* the rifle fire never ceased. The noise was superb. On the fourth day a regiment of Federal troops came—and everybody else went home. It was the best second act that had ever been staged, and was marred by only one unpleasant event. Three men were killed. It was true they were killed in a purely accidental encounter between scouting parties, but the incident shows that great care must be exercised in the future if this march is to become a permanent institution in West Virginia, as it now promises to be. . . .

You arise in your seat. Stay. There is another act, the great courtroom scene.

Hardly had the last miner handed his gun in than the Logan County grand jury met in special sessions. It indicted whole pay rolls. It indicted for murder, conspiracy, and unlawful assembly. Then it rested, met in regular session, and indicted some more. It met yet again, and to the hundreds of indictments already found, it added a score or so for treason. And so, in a few months, after a change of venue had been granted, court opened to try these cases. The court sat in the same room at Charles Town where John Brown had been convicted of treason, and oddly enough, the first case called was a treason case. Defendants and witnesses appeared by the hundreds. State police paraded in front of the courthouse carrying big pistols, and a lieutenant of State police got arrested and locked in the town hoose-gow for getting saucy with the town constable. Witnesses told gory stories for a month. Lawyers orated. Foamy spittle flew hither and yon, and flecked the coats of the jury. The first treason defendant was acquitted, but in the next month two miners were convicted of murder. Then another treason trial; the defendant was convicted and sentenced to ten years. By now the pastoral community of Charles Town was so rent with the controversy that it was impossible to get a jury. The trials were removed, once to Berkeley Springs, and yet again to Lewisburg.

Thus life in West Virginia in this year 1923. In addition to the big show there are innumerable little shows. In all the coal counties the plots, the vendettas, the murders, and the trials go on incessantly. The Federal court at Charleston is a never-ending round of restraining orders, injunctions, and citations for contempt. The sterile conflict overshadows and paralyzes everything else. Before it the State government is impotent. The State police, organized bona fide to enforce the law, are animated by no maturer ideal than to posture as moving-picture editions of the Canadian Mounted, i.e., to wear pretty uniforms, carry pistols, and growl sidewise that they always get their man. They are now quite as detested as the mine guards; the miners called them the "Governor's Cossacks," and charge openly that they are on the side of the operators.

The bustling little inner-loop-outer-loop cities are but centers where gossip is exchanged and new plots hatched. Their weekly luncheon clubs are but debating societies devoted to denying the conflict. Their newspapers are degraded win-an-auto sheets whereof every other writer is in the pay of one side or the other. The activities of the State university, with its farmers' short courses and summer camps for girls, whatever their actual merit, seem innocuous and pointless while the banging of the guns echoes and reechoes. Culture is at a standstill; the only theaters are movies that show five-reel shooting features; there are no libraries, no concerts.

The conflict mars also what might stand forth as achievement. For in these mountains industry is organized on a gigantic scale. To see it is to get the feeling of it: the great iron machinery of coal and oil, the never-ending railroads and strings of black steel cars, groaning and creaking toward destination. A plume of smoke "down the holler" and a locomotive comes stealing around the bend. You are drawn close to these big inanimate things. The locomotive ceases to be a terrifying pile of steam jets and puffing, and becomes "she"; you lean affectionately against her as you swap talk with the engineer and spit familiarly on her wheels. There is crude outdoor poetry about it. Similarly to the north. Thousands of acres of orchards grow incredible quantities of apples, which are stored in warehouses redolent of fruity perfumes and shipped to far places of the earth. But this is all enchanting for what it suggests, not for what it is. Back of it all are always the scowling and muttering that spoil it.

Futile indeed seems the $50,000,000 road program that is to civilize the State. For ever recurs the question: Is the State civilizable? The answer is not apparent yet. Possibly it would be well to remember that this new West Virginia of great enterprises is still quite young. It may have a touch of industrial indigestion. Or its malady may be more grave. Give it a century or so. Then possibly it will shoot the pianist and call for a new score.

WISCONSIN

A Voice from the Middle Border

ZONA GALE

OCTOBER 18, 1922

SHE SAID: "When we came to Wisconsin forty years ago we drove the ninety
miles from Milwaukee and settled here in the woods. We didn't have a plow. We
didn't have a ham. The neighbors lent him an ax and a saw and we begun. And
now we've got this eighty we're on. And the three forties next we give the boys
for wedding presents. They ain't all paid for yet. Ours'll be ours, though, before
we die." She and he are seventy-odd, made of brown horn and cord. To them
living means their "eighty."

A north county townsman said: "My wife and I have adopted two children
and she wants to take another. I laid aside above two thousand last year and I tell
her to go ahead—nothing like music in the home." And in another mood: "I tell
you, a man's got to do something for somebody else. Down and out, is he? Family
sick on his hands? Put me down for a tenner."

After the sixties, such was the State drama: New Englander, Scandinavian,
German pioneer or son of a pioneer paying for his eighty; or as prosperous
townsman saving for his home. Here and there a voice asking or pledging remedial aid. Farm, business, home, school, drone of legislature—and a crust or
a coin for the uncompensated. Beyond farm and town were the crash of falling
forests, clink of new-spiked rails, detonations from the iron counties, and the
occasional cry of a bewildered Red Man. All on a background of shadowed grain
and colored lakes and glossy pasture land.

Also there was a lullaby titled: "Do not do so-and-so lest capital be driven out
of the State." In a word, the drama and refrain of the old individualism. Already
forgotten were such stirrings as the cooperative settlements of the forties and the
Granger movement; and already aging was that young party of protest at slavery
and secession, the Republican Party, born at Ripon, Wisconsin, in 1854 and
christened in the Capitol Park at Madison.

Until the nineties. Then came La Follette. His story is one of the great ro-
mances of Wisconsin. His battles have now been fought in State after State but
in Wisconsin it was pioneer ground and principally a one-man conflict. It was

396

news to the people that they had not a representative government because of the convention system. It was news to the farmers and manufacturers and home-owners of the State that they were paying double the taxes paid by the railroads. It was news that in reporting gross earnings the railroads had not counted a mil-lion dollars annually in secret rebates. Spectacular collection of taxes on these rebates, abolishment of the whole rebate system, imposing of equal taxes at State valuation on holdings, and then rate regulation to prevent payment of in-creased taxes by increased carriage cost; and at last the Railroad Commission itself, following an earlier and abortive commission—all these came to Wiscon-sin through the one-man center of energy who could fill other men with con-viction and teach them the peril in which their government labored. Rocking up through the black prophecies came the laughter of the State when the Railway Commission books showed for the first five years of its operation a two-million-dollar reduction in rates but an increase of 18.45 per cent in new earnings of the roads of the State against 18.41 per cent increase in net earnings for all the roads of the nation. The other public utilities, soon shepherded into the commission, outran that record. Capital simply could not be driven out of the State! Mean-while the first full primary law in the United States had been written into the Wisconsin statutes.

Yet the story of the struggle to defeat this legislation is one of the saddest in Wisconsin records. The whole story of the opposing lobbies has been told in La Follette's autobiography and shows that Monte Carlo stages nothing more dev-astating than do the committee rooms of the capitols.

For a time Wisconsin lit new peaks at every legislative session. The commis-sion idea kindled a flame then new to our traditionized vision: that the deter-mining of conditions of certain relationships on a basis of legal precedent is fantastic and must be replaced by administrative interpretation on the basis of present economic and social fact. Followed a statute said in 1911 to be the great-est piece of labor legislation in the United States, the Industrial Commission to administer the new Workmen's Compensation Act and all other labor laws—the first instance in the country of the State assuming to control and regulate health and safety of the workers. Tax Commission, Dairy and Food Commission, Free Library Commission, State Insurance Department, State Banking Department for bank inspection, and Immigration Bureau of the Department of Agriculture (with a Chicago office) now all contribute to the humanizing of the State ma-chinery, to the stressing of human values in organized living. The Wisconsin Idea. The last commission, the Market Commission of 1919, to teach farmers to grade their own goods and market their own products and organize in cooper-ative groups, is designed ultimately to do for agriculture what the Industrial Commission does for industry. And to do more than that.

Not that cooperation in a quiet way has not already had growth in Wisconsin, which passed one of the first cooperative laws in the Union. Perhaps it is by spiritual inheritance from those five cooperative communities of Owenites and Fourierites—the Wisconsin Phalanx, Hunt's Colony, St. Nazianz, Spring Farm, and the Utilitarian Association, which had early dreamed their dream of relationship and died of institutionalization—that in 1917 there were in Wisconsin 1,536 cooperative creameries, cheese factories, produce companies, live-stock shipping associations and stores, besides 803 mutual telephone companies. These are soil for the flowering of that inevitable great growth so slow to root in America.

"Poor Wisconsin! So burdened by administrative commissions that the taxpayers move out of the State." One hears that occasionally from an editorial pen, a pen descended from that quill which used to be afraid of driving out capital. The answer which that pen will best understand is that not one dollar of the general property tax touches the Wisconsin commissions or boards or departments, for these are supported by the corporation taxes. (Railroad taxes, for example!) All the Capital expenses are worth pausing over. The legislature of 123 members cost $373 a day and has eighty-eight employees who are in the classified civil service. This sum is one-third that which some States pay smaller legislatures having two score more employees politically appointed. Of course by political appointments the commissions might be sabotaged, as is said to be happening now in New York State.

One hears occasionally too that Wisconsin is losing its progressivism. It is true that during the three administrations preceding the present, Wisconsin rather stood still. But nothing of importance was repealed. Indeed Wisconsin was the first State to ratify the Nineteenth Amendment; and to pass the Equal Rights Bill by which women are given equality before the law, with the safeguarding too of the protective legislation "which they now enjoy for the general welfare"—the eight-hour day and minimum-wage laws. The revolutionary rights to enter into equal partnership with her husband, to sue and be sued if she must, to make contracts unaided, have her residence declared to be where she actually lives, and to receive employment even though married are insured by this radical bill. By it lichened centuries of the old English common law are dropped. Can anybody say that the State is not progressive still?

Meanwhile something else had been happening in Wisconsin. A mile down a Madison street from the Greek dome of the new Capitol ($2,000,000 the dome alone cost, we tell you, and we add that the Governor's reception room is a replica of a room in the Doge's palace; but for the Doge we give no reason) stands an institution which makes every Wisconsin tax-payer either a psalmist or a prophet of peril. He ought to be a poet, for there is, we concede, nowhere in America a lovelier campus than that which lifts from Lake Mendota. Inscribed on a stone near its highest hall is that declaration of freedom made by the regents who had just tried Dr. Richard T. Ely for "economic heresy":

> We cannot for a moment believe that knowledge has reached its final goal or that the present constitution of society is perfect. . . . In all lines of investigation . . . the investigator should be absolutely free to follow the paths of truth wherever they may lead. Whatever may be the limitations which trammel inquiry elsewhere, we believe

the great State of Wisconsin should encourage that continual fearless sifting and winnowing by which alone truth can be found.

This cry of Tomorrow, adopted as a plank in one Republican State platform, is of course not always lived up to by capitol or university. Of late the halls of the university have been denied for the public appearance of the editor of *The Nation*, of Scott Nearing, and of Kate Richards O'Hare, who were obliged to speak somewhere else in Madison on those occasions—Mrs. O'Hare at the Capitol. And within five years both the faculty of the university and the State legislature have, not quite unanimously, formally censured Senator La Follette for his opposition to the entrance of the United States into the World War. But the dream is there and Wisconsin has had for that dream two wings, one political and one educational. Dr. Richard T. Ely's "curious new individualism, that the State is a necessary good whose duty is to preserve to men opportunities which they deserve and profit by" did as much for the young as progressive legislation did for the elders to make men socially conscious and to give them a right attitude toward public affairs. Dr. John R. Commons and Dr. E. A. Ross (the latter fresh from two boycotts of his own for "economic heresy") sifted and winnowed in political economy and sociology "on the hill," while La Follette and others sifted and and winnowed at the Capitol; and Frederic C. Howe sifted and winnowed at large. In those days were many giants. Some of the giants still survive.

Then McCarthy.[1] "I, a wandering student, seeking knowledge, came knocking at the great gates of the University of Wisconsin and it took me in, filled me with inspiration, and when I left its doors the kindly people of the State . . . gave me a man's work to do." The "man's work" was for one thing the Legislative Reference Library. For what was the use of progressive legislation if the new statutes were so loosely drawn that they failed to express the will of the people? And what was the use of expressing the will of the people if there were no trained servants to carry it out? McCarthy saw democracy failing at its source; legislators with ideas of public service thwarted because they could not find out how other States and nations handled those ideas; unscrupulous lawyers drawing up bills purposely unconstitutional; the openly recognized scheme of jokers; the farmer or grocer or country lawyer faced unprepared with the making of laws on every phase of life; and expected to vote on two thousand bills at a session. He came with his idea of a Legislative Reference Library. They laughed at him; much later they took him on sufferance in the attic of the Capitol; very early they introduced a bill to abolish him; then they accepted him. The idea has been adopted in State after State and at Washington—though at Washington they are slowly strangling the library by failure to make it appropriations. These two tasks which "McCarthy of Wisconsin" set for himself—the improving of statute law and the improving of public administration, so little spectacular, so ripe for drudgery are of the fabric of Wisconsin, present and to come. Some day his

[1]Charles McCarthy (1873–1921). [D. H. B.]

Society for Training for Public Service will not exist merely on paper as it does now; and the extended functioning of administrative experts may lead to nothing less than his idea of a new equity.

Also McCarthy's touch is on the continuation school laws—entrance into industry not dependent on age alone but on completion of eighth grade, part-time attendance obligatory up to *eighteen* years, and such schools required, with State aid, in towns of five thousand. And on the University Extension program which serves its thousands in spite of the reactionaries' slogan of: "This university-on-wheels business has got to stop." And McCarthy's trail led by the farms and through one administration the State Board of Public Affairs was transformed into a rural agency studying, with the university, European marketing systems, State loans to farmers, cooperative credit. The Marketing Commission was his dream. His death two years ago was as little a death as ever a man died. He is still saying about the Capitol his careless: "Well, it's something where there was nothing."

Something where there was nothing. But there must be soil. And even with leaders like these, preaching that democracy and representative government are never won to keep, how was it that Wisconsin proved such favorable soil for progressivism? They were the camera, but who made the plate? The plate was made by the spirit of liberty stirring in northern Europe in the late forties. In Scandinavia, Germany, Ireland, Poland, Belgium, Switzerland. In political refugees. In Carl Schurz and the revolutionists of 1848. Intellectual brothers to those of the New Englanders who would still have brewed tea in Boston harbor. And it was spiritual brothers to the Brook Farm folk who now founded those little cooperative commonwealths whose ideals, reinterpreted, recur among us like a motif. Migrant to America, they read a pamphlet printed by immigrants to say that Wisconsin, then just admitted to the Union, had a constitution favorable to a Free State and that here only a year was required for citizenship. But the whole northern Mississippi Valley was peopled with such immigrants.

"Not a plow . . . not a ham . . . they lent him an axe and a saw and he begun . . . I laid aside two thousand last year. . . . Something for somebody else. . . . Careful lest capital be driven from the State."

Yes, all that followed. Farm and business, home and school, caution, conformity, economy, and a charity crust for the uncompensated. The old individualism, drama and refrain. But beneath the fine old individualism slept the stuff of the pioneers, patriots who had not been afraid to mention it when their country was wrong. And when the cry for representative government reappeared not as a political slogan but as an economic and educational program something ancient, it seems, woke in the flesh of their children. "I have never doubted," said La Follette, "that, once the people understood, they would reclaim their government."

Something where there was nothing. A proper attitude toward public affairs. A torch brought by the pioneers and held by President John Bascom of the university, patiently urging the service which education must pay back to the State.

One of his pupils was the late President Charles Van Hise, who held the torch for a while. Another pupil was La Follette.

What else of Wisconsin? Always there is the still background of that stretching acreage of farms. And it isn't that $234,000,000 worth of milk was produced in the State in 1920; or 307,000,000 pounds of cheese and 95,000,000 of butter in 1919; it isn't this (though we like thus adroitly to get it in the conversation). It isn't that the university agricultural school has bred pedigreed grain with which it won the world's championship in 1910; or made corn and all kinds of fruit grow up Lake Superior way; or that it has brought research contributions to soil testing and marsh draining; or discovered five of the six tests used everywhere in dairying. It isn't these, after all. It is that the university and the capitol *care*. That they touch the people's life as it is lived. The Wisconsin Idea. The University Idea. And here it is, from Major Edward Fitzpatrick of the present Wisconsin Board of Education: "Wherever spirit grows by mysterious contact with spirit, in the passion to make knowledge serve human needs, there is the essence of the University Idea." No wonder that this board has lately become a social planning department and that there is now being outlined a State-wide educational program to make the progress of Wisconsin a course consciously planned for a decade to come.

Among the unacademic educational forces in the State should be named the Socialist Party with Victor Berger. Not only because, anonymous on the statute books, is many a measure which the Socialists urged years ago and saw others pass; nor because for years the Socialists have successfully governed Milwaukee as they do now, but because of their general service to the State in quickening the social consciousness.

What else of Wisconsin? A progressive Governor, renominated on a platform which includes the abolishing of the secrecy clause in the income-tax law; and in Governor Blaine's hands are figures and names which show that $1,500,000 in income-tax returns have been held back from the State in the last six years by certain corporations—and the work of auditing is barely begun. No wonder that for the first time in the political history of Wisconsin the Old Guard, the stalwart Republicans, are calling themselves "independent progressives," or "constructive progressives," or just progressives for short. "The sheep in the clothing of what he used to call a wolf," says an earnest wag.

And what else? A unique geological background of thrilling revelation and a rich Indian and French and Jesuit tradition. Thousands of acres of forest reserve—now that millions of the northern giants have been felled. A State Conservation Commission and a "Lovers of Our Native Landscape" preserving woods and granite cliffs and waterfronts—now that some of these waterfronts already bear a general resemblance to the burning ghats. A labyrinth of little towns with pathetic Main Street lists inscribed with names of boys fed to the old old Minotaur. A mass of the people still living the lives of the sixties—individualists, as we say, "egg and bird" ("Fine citizen. Tends exclusively to his own business"); turning a languid or a suspicious or an alarmed eye on social legislation (''Social or Socialist, what's the difference?'' And ''Don't 'civic' mean keeping the saloons shut?''); with women of three generations awake and aware of these dawns, pioneer suffragists or undergraduate utopists; and with other women repressed, overspecialized to housework, and that pendulum swinging to daughters neither repressed nor specialized. All the tawdriness of the sad scramble for pleasure in rides and reels, with hard-favored recreation halls and desultory pageants of commercial floats as our chief form of art expression. But also the schoolhouses open for non-partisan non-exclusive assembling of the people and this mandatory on all school boards. And the Wisconsin Players, a laboratory for the youth of the State to try themselves out, without cost, in the arts of the theater. A Milwaukee Art Society with a permanent exhibit by Wisconsin artists, an exhibit taken out in the autumn to the county fairs. A State Music Federation. Stephen Babcock, inventing the fat test for milk and refusing to patent it. A poet, William Ellery Leonard, whose voice and vision are for ''the prophets of the New, until the few are all.'' John Muir's birthplace. Ole Bull's house as the executive residence. Bill Nye's own town. Edna Ferber's laughter and Hamlin Garland's devotion celebrating the Middle Border. The home of Ringling's circus—and when of late Al Ringling died the legislature adjourned and (in the neighboring town where he began his show business with one dog in a crate) attended his funeral. Everywhere stir such revaluations as that, furthering sympathy, furthering reality.

In brief, the well-known human being, wistful that life be physically and spiritually beneficent to him and even to his kind. And lifting through the mechanism of government and education the Wisconsin spirit saying so that it is actually audible: ''Your hope is the State's task.''

But McCarthy's words are best: ''Well, where there was nothing there is something.''

WYOMING

A Maverick Citizenry

WALTER C. HAWES

JANUARY 16, 1924

W HEN THE roaring middle years of the nineteenth century were witnessing a mighty trekking to and fro of young and turbulent manhood in search of virgin lands or gold in these United States, one particular stretch of murderous desert in the western part of the territory of Dakotah baffled the quest of the frontiersman for anything worth development. For a full quarter of the century these torrents of humanity surged this way and that, to California, to Pike's Peak, to Nevada, to Montana, and all that while the district that was to be Wyoming was regarded only as a desolate place along the trails which men traversed for the sole purpose of reaching some place beyond. Twenty years of flood-tide emigration along the Oregon Trail left no residue save the soldiers in the military posts and the keepers of the road houses. Indeed had it not been for a break in the Rocky Mountains and a welling up of the plans which caught the eye of the searchers for easy passage to the Pacific Coast, there is no telling when the attention of men would have been turned this way.

It was this low place in the hills that brought to the district in the summer of 1867 the two creeping lines of steel which represented the westward progress of the first coast-to-coast railway. And keeping pace with the breaking plows of the contractors went the first towns of the district, the riotous "hells on wheels" that sprang up overnight and went as quickly, populated with the huge construction gangs and the motley horde which preyed upon them. At intervals behind this moving vanguard settlements sprang up on the division-point towns, permanent but almost as rough and ready as their mushroom predecessors.

The violence that prevailed in those towns during the first year made it certain that if continuous rail traffic was to be assured, there must be some seat of government nearer than the capitol of Dakotah Territory. And thus it was that Wyoming, child of the cross-continental trails, came into being as a unit of administration to serve the needs of the Union Pacific Railroad.

There being no other reason for the existence of the Territory, it was not unnatural that the railroad corporation regarded the new division of the United

403

Yellowstone National Park, Wyoming. "For a full quarter of the century these torrents of humanity surged this way and that, to California, to Pike's Peak, to Nevada, to Montana, and all that while the district that was to be Wyoming was regarded only as a desolate place along the trails which men traversed for the sole purpose of reaching some place beyond."

States much as it regarded the huge land grants to which the federal government had given its full title. By a shrewd manipulation of these land grants it secured legal possession of the immense coal deposits bordering its right-of-way which then seemed the only part of the Territory worth owning. For many decades it was common report that the Union Pacific was the power behind the throne in territorial politics, and results went to show that it had ways and means of exerting strong persuasion wherever its interests were vitally involved. Until the present year the assessments of Union Pacific properties in Wyoming were fractional as compared with the assessment of that corporation's properties in other States. In 1922 the line across the prairies of Nebraska was assessed at $133,155 per mile, while the same line in Wyoming, with long stretches of mountain construction and with tunnels and snowsheds costing millions, was assessed at $62,376.20 per mile. That same year a former division superintendent and known business ally of the Union Pacific running for governor on the single plank platform of economy and tax reduction was defeated by 723 votes. His defeat was followed by the appointment of a State board of equalization which ordered a sharp raise in the assessment of Union Pacific properties.

In the period immediately following construction no one was interested in disputing the suzerainty of the railroad. Viewed from the window of a railway coach the Territory seemed through most of its extent a land as desolate as the surface of an extinct planet. To the eye accustomed to the rational, water-molded topography of the East the land was beyond comprehension. A precipitately tilted ledge of rock would cut across the trail without reference to the rest of the landscape, and the route would skirt along its base to a V-shaped water-gap through which a bewildered river found its way. These rivers following circuitous routes through the bad lands eventually gave the State its value as one of the finest cattle ranges in the world. From the high central plateau seated like the cupola of a continent they radiate east, north, west, southwest like the spokes of a wheel, paying the State's tribute of waters to the Gulf of California and Puget Sound as well as to the Missouri and Mississippi on the east.

But it required someone other than a New York farmer's son to discover the land's value. Cattleman of the Texas and Panhandle ranges driving their herds hundreds of miles north to a railroad outlet found that the seemingly scanty grasses had a strength unknown to forage of more rainy lands. They soon were trailing hundreds of thousands of cattle here in the early summer to fatten on the nutritious Northern grasses and be shipped to market in the fall. Not a fence intervened along their route, and under ordinary conditions the cattle were brought the whole way for not more than $1 per head.

It was not until the middle seventies that the dangers from hostile Indians were removed and headquarters ranches were established. The perils were still so great that they were reflected in interest rates as high as from 24 to 36 per cent required by the Texas and Cheyenne banks. The result was that large stockselling companies were formed which enlisted capital in the Eastern States and in England and Scotland. As a consequence the range passed into foreign hands during the period of development.

Despite the ravings of the romanticists over the freedom and the larger manners of the days of the unfenced range, the plains cattle-industry of those days was no pure democracy. All conditions made for the success of the large outfit. Under the provisions of the federal land laws legal title to the range was out of the question save in small amounts beneath notice in a pastoral country. Consequently the range was no-man's land, and anyone who could get money could flood it with cattle. An estimate of that day states that a herd of 5,000 cattle could be maintained there for $1 per head, a herd of 10,000 for 75 or 80 cents per head, and a herd of 25,000 for not much over 50 cents per head the year round. Large herds, running as high as 75,000 head, became the rule. When the Wyoming Live Stock Association was formed in 1879 it was reputed to be the largest organized body of stockmen in the world, comprising 400 members representing over half the States in the Union and several foreign countries, and possessing stock and equipment valued well up toward $100,000,000. The foreign-owned companies employed foremen who were often stockholders and managed as many as 150 men. Only part of this force was resident on the range the year round; and every spring there was an influx of riders. After the beef round-ups in the fall these transients would "hole up" in the towns with the stake they had earned, or in many cases they went to Eastern States, where they followed more prosaic occupations during the winter.

This was the Wyoming beloved of the romanticist—a community of roistering young bachelors without a stake in the land and with little aim other than to enjoy the spice of adventure that went with the cattle industry. Among them prevailed the open-handed camaraderie of the adventurer. Even among their employers, while the reserves of the bank of nature were more than equal to the demands there was no reason for tight-fistedness or thieving. Thus it was that for a decade or less there prevailed an atmosphere of open-handed generosity and honorable dealings.

It was inevitable that this seemingly idyllic period should be no more than an evanescent phase of the land's development; and sober consideration will reveal that its perpetuation was not desirable. The life of the cow-hand alternated between long periods of hard work, when he was the very moderately paid employee of a large outfit, and brief seasons of hard dissipation in the sordid little cow towns composed of a store or two and several saloons about a loading chute. The social institutions of the country were crude. Well into the twentieth century the barkeepers outnumbered the doctors, lawyers, and ministers of the State combined. There were few decent women back in the range country and many reasons for not bringing them there.

When the abler men aspired to homes and outfits of their own they came into conflict with the interests already in control of the range. The syndicates discouraged ownership on the part of their employees, unless they wished to buy stock in the companies. It was true that an employee with a brand of his own could steal without limit from his employer. It was accordingly a rule with many companies that the employee with his own brand was blacklisted.

But the large concerns were unable to compete with these new rivals who had grown up in their employ and were the real cattlemen on whom they had depended for the rough and ready work. For once the man on the ground doing the work of production held the advantage, for he knew the industry from every angle. The chief weakness of the syndicates lay in their inability to get undisputed control of any considerable acreage. The homestead law allowed each man a title to 160 acres of land, to be acquired by actual residence. For a foreign company this was a poser. Twenty average acres of range land were required to maintain one cow the year round. If the outfit owned 5,000 cattle, which was a small herd in the open-range days, it needed the equivalent of 625 homesteads to run them on. The large companies laid their case before Congress, asking for legislation permitting long-term leases of large tracts of arid land as a matter of range conservation. There were strong arguments in favor of such legislation. Notwithstanding the large gross returns reported from later systems of mixed small ranching and farming, it seems probable that more clear money was taken from the country during the day of the large company than at any other time since. For the changes since have involved much costly controversy and expensive education, however valuable they may be in the long run. The odium attaching to the exploitation of the public lands by foreign capital was emphasized with good effect by the opponents of leasing, however, and the lawmakers were unwilling, for political reasons if for no other, to lay themselves open to that charge.

Overstocking and disorganization ensued, and the severe winter of 1886–87 was sufficient to bring the old order to an abrupt end. From 50 to 60 per cent of the cattle were lost that season before summer opened. Such companies as did not immediately go out of business reduced their operations to bedrock, and in the ensuing decade the number of cattle in Wyoming fell from 900,000 to 300,000.

At the close of the disorganized period the return of better times found the hated "nester," the small rancher, in full control. For a period of ten years the men who had grown up with the country and who had been identified with its development more than any other class of men before or since were in possession. At the close of that decade there were reported to be 3,200 horse and cattle raisers in the State, with herds ranging from 100 to 1,000. But even with these smaller holdings, the legal title to sufficient range was out of reach. They managed as best they could with gentlemen's agreements; several ranchers would fence in a tract for a common pasture. But the time came when these men, in their turn, found themselves helpless before a new invasion.

The new heir to the range was the homesteader who proposed to take the 160 acres allowed by law and make his living on it by agriculture. For him it seemed the federal government had been waiting as the rightful owner who was to develop the arid lands along a policy which it could sanction—the policy which had been tested in the fertile rain belt.

In reality the movement was engineered by land boomers who took advantage of the land fever which resulted from the prosperous farming period which came with the opening of the twentieth century. The boomer saw and grasped his golden opportunity to exploit the cheap lands of the West. He took up the systems, so called, of dry-farming developed by experimenters and expanded them in a literature that reeked with the patter of "dust mulches" and "subsoil packing" warranted to retain in gravel beds every drop of moisture and hold it the year round payable on demand. He acquired title to cheap railway lands, or he offered to "locate" settlers on homesteads for fees ranging from $25 to $100.

The wage slave and the tenant farmer of the East leaped hungrily to the bait, and there ensued that crusade of the innocents that shattered its ranks in vain against the stubborn desert. Heeding not the warnings of the experienced ranchers, which they held to be inspired by their selfish interest, and armed with a dry-farming manual furnished gratis by the promoter as a buckler against disaster, these knights errant of the soil essayed their high emprise of making a bushel of wheat grow where nature had produced but a tuft of bunch-grass.

During a few years conditions favored them. World War prices enabled settlers on the better lands to make ends meet and even show a margin of profit. But the fitting symbol of the whole movement was the shack which the homesteader built for his home. All houses in the dry-farming districts were "shacks" in name and most of them were that in fact. Mere little paper-lined shells they were, to be blown away at the first puff of disaster. When disaster did strike the farming industry in 1920, it transpired that the dry-farming movement was also a shell of another type, loaded with dynamite. Eastern loan companies had over-financed the movement, advancing $8, $10, even $12 per acre on lands that now go begging for purchasers at any price. It is true that these loan companies had managed to get usurious rates of interest by the expedient of withholding a good sum from the principal as a "commission" for making the loan. But that availed them nothing when the owner of the land elected to call the transaction a sale and decamped with the money, leaving the company to reimburse itself as best it might from the lands which it had accepted as security. The companies now hold the nests but the birds are flown. When the collapse came the dry-farmers who had been holding on precariously during the best years scattered to the four winds. A few restricted localities were favored with a soil adapted to producing crops under arid conditions, and here a remnant held on. A county agent whose business takes him into a number of dry-farming communities estimates that in the neighborhood of 10 per cent of the farmers who came in the boom period are left. In one section where originally 125 farmers settled there are five left; in another there are two left out of twenty-four. The 90 per cent who let go bettered their condition, and are now for the most part in the oil fields and railway towns, earning good wages and living better than at any time in their experience.

But he who concludes from the above recital that there is nothing left to do but to inscribe R.I.P. over the departed glories of the land is very much mistaken. For as the dry-farming industry was just about to burst like the overblown bubble it was, and as the live-stock industry was entering a temporary eclipse, a new dynamic more potent than was ever known in rangeland before entered this arena of seemingly spent forces. Far below the grass roots once considered the State's sole wealth the adventuring drills of the wild-catters discovered the miracle of petroleum. As early as the nineties there had been a small production from the shallow sand of Salt Creek, but it was not until 1914 that the presence of the deeper and richer sands was determined.

The first result was a rush of the oil companies for holdings, and a battle of giants ensued, from which the Standard group emerged victor. By virtue of its position as the owner of the only pipe-lines out of the fields in the early development, the Standard was able to throttle competition to an unusual degree. Crude prices in the Wyoming field were hammered down to a fraction of the mid-continent prices. When the product of the latter fields was selling for $3.50 per barrel during the war, the higher grade Salt Creek product was selling for around $2 per barrel. When mid-continent prices slumped to about $1, Salt Creek crude was selling for barely more than half that amount. When the independent company was not crowded to the wall by these methods, the Standard bored from within until it secured control of the majority of the stock.

In September, 1921, a faction of the independent operators under the lead of attorney George Brimmer of Rawlins demanded a special session of the legislature to enact laws curbing the monopolistic tendencies of large companies, but nothing was done, and the hold of the Standard on the oil industry of the State is practically complete.

As the oil was discovered almost entirely on Federal or State lands, the companies hold these lands under lease, paying royalties to those governments. As the laws require that the bids be open to competition, the companies sometimes fail to make previous arrangements, and there is spirited bidding. Such was the case with the famous Section 16, located in the heart of Salt Creek and owned by the State. When the date came to release in 1923, there entered the lists a defeated candidate who ascribed his downfall in the election of the previous year to Standard machinations. As a consequence the Standard interests were forced to raise the royalty for the lease of Section 16 from 35 per cent to 65 per cent of the production.

But an oil monopoly has ways and means of recouping such losses. The royalties paid to the State are largely recovered by higher charges on gasoline within the State's borders. Since the beginning of the industry, Wyoming gasoline has sold cheaper at Missouri River points than within the State. At the present time the gasoline that is selling in towns neighboring the oil fields at 21 cents per gallon is selling in Colorado at 16 cents. Glaring as this practice is, there is no concerted move to check it.

The discovery of oil did more, however, than to enrich a large corporation. It served to turn the attention of the entire State inward for the first time. At last there is a universal center of interest—Salt Creek. About that oil field and the young city of Casper which has developed from it there has crowded a population of 50,000, the first industrial center of any consequence in the State. Previously it had been a State without cities, a ragged fringe of settlements around a central desert. Economically the State had been as thoroughly partitioned into spheres of influence as ever was Poland or darkest Africa.

Due to the development of Salt Creek there is now under construction the first railway line designed to serve the interior needs of the State—the road being built by the Haskell interests from Sheridan to Casper, and is eventually to connect with the Union Pacific at Rawlins. A few days ago a request was filed for permission to build another railway north from Casper to the Montana line. Eventually Salt Creek seems destined to become the hub of a system of railways radiating to every region of the State, which will bind together all sections about this rich central empire. Then this meaningless geographical rectangle, this oblong satire on rational map-making, may become at last a unified commonwealth, a State among States, instead of a mere tribute payer to a usurious sisterhood. And then may arise the organized will to resist the exploitation of resources by monopolies without regard to the rights of the citizens.

Yet is there any assurance of such outcome? Will the imprisoned genii of the earth which were released through the casings with the roaring gas and thundering crude when the wild-catter's bit pierced the wealthy lower sands of Salt Creek effect any real social and political development? Or will the State merely experience a change of corporate allegiance, and become known as a province of Standard Oil?

CONTRIBUTORS

SHERWOOD ANDERSON (Ohio)   Anderson, born in Camden, Ohio, in 1876, launched his writing career in 1912, when he abruptly left his Ohio business for Chicago. His literary reputation among his contemporaries rested on the daring techniques through which he conveyed the psychic turbulence beneath placid appearances and his constant theme of the damage that the machine age inflicted on emotional life. Both are evident in his first success, *Winesburg, Ohio* (1919), and his collection of short stories, *The Triumph of the Egg* (1921). Among those who acknowledged his influence were Ernest Hemingway, William Faulkner, Van Wyck Brooks, and Waldo Frank.

MARY AUSTIN (Arizona)   Born in Illinois in 1868, Austin earned a reputation as an essayist of the West and an expert on Native American life with her *Land of Little Rain* (1903). Her novel *A Woman of Genius* (1912), which detailed the struggle of the protagonist with the restrictive culture of the Midwest, earned Austin acclaim in avant-garde circles, and prompted her move to the East. There she encountered the Fabian socialism and feminism that would mark her later work. Disenchanted by urban life, she left New York City in 1919 for Taos, New Mexico, where she continued writing sketches of the Southwest.

BEN LUCIEN BURMAN (Kentucky)   Burman's life and career were intimately tied to the state. Born in Covington in 1895, he left a career as a journalist to become a satirist of Southern mores. By the 1930s, his attitude toward the region had changed, and his nostalgic *Blow for a Landing* (1938), a sympathetic examination of the Kentucky of his youth, won the Southern Authors prize for the most distinguished book of the year.

JAMES M. CAIN (West Virginia)   Cain, who was born in Annapolis, Maryland, in 1892, worked for the Baltimore *Sun* and the New York *World* throughout the 1920s. In 1931 he devoted himself to the writing of fiction. The early influence of H. L. Mencken is evident in Cain's 1930 essays on politics in *The American Mercury* and in his crime novels, the best known of which are *The Postman Always Rings Twice* (1934), *Mildred Pierce* (1941), and *Double Indemnity* (1943).

HAYDEN CARRUTH (South Dakota)   As a young man Carruth moved with his family from Minnesota, where he was born in 1862, to the Dakota Territory. He gained fame as a humorist with the *Estelline Bell,* his newspaper; *Track's End* (1911), an adventure novel about a boy growing up in the Dakota Territory; and "The Postscript," his column for *Woman's Home Companion.*

WILLA SIBERT CATHER (Nebraska)   Born in Virginia in 1876, Cather moved at the age of seven to Nebraska, the site of some of her most memorable fiction. Managing editor of *McClure's* until 1913, Cather penned *O, Pioneers* (1913), *The Song of the Lark* (1915), *My Antonia* (1918), and *One of Ours* (1922; Pulitzer Prize), which evoke the struggle to tame the wild terrain of Nebraska and celebrate the value of tradition in halting the corrosiveness of twentieth-century progress. Her later important works include *The Professor's House* (1925) and *Death Comes for the Archbishop* (1927).

CHARLES H. CHAPMAN (Oregon)   A native of Wisconsin, where he was born in 1869, Chapman had an extraordinarily varied career. He received his Ph.D. from Johns Hopkins in 1891 and moved to Oregon, where he spent his first years in the state as a journalist. In 1893 he assumed the presidency of the University of Oregon. His administration was marked by quarrels over his enforcement of admissions standards for Eugene high school graduates, his discipline of athletes, and his shopping for groceries in Portland. These quarrels induced his resignation in 1897. A career of organizing and lecturing for the Industrial Workers of the World followed. In his later years Chapman returned to Oregon and his first love, agriculture.

LEONARD LANSON CLINE (Michigan)   Born in Bay City, Michigan, in 1893, Cline wrote for various Detroit newspapers until his death in 1929.

ROBERT CLOUTMAN DEXTER (Rhode Island)   Dexter entered social work in Providence after his graduation from Brown University in 1908. A professor of social work at Clark University and Skidmore College, Dexter wrote *Social Adjustment,* for many years the standard text on the subject.

THEODORE DREISER (Indiana)   Born in Terre Haute, Indiana, in 1871 to a poor German Catholic family, Dreiser worked at numerous newspaper jobs before he published his first novel, *Sister Carrie,* in 1900. Its pathbreaking naturalistic treatment of moral issues—not his publisher's prudishness, as Dreiser alleged—contributed to its failure with the reading public. A nervous breakdown ensued, and Dreiser did not publish again until *Jennie Gerhardt* (1911). These and his other notable works—*The Financier* (1912), *The Titan* (1914), *An American Tragedy* (1925)—reflected his incessant desire to discover the raw drives that propelled human behavior. The suppression of his sexually frank *The "Genius"* (1915) made him a hero to many literary rebels. During the 1920s Dreiser had friendly relations with the Communist party and wrote the pro-Soviet *Dreiser Looks at Russia* in 1928.

W. E. B. Du Bois (Georgia)   Editor from 1910 to 1932 of *The Crisis,* the journal of the National Association of the Advancement of Colored People, Du Bois was born in Great Barrington, Massachusetts, in 1868. He was a professor at Atlanta University when he published his innovative *Souls of Black Folk* (1903), which Henry James called the best American book of the year. In these essays he revised Reconstruction historiography, defended the value of both classical and folk knowledge, asserted to a white audience the numerous contributions of African-Americans to American life, challenged the accommodationist views of Booker T. Washington, and criticized the commercial ethic of southern Progressives. Until his death in Ghana in 1963, Du Bois alternately called for a multi-racial coalition of the oppressed and insisted that only through Pan-Africanism could blacks achieve a measure of justice.

C. L. Edson (Arkansas)   Edson was a southern humorist whose *Ballads of the Boys of Old K. U., Prairie Fire: An Epic Poem,* and *The Great American Ass* ridiculed southern customs.

George Clifton Edwards (Texas)   Born in Dallas in 1877, Edwards was a Socialist lawyer who represented Texas labor and radical organizations.

Arthur Fisher (Montana)   Fisher was born in Chicago in 1894. He taught law at the University of Montana in 1921–1922 until the local American Legion's protests against his liberal politics forced his dismissal. He edited *The New Northwest* in Missoula before returning to the practice of law.

Dorothy Canfield Fisher (Vermont)   Born in Kansas in 1879, Fisher moved to her ancestors' Vermont in 1907. A prolific author, she wrote more than fifty books. Her novels of the 1920s, of which *The Brimming Cup* (1921) and *The Homemaker* (1924) earned the most acclaim, dealt with the struggle of women to accept the limits of social life. Practicing the civic responsibility that she long extolled as an essential characteristic of Vermont life, Fisher was the first female member of the Vermont state board of education. Her final work, *Vermont Tradition: The Biography of an Outlook* (1953), developed at greater length her defense of the unique antimodernism of her state.

Douglas Freeman (Virginia)   Freeman, native of Lynchburg, Virginia, became the editor of the Richmond *News Leader* in 1915 at the age of twenty-nine.

In the course of establishing his reputation as one of the premier southern progressives, he devoted himself to the study of Virginia history. His biography of Robert E. Lee won the Pulitzer Prize in 1935.

ZONA GALE (Wisconsin)   Born in Portage, Wisconsin, in 1874 and educated at the University of Wisconsin, Gale wrote realist fiction rooted in Wisconsin village life. She won the Pulitzer Prize for the dramatization of her novel *Miss Lulu Brett* in 1921. Committed to Progressivism, Gale actively campaigned for Robert La Follette in the presidential election of 1924.

ERNEST GRUENING (New York I)   Born in New York City in 1887, Gruening was graduated from Harvard medical school, but chose instead a career in journalism. Managing editor of *The Nation* from 1921 to 1923, he was the moving force behind "These United States." Progressive and anti-imperialist in politics in the 1920s, Gruening stayed the course throughout his career. After he left the magazine, he served as national publicity director for the Progressive party in 1924, assistant secretary of the interior during the 1930s, and governor of Alaska. As senator he cast one of the two votes against the Tonkin Gulf Resolution, authorizing U.S. retaliation against North Vietnam.

WALTER C. HAWES (Wyoming)   A long-time resident of Wyoming, Hawes edited the Rock River *Review* and often wrote on Wyoming for national publications.

ROBERT HERRICK (Maine)   Born in Cambridge, Massachusetts, in 1868, Herrick combined a professorship of English at the University of Chicago with an active career as a novelist. He detailed the social decay at the root of modern life in such realist works as *The Memoirs of an American Citizen* (1905), *One Woman's Life* (1913), *Clark's Field* (1914), and *Waste* (1924). Owner of a vacation home in York, Maine, Herrick never ceased to consider himself a "pure-blooded New Englander."

MANLEY O. HUDSON (Missouri)   Hudson, born in 1886 in St. Charles County, Missouri, taught law at the University of Missouri. A specialist in international law, he served in the American delegation to Versailles and later in the Department of State.

EASLEY S. JONES (Colorado)   Born in Nebraska in 1884, Jones was a teacher in Boulder, Colorado, and author of high school and college composition textbooks.

REGINALD WRIGHT KAUFFMAN (Pennsylvania)   Kauffman, born in 1877 in Columbia, Pennsylvania, worked for numerous Philadelphia publications. His writings ranged from an exposé of the white slave trade to war dispatches from

France. An advocate of both suffragist and internationalist causes, Kauffman was a member of the Republican National Committee's mission to the World War I peace conference.

MURRAY E. KING (Utah)   Born in 1876, King was educated at the Mormon Academy in Fillmore and Brigham Young University, although he had by then renounced his Mormonism. After brief stints in teaching and reporting for various Utah papers, he became editor of the official organ of the Utah Federation of Labor. Committed to labor and progressive causes, King later joined the staff of *Socialist World/American Appeal* and served as an official of both the Nonpartisan League and the Farmer-Labor party's research bureau.

SINCLAIR LEWIS (Minnesota)   Lewis was born in Sauk Center, Minnesota, in 1885 and graduated from Yale in 1908. He began his career as a novelist with *Our Mr. Wren* (1914). During the 1920s he wrote, among other novels, *Main Street* (1920), *Babbitt* (1922), *Arrowsmith* (1925), and *Elmer Gantry* (1927). Lewis was awarded the Nobel Prize for literature in 1930. Long considered a parodist of middle-class manners and one of the leading advocates of the view of the twenties as repressive, Lewis ironically achieved wide popularity among the people he supposedly satirized, perhaps because his best work revealed an underside of decency and courage.

LUDWIG LEWISOHN (South Carolina)   Lewisohn emigrated in 1890, at the age of eight, from his native Germany to Charleston, where he attended college. After anti-Semitism and suspicions of his pacifism aborted his academic career, Lewisohn continued his championing of modern continental playwrights as editor and drama critic of *The Nation*. His turbulent marital life, which he frankly detailed in both autobiography and fiction, attracted national attention. Among his later contributions during the 1920s was his forceful argument against Jewish assimilation into American life, which he viewed as a surrender of uniqueness.

JOHN MACY (Massachusetts)   Literary editor of *The Nation* in 1922, Macy was born in 1877 in Detroit to a family that traced its Massachusetts roots to the colonial period. A socialist, he was literary editor of the Boston *Herald*. Married to Anne Sullivan, the famous teacher of Helen Keller, Macy was one of the prominent literary rebels of the 1910s. His *Spirit of American Literature* (1913) was a pioneer attack against the genteel tradition of letters.

ANNE MARTIN (Nevada)   Martin was born in the Nevada Territory in 1875 and taught history at the Nevada State University until she jettisoned academics for politics. She led Nevada's fight for equal suffrage and achieved national prominence when she assumed the chair of the National Woman's party. Adopting the feminist position that neither party served the interests of women, Martin ran as independent candidate for U.S. Senate in 1918 and 1920.

H. L. MENCKEN (Maryland)   Born in Baltimore in 1880, Mencken set the tone for much of the literary rebellion of the 1920s with his scathing columns in the Baltimore *Sun* and two magazines that he edited, *Smart Set* (1914–1923) and *The American Mercury* (1924–1933). Sworn enemy of American "Puritanism," fundamentalism, and the "booboisie" and champion of Friedrich Nietzsche, Mencken saw mediocrity and irrationality almost everywhere, an evaluation he maintained until his death in 1956.

E. E. MILLER (Tennessee)   Editor of the *Southern Agriculturist,* published in Nashville, Miller was a native of the state. Throughout the 1920s he wrote on agricultural issues for national publications.

HOWARD VINCENT O'BRIEN (Illinois)   Born in Chicago in 1888, O'Brien became a Chicago literary figure after service with the artillery in France during World War I. A novelist, travel writer, and political commentator, O'Brien was literary editor of the Chicago *Daily News* from 1928 to 1932, when he became a columnist for the paper.

RALPH D. PAINE (New Hampshire)   Paine moved to New Hampshire from Illinois, where he was born in 1871, and became well known as an author of sea stories and boys' books. An independent Republican, he served in the New Hampshire legislature until his death in 1925.

ROBERT GEORGE PATERSON (North Dakota)   Paterson observed the operations of the Nonpartisan League at firsthand as the legislative correspondent and city editor of the Fargo *Forum.*

BURTON RASCOE (Oklahoma)   Born in Kentucky in 1892, Rascoe worked in Oklahoma between 1908 and 1911 as a reporter for the Shawnee *Herald.* When he was dismissed from the Chicago *Tribune* in 1920 for an irreverent allusion to Mary Baker Eddy, the founder of Christian Science, he returned to his father's cotton plantation in Seminole, Oklahoma. A confidant of James Branch Cabell, who dedicated his *Jurgen* (1919) to him, and of Theodore Dreiser, whose biography he wrote in 1925, Rascoe returned to literary life in the mid-1920s as literary editor for the New York *Herald-Tribune.* Known in his day as an energetic and witty writer with a casual attitude toward accuracy, Rascoe specialized in literary histories and in new editions of literary classics.

BEULAH AMIDON RATLIFF (Mississippi)   Born the daughter of a North Dakota jurist in 1896, Ratliff associated with the Young America circle around *Seven Arts* magazine during the 1910s. After her marriage in 1919 she lived for two years in Mississippi. Later she was on the staff of *The Survey* and served as director of the National Consumers League.

DON C. SEITZ (Connecticut)   Seitz was born in Ohio in 1862 and had a long career as a New York journalist, primarily on the staff of Joseph Pulitzer's New York *World*, whose liberal, anti-imperialist policies Seitz was reputed to have shaped. A resident of Connecticut for thirty years, Seitz campaigned for female suffrage and political reform in the state. He was an avid biographer and historian, especially of journalists and political figures.

ELIZABETH SHEPLEY SERGEANT (New Mexico)   Born in Massachusetts in 1881, Sergeant was graduated from Bryn Mawr, where she earned honors for her writing. Sergeant combined journalism with social work. She spent most of her life in Boston and New York City, where she was a regular correspondent for *The New Republic*, for which she filed dispatches from France during World War I.

JOHAN J. SMERTENKO (Iowa)   Smertenko spent two and a half years in Iowa as the managing editor of *The Grinnell Review* and director of publicity for the Grinnell College endowment fund.

CLARA G. STILLMAN (Florida)   The sister of Ernest Gruening, Stillman was the author of *Samuel Butler: A Mid-Victorian Modern* (1932) and *Fairy Tales Near and Far* (1945).

M. R. STONE (Idaho)   Stone was an Idaho civil engineer who specialized in bridges and rail lines.

BASIL THOMPSON (Louisiana)   Born in 1892, Thompson was the editor of *The Double Dealer*, a monthly literary magazine in the tradition of Oscar Wilde, until his death in 1924.

ARTHUR WARNER (Delaware)   An editor of *The Nation* with Progressive sympathies, Warner conducted a special investigation for his article.

GEORGE P. WEST (California)   West's Progressive sympathies were manifest throughout his career, first as an aid to Senator Hiram Johnson of California during the 1910s, later as an independent journalist. In the 1920s West wrote for *The Nation, The Survey, The New Republic,* and *The American Mercury* on labor and radical issues and California politics.

ROBERT WHITAKER (Washington)   Born in Lancashire, England, in 1863, Whitaker was an ordained Baptist minister who was twice posted in Seattle (1888–1890 and 1922–1923). A charter member of the American Civil Liberties Union, he also published *The Gospel at Work in Modern Life* (1915), which drew upon the social gospel of Walter Rauschenbusch, and a collection of his poems.

WILLIAM ALLEN WHITE (Kansas)   White, born and reared in Eldorado, Kansas, was the publisher and editor of the Emporia *Gazette* until his death in 1944. He attracted national attention at the age of twenty-eight with his 1896 editorial "What's the Matter with Kansas?" in which he attacked Populism for its impractical programs and outlandish adherents. Attracted to the more respectable progressivism, White backed Theodore Roosevelt's 1912 presidential bid and was a member of the national committee of the Progressive party from 1912 to 1916.

EDMUND WILSON, JR. (New Jersey)   Born in Red Bank, New Jersey, the son of the state attorney general, in 1895, Wilson went on to become one of the nation's premier literary critics and essayists. His *Axel's Castle* (1931) was one of the first accessible explanations of twentieth-century European literary trends. Critic and editor for *Vanity Fair, The New Republic,* and *The New Yorker,* he was at the heart of the major literary debates of the mid-twentieth century. Among his major works are *The Wound and the Bow* (1941), on Freudian interpretation of literature; *To the Finland Station* (1940), on Marxism; and *Patriotic Gore* (1965), on the literature of the Civil War period.

ROBERT WATSON WINSTON (North Carolina)   Winston, who was born in 1860 in Windsor, North Carolina, practiced law in the state until his retirement in 1924. Specializing in business cases, he represented North Carolina against railroad companies, the American Tobacco Company in various antitrust actions, and the Progressive editor Josephus Daniels in a contempt suit in 1903. In his biographies of famous southerners and his 1937 autobiography, Winston repeatedly criticized those southern traditions that he believed prevented intellectual and economic growth.

CHARLES W. WOOD (New York II)   The son of a Methodist minister in Ogdensburg, New York, where he was born in 1880, Wood was a locomotive fireman until he won a writing contest sponsored by *Collier's* in 1908 and was inspired to try journalism. Wood worked in Syracuse and Schenectady before joining the staff of *The Masses* in 1916.

CLEMENT WOOD (Alabama)   Born in Tuscaloosa, Alabama, in 1888, Wood served as assistant city attorney in Birmingham until he began his writing career in New York City in 1914. Over the next thirty-six years Wood produced novels of southern race relations, biographies of Walt Whitman and the social theorist Lester Frank Ward, several books on dream interpretation, and political tracts, including *Don't Tread on Me—A Study of Aggressive Legal Action for Labor Unions* (1927), *Warren Gamaliel Harding: An American Comedy* (1932), and *Herbert Hoover: An American Tragedy* (1932).